INTRODUCTORY PLANT VIROLOGY

For graduate and post graduate students of General Botany, Microbiology, Plant Pathology and Plant Virology

D.P. TRIPATHI
Ph.D.
Department of Plant Pathology
C.S.A. University of Agriculture and Technology
KANPUR-208 002 (U.P.)

KALYANI PUBLISHERS
LUDHIANA - NEW DELHI - NOIDA (U.P.) - HYDERABAD
CHENNAI - KOLKATA - CUTTACK - GUWAHATI - KOCHI

KALYANI PUBLISHERS

Head Office

B-I/1292, Rajinder Nagar,
Ludhiana-141 008

Administration Offices :

4779, Ansari Road,
23, Daryaganj, **New Delhi**-110 002

Works

B-16, Sector 8, **Noida** (U.P.)

Branches

1, Mahalakshmi Street,
T. Nagar, **Chennai**-600 017

110/111, Bharatia Towers, Badambadi
Cuttack–753 009 (Orissa)

3-5-1108, Narayanaguda,
Hyderabad-500 029

10/2B, Ramanath Mazumdar Street,
Kolkata-700 009

Arunalaya, Saraswati Road,
Pan Bazar, **Guwahati**-781 001

Convent Road, **Kochi**-682 035

P-30661 03

Second Revised Edition 2007

Reprinted, 2020

TYPESETTING & DIAGRAMS

(IPV)

At Gautam Graphic Printers
Mai Hiran Gate, Jalandhar.

978-81-272-3968-8

PRINTED IN INDIA

At Kalyani Printings, B-15, Sector 8, NOIDA
and Published by Mrs. Usha Raj Kumar for
Kalyani Publishers, New Delhi-110 002

PREFACE

This book is intended chiefly for graduate and post graduate students of General botany, Microbiology, Plant pathology and Plant virology covering courses in Plant Virology prescribed by most of the Indian Universities. During the twenty first century, interest in Plant Virology has increased quite significantly due to the destructive nature of plant viruses that cause considerable damage to the economic crops every year. The main stimulus for wide scope of Plant Virology undoubtedly is due to the recent advances in molecular biology of plant viruses. Subject of Plant Virology has widened during last decade but there is no any complete book which may serve purpose of our students. Keeping in view the needs of the students, the book in hand entitled **'Introductory Plant Virology'** is being presented. It embodies—different chapters covering all the subject sub disciplines of Plant Virology. The book has been written in simple language and suitable illustrations have been given so as to make the book more useful for beginners and post graduate students alike.

The special mention has been made on different diseases of economic importance so as to popularize the students with different virus diseases. Safety is utmost requirement in laboratory while working with different expensive and sophisticated instruments, glassware, hot water bath, reagents, chemicals and media ; therefore, laboratory guidelines have also been given in the book for beginners.

Precautions have been taken to discuss each topic in systematic manner and avoid mistakes ; still omissions and mistakes are bound to be found in this attempt. I wish to express my deep sense of gratitude to the pioneers and authors whose illustrations and reviewed work have been fully utilized with some additions and modifications in preparation of this book.

I am extremely grateful to Dr. P.K. Singh, Vice Chancellor and Dr. K.D. Upadhyay, Dean (Agriculture), C.S. Azad University of Agriculture & Technology, Kanpur for acceleration in quality research, teaching and extension which inspired me to write this book.

I owe deep debt of gratitude to all the members of the Department of Plant Pathology, C.S.A. University of Agriculture and Technology, Kanpur (U.P.) alongwith Dr. M.S. Kulkarni, Associate Professor, College of Horticulture, Arabhavi, University of Agricultural Sciences, Dharwad (Karnataka) and Dr. A.P. Bhagat, Senior scientist, Rajendra Agricultural University, Bihar for necessary help they have given time to time.

Thankful acknowledgement is also due for the help and suggestions received from National Professor Anupam Varma, Dr. D.V. Singh (Head), Professor Y.S. Ahlawat, Dr. R.K. Jain., Dr. F.R. Niazi, Dr. N.K. Chakraborty, Dr. M. Dutta, Dr. Shelly Praveen, Dr. P. Ramchandran, Dr. V.G. Malathi, Dr. V.K. Baranwal, Dr. Jasbir Singh and Miss Sahana Majumdar of Division of Plant Pathology, Indian Agricultural Research Institute, New Delhi.

Sri Vibhuti Pandey, Mrs. Kalpanarani and Sri Sandeep Rajani who worked hard untiringly in making illustrations and assisting in typing of the manuscript, deserve words of special mention and appreciation.

At last but not least, I thank to M/s Kalyani Publishers for untiring efforts in bringing out the book in such a form timely. I hope the book in present form will fulfill the desirable needs of the students and teachers alike. Constructive suggestions from readers, if any, will be highly appreciated and incorporated in future editions of the book. The book is expected to receive wide acclaim through out the country.

Plant Virology Research Laboratory, **—D.P. Tripathi**
Department of Plant Pathology.
C.S. Azad University of Agriculture and Technology.
Kanpur (U.P.)

PREFACE

Second Edition

Research and training in Plant Virology in India has made rapid strides during recent years. The first edition of the book entitled 'Introductory Plant Virology' was written to provide a concise introduction of applied Plant Virology to the undergraduate and post graduate students of General botany, Microbiology, Plant Pathology and Plant Virology covering courses in Plant Virology prescribed by most of the Indian Universities. Keeping in mind the teaching requirements and demand of the book, it was desirable to update this book so as to provide recent information of advancements made in the field of Plant Virology.

In this edition, all the chapters of the book have been updated by incorporating research work scattered in various journals. Besides, four new chapters including three-dealing with virus like symptoms producing phytopathogenic organisms-Viroids, Phytoplasma and Spiroplasma ; and the fourth chapter, dealing with 'Diseases of medicinal plants' have been included, so as to make the book all in one.

I offer my felicitation to the scientists and pioneers working in the field of Plant Virology whose contributions have been utilized to bring out this updated edition. I am confident that this edition will prove very useful to the students as a text book and to the scientists as a valuable reference.

I am indebted to Dr. V.K. Suri, Vice Chancellor, Dr. A.N. Tiwari, Dean (Agriculture) and Dr. K.D. Upadhyay (ex Dean-Agriculture) of C.S. Azad University of Agriculture and Technology, Kanpur ; to all the members of Advanced Center of Plant Virology, Division of Mycology & Plant Pathology, Indian Agricultural Research Institute, New Delhi and to the members of Department of Plant Pathology C.S. Azad University of Agriculture and Technology, Kanpur for their help in different ways.

I hope the book will acclaim wide circulation through out the country.

D.P. TRIPATHI

e-mail : dptripathi1945@ rediffmail.com

Plant Virology Research Laboratory,
C.S.A University of Agriculture & Technology,
Kanpur–208002 (U.P.)

CONTENTS

Chapters	Pages

1

HISTORY OF PLANT VIRUSES

What are plant viruses, Characteristics of plant viruses, Difference among viruses and other cellular organisms, Difference between viruses and bacterial cells, Difference between viruses and plasmids, Viruses are living or non-living, Historical development of plant virology, Work done in India and economic impact of plant viruses.

Many of the plant diseases now known to be caused by viruses have been in existence for a very long time. It was only by the end of 19th century when work on diseases of plants caused by viruses started getting attention. As early as 1886, Adolf Mayer, who was Professor at Agricultural College and Director of Experimental Station at Wageningen in Netherlands, observed for the first time a highly contagious disease of tobacco which could infect healthy plants by injecting diseased leaf extract (sap) to leaf veins of healthy tobacco plants. Later in 1889, Dimitry Ivanovsky confirmed the findings of Mayer regarding sap transmissible nature of the disease. He also observed that sap of diseased plant remained transmissible even after filtering it through bacterial filter paper but he did not differentiated it from bacterium. In 1898, a Dutch Professor named Martinus Beijerinck differentiated it from bacterium and named *cantagium vivum fluidum*. He further concluded that *contagium vivum fluidum* was able to reproduce itself in living plants and referred it as virus. Beijerinck is, therefore, rightly considered as Father of Plant Virology which is a branch of botanical or agricultural science dealing with different aspects of plant viruses including diseases caused by them.

❍ What are plant viruses !

During the 18th century, a Dictionary referred the term virus having meaning the poison, venom and also a kind of watery matter. The term virus, the Latin word for poison or slimy liquid was used from centuries to mean any toxious entity. With the advancement of knowledge, Bawden (1950) working with viruses described a virus as an obligatory parasitic pathogen with dimensions of less than 200 nm. After few years, Lwoff and Tournier (1966) described five characteristics to explain the nature of a virus. Those characteristics were (1) Viruses possessed only one type of nucleic acid-ribonucleic acid (RNA) or deoxyribonucleic acid (DNA), (2) They reproduced from their sole nucleic acid, (3) They could not grow and were unable to divide by binary fission, (4) They did not contain any system to generate high potential energy and (5) They used ribosome of the host to carry on reproduction.

After few years, Matthews (1970) modified specific characteristics of viruses suggested by Lwoff and Tournier. He emphasized that (1) viruses possessed only one type of nucleic acid *i.e.* RNA or DNA as the genetic material, (2) genetic material could occur as one or more nucleic acid molecules encaged within a protective protein or lipoprotein shell. Each nucleic acid molecule may be encapsidated in a separate sheath or all nucleic acids may be encaged in the same particle, (3) they could replicate only in the presence of intracellular ribosome, transfer RNA and energy generating system within a suitable host under favourable environment, (4) some also require the presence of other viruses, (5) they could cause discase at least in one host under favourable environment.

It is difficult to formulate any one definition of viruses. Therefore, viruses may be defined keeping in view the cardinal properties usually considered characteristics of viruses. These are, first, their extremely small size which is below the resolving power of the ordinary microscope, secondly, their ability to pass through pores of a filter candle which is impermeable to visible bacteria, and thirdly, their inability to multiply in the absence of the living cell.

On the basis of the cardinal and general characteristics given above, Matthews (1981) defined plant viruses more specifically as under :

'A set of one or more nucleic acid template molecules normally encaged in a protective coat or coats of protein or lipoprotein which is able to organize its own replication only in suitable host cells. Within such cells virus production is (a) dependent on the host protein synthesizing machinery, (b) organized from pools of the required materials rather than by binary fission, and (c) located at sites which are not separated from the host cells.'

Gibbs and Harrison in 1976 explained viruses in such a way which include most of the viruses and viroids as smallest known pathogens. They attempted to define plant viruses in more comprehensive way as under :

'Viruses are transmissible parasites whose nucleic acid genome is less than 3×10^{-8} *Da in weight and that need ribosome and other components of the host cells for multiplication.'*

From above descriptions and explanations, it can be concluded that most of the scientists consider viruses having similar characteristics and biological relationships. Characteristics, their physiochemical properties and biological relationships described above are comprehensive enough to give a clear concept about the viruses. Therefore, the simplest, expressive and comprehensive definition of viruses may be given as under keeping in view the specific characteristics described by different scientists.

'Viruses are super molecular complexes that behave as living organisms in appropriate host cells where they replicate and cause diseases of different deseriptions. They consist of a nucleic acid core (DNA or RNA) surrounded by a protein capsid or in some cases a membraneous envelope.'

❍ Characteristics of viruses

Viruses have some distinguishing characteristics which may be summarized as under :

(1) Basically, the plant virus particles consist of infectious nucleic acid known as genome. Genome is usually found encapsidated within a protective coat or shell (Crick and Watson, 1956).

(2) The genome which carries the genetic information necessary for virus replication, is composed of ribonucleic acid (RNA) in most plant viruses but may consist of deoxyribonucleic acid (DNA) in members of *Caulimovirus* and *Geminivirus* groups. Both RNA and DNA may be found in some rare viruses as in *Rice tungru virus* (RTV).

(3) The viruses are macro molecules and differ from eukaryotes and prokaryotes. They behave as living organisms in appropriate host cells.

(4) The RNA and DNA present in viruses may be single stranded (ss) or double stranded (ds).

(5) They may give rise to variants through various kinds of changes in virus nucleic acid (Hull, 2002).

(6) Nucleic acid genome in RNA viruses may be composed of single molecular species (mono-partite). However, some RNA or DNA viruses may have two (bi-partite) or more molecular species of nucleic acid (multi-partite). Genomes with more than one molecular species of RNA usually require the presence of all the major genomic components for complete infectivity.

(7) Plant viruses vary considerably in the relative amount of nucleic acid and protein they contain. Viruses with isometric particles may contain 15-45% nucleic acid whereas viruses with rod shaped particles have only 5% nucleic acid.

(8) All viruses are obligate parasites. Their particles contain various amounts of ions, polyamines, enzymes and water in suspension.

(9) In addition to multi component genome, some other complex genomic systems may occur in some plant viruses. These control or modify the infection process as observed in case of satellite viruses. The term virus satellite was first used to describe the small spherical virus associated with *Tobacco necrosis virus* (Kassanis, 1962). In this virus the larger particles (30 nm in diameter) are able to replicte from their own nucleic acid genome ; however, the small particles function as satellite in the host plant and are dependent upon the whole virus genome for replication. *Tobacco* necrosis virus (TNV) and satellite tobacco necrosis virus (STNV) are not serologically related.

(10) Spread of viruses in plants is fundamental to most of the plant viruses. When a virus is introduced into the leaf epidermal or mesophyll tissues of a susceptible host plant by mechanical abrasion or by insect vector, a focus infection is established from where it invades neighbouring cells through the process of local spread.

(11) During local spread, the virus or its nucleic acid usually crosses the cell wall from infected to uninfected cells through the channel known as plasmodesmata. Plasmodesmata provides continuous intra-cellular connections through out the tissue of the plant. After infection, the plasmodesmata shows extensive modifications in its tissues such as increased width to facilitate accommodation of virus particles and increased plasmodermal tube in length so that it may invade the space of the two neighbouring cells in each direction distorting their plasma membrane.

(12) All the plant viruses are transmissible from diseased plant to healthy plants through the means of mechanical, biological or insect vectors.

(13) Most of the plant viruses have antigenic property to induce antibodies production in mammals.

(14) Plant viruses have capacity of mutability for developing virus strains.

(15) Plant viruses may be purified and crystallized. Their infectivity is retained even after crystallization.

(16) Viruses vary considerably in size and complexity. The genome can vary in size from single gene to more than 200 genes. For example, the genomes of nanoviruses and the satellite virus of *Tobacco necrosis virus* encode a single protein whereas many others may code for as many as 800 proteins.

(17) The majority of plant viruses possess minus (—) strand (messenger sense) ssRNA genomes. Viruses with dsRNA or minus (—) strand ssRNA package their RNA-dependent RNA polymerase in their virions so that mRNAs are transcribed from the viral genomes and released from the virions.

❍ Difference among Viruses and other Cellular Parasites

Three simplest kinds of parasitic cells namely, phytoplasmas, rickettsia and chlamydiae differ from plant viruses, remain invisible by light microscope and measure usually 150 to 300 nm in size. Phytoplasmas have bilayer membrane but no cell wall. They contain ribosome and DNA and replicate by binary fission. Some of them that infect vegetables may be grown *in vitro* and are inhibited by some antibiotics.

The rickettsia are small, non-motile bacteria, measuring about 300 nm in diameter. They have cell wall, plasma membrane and cytoplasm with ribosome and DNA strands. They are obligate parasites and are definitely cells because they multiply by binary fission.

The Chlamydiae include the simplest known kind of cells. They are obligate parasites and lack an energy generating system. They have two phases of their life cycle. Outside the host cell, they exist as infectious elementary bodies, measuring about 300 nm in diameter. Their bodies have no cell wall and are specialized for extra-cellular survival. The elementary body enters the host cell (phagocytosis) and within eight hours it is converted into a much larger infectious reticulate body which is bounded by a bilayer membrane derived from the host. The reticulate body divides by binary fission within this membrane, giving thousands of progeny within 40 to 60 hours.

❍ Difference between Viruses and Bacterial Cells

Viruses differ from all other cells and can be easily distinguished in following ways as observed by Matthews (1981) :

1. In viruses, there is lack of a continuous membrane separating viral parasite

and host during intracellular replication. However, cellular parasites that replicate inside a host cell appear always to be separated from host cell cytoplasm by a continuous bilayer membrane.

2. Absence of the protein synthesizing system in viruses.
3. Replication of viruses is by synthesis of a pool of components followed by assembly of many virus particles from the pool. In bacteria, even the simplest cell replicates by binary fission.

❍ Difference between Viruses and Plasmids

Plasmids are small circular molecules of DNA, usually found in bacteria that exist separate from the bacterial chromosomes. In nature, plasmids sometimes carry genes that are responsible for the spread of antibiotic resistance among bacteria. Viruses differ from plasmids in following respects :

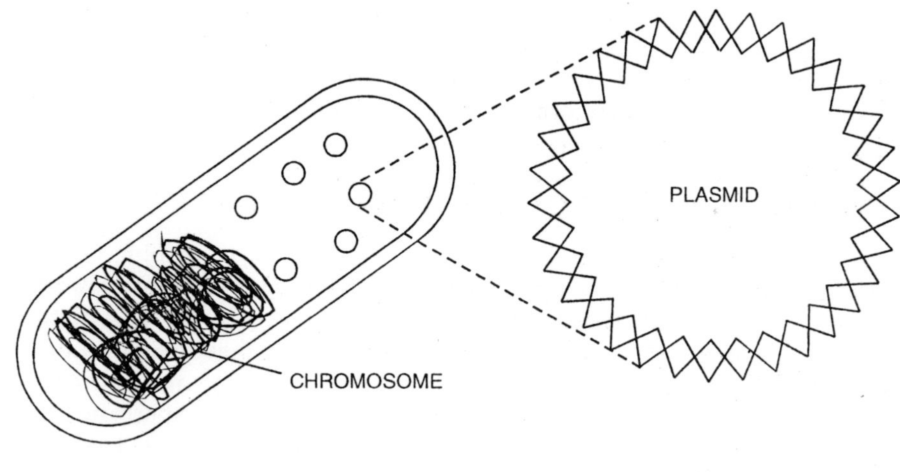

Fig. 1.1. Showing *E. Coli*—bacterium with plasmid as extra chromosomal DNA (diagramatic).

1. Normal viruses have a particle with a structure designed to protect the genetic material in the extra cellular environment and to facilitate entry into a new host cell.
2. Virus genomes are highly organized for specified virus functions of not known value to the host cell, whereas plasmids consist of bacterial genetic material often useful for survival of the host.
3. Viruses can cause death of cells or disease in the host plant but plasmids can not.

❍ Viruses are living or non-living

Arguments often arise as to whether viruses are living or non-living in nature. In this respect, Matthews listed three major criteria that separate all viruses from all cells ; first the viruses lack the protein synthesizing system, second-viruses multiply via synthesis of a pool of viral components followed by assembly into virions, and third-viruses lack a continuous bilayered membrane separating them from the hosts during multiplication. Further more, viruses lack the machinery of all living cells and so are dependent on living host cells for their multiplication.

On the basis stated above we can conclude that viruses do not fulfill the above three criteria so they are non-living. However, viruses like living cells, have nucleic acid genomes and are capable for mediating their own multiplication inside the host. Further more, viral genomes undergo mutation and are thus able to adopt some changes. Besides these, they are influenced by different physical environments including light, temperature and pH etc. With these attributes viruses may be considered as a part of living world leading a borrowed life. Even then, viruses are not considered as organisms because they can be crystallized in the laboratory and in that state may remain infective even after crystallization and thus behaving like chemical or molecule.

In this way viruses are non-living molecular pathogens outside the host which function as living organisms inside the host. As we are concerned with the host-pathogen relationship, therefore, we may consider viruses as living and their chemical or molecular existence outside the host may be assumed as their inactive period essential for survival.

HISTORICAL DEVELOPMENT OF PLANT VIROLOGY

During the 17th century in Holland, colour variegation or striping of tulip petals in plants infected with *Tulip mosaic virus* were much liked by then tulip growers because of their attractive colouration. History reveals that pictures painted by artists in those days illustrated the distinct symptoms of the petal break disease now known to be incited by viruses. Some of the common viral diseases although not recognized to be serious, were observed quite early but they could not get due importance before the studies made by Adolf Mayer who published his research work in 1986. Mayer named the disease as *Mosaikkankheit* (Mosaic like) for the mosaic like pattern on leaves of diseased plants. It was 1886 when the science of plant viruses—the **Plant Virology** is thought to have been born. The word virus at the beginning of 19th century included every thing from toxin to bacteria. In order to differentiate the new infectious agent causing mosaic, the term *filtrate virus* was used. The term filtrate virus survived for many years till the discovery of Mulvania (1926) & Smith and Doncaster (1935). They observed its ability to pass through a bacterial filter.

There were contradictory statements about the causal agent of tobacco mosaic type diseases. Some scientists implicated enzymes, some blamed on specific toxins while others believed that the disease was caused by defective nutrition of the young and the growing cells due to the lack of nitrogenous reserve food material accompanied by an abnormal increase in activity of oxidizing enzymes in the diseased plants.

Till the year 1935, the main emphasis in virus research was confined to the description of the disease, search for insect vectors and properties of the virus. The proteinaceous nature of the virus was first demonstrated by Stanley (1935) when he isolated *Tobacco mosaic virus* (TMV) in a crystalline form. Later in 1936, Bawden and his associates described the nature of TMV as nucleoprotein.

Important events in the development of Plant Virology may be summarized as under :

Iwanowski (1892) demonstraed that diseased sap of infected tobacco plants was infective even after it was passed through the bacterial proof filter. Beijerinck (1898) referred the name virus for the first time, therefore, he is considered as the Father of Plant Virology. Ball (1906 and 1917) demonstrated transmission of a virus disease by a leaf hopper (*Circulifer tenellus*). Nishimura (1918) demonstrated virus infected symptom-less plants. Schultz, Folsom and Murphy (1923) identified aphids as virus vectors. Carsner (1925) and Johnson (1926) observed mutability in viruses resulting in development of strains. Beale (1928) observed that plants infected with TMV contain a specific antigen. McKinney (1929) and Thung (1931) reported cross protection method of disease management. Smith (1931) reported use of indicator plants for the separation and identification of different viruses. Knolland and Ruska (1932) invented the use of Electron microscope. Gratia (1933) showed that plants infected with different viruses contained different specific antigens. Chester (1935-36) showed that different strains of TMV and *Potato virus X* could be distinguished serologically. He also demonstrated that serological methods could be used to obtain a rough estimate of virus concentration. In 1935, Stanley crystallized *Tobacco mosaic virus* and showed the presence of protein in virus. Bawden *et al* (1936) reported that TMV is a nucleoprotein. Bawden and Pirie (1937) purified and crystallized *Tomato bushy stunt virus* and observed its morphology as three dimensional crystals. Kunkel (1937) first observed multiplication of *Aster yellows* in leaf hopper vector. Kausche *et al* (1939) first recorded electron micrograph of TMV. Fuchsia (1940) studied transmission of *Rice dwarf virus*. Bernal and Fankuchen (1941) studied organization of TMV by X-ray diffraction. William and Wycoff (1944 and 1946) developed shadow casting technique of electron microscopy. Pease and Baker (1946) developed sectioning technique of electron microscopy. Brakke (1951 and 1953) developed technique entitled **Density gradient centrifugation.** Black and Brakke (1952) demonstrated that *Wound tumor virus* multiplies in its leaf hopper vector. Morel and Martin (1952) showed that virus free plants could be obtained from infected parents using meristem tip culture method. Kassnis (1954) demonstrated that virus could be eradicated from infected plants by high temperature treatments. Crick and Watson (1957) formulated general theory about structure of viral capsid. Brandes (1957 and 1964) developed leaf dip procedure of electron microscopy for identification of rod shaped viruses. Bancoft and kaesberg (1958) observed that *Alfalfa mosaic virus* is a multi component virus. Teakle (1960) observed transmission of *Tobacco necrosis virus* by zoospores of fungus–*Olpidium brassicae*. Anderer *et al* (1960) and Tsugita *et al* (1960) worked out sequence of amino acid arrangement in protein molecule of TMV coat protein. Klug and Finch (1960) confirmed that spherical viruses like *Turnip yellow mosaic, Tomato bushy stunt* and *Southern bean mosaic* are icosahedral in symmetry by X-ray diffraction studies. Kassanis and Nixon (1962) reported *Tobacco necrosis virus* as satellite virus. Black and Markham (1963) reported *Wound tumor virus* to contain double stranded RNA. Gierer and Schramm (1966) reported that infectivity of TMV resides in its RNA. Lister (1966, 1968) reported that the use of **density gradient centrifugation** and **acrylamide gel fractionation techniques** have allowed many viruses with multipartite genome to be characterised.

Fig. Pioneers in the field of Plant Virology.

Another important development has been the use of protein synthesizing system from wheat germ in which plant viral RNAs act as efficient messengers. Their use has allowed a beginning to be made on the mapping of the plant viral genomes by biochemical means.

Doi *et al* (1967) reported mycoplasma like organisms (now called as phytoplasmas), being the causal agents of plant diseases producing symptoms like viruses. Shepherd *et al* (1968) reported that *Cauliflower mosaic virus* contains DNA as nucleic acid. Butler (1970) and Wu and Bruening (1971) reported that capsids of *Turnip crinkle virus, Tomato bushy stunt virus* and *Cowpea mosaic virus* are composed of two or three types of polypeptide chains. Diener and Raymer (1967) and Diener and Smith (1971) reported that potato spindle tuber disease is caused by a free nucleic acid (viroids). Hirai and Wildman (1969) and Hagiladi *et al* (1975) reported that TMV inhibits transcription of chlorophyll. Harrison *et al* (1971) classified plant viruses into sixteen groups. Butler and Klug (1971), Ohno *et al* (1971) and Durham *et al* (1971) reported that double disc aggregates of TMV protein which sediment at 20-25 S interact with 5′-end of TMV RNA and initiate virus assembly. Franski (1973) created plant rhabdovirus group. Nienhaus and Sikora (1979) reported rickettsia like organisms as causal agents of plant diseases. Goheen *et al* (1973) reported that Pieree's disease of grapevine and alfalfa dwarf are caused by rickettsia like organisms. Hewitt *et al* (1958) and Grogen *et al* (1958) opened the way for possible control of a series of plant viral diseases by finding effective resistance and tolerance in varieties against viruses. Jonard *et al* (1975) and Guilley *et al* (1975) reported that replication initiating site of TMV RNA appears to be constituted by a sequence of 103 nucleotides that represent a part of the coat protein cistron. Clark and Adam (1977) developed *Enzyme linked immunosorbent assay* (ELISA) technique for detection of viruses. Dietzen *et al* (1982) reported use of monoclonal antibodies for detection of *Tobacco mosaic virus.*

In recent years, it has become increasingly apparent that effective control of virus diseases in a particular crop and in a given area usually requires an integration and continuing programme involving more than one kind of control measures.

WORK DONE IN INDIA

Research in plant virology has been done exclusively at Indian Agricultural Research Institute, New Delhi ; University of Agricultural Sciences, Bangalore (Karnataka) ; National Botanical Research Institute, Lucknow (U.P.) ; ICRISAT, Hyderabad (A.P) ; Central Potato Research Institute, Shimla (H.P.) and at various Agricultural Universities of the country. Some of the important contributions in the field of plant virology may be summarized as under :

V.V. Chenulu and S.P. Raychaudhary reported many important viral diseases of plants of economic importance. In 1958, Azad and Sehgal studied some important viral diseases and suggested control measures theirof. Viral and phytyoplasma's diseases of some temperate fruits were further studied by S.P. Raychaudhary, D.C. Sharma and V.K. Giri in 1971. Phyllody disease of Toria was recognized by Vasudeva and Sahambi (1955) and Kaushik *et al* (1978). They also studied symptomatology of *Mungbean yellow mosaic geminivirus* and observed the virus to be quisi-isometric in morphology and transmissible by whitefly. B.B. Nagaich and K.S. Bashishtha (1965) studied some additional virus diseases of temperate fruits in Shimla hills (H.P.). B.B. Nagaich and

S.M. Paul Khurana contributed management of viral diseases of potato. In West Bengal, Shankar Mukhopdhyay studied vector ecology of white fly transmitted viral diseases of vegetables and rice tungru disease. Work done by M.D. Misra on rice tungru is worth commendable. Works on control measures have also been done in our country. K.S. Bhargava and S.M.Paul Khurana (1969) identified efficacy of oil sprays in management of papaya mosaic disease. Khan and Mukhopdhyay (1985) studied the effect of cultural methods on the incidence of yellow vein mosaic disease of okra. Nagarajan and Ramkrishna (1971) studied cucumber viruses in Chennai and Pathak (1974) described seed borne plant viruses, their identification and diagnostic seed health testing. D.V.R. Reddy and his associates reported the occurrence of *Peanut mottle virus* and described its economic importance from International Crop Research Institute for Semi Arid Tropics (ICRISAT), Hyderabad. In Uttar Pradesh, K.S. Bhargava studied *Cucumber mosaic virus* and *Sugarcane mosaic virus* in detail. In order to manage different viral diseases, G.S. Verma and H.N. Verma contributed the importance of antiviral proteins.

Besides above works of significance, notable contributions have been made by S.P. Raychaudhary, Aupam Varma, Y.S. Ahlawat and R.K. Jain in the field of plant virology. They have reported a large number of plant viral diseases of economic importance. For extensive and advanced research in plant virology, an *Advanced Center of Plant Virology* was established at I.A.R.I., New Delhi in 1988. Research on different aspects of plant virology, chiefly the molecular studies of viruses is being done at this center. The center is also offering short term and long term training to virologists working in different parts of the country to accelerate research in the field of plant virology.

ECONOMIC IMPACT OF PLANT VIRUSES

Most except few economically important crop plants may become infected with viruses. Virus diseases affect adversely, causing reduction in yield and quality of the produce. The extent of losses depend on many factors and vary widely in different ways as summarized below :

1. Viruses seldom kill plants outright but viral disease outbreak during vulnerable stages of crop growth may cause crop failure. Vegetatively propagated crops like potato, sugarcane, banana and citrus trees may suffer severe loss if raised from infected propagating materials.
2. Effect of viruses on crop losses is usually sudden in annuals because damages are caused within the brief span of cropping season.
3. In perennials, the process of loss is slower and the effect may be more disastrous in the long run. The grower not only loses the immediate yield but also he is bound to invest for replacement of the diseased plants and wait for the returns till they become productive.
4. There are numerous examples of severe crop losses due to virus diseases. Nearly 75% of the sweet orange trees were destroyed by the *Citrus tristeza virus* at San Paul state in Brazil within a period of 12 years (Bos L., 1982).
5. *Cacao swollen shoot virus* has been a menace to the cacao plantation in West Africa years ago. In Ghana, more than 100 million cacao trees have been cut down since 1945 so as to stop the spread of the disease.

6. The nematode-borne *Grapevine fan leaf virus*, found in many parts of the world, have been observed to reduce yield of grapes by 10 to 20%.
7. Sugar beet crops in Europe and America have suffered serious losses due to *Sugar beet yellows* for many years. Total losses due to this disease in Britain were estimated to be about 1,000,000 tons in 1957.
8. The fungus borne *Wheat mosaic virus* and the mite borne *Wheat streak mosaic virus* have caused huge losses of wheat in some states of North America in certain years.
9. *Barley yellow dwarf virus* disease has proved to be a potential menace to wheat, barley and oats in many temperate countries with large scale outbreaks.
10. Virus diseases in potato remained a major constraint to potato cultivation in various parts of the world. In India, losses in potato yield have been estimated to be 20 to 35% due to *Potato leaf roll virus* and *Potato virus Y* as reported by Nagaich and Agarwal in 1969.
11. *Tomato mosaic virus* caused a loss of 15 to 20% in yield to the crop as reported by Broad Bent (1976).
12. Infection of vegetatively propagated crops is wide spread and often every plant of a particular cultivar may be infected with one or more viruses.
13. In cereal crops, serious losses were caused by viruses in wheat at Kansas, U.S.A. in 1953. It was estimated that losses of $3,000,000 and $14,000,000 were caused by soil borne *Wheat mosaic virus* and *Wheat mosaic streak virus* respectively.
14. Loss estimated due to mustard mosaic virus in Indian mustard was reported by Vasudeva (1950) to be as high as 30 to 40% in Delhi.
15. The incidence of *Tobacco leaf curl virus* has been recorded upto 100% and yield loss may be upto 70% depending on the age of the crop at which infection occurs. Usually the loss in yield was observed to be higher if the infection occurs in early growth stage of the crop.
16. In a survey conducted in 8 districts of Karnataka, it was observed that the incidence of *Tomato leaf curl virus* ranged from 17 to 53% and upto 100% in crop growth in July—November and in February—May respectively. In Haryana, the disease incidence was found to be 100% in tomato variety HS—101 while 20 to 60% disease incidence was reported in other varieties like Pusa dwarf, Gold ruby and Estopal. In another survey in West Bengal, incidence ranged from 1-30% (Baranwal, 1996).
17. In India, various viral diseases like Yellow vein mosaic of okra, Papaya leaf curl, Sterility mosaic of pigeon pea and Mungbean yellow mosaic etc are causing considerable loss to the crop every year.
18. Incidence of leaf curl of American cotton was recorded as high as 60-95% during the year 1996 (Puri *et al* 1996).

Besides above, viruses are known to cause losses in different ways. A partial list of diseases causing considerable loss to different crops of economic importance may be summarized in following table.

Table 1.1 Partial list of diseases causing considerable loss to different crops.

Crop	Name of the virus	Yield reduction as reported
Apple	Mosaic	60% when 80% plants were affected in region of Philippines
Banana	Bunchy top	5000 Ac
Broad bean	Pea enation	50% of crops in affected region
Cacao	Swollen shoot	50% of mature trees on 250 acres in Ghana before 1954
Cassava	Mosaic	11% of the crop in Africa before 1956
Cherry	Yellows	50% of the infected trees before 1953
Cotton	Leaf crumple	80% in some fields in Arizona before 1985
Grape vine	Leaf roll	5% in California until 1970, 8% in USA during 1950
Lettuce	Tomato spotted wilt, Beet yellow stunt Necrotic yellows	50-90% 50-85% in affected field before 1972 50% of crop in South Australia before 1963
Melons	Zuccini yellow mosaic and water melon mosaic disease.	40-50% in deserts valleys of Southern CA during 1984
Orange	Tristeza	10 K trees in three provinces in Spain before 1988
Peach	Mosaic	200 K trees in South west USA before 1953
Peanut	Groundnut rosette	560,00 tons in Nigeria in 1975
Potato	Mild mosaic and leaf roll diseases	In Maine with secondary PVX infection before 1951 and 3% in USA in 1950.
Rice	Tungru	1% in Malaysia in 1981 to 1984 and 100% in Indonesia in 1971
Soybean	Viruses	0.76% in Southern USA average for 1974-1994
Spinach	Beet western	2% in USA in 1950
Sugar beet	Yellows Yellow vein	5% in England 1970-73 6% in USA in 1950 9% in Great Britain 1946-1962
Tomato	Spotted wilt Cucumber mosaic	75-100% in Ohio and Hawaii during 1940 30-60%

Crop	Name of the virus	Yield reduction as reported
Wheat	Barley yellow dwarf Streak mosaic Soil borne wheat mosaic	10 bu/Ac in Judith Valley Montana in 1980 7% of crop in Kansas in 1947 20% of crop in areas of 13 fields in NB 1972- 1974
Maize	Mosaic	90% yield loss in Argentina during 1983

From above brief descriptions, it can be concluded that viral diseases cause significant loss in yield of the crop every year. There are records of yield increase when virus was not present in greenhouse and fields trials. The data on such increase in yield as presented below is based on the book entitled "*Plant Virus Disease Control*" published by American Phytopathological Society, St. Paul, Minnesota, USA. in 1998.

Table 1.2 Yield Increase among crops when virus was not present in green house and fields.

Crop	Virus	Yield increase with their parameters
Apple	*Russet ring virus*	60%
Barley	*Barley yellow dwarf virus*	45-65% in two rows and six rows vars. in Montana.
Cotton	*Cucumber mosaic virus*	27%, no bolls from plants inoculated young in field.
Lettuce	*Lettuce leaf roll virus*	44% seed yields in green house trials.
Pepper	A virus	11-56% in 5-years trials
Potato	A virus	65-92% plants planted with infected tubers
Rice	*Rice tungru virus*	12-90% among 7 vars. inoculated one week after soaking
Strawberry	*Vein banding* and latent "C"	88% by third year after inoculation.
Sweet potato	Virus complex	25-35% among 4 cultivars in 1978 trials.
Tomato	*Cucumber mosaic virus*	19-52% among 6 sites in 1987 tirals.
Wheat	*Barley yellow dwarf virus* *Seed-borne wheat mosaic virus*	40-90% among plants in susceptible vars. Inoculated early. 0-80% among 53 cultivars in 1952 trials.

Thus we can conclude that by avoiding the occurrence of plant viruses, we can procure increased yield and improved quality of the produce.

2

MORPHOLOGY AND STRUCTURE

Introduction, Virus composition, Protein shell or capsid, Functions of viral capsid protein, Distinguishing characters, Specific characteristics, Amino acids in protein, Conjugated protein, Nucleic acid in virus, RNA and DNA are polynucleotides, Structure of DNA viruses, Structure of RNA viruses, Atomic structure of viruses, Two kinds of symmetry in plant virus structure, Shape and dimensions of plant virus particles. Key concept of plant virus structure and importance of understanding virus structure.

Every virus particle usually consists of one nucleic acid molecule integrated into the protein shell (capsid) formed of many identical protein molecules. In some viruses an additional membrane called envelop usually composed of lipid or lipo-protein may also be found. The protein shell serves to protect and package the nucleic acid. It gives resistance to proteases and tolerance to temperature. Thus the nucleocapsid is the structure composed of nucleic acid surrounded by capsid which is usually regarded as complete and common virus particle which lacks envelop. The proteinaceous nature of virus was first demonstrated by Stanley (1935) when he isolated *Tobacco mosaic virus* (TMV) in a crystalline form. In 1936, Bawden and his associates described TMV as nucleo-protein as shown below :

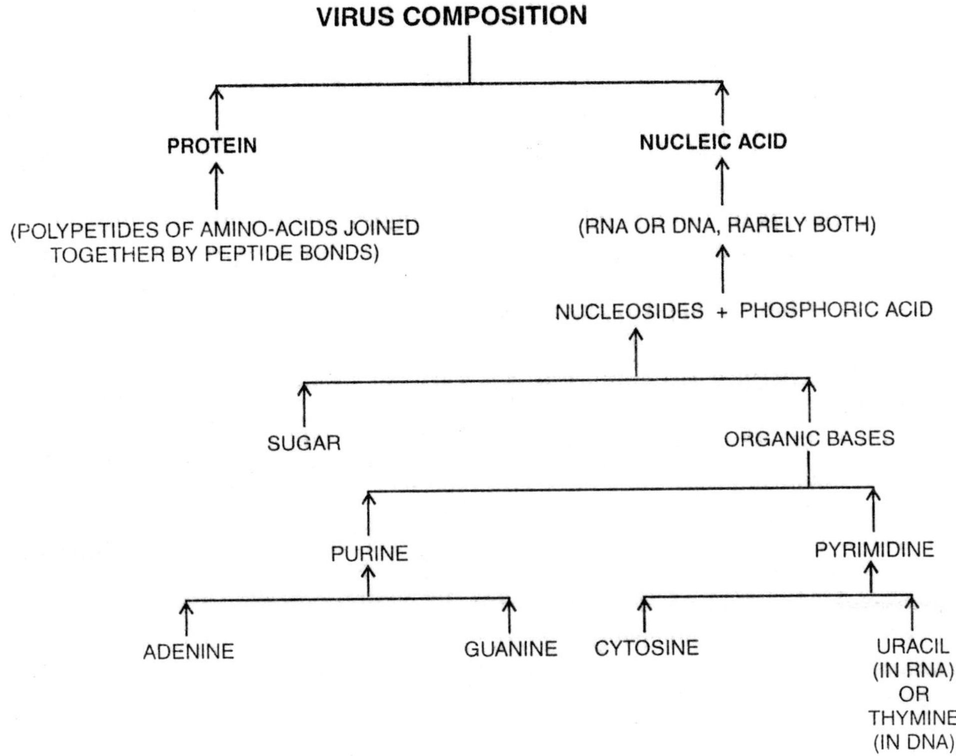

Fig. 2.1. Diagramatic representation of plant virus composition.

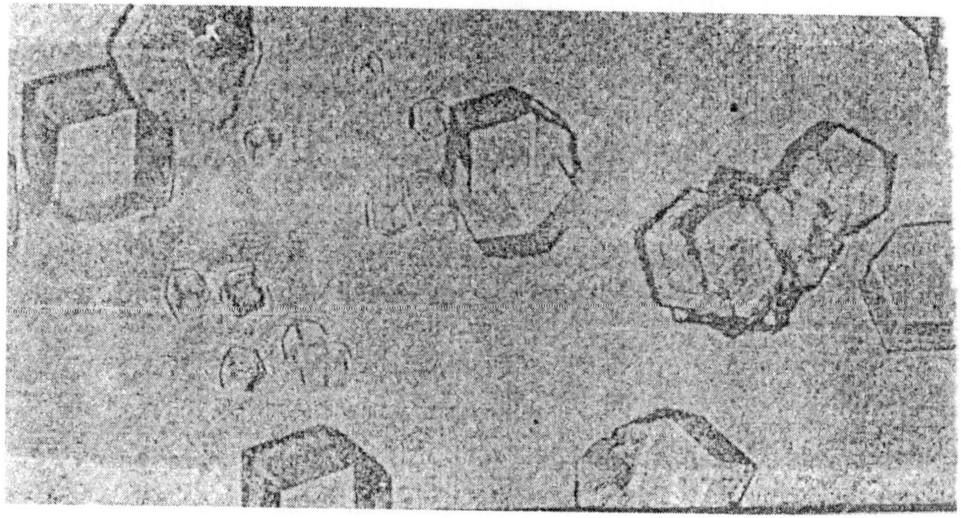

Fig. 2.2. Morphology of crystals of *Tomato bushy stunt* virus as seen under EM.

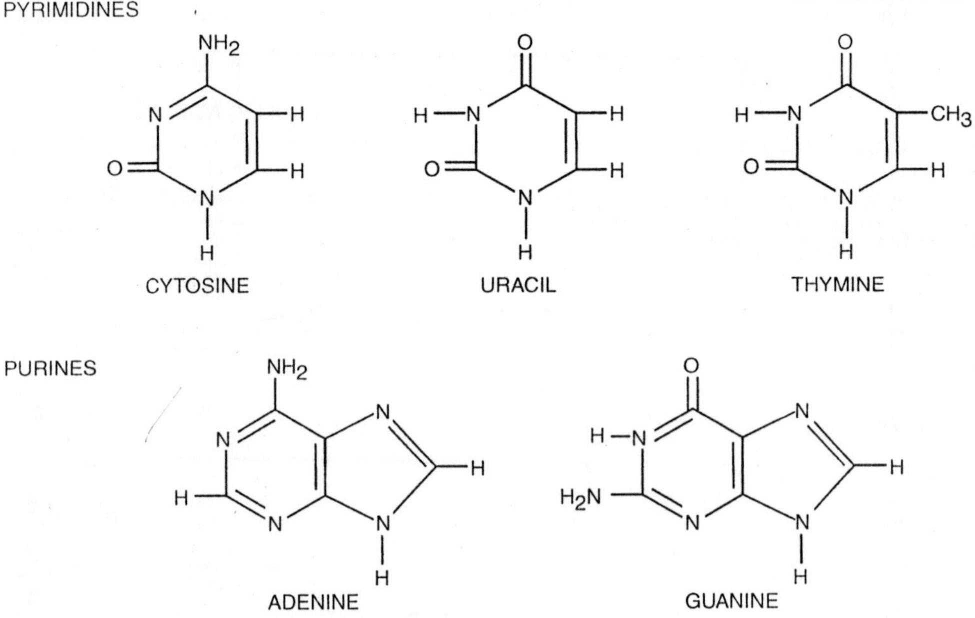

Fig. 2.3. Showing Chemical structure of adenine, guanine, cytocine, thymine and uracil,

❍ The Protein shell or Capsid

Crick and Watson (1956) were the first to suggest that protective protein coat of a virus was built up from a number of identical protein molecules or subunits packed together in a regular pattern. A protein molecule is the basic structural unit of the shell (capsid) of all the viruses. In helical viruses, protein subunits are joined together as individuals and in spherical viruses, 5 to 6 structural molecules are clustered together to form capsomers or clusters or groups. Structural units in both the helical and spherical viruses are also the morphological units.

❍ Function of Viral capsid proteins

The viral capsid proteins have some specific functions. Some most important functions of capsid proteins may be summarized in Table 2.1 as under :

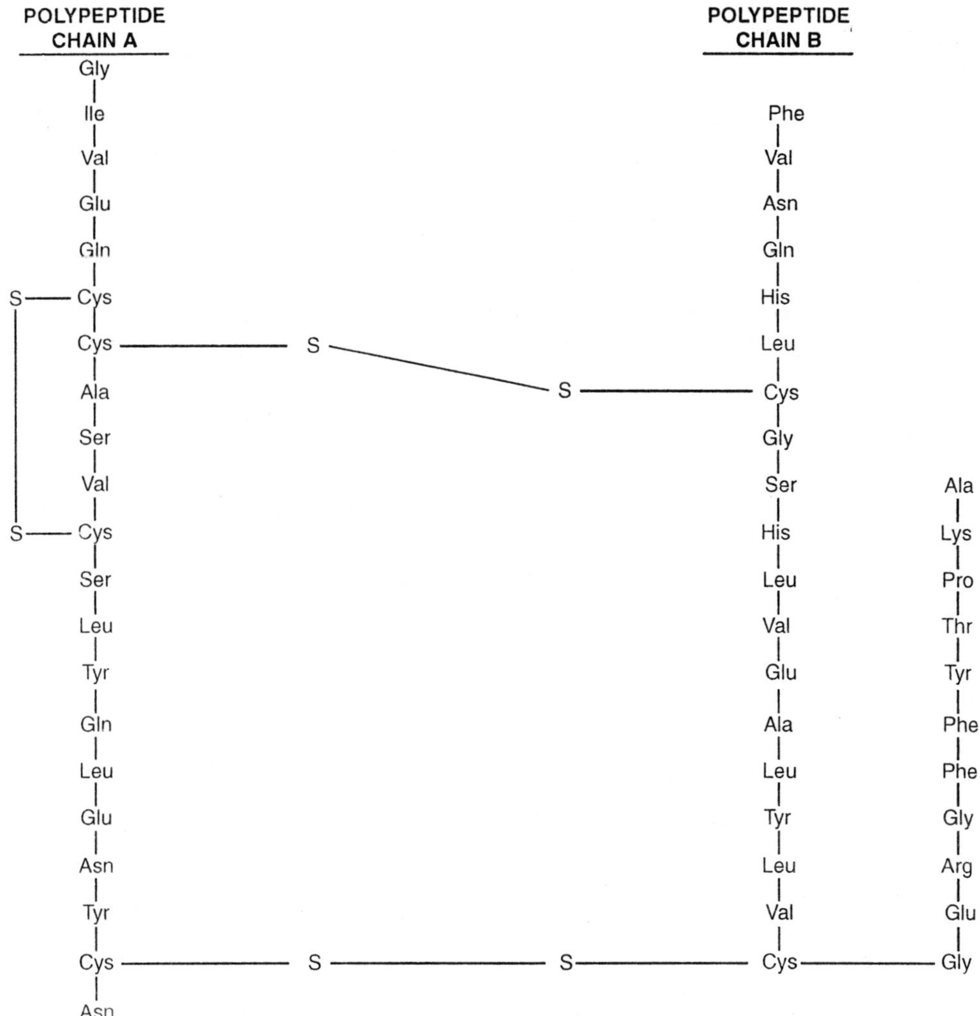

Fig. 2.4. Showing Chemical structure of a protein (beef insulin). The two polypeptide chains are linked through disulphide (-S-S-) bonds.

Table 2.1. **Specific functions of capsid protein surrounding the virus nucleic acid.**

Specific functions	Remarks about the functions
Assembly	Subunits usually assemble to form a protective shell for the nucleic acid.
Nucleic acid recognition and packing	Sub-units specifically package the viral nucleic acid.

Interaction with the host	(1) The capsid may participate in the viral infection process by binding to receptors and mediating cell entry in non-plant viruses. (2) Interactions between the virion and host cellular components may assist viral transport in plant viruses.
Mutations	Regions of some animal viruses are readily mutable producing changes in capsid structure that inhibit recognition by antibodies produced by previous infection or vaccination by another serotype.

❍ Distinguishing characteristics

1. Besides protecting delicate nucleic acid genomes, proteins provide the basis for serological determination of viruses. Proteins are condensation products of many amino acids linked by peptide bonds into linear macro molecules (Fig. 2.4).
2. Proteins are composed of about 150-600 or more residues of some 20 amino acids which are arranged in linear chain (Fig. 2.6).
3. The most plant viruses are built of one kind of protein sub-units.
4. A protein molecule is a poly-peptide chain formed by forging peptide linkage between constituent amino acid residues having four levels of structural organization (Fig. 2.5) as under.
   (*i*) Specific sequence of amino acids in a polypeptide chain is called primary structure (first level of protein organization).
   (*ii*) Spherical or spiral coiling of polypeptide chain represents secondary structure (second level of protein organization).
   (*iii*) Folding of polypeptide chain over itself represent tertiary structure (third level of protein organization).
   (*iv*) Besides, interrelationship and interaction of different poly peptide chains to one another in a complex protein is regarded as quaternary structure (fourth level of protein organization).
5. The structural complexity of protein increases from primary to tertiary structures due to the involvement of various types of bonds between different chemical groups. The primary structure of protein molecules results from strong covalent peptide bonds (- CO-NH-). In covalent bonding, a pair or pairs of electrons are shared equally between two atoms. The secondary and tertiary structures are formed by a few strong covalent disulphide (-S-S) bonds but mostly by a large number of weak hydrogen bonds (hydrogen atom-sharing electron with two oxygen atoms).
6. The linear polypeptide chain has two ends namely, a left handed amino or N-terminal end and right handed carboxyl or C- terminal end. The amino acids (nitrogenous) terminal end is more reactive than C-terminal end. The amino acids are joined sequentially beginning with N-terminal end and the synthesis proceeds towards C-terminus.

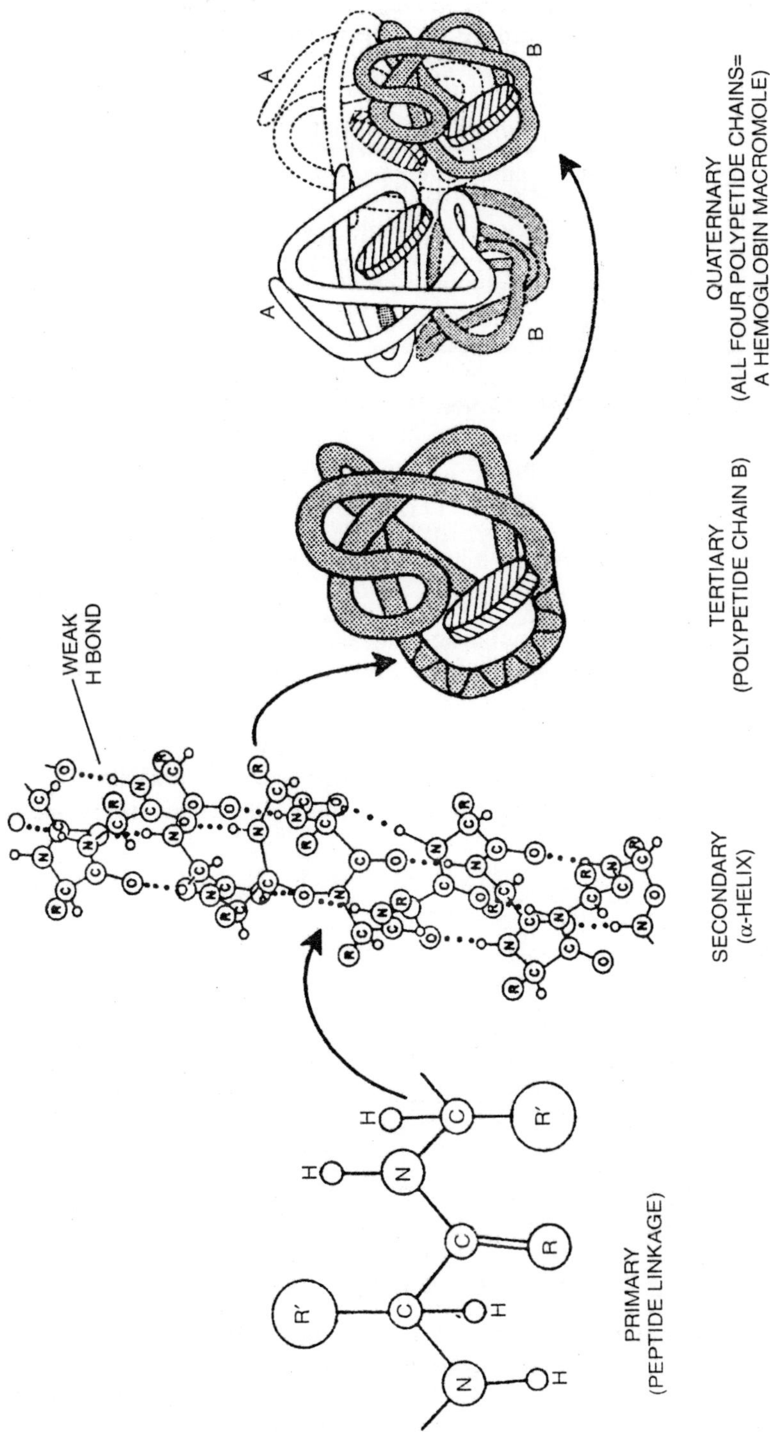

Fig. 2.5. Diagramatic representation of different levels of protein organization.

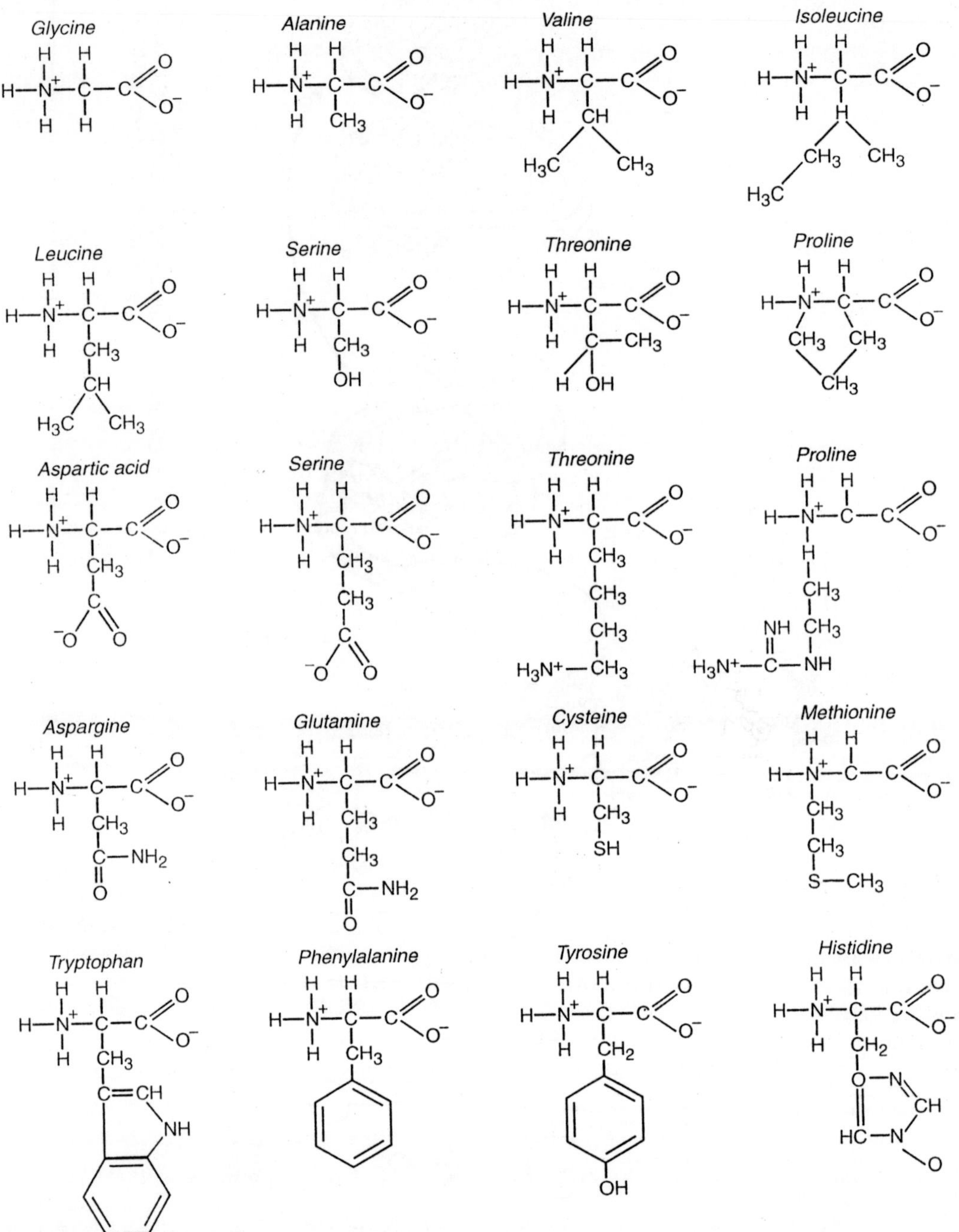

Fig. 2.6. Molecular structure of 20 important amino acids found in protein

7. The sequence of amino acids is determined by denaturing and cleaving of polypeptide chains using specific enzymes. Analysis of fragments is done by sequential removal and identifications of terminal amino acids.
8. During protein synthesis template is needed only for amino acid sequence.
9. When two dimensional primary structure of a polypeptide chain has been synthesized, it spontaneously and automatically folds up in a specific fashion to form the typical protein molecule.
10. The molecular weight of protein is estimated by ultracentrifugation and poly-acrylamide gel electrophoresis. The amino acid content is estimated by hydrolysis followed by chromatographic analysis.

❍ Specific Characteristics

Capsid protein does not differ in composition from other type of proteins in any fundamental way. However, in some cases some amino acids may be absent in virus protein. *Tobacco mosaic virus* (TMV) molecule lacks histidine and methionine which are found in others.

There are a few plant viruses such as *Potato yellow dwarf virus* and rhabdoviruses which contain complex protein configuration containing more than one type of poly-peptides resulting in quaternary structure. In rare cases, virus proteins are essential along with RNAs to cause infection as observed in some multipartite viruses like *Alfalfa mosaic virus* (Francki *et al*, 1985).

AMINO-ACIDS IN PROTEIN

Like other proteins, virus proteins are composed of amino acids. There are twenty different amino acids used as building block molecules for proteins. These amino acids are chemically different from each other but all of them possess (*i*) an amino (NH_2) group, (*ii*) a carboxyl (-COOH) group and (*iii*) the R group. The various R groups are responsible for the different properties of the amino acids (Fig. 2.6).

In all the 20 amino acids linkage is achieved through condensation. When amino acids join, the amino group of one forms a bond with the carboxyl group of the other. The resulting linkage is a peptide bond (-C-N-). The joining of amino acids such as valine-, glutamine-, tyrosine- and alanine result in a larger molecule called a polypeptide. When it has reached a length of 50 or so amino acids, it is generally regarded as a protein. The immense variety of proteins in living systems result from the kind of amino acids, their sequence in the polypeptide chains and also the three dimensional structure of the chain. The sequence of amino acids forms the structural backbone of proteins.

CONJUGATED PROTEINS

Proteins are often combined with non amino acid components to form conjugated proteins. Common example includes the nucleoproteins (nucleic acid + protein), the lipoprotein (lipids + protein), chromo proteins (pigments + proteins) and metalloid-proteins (heme or metal ions + protein). Heme is an iron-porphyrin substance in which four nitrogen containing pyrrole rings are linked to an iron (Fe) atom. Heme occurs in hemoglobin and in other biologically important pigments.

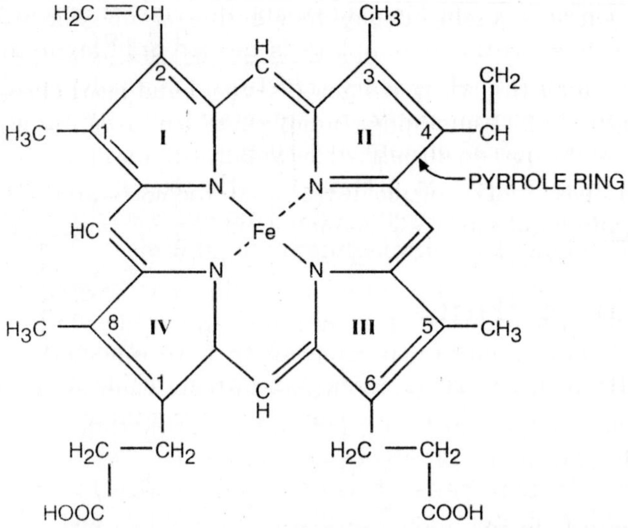

Fig. 2.7. Chemical structure of the heme molecule in which four nitrogen containing pyrrole rings with the central iron (Fe) atom is seen.

NUCLEIC ACIDS IN VIRUS

Nucleic acids are natural polymers. They fall into two major classes, namely, ribonucleic acids (RNA) and deoxyribonucleic acid (DNA), depending on whether their nucleotide components contain ribose or deoxyribose sugars. Another chemical difference between RNA and DNA involves the nitrogenous bases. Both the RNA and DNA contain four bases, in which three are common to both and only the fourth is found to be different. In RNA, uracil occurs but in DNA thymine is found in place of uracil. Nucleotides comprising RNA and DNA are as under :

RNA	
AMP	CMP
GMP	UMP

DNA	
dAMP	dCMP
dGMP	dTMP

In most of the plant viruses, the presence of ribonucleic acids (RNA) is very common whereas deoxyribonucleic acid (DNA) occurs in few viruses only. However, both RNA and DNA have also been observed in some plant viruses. The building block component of nucleic acids is called nucleotide. Each nucleotide consists of three substances which include (*i*) a nitrogenous base, (*ii*) a pentose sugar and (*iii*) a phosphate group. The nitrogenous bases fall into two groups—one is characterized by a purine ring and the other by the pyrimidine ring. Nucleotides are linked through their phosphate groups to form the poly-nucleotide strands characteristic of RNA and DNA. The bases project out from the sugar-phosphate backbone of the strands as shown below :

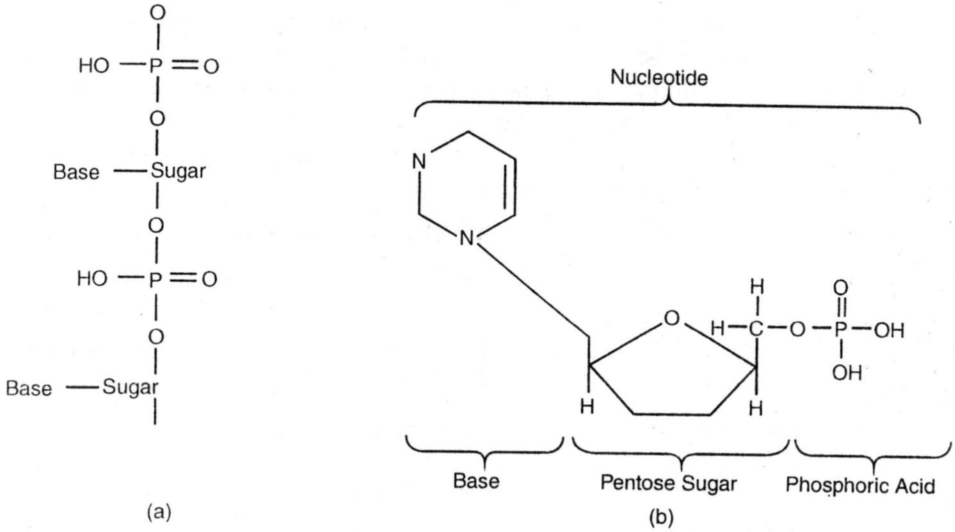

Fig. 2.8. (*a*) The sugar-phosphate backbone of nucleic acids.
(*b*) The basic chemical structure of a nucleotide

Purine (double-ring molecule) and pyrimidine (single-ring molecule) are two different types of heterocyclic and nitrogenous organic bases found in nucleic acids. Cytosine (C), thymine (T) and uracil (U) are the most common bases related with pyrimidine. Purine includes two types of bases known as adenine and guanine. Cytosine (C) and uracil (U) are found in RNA, whereas cytosine (C) and thymine (T) are found in DNA.

Adenine (A) and guanine (G) are the purines found both in RNA and DNA. The nucleotides vary in structure depending on their base and sugar components.

DNA AND RNA ARE POLY-NUCLEOTIDES

Deoxyribonucleic acid (DNA) and ribonucleic acid (RNA) are poly-nucleotides,

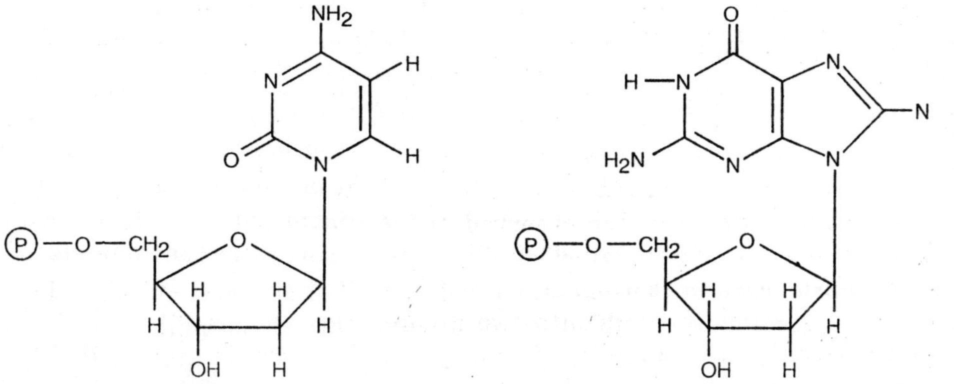

Fig. 2.9. Chemical structure of cytidine monophosphate (CMP) and Deoxyguanosine monophosphate (dGMP).

usually composed of many similar units of nucleotides. In deoxyribonucleic acid deoxyribose (2-deoxy D- ribose) and in ribonucleic acid (RNA) ribose (D-ribose) are found as pentose. Ribose has a hydroxyl (OH) group at positions 1′, 2′, 3′ and 5′, whereas deoxyribose lacks oxygen at 2 position. Eight different nucleotides as given below are commonly found in nucleic acids.

The nucleotides usually consist of several phosphate residues but in DNA and RNA, they are present only as monophosphates.

Base-sugar phosphate	Chemical name
Adenine-ribose-phosphate	Adenosine monophosphate (AMP)
Adenine-deoxyribose-phosphate	Deoxyadenosine monophosphate (dAMP)
Guanine-ribose-phosphate	Guanosine monophosphate (GMP)
Guanine-deoxyribose-phosphate	Deoxyguanosine monophosphate (dGMP)
Cytosine-ribose phosphate	Cytidine monophosphate (CMP)
Cytosine-deoxyribose-phosphate	Deoxycytidine monophosphate (dCMP)
Uracil-ribose-phosphate	Uridine monophosphate (UMP)
Thymine-deoxyribose-phosphate	Thymidinemonophosphate (dTMP)

POLYNUCLEOTIDE AND PHOSPHODIESTER BOND

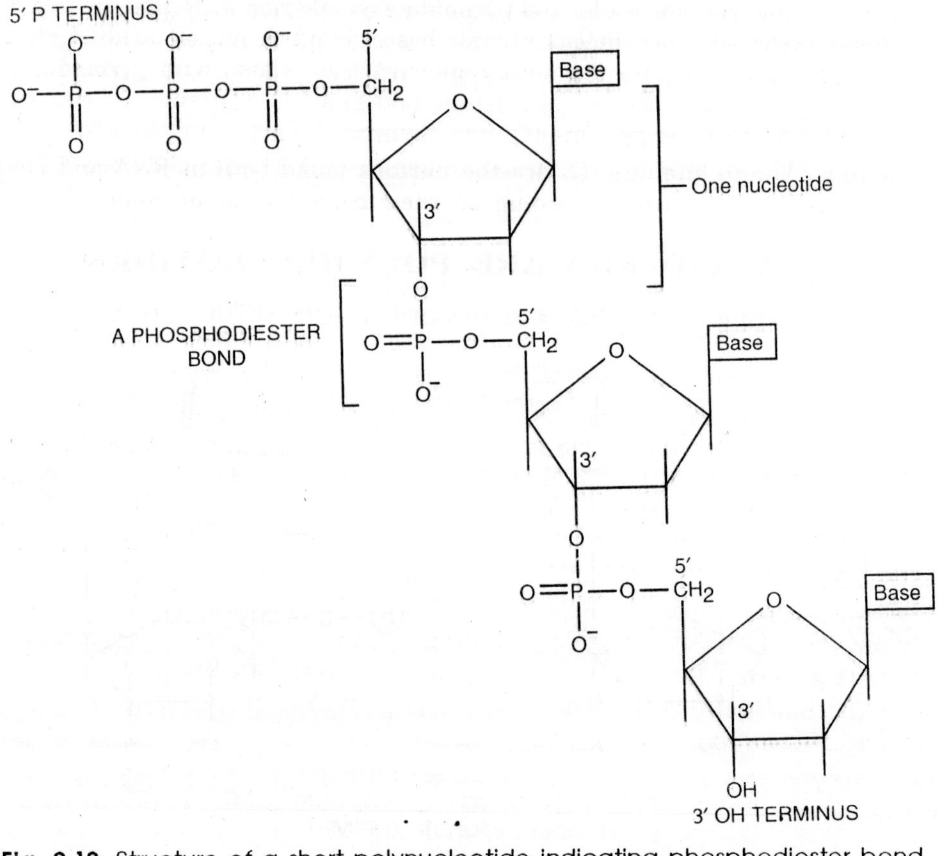

5′ P TERMINUS
One nucleotide
A PHOSPHODIESTER BOND
3′ OH TERMINUS

Fig. 2.10. Structure of a short polynucleotide indicating phosphodiester bond.

Individual nucleotides join together to form a polymer. This polymer is called as polynucleotide and is formed by attaching one nucleotide to another by way of phosphate group. The nucleotide monomers are linked together by joining the phosphate (α) group attached to the 5′ carbon of one nucleotide to the 3′ carbon of the next nucleotide in the chain. The linkage between the nucleotides in a polynucleotide is called a phosphodiester bond. In phosphodiaster bond, phospho-indicates the presence of phosphorus atom and diester refers to the two ester (C-O-P) bonds in each linkage. This may also be called as 3′–5′ phosphodiester bond.

The chemical distinction between the two ends means that polynucleotides have direction which can be looked on as 5′ to 3′ or 3′ to 5′. The direction of the nucleotide is important in molecular biology.

All plant viruses usually contain only one type of nucleic acid in each particle. The plant viruses except very few contain RNA as the nucleic acid. Most of the viruses are single stranded except few which are double stranded such as *Rice dwarf virus*.

STRUCTURE OF DNA IN VIRUSES

J. Watson and F. Crick in 1953, after studying X-ray diffraction, proposed that the DNA macromolecule actually consisted of two parallel polynucleotide strands winding in such a spiral manner which forms a double stranded helix. They observed that

(1) DNA double helix comprises of two polynucleotide chains.

(2) The nitrogenous bases are stacked on the inside of the helix, while sugar-phosphate forming the back-bone of the molecule is on the outside.

(3) The two polynucleotide chains interact by hydrogen bonding. There is a very strict combining rule for hydrogen bonding.

(4) Ten base pairs occur per turn of the helix. The spacing between the adjacent base pairs is 3.4 Å. The diameter of the helix is 20Å.

(5) The two strands of the double helix are anti-parallel. One polynucleotide chain is running in 5′ to 3′ direction and the other chain in 3′ to 5′ direction.

(6) The double helix has two different grooves—the major and the minor.

(7) The double helix is right handed and

(8) In two polynucleotide chains, base pairs are complementary.

The sequence of one strand determines the sequence of the other. The rule is that A base pairs with T and forms two hydrogen bonds. G base pairs with C and forms three hydrogen bonds (Fig. 2.11).

STRUCTURE OF RNA IN VIRUSES

The RNA is the genetic material in plant viruses. It controls the infectivity and codes for specific capsid protein of the virus. Virus RNA is thus typically regarded as a poly cistronic messenger which embodies information for 1000 to 2000 amino acids pertaining to a number of proteins. Infectivity is another important property of virus RNAs. Entire RNA molecule is required for causing infection. Any internal break destroys its infectivity. RNA gives a definite length and breadth to virus particles by its presence. Length of a virus is a genetically characterized character. It may also help to stabilize the shape and architectural structure of a virus, particularly in spherical viruses.

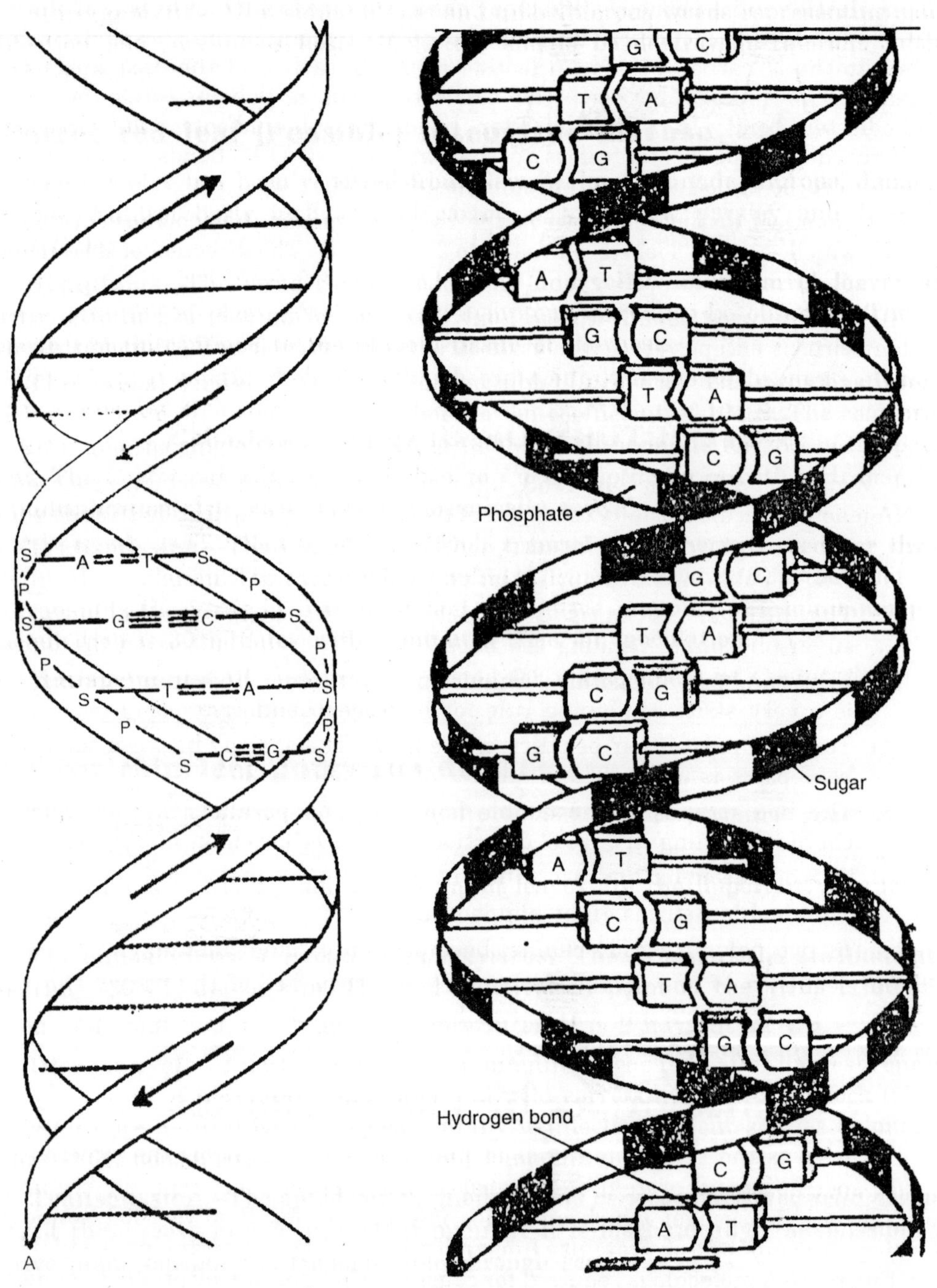

Fig. 2.11. Diagramatic Structure of double helix as proposed by J. Watson and F. Crick in 1953

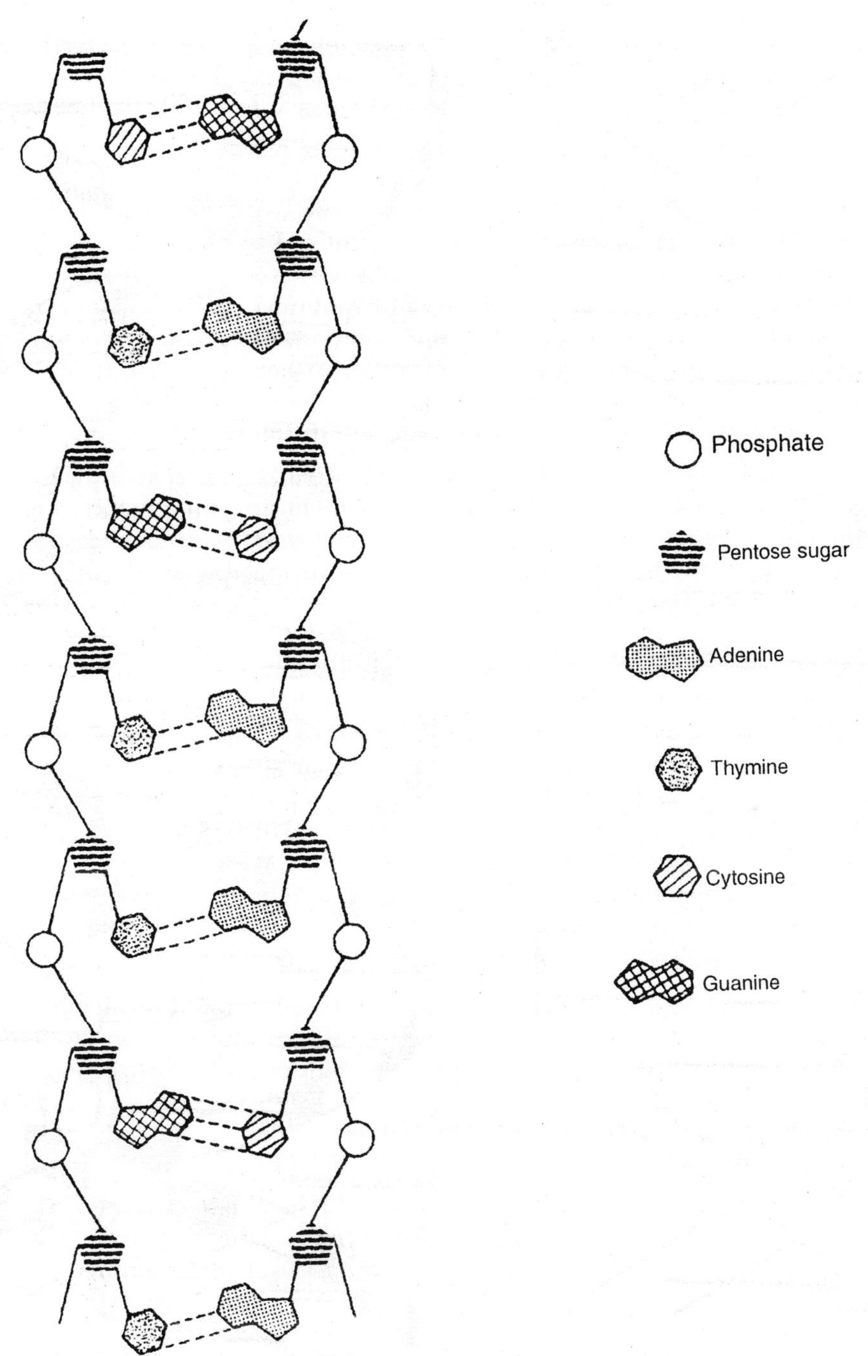

Fig. 2.12. Diagramatic representation of composition of a segment of double stranded DNA molecule cross linked by hydrogen bonds.

ATOMIC STRUCTURE OF VIRUSES

Professor Ming Luo of University of Alabama, USA has described architecture, atomic structure of both helical and spherical viruses, nucleic acid protein interaction and assembly of protein sub-units on the basis of work done in recent years.

❍ Architecture of Viruses

Viruses have two essential components—protein and nucleic acid. A closed capsid may be formed by one type or a few types of proteins to encapsulate the nucleic acid genome. The protein capsid usually has a helical symmetry as in filamentous or rod shaped viruses and icosahedral symmetry as in spherical viruses. The symmetry allows a small protein unit to assemble into a large particle. The helical symmetry is described by the diameter *d*, the pitch P, and the number of sub-units per turn. There are as many as capsid proteins as is necessary to cover the nucleic acid genome completely.

The icosahedral symmetry is defined by six fivefold axes, ten threefold axes and fifteen twofold axes. A number *T*, called the triangulation number indicates how many quasi-symmetrical sub-unit interactions there are within one asymmetrical region of the icosahendron. There are a total of 60 *T* copies of proteins in one icosahedral capsid. In some viruses, there is a membrane envelope wrapped around the protein-nucleic acid core which contains proteins on its surface.

❍ Atomic Structure of Helical Viruses

The intact TMV structure containing the nucleic acid may be determined by X-ray fiber diffraction experiments, as also that of Pf2 phage. The coat protein of TMV and Pf2 contain mainly α helices and the nucleic acid interacts with the coat protein with one base (Pf2) or three bases (TMV) per protein unit. The axis of the coat protein helix coincides with that of the nucleic acid. The TMV-RNA is inserted into the coat protein helix in the growing virus particle. The coat proteins of Pf2 are added one by one to the DNA helix emerging from the membrane.

❍ Atomic Structure of Spherical Viruses

Under appropriate conditions, spherical viruses without a membrane envelope form large single crystals. The atomic structure of such viruses can be determined by X-ray crystallography with the aid of super computers and synchrotron X-ray source.

❍ Nucleic Acid-protein Interactions

The viral nucleic acid genome is always packed inside the protein capsid. The structure of the nucleic acid can not be observed in single crystal X-ray diffraction experiment because of the random orientation of the icosahedral particles in the crystal. However, in rare cases, the nucleic acid might assume icosahedral symmetry by interacting with the protein capsid.

SHAPES AND DIMENSIONS OF VIRUS PARTICLES

On the basis of their shapes, viruses have been grouped in to three classes : helical, icosahedral and plant rhabdovirus (enveloped).

Helical viruses are invariably helical in symmetry and are also known as elongated viruses. Such viruses are longer in shape ranging from 180 to 1250 nm in length. The diameter of these viruses varies from 10-25 nm. All helical viruses are of two types in their morphology which are known as rod shaped and flexuous viruses. Rod shaped elongated viruses are stiff and straight like a rod, whereas flexuous viruses are flexible and thread like in appearance. *Tobacco rattle virus, Wheat mosaic virus* and *Barley stripe mosaic virus* are short rigid rod-shaped in appearance, measuring about 180-210 nm in length and 20-25 nm in diameter. Some of the flexuous viruses are *White clover mosaic virus* and *Water melon mosaic virus*.

Icosahedral viruses include *Rice dwarf virus*, satellite *Tobacco necrosis virus, Sugar beet curly top virus* and *Wound tumor virus*. Icosahedral viruses are equal in measurements and each face of the icosahendron is an equilateral triangle with isometric symmetry. Diameter of majority of icosahedral viruses ranges between 16-100 nm.

Rhabdoviruses also known as enveloped viruses usually represent many of the animal viruses. Only few viruses counted to be about 15, are known as plant viruses. Such viruses possess envelope. Viral envelop is a tri laminar membrane composed of lipids. These envelops help the viral particles to penetrate into the host cells. In such cases, enveloped nucleocapsids are found infectious and naked nucleocapsids remain not infectious to cause infection. Envelope gives stability to the virus and helps it to be infectious. Any sort of damage to the envelope may result in the loss of infectivity of the virus. Enveloped viruses are also known to be unstable in nature. Enveloped viruses are usually called as rhabdo virus because of their close resemblance with vesicular stomatitis virus. Gomphrena virus is an example of such viruses.

TWO KINDS OF SYMMETRY IN PLANT VIRUS STRUCTURE

Tobacco mosaic virus (TMV) illustrates the use of helical symmetry. The TMV is a narrow and rigid rod like virus, measuring 18×300 nm in size. The rod contains an axial channel that is 4 nm wide. The helical rod is comprised of 2,123 copies of the identical 17.5 KDa coat protein subunits surrounding a single stranded RNA composed of 6,131 nucleotides. The viral RNA lies within a groove in the surrounding protein helix. The groove is about half way between the interior channel of the rod and the rod's exterior surface. The pith of the TMV helix is 2.3 nm. There are a total of 130 helical turn per virion. One sequence of this tightly packed helical architecture is remarkable virion stability. This tight packing arrangement allows the TMV-RNA to be protected from nucleases and the TMV coat protein to be remarkably resistant to proteases.

Cowpea chlorotic mottle virus is a member of genus *Bromovirus* of the family Bromoviridae. The structure of this virus has been determined by both Cyro-electron microscopy and image reconstruction and by X-ray crystallography. The virus capsids contain 180 identical coat proteins sub units (19.8 K Da each) arranged with a T = 3 quasi-symmetry and organized in 20 hexametric and 12 pentameric capsomers. Coat protein subunit structure is characterized by the presence of N- and C- terminal 'arms' that extend away from the central, eight stranded anti parallel beta-barrel core. Each coat protein subunit consists of a canonical beta barrel fold from which long N-terminal and C- terminal arms extend in opposite direction. The N- and C- terminal arms facilitate the inter capsomers contacts. The arms in each sub-unit extend away from its capsomers of origin and interact with the 2-fold related sub-units in adjacent sub-unit.

The N-terminal arms provide additional stability for the interpenetrating C-terminal arms by "clamping" the arms between the beta-barrel module and the extended N-terminal arms. The N-terminal extension also appears to stabilize hexametric capsomers. A brief description of virus structures of members of some important families/groups having different sizes are being presented here for reference :

Table 2.2 **Structures of viruses belonging to different groups/families.**

Family/ group	Typical member	Genome Structure	Nucleo- capsid Proteins	Capsid symmetry	Size (nm)
Caulimovirus	*Cauliflower mosaic virus*	dsDNA 1-circular	420 copies 42 kDa	T = 7	50
Comoviruses	*Cowpea mosaic virus*	ssRNA(+) 2-linear	60 copies and 42 kDa	P = 3	28
Cryptovirus	*White clover cryptic virus*	dsRNA 2-3- linear	53-63 kDa	?	30-38
Cucumovirus	*Cucumber mosaic virus*	ssRNA(+) 3-linear	180 copies 24 kDa	T = 3	28
Dianthovirus	*Carnation ring spot virus*	ssRNA (+) 2- linear	40 kDa	?	34
Fabavirus	*Broad bean wilt virus*	ssRNA(+) 2-linear	27-43 kDa	?	30
Illarvirus	*Tobacco streak virus*	ssRNA (+) 3-linear	25 kDa	?	26-35
Luteovirus	*Barley yellow dwarf virus*	ssRNA (+)	24 kDa.	?	28
Machlovirus	*Maize chlorotic dwarf virus*	ssRNA (+) 1- linear	18-30 kDa	?	30
Necrovirus	*Tobacco necrosis virus*	ssRNA(+) 1-linear	180 copies 22 kDa	T = 3	28

From above description, it is evident that Cryo-EM, image reconstruction and X-crystallography of plant viruses have contributed to our understanding of plant virus structure. This detailed structural information not only provides us the valuable tools for viral disease diagnosis but also the knowledge to design and test new antiviral strategies based on modifying virion assembly, stability and disassembly.

KEY CONCEPTS OF PLANT VIRUS STRUCTURE

Plant virus structure has been examined for over 60 years which resulted in the emergence of several key concepts. Some important information regarding plant virus structure may be summarized as under :

1. All the viruses examined to date are built upon either helical or icosahedral symmetry arrays.
2. Most plant viruses utilize non-covalent interactions among coat protein subunits and between the coat protein units and the viral nucleic acid to control virion stability.
3. The most plant viral virions are not dependent on interactions with cell surface receptors to enter their host cells. In addition, plant viruses do not have mammalian like immune system which reduces the need for expression of highly variable structures on the surface of the virion.
4. Most plant viruses range in size from 26 nm to 300 nm. However, in their smallest dimension plant viruses seldom exceed 50 nm. A typical plant cell has enough volume to contain up to 10^9 particles and only some plant viruses approach this density as observed in *Tobacco mosaic virus* (TMV).
5. The unique features of plant cells dictate the mechanism of plant virus cell to cell movements, which is usually dependent on passage through host cell plasmodesmata that directly connect adjacent plant cells. Virus movement through the plasmodesmata in the infected leaf can either be accomplished as a viral nucleic acid-protein complex or as assembled infectious virions. Generally, long distance systematic movement through the plant's vascular system requires assembled virions.
6. Despite of their small size, different biophysical techniques are used to examine plant virus structure. These techniques include Electron microscopy (EM), X-ray crystallography, Neutral scattering, Raman spectroscopy, Ultra centrifugation and Gel electrophoresis. Over the past 50 years, EM and X-ray diffraction have been the most powerful and widely practised techniques for studying plant viruses. Direct visualization by EM has a practical resolution of 1-5 nm. Cryo-EM in combination with image reconstruction can be used to extend this resolution to 18-50 Å. However, X-ray diffraction techniques have the ability to examine virus structure at atomic resolution (2-3 Å).
7. All plant virions are assembled from repeating protein sub-units that are encoded by the viral genome. Genetic economy dictates that virions are made of many identical copies of one or relatively few kinds of proteins. In plant viruses this seldom exceeds three different sub-units. The requirement to use a repeating sub unit for assembling, the virion strongly favours the use of symmetrical architecture for maintaining similar protein-protein interfaces.
8. Nature has adapted virion structure to be based on the two types of architectures that allow for the largest virion built with the use of a repeating

sub-unit. Rod like viruses such as *Tobacco mosaic virus* (TMV) are based on a helical symmetry and spherical viruses such as *Cowpea chlorotic mottle virus* are based on icosahedral symmetry.

IMPORTANCE OF UNDERSTANDING VIRUS STRUCTURE

There are several reasons why an understanding of plant virus structure is important. Some important reasons may be described as under :

1. Plant viruses are responsible for more than 500 diseases of crops. It is certainly a gross under estimation of the correct number of plant diseases caused by viruses. The under estimation is due to the difficulty of diagnosing plant virus diseases based on host symptoms alone. Practically reliable viral disease diagnostics have become dependent on methods that directly detect viral components.
2. ELISA and polymerase chain reaction (PCR) are highly effective for the detection of suspected known species of viruses. They are not effective for the diagnosis of an unknown plant virus. Therefore, a plant virologist needs to have an appreciation of plant virus structure in order to identify an unknown virus.
3. Understanding to plant virus structure is important as it is a tool to understand the mechanisms and virion assembly and disassembly. An understanding of these viral processes is likely to lead to new and highly effective viral control measures in agricultural crops.
4. The success of engineered viral coat protein-mediated protection in plants is due to its ability to alter virion disassembly.
5. Knowledge of plant virus structure is essential so as to understand the mechanism of virus movement from cell to cell, long distance movement within the plant, one plant to other and also movement by vectors.
6. The host's response to infection is often mediated by the structural components of the virion, which is an infectious or non-infectious virus particle.
7. A detailed understanding of viral structure provides a model system for understanding the fundamental principles with the cellular macro molecular complex.

3

CLASSIFICATION OF PLANT VIRUSES

Importance of classification, Different systems of classification, Group concepts of classification, Some new groups of viruses, Current system of classification, Classification of viroids, Naming of viruses and viroids species.

As early as 1927, Johnson proposed a system of classification for naming and grouping of plant viruses on the basis that a virus should take the common name of the host with an appropriate number added with it. In this way, *Tobacco mosaic virus* was called as **tobacco virus 1**. After few years in 1937, Smith proposed that the name of the host should be Latinized and the generic name of the host be used to name a virus. Thus the **tobacco virus 1** became *Nicotiana Virus 1*. The common (vernacular) names of plant viruses were usually long, so the virologists soon started to abbreviate them, such as for *Tobacco mosaic virus* they used TMV. These abbreviations were not officially standardized, therefore, confusing situations raised several times in viruses like *Cucumber mosaic virus* and *Cauliflower mosaic virus*. Consequently, virologists used to write the full vernacular name of the virus followed by its abbreviation. In this case they used full vernacular name on the first occasion followed by its abbreviation in all other places of the publication. Most virologists now try to standardize abbreviated names in such a way as to minimize the confusion. They used CMV for *Cucumber mosaic virus* and used CaMV for *Cauliflower mosaic virus*. Recently virologists have started using modified abbreviations to name the viruses. They use BySpMV for *Barley stripe mosaic virus* and ByYStMV for *Barley yellow striate mosaic virus* as used by Suitic *et al* (2000) in their book entitled 'Handbook of Plant Virus Diseases', published by CRC Press, Washington DC.

❍ Importance of classification

Classification is the scientific grouping of biological entities according to their resemblance and differences. The aim of classification is to establish order in diversity and to provide insight into the mutual relationships. Suppose a newly detected virus is found related to an already described group of virus, the information may be useful in predicting its ecological affinities and possible vector group involved in field spread. Thus classification is important for understanding related viruses very well.

❍ Basis of classification

Classification is based on different characteristics of viruses as under :

1. **Morphology of virions**—Virions size, shape, presence or absence of an envelope, capsomeric symmetry and structure.

2. **Physical properties of virions**—Molecular mass of virions, buoyant density of virions, sedimentation coefficient, pH, stability, thermal stability, ions (Mg++, Mn++) stability, solvent stability, detergent stability and radiation stability.

3. **Genomic properties**—Type of nucleic acid -DNA or RNA, single stranded or double stranded, linear or circular, sense– positive, negative or ambisense, number of segments, presence or absence and type of 5′-terminal cap, presence or absence of 5′-terminal covalently linked polypeptide, presence or absence of 3′-terminal poly (A) tract (or other specific tract) and nucleotide sequence comparisons.

4. **Properties of proteins**—Number of proteins, their size and functional activities (especially virion transcriptase, reverse transcriptase, virion hemagglutinin, virion neuraminidase, virion fusion protein etc.).

5. **Lipids**—Presence or absence of lipids, nature of lipids.

6. **Carbohydrates**—Presence or absence of carbohydrates and their nature.

7. **Genome organization and replication**—Strategy of replication of nucleic acid, characteristics of transcription, translation and post-translational processing, site of accumulation of virion proteins, site of assembly, site of maturation and release, cytopathologies and inclusion bodies formation.

8. **Antigenic properties**—Serological relationships and mapping epitopes.

❍ Different Systems of Classifications

With the advancement of knowledge, the plant viruses were classified by different virologists in different following ways :

1. Classification based on morphology and particle size.
2. Group concept classification.
3. Current ICTV based classification.

❍ Classification based on morphology and particle size

Gibbs and Harrison (1976), Bos (1983) and Stevens (1983) classified viruses on the basis of their structure, morphology and particle size. They suggested classification of viruses as under :

I. Elongated or helical viruses II. Isometric viruses

III. Bacilliform or bullet-shaped viruses.

On the basis of morphology and size of particles, viruses have been grouped into three categories. Such categories are elongated or helical viruses, isometric viruses and bacilliform or bullet shaped viruses. Elongated viruses are of two types—(1) rigid rod shaped and (2) flexuous rod shaped. Rigid rod shaped viruses include two types of viruses like monopartite and multipartile. Monopartile virus group include only Tobamo virus group; however multipartite includes hordeiviruses, Tobraviruses soil borne wheat mosaic viruses and Peanut clump viruses. Flexuous rod shaped elongated viruses are single type in composition. It includes four groups of viruses all being monopartite in nature. These four groups are Potex viruses, potyviruses, carlaviruses and clostero- viruses.

Isometric viruses are four types and include single stranded RNA (ssRNA) viruses, double stranded RNA (dsRNA), single stranded DNA (dsDNA) and double stranded DNA (dsDNA) viruses. Isometric single stranded RNA viruses are three types—(1) monopartite viruses with six virus groups (2) multipartite viruses with seven virus groups and (3) enveloped viruses with single Tomato spotted wilt virus group. Double stranded RNA viruses include Reoviruses that consist of Phytoreoviruses and Fijii viruses. Similarly isometric single stranded DNA viruses include Geminivirus group and isometric double stranded DNA viruses include only caulimoviruses.

Bacilliform or bullet shaped viruses are two types—one type includes plant viruses without envelope and other type includes enveloped viruses consisting of single virus group Rhabdoviruses.

Keeping in mind the particle morphology and size, plant viruses described above may be summarized as under :

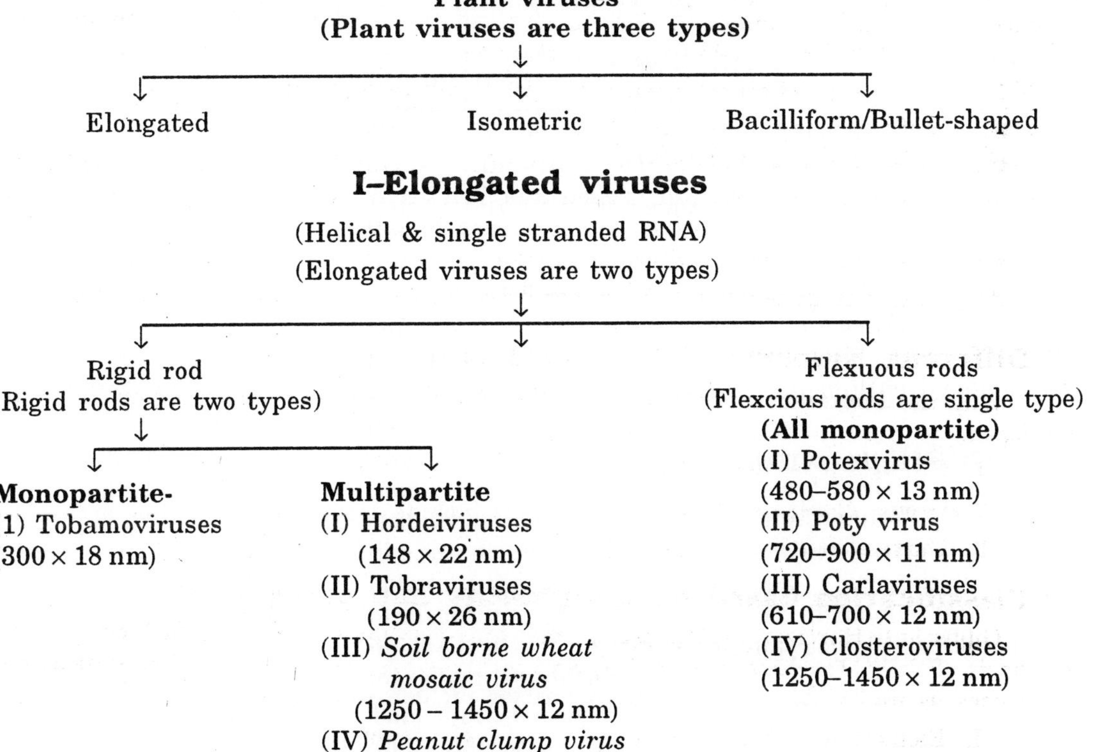

II Isometric viruses

(Isometric viruses are four types)

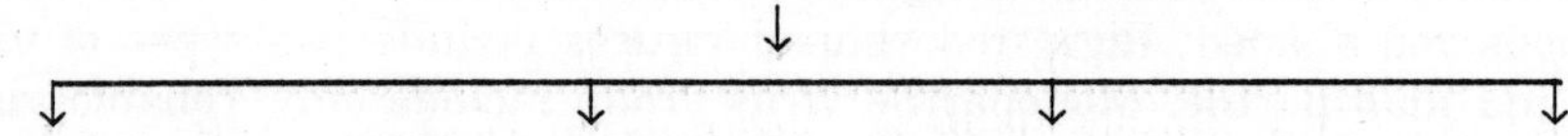

(1) Single stranded RNA (2) Double stranded RNA (3) Single stranded DNA (4) Double stranded DNA

❍ (1) Single-stranded RNA

(Isometric viruses with single stranded RNA are three types)

(a) Mono partite	**(b) Multipartite**	**(c) With-envelope**
(I) Tymoviruses (28 nm)	(1) Comoviruses (25-30 nm)	(1) Tomato spotted wilt viruses (80-85 nm)
(II) Tombusviruses (30 nm)	(II) Nepoviruses (28-30 nm)	
(III) Sovemoviruses (20 nm)	(III) Pea-enation viruses (28 nm)	
(IV) Tobacco-necrosis viruses (26 nm)	(IV) Dianthoviruses (31-34 nm)	
(V) Luteoviruses (20-24 nm)	(V) Cucumoviruses (20-30 nm)	
(VI) Machloviruses (30 nm)	(VI) Bromoviruses (26 nm)	
	(VII) -Ilaviruses (26-35 nm)	

❍ (II) Double-stranded RNA

(Isometric double stranded RNA viruses include Reoviruses that are two types)

Reoviruses

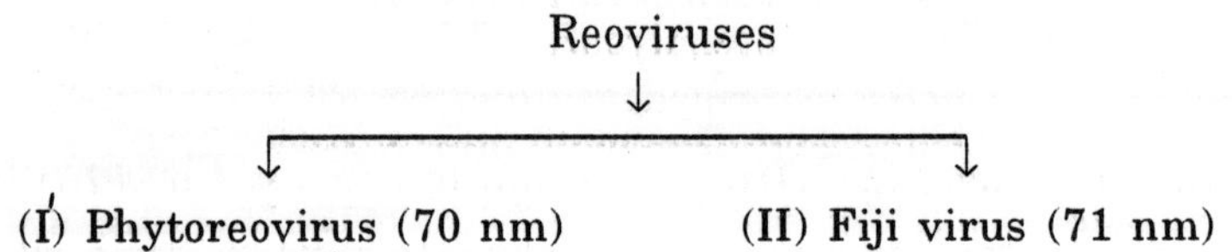

(I) Phytoreovirus (70 nm) (II) Fiji virus (71 nm)

❍ (III) Single-stranded DNA

(Isometric single stranded DNA viruses include Gemini viruses that are single type)

(I) Gemini viruses (28-30 nm)

❍ (IV) Double stranded DNA

(Isometric double stranded DNA viruses include Caulimoriruses that are single type)

(1) Caulimoviruses (50 nm)

III-Bacilliform or Bullet-shaped viruses

(Bacilliform or Bullet shaped viruses are two types)

(1) Without envelope	(2) With envelope
Example-*Alfalfa mosaic virus*	Example-Rhabdoviruses
(58 × 18 nm)	(200–350 × 75–79 nm)

MORPHOLOGY OF VIRUSES

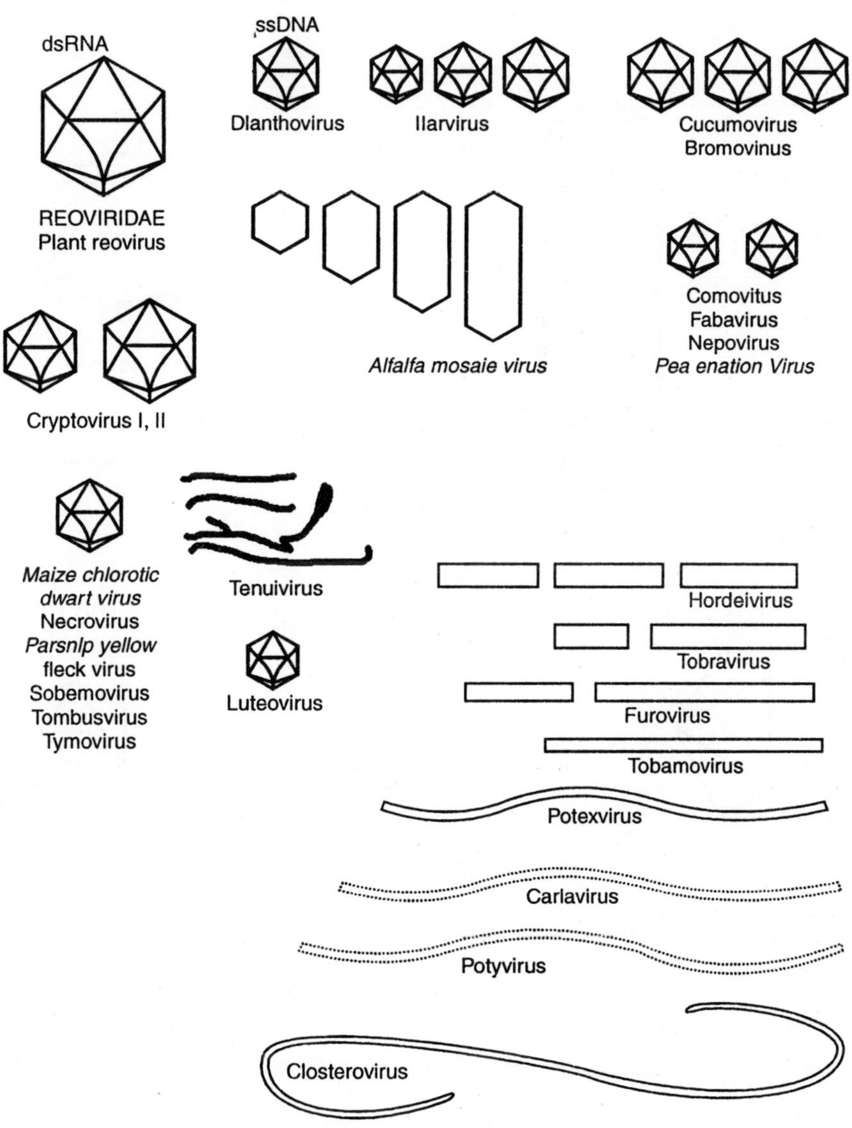

Fig. 3.1. Diagrammatic representation of families of viruses infecting plants.

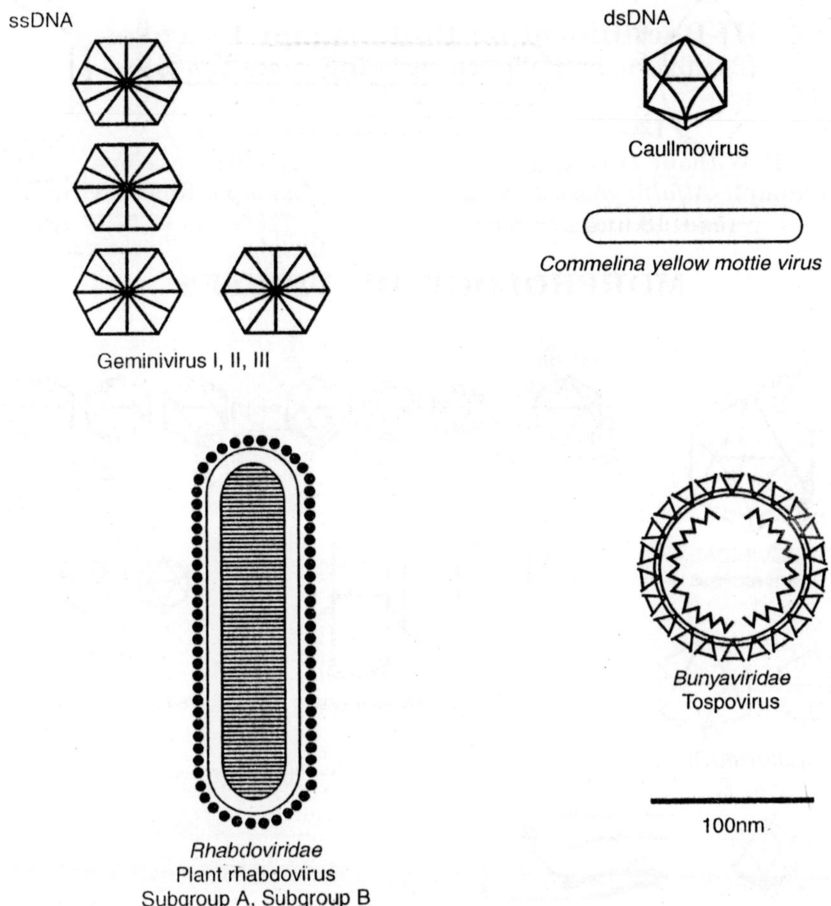

Fig. 3.2. Diagramatic representation of families of viruses infecting plants.

Fig. 3.3. Diagonmatic representation of the families of viruses infecting algae, fungi and protozoa, grouped on the basis of nature and standness.

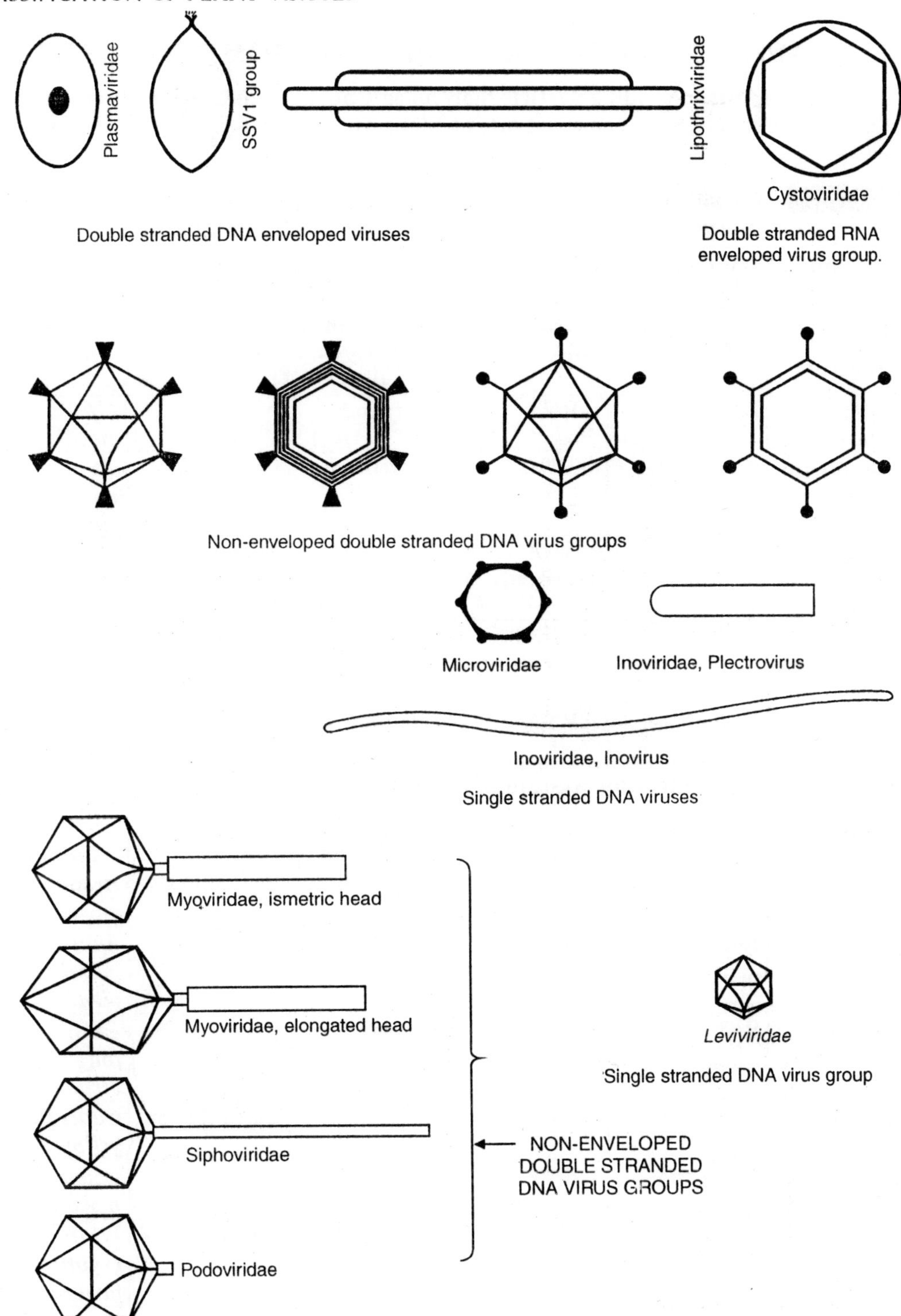

Fig. 3.4. Diagramatic representation of families of viruses infecting bacteria.

CHARACTERISTIC FEATURES OF SOME VIRUSES

For better understanding particle morphology, nucleic acid type, acid configuration, host and type members of some important plant virus groups/families have bee given below.

Table 3.1 **Classification and nomenclature of some plant viruses with their particle morphology, nucleic acid type and acid configuration.**

Family name not assigned by ICTV.

Name of group/ family	Particle morpho-logy	Nucleic Acid Type	Acid confi-guration configu-ration	Host	Type member
Alfalfa mosaic	Bacilliform	ssRNA	3+strands	Alfalfa	*Alfalfa mosaic virus*
Commelina yellow mottle	Bacilliform	dsDNA	1 circular	Comme-lina	*Commelina yellow mottle virus*
Maize chlorotic dwarf	Isometric	ssRNA 1+strand	1+strand	Maize	*Maize chlorotic dwarf virus*
Parsnip yellow fleck	Isometric	ssRNA	1+strand	Parsnip	*Parsnip yellow fleck virus*
Pea enation mosaic	Isometric	ssRNA	2strands	Pea	*Pea enation mosaic virus*

Family name already assigned by ICTV.

Name of group	Morpho-logy	Nucleic acid type	Acid confi-guration	Host	Type member
Bromo-virus	Icosahedral	ssRNA	3+strands	Brome grass	*Brome mosaic virus*
Capillo-virus	Rod	ssRNA	1+strand	Apple	*Apple stem growing virus*
Carlavirus	Rod	ssRNA	1+strand	Carnation	*Carnation ton latent virus*
Caulimo-virus	Isometric	dsDNA	Circular	Cauli-flower	*Cauli-flower yellows virus*
Comovirus	Isometric	ssRNA	1+strand	Cowpea	*Cowpea mosaic virus*
Crypto-virus	Isometric	dsRNA	2 segments	White clover	*White clover cryptic virus I & II*
Cucumo-virus	Isometric	ssRNA	3+strands	Cucumber	*Cucumber mosaic virus*

Name of group	Morphology	Nucleic acid type	Acid configuration	Host	Type member
Dianthovirus	Isometric	ssRNA	3+strands	Carnation	*Carnation ring spot virus*
Fabavirus	Isometric	ssRNA	3+strands	Broad bean	*Broad bean wilt virus*
Furovirus	Rod	ssRNA	2+strands	Wheat	*Soil borne wheat mosaic virus*
Geminivirus I	Isometric	ssDNA	1 circular	Maize	*Maize streak virus,*
II		ssDNA	1 circular	Sugar beet	*Beet curly top virus,*
III		ssDNA		Bean	*Bean, golden mosaic virus*
Hordeivirus	Helical	ssRNA	3+strands	Barley	*Barley stripe mosaic virus*
Ilarvirus	Isometric	ssRNA	3+strands	Tobacco	*Tobacco streak virus*
Luteovirus	Isometric	ssRNA	1+strand	Barley	*Barley yellow dwarf virus*
Marafivirus	Isometric	ssRNA	1+strand	Maize	*Maize-rayadofino virus*
Nepovirus	Isometric	ssRNA	2+strand	Tobacco	*Tobacco ring spot virus*
Potexvirus	Rod	ssRNA	1+strand	Potato	*Potato virus X*
Potyvirus	Rod	ssRNA	1+strand	Potato	*Potato virus Y*
Reoviridae	Icosahedral	dsRNA	10-12 Segments	—	*Wound tumor virus*
Rhaboviridae A	Bacilliform	ssRNA	1-strand	Lettuce	*Lettuce necrotic yellow virus*
B	Bacilliform	ssRNA	1-strand	Potato	*Potato yellow dwarf virus*
Sobemovirus	Icosahedral	ssRNA	1+strand	Bean	*Southern bean mosaic virus*

Name of group	Morphology	Nucleic acid type	Acid configuration	Host	Type member
Tenuivirus	Rod	ssRNA	4-strands	Rice	*Rice stripe virus*
Tobamovirus	Rod	ssRNA	1+strand	Tobacco	*Tobacco mosaic virus*
Tobravirus	Rod	ssRNA	2+strands	Tobacco	*Tobacco rattle virus*
Tombusvirus	Isometric	ssRNA	1+strand	Tomato	*Tomato bushy stunt virus*
Tymovirus	Icosahedral	ssRNA	1+strand	Turnip	*Turnip yellow mosaic virus*

Source—After Francki, R.I.B., *et al*, (1991) Classification and Nomenclature of Viruses. *Archives of Virology*. Supple. 2. Springer-Verlag.NY, 450 pp.

GROUP CONCEPT CLASSIFICATION

The first Plant Virus Sub-committee (PVS) of International Committee on taxonomy of Plant Viruses (ICTV) suggested different groups of plant viruses under the chairmanship of Harrison (1969).

Later on, some more groups were included. Summary of characteristics of important groups of viruses as approved by ICTV are being given as under :

(A) Viruses with single stranded RNA genome (ssRNA) without envelope.

(B) Viruses with ssRNA and particles enclosed in envelopes

(C) Viruses with ssDNA genome.

(D) Viruses with dsDNA genome

(E) Other angiosperm viruses.

Some most important characteristics of groups of viruses are being described here :

○ A. Viruses with ssRNA genome having non-enveloped particles

This group includes many important groups of isometric viruses such as Luteoviruses, Maize chlorotic dwarf viruses, Sovemoviruses, Tombusviruses, tobacco necrosis viruses, Tymoviruses, Comoviruses, Dianthoviruses, Nepoviruses, Alfalfa mosaic viruses, Bromoviruses, Cucumoviruses, Ilaviruses, Velvet viruses, Tobraviruses, Hordeiviruses, Potexviruses, Carlaviruses, Potyviruses and Closteroviruses etc.

(1) LUTEOVIRUS GROUP

The name of this group was derived from Latin world "luteus" meaning yellow. It produces yellowing symptoms on infected host. The genome of this group consists of monopartite ssRNA within isometric particles. *Barley yellow dwarf virus* is the **type**

member of this group. Other members of the group are *Beet mild yellows, Beet western yellows, Carrot red leaf, Legume yellows, Malva yellows, Pea leaf roll, Soybean dwarf* and *Turnip yellows*. Tentative members are *Beet yellow net, Celery yellows, Groundnut rosette assistor, Chickpea stunt, Grapevine ajinoshika leaf yellows, Milk vetch dwarf, Millet red leaf, Physalis mild chlorosis, Physalis vein blotch, Raspberry leaf curl, Ryegrass chlorotic streak, Tobacco vein distorting, Tobacco yellow net, Tobacco yellow vein assister, Tomato yellow net* and *Turnip latent virus.*

❍ Distinguishing characteristics :

1. The symptoms shown by naturally infected plants persist or disappear soon after infection and the plants apparently recover.
2. It is transmitted in nature by an insect vector belonging to Aphidae usually in persistent manner and retained even when the vector moulds but not multiplying in the vector. The virus is not transmitted in progeny. It does not require helper virus for transmission. Non-vector transmission is by grafting but not by contact and not by seed and pollen.
3. Particles are isometric, not enveloped, measuring 24-27 nm in size, profiles rounded and slightly angular with surface smooth. Usually leaf sap contains few particles.
4. The thermal inactivation point ranges between 45–75 C°, longevity *in vitro* 5-21 days and dilution end point 10^{-2} to 10^{-4}.
5. Chemically, the particles contain nucleic acid 16-37.8% (mean 28.5%), protein upto 84% (mean 73.1%), and single stranded RNA genome.
6. Particles are found in vascular parenchyma, phloem and plasmodesmata or in companion cell with some exception.
7. Virus preparations are highly immunogenic. Particles react in standard gel diffusion tests. No special conditions are required for serological tests. Also detectable by ISEM and ELISA.

The sequence of the genome of an isolate of *Barley yellow dwarf virus* shows the evidence of a modular origin of its genome. Its polymerase has clear sequence similarities with that of *Red clover necrotic mosaic dianthovirus*. Luteovirus virion proteins show a distinct sequence similarity to the virion proteins of *Tomato bushy stunt tombusvirus.*

(2) MAIZE CHLOROTIC DWARF VIRUS GROUP

The **type member** of this group is *Maize chlorotic dwarf virus.* The group is characterized by the presence of monopartite ssRNA genome contained in isometric particles of approximately 30 nm in diameter. The virus has very narrow range of hosts within the Graminae and is transmitted easily by leaf hoppers in a semi-persistent manner. It is not transmitted by sap inoculation.

(3) SOVEMOVIRUSES GROUP

The name was derived from southern bean mosaic and the **type member** is *Southern bean mosaic virus.* Group members have mono partite ssRNA genomes with isometric particles, measuring approximately 28 nm in diameter. Other members of the group are *Turnip rosette mosaic, Cocks foot mottle, Lucerne transient streak, Rice yellow mottle, Solanum nodiflorum mottle, Sowbane mosaic, Subterranean clover mottle, Velvet tobacco mottle* and *Blueberry shoestring virus*. Tentative members are *Cocksfoot mild mosaic, Ginger chlorotic, Olive latent-1* and *Panicum mosaic virus*.

❍ Distinguishing characteristics

(1) Virus particles have thermal inactivation point 70-90 C° (mean 82.7 C°). Longevity *in vitro* 20-365 days. Dilution end point 10^{-5} to 10^{-9}. The viruses are transmitted by an insect vector in nature usually belonging to Aphididae, Coleopteran or Cicadellidae. They are usually transmitted in semi-persistent manner and they do not require helper virus for transmission. Also transmissible by mechanical inoculation, by grafting, by seed but not by contact or pollen.

(2) Genome single stranded RNA, nucleic acid 18-21%, protein 79-82% and lipid 0%.

(3) Particles are found in mesophyll, epidermis, meristem, xylem, phloem and all parts of the host plant but rarely in cytoplasm, nucleus, mitochondria, chloroplasts or the cell vacuole.

(4) Preparations are usually strongly immunogenic or poorly immunogenic ; Particles react in standard gel diffusion tests. No special conditions are required for serological tests. Mixed liquid tests give granular precipitations. Also detectable by ELISA and solid phase radio-immune assay.

(5) The polymerase GDD motif and virious of the polymerase of Sovemoviruses show clear sequence similarities to similar genomic regions of the Luteoviruses and Comoviruses.

(4) TOMBUSVIRUSES GROUP

The name of this group was derived from tomato bushy stunt and the **type member** of this group is *Tomato bushy stunt virus*. The group members have mono-partite ssRNA genome with isometric and non-enveloped particles, measuring about 30 nm wide (27-34 nm) in neutral and acid stain or in presence of divalent cations. Other possible members of this group are *Artichoke mottle crinkle virus, Carnation Italian ring spot virus, Pelargonium leaf curl virus, Petunia asteroid mosaic virus, Egg plant mottled crinkle virus* and *Grapevine algerian latent virus*.

❍ Distinguishing characters

(1) Members are transmissible by mechanical inoculation by grafting, by seed and in some other members by contact. Members are not transmitted by pollen and insect vectors. They are soil-borne in nature.

(2) Virus particles have thermal inactivation point 75-90 C°. Longevity *in vitro* 23-490 days. Dilution end point 10^{-5} to 10^{-7}. Most stable at pH 5–6.5.

(3) Genome single stranded RNA. Nucleic acid 14-22% (mean 19.3%), protein 78-85% and lipid 1.4-1.7%.

(4) Particles are found in vascular parenchyma and in all other parts of the host cells including cytoplasm, nucleus, chloroplasts, mitochondria and vacuole.

(5) Serologically, virus preparations are strongly immunogenic. Particles react in standard gel diffusion tests. Mixed liquid tests give granular precipitates.

(6) Sequence similarities show Tombusviruses to be closely related to the Comoviruses and Sovemoviruses being more distantly to luteoviruses.

(5) TOBACCO NECROSIS VIRUSES GROUP

Tobacco necrosis virus is the **type member** of this group. Its isometric particles contain mono partite ssRNA. They are about 26-28 nm in diameter. *Cucumber necrosis virus* is a **possible member** of this group.

❍ Distinguishing characteristics

(1) The members of this group have worldwide host range and distribution.

(2) They are readily transmitted by sap inoculation and are also known to be transmitted in soil by zoospores of the fungus- *Olpidium brassicae.*

(3) They are not transmitted by seed, pollen and insect vectors.

(4) *Tobacco necrosis virus* acts as a helper to a satellite virus. The two members are not serologically related but share most of the biological properties.

(6) TYMOVIRUSES GROUP

The name was derived from turnip yellow mosaic. The **type member** of this group is *Turnip yellow mosaic virus.* The mono partite ssRNA genome is contained in isometric particles of 28-30 nm diameter. Other members of the group are *Andean potato latent, Belladona mottle, Cacao yellow mosaic, Clitoris yellow vein, Desmodium yellow mottle, Dulcamara mottle, Egg plant mosaic, Erysimum latent, Kennedya yellow mosaic, Okra mosaic, Onion yellow mosaic, Passion fruit yellow mosaic, Peanut yellow mottle, Physalis mosaic, Plantago mottle, Wild cucumber mosaic* and *Vandzeia necrotic mosaic virus.*

❍ Distinguishing characteristics

(1) The viruses are transmitted in nature usually by insect vectors belonging to coleopteran (beetles) in persistent manner. Non-vector transmission is by mechanical inoculation and by grafting. Transmission is very rare by contact between plants and by seeds but not by pollen.

(2) Particles are isometric and non-enveloped. Leaf sap contains many virus particles.

(3) Thermal inactivation point is 55-90 C°, longevity *in vitro* 7-100 days and dilution end point is 10^{-3} to 10^{-8}. They are composed of single stranded RNA genome with nucleic acid 35%, protein 65% and lipid 0%. Other compounds include polyamines mainly spermidine.

(4) Particles are found almost in all parts of the host plant such as cytoplasm, nucleus, chloroplasts, mitochondria and the cell vacuoles.

(5) Preparations are strongly immunogenic. Particles react in standard gel diffusion tests. Mixed liquid tests give granular precipitates. Also detectable by ELISA and ISEM.

(6) The GDD and nucleotide binding fold region of the replicases protein show that Tymovirus replicases have clear affinities with the tobamo/alpha virus polymerases super group, being closest to the potex viruses and carlaviruses.

(7) COMOVIRUSES GROUP

The name was derived from cowpea mosaic and the **type member** of the group is *Cowpea mosaic virus*. The genome consists of bi-partite ssRNA. The two types of RNA are contained in separate isometric particles, each measuring about 24 nm in diameter. Each type of particles is required for infection. Some other particles containing no RNA may also be present in the infected plants. Group members include *Andean potato mottle, Bean pod mottle, Bean rugose mosaic, Broad bean true mosaic, Cowpea severe mosaic, Glycine mosaic, Pea mild mosaic, Radish mosaic, Red clover mottle, Squash mosaic* and *Ullucus virus. Broad bean wilt virus is the possible member of this group.*

❍ Distinguishing characteristics

(1) The viruses of this group are usually transmitted in nature by the insect vectors belonging to coleopteran (beetles) in persistent manner. Also transmissible by mechanical inoculation by grafting, by contact and rarely by seed and by pollen to seed.

(2) Thermal inactivation point 55-80C°. Longevity *in-vitro* 2-112 days and dilution end point 10^{-3} to 10^{-8}. Genome is composed of single-stranded RNA with nucleic acid 25-35% and protein 65-75%. Other compounds include polyamines and spermidine.

(3) Members do not depend on other viruses for replication.

(8) DIANTHOVIRUSES GROUP

The name was derived from *Dianthus*, the generic name of carnation. The **type member** is *Carnation ring spot virus*. Group members have bipartite ssRNA genome but it is not known whether the two species are encapsidated separately or not. The isometric particles range between 31-34 nm in diameter. Other members of the group are *Red clover necrotic mosaic virus* and *Sweet clover necrotic mosaic virus*.

❍ Distinguishing characteristics

(1) The viruses are usually transmitted in nature without the aid of the specific vectors. Non-vector transmission includes mechanical inoculation by grafting and by contact of plants but not by seed or pollen.

(2) Thermal inactivation point 60-90 C° (mean 77.5 C°). Longevity *in-vitro* is 50-70 days (mean 60.8 days). Dilution end point is 10^{-5}. Particles are found in leaves, roots and all other parts of the host plant.

(3) Virus preparations are immunogenic or strongly immunogenic. Particles react in standard gel diffusion tests. Also detectable by ELISA and ISEM.

(4) The GDD region of the genome of *Red clover necrotic mosaic virus* shows clear homology with that of the *Barley yellow dwarf luteovirus.*

(9) NEPOVIRUSES GROUP

The name has been derived from nematode transmitted polyhedral shaped viruses. The **type member** of the group is *Tobacco ring spot virus*. Other members of the group include *Arabis mosaic, Artichoke Italian latent, Artichoke yellow ring spot, Blue berry leaf mottle, Cacao necrosis, Cassava American latent, Cassava green mottle, Cherry leaf roll, Cherry rasp leaf, Chicory yellow mottle, Grapevine Bulgarian latent, Grapevine chrome mosaic, Grapevine fan leaf, Hibiscus latent ring spot, Lucerne Australian latent, Peach rosette mosaic, Potato black ring spot, Raspberry ring spot, Strawberry latent ring spot, Tomato black ring* and *Tomato ring spot virus.* The angular isometric particles are 28 nm in diameter. The genome is bi-partite consisting of two ssRNA molecular species in distinct particles. Both types of particles are required for infection. A third particle containing no RNA is frequently detected in infected plants.

❍ Distinguishing characteristics

(1) They are usually transmitted in nature by nematodes belonging to Dorylamida. Some are also transmissible by aphids, beetles, thrips and mites in non-persistent manner or in semi-persistent manner.

(2) Non-vector transmission is by mechanical inoculation, by grafting, by seed, by pollen to seed and by pollen to pollinated plants (*Cherry leaf roll virus*) but not by contact between the plants.

(3) Thermal inactivation point 50-75C° (mean 60.4C°). Longevity *in vitro* is 1-70 days. Dilution end point 10^{-2} to 10^{-6}. Leaf sap contains many virus particles in early infection. Genome consists of single stranded RNA. Particles are found in leaves, roots, mesophyll, epidermis, meristem, vascular parenchyma and in all other parts of the host.

(4) Viral preparations are highly immunogenic or immunogenic. Particles react in standard gel diffusion tests. Also detectable by PHA, Latex, ISEM and ELISA.

(5) Nepoviruses share many features in Comoviruses. Both have bi-partite genome of similar composition with genome linked protein (VPg) at 5′-terminus and a poly A region at the 3′-terminus and similar translation strategies.

(10) ALFALFA MOSAIC VIRUS GROUP

The tripartite genome of the virus is composed of three larger molecular species of ssRNA. A fourth smaller species of RNA is also present and each is separately encapsidated. The three-layered RNA species are contained in the larger particles. The **type member** is *Alfalfa mosaic virus*. Other members are not well recognized. Tentative member is *Dog's mercury virus.*

❍ Distinguishing characteristics

(1) Members belonging to this group are usually transmitted in nature by insects belonging to Aphididae in non-persistent manner. Non-vector transmission

is by mechanical inoculation, by seed and by pollen to seed but not by contact between the plants.

(2) Virus particles are bacilliform and not enveloped. They measure usually 18 nm × 30 nm in size. Leaf sap contains many particles. Also found in all parts of the host.

(3) Viral preparations are poorly immunogenic. Particles react in standard gel diffusion tests. Mixed liquid tests give granular precipitations.

(4) Amino acid sequence encoded by RNA-1 and RNA-2 of *Alfalfa mosaic virus* shows clear sequence similarities with bromoviruses, cucumoviruses and ilarviruses.

(11) BROMOVIRUS GROUP

The name of this group has been derived from brome mosaic and the **type member** is the *Brome mosaic virus*. This group contains viruses with tripartite genome of ssRNA, encapsidated separately in isometric particles, measuring about 26 nm in diameter. Other members of the group are *Broad bean mottle, Cassia yellow blotch, Cowpea chlorotic mottle,* and *Melandrium yellow fleck virus.*

❍ Distinguishing characteristics

(1) Members are usually transmitted in nature by insect vectors belonging to coleopteran in persistent manner. Non-vector transmission is by mechanical inoculation, by grafting and rarely by seed but not by pollen.

(2) Thermal inactivation point 67-95 C°. Longevity *in vitro* is 1-44 days and dilution end point is 10^{-3} to 10^{-5}. The virus remains stable at pH –3.6.

(3) Particles are found in mesophyll, leaves and in all other parts of the host.

(4) Preparations are immunogenic or strongly immunogenic. Particles react in standard gel diffusion tests.

(5) Amino acid sequence encoded by RNA-1 and RNA-2 of *Brome mosaic virus* shows clear sequence similarities with parts of the genome of other alfalfa mosaic viruses, cucumoviruses, ilarviruses, tobamoviruses and tobraviruses.

(12) CUCUMOVIRUSES GROUP

The name was derived from cucumber mosaic and the **type member** of this group is *Cucumber mosaic virus*. The viruses of this group have tripartite genomes, encapsidated in three types of isometric particles, measuring about 28 nm in diameter. All three components are necessary for infection. Other definite members of the group are *Peanut stunt virus* and *Tomato aspermy virus. Cowpea ring spot virus* is known as possible member of this group.

❍ Distinguishing characteristics

(1) Members are transmitted in nature by insect vectors belonging to Aphididae in a non-persistent manner. Non-vector transmission is by mechanical inoculation, by grafting, by seed and by pollen to seed. They are not transmitted by contact.

(2) Thermal inactivation point is 66 C° and longevity *in-vitro* is 8-10 days.

(3) Preparations are immunogenic or strongly immunogenic. Particles react in standard gel diffusion tests. Also detectable by ISEM and ELISA.

(4) Amino acid sequences encoded by genome of *Cucumber mosaic virus* show clear sequence similarities with those encoded by the genomes of other alfalfa mosaic, bromoviruses and ilarviruses.

(13) ILARVIRUSES GROUP

The name of the group was derived from the isometric labile ring spot characteristic of the viruses of this group. The **type member** is *Tobacco streak virus*. All members of the group have a tripartite ssRNA genome, each contained in separate isometric particles which vary from 26-35 nm in diameter. All particles have the same density but their sedimentation rates differ because of their sizes. Group members include *Apple mosaic, Black raspberry latent, Citrus leaf rugose, Cherry rugose mosaic, Citrus variegation, Elm mottle, Danish plum line pattern, hop-A, hop-C, Lilac ring mottle, Prune dwarf, Hydrangea mosaic, North American plum line pattern, Pear ring spot, Prunus necrotic ring spot, Rose mosaic, Spinach latent* and *Tulare apple mosaic virus.* Name of some tentative members are *Pelargonium zonate spot, Raspberry bushy dwarf* and *Sun flower ring spot virus.*

❍ Distinguishing characteristics

(1) Members of the group are transmitted in nature by insect vectors belonging to Thysanoptera in a non-persistent manner. Some viruses are also transmitted without the help of any vector by unknown means. Non-vector transmission is by mechanical inoculation, by grafting, by seed, by pollen to seed and by pollen to pollinated plants but not by contact between plants.

(2) Thermal inactivation point of the virus is 45-65 C°, longevity *in vitro* 1-6 days and dilution end point is variable.

(3) Particles are usually isometric or bacilliform. They are pleomorphic and non-enveloped. They measure 20–38 nm × 12–35 nm in size.

(4) Profiles are rounded pleomorphic. Genome consists of single stranded RNA.

(5) Preparations are immunogenic or poorly immunogenic. Particles react in standard gel diffusion tests. Mixed liquid tests give granular precipitates. Also detectable by ELISA.

(6) Ilarviruses have a tripartite genome like other members of tricornaviruses.

(14) VELVET TOBACCO MOTTLE VIRUS GROUP

The **type member** of this group is *Velvet tobacco mottle virus*. This group has not yet been given approval as a group by ICTV. The genome consists of one molecule of linear ssRNA and a second molecule of circular ssRNA with viroids like structure. Both are required for infection. The particles are isometric, measuring about 30 nm in diameter. They have narrow host range and are readily transmitted by sap inoculation and by beetles. Other members of the group are *Lucerne transient streak, Solanum nodiflorum mottle* and *Subterranean clover mottle virus* (Matthews, 1982).

(15) TOBRAVIRUSES GROUP

The name of the group was derived from tobacco rattle and the **type member** of the Tobraviruses group is *Tobacco rattle virus*. The group has viruses with rigid rod shaped particles of two different lengths, measuring 180-215 nm and 46–114 nm × 21–23 nm in sizes respectively. The genome consists of one molecule of linear ssRNA and a second molecule of circular ssRNA with viroids like structure. Both are required for infectivity. Other members of the group are *Pea early browning* and *Pepper ring spot virus*.

❍ Distinguishing characteristics

(1) Member viruses are transmitted in nature by a nematode vector belonging to the Trichodoridae. Non-vector transmission is by mechanical inoculation, by grafting, by seed but not by contact between the plants and not by the pollen.

(2) Thermal inactivation point is 74-85 C°. Longevity *in vitro* is 25-183 days and dilution end point 10^{-4} to 10^{-6}.

(3) Preparations are strongly immunogenic. Particles react in standard gel diffusion tests. Also detectable by ISEM, ELISA, and Latex agglutination.

(4) The GDD region of the Tobraviruses seems most closely related to that of the Hordeiviruses.

(16) HORDEIVIRUSES GROUP

The name was derived from the Latin *Hordeum* meaning barley. The **type member** is *Barley stripe mosaic virus*. Group members are rigid rods particles in shape. They measure 100–150 nm × 20 nm in size. They have a single stranded RNA genome within particles of two to four different lengths depending on the strain. Particles of different lengths contain different RNA molecular species and two or three particle components are required for infectivity. The other members of the group are *Lychnis ring spot virus* and *Poa semi-latent virus*.

❍ Distinguishing characteristics

(1) Members of the group are transmitted in nature by unknown means. Non-vector transmission is by mechanical inoculation, by contact between the plants, by seed, by pollen to seed and by pollen to pollinated plants.

(2) Thermal inactivation point is 65-70 C°. Longevity *in vitro* 14-21 days. Dilution end point 10^{-2} to 10^{-3}. Particles are found in all the parts of the host plant.

(3) Preparations are immunogenic or strongly immunogenic. Particles react in standard gel diffusion tests. Mixed liquid tests give flocculent precipitates.

(4) The hordeivirus group and alfalfa mosaic viruses, bromoviruses, cucumoviruses and ilarviruses have tripartite genomes with a 5′-terminal cap.

(17) POTEX VIRUS GROUP

The name was derived from *Potato virus* X and the **type member** of the group is *Potato virus* X (PVX). The particles are flexuous rods of about 470-580 nm in length and 13 nm in width. The genome is a single species of ssRNA. Other member of the group are *Cactus X, Cassava common mosaic, Clover yellow mosaic, Cymbidium mosaic, Daphne X, Foxtail mosaic, Hydragia ring spot, Narcissus mosaic, Papaya mosaic, Pepino mosaic, Plantain mosaic X, Potato aucuba mosaic, Tulip X, Viola mottle, White clover mosaic, Wine berry latent* and *Zygocactus X virus*. Possible or tentative members are *Artichoke curly dwarf, Bamboo mosaic, Malva veinal necrosis, Potato aucuba mosaic* and *Rhododendron necrotic ring spot virus*.

❍ Distinguishing characteristics

(1) Members are transmitted in nature by unknown means. Non-vector transmission is by mechanical inoculation, by grafting, by contact but not by contact between the plants, not by seed and not by pollen.

(2) Viruses are filamentous and not enveloped. Thermal inactivation point is 55-100 C°, longevity *in vitro* is up to 365 days and dilution end point is 10^{-6} to 10^{-7}. Particles are found in mesophyll, epidermis, xylem and all other parts of the hosts.

(3) Preparations are immunogenic or strongly immunogenic. Particles react in standard gel diffusion tests. Also detectable by ELISA and ISEM.

(4) The GDD region of the replicases of potex viruses shows clear sequence similarities with those of carlaviruses and tymoviruses.

(18) CARLAVIRUSES GROUP

The name of this group was derived from carnation latent and **type member** is *Carnation latent virus*. The group has flexuous rod shaped particles, measuring 620-700 nm in length and 13 nm in width, containing a single species of RNA. Other members of the group are *Alfalfa latent, American hop latent, Cactus-2; Chrysanthemum B, Cowpea mild mottle, Eggplant mild mottle, Elder berry carlavirus, Selenium S, Hippeastrum latent, Honey suckle latent, Lily symptom less, Mulberry latent, Muskmelon vein necrosis, Narcissus latent, Passiflora latent, Pea streak, Poplar mosaic, Potato M, Potato S, Red clover vein mosaic* and *Shallot latent virus*. Tentative members are *Cassia mosaic, Chicory blotch, Cynodon mosaic, Elderberry A, Garlic mosaic, Nasturtium mosaic* and *White bryony mosaic virus*.

❍ Distinguishing characteristics

(1) Transmitted in nature by insect vectors belonging to the Aphididae in a non-persistent manner. Non-vector transmission is by mechanical inoculation, by grafting, by seed, rarely by pollen to pollinated plants and not by contact between the plants.

(2) Filamentous in morphology and not enveloped. Flexuous with longitudinal grooves. Thermal inactivation point is 50-80 C°, longevity *in vitro is* 1-8 days and dilution end point is 10^{-2} to 10^{-6}. Particles are found in mesophyll, epidermis, vascular parenchyma and palisade cells of the cytoplasm.

(3) Preparations are strongly immunogenic. Also detectable by ELISA, ISEM and micro precipitin tests.

(4) The GDD region of the replicases protein of potato S carlaviruses shows clear sequence similarities to the equivalent regions of potex and tymoviruses. The virion proteins of carlaviruses also show clear sequence similarities to those of potex viruses and poty viruses.

(19) POTY VIRUS GROUP

The name of the group was derived from Potato virus Y and the **type member** of the group is *Potato virus Y*. The particles of viruses of this group are usually flexuous and rod shaped in morphology. They measure about 680–900 nm × 11 nm in size. Group members include *Bean common mosaic, Bean yellow mosaic, Beet mosaic, Carnation vein mottle, Carrot thin leaf, Celery mosaic, Clover yellow vein, Cocksfoot streak, Cowpea aphid borne mosaic, Dasheen mosaic, Henbane mosaic, Hippeastrum mosaic, Iris mild mosaic, Leek yellow stripe, Lettuce mosaic, Onion yellow dwarf, Papaya ring spot, Parsnip mosaic, Passion fruit woodiness, Pea necrosis, Pea seed borne mosaic, Peanut mottle, Pepper mottle, Pepper veinal mottle, Plum pox, Potato A, Soybean mosaic, Sugarcane mosaic, Tobacco etch, Tulip breaking, Turnip mosaic, Watermelon mosaic, Wheat spindle streak mosaic, Wheat streak mosaic, Wheat yellow mosaic, Yam mosaic, Zucchini yellow fleck* and *Zucchini yellow mosaic virus*. Possible members are *Amaranthus mosaic, Anthoxanthum mosaic, Aquilegia mosaic, Artichoke latent, Carrot mosaic, Celery latent, Celery yellow mosaic, Chickpea distortion mosaic, Crinum datura 437, Datura mosaic, Dendrobium mosaic, Desmodium mosaic, Dioscorea trifida, Dock mottling mosaic, Fern ficus* and *Holcus streak, Indian pepper mottle, Isachne mosaic, Kenneedya Y, Maclura mosaic, Marigold mottle, Palm mosaic, Passion fruit ring spot, Primula mottle, Sweet potato latent, Sweet potato mild mottle, Sweet potato vein mosaic, Sweet potato yellow dwarf, Teasel mosaic, Wheat streak, White bryony mosaic* and *Wild potato mosaic virus*.

❍ Distinguishing characteristics

(1) Viruses of this group are transmitted in nature by the insect vectors belonging to Aphididae in a non-persistent manner. Non-vector transmission is by mechanical inoculation, by seed and rarely by pollen to seed but not by contact between the plants.

(2) Thermal inactivation point is 44-75 C°, longevity *in vitro* is usually 4-10 days and dilution end point is 10^{-1} to 10^{-6}. Particles are found in mesophyll, epidermis, leaves, roots, meristem and phloem.

(3) Preparations immunogenic or strongly immunogenic. Particles do not react in standard gel diffusion test. Mixed liquid tests give flocculent precipitates. Also detectable by ELISA, ISEM and Radio-immune assay.

(4) Genomic sequence comparisons indicate that much of the potyvirus genome has common ancestry with the genomes of the Comoviruses. However, the morphology of their virions indicates that they are probably not related to virion protein genes.

(20) CLOSTEROVIRUSES GROUP

The name of the group was derived from the Greek word Kloster, meaning spindle, because of the group's long thread like particles. **Type member** of the group is *Beet* *yellow virus*. Members have very long flexuous rod shaped particles, measuring 600–2000 nm × 10 nm in size. The genome consists of a single molecular species of ssRNA. Others members of the group include *Beet yellow stunt, Burdock yellows, Carnation necrotic fleck, Carrot yellow leaf, Clover yellows, Citrus tristeza, Festuca necrosis, Lilac chlorotic leaf spot, Wheat yellow leaf virus* and *Grapevine stem pitting virus*. Other possible members are *Apple chlorotic leaf spot, Apple stem growing, Heracleum latent* and *potato virus T*.

❍ Distinguishing characteristics

(1) Transmission in nature is by unknown means, usually by insect vectors belonging to the Aphididae or Pseudococcidae. They are transmitted in semi-persistent manner. Infectivity is lost when vector molts. Viruses of the group do not multiply in vectors. Not transmitted directly to progeny. Non-vector transmission is by mechanical inoculation with great difficulty. Transmission also by grafting but not by seed, contact and pollen.

(2) Non-enveloped and filamentous in structure. Particles are found in phloem, companion cells, epidermis, cytoplasm and nucleus.

(3) Thermal inactivation point is 40-60 C°, longevity *in vitro* is 1-6 days and dilution end point is 10^{-4} to 10^{-5}

(4) Preparations are immunogenic or poorly immunogenic. Particles do not react in standard gel diffusion tests but may react with *Grapevine stem pitting virus*. Mixed liquid tests give flocculent precipitates. Also detectable by ISEM.

SOME OTHER VIRUS GROUPS

(21) CRYPTOVIRUS GROUP

This name has been derived from the Greek Krypte meaning hidden. **Type member** is *white clover cryptic virus-1*. Viruses of this group consist of bipartite double stranded RNA genomes contained in isometric particles with rounded profiles of 30 nm. in chameter.

(22) REOVIRUS GROUP

Plant virus members includes Phytoreovirus genus the *type member* is *Wound tumour virus*. It consists of double stranded RNA genome that has of molecular species encapsidated with in an isometric particle measuring 70 nm. in diameter. Other two subgroups are Fijivirus and Rice ragged stunt virus sub groups.

(23) SATELLITE VIRUS GROUP

TYPE MEMBER of this group is *Tobacco neerosis satellite virus*. The genome consists of monopartite single stranded RNA, contained within isometric particles with rounded profiles, measuring 17 nm in diameter. The satellite virus depends upon co-infection with *Tobacco necrosis virus* for its replication. Other possible members are *Panicum mosaic satellite virus* and maize white line mosaic-satellite like virus. This group has not yet bean approved by the ICTV.

B. VIRUSES WITH ssRNA GENOME AND PARTICLES ENCLOSED IN ENVELOPES

(24) RHABDOVIRUS GROUP

The name of the group was derived from the Greek *rhabdos* meaning rod. The **type member** of this group is *Lettuce necrotic yellows virus*. This is one of the important virus groups that was classified earlier as a family Rhaboviridae. Other members of the family infect invertebrates and vertebrates. The plant virus members have bacilliform or bullet shaped particles, measuring 160–380 nm × 50–95 nm in size. The bullet shaped particles are thought to arise through breakage of bacilliform particles during sample preparation for electron microscopy. The particles consist of an outer membrane containing lipid and protein and an outer helically constructed core containing protein and single molecular species of ssRNA. Other members of the group are *Barley yellow striate mosaic, Beet leaf curl, Broccoli necrotic dwarf, Lucerne enation, Maize mosaic, Northern cereal mosaic, Potato yellow dwarf, Raspberry vein chlorosis, Rice transitory yellowing, Saw thistle yellow vein, Strawberry crinkle, Wheat* (American) *striate mosaic* and *Wheat chlorotic streak virus*. Tentative members of the group are *Chodrilla juncea stunting, Red clover mosaic, Clover enation, Oat striate, Pine apple chlorotic leaf streak, Rye grass bacilliform, Iris germanica leaf stripe, Lotus streak, Melon variegation* and *Zea maize virus*.

❍ Distinguishing characteristics

(1) Transmitted in nature by insect vectors belonging to Aphididae and Cicadellidae in persistent manner. Retained when vector moulds and multiplies in the vectors. Transmitted directly to progeny of vectors. Non-vector transmission is by mechanical inoculation and for some members by grafting but not by contact between plants, not by seed and not by pollen.

(2) Thermal inactivation point 40-75 C°, longevity *in vitro* up to 4 days and dilution end point varies from 10^{-2} to 10^{-5}.

(3) The matrix proteins of *Vesicular stomatitis virus* and *Influenza virus* show sequence similarities indicating a common origin for at least one gene of these negative strand RNA viruses with enveloped particles.

(25) TOMATO SPOTTED WILT VIRUSES

The **type member** of the group is *Tomato spotted wilt virus*. The particles of the virus are isometric, measuring about 85 nm in diameter. They are enclosed within a lipo protein envelope. The single stranded RNA genome is composed of at least four molecular species of RNA, but the RNA alone is not infectious. The nature of its relationship with the viral proteins has not so far been determined in detail. The group is also called as tospovirus group. It includes 13 known species including *Peanut bud necrosis virus*, *Peanut yellow spot virus* and *Peanut yellow mottle virus* etc. These viruses are mainly transmited by two thrips species—*Franklimiella occidentalis* and *F. fusca* they are also transmissible by mechanical means.

❍ Distinguishing Chracteristics

1. *Tomato spotted wilt virus* and *Peanut bud necrosis virus* have wide host range. They produce chlorotic spots and mild mottle symptoms. Necrotic nd chlorotic rings and streaks my develop in due course. Necrosis of terminl buds is usually observed when atmospheric temperature reaches above 30°C. Secondary symptoms include stunting and proliferation of axillary shoots with reduction of leaflets.
2. *Tomato spotted wilt virus* is transmitted by two species of thrips ; namely, *Frankliniella occidentalis* and *Frankliniella fusca*. However, and *Peanut bud necrosis virus* have been reported to be transmitted by *Thrips palmi.*
3. Complete nucleotide sequence of the two major tospoviruses—*Peanut bud necrosis virus* and *Tomato spotted wilt virus* infecting peanut has been reported.
4. Purified virus particles are non infectious. Virus particles are spherical, measuring 80-100 nm in diameter, usully surrounded by a glycoprotein rich lipid membrane. They encapsulate three species of RNA ; viz, small (S), medium (M) and large (L).
5. These three RNA species contains 3057, 4801 and 8911 nucleotides respectively in *Peanut bud necrosis virus* and 2916, 4821 and 8897 nucleotides respectively in *Tomato spotted wilt virus.*
6. Large RNA species is of negative polarity and medium and small RNA species are ambisense in character. They are bound nucleo-capsid protein molecule and code for six proteins-two glycoprotein, nucle-capsid protein and two non structural proteins (NSs and NSm).
7. Thermal inactivation point of both *Tomato spotted wilt virus* and *Peanut but necrosis virus* is 45°C for 10 minutes. Longevity *in vitro* is less than 5 hours at room temperature.

(26) REOVIRUSES GROUP

Reoviruses comprise the important virus group classified as a family Reoviridae. Besides viruses that infect plants, some viruses are known to infect invertebrates and vertebrates. The plant virus members are divided into two sub groups—the genus *Phytovirus* and genus *Fijivirus.* The **type member** of Phytoreovirus is *Wound tumour virus*. The genome consists of twelve segments encapsidated within an isometric particle, measuring approximately 70 nm in diameter.

❍ Distinguishing characteristics

(1) Members are transmitted by leaf hoppers in which they are propogative. They are not transmitted by sap inoculation. The other *Phytovirus* is *Rice dwarf virus.*

(2) Genus *Fijivirus* is characterized by the isometric particles similar to those of the *Phytoreovirus*. They measure approximately 70 nm in diameter. With a RNA genome divided into ten segments, they usually infect plants of graminae family.

(3) Other members of the group are *Sugarcane Fiji virus, Maize rough dwarf, Oat sterile dwarf, Rice black streak dwarf, Pangola stunt, Cereal tillering disease virus* and *Lolium enation virus. Rice ragged stunt virus* is a possible member of the group.

C. VIRUSES WITH SINGLE STRANDED DNA GENOME

(27) GEMINI VIRUS GROUP

The name was derived from the Latin *Gemini* meaning "twins". The **type member** is *Maize streak virus*. Members have unusual particle morphology as their particles mainly occur in pairs. Particles measure about 18-20 nm in size. The virus genome is ssDNA and is so far unique among plant viruses. They are mostly found in tropical areas where they cause considerable loss to the food and fiber crops. Some important members of the group are *Bean golden mosaic, Beet curly top, Cassava latent, Euphorbia mosaic, Tomato golden mosaic, Tomato yellow dwarf, Tobacco leaf curl, Tobacco yellow dwarf, Bean summer death* and *Mung bean yellow mosaic virus.*

D. VIRUSES WITH DOUBLE STRANDED DNA GENOME

(28) CAULIMOVIRUS GROUP

The name of the group was first derived from *Cauliflower mosaic virus*. Members of the group have a genome consisting of one molecule of dsDNA which has three discontinuities—two in one strand and one in the other. The genome is encapsidated in isometric particles, measuring about 50 nm in diameter. Other members of the group are *Carnation etched ring, Dahlia mosaic, Mirabilis mosaic* and *Strawberry vein banding virus.*

❍ Distinguishing characteristics

(1) They are transmitted in nature by the insect vector belonging to Aphididae in semi persistent manner. Non-vector transmission is by mechanical inoculation by grafting. They are not transmitted by contact between the plants, not by seed and not by pollen.

(2) Thermal inactivation point is 75-80 C°, longevity *in vitro* 1-32 days. Dilution end point 10^{-3} to 10^{-4}.

(3) Preparations are strongly immunogenic. Particles react in standard gel diffusion tests. Also detectable by ELISA, ISEM and Latex agglutination tests.

(4) The Caulimoviruses and badna-viruses have genomes of similar size and structure.

(5) The replication strategy of Caulimovirus is also distinctly different from most plant viruses. In the replication process a terminally redundant RNA is used as a template for the synthesis of the double stranded DNA by a virally encoded reverse transcriptase enzyme.

E. OTHER ANGIOSPERM VIRUSES

In addition to above groups, a number of other viruses have also been described in the CMI/AAB descriptions. They may be summarized as under :

(1) Apple stem grooving virus group includes *Apple grooving* and *Potato virus T*.

(2) Barley yellow mosaic virus group includes *Barley yellow mosaic, Oat mosaic, Rice necrosis mosaic* and *Wheat spindle streak mosaic virus*.

(3) Wheat streak mosaic virus group includes *Agropyron mosaic, Oat necrotic mottle, Rye grass mosaic* and *Wheat streak mosaic virus*.

All above three groups have viruses with rod shaped particles. Viruses with isometric particles have been included into cocks food mild mosaic virus group and oat blue dwarf virus group.

SOME NEWLY RECOGNIZED VIRUS GROUPS

(29) TENUIVIRUS GROUP

The Tenuiviruses are a relatively newly recognized group of plant viruses. However, the diseases caused by them are known since the early 1900s. There are mainly 5 Tenuiviruses such as *Rice stripe virus, Maize stripe virus, Rice hoja blanca virus, Rice grassy stunt virus* and *European wheat striate mosaic virus*.

❍ Distinguishing characteristics

1. Tenuiviruses are transmitted by specific Delphacid plant hoppers belonging to Homopterous and Delphacidae. They are not mechanically transmissible.
2. Host range is limited to monocotyledonous species.
3. Symptoms produced by them usually include leaf striping, white colouring of leaf stripes and stunting.
4. The name of the group has been derived from the slender filamentous structure.
5. Particles are thread like, very thin in diameter (8-10 nm) and often without defined length.

(30) NANOVIRUSES GROUP

Until the late 1980s, Gemini viruses were the only known group of plant viruses with a genome consisting of ssDNA. Following the discovery of a novel type of plant infectivity, ssDNA viruses such as *Banana bunchy top virus, Coconut foliar decay virus* and *Subterranean clover stunt virus* were recognised. They were initially assigned as tentative members to the family Circoviridae. The new group Nanoviruses has not been assigned yet to a virus family. It includes four species namely *Banana bunchy top virus, Falsabean necrotic yellow virus, Milk vetch dwarf virus* and *Sugarcane streak virus*.

❍ Distinguishing characteristics

(1) *Banana bunchy top virus* now widely occurs on Pacific Islands, Australia

and Indonesia has an erratic geographic distribution in southern Asia and Africa.

(2) *Banana bunchy top virus* infects bananas (*Musa* species) and closely related species within the Musaceae.

(3) Nanoviruses are strictly restricted to phloem tissue of their hosts.

(4) One aphid species—*Pentalonia nigronervosa* has been reported as its vector. Transmission by grafting has been reported but not through mechanical means and seed. The aphid requires short acquisition and inoculation access feeding periods of about 30 minutes.

(5) Nanoviruses possess small icosahedral virions (18-20 nm in diameter) made up of a single capsid protein of 19-20 kDa and circular ssDNA. The genome of the nanoviruses comprises several ssDNA components.

(6) Nanovirus virions have a sedimentation coefficient of about 46S. Virions are unstable in Cesium Chloride(C_sCl) and particles stability is not affected by freezing of tissue before virion extraction.

(7) Virions are strongly immunogenic. Most Nanovirus species are serologically distinct from one another. *Banana bunchy top virus* seems to be serologically unrelated to the other three Nanovirus species.

❍ Current Classification of Plant viruses

Prior to the current classification, most plant viruses were placed in different groups as described above. However, in few instances, some viruses belonging to vertebrates were classified into families and genera. In 1995 classification of 41 new genera were also recognized. Of which, 19 were classified into 7 new families. An unusual feature of that classification was that 22 genera were described but were not classified under families. These were unassigned genera. In 6th International Committee on Taxonomy of Viruses (ICTV) report, plant viruses were classified into genera and families. The 7th report of the ICTV listed a total of 904 plant viruses classified as members or tentative members in 70 genera.

Table 3.1 **Partial list of plant viruses named in alphabetical order and their abbreviations as used in the 7th ICTV report which has recently been published, is given below :**

Genome	Family	Genus	Type species (abbreviation)
dsDNA (reverse transcribing)	Caulimoviridae	*Caulimovirus*	*Cauliflower mosaic virus* (CaMV)
		SoyCMV-like viruses	*Soybean chlorotic mottle virus* (Soy MV)
		CVMV-like viruses	*Cassava vein mosaic virus* (CVMV)
		PVCV-like viruses	*Petunia vein clearing virus* (PVCV)
		Badnavirus	Commelina yellow mottle virus (Com YMV)

Genome	Family	Genus	Type species (abbreviation)
		RTBV-like viruses	*Rice tungru bacilliform virus* (RTBV)
ssDNA	Geminiviridae	*Mastrevirus*	*Maize streak virus* (MSV)
		Curtovirus	*Beet curly top virus*
		Begomovirus	*Bean golden mosaic virus*
	—	*Nanovirus*	*Subterranean clover stunt virus*
dsRNA	Reoviridae	*Phytoreovirus*	*Wound tumor virus*
		Fijivirus	*Fiji disease virus*
		Oryza virus	*Rice ragged stunt virus* (RRSV)
	Partutvirdae	*Alphacrypto virus*	*White clover cryptic virus*-1(WCCV-1)
		Betacryptovirus	*White clover cryptic virus*-2(WCCV-2)
	—	*Varicosa virus*	*Lettuce big-vein virus* (LBVV)
(-) **ssRNA**	Rhaboviridae	*Cytothabdovirus*	*Lettuce necrotic yellow virus* (LNYV)
		Nucleo rhabdovirus	*Potato yellow dwarf virus* (PYDV)
	Bunyaviridae	*Tospovirus*	*Tomato spotted wilt virus* (TSWV)
	—	*Tenuivirus*	*Rice stripe virus* (RSV)
	—	*Ophio virus*	*Citrus psorosis virus* (CSV)
(+) **ssRNA**	Bromoviridae	*Bromo virus*	*Brome mosaic virus* (BMV)
		Cucumo virus	*Cucumber mosaic virus* (CMV)
		Alfamo virus	*Alfalfa mosaic virus* (AMV)
		Ilavirus	*Prunus necrotic ring spot virus* (PNRSV)
		Oleavirus	*Olive latent virus* 2 (OLV-2)
	Closteroviridae	*Clostero virus*	*Beet yellows virus* (BYV)
		Crinivirus	*Lettuce infectious yellow virus* (LIYV)
	Comoviridae	*Como virus*	*Cowpea mosaic virus* (CMV)

Genome	Family	Genus	Type species (abbreviation)
	—	*Nepovirus*	*Tobacco ring spot virus* (TRSV)
	—	*Fabavirus*	*Broad bean wilt virus*-1 (BBWW-1)
	Luteoviridae	*Luteovirus*	*Barley yellow dwarf virus-PAV* (BYDV- PAV)
		Polero virus	*Potato leaf roll virus* (PLRV)
		Enamovirus	*Pea enation mosaic virus*-1 (PEMV-1)
	Potyviridae	*Potyvirus*	*Potato virus-Y* (PVY)
		Rymovirus	*Ryegrass mosaic virus* (RGMV)
		Bymovirus	*Barley yellow mosaic virus* (BaYMV)
		Macluravirus	*Maclura mosaic virus*
		Ipomovirus	*Sweet potato mild mosaic virus* (SPMMV)
		Tritimovirus	*Wheat streak mosaic virus* (WSMV)
	Sequiviridae	*Sequivirus*	*Parsnip yellow fleck virus* (PYFV)
		Waikavirus	*Rice tungru spherical virus* (RTSV)
	Tombusviridae	*Tombusvirus*	*Tomato bushy stunt virus* (TBSV)
		Carmovirus	*Carnation mottle virus* (CaMV)
		Necrovirus	*Tobacco necrosis virus-A* (TNV-A)
		Machlomovirus	*Maize chlorotic mottle virus* (MCMTV)
		Dianthovirus	*Carnation ring spot virus* (CRSV)
		Avenavirus	*Oat chlorotic stunt virus* (OCSV)
		Aureus virus	*Pothos latent virus* (PLV)
		Panicovirus	*Panicum mosaic virus* (PMV)
(+) ssRNA	—	*Tobravirus*	*Tobacco rattle virus* (TRV)
(+) ssRNA	—	*Tobamovirus*	*Tobacco mosaic virus* (TMV)

Genome	Family	Genus	Type species (abbreviation)
(+) ssRNA	—	*Hordeivirus*	*Barley stripe mosaic virus* (BSMV)
(+) ssRNA	—	*Furovirus*	*Soil-borne wheat mosaic virus* (SBWMV)
(+) ssRNA	—	*Pomovirus*	*Potato mop-top virus* (PMTV)
(+) ssRNA	—	*Pecluvirus*	*Peanut clump virus* (PCV)
(+) ssRNA	—	*Benyvirus*	*Beet necrotic yellow vein virus* (BNYVV)
(+) ssRNA	—	*Sobemo virus*	*Southern bean mosaic virus* (SBMV)
(+) ssRNA	—	*Marafivirus*	*Maize rayado fino virus* (MRFV)
(+) ssRNA	—	*Umbravirus*	*Carrot mottle virus* (CMoV)
(+) ssRNA	—	*Tymovirus*	*Turnip yellow mosaic virus* (TYMV)
(+) ssRNA	—	*Ourmiavirus*	*Ourmia melon virus* (OuMV)
(+) ssRNA	—	*Potex virus*	*Potato virus X*(PVX)
(+) ssRNA	—	*Carlavirus*	*Carnation latent virus* (CLV)
(+) ssRNA		*Foveaviruses*	*Apple stem pitting virus* (ASPV)
(+) ssRNA	—	*Allexivirus*	*Shallot virus X (Sh VX)*
(+) ssRNA	—	*Idaeovirus*	*Raspberry bushy dwarf virus* (RBDV)
(+) ssRNA	—	*Capillovirus*	*Apple stem grooving virus* (ASGV)
(+) ssRNA	—	*Trichovirus*	*Apple chlorotic leaf spot virus* (ACLSV)
(+) ssRNA	—	*Vitivirus*	*Grapevine virus A* (GVA).

*Total number of species in a family not assigned to a genus.

❍ Names of Virus and Viroid Species

Usually the names of order, families, sub families and genera are always printed in italics or underlined when writing and the first letter is always capitalized. The new rule of International Code of Virus Classification and Nomenclature is as under as per the suggestion of Mayo and Horzinck (1998). Under the rule, names of species are always printed in italics and first letter of the first word is capitalized. Other words are not capitalized unless they are proper noun or part of proper nouns. Examples of *Tobacco mosaic virus, Polio virus* and *Murray River encephalitis virus* may be cited here. In this case river is the proper noun.

The use of italics when referring to the name of a species as a taxonomic entity will clearly be a signal that it has the status of an official recognized species. Although the name of all the viruses both having official status and also those not yet classified have been italized in this text for maintaining the similarity in naming the viruses. A complete list of all the virus species that have been recognized so far can be found in the 7th ICTV Report published in April 2000 (Van Regenmortel *et al*, 2000). Scientific names in biology are usually Latin words, and the use of italics indicates their Latin origin. However, the International Committee of Virologists is strongly opposed to the introduction of Latin binomials for naming viruses and the nomenclature system developed by ICTV reflects this position.

In order to use the name of the virus, descriptions and lists have been adopted from the VIDE database, CAB International, University Press, Cambridge. Abbreviations used by most of the virologists which seem to be easy to adopt and understand by the readers, is being followed in this text. For example, T can be used to symbolize tobacco, tomato and turnip. In the text T is retained for tobacco, C is retained for cucumber and similarly many such words used by earlier scientists are being retained as it was used by different scientists earlier. Many acronyms have been changed in order to remove confusion among different abbreviations used to name the viruses. For example, M currently may indicate mosaic, mottle, mild and mottling. To get rid of confusion, Sutic *et al* (1999) used M for mosaic as used by earlier scientists, used Mt for mottle, used Md for mild and used Mg for mottling. Following this pattern, viruses and diseases may be abbreviated in following manner.

Maize dwarf mosaic virus	MDMV
Maize chlorotic dwarf walkavirus	MCDV
Maize rough dwarf fijivirus	MR$_G$DV
Maize mosaic rhabdovirus	MMV
Maize streak geminivirus	MS$_K$V
Maize white line mosaic virus	MWtLnMV
Maize chlorotic mottle machlomovirus	MCMtV
Maize rayado fino marafivirus	MRaFnV
Maize leaf fleck virus	MLFkV
Wheat striate mosaic rhadovirus	WS$_T$MV
Wheat American striate mosaic rhabdovirus	WAStMV
Wheat European striate mosaic rhabdovirus	WEStMV
Wheat soil-borne mosaic virus	WSoMV
Wheat streak mosaic potyvirus	WStMV
Wheat spindle streak mosaic virus	WS$_L$S$_K$MV
Wheat winter mosaic rhabdovirus	WWnMV
Wheat dwarf disease	WDDs
Wheat chlorotic streak rhabdovirus	WCSkV
Wheat yellow leaf closterovirus	WYLV
Barley stripe mosaic virus	BySpMV
Barley yellow dwarf virus	ByYDV

Barley yellow dwarf luteovirus	ByYDV
Barley yellow striate mosaic virus	ByStMV
Barley stripe mosaic hordeivirus	BySpMV
Barley yellow mosaic potyvirus	ByYMV
Barley yellow striate mosaic rhabdovirus	ByYS$_T$MV
Cereal tillering disease reovirus	CrTIDsV
Cearl chlorotic motle rhabdovirus	CrCMtV
Cereal northern mosaic virus	CrNnMV
Oat blue dwarf virus	O$_T$B$_L$DV
Oat sterile dwarf reovirus	O$_T$S$_R$DV
Oat pseudo-rosette virus	O$_T$P$_D$R$_O$V
Oat mosaic virus	O$_T$MV
Oat soil-borne stripe virus	O$_T$SoSpV
Oat striate mosaic virus	O$_T$StMV
Oat necrotic mottle virus	O$_T$NcMtV
Rice dwarf reovirus	RDV
Rice black-streaked dwarf reovirus	RBSkDV
Rice gall dwarf reovirus	RG$_L$DV
Rice ragged stunt reovirus	RR$_D$S$_N$V
Rice stripe tenuivirus	RSpV
Rice hoja blanca tenuivirus	RHBV
Rice grassy stunt tenuivirus	RG$_R$S$_N$V
Rice necrosis mosaic virus	RNMV
Rice transitory yellowing rhabdovirus	RTyYgV
Rice tungru waikavirus	RTgV
Rice yellow mottle sobemovirus	RYMtV
Sorghum mosaic potyvirus	S$_R$MV
Sorghum stunt mosaic virus	S$_R$S$_N$MV
Sorghum yellow banding virus	S$_R$YBaV
Sorghum chlorotic spot virus	S$_R$CSptV
Brome mosaic virus	BrMV
Cocksfoot mild mosaic virus	CkMdMV
Cocksfoot mottle sobemovirus	CkMtV
Cocksfoot streak potyvirus	CkSkV
Foxtail mosaic potexvirus	FxMV
Guinea grass mosaic potyvirus	GugMV
Ryegrass mottle virus	RgMtV
Ryegrass enation virus	RgEnV
Ryegrass mottle virus	RgMtV
Ryegrass mosaic potyvirus	RgMV
Ryegrass bacilliform rhabdovirus	RgBc V

Ryegrass cryptic virus	Rg Cc V
Johnsongrass mosaic potyvirus	JgMV
Alfalfa mosaic virus	AMV
Alfalfa latent carlavirus	ALtV
Lucern (Alfalfa) *Australian latent nepovirus*	AAaLtV
Lucern (Alfalfa) *transient streak sobemovirus*	ATtSkV
Red clover mottle comovirus	RClMtV
Red clover necrotic mosaic bromovirus	RClNcMV
Red clover vein mosaic carlavirus	*RClVMV*
Red clover chlorotic ringspot virus	RClCRsV
Clover yellow mosaic potexvirus	*ClYMV*
Clover yellow vein potyvirus	*ClYVV*
White clover mosaic potexvirus	WClMV
Pepper mild mottle tobamovirus	PpMdMtV
Pepper mottle potyvirus	*PpMtV*
Pepper veinal mottle potyvirus	PpVMtV
Tomato aspermy cucumovirus	TmAyV
Tomato black ring nepovirus	TmBRV
Tomato bushy stunt tombusvirus	TmBuSnV
Tomato golden mosaic geminivirus	*TmGMV*
Tomato mosaic tobamovirus	TmMV
Tomato ringspot nepovirus	TmRsV
Tomato spotted wilt virus	TmSpoWV
Eggplant mosaic tymovirus	EMV
Eggplant mottled dwarf rhabdovirus	EMtDV
Turnip mosaic virus (Syn.)	TuMV
Cauliflower mosaic caulimovirus	CfMV
Broccoli necrotic yellow rhabdovirus	BcNcYsV
Radish mosaic comovirus	RaMV
Radish yellow edge virus	RaYEgV
Turnip crinkle tombusvirus	TuCrV
Turnip rosette mosaic sobemovirus	TuRoMV
Turnip yellow mosaic tymovirus	TuYMV
Turnip yellows luteovirus	TuYsV
Onion yellow dwarf potyvirus	OYDV
Shallot latent carlavirus	ShLtV
Leak yellow stripe potyvirus	LkYStV
Garlic mosaic potyvirus	GcMV
Cucumber leafspot tombusvirus	CLsV
Cucumber mosaic cucumovirus	CMV
Cucumber necrosis necrovirus	CNV

Cucumber green mottle mosaic tobamovirus	CGnMtMV
Melon necrotic spot virus	MnNcSpoV
Watermelon mosaic potyvirus	WmMV
Squash mosaic comovirus	SqMV
Squash leaf curl geminivirus	SqLcV
Zucchini yellow mosaic potyvirus	ZYMV
Zucchini yellow fleck virus	ZYFkV
Bean common mosaic potyvirus	BCmMV
Bean yellow mosaic potyvirus	BYMV
Bean leaf roll luteovirus	BLrV
Bean southern mosaic sobemovirus	BSuMV
Pea (common) *mosaic virus*	PeCmMV
Pea early-browning tobravirus	PeElBrV
Pea enation mosaic virus	PeEnMV
Pea seed-borne mosaic potyvirus	PeSdBnMV
Pea streak carlavirus	PeSkV
Broad bean mottle bromovirus	BBMtV
Broad bean true mosaic comovirus	BBTMV
Broad bean wilt (possible) comovirus	BBWV
Cowpea aphid-borne mosaic potyvirus	CpApBnMV
Cowpea chlorotic mottle bromovirus	CpCMtV
Cowpea mosaic comovirus	CpMV
Cowpea severe mosaic comovirus	CpSeMV
Cowpea mild mottle carlavirus	CpMdMtV
Carrot mottle virus	CoMtV
Carrot red leaf (possible) luteovirus	CoReLV
Carrot thin leaf potyvirus	CoTnLV
Carrot latent rhabdovirus	CoLtV
Carrot mosaic potyvirus	CoMV
Carrot yellow leaf closterovirus	CoYLV
Celery mosaic poty virus	CeMV
Celery latent virus	CeLtV
Celery ringspot virus	CeRsV
Celery yellow net virus	CeYNtV
Celery yellow spot luteovirus	CeYSptV
Parsnip mosaic potyvirus	PnpMV
Parsnip yellow fleck virus	PnpYFkV
Artichoke Italian latent nepovirus	*AklLtV*
Artichoke vein banding nepovirus	AkVBaV
Artichoke yellow ringspot nepovirus	AkYRsV
Artichoke curly dwarf virus	AkCuDV

Artichoke latent nepovirus	AkLtV
Artichoke mottled crinkle tombusvirus	AkMtCrV
Lettuce mosaic potyvirus	LMV
Lettuce necrotic yellows rhabdovirus	LNcYsV
Lettuce big vein virus	LBiVV
Lettuce necrosis virus	LNV
Spinach latent ilarvirus	SLtV
Pea nut bud necrosis virus	PtBdNV
Pea nut clump pecluvirus	PtCpV
Peanut mottle potyvirus	PtMtV
Peanut stripe potyvirus	PtSpV
Peanut stunt cucumovirus	PtSnV
Peanut chlorotic streak caulimovirus	PtCStV
Groundnut rosette disease	*GtRoDs*
Potato leafroll luteovirus	PLrV
Potato potyvirus A	PVA
Potato carlavirus M	PVM
Potato carlavirus S	PVS
Potato potyvirus Y	PVY
Potato aucuba mosaic potex virus	PAcMV
Potato yellow dwarf rhabdovirus	PYDV
Potato spindle tuber viroid	PSlTbVd
Potato mop top tobamovirus	PMpTpV
Potato potexvirus X	PVX
Tobacco mosaic tobamovirus	*TMV*
Tobacco etch potyvirus	TE_HV
Tobacco vein mottling potyvirus	*TVMgV*
Tobacco yellow dwarf geminivirus	TYDV
Tobacco leaf curl geminivirus	TLCuV
Tobacco rattle tobravirus	TRtV
Tobacco ringspot nepovirus	TRsV
Tobacco necrosis virus (type)	TNV
Tobacco streak ilarvirus	TSkV
Beet curly top (possible) geminivirus	B_TCuTpV
Beet mosaic potyvirus	B_TMV
Beet necrotic yellow vein tobamovirus	B_TNcYVV
Beet western yellows luteovirus	B_TWsYsV
Beet yellows closterovirus	B_TYsV
Beet leaf curl rhabdovirus	B_TLCuV
Beet mild yellowing luteovirus	B_TMdYgV
Beet pseudo yellows virus	B_TPdYsV

Beet yellow net virus	B_TYNtV
Sugarcane mosaic virus	ScMV
Sugarcane serch disease	ScShDs
Sugarcane streak virus	ScSkV
Sugarcane chlorotic streak disease	ScCSkDs
Sugarcane striate mosaic disease	ScStMDs
Fiji disease reovirus	FiDsV
Sugarcane mild mosaic closterrovirus	ScMdMV
Sugarcane bacilliform badnavirus	ScBcV
Sugarcane yellow leaf luteovirus	*ScYLV*
Sunflower mosaic virus	SfMV
Soybean mosaic potyvirus	S_YMV
Soybean dwarf luteovirus	S_YDV
Soybean chlorotic mottle caulimovirus	S_YCMtV
Hop mosaic carlavirus	HMV
Hop latent carlavirus	HLtV
Hop stunt viroid	HSnVd
Hop chlorotic disease virus	HCDsV
Hop mosaic chlorosis virus	HMCsV
Apple mosaic ilarvirus	ApMV
Apple chlorotic leafspot closterovirus	ApCLsV
Apple tulare mosaic virus	ApTrMV
Apple leaf pucker disease	ApLPkDs
Apple green crinkle disease	ApGnCrDs
Apple ring spot disease	*ApRsDs*
Apple rough skin disease	ApRgSknDs
Apple star crack disease	ApStrCkDs
Apple scar skin viroid	ApScSknVd
Apple dapple viroid	ApDlVd
Apple stem grooving capillovirus	ApStmGgV
Apple stem pitting disease	ApStmPgDs
Apple platycarpa scaly bark disease	ApPcSyBkDs
Pear ring disease	PrRDs
Pear ring pattern mosaic disease	PrRPtMDs
Pear bud drop disease	PrBdDpDs
Pear stony pit disease	PrStnPiDs
Pear freckle pit disease	PrFrPiDs
Quince stunt disease	QSnDs
Quince sooty ringspot disease	QStyRsDs
Quince fruit deformation disease	QFtDnDs
Plum pox potyvirus	*PlPV*

Prunus dwarf ilarvirus	PsDV
Prunus necrotic ringspot ilarvirus	PsNcRsV
Plum line pattern virus	PlLnPtV
Plum fruit crinkle	PlFtCr
Peach leaf necrosis disease	PhLNDs
Peach rosette mosaic nepovirus	PhRoMV
Peach enation virus	PhEnV
Peach line pattern and leaf curl virus	PhLnPtLCV
Peach latent mosaic viroid	PhLtMVd
Peach asteroid spot disease	PhAsSpDs
Peach wart disease	PhWDs
Peach stubby twig disease	PhSbTwDs
Peach bark and wood grooving disease	PhBkWdGgDs
Peach oil blotch disease	PhOlBhDs
Peach seedling chlorosis disease	PhSgCsDs
Apricot ring pox disease	AtRPDs
Cherry leaf roll nepovirus	ChLrV
Cherry rasp leaf nepovirus	ChRpLV
Cherry green ring mottle disease	ChGnRMtDs
Cherry rusty mottle disease	ChRyMtDs
Cherry little cherry disease	ChLlChDs
Cherry twisted leaf disease	ChtdLDs
Cherry spur cherry disease	ShSprChDs
Cherry bark canker disease	ChBCnDs
Sour cherry green ring mottle disease	SChGnRMtDs
Walnut line pattern disease	WtLnPtDs
Walnut mosaic disease	WtMDs
Chestnut mosaic tobamovirus	CtMV
Banana bunchy top virus	BaByTpV
Banana bract mosaic potyvirus	BaBtMV
Citrus tristeza closterovirus	CsTzV
Citrus variegation ilarvirus	CsVgV
Citrus exocortis viroid	CsExVd
Citrus cachexia-xyloporosis disease	CsCXDs
Citrus concave gum disease	CsCgDs
Citrus cristacortis disease	CsCtDs
Citrus gummy bark disease	CsGmBkDs
Citrus psorosis disease	CsPsDs
Citrus ring spot disease	CsRsDs
Citrus vein enation disease	CsVEnDs
Olive latent ringspot nepovirus	OlLtRsV

Coconut cadang-cadang viroid	CcCcgVd
Papaya mosaic potexvirus	PaMV
Papaya ringspot potyvirus	PaRsV
Strawberry crinkle rhabdovirus	SbCrV
Strawberry mild yellow edge luteovirus	SbMdYEgV
Strawberry mottle virus	SbMtV
Strawberry vein banding caulimovirus	SbVBdV
Raspberry vein chlorosis rhabdovirus	RbVCsV
Raspberry bushy dwarf virus	RbBuDV
Black raspberry necrosis virus	BRbNV
Blueberry leaf mottle virus	BlbLMtV

4

PURIFICATIONS AND PROPERTIES

Plant virology laboratory, Basic rules and requirements, Usefulness of different steps in purification, Conditions for virus purification, Purification of different viruses, Protocol for purification of citrus mosaic badnavirus, Protocol for purification of potato virus Y, Density gradient, Sucrose density gradient, Dialysis of virus sample and study of physical properties of viruses.

PLANT VIROLOGY LABORATORY

❍ Basic Rules of Virology Laboratory

For efficient working, there should be a well-established plant virology laboratory attached with tissue culture laboratory, green house/glass house and well protected agricultural lands for field experiments. Besides these, cultural media room, autoclave room and cool room should also be fully established near the plant virology laboratory for proper research work. If a large number of students are working in the laboratory, they should be aware what to do and what to not and what are the different apparatus/instruments and equipment present in the laboratory ? How they are operated and what are their functions ? What are the chemicals which are used to prepare buffers, reagents, stains and other preparations ? How should the students enter to the laboratory and how should work ? Thus it is important for freshers including students, teachers, assistants and helpers to follow the fundamental rules and guidelines for efficient and safe working in the laboratory. Some of the important rules and guidelines may be summarized as under :

1. Always maintain aseptic conditions in the laboratory while doing different kinds of laboratory works, including purification, tissue culture, media preparation for growing plantlets, study of physical and biological properties etc. of the viruses.
2. Always wear an apron before entering the laboratory to get protected from contamination and laboratory hazards. Apron should always be kept well cleaned and washed.
3. Long hairs and nails etc. should be cut to normal to avoid contamination and chemical hazards and facilitate efficient working with different instruments, apparatus, chemicals, buffers and reagents.
4. Avoid keeping books, purses and bags etc. on working table so as to keep the working bench clean for efficient working.
5. Eating food, drinking water and other drinks as well as smoking and spitting in the working laboratory should be avoided to avoid contamination and infection from microorganisms. Never put pencil, pins, inoculating needle and thread in mouth, nose and ear, so as to avoid infection and adverse effect of chemicals due to contamination and carelessness.
6. Working benches should be cleaned regularly with ethanol (70%) or phenol (1 :100) and hands must be washed with soap in running tap water before and after the work performed in the laboratory.
7. Do not put your finger in nose and avoid its contact with lips and eyes and use quality gloves where necessary while handling the chemical solution, stains, reagents, buffers, ultra-voilet light, sprit lamp and different glassware etc.
8. Always keep the burner at proper distance from the organic solvents and it should be turned off soon after the use so as to avoid fire accidents. Always use flame sterilized inoculation needle/loop, scalpels and knife etc. in tissue culture laboratory. Handle rotors of the centrifuge sincerely with extra care.
9. Keep the chemicals, reagents and stock solutions etc. at their respective places.
10. Ask your teacher or laboratory technician for any difficulty and maintain proper record of the work done.

BASIC REQUIREMENTS OF VIROLOGY LABORATORY

❍ Partial list of common equipment along with names of some specific firms

Autoclave; Refrigerator; Balance electronic (micro and macro); Low speed centrifuge. Sorvall Instruments; Beckman's Ultra-centrifuge; Beckman's Optima L-90 K, Ultra-centrifuge; Roters 55.2 and SW 41 TI; Centrikon T-Ultra- centrifuge; Distillation Plant-USF Elga Prima & Maxima; Sigma 3 K-30 Model Table top centrifuge; Table top micro-centrifuge; Microfuges-refrigeratred and non-refrigerated; Ultra low freezer (Vertical); Ultra-freezer (—80°C) horigental; Freeze dry system; Deep freezers (—20°C and —80°C); pH meter-Wisdom Scientific Co. Inc. Edison, New Jersey, USA.; Erycomp-Thermo Cycler with power block-II system- Easycycler; Horigental gel electrophoresis unit with electro power pack; Vertical slab gel electrophoresis apparatus; Submarine gel electrophoresis set (tray comb of different sizes); Gel Doc Mega; Laminar air flow hood; Vortex mixer; Hot plate; Microwave oven; Automatic pipettes of variable volumes; Electronic pipettor; Shaker incubator with refrigeration; Stirring/shaking water bath (for different temperatures like 37 C°, 42 C°, 50 C°, 65 C°, 95 C° and boiling temperature; Hot air ovens Power pack; Hybridization oven; Scinitillation counter; Sequencing apparatus; Freeze dryers; ELISA reader; Suction pump and gel dryer.

❍ Supplies

Plastic wares; eppendorf tubes (1.5 ml, 0.5 ml); PCR tubes; tips (5 ml, 1 ml, 200 μl, 1-10 μl), sequencing loading tips; tip boxes; Petriplates; storage boxes, stands of different sizes; ELISA plates.

❍ Others

Latex gloves; plastic gloves; syringes; filters; filter holder, magnetic bars; pH paper; tooth picks; X-ray film; developer and fixer; X-ray cassettes; pestle and mortar; paper and polythene bags; markers; thread; rubber bands and wax coated labels.

Preparation of Chromic acid for cleaning Glassware

Care should be taken that the glassware which are used in virology laboratory are neat and clean. Chromic acid is widely used as cleaning agent for glassware. It is a mixture of sodium dichromate and concentrated sulphuric acid. Chromic acid possesses powerful oxidizing and solvent properties and is suitable for cleaning glassware.

METHOD OF PREPARATION

Weigh 5g of sodium or potassium dichromate ($K_2 Cr_2 O_7$ or $Na_2 Cr_2 O_7$) and dissolve it in 5 ml of distilled water in a beaker of 250 ml capacity. Add 100 ml of concentrated sulphuric acid (H_2SO_4) slowly and slowly, stirring it constantly. The mixture is allowed to cool at about 4C° and now store it in a dry glass stoppered bottle. It is ready to use. Use brush and tap water.

HOW TO USE WATER BATH

Water bath is an instrument that is used to provide constant temperature to a sample. It consists of an insulating box made up of steel fitted with electrode heating coil. The temperature is controlled through thermostat. In some of the water bath, platform rotates and such water bath is called as water bath shaker.

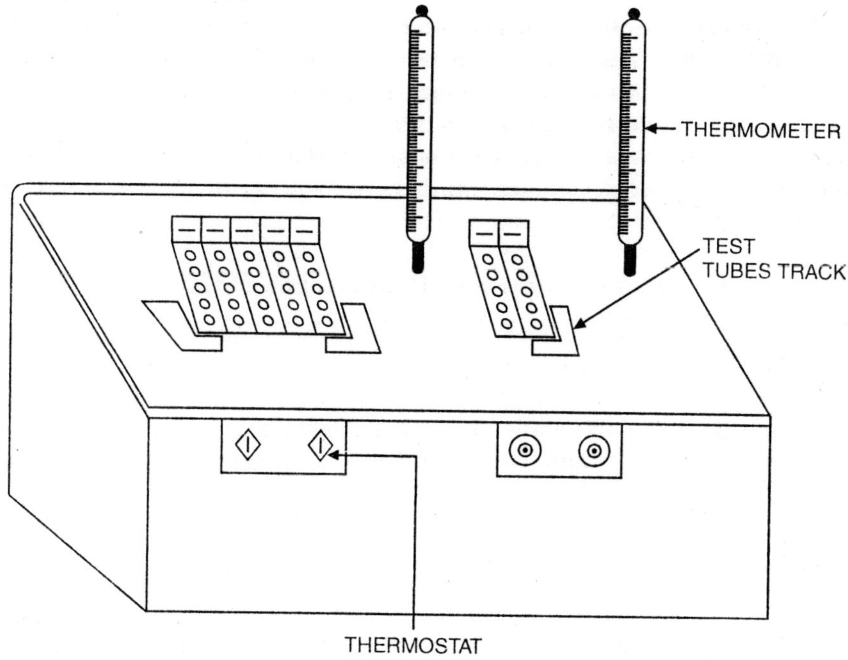

Fig. 4.1 Diagramatic representation of a Water bath incubator shaker.

HOW TO USE AUTOCLAVE

The autoclave is usually operated at 15 lb/inch^2 (1 kg/cm^2) steam pressure. The

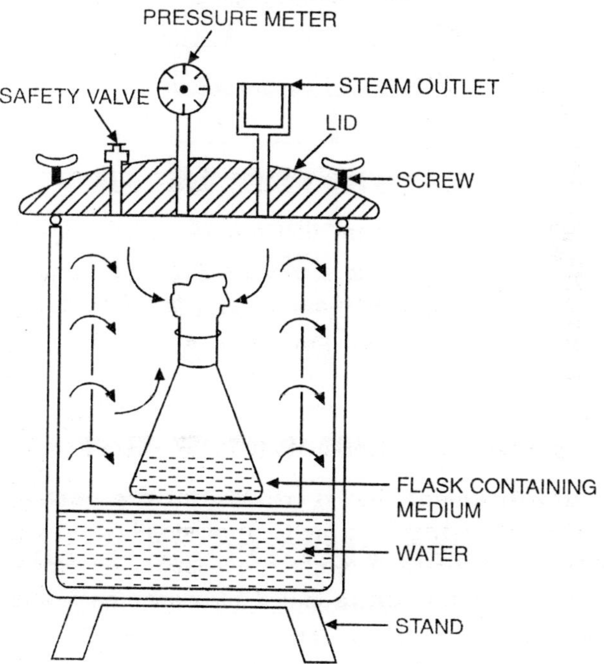

Fig. 4.2 Diagramatic representation of Autoclave.

killing action of heat can be done by using increase in steam in a closed system. The water boils at 100°C and the steam accumulates in a closed container resulting in increase in pressure. In autoclave, steam passes from below at the base. The side walls are heated by the steam jacket. It has a provision to record the pressure and temperature. The water level should be checked and kept to the normal level as desired and it should be completely evacuated and the steam must have access to the object to be sterilized.

HOW TO USE INCUBATOR

An incubator is an instrument that consists of copper/steel chamber, around which warm water or air is circulated by electric current by means of small gas flame. The temperature of the incubator is kept constant and is controlled by thermostat. The incubator is made up of double walled chamber adjusted to a desired temperature. It is done by using an external knob controlling the thermostat system. The door of the incubator should be opened when necessary.

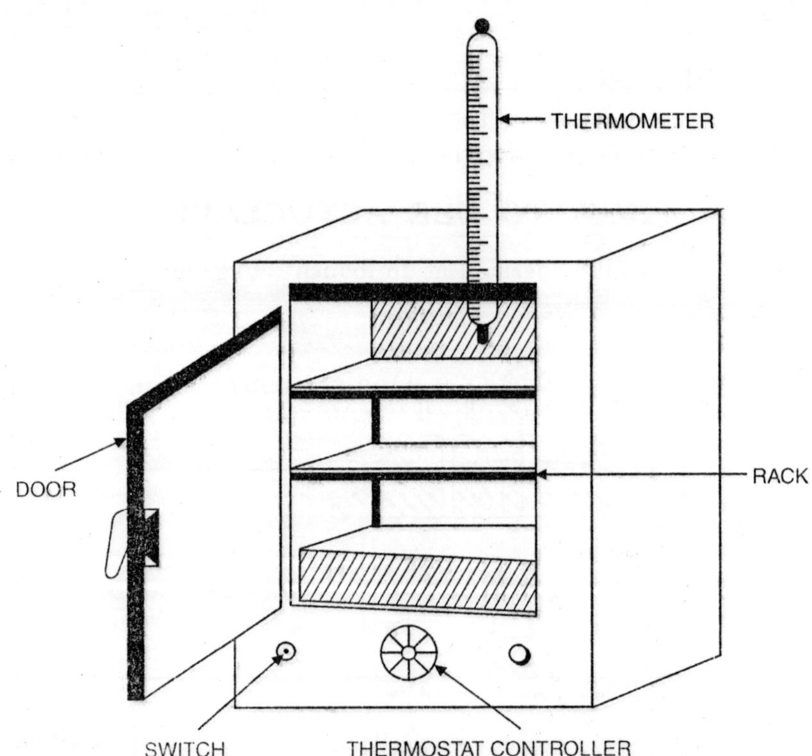

Fig. 4.3 Diagramatic representation of Incubator.

HOW TO USE ELECTRONIC BALANCE

For chemical and biological experiments, accurate amount of chemical should be weighted by using an electronic balance. There are several types of balances according to the requirement and the amount of material to be weighed. Balance may be single pan balance, chemical, analytical and electronic balance. Ultra micro balance can weigh the materials of 0.01 μg to 2.0 mg. Electric balance works in presence of electricity that shows digital display of weight. In electronic ultra micro balance, weights of different measurements are not required.

HOW TO USE SPECTROPHOTOMETER

Spectrometer is an instrument that utilizes light as a soure of radiation and measures changes in optical density or absorbance. It has three basic and principal parts—(1) The source of radiation (2) A unit for dispersing radiation at different wavelengths and (3) A device that detects the amount of radiation at different wavelengths.

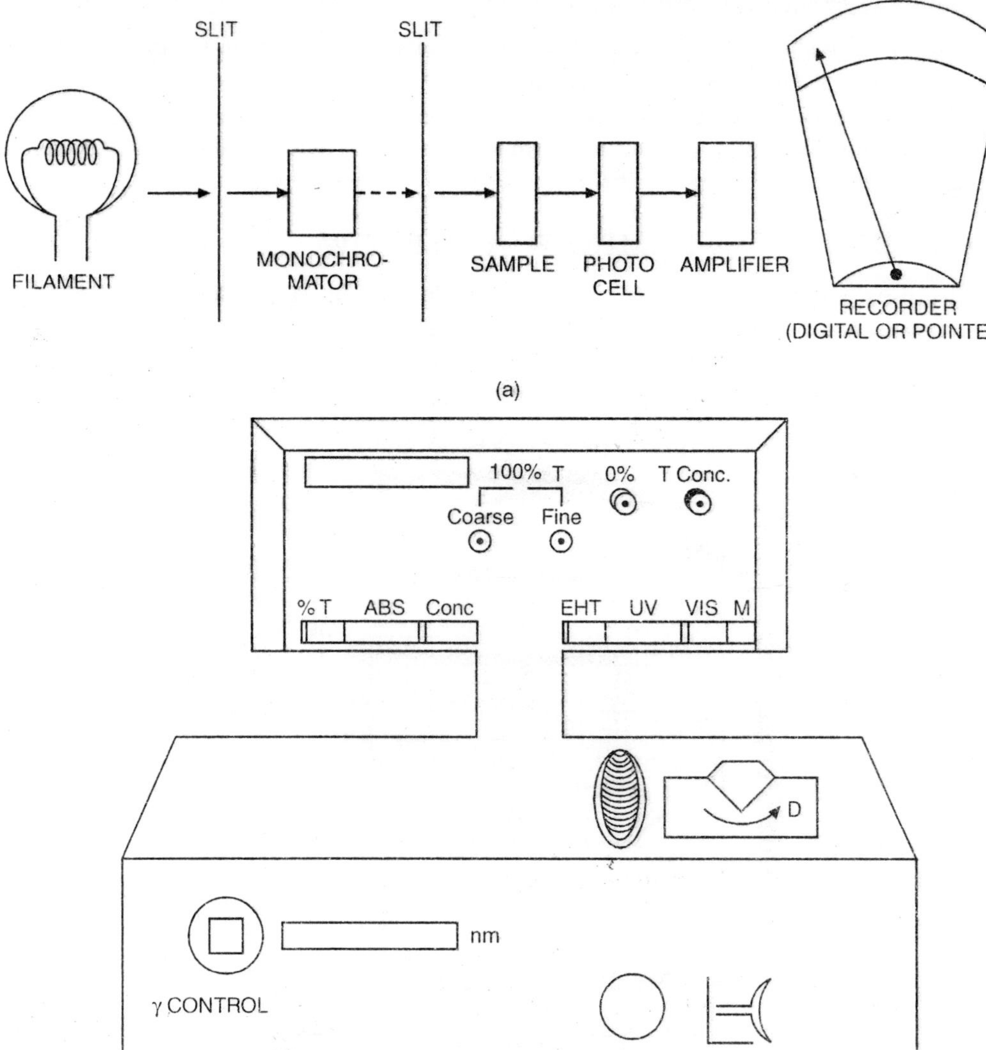

Fig. 4.4 Diagrammatic representation of UV Spectrophotometer. (*a*) Functioning of Spectrophotometer and (*b*) U.V. Visible Spectrophotometer

For quantitative estimation of absorbance of different concentrations of substances, absorbance may be measured following Beer's Law of Absorbance. The law explains that when a ray of monochromatic light passes through an absorbing medium, its intensity decreases exponentially as the concentration of absorbing medium increases. The mathematical expression of Beer's law may be represented as under :

$$\text{Log } Lo / 1 = K_C$$

where l_0 = Original intensity of light beam,

I = Intensity of beam passing through a solution, and

C = Concentration of the solution in moles/l.

K = Constant

A plot of absorbance (Y-axis) versus concentration (X-axis) yields a calibration curve. The theory may be used in quantitative estimation.

The spectrophotometer is of many types such as (1) *Visible range spectrophotometer,* (2) *UV visible spectrophotometer* and (3) *I R Spectrophotometer.* All the spectrophotometesr are used in different ways in laboratories.

LAMINAR AIR FLOW

Laminar air flow is an apparatus consisting of an air blower in the rear side of the chamber. I can produce air flow with uniform velocity along the paralle flow lines. Laminar air flow is a special kind of chamber that helps in transferring microbial cultures under aseptic conditions.

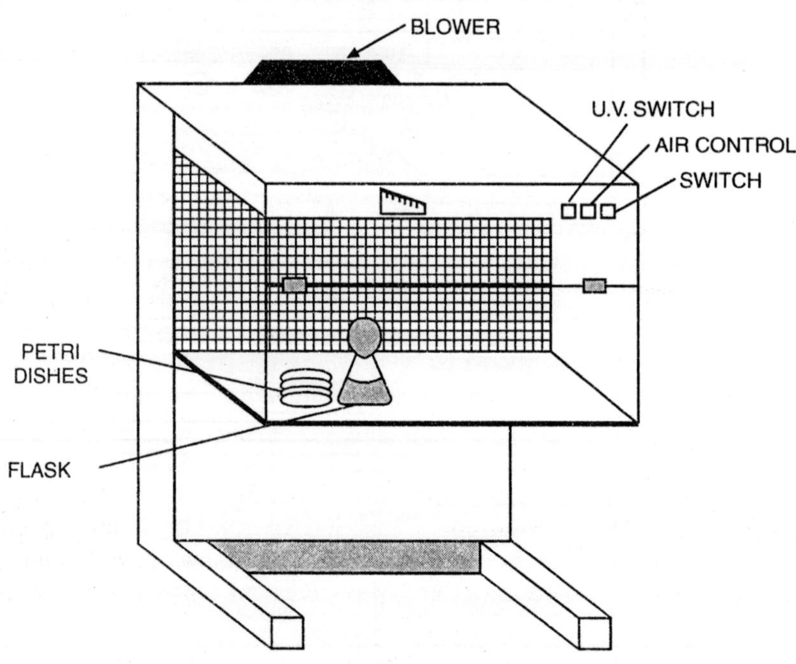

Fig. 4.5 Laminar airflow system

CENTRIFUGES AND THEIR USE

Centrifuges are the instruments which operate through the centrifugation technique. Centrifugation technique is based on molecular mass, shape and density of the particles. The rate of velocity at which particles sediment is proportional to the force rate and velocity of sedimentation applied forces. The centrifugal force is applied which induces the gravitational force of the materials present in a solution. The *centrifugal force acts in a direction away from the centre of the axis.* If the speed of rotation is faster, the force will be higher accordingly. The rate of sedimentation depends upon the applied centrifugal field (G). The G is the function of square of angular velocity (radians/sec.) of the rotor and the radial distance (r in cm) of the particles present from the axis of rotation.

$$G = \omega^2 r$$

Since, one resolution is equal to 2 radians,

$$\omega = 2\pi/60 \text{ resolution per minute}$$

Therefore $$G = \frac{2\pi\,(\text{revolution/minute})^2\, r}{(60)^2}$$

The centrifugal force is expressed as relative centrifugal field (RCF) in g unit (g = 9.8065 M/sec^{-2} or 980 cm sec^{-2}).

There are four main types of centrifuges namely, small bench centrifuge, refrigerated centrifuge, high speed centrifuge and ultracentrifuge etc.

PURIFICATION OF VIRUSES

Isolation and purification of plant viruses are the important and foremost steps for studies on host range, physical and chemical properties, electron microscopy and molecular aspects including genomic organisation. The cumulative information is pre-requisite for identification of the virus. The aim of purification of viruses is to separate the non-virus materials of a plant from the virus. Highly purified preparations are essential in chemical analysis of the viruses but less pure virus will often suffice to produce an antiserum. Thus general principle of virus purification may be explained as *"Purified virus preparations are essential to study the biophysio-chemical properties of the viruses. Techniques for purification aim at the separation of virus from host constituents without affecting the structure and infectivity of the virus to be purified."*

Usually purification includes mincing of the plant material and then removing large fragments of cells by centrifuging at low speed. After this, the virus is sedimented by centrifuging at high speed. The supernatant is removed and the virus containing pellet is dissolved in a buffer solution. Centrifugation again at low speed is done for sedimenting non-virus materials. By repeating the low speed and high speed centrigutation (differential centrifugation), the virus may become free from non-virus components.

Besides sedimentation of virus by high speed centrifugation, it is possible to precipitate the virus by adding chemicals to the virus containing solution and to sediment it by low speed centrifugation. Organic solvents which help to separate the virus from non-virus material can also be added to the sap.

Density gradient centrifugation may be included as one step in the purification procedure to separate particles which do not differ much in sedimentation rate.

❍ Usefulness of the different steps of purification

(1) Both crude and purified virus preparations can be used on test plants and to measure the relative concentration of the virus. Aggregation of virus is measured as loss of virus. Inactive virus and impurities are not measured at all.

(2) Serology may measure the concentration of virus. Impurities are also measured if tested with an antiserum prepared with proteins of healthy plants.

(3) Spectrophotometer is used for measurement of the absorption spectrum which may indicate the presence of proteins and nucleic acid but does not show that the absorption is caused by the presence of virus. Nevertheless, this method gives a good impression of the total quantity of absorbing material present.

(4) Electron microscopy applied as negative staining, shows shape, size and quantities of virus particles and impurities. This method can be performed with in minutes.

(5) Viruses are colourless. Dry weight measurement provides the weight of the viruses together with impurities.

CONDITIONS FOR VIRUS PURIFICATION

The wise way to proceed with the purification of a given virus is first to collect all the available information about it and then to devise a procedure. The common steps in the isolation of many viruses are as under :

(1) Culturing of biologically pure virus in a host.

(2) The host should contain less interfering compounds and should be able to grow in shorter time supported with high concentration of virus.

(3) The virus must be extracted into a liquid medium with the chances of minimum loss of infectivity.

(4) The extract should be clarified to remove as much host material as possible without loss of virus.

(5) Concentration of the virus in the clarified extract should be done by differential centrifugation or by chemical precipitation.

(6) Further purification varies from virus to virus.

PURIFICATION OF DIFFERENT VIRUSES

Procedure for purification of some viruses is being given as under :

PURIFICATION OF CITRUS MOSAIC BADNA VIRUS

This virus was first reported in India by Y.S. Ahalawat (1996). Characteristic symptoms of the disease were observed as bright yellow mottling of leaves associated with vein banding and mosaic pattern. When seen under electron microscope, purified preparation showed the presence of non-envelope bacilliform particles, measuring about 30 nm × 150 nm in size typical of badnavirus. Ultra thin section also showed bacilliform virion in cytoplasm. The virus was observed to be serologically related with badna viruses.

❍ Protocol

(1) Took 100 g of symptomatic citrus leaves, washed thoroughly and dried in shadow then powered in liquid nitrogen.
(100 g of leaves from mosambi plant showing symptoms of disease should be collected from the infected host. Washed it properly with tap water to remove dirt etc. After washing leaves, it should be spread on blotting papers so as to evaporate the water. Leaves after this are crushed in the mortar with the help of pestle to make thin powder by using liquid nitrogen.)

(2) Mix the leaf powder in two vol. of 50 m M tricitrate buffer (pH-7.4) and homogenate was filtered through double layered muslin cloth.
(Tris citrate buffer 2 vol. of 50 mM should be prepared by mixing 10 ml of tris citrate into 190 ml of distilled water. 200 ml of this dilution is used to dissolve 100 g powdered leaves. After mixing 200 ml of diluted buffer as stated above, the solution was mixed thoroughly and stirred for making homogeneous solution. Get it filtered).

(3) Clarify the filtrate by low speed centrifugation (10,000 rpm for 10 minutes) after adding 25% chloroform (v/v) and allowed the extract for 10 minutes at 4C° while stirring.
(In above solution 50 ml of chloroform i.e. 25% of the volume, should be added and mixed properly by stirring. The solution should now be poured in the low centrifugation tubes. By putting these tubes in proper rotor, centrifuge it at 10,000 rpm for 10 minutes maintained at 4C°. After centrifugation, the supernatant should be collected in a beaker and place it in ice bucket. Discard the pellets).

(4) The virus should be pelleted by high speed centrifugation at 36,000 rpm for 60 minutes.
(The supermatant should be filled in 6 centrifuge tubes with precaution that there should be no bubble in any of the centrifuge tubes. Weigh these tubes and place them in rotor accordingly to maintain the balance as safety measures. There should be no significant difference among the weight of the tubes. Now ultracentrifugation is given at 43,000 rpm for 60 minutes at 4C°).

(5) Dissolve the pellet in 10m M phosphate buffer (pH-7.2) and clarify again by low speed centrifugation.
(Phosphate buffer of 0.01 M strength is used at the rate of 200 μl per pellete to dissolve it. Dissolved pelletes should be collected in microfuge tubes and should be preserved in ice box).

(6) Give the sample for EM examination.
(Both the tubes should be spinned for a short period. One of the samples should be used for EM examination).

❍ Observation

When seen under electron microscope, bacilliform particles characteristic of citrus mosaic badnavirus is anticipated to be seen.

OTHER PROTOCOL FOR PURIFICATION OF CITRUS MOSAIC BADNAVIRUS

Citrus mosaic badna virus may be purified by other method also as given below:

(1) Take 50 g of diseased leaf sample, wash properly, get dried on blotting paper in the laboratory and cut it in small pieces. Such pieces should be crushed so as to make thin powder by grinding them in mortar with pestle using liquid nitrogen.

(2) Add 150 ml (three times) citrate buffer (0.1 M citrate buffer) (pH-5.9) and add 1.0 g cellulose enzyme to it. Mix it properly.

(3) Incubate the mixture at 37C° for 2.15 hours in Lab therm incubator. After incubation, filter the mixture by double layered muslin cloth. Collect the filtrate in beaker and place in ice bucket.

(4) Centrifuge the solution at 8,000 rpm at 4C° for 15 minutes. The supernatant thus obtained will be approximately 190 ml in volume. Place it in cool room overnight.

(5) Add 7% PEG (polyethylene glycerol) (13.3 g) to the supernatant and mix 0.2M NaCl (2.22 g) and 1.9 ml Triton X-100 (1%) to it.

(6) Mix the mixture for 1.30 hours by magnetic strirrer and after that keep it in incubator for 2 hours at room temperature.

(7) Above mixture should be filled in centrifuge tubes for giving low speed centrifugation at the speed of 12,000 rpm for 10 minutes. Discard the supernatant and use pellets.

(8) Resuspend the pellets in citrate buffer. Add 0.1M citrate buffer (pH-5.9) and filled the suspension to centrifuge tubes leaving no air bubble at all. There should be no significant difference among the weights of the filled tubes. Suspension in tubes should be centrifuged at 36,000 rpm for 2.5 hours at 4°C.

(9) Discard the supernatant and use the pellets. Dissolve the pellets in least possible volume of citrate buffer (100-300 μl, 0.1 M and pH-5.9) keeping them in 2 microfuge tubes.

(10) Both the microfuge tubes should be spinned for a short period in table top centrifuge.

(11) A sample should be examined under EM.

Observation. Particles of the virus will be seen.

❍ Protocol for *Potato virus* Y (PVY) purification

(1) After 2 to 3 weeks of inoculation, diseased leaves samples should be homogenized in two volumes (w/v) of 0.5 M borate buffer pH-8.0 containing 0.2 M urea and 0.15% thioglyconic acid.

(2) Pass the homogenate through double layer muslin cloth and emulsify with one half volume (w/v) each of chloroform and carbon tetrachloride by stirring for 15 minutes.

(3) Centrifuge the mixture at 5,000 g for 10 minutes.

(4) Pass the supernatant through Whatman's filter paper. Add PEG 6000 and NaCl to a final concentration of 4 and 1.75% (w/v) respectively.

(5) Allow the mixture to stand for 1 hour at 4C° after stirring for 30 minutes.

(6) Centrifuge the contents at 8,000 g for 12 minutes.

(7) Resuspend the precipitate in one fifth of the original volume of 0.5 M borate buffer pH-8.0. Incubate overnight giving slow agitation at 4C°.

(8) Next day, centrifuge the material at 5,000 g for 10 minutes and discard the pellet.

(9) Make a layer of supernatant over 30% sucrose (w/v) in 0.5 M borate buffer per centrifuge tube and centrifuge at the speed of 80,000 g for 2 hours in Beckman 55.2 Ti rotor.

(10) Resuspend the pellets in 0.05 M borate buffer containing 5 mM EDTA as re-suspension buffer.

(11) Repeat differential centrifugation steps, if required.

(12) Further purification may be done by sucrose-density gradient centrifugation (10-40% prepared in re-suspension buffer) for 2 hours at 25,000 rpm in Beckman SW 41 Ti rotor.

(13) Virus peak fractions were collected by passing the contents of tube through ISCO density gradient fractionators. With the help of a syringe collect virus containing zone.

(14) Dialyze fractions overnight at 4C° (with 3 changes) against 0.05 M borate buffer pH-8.0 containing 5 mM EDTA.

(15) Centrifuge at the speed 80,000 g for 2 hours in a Beckman 52.2 Ti rotor.

(16) Re-suspend the pellets in small volume of re-suspension buffer and examine under EM.

❍ Density gradient in purification

Density gradient is a column of fluid that increases in density from the top of the centrifuge tube to the bottom. Density graident centrifugation involves sedimenting a virus sample through a density gradient. As different particles move through the density gradient, they separate into discrete bands. Density gradient can be formed with densest layer on the bottom. Each layer has a different density and the virus sample is loaded on the top of the performed gradient. There is a wide variety of materials used to make density gradient.

SUCROSE DENSITY GRADIENT

Sucrose is often used to perform gradient. Cesium chloride is a salt that forms a gradient spontaneously when in a centrifuged field. The medium chosen must be compatible with the sample and must have sufficient range of densities to separate all the components of the sample. Usually buffers are used as medium to make solution of different concentrations.

In sucrose density gradient, solutions of different concentrations viz., 10%, 20% and 30% are prepared in buffer solution (phosphate buffer 0.01M). First of all 3 ml of 30% sucrose solution is filled in two distinct transparent gradient tubes. Above it, 3 ml of 20% sucrose solution is poured in both the tubes. Onto it 2.5 ml of 10% sucrose solution and again above this 2.5 ml of phosphate buffer (no sucrose) should be poured in both the tubes. Now at the top, 2 ml of virus sample is poured on each of the gradient tubes. When pouring the solution of different concentrations, precautions are taken so that different layers of different concentrations may not mix with each other. These tubes should be kept for some time at room temperature.

Now these tubes should be centrifuged at 40,000 rpm for 4.30 hours. After centrifugation these tubes are examined for the presence of virus containing bands in light. Pick up the virus containing band with the help of a needle and syringe. Get it examined under EM.

DIALYSIS OF THE VIRUS SAMPLE

Dialysis is a separation process that use membranes similar to those used for ultra-filtration. Dialysis is based on differences in the concentrations of solutes between one side of the membrane and the other. Solute molecules that are small enough to pass through the pores of the membrane will diffuse from the side with higher concentration to the side with low concentration. The distinctive feature of the dialysis is that differences in solute concentration provide the 'driving force'. Dialysis does not require pumps or a vacuum to force material through the pores of the membrane.

❍ Methodology

Sample containing virus particles and sucrose is dialyzed to obtain sucrose free virus sample. First of all such solution is filled in dialysis membrane bag and both the open sides of membrane bag are tied properly. The bag so prepared is hanged in phosphate buffer (0.01 M) in accordance with the proper procedure. It is now placed on stirrer plate for 8 hours by putting the magnetic stirrer inside the beaker containing buffer solution with the precaution that it should not touch the bag. Dialysis is done giving three changes.

❍ Observation

After dialysis the sucrose free concentrated virus sample should be taken out of the dialysis membrane bag for examination under electron microscope.

STUDYING PHYSICAL PROPERTIES OF VIRUSES

With physical and chemical assay methods the total viral nucleoprotein can be measured. The local lesion assay only indicates that one sample is more infective than the other. Over the other methods, the local lesion method has the advantage that it can be used for measuring the virus concentration in crude sap.

❍ Virus concentration

There is direct relationship between the number of lesions and concentration of infective virus. The number of lesions produced on the host varies among plants and among leaves. There is little difference between the reaction of opposite halves of the same leaf and in plants with opposite pair of leaves between the leaves or half leaves of each pair. To minimize these variations each inoculum is inoculated to a number of leaves or half leaves (Bawden, 1964; Roberts, 1964).

❍ Dilution end point determination

The dilution end point is generally reported as being between two dilutions *i.e.* between the higher dilution that was still infectious and the next higher one. The test is performed by inoculating local lesion test plants with sap diluted repeatedly × 10. In case the local lesion host plant is not known, at least 5 plants which react systemically should be inoculated with each sample. Procedure is as under.

❍ Requirements

Mortar and pestle, a piece of cheese cloth, beaker, pipettes, measuring pipette 10 ml, evaporating dishes with flat bottom and leaves infected with virus.

❍ Procedure

Grind the leaves in a mortar and collect extract by passing through cheese cloth. Make dilutions. Make dilutions as undiluted, 10^{-1}, 10^{-2}, 10^{-3}, 10^{-4}, 10^{-5}, 10^{-6} and 10^{-7}. Put the 8 test tubes in a row in a test tube rack and fill 7 of these with 9 ml water with the help of a pipette. Pour 1 ml sap in the second test tube to make dilution 10^{-1}. Mix it thoroughly and add 1 ml of this dilution (10^{-1}) to the third test tube to make the dilution 10^{-2}. Repeat the procedure till 10^{-7}. Inoculate the sap to the host to test infectivity. Compare the dilution end point value obtained with that available in the literature (Smith, 1997; Klinkowski, 1968; Gibbs, 1970).

❍ Thermal Inactivation point determination

The most commonly accepted definition of the thermal inactivation point of a virus in crude juice is *the temperature required for the complete inactivation of a virus in untreated crude juice during a ten minutes exposure*. The term is used to state one temperature as the inactivation temperature or to mention two temperatures in between which the virus is inactivated completely (Ross, 1964; Bawden, 1964; Smith, 1972). Experiments may be done by heating the crude juice to 50, 60, 70, 80, 90 and 100°C. In the range of inactivation, the experiment is repeated at 5 C° intervals. Field experiments may be included by counting the local lesions which result from the inoculation of each samples.

❍ Requirements

Mortar and pestle, piece of cheese cloth, water bath with test tube plate, thermometer to measure 0—100°C test tubes, pipette measuring 10 ml, evaporating dishes with flat bottom and leaves infected with virus.

❍ Methodoloy

Grind desirable quantity of infected leaves in a mortar and press the sap through cheese cloth. Pour the sap in a shallow dish and fill the pipette with sap. Take care that only the tip of the pipette should come in contact with the sap. Pipette 2 ml of the sap in each of the 8 test tubes. Prevent the sap contaminating the upper part of the tube. Fill the water bath with water until the level is at least 3 cm above the level of the sap in the test tube. Heat the water in the bath to different temperatures viz., untreated (about 20°C), 40°C, 50°C, 60°C, 70°C, 8°C, 90°C and 100°C. When the water in the bath reaches the lowest temperature, put one tube in the rack of the bath. Place a thermometer close to the tube at the same level. By adjusting the flame maintain this temperature for 10 minutes. Remove the tube from the bath after 10 minutes and cool it in running water. After heating the bath to the next temperature treat a second tube in the same manner. When all tubes have been treated, inoculate the test plants with the different samples treated with different temperatures.

❍ Observation

Count the number of lesions and sum of each sample. Note the thermal inactivation point and compare it with the value with those reported in literature.

❍ **Longevity *in vitro* (ageing) determination**

Longevity *in vitro* may be defined as the time expressed in days, weeks or hours for which the virus in crude juice kept at room temperature remains infectious. It is usual to store the crude juice in closed tubes and to test a sample on test plants at a series of intervals. It is rough test because the room temperature varies from 25-28C°. Ross (1964) recommended 20-22C° as room temperature for testing longevity *in vitro*. Longevity depends on the original concentration of crude juice and the properties of the sap. Therefore, the test is of limited value for identification of virus. With an unknown virus, preliminary tests will show if the virus is inactivated after hours, days, weeks or months of storage at room temperature.

❍ Requirement

Mortar and pestle, piece of cheese cloth, 2 ml pipette, test tubes with test tube rack, virus infected leaves.

❍ Methodology

Grind 50 g infected leaves and get the juice filtered with cheese cloth. Pipette 2 ml of sap to each test tube. Close the tubes with a stopper or aluminium foil. Preserve the tubes for different time. After the prescribed times, the test plants or leaves are inoculated with the sample. Testing is complicated because of the long duration of the experiment.

❍ Observation

Count the number of lesions and sum for each sample. Corrections can be made by comparing with standards. Record the longevity of the virus *in vitro*.

5

PATHOGENICITY AND REPLICATION

✉ ***Introduction, How does virus cause infection, Early events in plants virus infection, Virus multiplication, Replication of RNA viruses, Replication of DNA viruses. Generalized outline for the replication of a small ss positive sense RNA virus.***

Some plant viruses such as *Tobacco mosaic virus* and *Cucumber green mottle mosaic virus* are produced in high concentration and are so stable out side their host plants that they can easily survive there for considerable time. Reaching of virus sap to the surface of a host plant is usually called 'contamination'. The virus particles may enter healthy plants during wounding resulted due to some reasons especially by the implements, animals and insects. Viruses are also transmitted artificially by rubbing leaves of hosts with the sap of the diseased plants in presence of an abrasive which produces small wounds or by deliberately using certain insects. Such artificial introduction is called inoculation.

In some cases, the virus get established upon entry, multiples and starts to move from cell to cell but infected cells rapidly die causing a check for virus spread any more. In some pathogens like *Cucumber mosaic virus*, recovery of symptoms may be practically observed but such recovered plants always remain infected for the rest of their lives.

Pathogenicity of the virus depends upon the aggressiveness or infectivity (readiness to infect and invade the host and multiply therein) and on its virulence. The proneness to disease depends on susceptibility of the host to accept the virus and assist in multiplication and internal spread.

KOCH'S POSTULATES

Rules by Robert Koch to prove the pathogenicity of a microorganism were modified for plant viruses are : (1) isolation of the virus from a diseased host; (2) cultivation of the virus in experimental hosts or cells; (3) purification followed by the incoulation of the filtered or purified virus; (4) production of a comparable disease symptoms like the original on related host species following inoculation with the processed virus; and (5) re-isolation of the same virus.

EARLY EVENTS IN PLANT VIRUS INFECTION

The early events in virus infection involves three steps-(1) absorption on the host surface, (2) penetration or entry into the host cell, and (3) un coating or disassembly of virus particles for replication and spread. The initial contact of the virus particle and the host is usually referred to as absorption on entry. The process during which the virion or its nucleic acid passes into the cytoplasm of the cell is called as the penetration or entry. *Un-coating is the removal of various components of the mature virions and subsequent release of viral genome and other constituents which play role in establishing infection.* Unlike animal viruses and bacteriophages, wounding is essential for initial entry of the virus in plant.

It seems rather unlikely that plant viruses contain specific attachment protein or their coat proteins are involved in recognition phenomena. However, few plant viruses such as *Tomato spotted wilt virus* has been reported to contain two types of capsid proteins which are thought to interact with cell receptors.

Inside the host, viral nucleic acid inhibits the synthesis of host cell protein and host RNA by some mechanism. The virus completely depends on host cell for supply and structural machinery for its replication.

VIRUS MULTIPLICATION

The nucleic acid is a virion that contains only a few of the genes needed for the synthesis of new viruses. These includes genes for the virion structural components such as capsid, protein and the genes for a few of the enzymes used in the viral life cycle. These enzymes are synthesized and function only when the virus is with in the host cell. Viral enzymes are entirely concerned with the replicating or processing viral nucleic acid. Enzymes needed for protein synthesis, ribosomes, tRNA and energy production are supplied by the host cells and are used for synthesizing viral proteins including viral enzymes.

Thus for a virus to multiply, it must invade the host cell and take over the host metabolic machinery. A single virion can give rise to several or even thousand of similar viruses in a single host cell.

RNA Virus Replication

Theo W. Dreher of Oregon State University, USA has described RNA virus replication. More than three quarters of plant viruses have positive(+) sense RNA genomes, that is genomes for which the encapsidated virion RNA serves both as template for RNA replication and as messenger RNA encoding viral proteins. In contrast to positive strand (RNA viruses with double(—) standard or negative sense RNA genomes), RNA viruses, those viruses must carry active RNA polymerase within their virions, and the first event within an inoculated cell in the production of viral messenger RNA encoding the essential viral proteins. This step is skipped in case of positive-strand RNA viruses, since their genome RNAs can be immediately translated to yield viral proteins.

Sequence similarities among the RNA-dependant RNA polymerase (RdRps) encoded by all positive-strand RNA viruses-those infecting plants, animals and bacteria-indicate that the RdRp genes of these viruses are all derived from a single ancestor. There are further relationships among subsets of positive-strand RNA viruses through conserved proteins that function in genome replication. Such conservation of essential proteins reflects broad commonalities in the replication schemes for these viruses. The replication cycle for all positive- strand RNA viruses consists of negative-strand (anti-genome) synthesis using the inoculum genomes as templates, followed by the synthesis of an excess of positive-sense progeny strands (amplification). Double stranded genome length RNA can be isolated from infections of most, if not all, positive strand RNA viruses, but free or partially hybridized negative-strands are thought to be the active replication intermediates. In some viruses, one or more positive-sense subgenomic RNAs (specialized mRNAs representing part of the genome) are also synthesized from negative-sense templates. The synthesis of RNA occurs by *de novo* initiation of product strands in many viruses, and in many cases the product strands acquire 5′ caps like those of eukaryotic mRNAs. In those viruses with genome-linked protein (VPg), RNA synthesis probably begins with the use of the VPg as a primer. Positive-strand RNA viruses replicate in the cytoplasm in association with membranes and are thought to recruit host proteins to assist or regulate RNA synthesis. Host RdRp activity that is present in uninfected plants is not thought to participate in the replication of viral RNA genomes.

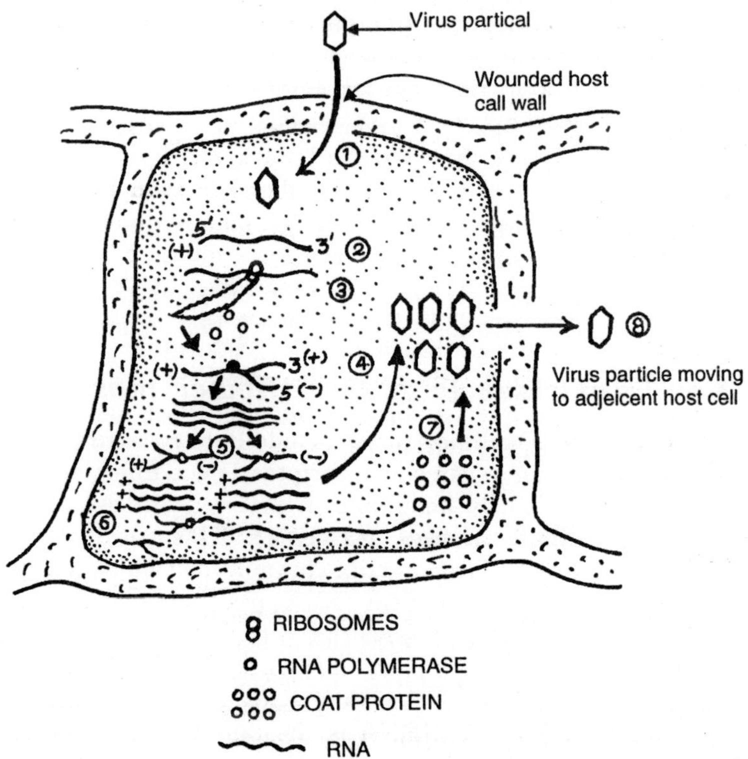

Fig. 5.1 Showing diagramatic representation of generalized outline for replication of a small ss Positive sense RNA virus.

Replication of a possitive sense single stranded RNA (+)ssRNA virus may be gneralized as under. Generalized out line for replication of a small single stranded positive sense RNA has been represented above (Fig. 5.1).

(1) The virus particle enters the cell through a wound made in the cell wall. (2) The RNA escapes from the protein coat. (3) The infecting RNA becomes associated with host ribosome and a viral specific, RNA dependant RNA polymerase is synthesized. (4) The polymerase synthesizes negative sense genomic length strands of RNA. (5) The polymerase then synthesizes genomic size RNA copies and coat protein mRNAs using an internal initiation site on the genomic negative sense RNA. (6) Host cell ribosome synthesizes large numbers of coat protein molecules using the coat mRNAs. (7) Coat protein is assembled around genomic RNA molecules to produce progeny virus particles, which accumulate in the cell. (8) A few particles migrate to neighboring cells through plasmodesmata.

DNA VIRUS REPLICATION

DNA virus replication has been explained by Roger Hull of Norwich Research Park, U.K. There are three groups of plant viruses with DNA genomes-the Caulimoviridae, the Geminiviridae and the Nanoviruses. The family Caulimoviridae comprises 6 genera distinguished by genome organisation and particle shape. The particles are either isometric or bacilliform and each contains a single molecule of double stranded DNA (dsDNA) of about 7.2 to 8.0 kbp. with one or more discontinuity in each strand.

There are 3 genera of family Geminiviridae also distinguished by genome organisation and transmission vector. They all have circular single stranded DNA (ssDNA) genomes of about 2.5 to 3.0 kbp. encapsidated in twin icosahedral (geminate) in most members of the genus *Begomovirus*. The genome is divided between two DNA molecules and members of the other two genera have single DNA species.

The Nanoviruses are a newly proposed group of isometric viruses that contain at least 6 small circular DNA strands each about 1.0 kbp in size.

○ Family. Caulimoviridae (e.g. *Cauliflower mosaic virus*)

Members of the families Caulimoviridae include Para retroviruses which replicate via an RNA intermediate using reverse transcriptase. On infection of the plant the virus particles are disassembled by an unknown process and the virion DNA enters the nucleus in which the discontinuities are sealed. This covalently closed circular DNA associates with histones to form a mini-chromosome which is the template for transcription by the host DNA-dependent RNA polymerase. Two transcripts are produced, a more than genome length transcript with terminal redundancy termed as the 35 S RNA and the 19 S RNA which is the mRNA for one of the genes. All members of the family produce an analogue of the 35 S RNA but some do not transcribe an analogue of the 19 S RNA. The 35 S RNA is the template for reverse transcription and is also the polycistronic *mRNA* for at least some of the products. On entering the cytoplasm various gene products are translated from this RNA (and also from other viral mRNAs and spliced products of the 35 S RNA). Among the gene products are the reverse transcriptase (RT) and ribonuclease H (RNase H), which are the enzymes involved in converting the 35 S RNA to dsDNA. Synthesis of the first DNA strand, the (—) strand DNA is primed at a site about 500-700 nucleotides from the 5′ end of the 35 S RNA where there is a sequence complementary to the 3′ end of tRNA met in it. Using this primer the RT catalyses the synthesis of DNA towards the 5′ end of the 35 S RNA and RNase H removes the RNA moiety of the DNA-RNA duplex thus formed. This reveals newly formed DNA sequence with complimentarily to the terminal redundancy of the 35 S RNA which then links or strand-switches to the 3′ end of this RNA. Thus (—) strand DNA synthesis can continue on the 35 S RNA template. During the digestion of RNA moiety by RNase H, purine rich regions are left at specfic sites which become primers for (+) stand DNA synthesis, also by the RT enzyme. Synthesis of both the (—) and (+) strands continues with a further strand-switch when the (—) strand reaches the original tRNA priming site. When the advancing strands reach the primary sites for both (—) and (+) strand synthesis, there is a limited strand displacement, usually of a few 10 s of nucleotides, before the RT ceases functioning. This results in discontinuities in the DNA strand which are at specific sites (the primary sites) and usually comprises "triple stranded" DNA. The newly synthesized dsDNA is then encapsidated to form new virus particles.

❍ Family Geminiviridae

Three genera of family Geminiviridae have similar replication strategies, using a rolling circle replication system to amplify the ssDNA and to produce dsDNAs which serve as replication and transcription intermediates. In the first phase of rolling circle, the single stranded virion (+) sense DNA is the template for the synthesis of (—) stand DNA thought to be printed by an RNA molecule to produce the double stranded replicative form. This leads to the second step in which the replicative form provides the template for the synthesis of single stranded (+) strand DNA which is primed by a site specific nick within a conserved hair pin motif. Plus (+) strands of virion length are produced and legated to give the circular encapsidated form.

Gemini viruses do not encode any protein with similarity to known DNA polymerases, and it is likely that host DNA polymerases are used for DNA replication. These viruses encode a gene product- Rep, which induces the expression of the host DNA synthesis protein(s). This protein contains the amino acid sequence motif *EXCEL (L = Lucine, X* = any amino acid, C =Cystein, E = Glutamic acid) which is associated with proteins that interact with members of the retinoblastoma family of protein, thus stimulating cellular DNA synthesis.

Gemini viruses encode 3 proteins involved in their DNA replication and expression The Rep protein mentioned previously is also involved in the ssDNA deavage step of rolling circle replication and in the legation of the (+) strands to give the circular encapsidated form. The Rep accessory factor acts with the Rep protein in enhancing DNA replication and the activator protein regulates virion-sense transcription.

NANOVIRUSES

The replication of the ssDNA genomes of nanoviruses is thought to be very similar to that of Gemini viruses. Detailed studies have been made of *Banana bunchy top virus*, which has 6 genome segments. *DNA-1* encodes a protein of 32-33 kDA, which has amino acid sequence motifs similar to those of Gemini viruses Rep protein and which has nicking and joining activity. DNA-1 also has a small internal ORF encoding a protein of 5 kDa. DNA-5 encodes a protein of 19 kDa which contains the LXCXE motif found in the geminivirus Rep proteins and which mediates stimulation of cellular DNA synthesis by interaction with members of the retinoblastoma protein family. All the DNA species except DNA-3 have an endogenous promoter, that on DNA-5 being the most active.

On the entry to the initially infected cell, there is endogenous DNA polymerase activity to convert the ssDNA-5 to a double stranded form, which is then transcribed to give the 19 kDa protein that switches the cell from G to S phase. This then leads to the replication and transcription of other viral genomic DNAs including DNA-1 which is translated to give the Rep protein. The 5 kDa protein from internal ORF of DNA-1 is essential in conjunction with the Rep protein for excision and relegation in the rolling circle replication.

6

VIRUS DETECTION TECHNIQUES

✉ ***Different methods of virus detection, Biological assays, Diagnostic symptoms of virus diseases, Diagnosis by inclusion bodies, Diagnosis by internal symptoms, Latent infection, Phytotoxaemia, Factors affecting virus induced symptoms.***

Plant viruses can not penetrate the surface of their host and can gain entry to the tissues only through wounds. In nature, the commonest and the most important means of tansmission are through various biological methods which perform the role of introducing viruses into plant tissues to initiate infection. These methods are called biological methods of transmission and biotic agents responsible to transmit viruses are called vectors. Viruses are sometimes naturally transmitted to healthy plants when shoots or leaves of healthy and diseased plants rub together. The wounds caused by such rubbing usually may come in contact of viruses initiating infection. Virus transmission experiments show difference between viruses with regard to transmission characteristics and give valuable hints about their field spread and epidemiology.

DIFFERENT METHODS OF VIRUS DETECTION

There are different methods of detection of viruses. Some of the important methods which are used frequently may be classified as under

1. **Biological methods of detection.** Such methods usually include biological assays, host range studies, symptomatological studies, mechanical transmission studies, vector transmission studies and use of indicator plants for virus detection.
2. **Serological methods of detection.**
3. **Nucleic acid based methods of detection.**
4. **Electron microscopy.**

All the above methods will be described in detail with their practical application in plant virology.

BIOLOGICAL ASSAYS

Biological assays involve methods used to measure and determine the biological properties of a virus pathogen. These biological assays which involve host range studies, indicator plants and differential hosts are useful in virus detection. These are important in defining the virus nature of a suspected disease and also for the identification, differentiation and characterization of a virus isolate at the species or strain level.

❍ Host-range studies

A host range represents listing of species that are susceptible to a given virus. Such a list may also include species that are resistant to the virus. The natural host range is based on such host plant species usually infected under natural conditions. The experimental host range is based on such host species usually infected during experimental inoculations under controlled laboratory conditions. A new isolate is tested by inoculating a selected number of plant species known as indicator plants under green house conditions and by comparing the symptomatology with those of established viruses. The host range and symptomatology are the first criteria for the recognition

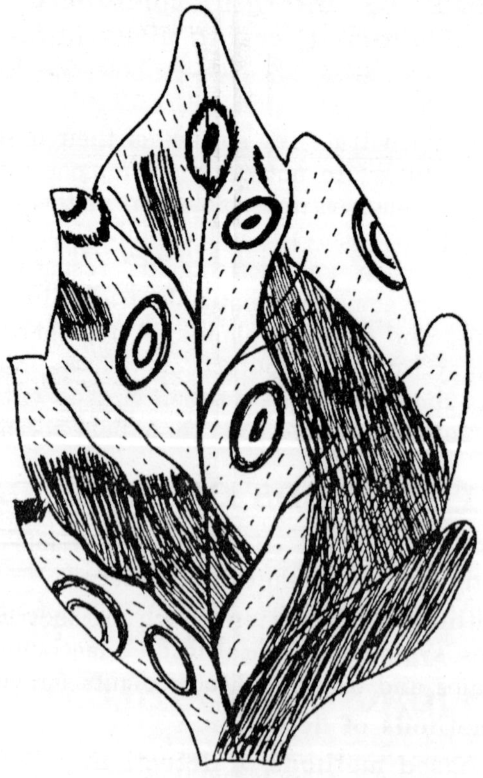

Fig. 6.1 Concentric rings and diamond-shaped symptoms on *Solanum nigrum* incited by *Tomato spotted wilt virus*

Fig. 6.2 Showing *Solanum nigrum* as indicator plant without disease symptom.

of specific viruses. On the basis of the characteristic symptoms, viruses are tentatively identified because of the fact that reliance on biological characteristics alone for virus recognition may lead to confusion as different viruses may produce similar symptoms in certain hosts. The utility of host range studies is contingent upon how readily the virus in question can be transmitted from one plant to the other under experimental conditions. Some viruses are not readily transmitted mechanically. For these viruses other means such as insect vectors and graft transmission may be necessary to conduct host range studies. Some complications of mechanical inoculation during host range studies may be experienced as certain plant species may contain certain inhibitors for infection or viral inactivation components. The host range studies must also include the possibility of latent infections.

Differential hosts are useful for separating one virus from a mixture of viral strains or a mixture of viruses. Such hosts are susceptible to certain viruses but not to others. Differential hosts have been used to identify viral strains and viral pathotypes. Indicator host plants are experimental hosts that under controlled conditions develop consistent and distinguishing disease symptoms when inoculated with particular viruses. Detailed list of indicator plants are in existence for many viral diseases. Such lists of indicator plants are useful particularly in diagnosing certain viral diseases in woody fruit plants.

Table 6.1. List of Susceptible laboratory host plants commonly used for virus studies

1. Family-Solanaeeae. *Nicotiana tabacum, N. glutinosa, Petunia hybrida* and *Nicotiana clevelandii.*

2. Chenopodiaceae. *Chenopodium quinoa, C. amaranticolor, Phasiolus vulgaris, Vicia fabae* and *Vigna sinensis.*

3. Cruciferae. *Brassica perviridis, Cucumis sativus and Cucurvita pepo.*

Local lesion symptoms are the result of a restricted virus infection, whereas systemic infections result in spread of virus from the site of infection to all parts of the host. In local lesion symptoms, the virus does not spread significantly from the site of infection. Such symptoms are the result of host response to virus infection. Local lesions may be necrotic as a result of the cell death or chlorotic as a result of chloroplast breakdown in cells surrounding virus infection. Local lesions may be diagnostic for certain viruses. Virus infectivity is measured by the number of local lesions induced by the mechanical transmission of a virus preparation. Presumably each lesion is the representative of infection by a single infectious unit of a sufficiently diluted virus preparation. If local lesion hosts are not available, infectivity assays are sometimes conducted by inoculating a group of plants with a dilution series of virus preparations and in this case assessment of the assays are based on determining the percentage of plants infected.

DIAGNOSTIC SYMPTOMS OF VIRUS DISEASES

Viral infection affects the metabolism and the growth of a susceptible host plant and usually disturbs normal functions of the infected host. The changes may be macroscopic which may be visible on leaves and other parts of the host plant or there may be internal changes in plant tissues usually seen only by the light or electron microscope. Such morphological changes are known as symptoms. Symptomatology is the orderly study of symptoms. Such studies provide first clue about possible infection and in many cases help to ascertain the virus involved. Further, symptoms produced in different plants by artificial inoculations may be of considerable diagnostic value. *Different viruses usually produce different symptoms on different plants.* Virus like symptoms may also be caused by other plant pathogens such as viroids, phytoplasmas and rickettsia like organisms. Likewise, the symptoms of nutritional imbalances and due to toxic components of arthropod saliva are often similar enough to appear as virus like maladies. Viruses produce a wide range of symptoms which may be grouped into three main categories.

(1) **External symptoms** (2) **Internal symptoms** (3) **Latent infections**

(1) EXTERNAL SYMPTOMS

External symptoms have further been sub-divided into three categories viz.

(a) *Primary symptoms* **(b)** *Systemic symptoms* **(c)** *Disease Syndrome.*

Primary symptoms are the result of the local reaction at the place of inoculation. These are usually of two kinds–local lesions and clearing of veins. Local lesions appear in the form of spots or rings. In vein clearing there is chlorosis of tissues or in the adjacent tissues to the veins. Frequently, a broad band of chlorotic tissue appears along the veins. These two primary symptoms-the vein clearing and the vein banding may disappear as the disease spreads or may remain present as major symptoms.

Secondary or systemic symptoms are produceed by secondary or systemic infection by the virus. Such symptoms consist of visible macroscopic changes and those changes that internally occur in the form of abnormal cell structures.

The occurrence of more than one type of symptoms in a diseased host is clled as a syndrome. Similarly, commulative symptoms produced by more than one type of virus or pathogen is referred as synergism.

Systemic symptoms usually appear with following characteristics :

(*i*) Colour deviation (*ii*) Necrosis (*iii*) Abnormalities in shape and size of the plant parts.

❍ Colour deviation in leaves

Deviation in colour is frequently observed in virus infected plants. Such deviations are usually seen in leaves, stems, flowers, seeds and fruits which may be observed in different kinds such as

Mosaic spotting which appears on leaves, blossoms and sometimes other parts of the plants resulting in manifestation of irregular spots or patches of light green, yellow or even white in colour. Such chlorotic areas may be circular or irregular, varying in size and are known as mosaic.

Ring spotting. Such symptoms appear as localized chlorotic or necrotic spots on leaves and are circular in shape. Sometimes necrosis and normal green areas appear in rings alternately. The rings are concentric to the central spot.

Chlorosis. It is characterized by the loss of chlorophyll and appearance of uniform yellowing on whole or some parts of leaves.

Distortion. It is the rolling and crinking of leaves caused by retarded growth of the veins which is termed as distortion.

Mottling. Evenly distributed patches of light or dark green forming uniform pattern such as in canna.

Variegation. Patches of chlorotic green or other colours as seen in abutilon mosaic on abutilon.

Vein flecking. Water soaked effect seen on the back of the leaf corresponding to vein cleared areas as seen in citrus tristeza on lime.

Vein banding. More green or yellow areas are seen around the vein such as cowpea vein banding on cowpea.

Yellow vein mosaic. Veins and veinlets turn yellow forming net like pattern as seen in yellow vein mosaic of okra.

Yellow mosaic. Entire leaf turns golden yellow as seen in mungbean.

❍ Colour deviation in stems

Colour deviation is also seen in stems in different diseases incited by viruses. Example of sweet pea enation may be cited here.

❍ Colour deviation in flowers

Colour breaking is characterized by discontinuous streaks of off light and dark colour as observed in *Bean yellow mosaic virus* on gladiolus and Canna mottle virus on canna.

Greening or Virescence. Characterized by turning of flowers to green and modified to leaf like in structure as observed in cotton virescence on cotton incited by phytoplasma.

❍ Colour deviation in fruits and seeds

Dark green patches in cucumber due to CMV infection. Papaya produces water soaked rings caused by *Papaya ring spot virus*.

On soybean seeds, speeks and mottle are seen which are caused by *Soybean mosaic virus*.

❍ Necrosis in leaves and fruits

Necrotic spots on leaves. Brown and red or black necrotic spots are observed in different viral diseases *e.g. Tobacco ring spot virus* on tobacco and concentric rings it on nasturtium due to *Nasturtium ring spot virus.* Apple ring spot due to *Apple ring spot virus* and necrotic spot on plum due to *Plum pox virus* are important symptoms.

❍ **Abnormalities in leaf shape, size and growth**

Leaf lamina between veins is poorly developed or not developed at all giving abnormal form of leaf and shoe string like symptoms may be formed as found in papaya ring spot disease in papaya.

Leaf out growths of variable size on the ventral surface of the veins called enation as found in Hibiscus leaf enation and tobacco leaf enation due to *Tobacco leaf curl virus.*

Blisters is seen in cucurbits due to *Cucumber mosaic virus* and on *Nicotiana tabacum* due to *Tobacco mosaic virus* (TMV).

Cupping—cup like structures are formed due to CMV on sponge guard.

Curling of lamina as found in Tomato leaf curl and chilli leaf curl. Leaves and petioles are twisted as seen in papaya leaf curl. Leaf roll is characterized by downward rolling such as in potato leaf roll and tobacco leaf roll. Reduction of leaf size and shape are found in little leaf of brinjal caused by phytoplasma. Individual leaves are greatly reduced in size as seen in papaya ring spot virus disease in papaya and in CMV infected cucurbits and tomato.

Proliferation–many small depressions of lateral buds may be seen in sunhemp. Phyllody (phytoplasma) is proliferation as seen in sesame.

Bushy appearance is seen in grassy shoot of sugarcane.

❍ Stem pitting

After removal of bark stem shows many small depressions as observed in citrus tristeza infected with *Citrus tristeza virus*.

❍ Bark scaling and cracking

Due to virus infection scaling of bark as found in citrus psorosis and bark cracking as in citrus exocortis caused by viroids are seen.

❍ Modification of flowers in vegetative shoots

In some cases, flowers are modified in a vegetative shoots as found in sunhemp and vinca phyllody. Similarly production of cluster of thin wiry shoots is called witches broom as in mosaic of papaya.

(2) INTERNAL SYMPTOMS

Various changes in histology of virus infected plant parts especially leaves, petioles and stems are caused by virus infection. Such histological changes or abnormalities can be categorized in mainly three groups, namely.

(1) Necrosis or death of cells
(2) Hyperplasia or excessive growth
(3) Hypoplasia or reduced growth differentiation of cell.

Hypoplasia resulting in thinner lamina is found usually associated with mosaic symptoms being more evident in yellow region of mosaic pattern. The reduction in number of chloroplasts, less differentiation of mesophyll cells and fewer in number with no intercellular spaces may be observed in yellow regions of mosaic pattern. In some cases, vein clearing symptoms, enlargement of tissues near the veins and absence of chlorophyll are observed.

The *histo-pathological changes* in phloem cells such as in potato infected with *Potato leaf roll virus*, occur in the form of necrosis of phloem vessels. In swollen shoot of cacao, the cells are generally normal but the swelling of shoots is due to the excessive production of xylem cells. Proliferation and necrosis of phloem cells have been frequently observed incited by geminivirus causing tobacco leaf curl. In mosaic infected leaves, the size and number of starch grains are reduced. There remains accumulation of starch in sugar-beets and potato infected with sugar-beet curly top and leaf roll viruses respectively.

Necrosis or streak symptoms cause drastic cytological changes in cells as they approach to death. However, how viruses do kill the cells is not yet known, since any enzymes or toxin is involved in virus pathogenicity.

Ultra structural changes have been observed in the plants infected with a specific group of whitefly transmitted Gemini viruses. In such cases altered nuclei are recognized by their uniformly distributed granular texture, reduction of chromatin, peripheral changes and apparent absence of nuclei.

Such ultra-structural changes might be a diagnostic feature in diseases caused by ssDNA viruses such as Gemini viruses. Such changes have not been observed in diseases caused by any other group of plant viruses.

❍ Diagnostic inclusion bodies

The development of inclusion bodies in virus infected cells is the major cytoplasmic effect found either in the cytoplasm or in the nucleus. They may be aggregates of virus particles in more or less crystalline array or of virus induced protein or other materials in such array. Inclusion bodies have been categorized on the basis of morphology and their composition as under :

(1) *Angled layer aggregates*—consists of elongated elements either single or in bundles of varying sizes.

(2) *Complex inclusions*—composed of virus particles, host organelles and virus induced proteins.

(3) *Cylindrical inclusions*—These appear in pin-wheels with attached scrolls as observed in Potyviruses. In longitudinal section they appear in bundles.

(4) *Crystalloid inclusions*—inclusion bodies usually consist of crystal form of viruses.

(5) *Hexagonal crystals*—Inclusion bodies are aggregates of virus particles being composed of many monolayers in thickness. They appear hexagonal from top view and square to rectangular from side view. They are usually seen in diseases incited by Tobamoviruses.

(6) *Laminated aggregates*—In the light microscope, these inclusion bodies appear as linear structure which are resolved in to plates while changing the focus.

(7) *Laminated inclusion components*—These inclusions are usually associated with Potexviruses. In electron microscope, they appear beaded or as smooth sheets which are straight or curved in shape.

(8) *Paracrystals*—They appear as true crystals in the form of middle or looped in structure.

(9) *Pin wheels*—In poty viruses such pin wheels are charactristics. In cross sections the central core appears cylindrical and the groups of curved arms appear to be attached with the central core.

(10) *Rounded plates*—These inclusions are usually seem in some of the Tobamoviruses. They are round to oval with irregular outlines. When seen to the top, these appear to be made up of many concentric rings of varying diameter.

(11) *Scroll*—The extended arms of pin wheels are rolled in such a way that they appear as of scroll structures.

(12) *X-bodies*—These bodies are usually found associated with some of the Tobamoviruses. They consist of virus particles and host organelles such as ribosome, endoplasmic reticulum and golgi bodies.

Inclusion bodies are visible under the light microscope in unstained tissue but staining facilitates their detection. Several simple and rapid staining methods are advised in which fresh epidermal stripes are immersed in solution. Staining with phloxine 0.5% dissolved in water for 1 to 2 minutes may be prepared and used for better results.

❍ Diagnosis by internal symptoms

Different kinds of changes are usually observed. With the help of these changes different diseases may be diagnosed. Such changes are of two types :

(1) Modification in normal cells and their contents.

(2) Microscopically visible inclusion bodies are usually produced in cytoplasm of diseased cells and sometimes in nucleus.

❍ Study of internal anatomy of virus infected leaves

❍ Requirements

(*i*) Infected leaf and healthy leaf, (*ii*) Razor or blade, (*iii*) Watch glasses, (*iv*) Carrot or potato, (*v*) Slides (*vi*) Cover slips, (*vii*) Blotting paper (*viii*) Light microscope, (*ix*) 1.0% Phloxin solution (*x*) 1.0% Trypan blue solution.

❍ Procedure

Cut cross section of healthy and infected leaves. Mount on slide and observe under microscope.

❍ Observations

In mosaic infected tissue chlorotic areas are thinner, palisade cells become round instead of normal tubular shape with fewer and smaller chloroplasts than usual. Chloroplasts are granular and lighter in colour. Increase in intercellular spaces and degeneration of some spongy cells are seen. In healthy leaves, normal anatomy of tissue is seen.

❍ Study of inclusion bodies under light microscope

❍ Requirements

(*i*) Infected leaves of tobacco (TMV) (*ii*) Cowpea leaves infected from *cowpea mosaic virus.* (*iii*) Diamorphotheca mosaic infected sample (*iv*) Healthy leaves of above plants (*v*) Watch glass, slides and cover slips (*vi*) Blotting paper (*vii*) Glycerine and forceps (*viii*) Light microscope (*ix*) Razor or blade (*x*) 1.0% aqueous solution of phloxin and (*xi*) 0.5% trypan blue aqueous solution.

❍ Procedure

Take out epidermal peels of infected and healthy leaves from the ventral surface. (2) Keep the peels in phloxin+trypan blue (1:1) in watch glass for 5 minutes. (3) Wash with distilled water to remove excess stain. (4) Mount in water/glycerine.

❍ Observation

Nucleus takes purple stain and inclusion bodies appear pink in colour. TMV produces middle shaped and hexagonal crystalline inclusions in epidermal cells. In cowpea mosaic amorphous mass in the cytoplasm of epidermal cells are seen. In Diamorphotheca mosaic virus disease bipolar and round inclusions attached on either ends of the nuclei are seen in all epidermal cells. In healthy peels clear cytoplasm and distinct nucleus are observed.

(3) LATENT INFECTION OR LACK OF SYMPTOM EXPRESSION

Some viruses are known to remain present within the susceptible hosts and multiply therein but induce no visible symptoms on the hosts. Such phenomenon is known as latency or latent infection. A latent virus may generally be detected by back inoculation to a susceptible host or by serological assay. In strict sense, the term latency and masking are not synonymous. Under certain conditions, the symptoms of infection may be masked and with the change of conditions the symptoms reappear. It is thus a temporarily phase. On the other hand, the latency is the total absence of visible symptoms over the entire range of environmental conditions to which the virus and host are exposed. Lack of obvious symptoms, however, does not necessarily mean that latent infection has no adverse effect on yield. The yield loss is likely to be overlooked unless detected by yield comparisons with plants known to be virus free. Latent virus infection presents special problems in tackling virus diseases. Plants with latent infection can not be easily detected for rouging. The latent infection is worse when a latent virus is seed-borne or vector transmitted. Such infections are worse most when occurred in stone fruits.

PHYTOTOXAEMIA

The term *Phytotoxaemia is referred to the toxic effect induced by the salivary components secreted by the arthropods especially while feeding.*

A few toxins induced symptoms may be categorized as under :

1. Local lessions such as leaf spotting diffused chlorotic spots at the feeding points.
2. Local lessions with development of characteristic cankers, cork formation, fruit scab and leaf drop streaks as secondary symptoms.
3. Tissue malformation such as leaf curling, rosetting, witches broom, proliferation, hopper burn, phyllody and gummosis.
4. Systemic effects are manifested as vein clearing, leaf streaking, growth depression, tissue necrosis and wilting etc.

❍ Factors affecting virus induced symptoms

Although the expression of virus induced symptoms is primarily governed by the genetic constitution of the virus and the host plant. However, expression of symptoms is secondarily influenced by both biotic and abiotic factors as described beow :

Abiotic factors include factors like temperature, light and humidity which are responsible for development of symptoms to a certain extent.

1. *Temperature*–Different temperature levels affect the severity and type of

symptoms in different virus infected plants. Symptoms of sugar beet yellows and potato leaf roll are observed to be more pronounced during summar than in winter. Similarly virus causing mosaic or ring spot symptoms such as potato virus X, tobacco necrosis and tobacco etch are known to cause severe symptoms during winter but not in summer.

2. *Light.*–High light intensities and low light intensities have significant effect on appearance of disease symptoms. The symptoms produced by *Cucumber mosaic virus* are much less severe under high light intensities than in lower ones.

3. *Humidity*–Although the effect of humidity on symptom expression has not been studied in much detail, yet there are evidences that high percentage of humidity favours plant growth and enhances plant susceptibility to virus infection.

Biotic factors 1. *Infection by other agents.* The mixed infection of two viruses produces more severe symptoms than produced by any one of the two as observed in the potato rugose mosaic due to mixed infection of *Potato virus X* and *Potato virus Y*. Many strains of *Tobacco mosaic virus* (TMV) produce only mosaic symptom in tomato but in combination with *Potato virus X*, a severe streak symptom develops which kills the infected plants.

2. Interactions of viruses with fungi, bacteria and namatodes usually increase host plant susceptibility to viruses and have been observed to enhance the severity of the virus diseases. Bottle gourd infected with *Cucumber green mottle mosaic virus* and *Water melon mosaic virus* develop mosaic pattern. However, blistering and stunting which become more severe if the bottle guard plants are also infected with powdery mildew fungus and root knot nematode.

VIRUS DIAGNOSIS THROUGH DOUBLE STRANDED RNA ANALYSIS

Analysis of double stranded (ds) RNA isolated from infected plants has been used as a basis for plant virus diagnosis. Morris and Dodds (1979) developed a method for the isolation and detection of dsRNAs from plants infected with RNA virues. They observed that the double stranded RNA banding patterns in gel electrophoresis were characteristic of many viruses. These double stranded RNAs represent replicative forms of the viral genomes and are not normally found in healthy plants.

❍ Advantages

1. This method is applicable in situations where unstable viruses, mixed infections or viruses in woody plants are being dealt with.
2. This technique has been found invaluable in studies involving the Closteroviruses, *Citrus tristeza virus* because this virus is difficult to purify, although the ds RNAs for this virus have been readily isolated and used for characterization studies of the genomic RNA and sub genomic RNAs as observed by Mawassi *et al* (1995). Viruses difficult to purify, ds RNAs extracted from virus infected tissues can be used as templates for gene cloning.

7

TRANSMISSION OF VIRUSES

Sap transmission, Method of sap inoculation, Method of graft transmission, Transmission through wedge grafting, Leaf patch grafting, Transmission through budding in citrus, Dodder transmission, Seed and pollen transmission, Transmission through insect vectors, Virus-vector relationship, Method of injury by insect vectors, Mode of vector transmission

A plant virus may be inoculated by mechanical and biological methods. Mechanical methods require preparation of inoculum and deposition of it to susceptible sites of the host manually. *Mechanical transmission* is thus the manual transfer and deposition of biologically active virus to a suitable site in the living cells by sub-lethal wounding or abrasion. This may be achieved either by inoculating infectious sap on healthy host directly or by grafting an infected tissue. *Biological transmission*, on the other hand, does not require preparation of inoculum, but is mediated by some organism carrying or containing virus. Such agents are insects, nematodes, fungi, dodder and organelles such as pollen and seed.

❍ Methods of mechanical transmission

Two methods of mechanical transmission are very commonly used; these are sap transmission and graft transmission. Transmission through sap of infected plants is the simple method of experimental inoculation. Sap inoculation, however, is not possible in viruses which seem to be restricted to the xylem and phloem. The success of mechanical transmission through sap chiefly depends on the source of inoculum, method of the preparation of incoulum, stability of the extracted virus and also on the test plants. Environmental factors such as light, temperature and humidity may also have considerable influence on sap inoculation.

I–SAP TRANSMISSION

Following factors are considered to be important for successful sap transmission of viruses.

(1) Younger leaves with characteristic symptoms of the virus should be preferred because higher concentration of virus is known to be found in such leaves in most cases.

(2) In some other cases, other parts of the plant except leaves may serve as better source of virus. In soil borne *Tobacco necrosis virus*, the roots of infected plants usually serve a better source of virus for sap inoculation. Similarly, the flowers in cucumber mosaic and both the barks and flower's petals in citrus tristeza and apple mosaic are the appropriate sources of viruses.

(3) Method of preparation of inoculum is also important to have the maximum virus concentration. Host metabolites and cellular debris are usually released simultaneously with the virus during extraction. Some of the compounds thus released may inactivate or inhibit the infectivity of the virus in question. Therefore, it is necessary to grind the leaf sample in a suitable buffer and use other additives to maintain pH so as to remove inhibitors and inactivators.

(4) Different species of host plants are required for studying different aspects like detection, culturing and infectivity assay of same virus.

(5) Many plant viruses are highly specific in their infectivity. Some plant species are susceptible to many viruses.

(6) The most frequently used hosts are *Chenopodium amaranticolor, C. quinoa, Cucumis sativus, Nicotiana glutinosa, N. tabacum, Petunia hybrida, Phaseolus vulgaris, Vicia fabae, V. sinensis* and *Gomphrena globosa*. Such laboratory test plants are often better than the natural hosts as virus donors and are easier to grow and maintain.

(7) In cucurbitaceous plants, the seeding cotyledons are more susceptible than the leaves. Similarly, in *Phaseolus vulgaris,* the primary leaves are more susceptible than the trifoliate leaves.

(8) Numerous ways of inoculation are used in practice. First of all, TMV sap was inoculated by injecting sap of infected plants into healthy ones by using capillary glass syringe with needle. Some other methods like use of micro syringe and ultrasonic devices are also used in some cases. Now a days, sap inoculation by rubbing is the most consistent practice used in inoculation. The simple procedure may be summaized as under :

METHOD OF SAP INOCULATION

❍ Requirements :

Young symptomatic leaves, test plants, carborundum on celite powder, pestle and mortar, phosphate buffer, cotton pad and muslin cloth.

❍ Procedure for sap inoculation experiment of *Cucumber mosaic virus*

(1) Symptomatic young leaves should be collected from diseased plant. In the

laboratory such leaves are washed properly and gently blotted dry with tissue/blotting paper. Weight of such leaves is taken and recorded.

(2) Phosphate buffer (0.1M and pH-7.4) is taken equal to (w/v) the weight of the leaves. The leaves are now grinded in sterlized pestle and mortar. Use of liquid nitrogen is preferred particularly for hard and fibrous tissue. In such case phosphate buffer is mixed after proper grinding.

(3) After thorough grinding the whole leaf pulp is pressed through double layered muslin cloth to get filtered standard extract of the leaves.

(4) Now on the leaves of the test plants, carborundum or celite powder is lightly dusted to cause injury on the leaves to be inoculated.

(5) Cotton pad soaked in such standard extract is rubbed on the leaves of test plants by supporting the leaf from the central surface below with a piece of card board in one direction only from the petiole on the apex of the leaf.

(6) After inoculation, inoculated leaves are washed with water in order to remove excessive inocula and carborundum or celite powder. For this purpose a wash bottle should be used.

(7) Inoculated plants are kept in the glass house for observation.

❍ Observations

After 10 to 15 days the characteristic symptoms may appear on young leaves of inoculated plants.

II–METHOD OF GRAFT TRANSMISSION

Grafting is an usual horticultural practice used especially in fruit trees for establishing organic union between the cut surfaces of tissues of two different plants. This practice is more popular in citrus, apple, pear, cherry, plum and other woody ornamentals. Various parts of the plant usually buds, tubers and stems etc. are used for grafting. Several viruses are known to be transmitted by grafting, therefore, grafting was very widely used earlier for experimental transmission of virus diseases which could not be transmitted through sap or other means. It is still useful but its use is mostly restricted to woody plants only (Fig. 7.1 to Fig. 7.6).

Although inter specific and inter generic grafts are often possible but grafts between taxonomically distinct species are much less likely to be successful. However, virus transmission without a good organic union between dissimilar species such as *Chenopodium amaranticolor* and grapevine by approach graft is usually observed to be successful experimentally. Thus in plant virology special technique of grafting have been developed which are not usually used in plant propagation. Wedge grafting, leaf patch grafting and budding are common methods used frequently in plant virology.

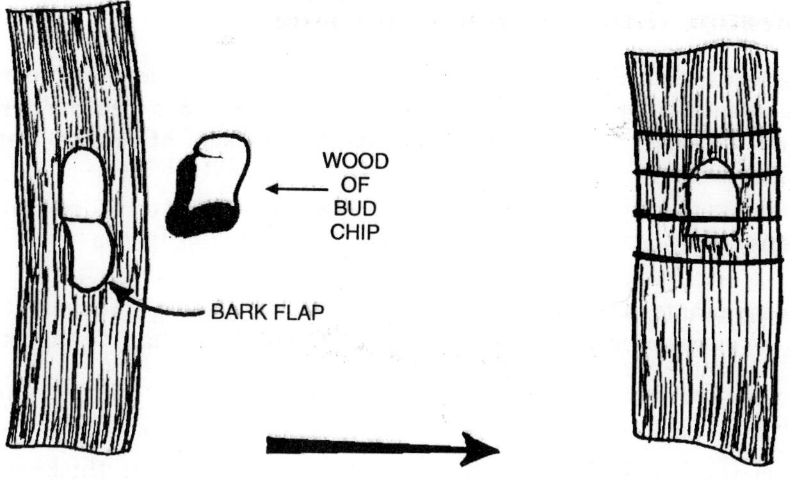

Fig. 7.1 Clip grafting

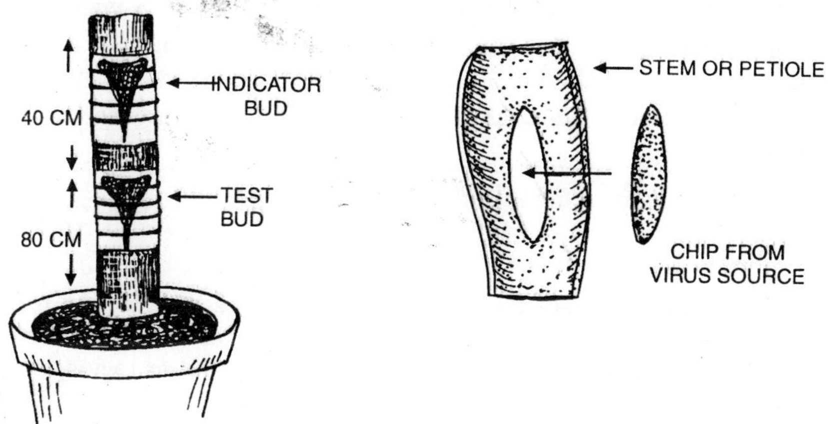

Fig. 7.2 Bud grafting

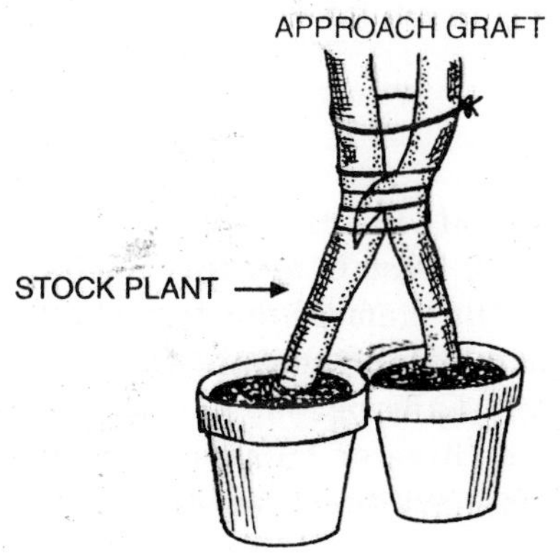

Fig. 7.3 Approach grafting

❍ Transmission through wedge grafting

In herbaceous plants such as tobacco infected with *Tobacco leaf curl virus*, a twig from the infected plant is taken as scion and grafted on a healthy test plant of similar age and thickness used as stock. Graft transmission of tomato leaf roll may be performed as under :

❍ Requirements

(1) Healthy plants of tomato (2) diseased plants of the same thickness (3) Grafting budding knife (4) pieces of muslin cloths (5) cotton (6) polythene bag (7) tag and marker.

❍ Procedure

(*a*) Select the healthy stock and diseased scion of the same thickness.

(*b*) Remove the upper portion of the stock and a 'V'-shaped cleft was made on it.

(*c*) Cut the lower portion of the diseased scion and make a wedge at the end.

(*d*) Fit the wedge of the scion in the cleft of the stock and tie with a piece of cloth.

(*e*) Wrap a wet cotton piece at the joint for union and cover the plant with bell-jar.

(*f*) Tie label showing date of inoculation.

❍ Observations

This method is most widely used both in herbaceous and woody plants. It is widely used for transmission of citrus viruses. After such grafting, the newly emerging leaves from the stock region begin to show the symptoms as on scion, the virus is assumed to be transmitted successfully.

❍ Leaf patch grafting

This method is particularly used for transmission studies of citrus and other temperate fruit viruses.

❍ Procedure

(1) A patch of leaf or bark of infected plant tree (patch size depending on the girth of test plant which is at least 6 months old) is taken. (2) A similar size patch is marked with a knife on the stem of the test plant. Three sides of the patch are loosened and the test patch is placed beneath the bark of the plant. Gently the patch is inserted and the flap hanging out is used to cover the patch and then whole is tied. (3) In this method three or four such patches can be put on the same stem at different places. (4) After grafting, the plants are maintained in the green house.

❍ Tongue and bottle grafting

These two methods are also used for transmission studies. Methods have been represented diagramatically below.

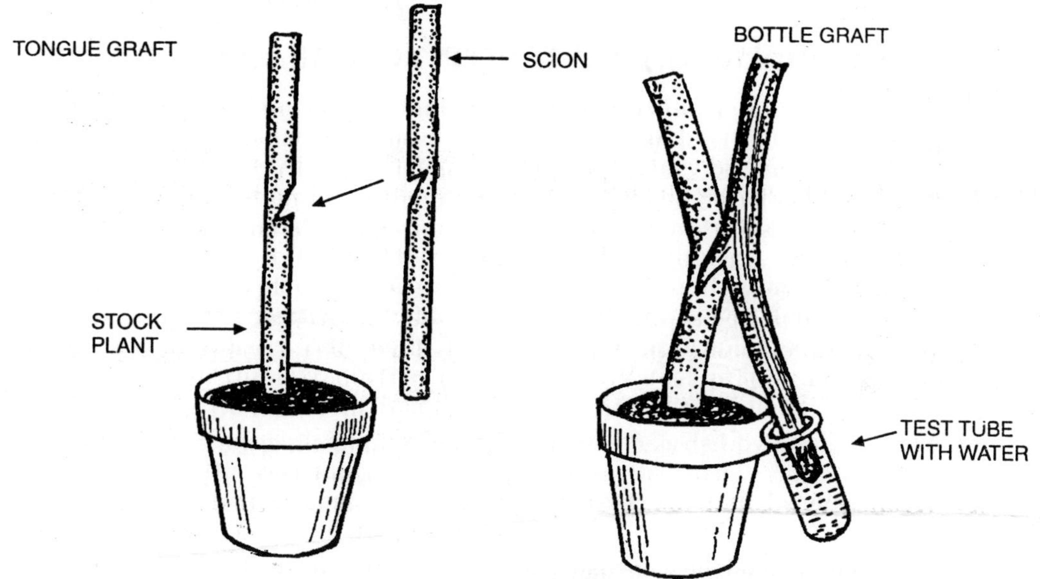

Fig. 7.4 Tongue and bottle grafting

❍ Transmission by budding in citrus

❍ Procedure

(1) Buds are obtained from twig of citrus plant bearing mature buds and are cut with a knife. (2) Woody portion from the bud is removed carefully. (3) On the healthy nursery plant of citrus, T-shaped cut *i.e.* first a transverse and then a longitudinal incision are made which should be superficial. (4) The test bud is then put inside the bark flap of the plant in such a way that only the bud remains emerged and bark portion of the bud remains covered with the flap. (5) Grafted portion of the stem is tied with a polythene strip bearing the bud exposed.

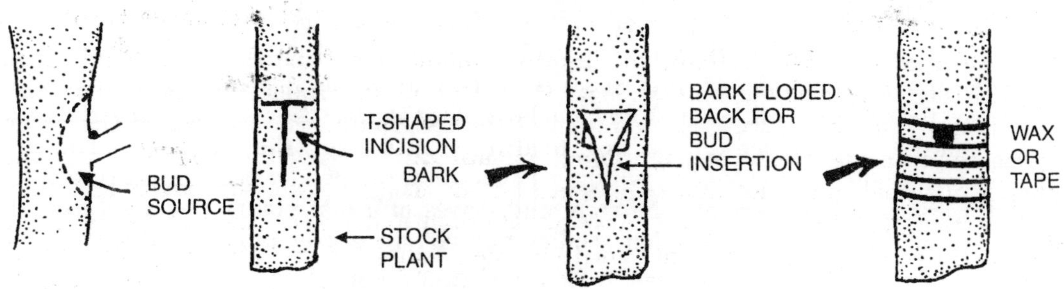

Fig. 7.5 Process of bud grafting

❍ Leaflet grafting

Certain viruses may be transmitted by leaflet grafting method. This method has been represented diagramatically below.

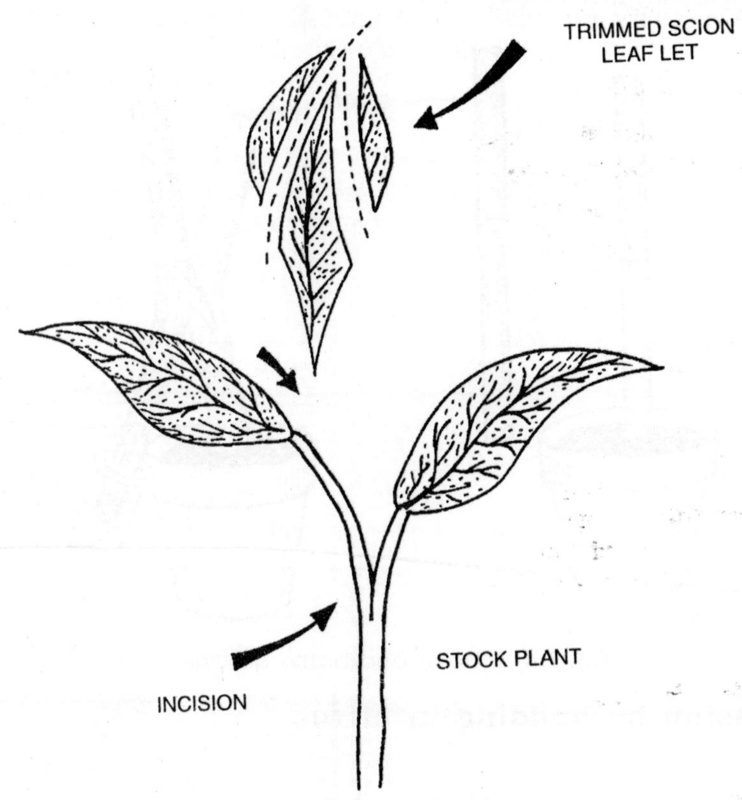

Fig. 7.6 Leaflet grafting

III–DODDER TRANSMISSION

Dodder transmission is an effective method of virus transmission in nature and in the green houses. Different viruses may be transmitted by dodder to plants that do not show transmission by grafting because of the incompatibility of the tissues. This method is valuable particularly when mechanical and vector transmission does not succeed. Dodder (*Cuscuta* species) is a genus belonging to the family Convolvuaceae of leafless elongated wiry herbs that are deficient in chlorophyll and are parasitic on other chlorophyllous plants. Dodder absorbs food from the host by means of haustoria and viruses too are transmitted from the one host plant to the other. Under experiment, viruses can be transmitted by putting healthy plants near the diseased ones. In transmission studies with dodder, winding cut sprouts of dodder may be initiated to grow on a diseased plant around the stem and leaves of a test plant. Several *Cuscuta* species are suitable for transmission studies but not all are equally effective.

Out of 20 species of dodder tested for experimental transmission, *Cuscuta compestris, C. subinclusa* and *C. refloxa* are being commonly used to transmit different viruses and phytoplasmas. These species have wide host range. Therefore, they are very useful in experimental virology. Dodder seeds may be germinated on the soil containing seeding of the host plant. The germinated dodder seed is placed in leaf axle of infected host. When it establishes, its shoots are trained on the test plant to be infected. CMV and TRV are usually used for a test. *Bean yellow mosaic virus* (BYMV) and *Potato virus* X (PVX) are not dodder transmissible.

❍ Procedure

(*a*) Put seeds of *Cuscuta subinclusa* on moist filter paper in a petri dish.

(*b*) Place seedlings with a stem of 2-4 cms in contact with the stem or petiole of the host plant. Do this in a humid plant chamber or immerse the root like 'peg' in a very small tube of water.

(*c*) *Beta vulgaris* and *Vicia fabae* (plants without many hairs) are suitable for development.

(*d*) Before starting of flowering, transfer stems (with a tip) of 10-20 cms length to a new host plant to keep the dodder in a vegetative stage.

(*e*) The dodder is inoculated by a virus by placing a seedling or stem of 10-20 cms. on the diseased host plant. Take care that the tip of the stem touches the host.

(*f*) After two weeks or later, train a dodder shoot against a test plant or cut a shoot of 10-20 cms and wind it round the test plant.

Transmission by dodder is just a passive transport of the virus since its multiplication in the dodder is not essential. However, transmission is more efficient if the virus/phytoplasma multiplies in the dodder itself. One precaution that is necessary for experimental transmission with dodder is to check the dodder plant for the presence of dodder latent virus. The virus is seed-borne and symptom less in *Cuscuta compestris* but produces symptoms in some species of plants parasitized by dodder.

IV–SEED AND POLLEN TRANSMISSION

Some viruses are carried on the seed coat (testa) as surface contaminants such as TMV on tomato seed. Some other viruses, however, may be carried in the embryo. Since the embryo and endosperm are formed within the embryo-sac after fertilization having no direct vascular connection and cellular contact with the mother plant, embryo infection has essentially to occur before flowering and formation of female gametes.

Factors involved in seed and pollen transmission

(1) Some viruses but not all have the ability to pass through or multiply in the meristematic tissue within the developing ovules.

(2) Some viruses may enter the seedling tissue through cells injured during the transplanting process.

(3) Different strains of virus may vary in their ability to be transmitted through seed. Seed transmission of different strains of *Barley stripe mosaic virus* in differnt barley and wheat cultivars were found to vary from 0% to 53%.

(4) A virus which is seed transmitted in one host may not be seed-borne in others. Differnt cultivars of a plant may vary widely in this respect.

(5) Virus transmission is greatly influenced by different temperatures. Transmission of *Barley stripe mosaic virus* is known to occur more through barley seeds grown at 20-24C° in comparison to the higher or lower temperatures.

(6) Most of the nematode-borne viruses, usually cause high proportions of infected seeds in infected mother plant.

(7) True seed-borne viruses seem to persist as long as the seed remains viable.

(8) Seedlings developing from infected seeds usually do not show detectable symptoms. However, some seed-borne viruses can be detected by inoculating indicator plants with extracts of embryo or pollen.

(9) The pollen-borne viruses seem to enter the ovule along with male gametes through the pollen tube as it grows into the embryo sac.

(10) A larger portion of transmission of *Bean common mosaic virus* in bean seed occurs when healthy flowers are pollinated with pollen from infected plants.

V–TRANSMISSION THROUGH INSECT VECTORS

About 94% or more of the plant virus vectors are arthropods and nearly 99% of those arthropod vectors are insects. Among all vectors more than 80% vectors of plant viruses belong to order-Homeptera. Order Homoptera includes many groups and each group of which contains many vector species. The Homopetera vectors belong to two broad groups namely, the **Auchenorrhyncha** and **Sternorrhyncha** which differ mainly by the position of the rostrum. The rostrum is the beak-like structure harboring the stylets. In **Auchenorrhyncha** to which the leaf hoppers and plant hoppers belong, the rostrum arises from the head.

In **Sternorrhyncha,** the rostrum arises ventrally from the chest which includes aphids, white flies, coccids and psyllids. The beetles are quite a dominant vector group with 74 species transmitting about 45 known viruses. The thrips (Thysanoptera) have rasping and sucking type of mouth parts with a very few vector species. Mites, the only non-insect group of arthropod-vectors have puncturing and sucking mouth parts. The aphids maintain largest group with the maximum number of vector species transmitting more viruses than others. The leaf hoppers rank second being much closer to aphids. Among whitefly vectors-*Bemisia tabaci* is the sole representative and stands second to aphid vector representative–*Myzus persicae* in respect to the number of diseases transmitted. The thrips usually transmit only one disease-the bud necrosis of groundnut caused by *Peanut bud necrosis virus*. Some coccid species are known vectors being a menace to the precious cacao plantation causing swollen shoot disease in West Africa.

❍ Virus vector relationship

The characteristics of transmission of different viruses by their vectors vary considerably. Some viruses may be acquired by its vectors from diseased plant within seconds and the vectors can infect the healthy plants immediately. Similarly some other viruses are acquired after a long time by its vectors and such vectors may remain infective for years. In this way virus vector relationships are important in studying transmission of viruses. Various terms are usually used in connection with experiments to determine the relationship between viruses and their vectors especially the insect vectors. Some of the common terms are being explained as under :

1. Acquisition feeding period. The time required by the vector for feeding on virus source plant to acquire the virus is known as acquisition feeding period.

2. Acquisition access period. The period of time a virus free vector is allowed access to a source of the virus is called acquisition access period.

3. Inoculation access period. The time for which virus carrying vector is allowed access to a virus free plant for inoculation is called inoculation access period.

4. Inoculation feeding period. The time for which a virus carrying vector actually feeds on a virus free plant for inoculation is known as inoculation feeding period.

5. Acquisition threshold period. The minimum period of time required by a vector to acquire virus from a diseased source plant is called acquisition threshold period.

6. Inoculation threshold period. The minimum time desired by a vector to inoculate virus to the virus free test plant is called inoculation threshold period.

7. Latent period. The period from acquisition of virus by the vector till the time the vector becomes capable to transmit the virus to healthy plants is called latent period.

8. Transmission threshhold period. The minimum time required by the vector to acquire a virus and inoculate the virus free plant with it, is called transmission threshold period.

9. Serial transfer. The transfer of a vector to a series of virus free plants one after another, is called serial transfer. The duration of exposing a plant and the interval of transfers depend on the discretion of the person conducting the experiment. Serial transfer experiments are done to determine the period for which a vector remains infective.

10. Transtadial passage. The passage of the virus through molting or in other words, the vector remains infective after molting.

11. Transovarial passage. When a virus passed to the progeny through egg of the infective vector.

METHODS OF VECTOR INJURY

Insect vectors destroy or damage all kinds of growing plants in different ways. Virus penetrates within the cell through the injury caused and virus retained by the vectors. Vectors damage the plants in following ways :

(*a*) By chewing leaves, buds, stems barks or fruits of the plant.

(*b*) By boring or tunneling in the bark, stem fruits, nuts, seeds or twigs.

(*c*) By causing cancerous growths on plants within which they live and feed.

(*d*) By attacking roots and underground stems in any of the above ways.

(*e*) By laying the eggs in some parts of the plant.

(*f*) By taking parts of the plant for the construction of the nests or shelters.

METHODS OF INJURY BY VECTORS

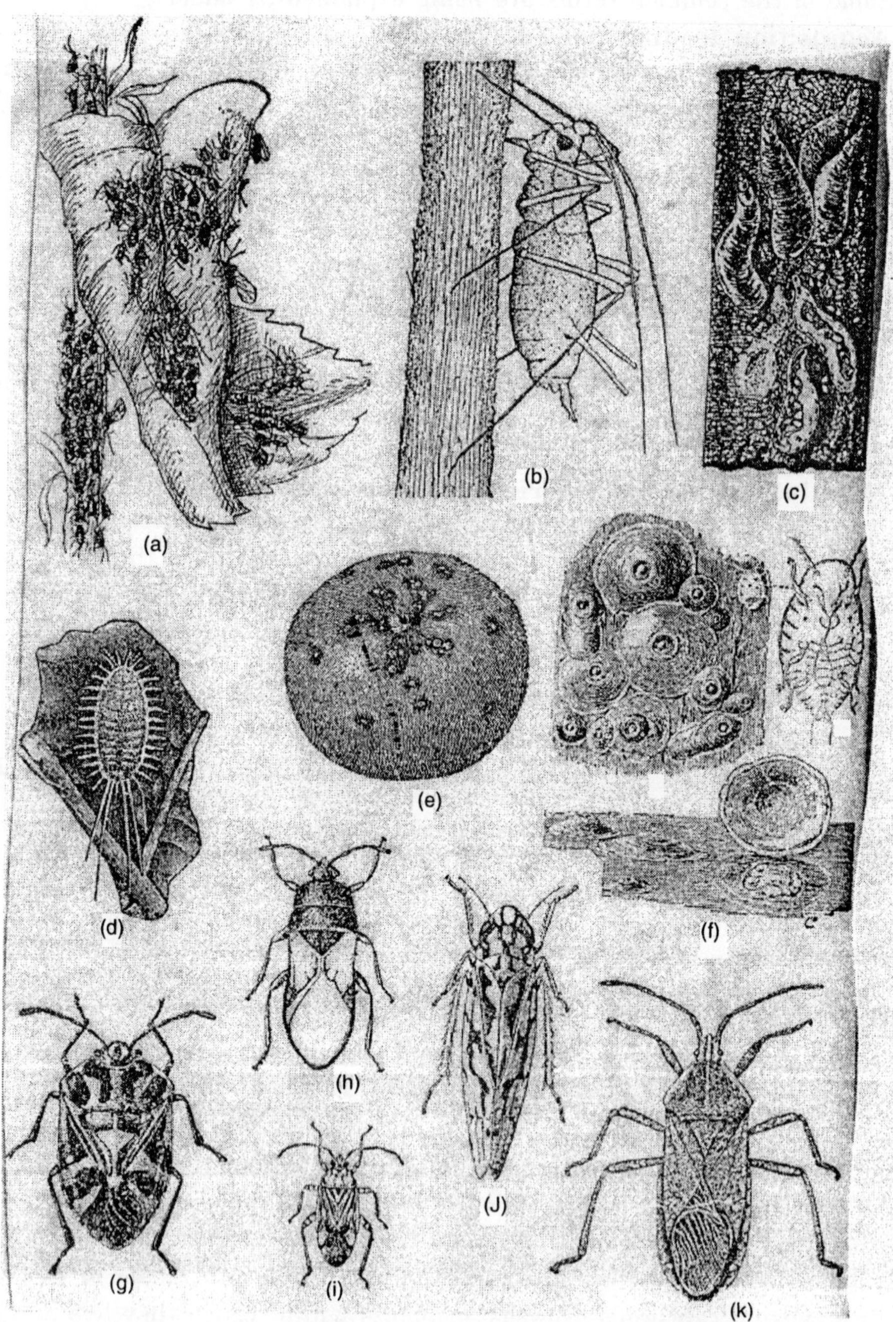

Fig. 7.7 Common plant feeding infects with piercing and sucking type of mouth parts. (a)-Aphids clustered on stem and leaf, (b)-feeding of aphid, (c)-Shell scals on bark, (d)-Long tailed mealy bug on leaf. (e) and (f) Scale insect on apple fruit, (g) Cabbage bug, (h) Spinach bug, (i) Plant bug, (j) Grape leaf hopper, (k) Squash bug.

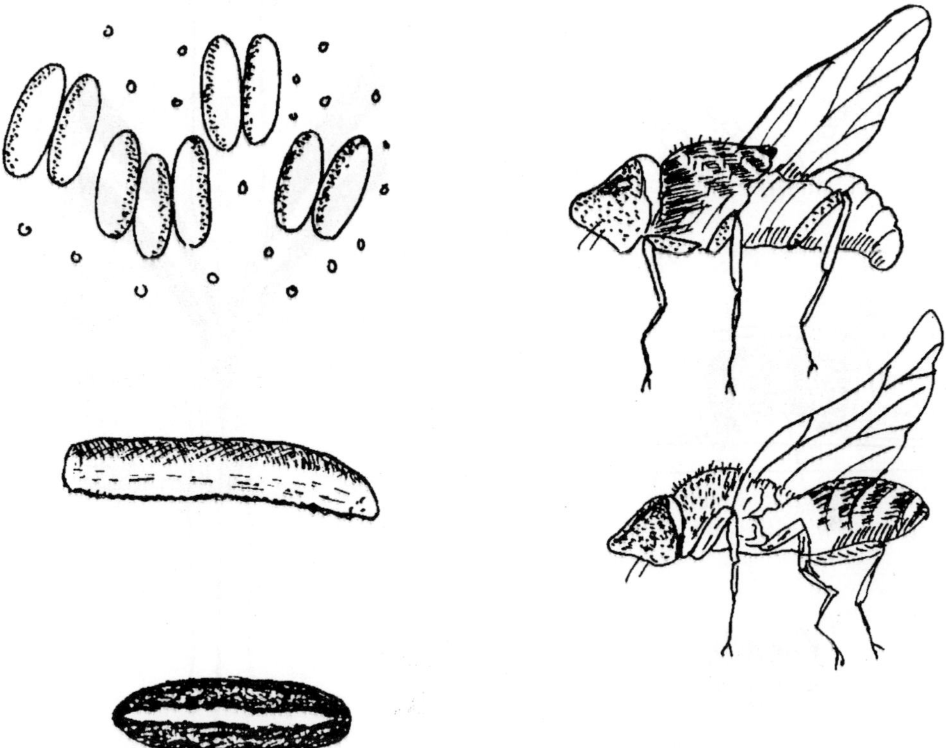

Fig. 7.8. Egg, larvae and adult of spinach leaf miner

(g) By disseminating pathogens including fungi, bacteria and viruses, injecting them into the tissues of the plant as they feed carrying them into their tunnels, or making wounds through which such disease causing agents gain entrance.

(h) By bringing about cross fertilization in certain plants and thus transmitting many viruses by pollen.

❍ Injury by chewing insects

Nearly all the injury caused by vectors result directly or indirectly from their attempts to secure food. Vectors take their food in a variety of ways. A primitive and very important method is by chewing off the external parts of a plant, grinding them up and swallowing the solid and liquid parts together by taking infinitely smaller bites. Such insect vectors are called chewing insects. Cabbageworms, armyworms, grasshoppers, the colorado potato beetle, the pear-slug and the cankerworm are common examples of such kinds of insects (Fig. 7.7, 7.8 and 7.9).

❍ Injury by piercing-sucking insects

A very important way in which vectors feed on growing plants is by piercing the epidermis and sucking out the sap from the cells within. In this case only

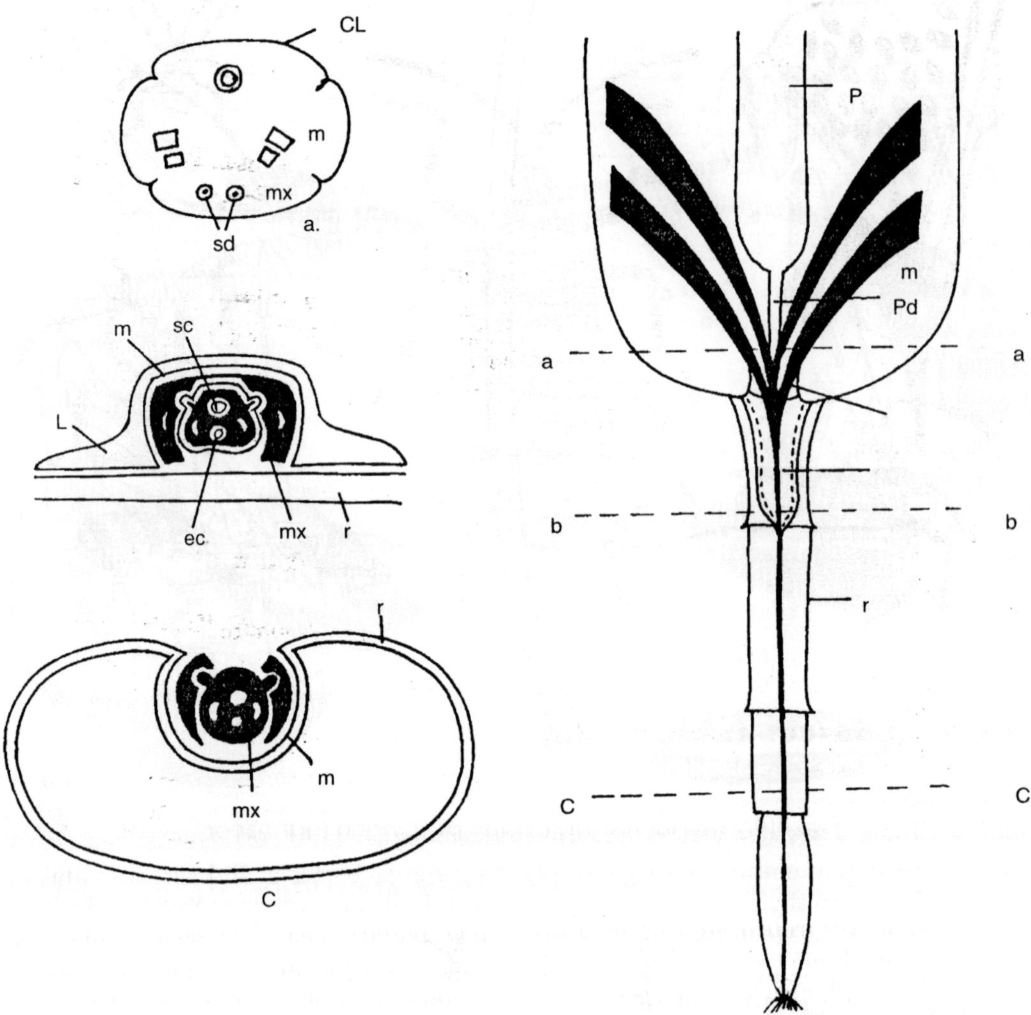

Fig. 7.9 Mouth part and adjacent region of the head of a Hemipterous insect. *cl*, clypeus; *ec*, ejection canal with salivary duct; *l*, labrum; *m*, mandible; *mx*, maxilla; *p*, pharynx; *pd*, pharyngeal duct; *r*, rostrum; *sd*, salivary ducts; *sc*, suction canal with pharynge duct.

internal and the liquid portions of the plant are swallowed, although the insect vectors remain externally on the plants. Such insects we usually called as piercing and sucking insects. This work is accomplished by means of externally slender and sharp pointed portion of the beak which is thrust into the plant and through which plant sap is sucked. The hole made by the beak is so small that it is never seen, but the withdrawal of the sap results in dissemination of the virus sometimes resulting in minute spotting. Aphids, scale insects, the chinch bug, the harlequin cabbage bug, leaf hoppers and plant bugs are well known examples of piercing and sucking insects (Fig. 7.10).

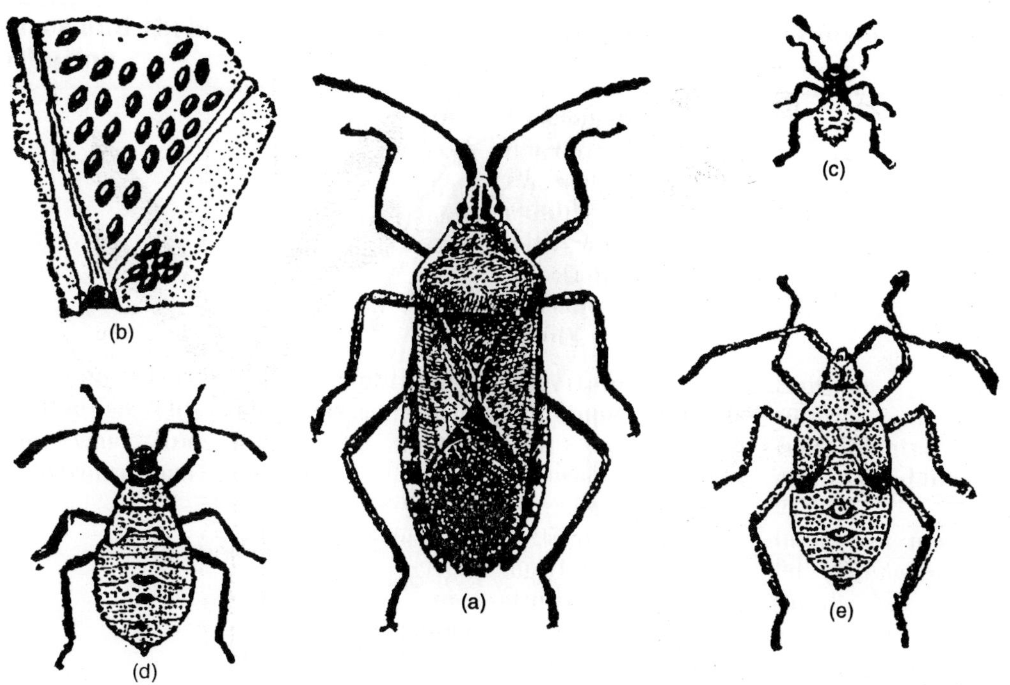

Fig. 7.10. Stages of squash bug (*a*) adult (*b*) eggs (*c*) nymps (*d*) & (e) nymphs.

❍ Mode of insect transmission

Plant viruses transmitted by insects may be divided into three categories, namely– non-persistent, semi-persistent and persistent. Persistent viruses are also called as circulative viruses. The persistent (circulative) viruses may be further divided into propogative and non-propogative types depending on whether they multiply in the vector or not.

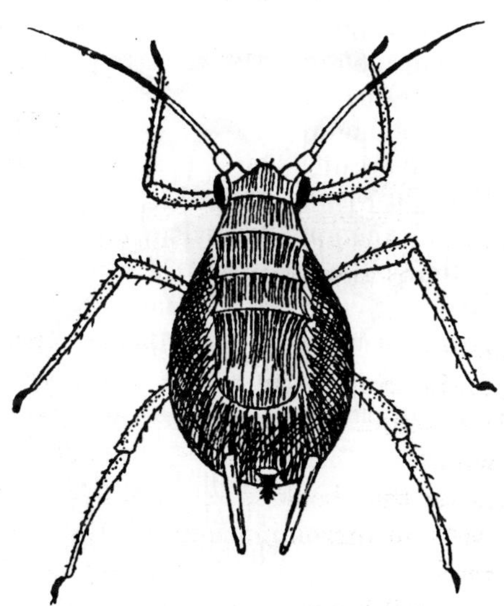

Fig. 7.11. Diagramatic represention of morphology of *Myzus persicae*.

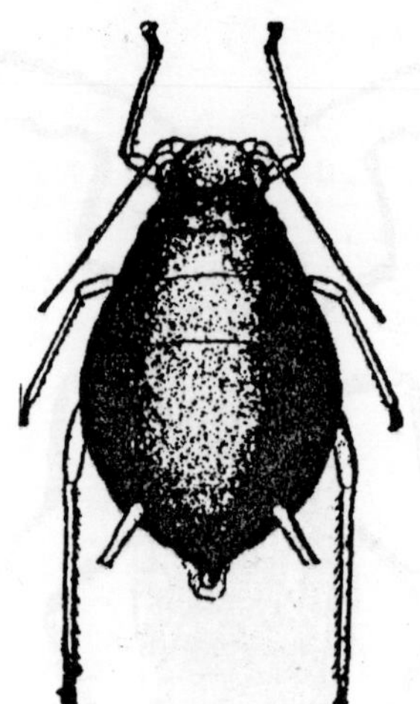

Fig. 7.12. Diagramatic representation of morphology of Strawberry root aphid.

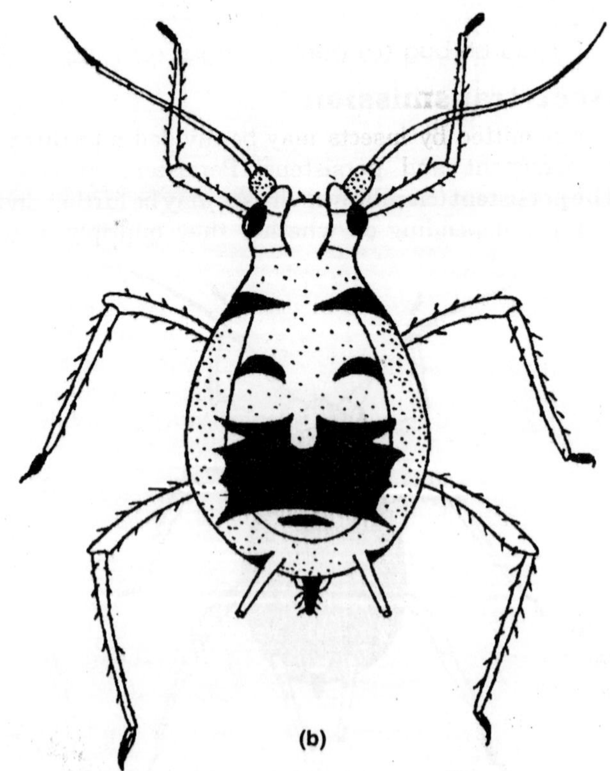

Fig. 7.13. Morphological characteristics of *Myzus circumflexus*

Persistent viruses are those who multiply in the body of the vector and thus they are retained in the body of such vectors for longer period than that of non-persistent viruses.

Non-persistent viruses are those which are acquired by the vectors after short period of feeding, retained for some time and are transmitted within short period which may be from few seconds to few hours (15 seconds to 2 hours). Out of 250 aphid borne viruses, most of them are non-persistent viruses. Banana mosaic, barley mosaic, bean mosaic, cardamom crinkle, chilli mosaic, pea mosaic, papaya ring spot, potato virus A and papaya virus Y are important aphid-borne non-persistent viruses. Most of the viruses transmitted by leaf hoppers and plant hoppers are persistent in nature except rice tungru virus transmitted by *Nephotettix implicata*. The viruses usually transmitted in non-persistent manner belong to potyvirus, caulimovirus and alfalfavirus groups. Members belonging to these groups include both helical and isometric DNA and RNA viruses having mono-,bi-, and tri-partite genomes.

❍ Characteristics of non-persistent viruses

(1) Different strains of the same virus may vary in efficiency to be transmitted by different vector species.

(2) Some strains of a virus transmissible in non-persistent manner by aphids may not be transmitted by aphids at all.

(3) The essential mechanism of transmission involves attachment of virus or absorption of viruses by the stylets-labial complex.

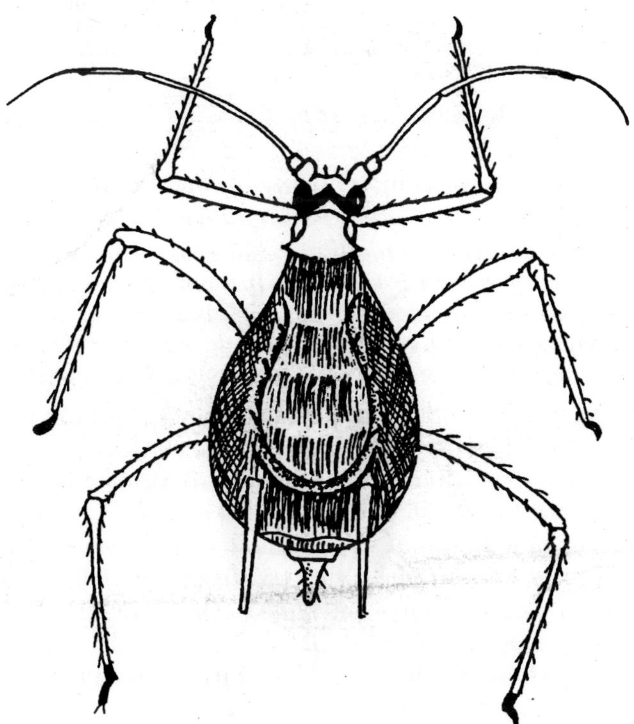

Fig. 7.14. Showing morphology of *Macrosiphon* Species.

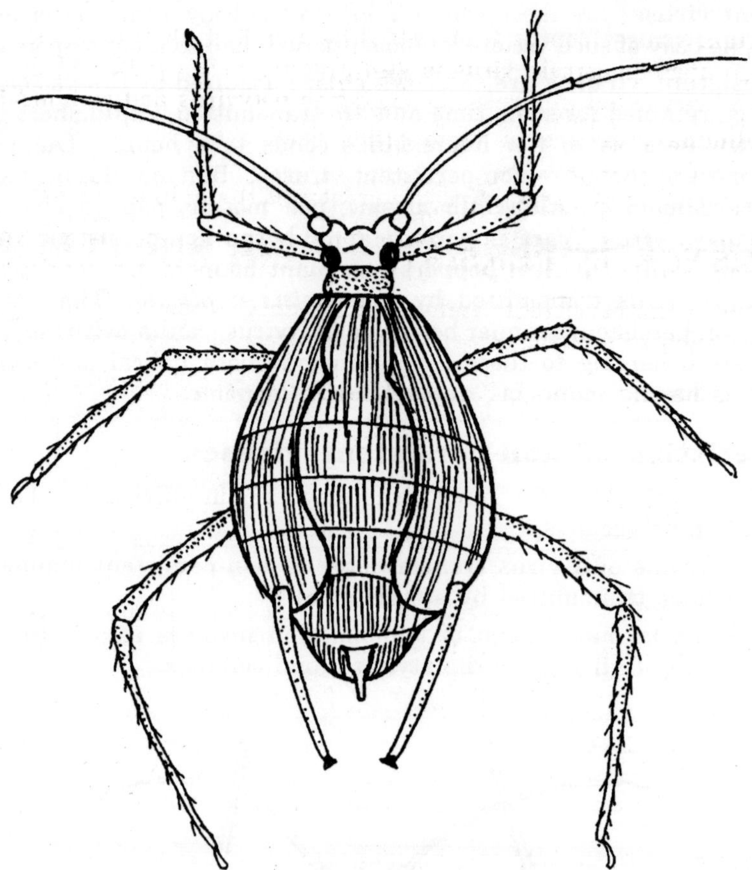

Fig. 7.15. Showing morphology of *Myzus pseudosolani.*

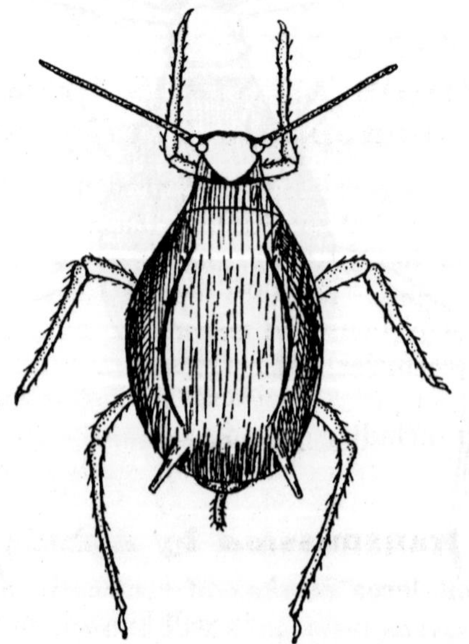

Fig. 7.16. Morphology of *Aphis rhamni*

(4) Certain viruses can be transmitted by aphids in non- persistent manner only when another certain virus is also present in the source plant. Such factors have been found in viruses belonging to potyvirus and caulimovirus groups.

(5) Preliminary fasting of vectors has been observed to improve acquisition efficiency.

(6) The rate of loss of infectivity is greater if the aphids are fed than if fasted.

DIFFERENCE IN PERSISTENT AND NON-PERSISTENT

Persistant, semi-persistent and non-persistent viruses differ significantly in different ways. Such differences may be summarized in following Table 7.1.

Table 7.1 **Difference among Persistent, Semi-persistent and Non-persistent viruses**

Properties	Non-persistent	Semi-persistent	Non-propagative	Propagative
Pre-acquisition feeding	Required	Not-required	Not-required	Not-required
Acquisition Time	More than one minute	Less than 30 minutes	Many hours	Many hours
Latent period	Nil	Nil	Hours to days	Hours to days
Persistence	One hour	More than 100 hours	Several days	Whole life
Retention after molting	Nil	Nil	Positive	Positive
Transovarial viral transmission	No	No	No	Yes
Mechanical transmission	Yes	Yes	Yes	No

APHIDS AS VIRUS VECTORS
(Order Homoptera, Family Aphididae)

Aphids constitute the largest group of plant virus vectors. More than 4000 species of aphids are known but only 200 species have been identified as vectors transmitting different plant viruses. In India, about 38 species of aphids have been identified as virus vectors transmitting about 70% of the viruses known to cause diseases of economic importance. The most conspicuous and distinctive character of aphids is the presence of the pair of siphunculi (cornicles), placed dorso-laterally on the 5th or 6th abdominal segment. Aphid-transmitted viruses cause severe losses through out the world, infecting numerous economic plants including cereals, legumes, vegetables, fruits and ornamentals (Fig. 7.11 to 7.16).

❍ Study of Virus transmission by Aphids

Aphids can transmit large number of viruses in plants both in persistent and non-persistent manner. *Myzus persicae* is well known and can transmit both the types of viruses *i.e.* persistent (*Potato leaf roll*) and non-persistent (Potato *virus Y*).

❍ Requirement

(1) Aphid culture (2) Test plant (3) Fine hair brush (4) Glass chimenys (5) Petri plates (6) Insecticide and a hand sprayer (7) Hands lens.

❍ Procedure

(1) From pure culture, aphids are collected and put in the glass vials for pre-acquisition fasting.

(2) After 2 hours of pre-acquisition fasting aphids are placed on virus infected leaf for 5-10 minutes for acqusition feeding. Stylet feeding may be observed under stereoscopic binocular.

(3) With the help of a fine hair brush these aphids are reared one by one on test seedlings. Ten aphids per seedling are used for this study.

(4) Such seedlings are covered with cages after acquisition access and placed in dark chamber overnight.

(5) Next day these seedlings are sprayed with the insecticide (such as metasystox 0.01%) to kill the aphids. Now the seedlings are placed in a glass house.

❍ Observations

Daily observations for appearance of diagnostic symptoms will be taken and percentage transmission of the virus on test seedlings will be recorded.

WHITEFLIES AS VIRUS VECTORS
(Order Homoptera, Family Aleyrodidae)

Whiteflies belong to the family Aleyrodidae of the order Homoptera and are placed in Sternorrhyncha along with aphids, coccids and psyllids. The family is small comprising about 1156 species belonging to 126 genera. The aleyroids differ from sternrrhynchans in the position of anus and associated structures. The anus opens on the dorsal surface of the abdomen, ventrally to a tongue like projection called *lingual*. They lie in a shallow depression called vasiform orifice which is partially covered dorsally by the operculum. Females differ from the males by their bigger and broader abdomen which does not taper posteriorly as in males. The number of eggs laid by a single female may exceed to 300 eggs. *Bemisia tabaci, Bemisia argenitifolii, Trialurodes abutiloneus* and *T.vaporariorum* are known to transmit different plant viruses. Of these *Bemisia tobaci* is economically most important as it transmits a large number of viruses mostly belonging to geminivirus group. *Bemisia tabaci* is capable of laying unfertilized eggs but these develop into males only. *Bemisia tabaci* is also capable of colonizing on numerous cultivated plants and weeds under favourable environmental conditions. Temperature above 32°C is not suitable for reproduction. Low humidity during hot weather has been reported to be highly determinant to immature stages. The species appear to be less sensitive to high humidity.

White flies are usually phloem feeders. They derive their food as amino acids and carbohydrates directly from the food transport system of the host plants. The stylet passes intercellularly through epidermis, mesophyll and finally to vascular tissues. This type of feeding behaviour is an effective means of acquiring and subsequently transmitting phloem-borne geminiviruses. A partial list of diseases transmitted by whiteflies has been given in following Table 7.2.

Table 7.2 A partial list of diseases transmitted by whiteflies.

Abutilon mosaic, African cassava mosaic, bean dwarf mosaic, bean golden mosaic. okra yellow vein mosaic, cotton leaf crumple, croton yellow mosaic, dolichos yellow mosaic. egg plant yellow mosaic, eupatorium yellow vein mosaic, euphorbia mosaic, Indian cassava mosaic, melon leaf curl, mungbean yellow mosaic, soybean crinkle leaf, squash leaf curl, tobacco leaf curl, tomato golden mosaic, tomato yellow leaf curl and potato yellow mosaic.

❍ Study of Virus transmission by whitefly

Bemisia tabaci is a very common whitefly and most of the Gemini viruses are transmitted by this whitefly in a semi-persistent manner.

❍ Requirements

(1) Whitefly culture (2) test plants (3) aspirator (4) cages designed for whitefly transmission (5) hand sprayer and (6) insecticide.

❍ Procedure

1. Healthy whitefly cultures are maintained in net house on *Nicotiana gluca* Graham.
2. With the help of aspirator 100 whiteflies are collected and released on virus infected leaves under specially fabricated glass tubes for acquisition of the virus.
3. These whiteflies are allowed to feed on test plants under controlled condition overnight. Ten test plants are used in the study and 10 white flies are used per test plant.
4. Next day seedlings should be sprayed with any suitable insecticide to kill the whiteflies after incoulation feeding.
5. Test seedlings were placed in special chamber for proper growth of the plant.

❍ Observations

Transmission percentage was recorded by observing characteristic symptoms produced on test plants.

MEALY BUGS AS VIRUS VECTORS

The mealy bugs belong to the family Pseudococcidae of super family Coccoidea having virus vector species. The mealy bugs owe their name due to the milky appearance as they are dusted all over with white powdery material. An important morphologial character of this family is the presence of segmented tarsi with a single claw. The females are wingless and hence their movement is restricted to crawling. They are phloem feeders and males are very small in appearance having single pair of wings and without mouthparts. Eighteen species of mealy bugs have been reported as vectors. The four viruses affecting cacao plantations are transmitted by mealy bugs. *Planococcoides njolensis* and *P. citri* are important vector species transmitting most of the viruses in this group. Nymphs are more efficient vectors than adults. Starved mealy bugs acquire virus more efficiently than non-starved ones. Acquisition feeding periods of 48-72 hours and inoculation feeding for 3-4 hours result in maximum transmission (Fig. 7.15 and Fig. 7.7d).

Fig. 7.15. Four common species of mealy bugs.

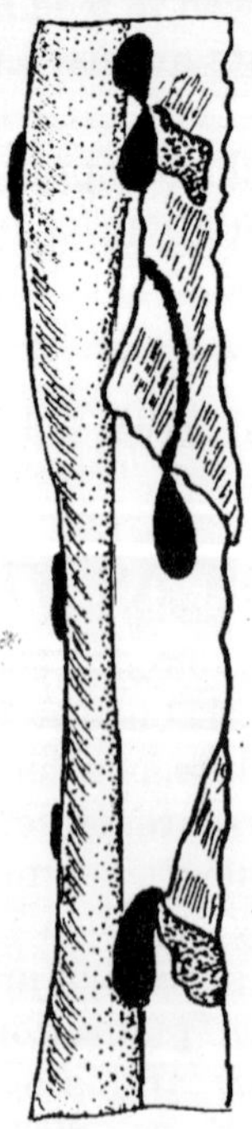

Fig. 7.16 Twig infected with shell scale insect

PSYLLIDS AS VIRUS VECTORS

The psyllids belong to the Homopetera family Psyllidae. Approximately 1500 species are known to occur and out of that 6 have incriminated as virus vectors. Three economically important diseases namely, pear decline, citrus greening and proliferation of carrots are known to be transmitted by these vectors.

LEAF HOPPERS AND PLANT HOPPERS AS VIRUS VECTORS

The leaf hoppers and plant hoppers belong to Auchenorrhycha and differ from aphids, whiteflies, psyllids and cocids by the position of rostrum arises from the head in Auchenorrhyncha. The leaf hoppers can be distinguished from the plant hoppers by some easily recognizable characters. In leaf hoppers the vertex is smooth and convex and sometimes obtuse angled with compound eyes at the extremes. The antennae are thin and minute, bristle-like in shape with two small basal segments. The forewings are non-transparent and variously colored. Plant hoppers on the other hand, have a narrow rectangular front between segments reduced to a thin filament. Their fore-and hind wings are usually hyaline or membranous and less colourful than those of leaf hoppers. The plant hoppers are not as dominant as the leaf hoppers in respect of the number of vector species and the number of plant viruses transmitted by them. Leaf hoppers and plant hoppers transmit several viruses of economic importance. About 15,000 species of leaf hoppers belonging to 2000 genera are known as virus vectors. The identification of leaf hoppers are based on many characters such as size and coloration, which are used widely in taxonomy and are diagnostic in many instances (Fig. 7.17).

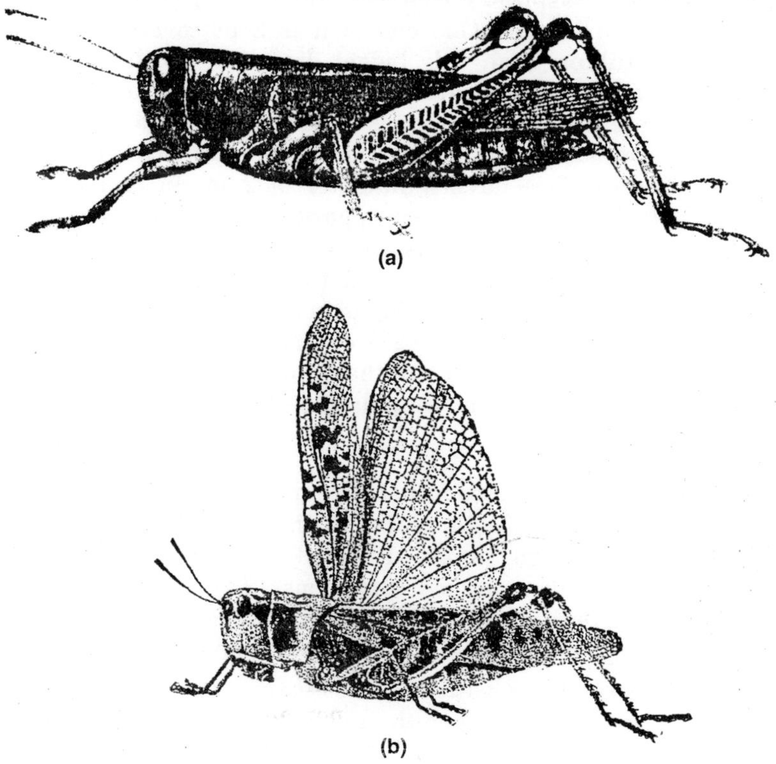

(a)

(b)

Fig. 7.17 (a) Adult grass hopper (b) Clear winged grass hopper

Leaf hoppers and plant hoppers are generally abundant during wet season and are found in lesser number when conditions become dry. The hoppers in general are phloem feeders but many species exploit xylem and mesophyll and occasionally all three tissues.

STUDY OF VIRUS TRANSMISSION OF LEAF HOPPERS

Tungru virus of rice was taken for this experiment. As known to all, tungru disease is caused by two different viruses which are morphologically and genomically different from each other. The one of the two viruses is spherical in shape called *Rice tungru spherical virus* (RTSV) and the other is known as *Rice tungru bacilliform virus* (RTBV). RTSV has single straded RNA genome and RTBV owns double stranded DNA genome. RTSV is transmitted independently by the vector namely, *Nephotettix virescens* while RTBV is transmitted only when the vector first acquires RTSV. Virus vector relationship is of semi-persistent type.

❍ Requirements

(1) Catcher

(2) Transmission cages

(3) Transfer chamber

(4) Tungru infected plants and

(5) Healthy rice seedlings are required for the experiment.

Catcher is a simple aspirator consisting of a glass tube measuring 0.7-0.8 cm in diameter and 12 cm in length. One end of it is kept covered by muslin cloth and inserted into a plastic tubing of slightly bigger diameter which measure about 75 cm in length. With this catcher insects are sucked from the open end of the plastic tube. Polymethyl methacrylate cages are used as **transmission cages** to encage the leaf hoppers for both the acquisition and inoculation feeding on rice seedlings. These cages are made of two different sizes having diameter of 2.54 cm and 7.62 cm. The body of the cages is provided with air vents on opposite sides being covered with 60 mesh nylon net. Nylon net is also used to cover the top of the cages in order to avoid accumulation of moisture and provide ventilation. **Transfer chamber** is used for performing all operations regarding handling of vectors. Transfer chamber is composed of rectangular wooden chamber measuring 2′ × 4′ × 1.4′ in size. Sliding glass doors having two panels are manipulated carefully on the front of the chamber to make enough room for the hands to be inserted for handling the vectors.

❍ Procedure

(1) Green hoppers are collected from the rearing cage. A batch of non-viruliferous green leaf hoppers (*Nephotettix virescens*) is encaged in a Polymethyl methacrylate cage on tungru infected rice variety TN-1 plants showing characteristic tungru disease symptoms. The shortest acquisition feeding has been reported to be 5 minutes but to be sure the hoppers are allowed an acquisition feeding access period of 6 hours.

(2) After the expiry of acquisition access feeding period, the viruliferous hoppers are encaged on individual healthy seedlings of usually 15 days old test plants @ 3 leaf hoppers per plant. In the pot all healthy seedlings are inoculated except one central seedling as control. Although only one leaf hopper can transfer

the virus but to be sure 3 hoppers per plant were used in this experiment. Similarly shortest inoculation feeding period of 7 minutes is reported but in this experiment inoculation feeding access of 18 hours is given.

(3) These inoculated plants are kept under glass house conditions for observation of sequence of symptoms.

❍ Observations

The inoculated plants will show characteristic symptoms of the disease after 5-8 days. Characteristic, symptoms of the disease are :

(1) spreading habit of plants.

(2) stunting.

(3) development of orange colour from tips to downwards on leaves.

(4) reduction in tillering, and

(5) chaffy grain formation.

❍ Precautions

Precautions should be taken while releasing insects on the encaged plants. They should be released by tapping the glass tubes and blowing should be avoided as it may cause injury to insects. Male hoppers and nymphs should be preferred in the experiment to avoid egg laying on the inoculated plants.

THRIPS AS VIRUS VECTORS

Thrips are generally minute and slender insects, living in flowers, leaf sheaths

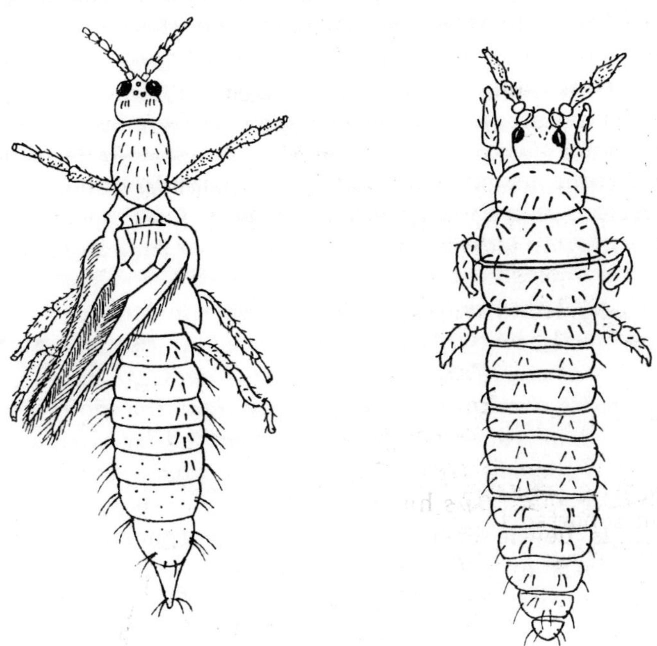

Fig. 7.18 (*a*) Adult female and (*b*) Second stage tarvae of *Thrips tabaci*

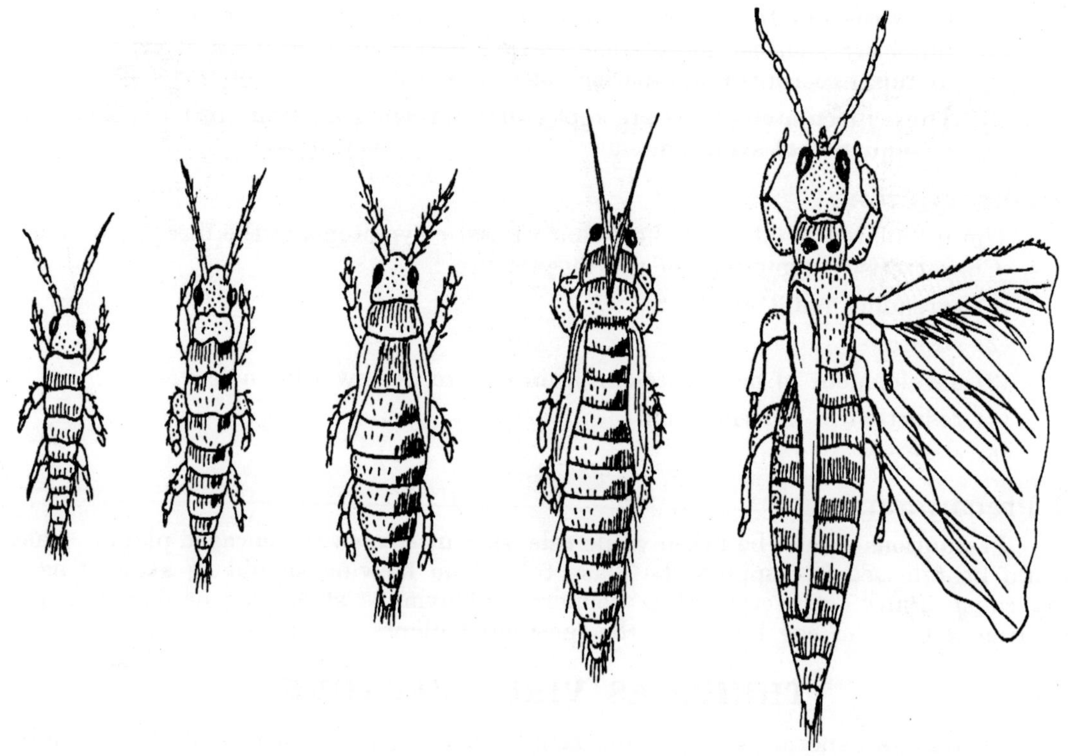

Fig. 7.19 Morphology of green house thrips.

and on other parts of the plant. They belong to order Thysanoptera having bristle wings. Full developed wings are narrow and membranous with fringe of long hairs around the margin. There is complete lack of right mandible. Left mandible is elongated and pointed. The maxillary stylets are elongated which look C-shaped in cross-section. The two maxillae fit together to form a tube with sub apical aperture and food is sucked through this tube.

Thrips are usually found restricted to the epidermal tissues or a few layers of mesophyll. They are not known to feed on the vascular tissues. So far 5 species of thrips namely *Thrips tabaci, Frankliniclla schulltazei, F. fusca, F. occidentalis* and *Scirtothrips dorsalis* are known to transmit *Tomato spotted wilt virus.* Two other viruses have been reported to be transmitted by thrips. *Thrips tabaci* has been reported to transm it *Groundnut bud necrosis virus* and *Tobacco ring spot virus. Tobacco ring spot virus* has nematode vector as well. Similarly *Cowpea mosaic virus* which is beetle borne in nature has reportedly been transmitted by *Seriothrips occipitalis* and *Taeniothrips sjostedti.* The virus is retained for weeks and often for life in thrips. There is no report of passage of virus through eggs of its vectors.

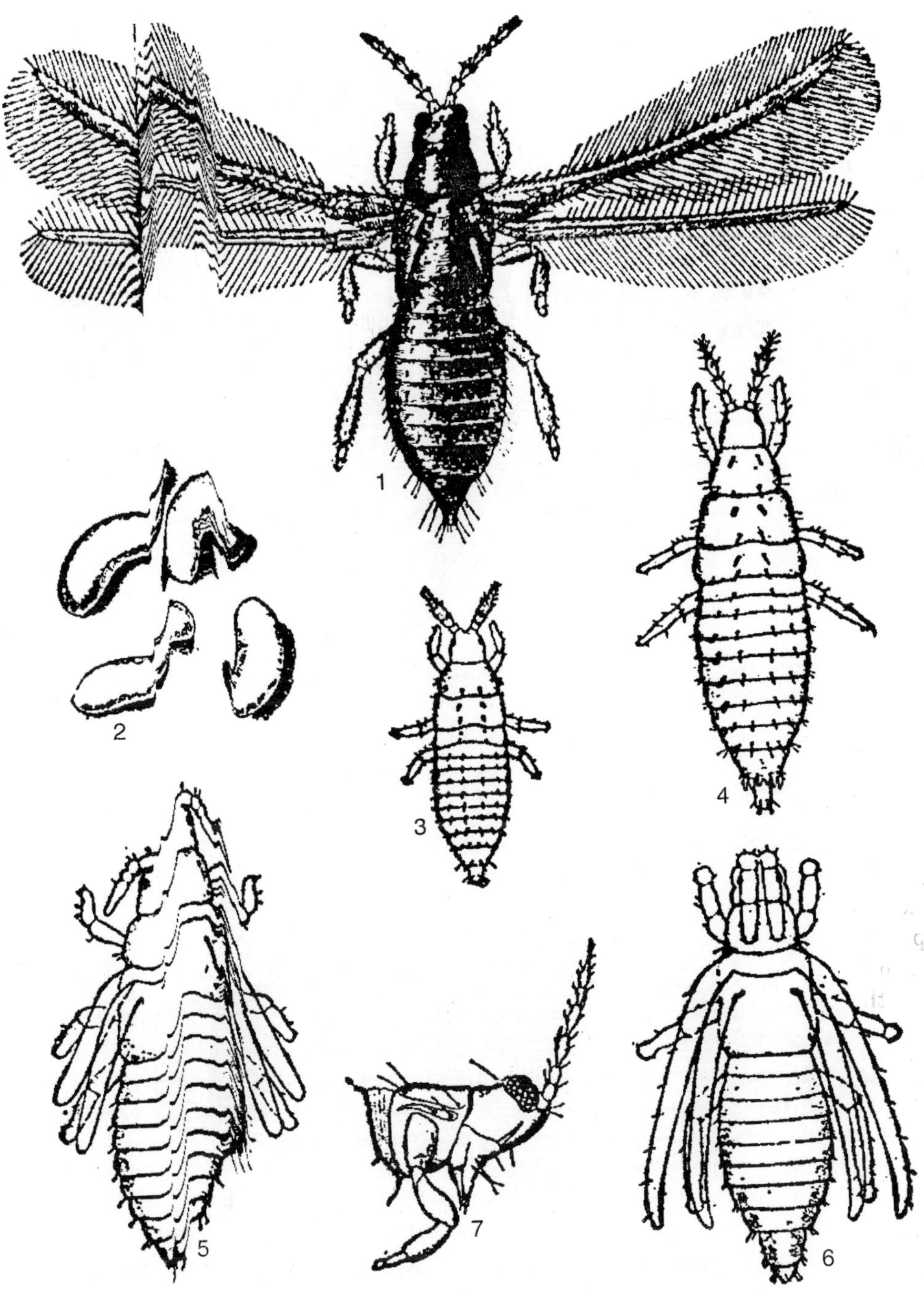

Fig. 7.20 Thrips showing 1-adult, 2-eggs, 3-first instar nymph, 4- second instal nymph, 5-Third instar nymph, 6-Last instar nymph and 7- Adult from the side

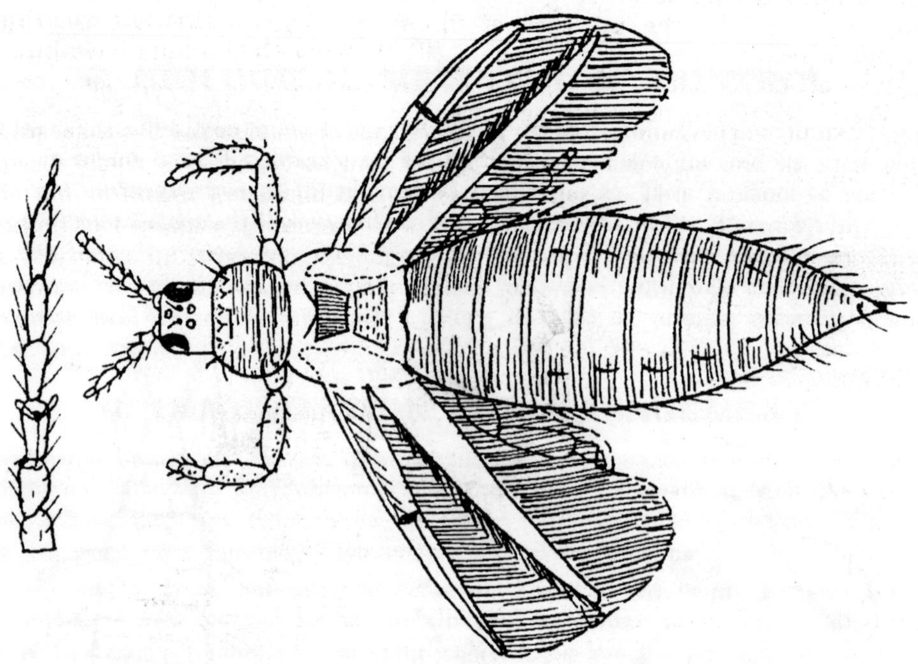

Fig. 7.21 The Thrips—*Frankliniella insularis*—a popular vector in Australia

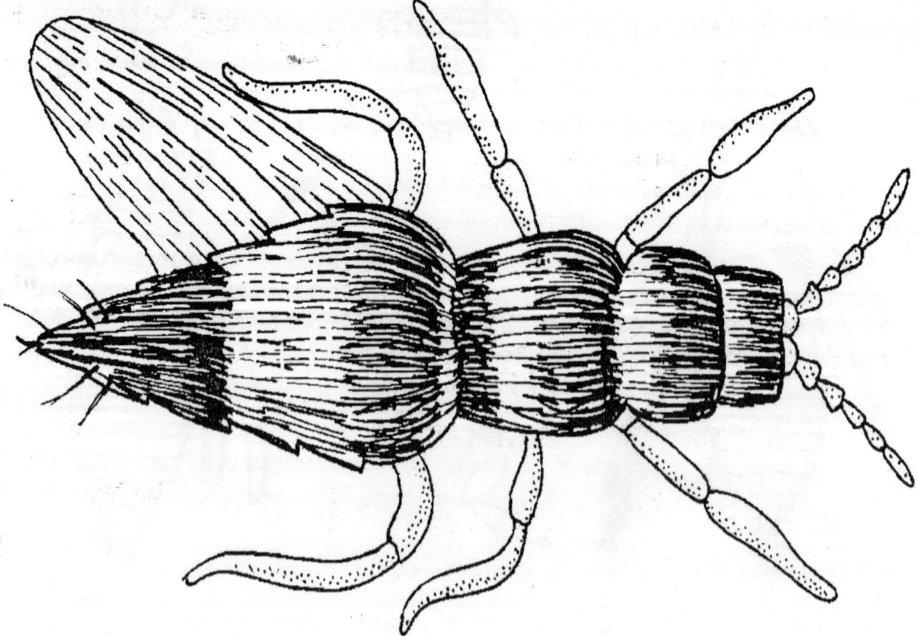

Fig. 7.22 *Thrips tabaci*—a popular insect vector as found especially in Europe

BEETLES AS VIRUS VECTORS

The beetles belong to order Coleoptera which is the largest group of insects. They are recognized by the presence of fore-wings. The hind-wings are thin and membranous which are real organs of flight. Both larvae and adults have biting and chewing type of mouth parts. More than 74 species of beetles have been reported as vectors. Vector species usually belong to family Chrysomelidae which contain large number of virus tansmitting genera namely, *Ceratoma, Diabrotica, Acalymma, Phaedon, Phyllotreta* and *Epitrix* etc.

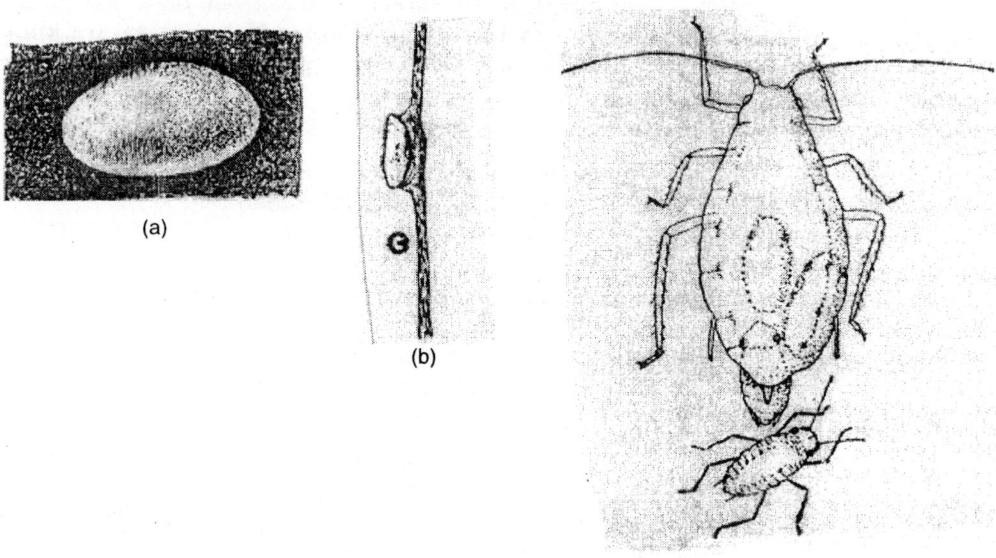

Fig. 7.23 Egg of beetle (*a* and *b*), A wingless green bug giving birth to living young parthenogenitically (*c*).

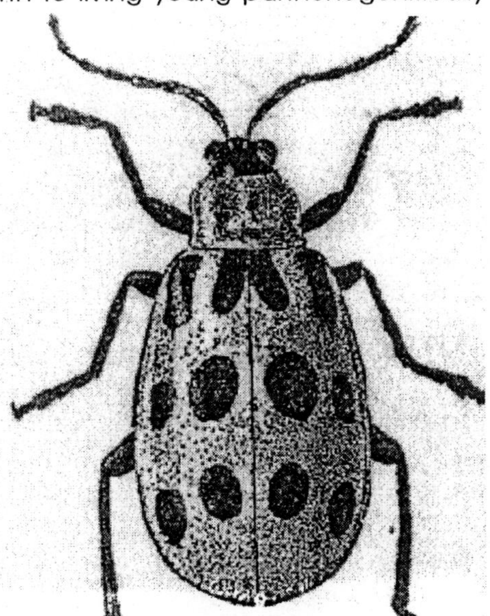

Fig. 7.24. Spotted cucumber beetle.

The beetles are known to transmit more than 45 plant viruses mostly belonging to comovirus, tymovirus, bromovirus and sobemovirus groups affecting plants of families Leguminosae, Cruciferae, Cucurbitaceae and Solanaceae. Although viruses are acquired by the beetles within few minutes but increased acquisition feeding periods generally result in increased transmission.

LACE BUGS AND MITES AS VIRUS VECTORS

Two species of lace bugs belonging to Piesmidae of order Heteroptera are known to transmit two viruses of sugar beet. *Piesma cinereum* transmits *Sugar beet savoy virus* in North America and *Piesma quadratum* transmits *Sugar beet leaf curl virus* in Europe. The nymphs can acquire the virus but can inoculate only when they become adults.

Mites are also important in virus transmission. They belong to the class Arachnida and are the only non-insect arthropod vectors of plant viruses. They are worm-like and very small in morphology. The adults usually measure about 0.2 mm in length.

They possess only four legs with modified mouth parts for piercing and sucking the sap of the plant. Mites usually feed on leaves, buds and other tender parts of the plant.

Only three plant viruses namely *Wheat streak mosaic virus, Agropyron mosaic virus* and *Rye grass mosaic virus* were definitely known to be transmitted by mites. These viruses are flexuous rods measuring about 700 nm in length. The vector species usually complete their life cycles in 7-10 days. Males are rare and parthenogenetic reproduction may result in very rapid build up of populations under favourable condition. Four species of mites which belong to genera *Aceria* and *Abacarus* are well known. Sterility mosaic of pigeonpea is known to be transmitted by *Aceria* species.

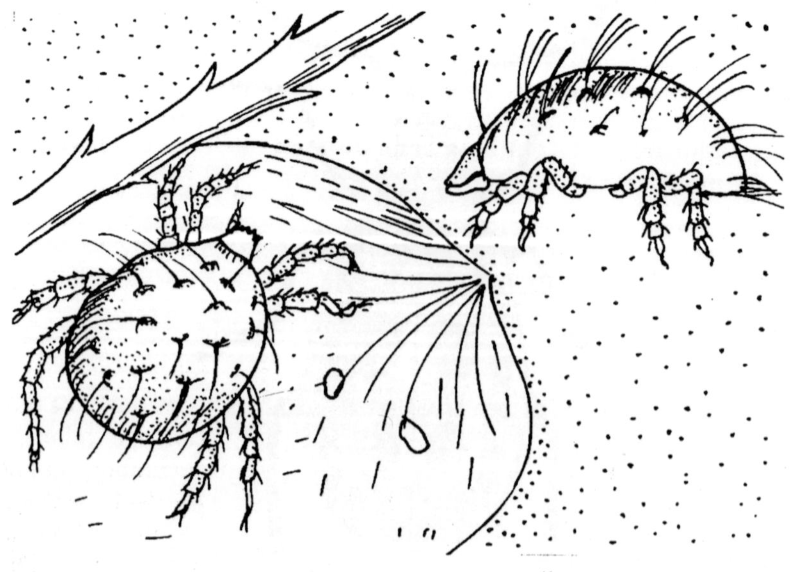

Fig. 7.25 The citrus red mites

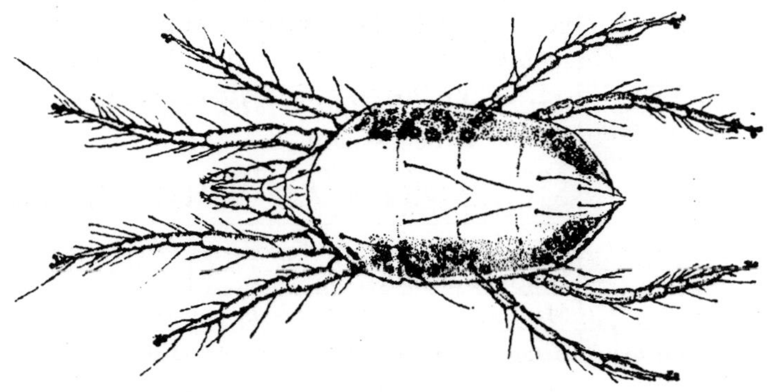

Fig. 7.26. Morphology of a mite.

NAMATODES AS VIRUS VECTORS

The namatode vectors are soil inhabiting ecto-parasites which feed on the roots, especially the root tips. Members of genera *Longidorus* and *Xiphinema* (family-Longidoridae) whose adults measure about 2-12 mm in length, are known to transmit polyhedral nepoviruses such as *Grapevine fan leaf virus*, *Arabis mosaic virus* and *Tomato ring spot virus*. *Trichodorus* and *Paratrichodorus* species which measure upto 2 mm in length usually transmit the straight tubular tobraviruses such as tobacco rattle and pea early browning viruses. Members of these four vector genera are known to be found widely in distribution. *Longidorus* species are more prevalent in temperate and *Xiphinema* species are more prevalent in the tropics. Eight species of *Longidorus* and seven of *Xiphinema* have been implicated in transmitting plant viruses.

A partial list of important nematode species proved to be vectors may be summarized as under :

Table. 7.3. **Nematode species and viruses transmitted by them.**

Nematode vectors	Virus transmitted	Host plants
Species transmitting nepoviruses		
Longidorus apulus	*Artichoke Italian virus* (Indian strain)	Artichoke (*Cynara cardunculus*)
L. arthensis	*Cherry rosette virus*	Cherry
L attenuatus	*Tomato black ring spot virus*	A wide host range such as alfalfa. Artichoke, beans, cabbage, celery, cucumber, gladiolus. Gra pe, leek, lettuce, onion, peach, phlox, potato, pumpkin, raspberry, strawberry etc.

Nematode vectors	Virus transmitted	Host plants
L. diadecturus	*Peach rosette mosaic virus*	Peach and plum.
L. elongates	*Raspbrry ring spot virus* (Scottish strain)	A wide host range.
L. fasciatus	*Artichoke Italian latent virus,* Greek strain *Tomato black ring virus,* Scottish strain	Artichoke and chicory As in *L. attenuatus*
L. macrosoma	*Raspberry ring spot virus,* English strain	As in L. attenuatus
L. martini	*Mulberry ring spot virus*	Mulberry in Japan.
Paralongidorus maximus	*Raspberry ring spot virus* grapevine strain	Raspberry and red currant
Xiphinema americanum	*Cherry rasp leaf virus, Peach rosette mosaic virus, Tobacco ring spot virus* and *Tomato ring spot virus*	A wide host range such as almond, American spearmint, apple, artichoke, autumn crocus, beans, black berry, blueberry, cherry, chickweed and cucumber etc.
X. diversicaudatum	*Arabis mosaic virus Strawberry latent ring spot virus*	A wide host range of woody and herbaceous plants including barley, begonia, carnation, celery, cherry, crocus, cucumber, gladiolus, grape, hops, lily, narcissus, peach, raspberry, roses, strawberry and tulip. Black currant, celery, cherry, olive, peach. plum, raspberry and rose
X. italiae	*Grapevine fan leaf virus*	Citrus, conifers, grape, mulberry, olive and raspberry
Species transmitting tobraviruses		
Paratrichodorus allius	*Tobacco rattle virus*	More than 400 woody and herbaceous plants, Weeds and their wild plants, asters, cereals, corn, crocus, gladiolus, grasses, lettuce, lily, orchids, petunia, phlox and tulip.

Nematode vectors	Virus transmitted	Host plants
P. anemones	*Pea early browning virus*	Alfalfa and pea.
P. minor	*Tobacco rattle virus*	Different host plants for different nematode species.
P. nanus	*Tobacco rattle virus*	
P. pachydermus	*Pea early browing*, Tobacco *rattle virus*	
P. tansaniensis	*Tobacco rattle virus*	
P. teres	Pea *early browing*, Tobacco *rattle virus*	
P. tunisiensis	Tobacco *rattle virus*	

+*Adapted from Taylor and Brown* (1997)

❍ Test Procedure for Virus transmission

In order to establish that a nematode is a vector of a virus, following conditions are essential to be fulfilled.

(1) The nematode must ingest the virus from the source plant.

(2) It must retain the virus which it later ejects into a bait plant.

(3) It must infect the bait plant with the virus.

(4) Contamination of the bait plant with the virus from some other source and transmission by an alternative vector has been shown not to have occurred.

A highly specific relationship takes place between a nematode vector and the virus or viruses it transmits. This specificity is a genetically determined recognition process between vector and the virus. It is a consequence of the nature, site and mechanism of virus particle retention within the nematode vector. It is determined by the nematode's ability to retain virus particles at specific sites within the feeding apparatus for a period of days, weeks or months. *Paratrichodorus, Trichodorus* and *Xiphinema* species can retain their respective viruses for periods of 8-12 months when stored in moist free soil. Viruses are less persistent in *Longidorus* species as its retains viruses for less than two months. Nematode vectors that feed on plant roots can transmit viruses in all developmental stages. In general, increasing the acquisition and transmission access periods from hours to several weeks increase the frequency of transmission. For example, *Xiphinema americanum* is known to transfer the virus in an hour or less than this. In laboratory and glass house studies, the rate of transmission of viruses by the nematode vectors is affected by temperature, soil moisture, the bait plant, the population and developmental stages of the nematodes. Virus isolate and the size of plot have also been found to affect the transmission.

SITES OF VIRUS RETENTION IN NEMATODE

As observed under Electron microscopy, viruses are found attached mainly to the cuticular lining of the odontostyle and the anterior region of the alimentary tract of the nematode vectors. They are shed with the cuticle when the nematode molts. Taylor and Brown (1997) have identified following sites of virus retention in nematode vectors :

(1) The inner surface of the odontostyle as observed in *Longidorus arthensis, L. elongatus, L. fasciatus* and *L. macrosoma*.

(2) The cuticle lining of lumen of odontophore and the esophagus (*Xiphinema americanum*).

(3) The esophageal lumen with virus particles absorbed to the cuticular lining along the entire length of lumen. Example *Tobacco rattle virus* in *Paratrichodorus pachydermus* and *Trichodorus similes*.

(4) The triangular section of lumen adjacent to the anterior end of the guide ring (Example, *Longidorus macrosoma*).

It has been observed that differences in the efficiency of transmission by nematode vectors are related to the intimate interaction between the nematode and the virus strain. Primary requirement for virus transmission by nematodes is the compatibility between virus and vector at the site of retention in the nematode. The mechanism of virus retention within nematode is not well known.

❍ Fungi as Virus Vectors

Earlier *Pythium ultimum* and *Synchytrium endobioticum* were known virus vectors and currently there are unconfirmed reports that species of *Puccinia* transmit the potyvirus *Maize dwarf mosaic virus* and the bromovirus *Brome mosaic virus*. However, only few species namely, *Olpidium bornovans, O. brassicae, Polymyxa betae, P. graminis* and *Spongospora subterranean* are important vectors and all these are soil inhabiting. The role of fungi as plant virus vectors was first discovered by Teakle (1960). Most of the fungi known to be virus vectors usually belong to chytrids (family-Olpidaceae) or the plasmodiophorids (family- Plasmodiophoraceae). These fungi are usually obligate parasites infesting roots in cool and wet soil. Viruses transmitted by fungi are more prevalent in temperate regions. In chytrids, three species namely, *Olpidium brassicae, O. barnovanus* and *Synchytrium endobioticum* are known as vectors of viruses. These three species have zoospores which are posteriorly uniflagilate with characteristic 'jerky' movement and are characterized by single celled resting spores. In plasmodiophorids also only three species viz. *Polymyxa graminis, P. betae* and *Spongospora subterranean* are important transmitters. These species have biflagellate zoospores and form single celled resting spores. All these species are obligate parasites on plant roots having similar developmental stages. These fungi tend to infect epidermal cells or root hairs near the root tips and then produce zoosporangia containing many zoospores which are released into the soil water surrounding the infected root from the zoosporangia through exit tubes under favourable conditions. These zoospores drift or swim to the surface of another root, withdraw their flagella and function as under :

1. Thin walled zoospore cysts which may germinate producing infection tube under suitable conditions and zoospore protoplasm enters the and after a few days.
2. The zoospore contents develop into a thin-walled zoosporangium producing many more zoospores that can be released into the root/soil environment through exit tubes; or
3. Produce a thin-walled zoosporangium and the zoospores produce a thick walled resting zoosporangium.
4. These resting spores are very resistant to dry weather and may remain viable in decaying root material for long periods of years. Under favourable

conditions these spores germinate to release new zoospores and cause infection.

Zoospores transmit viruses in two ways. (1) **Non-persistent transmission** in which the virus particles appear to enter the zoospore through the infection tube but they do not enter the resting spore during its formation; (2) **Persistent Transmission** in which viruses are acquired by fungi from virus infected plant cells and persist in the resting spores of these fungi. These resting spores and the virus they contain remain viable for years and even in air dried soils. These viruses are released with zoospores on germination. At least three isometric viruses namely, *Tobacco necrosis virus* (*Olpidium brassicae*), *Cucumber necrosis virus* (*O. radicale*), *Lettuce big vein virus* (*O. brassicae*) are known to be transmitted by these species. Similarly, *Polymyxa graminis* transmits wheat mosaic, *P. betae* transmits *Beet necotric yellow vein virus* and *Spongospora subterranean* transmits *Potato mop top virus*.

Nearly thirty soil born viruses and virus like agents are known to be transmitted by different species of fungal vectors. Ten polyhedral viruses out of which nine belong to the family Tombusviridae are acquired *in vitro* by *Olpidium* species. More than eighteen rod-shaped viruses belonging to different virus groups are acquired *in vitro*. They survive within the resting spores of the vectors namely, *Olpidium brassicae*, *Polymyxa graminis*, *P. betae* and *Spongospora subterranea*. A partial list of some important fungal species transmitting different viruses is listed in following table.

Table. 7.4. Different fungal vectors and viruses transmitted by them.

Name of vectors	Virus transmitted	Virus genera	Virus morphology
Chytrids			
Olpidium bornovanus	*Chenopodium necrosis virus*	*Necrovirus*	Isometric
O. bornovanus	*Cucumber leaf spot virus*	*Aureusvirus*	Isometric
O. bornovanus	*Cucumber necrosis virus*	*Tombusvirus*	Isometric
O. bornovanus	*Cucumber seed borne virus*	*Carmovirus*	Isometric
O. brassicae	*Freesia leaf necrosis virus*	*Varicosavirus*	Unknown
O. brassicae	*Lettuce big vein virus*	*Varicosavirus*	Rod
O. brassicae	*Lettuce ring necrosis virus*	*Varicosavirus*	Rod
O. brassicae	*Lisianthus necrosis virus*	*Necrovirus*	Isometric
O. brassicae	*Melon necrotic spot virus*	*Carmovirus*	Isometric
O. brassicae	*Red clover necrotic mosaic*	*Dianthovirus*	Isometric

Name of vectors	Virus transmitted	Virus genera	Virus morphology
O. brassicae	*Tobacco necrosis virus*	*Necrovirus*	Isometric
O. brassicae	*Tobacco necrosis satellite virus*	Unclassified	Isometric
O. brassicae	*Tobacco stunt virus*	*Varicosavirus*	Rod
Plasmodiophorids			
Polymyxa betae	*Beet soil-borne virus*	*Pomovirus*	Rod
Polymyxa graminis	*Barley mild mosaic virus*	*Bymovirus*	Filament
Polymyxa graminis	*Barley yellow mosaic virus*	*Bymovirus*	Filament
Polymyxa graminis	*Broad bean necrosis virus*	*Pomovirus*	Rod
Polymyxa graminis	*Indian peanut clump virus*	*Pecluvirus*	Rod
Polymyxa graminis	*Oat golden stripe virus*	*Furovirus*	Rod
Polymyxa graminis	*Oat mosaic virus*	*Bymovirus*	Filament
Polymyxa graminis	*Peanut clump virus*	*Pecluvirus*	Rod
Polymyxa graminis	*Rice stripe necrosis virus*	*Furovirus*	Rod
Polymyxa graminis	*Wheat soil-borne mosaic virus*	*Furovirus*	Filament
Polymyxa graminis	*Wheat yellow mosaic virus*	*Bymovirus*	Filament
Spongospora subterranea	*Potato mop top virus*	*Pomovirus*	Rod
Spongospora subterranea	*Watercress chlorotic leafspot virus*	unclassfieid	unknown
Spongospora subterranea	*Watercress yellow spot virus*	unassigned	unknown

8

SEROLOGICAL METHODS

Introduction, Antigens and antibodies, Different types of antibodies, Production of antibodies/antiserum, Production of monoclonal antibodies, Determination of antiserum titer, Micro precipition tests, Immunodiffusion tests, Agglutination tests, ELISA, Flow chart of DOC-ELISA, Direct tissue blot immunobinding assay, Immunofluorescence and other serological techniques.

Serology is that branch of science which deals with immunology and reaction pertaining to preparation and use of serum. In medical science, immunological techniques are widely used since many years by preparing antiserum to overcome the diseases like small pox, chicken pox and hydrophobia etc. In crop protection, immunological techniques can aid successfully since they permit early detection and correct identification of important pathogens in agriculture, horticulture and forestry. Immunological techniques are used extensively for quick and accurate detection of those pathogens which cause diseases with variable or latent symptoms on the host plant. Most destructive diseases, if recognized in host tissue at an early stage, suitable curative measures may be adopted to manage the disease by effective interception and destruction.

With regard to detection of plant viruses, antibodies are the most important serum components. The basis for serological detection of plant viruses lies in the fact that antibodies are produced in vertebrate animals after they are injected with plant virus antigens (virus-specified proteins) and that these antibodies combine specifically with epitopes (antigenic determinants) on the virus specified proteins. Epitopes react with complementary and specific combining sites called **paratopes** on the antibody molecule. Antigenic determinants or **epitopes** are those parts of a viral protein that react specifically with antibodies to the protein.

❍ Essentials for Serological Studies

There are two essentials for serological studies. These are (1) *Antigen* and (2) *Antibody*. **Antigen** is any substance which when introduced parenterally in the system of warm blooded animal; it stimulates the production of antibodies with which it reacts specifically. Thus antigen has two properties—(1) It must have the power of stimulating the production of an antibody and (2) It must react specifically with that antibody. **Antibody** is any substance which makes its appearance in the blood serum of animal in response to the stimulus provided by the antigens. **Serum** is the fluid which separates the white and red corpuscles from rest of the blood. Serum containing the antibodies is separated from the remaining blood components are referred as **antiserum**. Antibodies may be explained in other words as the altered globulins of the blood serum of animal in response to the stimulus provided by the antigen. These antibodies are characterized by being able to combine *in vitro* with the antigens used in these production to exhibit some visible reaction. The serum containing the antibody is called antiserum. Haptens or half antigens are incomplete antigens which have the ability to combine with the antibody *in vitro* but not have the ability to produce antibody *in vivo*. The capacity of an antigen to react specifically with an antibody is referred to as antigenic reactivity which is of course the main mechanism of acquired immunity in animals and men against infectious diseases. Study of the science of mechanism of acquired immunity is called as **immunology.** The antibody circulates in the blood stream and is capable of binding with immobilizing any of the same antigen that re-enters the blood stream.

❍ Characterization of Plant Viruses

Most of the plant viruses are effective antigens when injected into a suitable animal usually a rabbit which stimulate the production of antibodies that can be used in various serological tests. The serum containing the antibodies is separated from the remaining blood components and is referred to as antiserum. Serological tests have become widely applicable for the detection, diagnosis and characterization of plant viruses. Since Helen Purdy Beale (1931) used serology for detection of *Tobacco mosaic virus*, these techniques, now used for the detection of plant viruses have been adapted mostly from procedures developed in medical microbiology. Liquid precipitation techniques, wherein viruses combine with their specific antibodies form visible precipitants, were widely used for many years. During the period between 1960 and 1970 precipitation techniques conducted in agar gels (immuno-diffusion tests) also became widely applicable. Since the late 1970s, enzyme-linked immunosorbent assay (ELISA), various immunoblotting methods and immuno-electron microscopic procedures were developed.

❍ Basic Requirements for Serological Tests

The basic requirements for serological tests include having at least one antiserum suitable for the purposes and techniques for the study. Testing of normal serum can be useful in helping to detect nonspecific reactions that sometimes occur. The necessary antigens include the sample(s) to be assayed, a positive control consisting of a reactive source of the virus antigen used in preparing the antiserum and samples from non-infected plants to serve as negative controls.

❍ Different types of antibodies

As stated above antibodies belong to a group of protein y-globulins. The specific component of antiserum is made up of globulins and the type and amount of these determines the quality of antiserum. Antibody molecules have been classified into five classes namely, IgG, IgA, IgM, IgD and IgE. IgG primarily induced by protein antigens constitute about 80% of the antibody serum. In serological detection of plant viruses, two types are very popular in use. The main type is IgG fraction of the antiserum most effectively used in the techniques like ELISA, DIBA and ISEM. IgG has the molecular weight of about 150 000 and a sedimentation coefficient of 6.5 S. It is composed of two long or heavy and two short or light chains of 50,000-70,000 and of about 23,000 respectively. Each antibody has two binding sites. The other IgM (antibody) is a pentamer with bigger molecules. Its molecular weight is about 800 000 and sedimentation coefficient is about 19 S. It is the first kind of antibody produced after provocation by antigen but it usually disappears in a couple of weeks.

The highest dilution factor of the antiserum preparation reacting with virus is called **titer** of the antiserum. An antiserum with a titer of 1024 contains four times as many antibodies as one with a titer of 256. Thus antiserum can be used to measure concentration of virus.

PRODUCTION OF ANTIBODIES/ANTISERUM

In order to prepare antibodies/antiserum three conditions are essentials. These conditions are as follows :

1. Collection of infected plant
2. Purification of desired virus
3. Preparation of virus sample.

For purification of desired virus, first of all mechanical inoculation is done in such a host plant which has not any other injury or does not contain any injurious substances. Such host plants should grow easily and quickly. It should contain sufficient virus. Besides above characteristics such bost plants should be delicate and work as indicator plants. Host plants should not contain tannins, gums, latex or phenolic compounds as these substances and compounds interfere with the purification of the virus. At the time of peak virus concentration, the best suited part which contains maximum concentration of virus is harvested.

This harvested virus infected material is homogenized in such a way that maximizes the release of virus using suitable buffer. Suitable additives are also used if necessary to prevent virus inactivation. After homogenizing the host material, the sap is filtered by using double layered muslin cloth. The sap so obtained is further clarified by different methods which include centrifugation, heating, freezing and addition of suitable organic solvents. Next step in virus purification is to concentrate the virus by centrifugation or by other methods available and suitable to that particular virus. Precipitation with suitable salts is also done in some virus purification. Alternate cycles of high and low speed centrifugation will eliminate most of the non-virus larger particles. After this, rate-zonal-density gradient centrifugation should be given to remove contaminating materials leaving a pure virus preparation.

❍ Essentials of purification

Following conditions are essential for purification of viruses :

1. Virus characteristics should be well defined.
2. Extract of the infected plant should contain sufficient virus particles.
3. Virus particles should differ from rest of the constituents.
4. Virus should be stable enough to survive during various treatments.
5. A local lesion host (indicator) is desired.
6. The host plant should be free from other infection and should be suitable to be mechanically inoculated with the virus in question.

Typically antiserum is prepared in rabbits or mice but other animals such as goats and chickens can also be used for such preparation.

Polyclonal antiserum is composed of a variety of antibodies, each of which reacts with its own complementary epitope.

❍ Production of polyclonal antiserum

An immunization procedure for production of polyclonal antiserum in a rabbit may be summarized as under :

❍ Procedure

1. Serum is collected before immunization for use as control in certain tests. This pre-immune serum is called normal serum.
2. The plant virus purified (antigen) is injected in a rabbit intramuscularly two or three times at weekly intervals.
3. A total of 1-2 mg of virus, usually divided among several sites, could be administered at each date in the schedule.
4. The antigen is emulsified with an adjuvant before the intramuscular injection, which helps to boost the immune response.
5. About three to four weeks after the first injection, antiserum is collected and is tested for reactivity and specificity.
6. Additional collections are made every 1-2 weeks for several weeks and then a booster injection should be administered when serum titer falls.
7. The booster injection usually results in a rise in the production of antibodies within a few days.

The population of antibodies produced in an animal varies significantly. So that individual collections of polyclonal antiserum may vary in their reactivations. Depending on the objectives on the antigen and on the response of the animal, a useful antiserum could be obtained several months after the first injection. Antiserum so obtained should be preserved in antimicrobial glycerol (1 vol. glycerol/1 vol. antiserum). It may be preserved by adding 0.02 to 0.1 percent sodium azide which is suitable for short term storage. It is better to preserve antiserum in small sealed ampoules after freeze drying.

PRODUCTION OF MONOCLONAL ANTIBODY

A monoclonal antibody consists of a single type of antibody that reacts with a specific epitope. Mice are usually employed for development of monoclonal antibodies.

After a series of injections and verification of its response, mouse spleens are collected and antibody secreting cells are extracted and fused. Production of monoclonal antibodies (MAbs) by hybridoma technique was established by George Kohler and Cesar Milstein in 1975. This technique provided a revolutionary advancement in monoclonal antibody production. The property of specific antibody secretion derived from spleen cells has the ability to grow continuously in cell culture from the myeloma cells. Cloning and further selection of hybridoma allows the development of monoclonal antibodies of identical specificity and desired activity against a unique epitope of the immunizing antigen.

❍ Methodology of MAbs production

Method of production of monoclonal antibodies involves immunization of mice with antigen, growing myeloma cell line, fusion of myeloma and spleen cells, screening, selection, cloning and expansion of cell lines and cryo-preservation of hybridoma and monoclonal cell lines. Each of these steps are crucial for the success in monoclonal antibodies production. In this connection, it is also important to note that production of MAbs depends not only on the generation of numerous hybridoma cell lines and on the immune state of the spleen-donor animals but also on the knowledge and efficiency of basic culture under aseptic conditions. The immunoassay for screening antibody activity in hybridoma culture, supernatant is the key for success in hybridoma production.

Compared with conventional polyclonal antibody production, hybridoma technology has the potential of producing unlimited quantities of the same antibody in a reproducible manner. Another significant advantage of this novel technique is the ability to produce monoclonal antibodies against any antigenic determinant even when impure antigen or antigen mixtures are used as immunogenic.

❍ Applications of monoclonal antibodies

Monoclonal antibodies are being widely used in plant virology as they have been produced against more than 40 plant viruses representing more than ten taxonomic groups. MAbs have been found very useful for the identification of plant viruses and determining the degree of similarity between the members of the various groups of viruses. In addition to this, monoclonal antibodies are useful for studying the structural and functional aspects of gene products. MAbs have been proved to be the ideal serological reagent for investigating the antigenic relationships between viral protein at group, virus strain and serotype levels.

❍ Determination of antiserum titer

The titer of the antiserum is the highest dilution of the antiserum that reacts with its own homologous virus. It is usually determined by precipitation tube test. Tests are carried out in small thin walled glass tubes usually of 7 mm diameter. In usual practice, a two fold dilution series of one reactant (normally the antiserum) is added to a constant dilution of the other reactant. A 0.9 per cent solution of sodium chloride is normally used to dilute the antiserum and antigen. Usually 0.5 ml of purified virus and a similar volume of antiserum are mixed in the tube and thereafter it is incubated at 37°C in a water bath. The tubes are placed in water bath in such a way that half the content of the tubes remain below the surface of the water and remaining half above the surface of the water. It helps to speed up the rate of precipitation. Precipitations are observed at regular intervals. The highest dilution at which precipitation has occurred gives the titer. Precipitation tube tests may be summarized as under :

❍ Procedure

1. The tests are carried out in thin walled glass tubes. A dilution series of antiserum is mixed with a constant dilution of virus. Solution of 0.9% sodium chloride is used for making dilution.
2. In each 0.5 ml of antiserum dilution, 0.5 ml of partially purified virus is added in different tubes. Shake each tube for few seconds to mix the reactants and then incubate the tubes at 37°C in a water bath.
3. Observe each tube at interval of 10 minutes against a black background and record the intensity of the precipitation reactions in accordance with the following scoring system.

   (*a*) – means no reaction.

   (*b*) + – means precipitation barely visible.

   (*c*) + slight precipitation

   (*d*) ++ moderate precipitation

   (*e*) +++ heavy precipitation

   (*f*) ++++ very heavy precipitation

Isometric viruses produce fine granular precipitates whereas elongated viruses produce flocculent precipitates. The precipitation can easily be observed by holding the tube over a light source against a black background.

❍ Observations

The tubes whose contents precipitate most rapidly contain a mixture of antigen and antiserum in optimal proportion. The greatest antiserum dilution end point to produce a precipitate with virus dilution is the antiserum titer. In the same fashion titer of virus dilution can also be titrated.

❍ Precuations

It is desirable to include healthy plant crude sap and normal serum (removed from rabbit before injection) in the experiment as control. Good result is often obtained in case of partially purified virus having dilution of 1/5 and highest dilution of antiserum to be 1/1024. If the antiserum has been stored in 50% glycerol, this dilution would represent a titer 01/2048. The tube precipitin test can also be used to investigate relationship between viruses. Closely related viruses with most of their antigenic determinants in common will behave similarly with an antiserum to one of them. The titer determined may differ only by one or two dilution steps.

MICROPRECIPITIN TESTS

❍ **Micro Precipitin tests**

Micro precipitin test is the modification of tube precipitation test. It retains both the sensitivty and versatility. The test is very economical in the use of both the antiserum and the antigen. Single drop of the reactants are mixed in micro precipitin test. A grid titration is set up with a Petri dish and drops of mixed reactants are accommodated within the spaces of the grid.

❍ Requirements

Materials required for micro precipitin test are (1) a new plastic Petri dish (2) wax pencil/graph paper (3) diluents (0.85% saline or PBS) (4) autoclaved suitable tubes for preparation of antigen and antiserum dilutions (5) hand pipettes with disposable tips of 5 to 200 μl and 200 to 1000 μl (6) antiserum and normal serum (7) clarified virus containing sap extract (8) clarified healthy sap extract, and (9) mineral oil (Boot's liquid paraffin BP).

❍ Test procedure

1. Prepare a grid consisting of 8 mm squares. It may be done by wax pencil inside the Petri dish or on separate graph paper attached to the base of the dish. The use of wax paper is preferable. A separate record grid should also be prepared in which the locations of different dilutions may be recorded. In a standard sized Petri dish (90 mm diameter), a total number of $7 \times 7 = 49$ equal squares may be made. A full comparison including normal serum and healthy controls will, therefore, require two Petri dishes.
2. Two appropriate series of different dilutions for virus sap and antiserum are made separately using diluents. About 10 μl of each dilution of each component (virus containing sap and antiserum) is required for each combination to fill the spaces. A total of 490 μl or 500 μl of each component would be sufficient for 49 squares as stated above.
3. Place 10 μl of each dilution (antigen and antiserum) to each space in the grid as designated on the separate test grid.
4. Control drops were also placed.
5. Carefully flooded the dish with mineral oil (viscous paraffin oil) from one edge until all is covered. Care should be taken to avoid disturbing the drops.
6. Now transfer the Petri plates to the incubator and incubate them at 37°C for two hours.

❍ Observations

When examined with Stereo-microscope with top light and black background, precipitation reactions will be visible. After incubation Petri plates were transferred to a refrigerator and reactions were read after storage overnight. Reactions were recorded as suggested for tube precipitation tests.

IMMUNO-DIFFUSION TESTS

Immunodiffusion test is a serological proceedure in which the antigen-antibody reaction is carried out by allowing the reactants to diffuse in gel.

In these tests, the antibody-antigen reaction is carried out in a gel instead of liquid. Agar gel at suitable concentration may be used. The smaller isometric viruses diffuse through the gel without pretreatment. The longer rod shaped viruses are degraded in to smaller units before they diffuse to give a successful reaction. The gel-double diffusion test usually referred to as Ouchterlony test, is most widely used test in plant virology. Thin agar or agarose gel layers are prepared on glass slides or Petri dishes and suitably arranged wells are cut to accommodate the reactants. When the reactants meet in optimal proportions, precipitation lines are formed. As the test are two dimensional, several virus antigens and antiserum can be compared in one test.

❍ Requirements

(1) Glass slides or flat-bottomed new Petri dishes, (2) Sodium azide (avoid contact with skin and mouth), (3) Sodium chloride, (4) Cork borer, (5) Saline (0.85%) or PBS, (7) 0.07 M phosphate buffer pH-7.0, (9) Thioglycollic acid.

❍ Test procedure

1. Take 1.0 g agarose and 0.85 g sodium chloride in 100 ml of distilled water. Boil it and allow to cool to approximately 50°C and then add 0.02g sodium azide. Maintain agarose in water bath.
2. Pipette (not mouth pipetting) an appropriate amount of agarose onto glass slides (7 ml) or Petri dishes.
3. Now allow to solidify standing slides or Petri dishes on a leveled surface.
4. Poured slides or Petri dishes may be stored in humid chamber or at 4°C.
5. Using a cork borer, cut wells in the gel according to a pre-determined pattern.
6. Distance between wells should be 2-4 mm. Remove the Gel plugs by using suction. Care should be taken when extracting the agarose plug in order to avoid any short of damage to the edges of the wells.
7. Wells should be cut in agarose immediately before use to avoid accumulation of unnecessary liquid in them.
8. Now prepare several dilutions of antiserum with saline or PBS.
9. Extract the sap in a minimum amount of buffer and make dilutions of different known concentratoin. Use healthy sap of the same plant as control.
10. Now add reactants to wells in the prescribed and desired pattern and note the arrangement.
11. Incubate the dish and slide at room temperature ensuring that the reactants do not dry out. In order to keep the tests moist, damp filter paper circle may be kept inside the lid. Covering the gel surface with a layer of liquid paraffin or light mineral oil may also be done to keep the tests moist.

❍ Observations

Precipitation lines often become apparent with in 24-48 hours but incubation may be needed for longer period. Possible reactions may be interpreted as under :

1. **Straight line.** A straight line equidistant from antiserum and antigen usually occur when the antiserum contains antibodies against fraction 1 protein, which is present in both healthy and diseased sap and diffuse at the same rate as antibody molecules.

2. **Lines nearer to the antigen well curving around it.** It indicates that viruses are diffusing more slowly than antibodies.

3. **Lines nearer to the anti-serum.** It indicates that rapid diffusion of virus fragments has occurred.

4. **Double lines.** It indicates the presence of two components in the antigen well to which there are antibodies in the antiserum.

5. **Cross lines.** When the antigens have no common determinants although the antiserum contains antibodies of both.

6. **Precipitalion lines join.** When identical antigen reacts with their homologous antiserum, the ends of the precipitation lines join and do not cross.

7. **Spur formation.** When the antigens have some determinants in common e.g., with related virus strains and the antiserum is prepared against one of the antigen. A spur will form where the lines of precipitate will meet. Antibodies specific to the homologous antigen diffuse through the heterogonous antigen precipitate line.

Long and filamentous virus particles do not diffuse through the gels. In case of other viruses some diffuse through low concentration gels. Therefore, in long and filamentous viruses, particles are broken into smaller fragments which may diffuse by ultrasonic vibration or use of detergents. Fragmentation is known to change the antigenic character of viruses.

AGGLUTINATION TESTS

In serological agglutination tests, the antibody or virus antigen is absorbed on the larger particles. A positive reaction causes these larger particles to clump and so the antibody-antigen reaction is amplified. Slide agglutination test or chloroplast agglutination test has been very useful in the past for rapid detection of virus infected potatoes in the field. In this test virus infected crude sap is mixed with antiserum on a glass slide. If the reaction is positive, the chloroplasts and other sap debris will clump together.

Another useful agglutination test is the latex particles test. This test is highly sensitive and reported to be 100 to 1000 times more sensitive than micro precipitin tests.

Latex test offers a quick sensitive confirmatory test for establishing virus identity. Precipitation and agglutination tests are disadvantageous, expensive and require many test plants sap. Until the development of labelled antibody techniques, routine detection of some viruses was very difficult.

ENZYME-LINKED IMMUNOSORBENT ASSAY (ELISA)

ELISA is a serological test in which the sensitivity of the antibody-antigen reaction is increased by attaching an enzyme to one of the two reactions.

The enzyme-linked immunosorbent assay (ELISA) was initially applied for plant virus detection by M. F. Clark and A.N. Adams (1976). The original technique and modifications of it have collectively made ELISA one of the most widely applied methods for detection of plant viruses. A positive reaction is detected in the final stage of test when a colourless substrate undergoes a chemical change to give a coloured product as a result of exposure to an enzyme conjugated to antibody. The degree of reactivity can be measured spectrophotometrically with a special microplate reader designed to accommodate the 96-well plates. Results are interpreted by the relative reactiveness of different viruses.

The ELISA method is used extensively for diagnosis and detection of viruses and other pathogens in medicine and biomedical research. It has become a widely used technique in practical plant virology especially for the virus identification, virus taxonomy, epidemiology and virus disease management. The wide use of ELISA is also due to the commercial availability of reactants e.g., enzyme conjugates, preweighed substrates, equipment such as readers, ELISA plates, washing devices and tissue grinders etc.

❍ Advantages of ELISA techniques

1. Extreme sensitivity
2. Application in large number of samples.
3. It is semi-automatic technique.
4. It is economical in use of high cost antiserum.
5. It is quantitable.
6. It is independent of virus morphology and virus concentration.

❍ Different variations in ELISA

Three variations in ELISA have been described in plant virology. In all three variations carbonate buffer pH 9.6 is used in first step for suspension of antibodies or antigens.

❍ ELISA variation-1 (Double-antibody sandwich ELISA)

This method usually known as Direct double-antibody sandwich ELISA, was first described in detail by Clark and Adams in 1977. It consists of following steps as under:

Step-1. Purified antibody suspended in carbonate buffer (pH 9.6) is placed in the wells of plastic plate for at least one hour to coat the wells. The plates are then washed to remove buffer and unbound antibody.

Step-2. Virus antigen e.g., purified antigen or buffered extracts from infected plants, is added to selected wells. Extracts from non-inoculated virus free plants are added to other wells as negative controls. After incubation the plates are washed. When virus antigen is present, it reacts with and binds specifically to the antibody attached to the plastic. No antigen is bound in the wells containing extracts from healthy plants if the antiserum is specific for the virus.

Step-3. Enzyme (alkaline phosphate) conjugated to the same antibody used in the first step is added and incubated. If the virus antigen is present, antibody conjugated to the enzyme combines with the antigen. Therefore, the enzyme conjugate is bound in wells containing virus antigen and not in wells that contained extract from healthy plants. Unbound enzyme conjugate is removed through washing.

Step-4. The substrate *p*-nitrophenyl phosphate is added and incubated. The substrate in wells of positive samples turns yellow because the enzyme conjugate is present. However, the substrate in the wells of negative control samples remains colourless because the enzyme conjugate is not present. Samples may be assessed by measuring absorbency at a wavelength of 405 nm with a commercial ELISA plate reader. Visual assessments of the reaction are also useful.

The direct double-antibody sandwich technique is often more strain-specific than the indirect tests.

❍ Standardized double antibody sandwich ELISA

Flow chart of double antibody sandwich ELISA

Add 200 µl purified y-globulin in coating buffer to each well

↓

Incubate for 1 to 4 hours at 37°C

↓

Wash with PBS-T

↓

Add 200 µl test sample
(For citrus, grind 1 part tissue in 10-20 parts PBS-T + 2% PVP-40
or other suitable buffer)

↓

Incubate overnight at 6°C or 2 to 4 hours at 30°C

↓

Wash with PBS-T

↓

Add 200 µl enzymes labeled y-globulin diluted in conjugate buffer to an appropriate concentration (Usually 1/500 to 1/5000)

↓

Incubate for 1 to 4 hours at 30°C

↓

Wash with PBS-T

↓

Add 200 µl p-Niitrophenyl phosphate substrate 0.6-1.0 mg/ml in diethanolamine buffer

↓

Incubate for 0.5 to 2 hours at room temperature

↓

Stop reaction with 50 µl 3.0M NaOH

Visual assessment Photometric measurement at 405 nm

❍ Recomendations

1. Use reliable positive control in each plate.
2. Pre-test enzyme conjugate on substrate.
3. Check purified y-globulin for antigen specific y-globulins.
4. Use reliable negative control each plate. Absorb antiserum against healthy plant extract. Use fresh substrate and check for spontaneous colour change. Cover the plates properly.

5. Use extra wash step, handle plates carefully with lids on, use pre-determined loading pattern before loading. Blot top of plate after rinsing.
6. Use enzyme conjugate and substrate concentrations that will give OD_{405} of about 1.0 in 30-60 min with good antigen source and combination of incubation conditions selected.

DIRECT ANTIGEN COATING-ELISA (DAC-ELISA)

The double antibody sandwich ELISA (DAS-ELISA) as described above has been the most popular ELISA procedure for plant virus detection. However, for those laboratories engaged in the detection of large number of viruses, another form of ELISA *i.e.*, direct antigen coated ELISA (DAC-ELISA, indirect procedure) is preferable.

❍ Requirements

ELISA test can be performed in a laboratory with rudimentary equipment facilities such as pH meter, electronic balance, incubator, refrigerator, low speed centrifuge, magnetic strirrer, pestle and mortar and basic laboratory glass wares. Besides these, polystyrene microtitre plates (96 wells), virus infected and healthy plant samples, antiserum, enzyme-labelled antirabbit immunoglobulin and solutions/buffers.

Flow chart of DAC-ELISA

Add 20 µl test/control samples extracted/diluted in coating buffer, containing 2% (w/v) PVP to each well of the microtitre plate. Cover the plate and incubate at 37°C for 1/2 to 1.0 hour.

↓

Empty and wash the plate by flooding the wells with PBS-T for about 3 min. Repeat wash and soak operation thrice, then empty plate and shake out residual liquid draining on a paper towel.

↓

Add 200 µl blocking solution to each well. Incubate at 37°C for 1 hour to block polystyrene well reactive surfaces.

↓

Wash the plate three times as explained above step

Add 200 µl crude antiserum (primary antibody) diluted in PBS-TPO to each well. Incubate at 37°C for two hours or overnight at 4°C.

↓

Wash the plate three times as above

↓

Add 200 µl enzyme-labelled (alkaline phosphatase, ALP) antirabbit IgG (secondary antibody) diluted in PBS-TPO to each well.
Incubate at 37°C for 2 hours or overnight at 4°C.

↓

Wash the plate three times as above.

↓

Add 200 μl freshly prepared subtrate (parantitro-phenyl phosphate PNPP, 0.5-1.0 mg/ml) to each well. Incubate at room temperature 1-2 hours or more to observe reaction.

↓

Terminate reaction (if necessary) with 50 μl 3M NaOH to each well.

↓

Assess enzyme-mediated colour reaction either by visual observation or by measuring absorbance at 405 nm. Samples are recorded as infective or positive whose ELISA values exceed the healthy sample value by 2 to 3 times.

↓

Draw test plan in checker board format and determine optimal dilutions of various reagents to be used.

↓

Include both positive and negative reference samples to validate the assay.

❍ Observation

The positive samples show yellow colour after adding the substrate. The wells of the plate were measured for the OD at 405 nm in an ELISA reader and samples with 3 times of the OD of the healthy control were considered as positive.

ELISA VARIATION-2

Plate-trapped ELISA with antigen added in first step

Step-1. The wells are coated with antigen (purified antigens or extracts from plant) prepared in carbonate buffer. Plates are incubated and washed.

Step-2. Rabbit polyclonal antiserum containing antibody to the virus is diluted in phosphate buffered saline containing surfactant and added to the wells. After incubation the plates are washed. In wells the reactive virus antigen, the antibody is bound to the antigen. In wells where antigen from healthy plants was used as a control, the antibody to the virus does not bind to the host antigens and the antibody is removed by washing.

Step-3. Goat anti-rabit immunoglobulin conjugated with alkaline phosphate is added. This conjugate is available commercially. In wells that contain virus antigen, the goat anti-rabbit antibody-enzyme conjugate binds with rabbit antivirus antibody that had been trapped in step 2. After incubation and washing, this bound conjugate remains in the wells, but the unbound conjugate is removed by washing in wells treated with extracts from healthy plants.

Step-4. Substrate is added and the wells containing virus antigen show a positive reaction by the appearance of yellow colour, which is read as in step 4 of ELISA variation.

❍ Advantages

There are two important advantages of the ELISA variation 2. (1) Crude antiserum to the virus can be used and (2) Same commercially available enzyme-antibody conjugate can be used for detection of various viruses. (3) Thus it eliminates the need for the purification of antibody and the preparation of a separate conjugate for each system to be tested.

ELISA VARIATION-3

Indirect ELISA with polyclonal and monoclonal antibodies

Step-1. Polyclonal rabbit antiserum or purified antibody to the virus is diluted in carbonate buffer and added to the wells to coat them. The plates are incubated and washed.

Step-2. Extracts from infected plants are added to selected wells and extracts from non-infected plants are placed in other wells as controls. Incubate and wash.

Step-3. Monoclonal antibody to the virus is diluted and added to the wells. Incubate and wash.

Step-4. Goat anti-mouse immunoglobulin-alkaline phosphatase conjugate is added. Incubate and wash.

Step-5. Add substrate, incubate and read results. Positive reactions are indicated by the appearance of the yellow colour. The reading is taken with a micro-plate reader.

❍ Advantages

This procedure is an effective means of combining the broad reactivity of polyclonal antibody in the trapping phase with the varying specificities of a panel of monoclonal antibodies. Commercially prepared goat anti-mouse immunoglobulin-enzyme conjugates are available and are widely used.

ESSENTIALS OF DAS-ELISA

The double antibody sandwich (DAS) ELISA technique is most frequently employed for detection of plant viruses. The technique requires the followings :

1. Purification of gamma globulin (IgG),
2. Gamma globulin conjugation prior to beginning the test process.

Prepared globulins and conjugates specific to a small range of viruses can be obtained from the market. However, the purification and the conjugation procedures are relatively simple and can be carried out within the laboratory.

❍ **Preparation and purification of gamma globulin (IgG)**

For preparation and purification of gamma globulin (IgG) following materials are required :

(1) Whole antiserum (2) Neutral saturated ammonium sulphate (3) Phosphate buffered saline (PBS) (4) Dialysis tubing (7 mm) (5) Pre-equilibrated DE 52 cellulose column (6) Dimethyldichloro saline solution (BDH Chemicals) (7) Suitable tube for mixing, centrifugation and storage (8) Table top centrifuge and (9) Pipettes (1μl to 10 ml).

❍ Procedure for purification of IgG

1. Take 1.0 ml of antiserum and add 9.0 ml of distilled water in it.
2. Add 10.0 ml of saturated ammonium sulphate drop by drop to the above.

3. Incubate it for 30-60 minutes at room temperature to precipitate.
4. Centrifuge to (3) at low speed (3000-4000 rpm) for 15 minutes and collect precipitate.
5. Dissolve the precipitate in 2.0 ml of 1/2 strength of PBS (phosphate buffered saline).
6. Dialyze 3 times against at least 500.0 ml of 1/2 strength of phosphate buffered saline (PBS) for a period of 4.0 hours in each case at 4°C. Use low cut off dialysis tubing (7mm).
7. Use a Bio-rad 7 mm I.D. Econo column with a stop cock attached (a broken 10.0 ml pipette may also work as a column). Add approximately 5-10 ml of pre-equilibrated DE 52 cellulose. The cellulose slurry is poured down the side of the inside of the column to avoid air bubble formation. Allow the cellulose to settle. The column height should be approximately 7.0 cm. It is important to note that column is equilibrated with 1/2 strength PBS. When the pH of the ingoing buffer (1/2 strength PBS) matches the pH of the effluent, level the top of the cellulose. Add liquid carefully to side of column so that cellulose is not disturbed once packed. After equilibration adjust buffer level to top of cellulose column.

❍ Filtration

The salt-fractionated (S-F) serum is added drop-wise to the pre- equilibrated cellulose column. Run column until S-F serum level is at the top of the cellulose in column (begin collecting effluent as soon as column is started). Add 10-15 ml of 1/2 strength PBS carefully to column and continue collecting effluent until 12 ml fractions have been collected.

❍ Evaluation

Monitor the optical density of the effluent (each tube separately) at 280 nm on a Spectrophotometer with 1/2 strength PBS as reference. Combine tubes with OD_{280} values above 0.8 and adjust strength (using 1/2-strength PBS) of y-globulin to read approximately 1.4 OD units (about 1/2 ml/12 ml). If OD of combined fractions is less than 1.4, calculate globulin concentration as value read/1.4 = mg/ml.

❍ Storage

Store purified in silicone-treated (pre-treat with dimethyl-dichloro- saline as per manufacturer's recommendation) stoppered plastic or glass tubes at 4°C.

Antiserum of high titer is preferable but not essential. In most cases, partly purified IgG is used for ELISA. In some other cases ammonium sulphate precipitated gamma globulin has been sufficently successful without further purification by cellulose filtration.

❍ **Preparation of enzyme conjugate**

Following materials are required for preparation of enzyme conjugate :

1. Alkaline phosphatase (obtainable from the market–Sigma).
2. Gamma globulin (1 mg ml^{-1} concentration).

3. Glutaraldehyde solution (25% as prepared for Electron microscopy) (BDH Chemicals).
4. Dialysis tubing.
5. Phosphate buffered saline (PBS).
6. Bovine serum albumin powder (Sigma London, Chemical Co Ltd.)

❍ Procedure

1. Centrifuge 1.0 ml (equivalent to 5 mg or 5000 units) precipitate (alkaline phosphate) at the rate of 3000 too 4000 rpm for 10 minutes. Precipitate and preserve.
2. Dissolve precipitate directly in 2 ml (= 2 mg) purified gamma globulin.
3. Dialyze three times against 5000 ml PBS (4 hours each at 4°C).
4. Add fresh glutaraldehyde solution in 0.05% final concentration and mix well.
5. Incubate for 4 hours at room temperature during which a very faint yellow brown colour should develop.
6. Dialyze three times, 4 hours each against 500 ml PBS to remove glutaraldehyde.
7. Add bovine serum albumin to give a concentration of 5 mg ml^{-1} and store at 4°C in the refrigerator.

❍ **Direct Tissue Blot Immunobinding Assay**

It is useful technique for detection of phloem borne viruses infecting woody and perennial crop. Unlike DIBA, the ooze from the infected tissue is directly blotted or impressed on the nitocellular membrane by cutting the edge of the twig. The technique is particularly advantageous for mass screening of field trees. The samples can be blotted on the NC membrane in the field and then subjected to further testing in the laboratory as and when possible. The membrane can be maintained to another laboratory for testing in the absence of facility in remote areas.

❍ Requirement

Infected and healthy test twings, NC membrane, Bovine serum, Albumin (BSA), PBS-T buffer, Monoclonal antibody, Normal rabbit serum, Goat-anti-mouse (biotin labeled), Streptavidin, BCIP, NBT, Substrate buffer, Stop solution (10 mM Tris-HCl, 1m M EDTA, pH-7.5).

❍ Procedure

1. Pre-mark the paper using a ball point pen. Mark off in 1.0 cm increments.
2. Cut 20th ends of the tissue using a razor blade. Press each cut end in the pre-marked area of the paper. If the tissue is too juicy then blot again without making another cut. If we need to use the same piece of tissue for another test sample and it is dry, then it is desirable to cut the end again before we blot to the paper. A healthy and a virus infected control is must to be included in the test.
3. Allow the samples to dry for at least 30 minutes.

4. Place the paper in a flat container and block using 1% BSA in PBS (pH-7.5). Place at 4-6 C° for at least 2 hours or overnight.
5. Wash the paper in the container with PBS-T (pH-7.4) three times. Agitation is recommended to wash the entire blot.
6. Add the monoclonal antibody diluted with 1% normal serum. Place the container on a shaker for 1-2 hours at room temperature.
7. Wash three times in PBS-T as in step 5.
8. Block with 1% BSA for 30 minutes at room temperature.
9. Add goat anti-mouse (biotinylated) conjugate at the suggested dilution. Incubate 1-2 hours on the shaker at room temperature.
10. Wash three times with PBS-T as in step 5.
11. Block with 1% BSA for 20 minutes at room temperature.

    (Blocking with 1% BSA may not be necessary in between every step. The dilution of the antibody in normal serum may be sufficient to avoid any back ground staining. However, preliminary testing may be necessary for this determination. The most important blocking step with 1% BSA is after the initial tissue blots have been made).
12. Add Streptavidin at the suggested dilution in PBS. Incubate at room temperature for 30 minutes.
13. Mix the substrate (BCIP and NBT) in 0.1 M Tris (pH-9.5) which contains 0.1 M NaCl and 0.005 M MgCl.

    (Nitro blue tetrazolium-NBT can be dissolved in N, N-Dimethyl formamide (MDF) at a concentration of 7.5 mg/ml and Bromo Chloro- Indolyl-Phosphate (BCIP) at 50 mg/ml in DMF. Store the stock solutions in amber bottles and should be kept refrigerated. Add NBT to 0.33 mg/ml and BCIP to 0.175 mg/ml to the substrate buffer (0.1M Tris-BCIP, 0.1M NaCl, 5 mM MgCl) just before use.

(**Caution :** DMF is toxic and probably carcinogenic and can be absorbed through skin. Avoid breathing of the fumes and wear gloves to dispense.)

❍ Observation

1. Wait for a colour change on the blot. It is advisable to observe the colour change under a stereoscope. The positive and negative internal controls will be the determining factors as to when to stop the reaction. The reactions should be stopped when a strong reaction develops. Do not let the substrate stay on too long.
2. The blot is rated as positive when judged against healthy and virus controls. A positive blot will have areas of deep staining in the phloem areas similar to inclusion staining.
3. The healthy blot will not contain stained areas in the phloem.

❍ Dot-immuno-Binding Assay (DIBA)

It is a simple dot-blot-immuno-assay wherein antigen suspensions (1-5 µl each) are applied directly to the nitrocellulose/nylon membranes without prior electrophoretic separation. It is also called as dot-ELISA *i.e.* ELISA on membranes. This technique is useful for detection of many plant viruses. This technique is less time consuming, expensive and labour intensive than conventional ELISA procedures.

❍ Requirements

Incubator, pH meter, balance, refrigerator, low speed centrifuge, magnetic stirrer, pestle and mortar and basic glass-wares. Virus infected healthy samples, nitrocellulose (NCM) or nylon membrane, antiserum and enzyme labelled anti-rabbit immunoglobulin (IgG).

❍ Procedure

1. Extract tissue 1:10 (w/v) in antigen extraction buffer and express through cheese cloth.
2. Pipette 0.8 ml expressed sap into a 1.5 ml eppendorf tube. Add 0.4 ml $CHCl_3$, vortex and centrifuge in low speed centrifuge for 2 minutes.
3. Pipette 200 μl clarified sap (upper aqueous layer) into 800 μl antigen extraction buffer and vortex.

   (Antigen extraction buffer is prepared by adding 11.25 g diethyl dithiocarbonate (DIECA) to 1 litre TBS).
4. Put on gloves, cut a desired size piece of NCM and draw a lattice of squares of 1 × 1 cm each with a soft lead pencil. Use forceps for handling the membrane.
5. Wet the NCM by floating it on TBS and then air dry. Spot the test/control samples (5-10 μl) by hand.

   (TBS means Tris-buffer saline. It is used as stock solution and is prepared by using 0.02M Tris 4.48g and 0.5M NaCl 58.48g. pH is adjusted at 7.5 with 1 M HCl making the vol. 2 litre.)
6. Allow NCM to air dry and immerse in blocking solution with gentle oscillation for 1 hour at room temperature or overnight at 4°C.

   (TBS-SDM is blocking solution and is prepared by adding 5.0g spray dried milk (SDM) to 100 ml TBS)
7. Rinse once in TBS for 10 minutes.
8. Incubate for 1 hour at room temperature or overnight at 4°C in crude antiserum (primary antibody) diluted in TBS-SDM.
9. Rinse thrice in TBS for 10 minutes each.
10. Incubate for 1 hour at room temperature or overnight at 4°C in secondary antibody (enzyme-linked antirabbit IgG) diluted in TBS-SDM.
11. Rinse thrice in TBS for 10 minutes each.
12. Incubate in substrate solution at room temperature in dark and watch for colour development. Good colour development may take 5-10 minutes.

    (Substrate solution is prepared by mixing solution A and solution B. Solution A is prepared by Nitro blue tetrazolium (NBT) 75 mg mixed in 1 ml DMF and solution B is prepared by mixing Bromo Chloro Indolyl Phosphate (BCIP) into 1 ml DMFA. Store solution A and B refrigerated in amber bottles. Add NBT to 0.33 mg/ml and BCIP to 0.175 mg/ml to the substrate buffer just before use.)

13. Rinse thrice in the fixing solution for 10 minutes each and then air dry NCM between Whatman filter paper sheets.

❍ Observation

Assess the results by visual observation by comparing the intensity of purple colour by using densitometer. Photograph NCM (dry or wet) and store protected from light.

❍ **Trapping of virus particles or ISEM**

Techniques involving the visualization of the antibody-antigen reaction in the electron microscope is called as Immuno-sorbent electron microscopy (ISEM).

In this technique antibodies to viruses are absorbed to specimen support films on electron microscope grids. The trapping technique is also called as serologically specific electron microscopy or immuno-sorbent electron microscopy (ISEM).

❍ Procedure

(1) The antiserum is diluted to a suitable concentration before use. (2) Extracts from infected plants are added to the prepared support films. (3) The virus particles combine specifically with the absorbed antibodies. (4) After washing, specimens are stained with uranyl acetate and examined under electron microscope.

❍ Observation

The number of virus particles on antiserum treated films is observed significantly increased.

❍ **Decoration of virus particles**

Decoration method is also very common serological technique in which virus particles are absorbed to the films on electron microscope grids and then treated with antibody. The antibody combines with the virus particles and builds up a layer around the virus. The layer can then be detected by a dark halo around the particles as a result of staining with uranil acetate. This method of decoration is sometimes combined with the trapping technique.

❍ **Immunofluorescence (IF)**

The nature of the antigen carrying the epitopes recognized by the antigen specific monoclonal or polyclonal antibodies is determined by immunofluorescence (IF). The principle involved is the specific binding of antigen and antibody which can be determined in section or plant sap taken from infected plants using Fluoresce in isothiocyanate (FITC) labelled goat, anti, mouse/rabbit immuno-globulins.

❍ Importance

(1) The test is used to detect the phloem limited viruses and Fastidious prokaryotes, and

(2) To locate the pathogen in plant tissue.

❍ Requirement

Freeze-microtone, Binocular microscope, Cavity slides/glass slides, Razor/blade, Incubator, Antigen, Specific poly and monoclonal antibodies, Anti-mouse/rabbit IgG conjugated with FITC (Sigma) and Evan's blue.

❍ Procedure

(1) Make 3-4 mm long pieces of midribs of test sample (leaves).

(2) Cut 10 μm thin sections in a freeze microtone in ice blocks.

(3) Select the appropriate sections having intact vascular bundles under a binocular microscope and place them in cavity slides.

(4) Incubate slides at 55°C for 90 minutes.

(5) After incubation cover each section with a drop of specific antiserum.

(6) Incubate at room temperature for 1 hour.

(7) Wash thrice in PBS-T using a pasteurized pipette (PBS-T = PBS + 0.05% Tween 20).

(8) Drop 15 μl of conjugate (1 ml PBS + 10 μl anti-mouse/rabbit IgG conjugated with FITC (Sigma Chemicals) + 10 μl Evan's blue) over each section.

(9) Incubate in dark for 30 minutes.

(10) Mount in glycerine 1:1 (v/v) in PBS.

(11) Observe under fluorescent microscope at × 40 magnification.

(12) Chop midrib of 5 leaves each of healthy and diseased samples with a blade in a Petri plate in 2 ml PBS-600. (for 500 ml PBS-600 pH-7.4 dissolve 9.828 g $NaCl_2$, 0.9526 g KH_2PO_4, 1.4325g $Na_2 HPO_4 . 12H_2O$ PBS-T).

(13) Remove extract with the help of a syringe and put in an eppendorf tube.

(14) Centrifuge 14000 rpm for 10 minutes.

(15) Dissolve the pellet in 200 μl of antigen specific monoclonal antibodies.

(16) Incubate at room temperature for 40 minutes.

(17) Add 1 ml PBS after incubation and centrifuge as before.

(18) Dissolve the pellet in 20 μl conjugate (same as with sections).

(19) Incubate at room temperature for 30 minutes.

(20) Add 1 ml PBS and centrifuge as before washing.

(21) Emulsify the final pellet in 2 μl of glycerol and mount on a microscope slide.

(22) Observe under fluorescent microscope at × 100 magnification.

❍ Observations

Apple green fluorescence will be observed in affected issue of the section especially in phloem limited fastidious prokaryotes, whereas the healthy tissues will show dark red colour. Typical round and elongated forms of pathogen with apple green fluorescence will be seen as against the red colour with healthy extracts.

OTHER SEROLOGICAL TECHNIQUES

The techniques described above represent examples of the major serological techniques used frequently in virology. Besides these, there are a number of other techniques also which are used occasionally in plant virology. Such techniques include immuno-electrophoresis and radio-immunoassays. Radio-immuno-assays involve the use of radio-actively labelled antibodies or antigens. Radio-immuno-sorbent assays involves the detection of ^{125}I labelled antibodies or tritium labelled antibodies complexes with antigen in solid phase tests.

❍ Applications and trends

Serology is used for many purposes in plant virology. Applications in molecular biology of plant viruses include (1) the immuno-screening of cDNA libraries, (2) trapping of virus for polymerase chain reaction (immuno- capture-polymerase chain reaction), (3) analysis of transgenic plants from protein expression, (4) analysis of *in vitro* translation products to aid genetic mapping of viruses.

The sequencing of plant virus nucleic acids and proteins has tended to replace serology as a means of comparing viruses in taxonomic studies. Similarly, nucleic acid based probes are widely used for diagnostic purposes. Even then, serology continues to be used extensively for diagnostic and detection studies because of the availability of numerous antibody probes and also because of the broad applicability and effectiveness of serological methods.

9

NUCLEIC ACID BASED TECHNIQUES

Agarose gel electrophoresis, Characteristics features; Isolation of DNA from plant tissue, DNeasy plant mini kit for DNA isolation from plant tissue, Procedure for isolation; Principles of nucleic acid hybridization; What are plasmids, Principles and procedure for plasmid isolation; Plymerase chain reaction, Procedure for Polymerase chain reaction; R-PAGE Gel electrophoresis and Post-transcriptional gene silencing

Different techniques are commonly used as nucleic acid based techniques for detection of plant viruses. The most common and useful techniques are agarose gel electrophoresis, isolation of DNA, nucleic acid hybridization, plasmid isolation, polymerase chain reaction, return polyacrylamide gel electrophoresis (R-PAGE) and post-transcriptional gene silencing. These techniques are being described here in some detail.

AGAROSE GEL ELECTROPHORESIS

This technique is frequently used in molecular biology to separate DNA fragments and to assess the quality and quantity of DNA.

❍ Principles

Since all virus particles carry a positive or negative charge on their outer protein surface ; therefore, particles migrate in an electric field. This movements is called as electrophoresis.

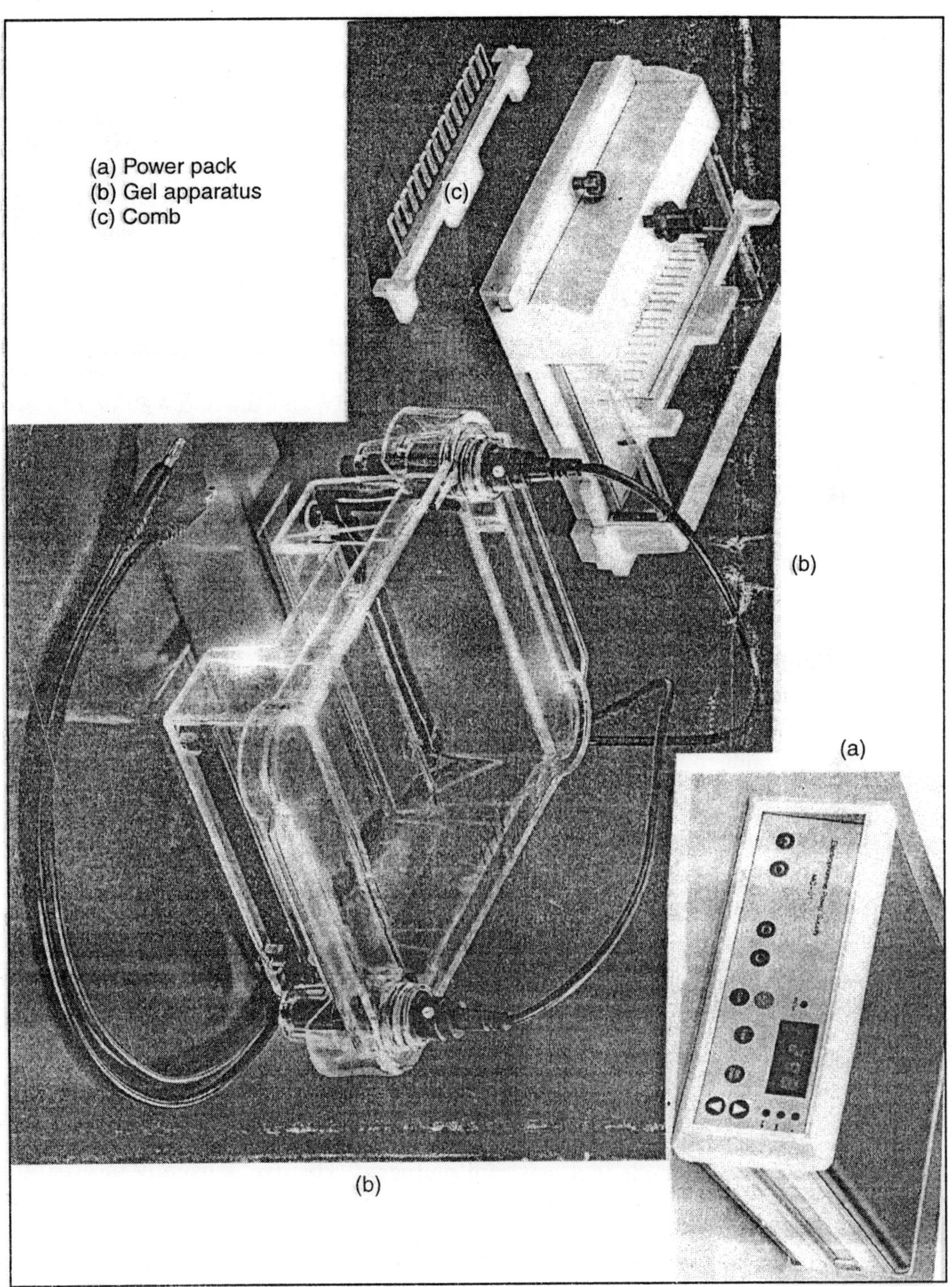

Fig. 9.1. Diagrammatic representation of Gel Electrophoresis unit

In gel electrophoresis, the gel is made from agarose, a highly purified form of the polysaccharide that is used to make agar plates on which bacteria are usually grown. The gel is immersed in buffer and the DNA fragments are loaded on to a well at one end of the gel and made it to move through the gel by the application of electric current. DNA is negatively charged, therefore, it moves towards the positive anode. However, the polysaccharide mix of the gel retards the DNA by a process of sieving, so that small fragments move faster and these fragments separate according to size. The DNA is visualized by adding ethidium bromide (EtBr), a fluroescent molecule which interact with the DNA bases, expanding the length of linear and nicked circular DNA molecules and making them more rigid. When ethidium bromide is added, UV radiation at 254 nm is absorbed by the DNA and transmitted to the bound dye. The energy is re-emitted at 590 nm in the red orange region of the spectrum. Ethidium bromide is a powerful mutagen and hence the gel should be handled carefully with the gloves. The DNA bands can be visualized under UV and the data can be recorded by gel documentation appliances.

❍ Characteristic features of gel electrophoresis

1. The molecular weight of the DNA

The migration rate is inversely proportionate to the molecular weight

2. Agarose concentration

The migration rate is inversely proportionate to the agarose concentration.

3. Conformation of the DNA

Linear form travels slowest and the super coiled form travels fastest.

4. Applied voltage

Typical value 5 volts per cm. The heat generated during electrophoresis is dissipated by the buffer.

❍ Other characteristics of gel electrophoresis

(1) DNA being poly anionic at neutral pH, it migrates towards the anode.

(2) The loading dye for DNA contains glycerol, which gives density to help the sample sinks to the bottom of the well. Marker dyes xylene cyanol and bromophenol blue moves at par with 300-400 bp DNA and Xylene cyanol with 2-3 kb DNA.

(3) The DNA is visualized by adding ethidium bromide, a fluorescent molecule which interacts with the DNA bases. To 0.8% agarose gel, add ethidium bromide 0.5 μg/ml concentration. UV radiation at 254 nm is absorbed by the DNA and transmitted to the bound dye. The energy is re-emitted at 590 nm in the red orange region of the spectrum.

(4) Ethidium bromide is a powerful mutagen. The dye is usually incorporated into the gel or conversely the gel is stained after running by soaking in a solution of ethidium bromide.

(5) The usual senility of detection is 0.1 μg of DNA.

(6) The gel will run along with a molecular weight marker, a wide range of which are commercially available.

❍ Procedure

1. Prepare 1% agarose gel in Tris-acetate EDTA buffer (1 X TAE) containing ethidium bromide.
2. To 1.0g of agarose, add 100 ml of 1 X TAE. Heat until dissolved. Cool the gel to 50°C and add ethidium bromide (0.5 μg/ml) before pouring into the gel apparatus.
3. Wash the gel casting tray and comb with water to remove dirt.
4. Place the apparatus on a leveled surface and check with the spirit level to adjust level.
5. Choose appropriate comb (commonly 12 slots) and fix into position.
6. Pour the gel onto the apparatus and allow it to cool and set.
7. After the gel has set firmly, pour little amount of buffer and remove the comb gently. Take care not to drag the comb and break the gel.
8. Immerse the gel slowly into the gel tank. Add sufficient amount of 1 X TAE buffer. Connect the electrode and check the current. Always check the electrical connections before loading the sample.
9. Load the sample into wells carefully.
10. Always load an aliquot of standard molecular weight marker along with the samples. It will help in assessing the size of the DNA fragment by comparing with the electrophoretic mobility.

❍ Anticipated results

Depending upon its confirmation and size, the DNA fragments will move as discrete bands. The ethidium bromide interacted with the DNA fragments will make it to emit pink fluorescence under UV lamp, which can be recorded in any gel documentation system.

ISOLATION OF DNA FROM PLANT TISSUE

The structure of DNA based on X-ray crystallographic analysis, established beyond all doubt that DNA is the genetic material. The model provided a ready explaination for how DNA could have biological specificity and self replicate to produce two faithful copies of itself. The structure proposed by Watson and Crick is now famous.

The DNA molecule is composed of two polynucleotide chains running in antiparallel direction and intertwined in the form of a regular helix with a diameter of 20 Angstrom. It is now clear that hereditary information was carried as the sequence of bases in a polynucleotide chain. This information was duplicated for progeny cells by opening up of the two DNA strands and synthesizing new polynucleotide chains whose sequence was complementary to the strand being copied.

ISOLATION OF DNA USING DN-EASY MINI-KIT

DNA may be isolated from plant tissue with the DNeasy plant mini-kit as described below. In this isolation experiment, citrus leaf was taken to isolate the DNA from the plant tissue.

❍ Procedure

1. Grind plant tissue with liquid nitrogen to a fine powder using a mortar and pestle. Transfer the tissue and liquid nitrogen to an appropriate sized tube and allow the liquid nitrogen to evaporate. Do not allow the sample to thaw. Continue immediately to Step 2.
2. Add 400 µl of buffer AP-1 and 4 µl of RNase. A stock solution (100 mg/ml) to a maximum of 100 mg of ground (wet weight) or 20 mg (dried) plant and vortex vigorously.

   (No tissue clumps should be visible. Vortex or pipette further to remove any dumps. Clumped tissue will not lyse properly and will therefore result in a lower yield of DNA. In rare case where clumps can not be removed by pipetting and vortexing, a disposable micropestle may be used. Buffer AP-1 and RNase-A should not be mixed prior to use.)
3. Incubate the mixture for 10 minutes at 65°C and mix 2-3 times during incubation by inverting tube. (*this step lyses the cells*).
4. Add 130 µl of buffer AP-2 to the lysate and mix. Now incubate it for 5 minutes on ice.

   (This step precipitates detergent, proteins and polysaccharides). **Optional**–Centrifuge the lysate for 5 minutes at full speed.
5. Apply the lysate to the Q1 Ashredder spin column(lilac) sitting in a 2 ml collection tube and centrifuge for 2 minutes at maximum speed.

   (It may be necessary to cut the end of the pipette tip to apply the lysate to the QIAshredder column. QIAshredder removes most precipitates and cell debris, but a small amount will pass through and form a pellet in the collection tube. This pipette should not be disturbed in Step 6).
6. Transfer flow through fraction from step 5 to a new tube (not supplied with the kit) without disturbing the cell debris pellet.

   (Typically 450 µl of lysate is recovered. For some plant species less lysate is recovered. In this case vol. is determined for the next step.)
7. Add 1.5 vol. of buffer AP-3/E to the cleaned lysate and mix by pipetting.

   (To 450 µl lysate added 675 µl buffer AP-3/E. Reduced the amount of buffer accordingly if less lysate is recovered. A precipitate is formed when ethanol is added but it does not affect the DNeasy procedure. It is important to pipette buffer AP-3/E directly onto the cleared lysate and mix immediately. It is also necessary to be ensured that ethanol has been added to buffer AP-3/E).
8. Apply 650 µl of the mixture from Step 7, including precipitates which have formed to the DNeasy mini spin column sitting in a two ml collection tube (supplied). Centrifuge for 1 minute at 8000 rpm. Discard flow through.
9. Repeat step 8 with remaining sample. Discard flow through and collection tube.
10. Place DNeasy column in a new 2 ml collection tube (supplied), add 500 µl buffer AW to the DNeasy column and centrifuge for 1 minute at 8000 rpm. Discard flow through and reuse the collection tube in step 11.

    (It is essential to be ensure that ethanol has been added to buffer.)

11. Add 500 μl buffer AW to the DNeasy column and centrifuge for 2 minutes at maximum speed to dry the membrane.

    (It is important to dry the membrane of DNeasy column since residual ethanol may interfere with subsequent reactions. This spin ensures that no residual ethanol is carried over during elution. Discard flow through and collection tube.

    After washing with buffer AW, the DNeasy mini spin column membrane is usually only slightly coloured. In the rare case the membrane remains significantly coloured after washing with buffer AW.

    Following the spin, DNeasy column is removed from collection tube carefully so that the column may not contact the flow through as this will result in carry over the ethanol).

12. Transfer the DNeasy column to a 1.5 ml or 2.0 ml micro centrifuge tube (not supplied) and pipette 100 μl of preheated (65°C) buffer AE directly on to the DNeasy membrane. Incubate for 5 minutes at room temperature and then centrifuge for 1 minute at 8000 rpm to elute.

    (Elution with 50 μl instead of 100 μl increases the final DNA concentration in elute significantly, but also reduces over all DNA yield. If larger amount of DNA is loaded, eluting with 200 μl instead of 100 μl increases yield).

13. Repeat elution Step 12 as described.

    (A new micro centrifuge tube can be used for the second elution step to prevent dilution of the final elute. Alternatively, the micro centrifuge tube can be reused for the second elution step to combine the eluate. It is important to note that more than 200 μl should not be eluted into a 1.5 ml micro centrifuge tube because the DNeasy column will contact to elute.)

❍ Observation

Prepare gel in TAE buffer by adding 1% agarose. DNA will be seen under UV Transilluminator. DNA bands will be seen clearly.

NUCLEIC ACID HYBRIDIZATION

The Watson and Crick model for the structure of double stranded (ds) DNA showed that the two strands were held together by hydrogen bonds between specific complementary bases-adenine (A), thymine (T), cytosine (C) and guanine (G). Interaction of base pairing is the basis of all molecular hybridization. The ability to use various physical and chemical procedures to disrupt base pairing and separate the strands (called as melting or denaturing the nucleic acid) and then to reinstate base pairing (called re-naturation, re-association or hybridization) enabled the various factors controlling the stability of the duplex to be examined. Although diagnosis of plant pathogens now involves mixed-phase hybridization with the target immobilized on a solid matrix, even then the theory developed for liquid-liquid hybridization is still very relevant.

❍ Denaturation

Double stranded (ds) nucleic acid usually denatures at high temperatures. Strand separation takes place over a relatively narrow range of temperatures. The temperature at which more than 50% of the sequences are denatured is called the *melting temperature* (Tm). The main factors affecting the melting temperature are the composition of the nucleic acid, the concentration of salt, pH of the solution and the presence of materials which can disrupt the hydrogen bonding. Some organic solvents such as formamide, dimethyl formamide, dimethyl sulphoxide and urea are known to lower the melting temperature (Tm). The melting temperature of double stranded RNA is significantly higher than that of double stranded DNA.

❍ Re-association (Hybridization)

The main factors affecting the rate of re-association includes temperature, salt concentration, fragment length, concentration of nucleic acid, RNA-DNA hybridization and probe stranded- ness. Single stranded (ss) probes overcome many of these problems. However, if 32p-labelled ss probe are used at concentrations above 100 mg/ml, binding may occur immediately.

❍ Stringency

The term is used to explain the effect of hybridization and wash conditions on the interaction between complementary nucleic acids which may be incompletely matched. The use of different stringencies is one of the more powerful tools of the hybridization technology.

❍ **Principles of nucleic acid hybridization**

Recent advances in recombinant DNA technology had led to clear understanding of plant viruses at nucleic acid level. Now the complete sequence, gene consent, gene arrangement of DNA and RNA viruses are well established. Earlier the coat protein gene product was used extensively by serological techniques for detection and differentiation. As the coat protein gene is only a fraction of the viral genome, therefore, specific detection was too difficult.

Nucleic acid hybridization technique involves the hybridization of labelled probes to cellulose nitrate bound nucleic acid that were spotted directly or transferred after fraction by electrophoresis on agarose gel (Southern transfer). Depending on the extent of homology between the viral nucleic acids immobilized on the cellulose nitrate and the nucleic acid in the probe, hybridization is retained which can be assessed by autoradiography.

❍ Requirements

Nitrocellulose or nylon membrane, automatic pipettes, tips,eppendorf tubes, microfuge, vacuum oven, shaking water bath, plate-farm shaker, plastic trays, latex gloves, lucite screen, big thick gauge polythene bags, bag sealer, Whatman 3M filter paper, blotting paper, X-ray cassette with intensifying screen, X-ray film, X-ray developer and fixative.

❍ Southern transfer

(1) The DNA is transferred from the gel after being denatured and neutralized through the buffer by capillary action onto the membrane.

(2) Once transfer has taken place to the membrane, it becomes a replica of the gel.

(3) The DNA should be denatured to make it single stranded to allow the probe to bind to it.

(4) The technique of transferring the DNA from the gel to a nylon/nitrocellulose membrane was first devised by Southern in 1975.

❍ Procedure

Procedure suggested and used at IARI is as under :

(1) Trim off the agarose gel above the loading wells, the regions not having any DNA to fix the orientation, make a slanting cut on the left hand corner.

(2) Take measurement of the gel.

(3) Soak the gel for 10 minutes in several volumes of 0.2N HCl. By this, DNA is partially hydrolyzed, can pass through the gel even if it gets dried. The resulting fragments get transferred efficiently. Avoid depurination for a longer time.

(4) Rinse it in de-ionized water.

(5) Soak the gel in a tray with denaturation solution with constant gentle agitation.

(6) After 45 minutes, pour the denaturation solution out and add neutralization solution. Soak the gel for 30 minutes with constant gentle agitation.

(7) While the gel is soaking, cut the membrane as per the gel measurement, trim off the membrane on the upper left hand corner. Handle the membrane with gloves and forceps. Don't tough it by hands.

(8) Soak the membrane in SDW for two minutes.

(9) Soak the membrane in 10xSSC for 15-20 minutes.

(10) Pour transfer buffer in a tray and set the transfer. Keep a glass plate across the tray and keep a 3M Whatman filter paper as a wick. Reverse the gel and keep it on a wick. Put the membrane on the gel carefully. Roll a pipette over it to remove air bubble. The left cut corner of the membrane should coincide with that of the gel. Put three sheets of Whatman paper cut to size. Put stacks of blotting paper on it. Every time take care to avoid air bubble. Put 500g to 1.0 kg weight to give pressure. Allow the transfer to take place overnight.

(11) Next day, remove the assembly with the forceps.

(12) Soak the membrane in 6 x SSC for 5 minutes to remove the agarose pieces.

(13) Dry the membrane. Immobilize the DNA by baking at 80°C for two hours. If nitrocellulose membrane is used, it must be baked in vacuum.

❍ **Hybridization with a probe**

❍ Procedure

(1) Denature the DNA at 100°C for 5 minutes. Now mix the following immediately :

(2) Denatured DNA 1μl (30-50 mg of DNA)

Primer (Random hexa-nucleotides) (100 mg/μl)	1 μl
10 × labelling buffer	5 μl
d NTP (10 m M dATP, d GTP, d TTP)	2.0 μl
Dithiothreitol (DTT) (20m M)	2.5 μl
Nuclease free BSA	2.0 μl
(alpha P) d CTP (4000 ci/mmol)	1.0 μl
Klenow (DNA Pol I) (3U)	1.0 μl
SDW	34.5 μl
	50.0 μl

(3) Incubate at 37°C for two hours.

❍ Probe preparation

The DNA is labelled by random primer labelling. Probe will be made by random primer labelling method, wherein, to the DNA fragment, random primers are added with one radioactive (d ATP or d CTP), and three other non-radioactive d NTPs. In the presence of Klenow, new strands are synthesized, which will have incorporation of radioactive d NTP.

❍ Pre-hybridization

The spaces in the membrane where DNA is not bound should be blocked to avoid non-specific binding of probe. This is done by immersing the membrane in a solution containing large molecular weight DNA or RNA along with detergent and dispersing agent.

Keep the membrane in one of the large glass cylinders of a hybridization oven. Balance with another cylinder. Add pre- hybridization solution in both the cylinders. The SDS in the pre-hybridization solution reduces non-specific probe binding and prevents nuclease activity. The yeast mRNA acts as blocking agent. Cylinders are rotated to facilitate uniform spreading of the solution.

❍ Hybridization

After 4 hours, add the probe into the pre-hybridization solution. Before adding the probe it should be denatured by boiling (Poke a vent hole in the tube before putting it in the water bath). Normally, probe is added at 0.5 X 10^6 cpm/ml of hybridization solution. Allow over night incubation at 65°C.

❍ **Useful tips and facts**

(1) A combination of temperature and salt concentration should be chosen for hybridization.

(2) The washing condition is considered as stringent when the temperature of washing is less than 65°C and the salt concentration is very low (0.2 SSC).

(3) The temperature and salt condition should be determined in preliminary experiments. Higher the sequence homology between the probe and the immobilized DNA, the pairing will be retained even at high temperature and low ionic strength of washing. This fact is used in finding out relatedness between different DNA fragments.

(4) Nucleic acid hybridization is also used in the detection and diagnosis of plant pathogens.

❍ Washing the blots

(1) Next day morning, pour hybridization solution and add 30 ml washing solution. It is done to remove any unbound probe.

(2) Rotate the cylinders and repeat the washing for two more times.

(3) Take the membrane out by forceps and dry it out on the paper towels.

❍ **Detection by Auto-radiography**

The particle emitted from a radioactive atom activates a photographic emulsion much like light or X-rays. If the photographic emulsion is brought into close contact with a radioactive source, the particles emitted by the source leave tiny, black silver grains in the emulsion after photographic development.

❍ Procedure

(1) Wrap up the membrane in a cling film and put it in an X-ray film cassette. Put the membrane in between intensifying screen to intensify the signal.

(2) Orient the X-ray film in dark by cutting off at the upper left hand corner and press it against the membrane.

(3) Keep at –20°C for 24 to 48 hours.

(4) Develop the X-ray film in dark as per the manufacturer's recommendation to detect hybridization pattern.

DOT-BLOT HYBRIDIZATION

Detection of a very small amount of virus in the plant material is possible by nucleic acid hybridization tests. In this technique, the nucleic acid from the plant material is irreversibly bound to a nitro-cellulose membrane (NCM) and is allowed to hybridize with radio-labelled probe of a virus suspected to be present in the sample. Positive hybridization indicates the presence of suspected virus in the test samples.

❍ **Procedure**

❍ Preparation of membrane

(1) Cut required amount of membrane by handling it with gloves. Mark 1.0 cm squares using soft pencil. Cut one edge to indicate orientation.

(2) Soak NCM in water, then in 20 X SSPE or 20 X SSC for 5 minutes.

(3) Drain off fluid and spread on clean blotting paper. Dot the samples as quickly as possible.

❍ Sample preparation

(1) Grind 1.0 g of leaf in 1.0 ml of TE buffer and filter it through muslin. *(Take 200 μl of this extract and add 50 μl of 0.5 N NaOH. Incubate at room temperature for 10 minutes.)*

(2) Add 25 μl 3M sodium acetate pH 5.0.

(3) Make dilution of 1:10 and 1:100 in TE.

(4) Dot carefully 2.5 to 5 μl of samples in each square in the membrane, keeping the dot as small as possible.

(5) Note the format in which samples have been dotted.

(6) Both the negative (healthy) and positive (virus infected diseased plant) sample should always be included in the tests for comparison.

(7) Air dry filters and bake in vacuum over for 80°C for 2 hours.

❍ Probe Production—Random Primer Method

Mix the following in the order in Eppendorf tube. Take care to protect yourself from radiation by using lab coat, gloves and lucite screen.

Water	33 μl
Oligolabelling buffer	10 μl
Bovine serum albumin	2 μl
Template DNAs	1 μl
32p—dCTP	3 μl
Klenow enzyme	1 μl
Total	50 μl

Note. Incubate behind the lucite screen at room temperature overnight. Stop reaction by adding 2 μl of 1 mM EDTA.

❍ Pre-hybridization

Calculate the volume of solution required at the rate of 1 ml/square cm of blot for bags.

For 10 ml mixture

Water	6.3 ml
50 × Denhardt's solution	0.8 ml
10 mg/ml sanicated salmon sperm DNA	0.1 ml
20 × SSC	25.0 ml
10% SDS	0.3 ml

Heat at 100°C in boiling water bath for 90 seconds. Put into the bag and seal. Take care to avoid air bubbles. Incubate in shaking water bath at 65°C.

❍ Hybridization

Add probe at the rate of 1×10^6 cpm/ml of solution. Denature probe by boiling for 5 minutes on water bath. Add to the bag and seal. Incubate in shaking water bath at 65°C over night.

❍ Washing

(1) Take out the blot by carefully cutting the bag.

(2) Discard the solution with the radioactive probe into radioactive waste.

(3) Transfer the blot to a plastic tray filled with washing solution.

(4) Wash with 2 X SSC with 0.1% SDS at 65°C on a platfarm shaker with moderate agitation. Each washing should be of 15-20 minutes.

(5) After two washes blot off excess liquid. Dry it on a paper towel placed between two layers of thin polythene sheet.

(6) In dark room place X-ray film on top, close cassette and place at –70°C over night. Develop autoradiogram.

❍ Observation

Dark spot or band in the X-ray film indicates the positive hybridization.

PLASMID ISOLATION

By the mid-1970s, the broad outline of how genetic information flows from DNA or RNA to protein was understood. It was possible at this time to put some pure DNA in a test tube along with the necessary enzymes and reagents and have the DNA transcribed into RNA and the RNA translated into protein-without using an intact cell. It is now possible to extract a gene from a cell, change it at will and put it back into the same or in a different cell to get a genetically engineered life form. A key discovery in this regard was that of certain enzymes which could cut DNA at very precise locations. These are called restriction enzymes. These molecular scissors are found in many bacterial species which use them to get rid of foreign viral DNA.

❍ **What are plasmids ?**

Plasmids are small circular extra chromosomal DNA molecules of small size (in the average range of 5-10 kilo bases, compared with the size of an average chromosome which may be of several kilo bases). They are known to exist in many bacteria and in some higher organisms too. A very large number of different kinds of plasmids are found in nature. Some are larger in size than others. Some are present in multiple copies in the host cell, while others may exist as a single copy. Several of the bacterial plasmids carry genes for drug resistance on them. Cell which contain these plasmids are resistant to the corresponding drugs, most of which are commonly used antibiotics such as Penicillin, Chloramphenicol and Tetracycline. The plasmid which can serve effective role in molecular biology especially in gene manipulation is one that is small in size, exists in high copy number per cell and carries one or two drugs resistant genes on it.

❍ Use of plasmids in the laboratory

In the laboratory, the molecular scientists can modify plasmids and use them to carry genes of interest into host bacteria. Once inside the bacteria, the plasmids multiply as the bacteria divide. These plasmids can be isolated from the host bacteria using various techniques.

❍ Mini-preparation procedure to isolate plasmids from host bacteria

❍ The solutions

L.B. (Luria Broth (1L)

10 g tryptone

5 g yeast extract

5 g NaCl

sterilized by autoclaving

GTE buffer

25 mM tris HCl (pH 8.0)

10 mM EDTA

50 mM glucose

Potassium acetate/acetic acid

60 ml of 5 M Potassium acetate

11.5 ml of glacial acetic acid

28.5 ml of H_2O

SDS/NaOH

1% SDS

0.2 N NaOH

TE buffer

1 mM Tris HCl (pH 7.5-8.0)

1 mM EDTA

❍ Procedure

1. Grow the plasmid containing bacterial culture overnight in L.B. medium.

(L.B. medium contains nutrients for bacterial growth).

2. Remove 1.5 ml of the culture and spin down the cells in a microfuge.

3. Discard the supernatant and resuspend completely the cell in 100 μl of ice cold GTE buffer.

(The buffer is kept cold to inhibit nucleases released during the procedure. GTE buffer contains Tris to maintain proper pH-8.0. EDTA to bind divalent cations (Mg^{++}, Ca^{++}) in the lipid bilayer and glucose which may act as an osmotic support or may help to prevent cells from clumping).

4. Add 200μl of SDS/NaOH and mix gently.

(The bacterial cells are lysed by the SDS, which stabilizes the membrane lipids and cellular proteins. The base denatures both the chromosomal and plasmid DNA. The strands of the circular plasmid's DNA remain inter twined. The suspension is mixed gently to avoid shearing the chromosomal DNA.

5. Set on ice for 10 minutes

(This resting step allows time for the SDS/NaOH to contact all the cells and the processes in step 4 to go to completion).

6. Add 150 μl of cold potassium acetate/glacial acetic acid and mix gently. A white precipitate will appear.

(The acetic acid neutralizes the sodium hydroxide added in step 4 allowing the DNA to renature. The potassium acetate causes the SDS to precipitate along with associated proteins and lipids. The large chromosomal DNA strands renature partially into a tangled web that precipitates along with the SDS complex. In contrast, the small coiled renatured plasmid remain suspended. In this step, therefore, they are suspended from chromosomal DNA, many proteins and the detergent).

7. Centrifuge the mixture and save the supernatant

(The discarded precipitate contains cellular material, linear DNA, protein and detergent. The supernatant contains the suspended plasmids).

8. Remove 400 μl of the supernatant; add equal vol. of isopropanol and mix.

(Isopropanol, like ethanol precipitates DNA. Isopropanol is used here because a smaller volume of isopropanol is required than ethanol. The alcohol quickly precipitate DNA and more slowly precipitates proteins. This step is done quickly).

9. Centrifuge and save the pellet

(The alcohol precipitated plasmid DNA is in pellet).

10. Wash the pellet in 200 μl of 100% ethanol

(Although isopropanol precipitated the DNA in the preceding step, an ethanol wash helps to remove extra salts and other unwanted contamination).

11. Centrifuge and save the pellet

12. Resuspend the pellet in 1.5 μl of Tris/EDTA buffer (TE).

(TE is often used for short term storage of DNA. Tris maintains pH, whereas EDTA relates divalent cations to inhibit nuclease activity).

❍ Anticipated results

Ethidium bromide is a fluorescent dye used to visualize nucleic acid in agarose gel. It acts inserting itself in to DNA molecules. 1% agarose gel was prepared and the DNA bands were observed.

POLYMERASE CHAIN REACTION (PCR)

The polymerase chain reaction (PCR) is a primer mediated enzymatic amplification of a DNA segment lying between two regions of known sequences. The polymerase chain reaction may be described as 'the process comprises treating separate complementary strands of the (target) nucleic acid with a molar excess of two oligonucleotide primers and extending the primers to form complementary primer extension products that act as templates for synthesizing the desired nucleic acid sequence'. In other words P.C.R. may be explained *'as a method used to copy a specific region of DNA many thousands of time. In this technique, DNA molecule is not cloned in a bacterial plasmid or virus. The only requirement is that the sequence at the borders of the selected DNA region must be known so that two short oligonucleotides can anneal to the target DNA mlecule for amplification.*

Kerry Mullis received the Nobel Prize for Chemistry (1993) for the discovery of PCR. The seeds of PCR began as a early as 1955 with the discovery of Nobel Laureate Arthur Kornberg, who discovered a cellular enzyme called *DNA Polymerase*. DNA polymerases serve several natural functions, including the repair and replication of DNA. After the introduction of the automated DNA thermal cyclers in 1989, PCR has been established as one of the most substantial technical advances in molecular biology.

❍ Applications and importance

(1) PCR is currently applicable in the areas of disease diagnosis, detection of pathogens, detection of DNA in all samples, DNA comparisons, high efficiency cloning of genomic sequences and many other areas.

(2) PCR has its usefulness in basic molecular, biological and clinical research.

(3) Besides these, PCR is useful in forensics, evolutionary studies, genome projects and plant pathology.

(4) The significance of PCR lies in its ability to amplify *in vitro* a specific DNA or cDNA sequences from trace amounts in a complex template.

(5) Now it is possible to amplify specific DNA or cDNA sequences from as short as 50 bp to more than 10,000 bp in length. With an automated DNA thermal cycler, 10^6 to 10^9– fold amplification may be carried out in a few hours.

(6) PCR has very high specificity and fidelity, which allows for the discrimination of sequences that differ by as little as a single nucleotide mutations.

(7) PCR has also been used for the detection of plant viruses from their vectors such as aphids, mealybugs, whiteflies, thrips, leafhoppers and nematodes.

(8) Very interesting and important approach for PCR-based detection says is the development of 'Multiplex PCR', a technique that allows the simultaneous amplification of several viroids or viruses using a mixture of specific primer pairs.

(9) PCR amplification of plant viruses and viroids has been used for screening transgenic plants, molecular cloning of pathogen genomes, nucleotide sequencing of pathogens and studying host-pathogen-vector interactions.

(10) PCR may be used for searching pathgens in water and soil samples.

❍ **The PCR reaction**

RNA virus genomes and viroids require the introduction of an RT step before the PCR amplification process (RT-PCR). The two most frequently used enzymes to perform this RT step are the reverse transcriptases (RTases). The PCR reaction is based on the annealing and enzymatic extension of two oligonucleotide primers (each usually 16 to 30 nucleotides in length) that flank the target region in a duplex DNA by means of a 'thermo resistant' DNA polymerase that will retain enzymatic activity at [illegible] temperatures.

❍ Three phases of PCR cycles

There are three phases of PCR cycles as under :

(1) Denaturation. In phase-1 the two strands of parent DNA molecule that include the sequence of interest are separated by heating to about 94°C.

(2) Primer annealing. In the second phase the reaction mixture is quickly cooled to around 72°C and the single stranded DNA hybridizes with the primer.

(3) Primer extension. In the third phase, the thermo-stable enzyme *Taq 1 DNA polymerase* is able to copy the DNA region of interest, beginning from the locations where the primers have bound.

Typically, the reaction mixture is first heated (DNA denaturation) and subsequently cooled (DNA annealing) in cycles of 30 seconds to a few minutes in length for each heating or cooling period. Heating the mixture separates the double-stranded DNA into two single strands. When the mixture cools, each primer hybridizes to its separated complementary DNA strand. Each of the annealed primers is then enzymatically extended on the template strand into a new DNA strand by the thermostable DNA polymerase. These three steps (denaturation, primer annealing and primer extension) which are carried out at different temperature ranges, represent a single PCR cycle. The next cycle of heating separates the copies from the original strands and both become templates for a new round of DNA synthesis. As a result of repeated cycles, the target DNA is amplified exponentially in a chain reaction.

❍ Essentials for PCR

(1) Oligomer primers. Primers for PCR should be 16-24 nucleotides long and are generally referred as Primer 1 and Primer 2 for the two ends of target sequence. Usually primers are used at a concentration of 1 μM which is sufficient for at least 30 cycles of amplifications.

(2) Amplification buffer. The standard buffer contains 500 mM KCl, 100 mM Tris-HCl (pH-8.0) and 20 M $MgCl_2$.

(3) Deoxyribonucleoside triphosphate. dNTPs are used at a saturating concentration of 200 μM for each dNTP.

(4) Target sequence. Template DNA containing the target sequence can be added in a single or double stranded form. Linear target sequences are amplified better as compared to close circular DNAs.

(5) *Taq* DNA polymerase. Two forms of *Taq* DNA polymerase is most frequently used as preferred enzyme.

❍ Procedure for Polymerase chain reaction (PCR)

(1) Isolate the plant DNA.

(2) Add the reagents in 0.2 ml micro-centrifuge (PCR) tube and place it on ice.

(3) Mix the following one by one.

Sterile water	10.5 μl
10 × PCR buffer	2.0 μl
d NTP Mix (10 mM)	1.0 μl

$MgCl_2$ (25 mM)	2.0 μl
Primer (forward) (10 p Mol)	1.0 μl
Primer (reverse) (10 p Mol)	1.0 μl
Template DNA (10 μg)	2.0 μl

(4) Give short spin and then add *Taq* DNA Polymerase (3 units) 0.5 μl. Total volume = 20 μl. (*Taq* DNA Polymerase is usually stored in special box at —20°C).

(5) Prepare cocktail of components as stated above. Keep one tube with each cocktail without plant DNA as control.

(6) Mix well and spin briefly to PCR microfuge tubes including control.

(7) Place the tubes in PCR thermocycler block and set the machine for following cycling conditions.

Steps	Temperatures	Time	Cycles
Step 1	94 C°	2 minutes	1 cycle
Step 2	94 C°	1 minute	
	55 C°	1 minute	25-30 cycles
	72 C°	1 minute	
Step 3	72 C°	5 minutes	
Step 4	4 C°	end	

(8) After amplification add 2.5 μl of tracking dye in sample and store at 4°C.

(9) Prepare agarose gel of 1.2%. Load the samples carefully in the wells and add suitable molecular weight marker (1 kb ladder) in one of the lanes.

(10) The gel was stained with ethidium bromide and then electrophoresis was carried out at a constant voltage of 50 volts. Take the photograph.

❍ Agarose Gel analysis of PCR products

1. Prepare 1.2% agarose gel in 0.5 X TBE buffer. Allow the agarose solution to cool in a water bath and add 5μl of 10 mg/ml ethidium bromide.
2. Cast a mini gel by pouring the agarose solution into a suitable gel mould with a suitable well forming comb. A 5 × 7.5 cm gel can be used to separate upto 15 samples.
3. Withdraw a 5-10 μl sample of the PCR reaction and add water and traching dye. Spin the sample.
4. Store the remaining sample at 4°C or in ice.
5. Once the agarose gel has set, remove the slot former and submerge the gel in a flat-bed tank containing 0.5 × TBE buffer so that the gel is covered by 2 mm of buffer.
6. Load the samples and suitable molecular weight markers, then do electrophoresis at 50V for 60 minutes.

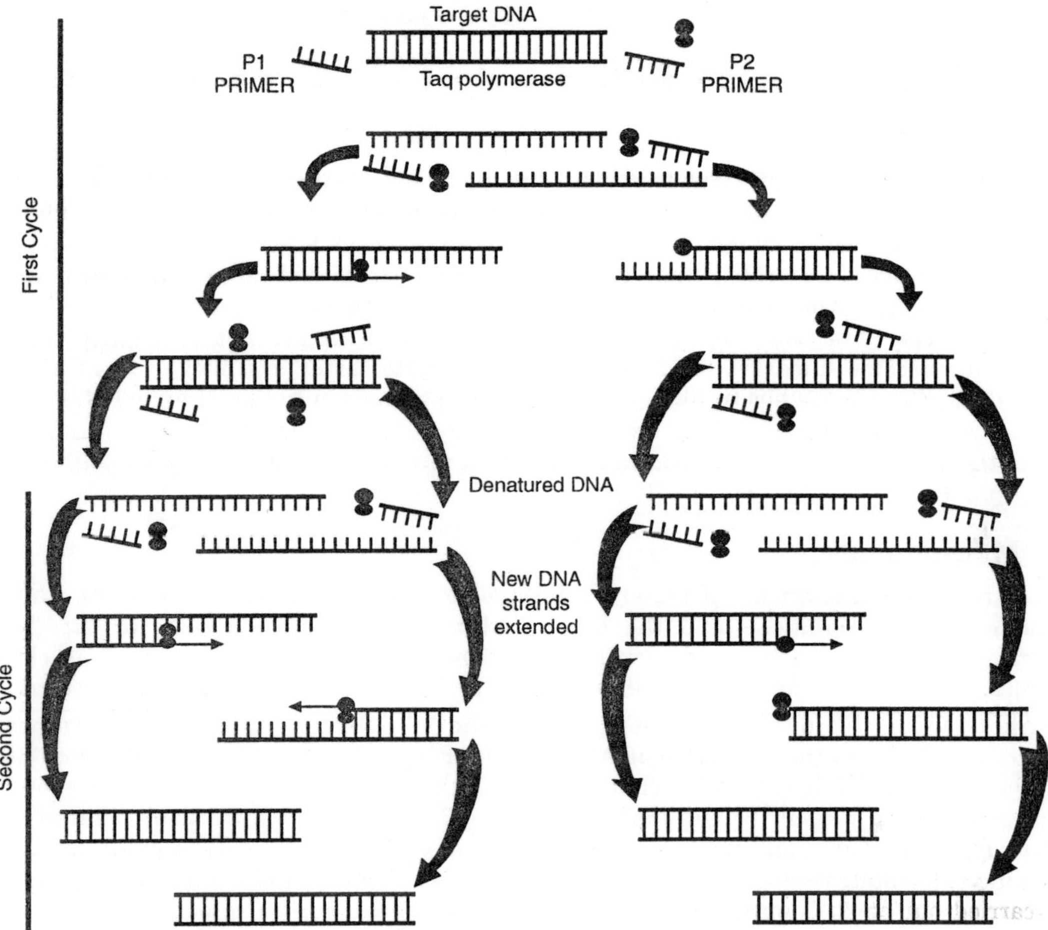

Fig. 9.2 Diagrammatic representation of polymerase chain reaction

❍ Observations

The band of the DNA fragment at expected base pair length may be observed as prominent fluorescing indicating amplification. Its molecular weight was determined by comparing with the molecular weight marker run on the same gel.

❍ Precautions

1. Use a fresh pair of gloves prior to starting the experiment.
2. Use fresh, sterile pipette tips, PCR tubes and fresh prepared buffers.
3. Do not use PCR reagents and solutions in any other experiments.
4. Add all components of PCR reaction before adding the template DNA.
5. Keep the level of EDTA in template DNA solution as low as possible.
6. Do not use excess of DNA polymerase and use dNTPs at saturating concentrations (200 µm for each dNTPs).
7. Start the PCR cycling process within 30 minutes after adding $MgCl_2$.

DETECTION OF VIROIDS

Return polyacrylamide gel electrophoresis (R-PAGE)

❍ Principles

R-PAGE is a modified form of bi-directional gel electrophoresis developed for viroid detection. Test nucleic acid sample is electrophoreses under non-denaturing condition followed continuously by denaturation with high heat and low salt buffer. Due to denaturation by low morality and high temperature, viroids molecules lose their double stranded configuration, become single stranded circular forms and migrate very slowly in the reverse direction. On the other hand, RNAs which are not covalently closed molecules become linear when denatured and migrate faster and move ahead of the viroids bands. On the electrophorograms, the lowest bands only the circular RNA. The viroid band is about 1.8 to 2 cm lower than any host RNA band visible in non-infected plant tissue. The R-PAGE method can thus detect viroids of different sizes from different crop plants.

❍ Methodology

In this assay, nucleic acids are subjected to two electrophoretic runs–one under non-denaturing conditions and the other under denaturing conditions. In the first electrophoresis with a high salt buffer, the viroids band is allowed to move as close to the gel front as possible without losing it. A dye, xylene cyanol FF_1, is used as a marker. When this dye reaches the gel front, the 7S RNA and viroids bands are near the edge. By then, the smaller molecular weight RNAs (5S and 4S) have migrated out of the gel into the lower buffer chamber. After the first electrophoresis, the buffer is exchanged for a low salt boiling buffer. Heated (87-90°C) buffer in desirable quantity is poured into the lower and upper electrophoresis chambers and allowed to stand for 5-10 minutes to facilitate viroids denaturation. The polarity is reversed and second electrophoresis is carried out at 70°C until the xylene cyanol is out of the gel (in return direction).

❍ Requirements

Young leaves with characteristic symptoms, pestle and mortar, liquid nitrogen, extraction buffer as desired, chloroform, isoamyl alcohol, Tris saturated phenol, bentomite, alcohol, low speed centrifuge.

❍ **Procedure**

❍ Nucleic acid extraction

Two procedures are used for extraction of total nucleic acid (NA) as described in Flow Chart A and B.

❍ Flow Chart A

Weigh 5 g of leaf tissue (H/D).

↓

Wash, blot, cut into small pieces, homogenize in chilled pestle and mortar using 2 vol. buffer (0.1 M Tris, 0.01 M EDTA, 0.1 M NaCl, 1% SDS containing 5 m M DTT and DIECA.

Add 3 vol. $CHCl_3$ isoamyl alcohol (24:1), 3 vol. of Tris saturated phenol pH-7.0

Leave at room temperature (RT) for 10-15 minutes shaking in between.

Centrifuge at 8,500 rpm, at 4°C for 15-20 minutes.

Add 0.5 vol. ammonium acetate 7.5 M, pH-7.0, 2.5 vol. absolute alcohol to supernatant. Incubate at—20°C over night (O/N).

Centrifuge at 8500 rpm at 4°C for 20 minutes.

↓

Dissolve pellet in sterile distilled water (10 μl/g tissue). Sample is ready to test.

❍ Flow Chart B

Weigh 5 g leaf tissue (H/D).

Wash, blot cut into small pieces, homogenize in a chilled pestle and mortar with 3 vol. buffer (0.5 M NH_4OH, 0.01 M EDTA pH 7, 0.5 M LiCl, 0.003% purified bentonite).

↓

Add 4 vol. of Tris or water saturated phenol.

Centrifuge at 8500 rpm at 4°C for 15 minutes.

Add 2 vol. absolute alcohol (EtOH), 0.5 vol. 4M sodium acetate to aqueous phase, keep at—20°C over night.

Centrifuge at 8500 rpm at 4°C for 15 minutes.

Dissolve pellet in sterile distilled water (10 μl/g tissue).

❍ Isolation of low molecular weight RNA (*LMW-RNA*)

Isolation of LMW-RNA from NA is done by column chromatography using CF-11 cellulose powder.

❍ Procedure

(1) CF-11 cellulose (Whatman) in proportion of 1g/5g fresh weight tissue is taken, stir well with 100 ml of sterile distilled water and keep undisturbed for 5 minutes.

(2) Water is drained off and this step is repeated twice.

(3) The cellulose was then shaken with STE : EtOH (65:35) twice. The cellulose slurry in STE : EtOH is applied on to plastic column with mira cloth filter at the end of the column.

(4) Each column is then equilibrated with 10-12 ml of STE : EtOH.

(5) Samples are dissolved in STE : EtOH (1ml/g fresh weight of tissue), loaded on the top of the column gently and after that it is absorbed. The column is washed with 10-12 ml of STE-EtOH until a clear eluate is obtained.

(6) Finally nucleic acid is eluted by adding 2-3 ml of STE buffer (without EtOH) and then eluate is precipitated as before.

❍ Gel Electrophoresis

Polyacrylamide vertical gels were used for electrophoretic separation of LMW-RNA under non-denaturing and denaturing conditions of run.

❍ Non-denaturing conditions

(1) Test LMW-RNA samples were electrophoreses in 5% Polyacrylamide native gel (acrylamide : bisacrylamide 29:1) in vertical slabs in TBE buffer.

(2) Electrophoresis was carried out at RT with 1X TBE as running buffer using a power source set at 46 mA (constant current) for 2.5 hours.

(3) 12 μl test nucleic acids were loaded in the slots mixed with 4 μl of bromophenol blue-xylene cyanol (tracking dye) prepared in 40% glycerol sucrose (MB grade).

❍ Denaturing conditions

R-PAGE is bidirectional gel electrophoresis under denaturing conditions.

1. The first run is done at 46 mA for 2 to 2.5 hours using TBE (1X) as running buffer.
2. The same gel is re-run by replacing the TBE (1X) with TBE (0.8 X) at 70°C in reverse polarity for 1.5 to 2.0 hours.
3. Electrophoresis unit was connected to water circulator bath set at 70°C and maintained so during the entire run. The low ionic strength of the buffer and high temperature created the denaturing conditions.

❍ Visualization of RNA bands

For visualization of bands, the gels were stained either in ethidium bromide or silver nitrate.

❍ Staining with ethidium bromide (EtBr)

The gels are stained with 10 mg/ml EtBr for 15 minutes. It is examined under photodyne Trans illuminator directly under UV light.

❍ Staining with silver nitrate

(1) Immerse gel in fixative 1 and leave at room temperature for 1 hour in a reciprocal shaker or incubate overnight.

(2) Transfer the gel to fixative II for 30 minutes or 1 hour at room temperature.
(3) Stain the gel with silver nitrate (0.2%) for 1 hour.
(4) Wash 2-4 times with sterile DDW.
(5) Transfer to developer solution 1, for 2-3 minutes until golden brown colour begins to appear.
(6) Transfer to developer solution 2, for 2-3 minutes until resolution of bands is clear.
(7) Preserve the gel in 5% acetic acid.

❍ Observation

The presence of viroids bands in infected samples were seen as low molecular weight RNA appearing lowest in the return gel. The RNA from band can be extracted, purified and used for cloning.

❍ **Solutions used**

STE buffer

0.1M NaCl, 0.001 M EDTA, 0.5 M Tris-HCl, adjut pH to 7.5 with HCl.

Polyacrylamide gel electrophoresis (PAGE)

30.0 g acrylamide 0.8 g N, N′-methylene bisacylamide, distilled water to make vol. upto 100 ml, filtered through Whatman filter paper No. 1.

TBE buffer

89 m M Tris, 89 m M boric acid, 2.5 m M EDTA, adjust pH-8.3 with Tris and make up the volume.

TEMED (N, N, N′ *, N′-tetramethylethylenediamine)*

Electrophoresis grade

❍ Staining

Fixative I : 5% glacial acetic acid in 25% EtOH.

Fixative II : 1% glacial acetic acid in 1% EtOH.

Silver : 0.2% silver nitrate dissolved in DDW.

❍ Developer

Solution I : 4.1% KOH containing 75% formaldehyde in DDW.

Solution II : 0.74% Na_2CO_3 dissolved in DDW.

❍ Preservative

5% glacial acetic acid.

❍ Precautions

(1) Use of plastic gloves from the first step onwards is essential.
(2) All glassware, plastic ware and other articles used must be thoroughly autoclaved or baked after rinsing with DEPC treated water.

(3) Extra care must be taken while handling phenol, lithium chloride, acrylamide and silver stain.

(4) Water should be free from chlorides.

POST TRANSCRIPTIONAL GENE SILENCING

❍ Protein mediated resistance

Post transcriptional gene silencing is a new concept to understand plant defense against viruses. As known to date, there are two important methods for developing genetically engineered resistance, depending upon the sources of genes used. The gene in one approach can be obtained from pathogen virus itself and in the other approach is to obtain resistant gene from any other sources. The former, known as the pathogen derived resistance, was first explained by Sanford and Johnston (1985). They suggested a part or complete viral gene to be introduced into on plant. The success of coat protein mediated resistance (CPMR) was initiated earlier by Powel Abel *et al* (1986). Now CPMR is being practised against several plant RNA viruses. In such cases, the coat protein gene is expressed and accumulation of protein plays a specific role in conferring protection. Therefore, approaches are referred to as protein mediated resistance.

❍ Post transcriptional gene silencing

In contrast to it, in some of the transgenic experiments, resistance was observed even when non-coding regions untranslatable RNA sequences and antisense RNA were used. The molecular mechanism behind this protection is now understood and is referred to as Post transcriptional gene silencing (PTGS).

❍ Mechanism

Post transcriptional gene silencing is a specific RNA degradation mechanism of any organism that takes care of aberrant unwanted excess RNA or foreign RNA in the cells. When PTGS is associated with viral RNA, it is called 'Viral induced gene silencing (VIGS)'. It is usually observed when plants show recovery from symptoms as in case of *Potato virus X*. When this virus infects *Nicotiana benthamiana*, the plant develops initial symptoms of viral infection at inoculated region. After some time the plants show signs of recovery and newly emerging leaves are free from PVX. Hamilton and Baulcomb (1999) reported that viral replicative RNA forms are degraded during the recovery. The resistance of the recovered leaves to the challenging virus is dependent on sequence homology between the viruses. This gene silence is called homology dependent gene silencing (HdGS).

❍ Functions of PTGS

In plants, PTGS functions as a natural defense mechanism against viruses. For the majority of the transgenic plants showing pathogen derived resistance, PTGS may well explain the mechanism of resistance. If transgenic plants get infected by viruses having homologous sequences, PTGS operates.

❍ Applications in management of virus diseases

Gene silencing in plants could have evolved as response to selection pressure by pathogenic viruses. Many plant viruses encode proteins that can suppress PTGS. If gene silencing is a natural defense mechanism of plants, the suppression of gene silencing is the counter strategy developed by the viruses. The mechanism in intervention between these two could lead to adopting PTGS strategy for management of virus diseases.

10

ELECTRON MICROSCOPY

Introduction, Common terminology, Advantage of Electron microscopy, Principles of Electron microscopy, Negative staining, How to prepare the grid, Methods in Electron microscopy, Leaf dip preparation, ISEM and Decoration in Electron microscopy.

❍ Introduction

The human eyes can see exceedingly tiny objects under special conditions. As for example, the particles of dust visible in the path of a light ray shining through an otherwise darkened room may be as small as 1.0 μm in diameter. However, particles smaller than this can not be visible to the naked eye. Such smaller particles are seen by the help of microscope. The microscope is an optical instrument designed to allow such smaller particles to be seen with the eye. The instrument literally extends our power of observation and enables us to explore the world of the 'invisible' through its ability of magnification.

The microscope produces an image (a picture) of an object that becomes magnified or enlarged as it is transmitted through two or more optical lenses. In the light microscope, a beam of visible light produces an image that is magnified by glass optical lenses.

Electron microscope (EM) in contrast to light microscope, is an optical instrument in which a beam of electrons is used to form a greatly enlarged image of an extremely small object through a series of electromagnetic lenses. Extremely small negatively-charged electrons given off by heated tungsten wire filament can be accelerated by high voltage to produce coherent electron beam as in cathode ray tube or oscilloscope and can be focussed by an electric field. The electric field of a dough nut-shaped electromagnet surrounding the electron beam acts just like the glass lens which focusses the light beam on the specimen. Electromagnet is used as the objective lens to form a highly magnified image of the specimen and by using one or more electromagnetic lenses, the image of the specimen is further magnified many times onto a phosphorescent viewing screen or photographic plate. Magnification is increased by strengthening the projector lenses by increasing the current through the electromagnets. Since the electrons are very much smaller than air molecules, therefore, high vacuum inside the stack of 'electromagnetic doughnuts' is essential so as to allow a free path for the electrons from the filament to the viewing screen. The specimen to be examined, must be ultra thin to allow some electrons to pass through to form an image, otherwise only the outlines of the objects are discernible.

Special methods have been developed to observe very small particles and their solid surfaces. In order to observe fine structures within the cell, tissues and organisms to be observed must be fixed, held at proper place and sliced over a hundred times thinner than a sheet of tissue paper. The slicing is done with the **'ultra microtome'** using an angular broken edge of plate glass. Both particles and ultra thin sections are held in the electron beam on a plastic film, thin enough to be transparent to the electrons. The film is held by a miniature wire mesh screen (grid) measuring about 3 mm in diameter. The grid in held in a movable holder for observation in the EM. The film, Grid and holder are analogous to the glass slide and movable stage of the light microscope.

❍ Common terminology

Word focus, resolution, magnification, sectioning, fixation and staining are most frequently used. An understanding of such terms is essential for better understanding of the subject.

Focus—The lens of human eye is able to adjust automatically (focus) to the object being viewed. Such adjustment which enables us to view an object is called 'focus'. Light microscopes are equipped with a mechanical adjustment that moves the lenses either toward or away from the object. In electron microscope electromagnetic lenses focus the image.

Resolution—The ability to distinguish two objects as separate entities is called resolution. As known to all of us that magnification is not the main object of microscopy. Resolving power is generally expressed as the size of the smallest object distinguishable.

Thus we can say that the resolving power of the human eye is about 0.1 mm or 100 μm. If two objects are so small or lie so close together that they can not be distinguished as separate. It means that such objects are beyond the resolving power of our eye.

Magnification—Resolving power limits the effective magnification of a microscope. The strong resolving power of an electron microscope permits direct magnification of over 100,000X, whereas a good light microscope can magnify the same object only about 1000X (times). Greatly increased resolving and magnifying power of the electron microscope enables to biologists to see smallest molecules which were previously known to occur through biochemical studies only.

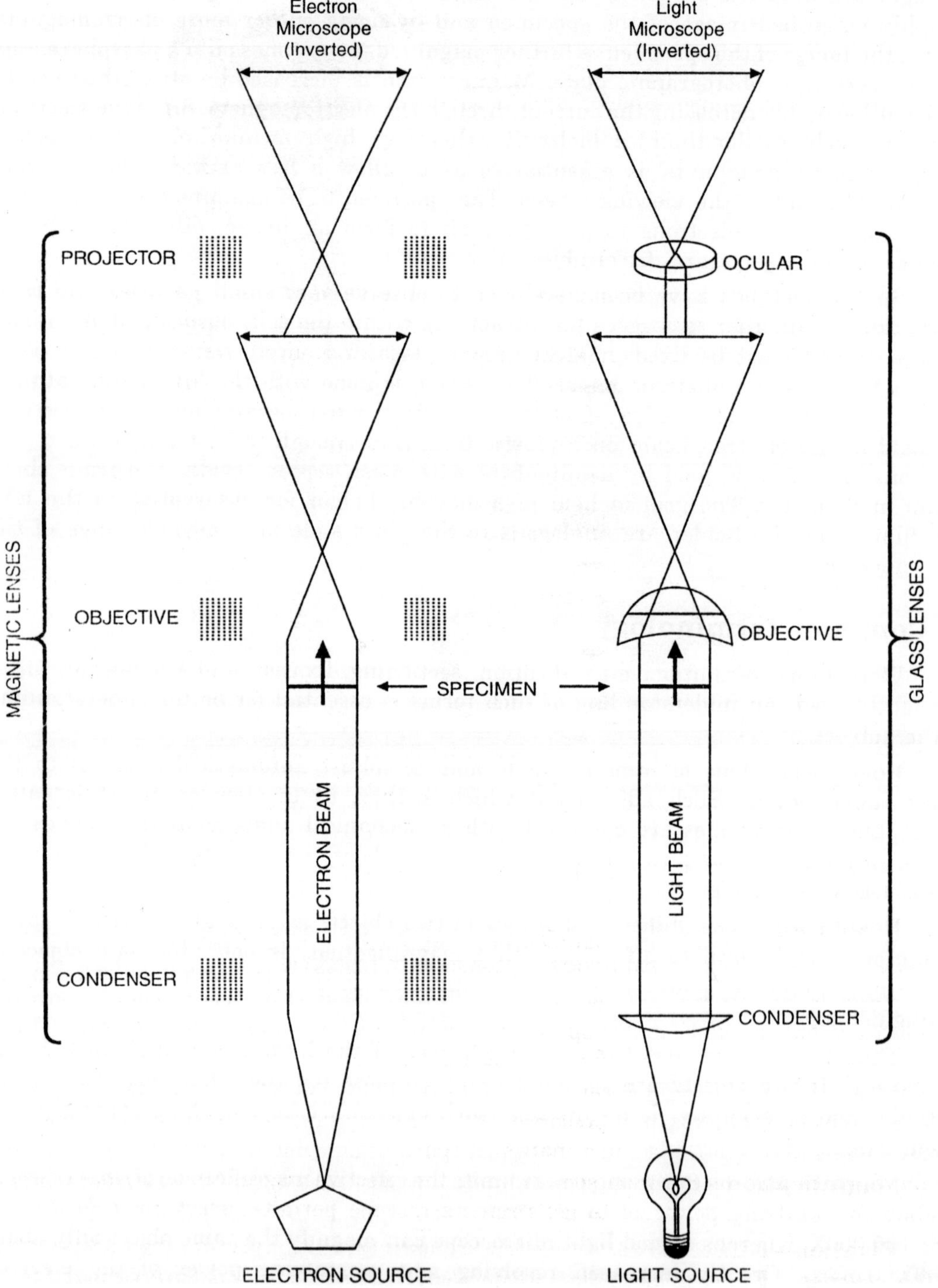

Fig. 10.1. Diagrammatic representation showing comparison of the optical system of the light and electron microscope.

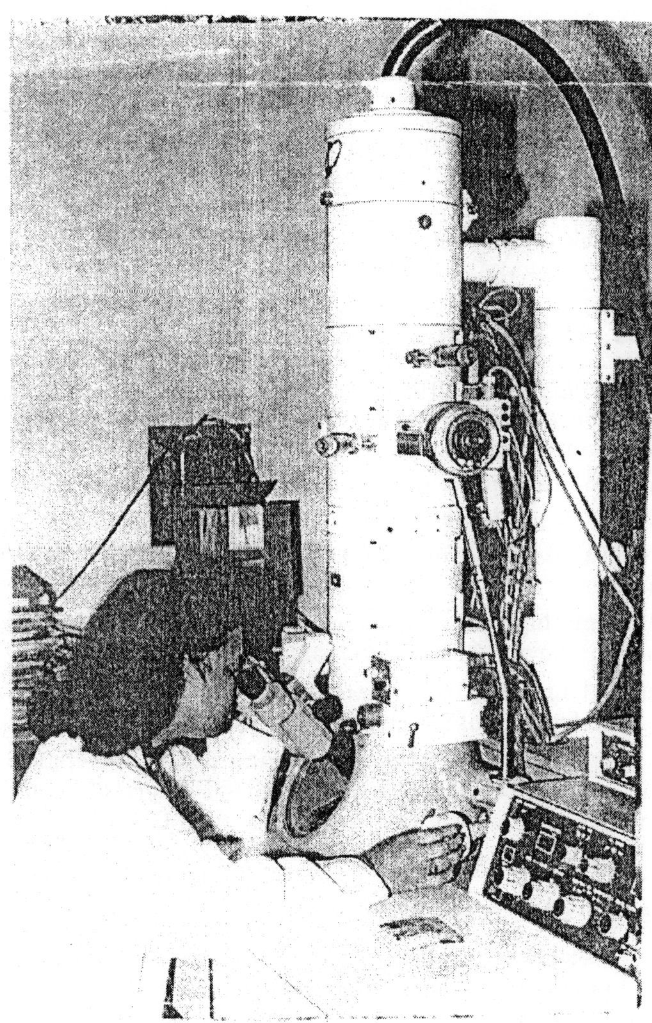

Fig. 10.2. Diagrammatic representation showing general morphology of Electron microscope.

Sectioning—In order to see any object through microscope, a common preparative technique is to cut (section) the specimen thinnest so as to observe it under light or electron microscope. Much thinnest section is cut by the microtome, an instrument similar to a butcher's meat slicer. A specimen is prepared for sectioning by placing it in a solution that kills and preserve (fix) it. The specimen is then dehydrated to remove water and embedded in a material (paraffin or plastic) that can be sectioned easily. Section may be cut with steel knives for light microscope but extremely sharp or diamond knives are needed to get thinnest section for electron microscopy.

Fixation—Different fixation agents are used for initial preservation and fixation of the specimen. Fixation is an important factor in microscopical observations.

Staining— Fixed specimens usually yield microscopical image of low contrast, therefore, stains are often employed for various structures. Light microscopical stains are usually dyes that impart various colours. In electron microscopy heavy metals are used as stains that decrease the ability of electrons to penetrate, thereby producing contrast.

It is important to know that object to be seen under EM must be dead and dehydrated for observation by transmission electron microscopy because they are observed in a vacuum, which is necessary for the beam of electrons. Specimens must also be very thin (0.1 μm thick or less) as electrons have a very low penetrating power through solid material.

❍ Advantages of Electron microscope

(1) Visualization of plant viruses on an electron microscope may be extremely useful for detecting previously unknown viruses occurring in diseased plant, even for which no antiserum is available.

(2) Electron microscopy is used for the tentative identification of known viruses based on size and shape.

(3) It is useful for determining serological relationships using virus-antibody combinations.

(4) Rapid EM methods can be used to monitor the steps in development of purification routines for newly discovered viruses.

(5) It is useful to verify the relative concentration of virus based on UV scans and peaks from density gradients.

(6) Virus particles, virus induced inclusion bodies, cytopathologies indicative of specific viral infections can be visualized directly in plant tissues prepared by a variety of techniques involving chemical or cryofixation, embedding and ultra thin sectioning.

❍ Principles of electron microscopy

Electron microscopy techniques for the diagnosis of viruses involve visualization of individual virus particles isolated from infected tissue. As known to us that viruses are macromolecules and are translucent to the electrons of EM and therefore they are invisible. In order to be visualized in the electron microscope, viruses and other biological structures must be made electron- dense by the attachment of heavy metal ions to deflect and scatter the electrons to create contrast and produce a visible image on a fluorescent screen or photographic negative. As the electron microscope image is produced by creating contrast by the selective addition of electron-dense metal ions, the process is referred as staining of specimen. When metal ions attach directly to the virus, they form a positive image when viewed.

❍ Negative staining

The usefulness of negative staining method was first discovered accidentally by C.E. Hall (1955). Hall reported that visibility of virus particles could be enhanced by surrounding the particles with electron-dense material rather than impregnating them. Negative staining of virus resulted in more realistic image and was quickly developed to be used in plant virus identification.

To visualize virus particles, the sample must be adhered to an electron microscope specimen grid which is usually a copper disc measuring 3 mm with a lattice work of holes. Such grids are produced in electron microscope laboratories or can be purchased ready made from the supplier's catalogs. The grid functions as support to the specimen much like the glass slide used in light microscope.

❍ Negative stains commonly used

Several different negative stains are used. For routine work, 1- 2% uranyl accetate (UA) is made in distilled water (pH-3.5-4.0). Most plant viruses are stable in UA and results in high resolution image giving good details about the morphology of the virus particles. However, UA should not be mixed directly with plant sap or with phosphate buffer because it causes precipitation of UA. Besides this, viruses incubated for too long time with UA tend to be positively stained. Phosphotungstic acid (PTA) is another negative stain. This stain works well at different pH levels with different buffers. However, this stain is known to cause artifacts. PTA is used as 1-2% solution made in phosphate buffer and pH is usually adjusted with NaOH. Ammonium molybdate (AM) used as stain is stable in light. It can be used with many buffers and works at different pH range (5-9). Image contrast with AM is less than the other stains. In immunologic electron microscopy AM is preferred.

❍ How to prepare the grid ?

In order to prepare the grid for viewing and for visualization of virus particles, the solution containing sample is allowed to incubate on a grid for several minutes. During this time the virus particles usually adhere to the carbon coated grid surfaces. The grid is now rinsed with distilled water and then is incubated with the staining solution for several minutes. After this, the grid is wicked dry with a wedge of filter paper and air dried before viewing. It is important to note that grid should not dry completely until the last step. To incubate the sample on the coated grid surface, drops of each solution are placed in wells of plastic micro well miniplates designed for tissue typing. Each well holds 10-20 μl of liquid. Now the grids are floated with the coated side down on top of the drops at each step.

The type of buffer used for extraction, morality and pH of the buffer, concentration of sample and the type of stain to be used must be determined to optimize host plant and virus combination.

❍ **Methods in Electron microscopy**

Different methods are commonly used in electron microscopic studies. Thes methods are leaf dip preparation, ISEM (Immunosorbent electron microscopy), trappin and decoration.

❍ Procedure for leaf dips preparation

(1) Grind an virus infected leaf, measuring about 2-3 mm in diameter over a clean glass slide in phosphate buffer (0.07M, pH 6.5).

(2) Place 10 μl of sap homogenate on parafilm or a waxed slide.

(3) Place an EM carbon-coated grid (film-slide downward) on the surface of the droplet, ensuring that the grid surface becomes wet. Incubate for 2-10 minutes at room temperature.

(4) Pick up the grid by its edge with the help of fine forceps and wash the grid from the filmed surface using continuous flow of 10-15 drops of double distilled water (DDW) to remove the sap.
(5) Add 2-4 drops of 2% uranyl acetate (UA) on the filmed surface of the grid carefully.
(6) Remove excess stain with a stripe of filter paper and allow the grid to dry.
(7) Observe the specimen under EM.

IMMUNOSORBENT ELECTRON MICROSCOPY (ISEM)

Immunosorbent electron microscopy (ISEM) is an important diagnostic technique developed by Derrick (1973). In this technique, an EM support film is first coated with antibodies which can trap the virus particles from a solution containing them. ISEM is used for two main purposes, (1) to trap comparatively large number of particles on the grid with less amount of host material, and (2) to detect individual viruses from a mixture of two or more viruses by decoration.

❍ Principles

The virus specific antibody is initially coated on the grids on which samples are mounted. The viruses present in the sample get trapped and concentrated in one place making it easy to visualize. If it is further treated with antiserum of related virus, the binding of antibody gives rise electron dence 'decoration' around the particles.

DECORATION IN ELECTRON MICROSCOPY

Decoration is the name of the phenomenon in which the virus particles are made visible by being absorbed to the film on the grid. Specific trapping requires treatment of the grid with antiserum by floating it on a drop of dilute virus antiserum as described below. The technique has greatly increased the sensitivity of electron microscopical detection of plant viruses. It may lead to a ten fold increase in number of virus particles on the grid and has been claimed to be as sensitive as local lesion assays. Additional decoration may be needed to prove the identity of the virus. Trapping may be insufficient when antiserum is used against a strain differing in serological differentiation index by more than three.

❍ Procedure for trapping

(1) Float the carbon coated grids as described earlier over a drop of 10 μl of antiserum diluted in phosphate buffer (1:1000) and incubate the grids for half an hour at 37C°.
(2) Wash the grids for 10-15 min. in phosphate buffer.
(3) Drain the grids and then place them over a drop of 10 μl of extract containing virus. Incubate them for 45 min. at room temperature.
(4) Remove the grids, wash with approximately 20 drops of double distilled water.
(5) Stain with 2-4 drops of 2% freshly prepared uranyl acetate solution.
(6) Drain the grid to dry and examine in EM at 20,000 magnifications.
(7) Count the number of particles from 10 different areas of the grid and compare with a grid prepared by leaf dip preparation.

❍ Procedure for decoration

(1) Repeat first four steps of the leaf dip preparation except that the washing at fourth step will be done in phosphate buffer.

(2) Again put the grid over specific antibodies for 30 minutes at room temperature.

(3) Wash the grid as done earlier with DDW and stain with 2% uranyl acetate solution and mount as earlier.

(4) Control will be same as with trapping procedure.

❍ Observations

In leaf dip preparation only a few particles may be visible and in trapping several particles will be seen. In decoration specific antibody halo around the virus particle will be clearly visible. The intensity of decoration depends on the concentration of appropriate antibodies in the antiserum.

11

VIROIDS AND PLANT DISEASES

✉ ***Structure and morphology, characteristic symptoms, replication in plant hosts, mode of transmission, cell to cell movement, classification of viroids, viroids and plant diseases, potato spindle tuber viroid disease, hop stunt viroid disease, citrus exocortis viroid disease, coconut cadang-cadang viroid disease, peach latent mosaic viroid disease , avocado sunblotch viroid disease , apple scar skin viroid disease and apple dapple viroid disease.***

VIROIDS AS PLANT PATHOGENS

Some of the diseases now known to be caused by viroids, have been known for many years. The causal agents of such diseases were viroids. However, nature and morphology of viroids were not described until 1971. Diener (1971) working with potato spindle tuber disease, observed that the causal agent of this disease was non-encapsidated RNA of low molecular weight. He called it viroid. Viroids are the smallest and the simplest known agents who cause infectious diseases to many plants producing symptoms identical to the viruses. Despite their smallest size (1.1-1.3 x 105 mol. weight) having 246-399 nucleotides, viroids are able to replicate in susceptible host plants. *Viroids are highly structured and circular in morphology, consisting of single stranded (ss) RNAs and lacking both the protein capsid and detectable messenger RNA activity.* Diener first used and described the term viroid as the pathogen of such disease. He explained the difference between the viroids and the viruses in following five fundamentals :

❍ Difference between vioids and viruses

1. Viroid as pathogen exists *in vitro* as un-encapsidated RNA. They are smallest

known agents, causing infectious diseases to several economically dicotyledonous and monocotyledonous plants.

2. Virus-like particles are not detectable in infected tissue.
3. The infectious RNA is of low molecular weight.
4. Despite its small size, the infectious RNA replicates autonomously and no helper virus is required.
5. The infectious RNA consists of a unique molecular species.

All the viroids discovered so far have been isolated from higher plants. More than two dozens viroids are now known and most of them cause economically important diseases to economic plants. Some common diseases incited by viroids are Potato spindle tuber viroid disease, Apple scar skin viroid disease, Peach latent mosaic viroid disease, Citrus exocortis viroid disease, and Coconut cadang cadang viroid disease.

❍ Structure and morphology

1. Viroids possess rather unusual properties for ss RNAs e.g. a pronounced resistance to digestion by ribonuclease and a highly cooperative thermal denaturation profile.
2. All known viroids are composed of ribonucleic acid of low molecular weight. All viroids lack protein coat and apparently exist as free RNA. Characteristically, viroids are composed of single stranded and circular RNAs that contain 246-399 unmodified nucleotides and lack any unusual 2', 5'-phosphodiester bonds or 2'- phosphate moieties.
3. They have been classified into two important families- Pospioviroidae and Avsunviroidae.
4. No virus like particles can be identified by EM in infected tissues. Viroids have some sequence similarities and about 27 distinct viroids have been recognized.
5. No viroids is known to code for a protein.

❍ Characteristic symptoms

1. Symptoms produced by viroids are similar to the symptoms incited by viruses. Symptoms produced by viroids are stunting, mottling, leaf distortion and necrosis.
2. Symptom expression is usually optimal at relatively higher temperatures that promote viroids replication.
3. Stunting and leaf epinasty (downward curling of leaf lamina resulting from unbalanced growth within the various cell layers) are often considered as the classic symptoms of viroids infection. Other commonly observed symptoms include vein clearing, veinal discoloration, necrosis and appearance of localized chlorotic or necrotic spots or mottling on the foliage.
4. Viroids infections are also observed accompanied by a number of cystopathic effects including chloroplast and cell wall abnormalities along with formation of membranous structures known as 'plasmalemmasomes' or 'paramural bodies' in the cytoplasm. Accumulation of electron-dense deposits in both chloroplast and cytoplasm can also be seen.

❍ Pathogenic to plants only

1. No any viroid is known to cause any disease in animals and human beings.

They cause diseases in plants. Only one or two base changes at specific sites of the viroids may be sufficicient to change the disease intensity.

2. Several viroids diseases of plants are of considerable importance, posing a potential threat to economic crops. Coconut cadang cadang disease has killed over 30 million palms in the Philippines since it was first recognized. Similarly many other viroids are causing considerable loss every year.
3. Viroids infection appear to cause no gross changes in host nucleic acid metabolism. They are highly resistant to heat and ultraviolet ionizing radiations.

❍ Replication in plant hosts

1. Viroids replication is believed to proceed via a 'rolling circle' mechanism involving the synthesis of a minus strand RNA template. Replication occurs in the nucleus (PSTVd and other members of the Ausunviridae). Viroids replicate by direct RNA copying in which all components required for viroids replication including RNA polymerase are provided by the pre-existing host nucleic acid synthesizing enzymes. A variety of multi-meric plus and minus strand viroids RNAs have been detected from infected cells.
2. Viroids replication may involve as many as six separate steps; that is, synthesis of multimeric (-) RNAs and (+) RNAs, cleavage of these multimeric RNAs and circularization of the resulting linear (-) RNA and (+) RNA monomers.

❍ Mode of transmission

1. All the viroids are mechanically and naturally transmissible from plants to plants. Many natural hosts of viroids are either vegetative propagated (potato and chrysanthemum) or plants that are subjected to repeated grafting or pruning operations (citrus, grapevine and many Prunus species). Potato spindle tuber viroid, Avocado Sun blotch viroid and Coleus blumei viroid can be vertically transmitted through pollen and/or true seed.
2. Commonly used techniques for experimental transmission of viroids include methods like standard leaf abrasion method, agro-inoculation method and agro-transformation method.
3. In razor slashing, phloem tissue in the petiole is inoculated via cuts made with a razor blade previously dipped in to the inoculums. *Potato spindle tuber viroid* and *Hop stunt viroid* have also been experimentally transmitted by agro-inoculation and agro-transformation techniques. In these techniques, a modified *Agrobacterium tumefaciens* Ti plasmid is used to introduce full length viroids c DNN into the potential host cell.

❍ Cell to cell movement

Viroids are known to move rapidly from cell to cell via plasmodesmata of the host plant but long distance movement is done through phloem. They are easily transmitted by sap, pollen and seed. However, no specific insect vector and no soil transmission have been reported.

CLASSIFICATION OF VIROIDS

Recently on the basis of nucleotide sequence features, it has been possible to devise a family/genus classification of viroids. Seventh Report on the International Committee on Taxonomy of Viruses proposed classification of viroids as described below:

Table 11.1 **Classification of viroids as proposed by R. Flores *et al.* (1998) in the 7th Report of the International Committee on Taxonomy of Viruses.**

Family	Genus	Species	Abbreviation	Nucleotides
Pospiviroidae	*Pospiviroids*	*Chrysanthem um stunt viroids*	CSVd	354-356
		Citrus exocortis viroid	CEVd	368-375
		Columnea latent viroid	CLVd	370-373
		Iresine viroid	IrVd	370
		Mexican papita viroid	MPVd	359-360
		Potato spindle tuber viroid	PSTVd	358-361
		Tomato apical stunt viroid	TASVd	360-363
		Tomato planta macho viroid	TPMVd	359-360
	Cocadviroids	*Citrus viroid IV*	CVd-IV	284
		Coconut cadang cadang viroid	CCCVd	246-247
		Coconut tinangaj viroids	CTiVd	254
		Hop latent viroid	HLV	256
	Hostuviroids	*Hop stunt viroid*	HSVd	294-303
	Apscaviroids	*Apple dimple fruit viroids*	ADFVd	306
		Apple scar skin viroid	ASSVd	329-334
		Australian grapevine viroid	AGVd	369
		Citrus bent leaf viroids	CBLVd	315, 318
		Citrus viroid III	CVd-III	294, 297
		Grapevine yellow speckle viroid 1	GYSVd 1	368-369

		Grapevine yellow speckle viroid 2	GYSVd 2	365
		Pear blister canker viroid	PBCVd	315
	Coleviroids	*Coleus blumei viroid 1*	CbVd1	248-251
		Coleus blumei viroid 2	CbVd2	301
		Coleus blumei viroid 3	CbVd3	361-364
Ausunviroidae	*Ausunviroids*	*Avocado sun blotch viroid*	ASBVd	246-251
	Pelamoviroids	*Chrysanthemum chlorotic mottle viroid*	CChMVd	398, 399
		Peach latent mosaic viroid	PLMVd	336-337

VIROIDS AND PLANT DISEASES

❍ Potato spindle tuber viroid disease

The disease is now widespread. The disease was first recorded in North America and Canada. It was also observed in Poland, former U.S.S.R., Turley and many Asian countries.

Symptoms. (1) Appearance of smaller leaflets with fluted margins and sharper angles between stems and petioles are usually observed. (2) The tubers become elongated with more eyes on the prominently developed surfaces. (3) Only fewer tubers are formed in infected plants. (4) On infected potato plants, rugosity and lateral twisting of leaflets along with progressive necrosis in the vascular tissues are observed. (5) Infected plants may remain stunted.

The causal viroid- *Potato spindle tuber viroid.* The viroid consists of a naked and single stranded RNA with out coat protein. The viroid contains 359 nucleotides covalently closed in circular molecules of 120 kDa. The viroid has been grouped with *Citrus exocortis viroid* and *Chrysanthemum stunt viroid.*

Disease cycle -The viroid is preserved in infected tubers which represent permanent source of infection. It is transmitted mechanically during tuber cutting for planting and by contact between diseased and healthy plants. In nature, the viroid is transmitted by seed and only by natural host. It may, however, infect tomato producing characteristic symptoms in some cultivars.

Management- Selection and production of healthy seed tubers is important measure to be practiced for the management of disease. Viroid free seed should be obtained from low temperature treatment and meristems tip culture.

❍ Hop stunt viroid disease

This disease is well known to occur in Japan.

Symptoms- Characteristic symptoms of the disease are yellowing and curling of upper leaves. As a result of the disease, internodes are shortened and plants usually remain stunted with characteristic smaller cones formation.

Causal viroids- *Hop stunt viroid*. The viroid consists of covalntly closed circular single stranded RNA genome composed of 297 nucleotides. In infective crude cucumber sap, the thermal inactivation point of the viroid is 84°C and longevity *in vitro* is 3 days at 4°C.

Disease cycle- The viroid is known to be preserved in infected hop plants. It is transmitted by propagative shoots when planted in new gardens. The disease is not seed and vector transmissible. However, it is known to be mechanically transmissible by sap inoculation.

Management- In order to manage the disease, infected planting stocks should be avoided to use as planting material in new garden.

❍ Citrus exocortis viroid disease

The disease is widespread in all citrus growing regions of the world, especially in countries like South America, Australia, North America and Northern America.

Symptoms -Virulent strain of the virus causes severe symptoms in plants grafted onto susceptible rootstocks. Main stem disorders are cracking, scaling and dropping of barks. Shoots of infected plants are found stunted with shortened internodes. Leaves are observed to be chlorotic. Usually all disorders occur in rapid sequence, resulting in necrosis and death of the infected rootstock tissues.

Causal viroids- *Citrus exocortis viroid.* It consists of ribonucleic acid without a protein coat. The RNA is single stranded, covalently closed and circular with a known sequence of 371 nucleotides. Thermal inactivation point is 90 to 100°C.

Host range- Natural hosts are sweet orange, lemon, mandarin, grapefruit, sour orange, lime, trifoliate orange and many other species of citrus. Experimental hosts are *Solanum tuberosum, Lycopersicon lycopersicum* and *Petunia hybrida* etc.

Disease cycle- The causal viroid is found permanently present in infected citrus and herbaceous hosts. It is transmitted by the infected plant sap, both with artificial inoculation and infected cutting tools. Primary mode of transmission is infected planting material. No insect vector is known.

Management- Healthy viroid free planting materials should be used in plantation. All tools should be disinfected by dipping into 10 to 15% NaOCl.

❍ Coconut cadang-cadang viroid disease

Coconut (*Cocos nucifera*) cadang-cadang disease is widespread in the Central Philippines. It causes massive coconut tree death, endangering its production. The latest report indicates that 30 million palm trees have been lost since the discovery of this disease.

Symptoms- Characteristic symptoms of the disease usually occur in all organs of the infected plants including the roots. A yellow-bronze colouration appears on the lower two third of fronds and small chlorotic spots gradually merge and form chlorotic mottle on the third and fourth fronds below the spear leaf. Nuts grow slowly and are deformed in morphology. Inflorescences become necrotic and sterile. In fected trees usually die in 8 to 16 years after the appearance of the symptoms.

Causal viroid - *Coconut cadang-cadang viroid.* The causal viroid consists of a circular or linear single stranded RNA occurring in monometric and diametric forms of 246 nucleotides. It has been reported that all sequenced isolates of the viroid have the same minimal nucleotide sequence.

Disease cycle- Coconut is the well known host of the virus. The natural mode of pathogenesis is not well known. The viroid is seed transmitted and also transmitted mechanically by some special procedure.

❍ Peach latent mosaic viroid disease

Peach latent mosaic viroid disease was first observed in France in peach cvs introduced from North America. Its etiology remained unknown for longer time. Flores *et al.* (1991) showed for the first time that the causal agent of the disease was a viroid. They proposed the name as peach latent mosaic viroid. The GF-305 peach seedlings (indicator plants) from which the viroid RNA was isolated, were experimentally infected with purified preparations of the viroid.

Symptoms- Leaves in infected trees were observed to develop more slowly. In due course, typical mosaic symptoms with characteristic vein banding were observed. The shoots were found to grow slowly with shortened internodes and delayed flowering and fruit ripening. Fruits remained smaller and distorted.

Causal viroids- *Peach latent mosaic viroid.*

Disease cycle- Peach is the natural and only viroid host. Other *Prunus* species are immune. In the GF-305 peach cv., the viroid can be detected in roots, leaves, young shoots, old branches and barks. Its seedlings were found to be excellent viroid indicator plants. *Myzus persicae* and possibly other aphids transmit the disease in peach orchards. However, the viroid has not been detected in seed. No proof exists of its mechanical transmission by pruning tools.

Management- Primary measures for prevention of infection include the use of viroid free planting materials. Besides, removal and destruction of infected trees, especially in young orchards should also be done.

❍ Avocado sunblotch viroid disease

The disease was first observed in California in 1928 and later in Florida. The disease is now known to occur is in countries where avocado (*Persea americana*) is grown. Such countries include Australia, Israel, Peru, South Africa, U.S.A. and Venczuela. This viroid usually infects only a few plants in the family -Lauraceae. Since beginning the cultivation of avocado in south Europe, regular inspections are done for detection and avoidance of the disease.

Symptoms- Different symptoms are known to occur on infected avocado stems. However, symptom-less infection are most frequently observed. Yellow streaks on green stems and branches are found as diagnostic symptoms. Red streaks on the fruits may also be observed. Infected fruits remain green up to maturity. The streaks usually become bright red on the fruits and then turn black or purple at maturity. Vein chlorosis and slight deformations on leaves may also be seen.

Causal viroid - *Avocadosun blotch viroid.*

Disease cycle- The pathogen survives naturally in infected avocado stems. The disease is seed transmissible. Infected seedlings from such seeds usually transmit the disease. The viroid is also graft transmissible. This viroid has been reported to be transmitted mechanically from avocado to avocado by a razor -slash technique that was also successful in transmitting it from infected fruit extract into healthy avocado plants. It has also been transmitted experimentally through pollen with bees as pollinators.

Management - Detection of the associated viroid is essential to be done. Detection can be done by graft transmission to healthy avocado seedlings or with the use of laboratory methods like PAGE and molecular hybridization using specific complementary DNA. Healthy plants should be chosen for seed, rootstocks and bud-wood sources.

❍ Apple scar skin viroid disease and apple dapple viroid disease

Apple scar skin and apple dapple were previously considered as two distinct viroids diseases; however, it is now known to be incited by homologous variants caused by a viroid. Both diseases were described in Canada, North America, Australia, Japan and Europe. Apple was the only known natural host of the disease; however, this viroid causes latent infection in many pear cultivars.

Symptoms- The characteristic symptoms of the disease are commonly seen as apple scar skin symptoms that appear on fruits about six weeks after fruit setting. This symptom spreads radically or irregularly on the fruit surfaces of the affected plants. As a result of the disease, fruit surfaces become corky in texture accompanied by an absence of natural fruit pigmentation. Such fruits may remain small that never reach to the maturity.

Causal viroids- *Apple scar skin viroid* and *Apple dapple viroid. Apple scar skin viroid* has also been detected by using a reverse transcription -polymerase chain reaction assay. A conserved 330 nucleotide sequence has been determined in the structure of this viroid.

Transmission- Sugar crab apple cvs are suitable indicators for rapid biological detection of these viroids. Both of these viroids are transmitted with vegetative plant parts. Apple seed is also infected. Presence of viroids in anthers, petals, receptacles, seed coats, cotyledons, embryos, leaves, barks and roots are sources of infection.

Management- The use of viroids free planting material is the main method for elimination of infection in apple production.

12

PHYTOPLASMA AND PLANT DISEASES

- ***Definition, general characteristics, differences between phytoplasmas and mycoplasmas; methods of detection - direct culture with media, indirect tests; molecular characteristics, serological characteristics, structural characteristics and genomics; phytoplasmas transmission, phytoplasmas pathogenesis, causation of diseases in plants, host range of phytoplasmas; identification of phytoplasmas ,phytoplasmas in cellular environments; nomenclature and classification, different groups of phytoplasmas- Aster yellows group, Peanut WB group, X-disease group, Coconut lethal yellows group, Pigeon pea witches'-broom group, Elm yellows group, Clover proliferation group, Ash yellows group, witches'-broom group, Apple proliferation group, rice yellow dwarf group, stolbur group, Mexican periwinkle virescence group, bermuda white leaf group, hibiscus witches'-broom group; unclassified phytoplasmas and some other Phytoplasma species; diseases incited by phytoplasmas-Aster yellows disease, papaya bunchy top disease, X-disease in peaches, strawberries leaf variegation, tomato yellows disease, purple-top disease of tomato, yellows diseases of monarda and echinacea,, potato purple-top wilt , grassy shoot disease of sugarcane, little leaf of eggplant, sandal spike disease, citrus greening disease, sesamum phyllody disease, , witches'-broom disease of bean, witches' broom diseases of red***

clover, stunt disease of bushes, prunus X disease, peach yellows disease, peach vein clearing disease, peach rosette disease, peach red suture disease, molieres disease, cherry decline disease, cherry blossom anomaly disease, cherry albino disease, Apricot chlorotic leaf roll disease, Some other phytoplasmal diseases - Witches' broom of Chinese jujube, marginal flavescence of potato and withes broom of potato disease.

PHYTOPLASMA AS PLANT PATHOGEN

Phytoplasmas are quite different from viruses, however, they produce symptoms like viruses. Therefore, brief description of phytoplasmas is essential.

Mycoplasmas are well known to cause diseases in human beings, animals and insects for many years; however, there association with the diseases of plants were reported only some years earlier. Mycoplasma like organisms, causing diseases in plants are called as phytoplasmas. In 1994, an article was published in the International Journal of Systematic Bacteriology that changed the trivial name of mycoplasma like organisms (MLOs) associated with the plant diseases to phytoplasma. Phytoplasmas are unique and intractable group of plant pathogens. They cause important diseases in a broad range of annual and perennial host plants. Phytoplasmas may be defined as under-

'Phytoplasmas are cell wall-less plant and insect pathogenic prokaryotes belonging to class mollicutes. They usually remain confined in the phloem tissues of the affected plants and are transmitted by grafting, dodder and insects but not by mechanical means. Characteristically, they are identical with or similar to the members of order-Mycoplasmatales and have been found to cause more than 75 distinct diseases in more than 200 plant species and a large number of arthropods.'

❍ General Characteristics

1. Symptoms produced by Phytoplasmas are yellowing and bronzing of foliage, growth abnormalities including proliferation of axillary shoots, shortening of internodes and reduction of leaf area and morphological change in floral parts resulting in sterility.
2. Gradual yellowing or reddening of leaves. Yellowing and characteristic phyllody and witches' broom appearance of infected plants are the distinguishing characters incited by phytoplasmas.
3. Phytoplasmas are known to remain restricted to the phloem sieve elements of infected plants where they are generally present in low concentration.
4. Pathogenicity of the phytoplasmas as causal pathogens has not been observed to be proved in accordance with the Koch's postulates.
5. Attempts to isolate and cultivate phytoplasmas (MLOs) on artificial nutrients media has been unsuccessful.
6. Phytoplasmas are known to be transmitted by grafting, dodder and insects but not by mechanical means.
7. Phytoplasmas are susceptible to tetracycline but not penicillin antibiotics.

8. Phytoplasmas have been extracted from host plants and from their vectors in pure form and from most of them antisera have been prepared.
9. Specific antibodies and DNA probes have become very useful in the detection and identification of phytoplasmas as pathogens.
10. Leafhoppers, plant hoppers and psyllids are important vectors responsible for the transmission of phytoplasmas.

❍ Differences between phytoplasmas and mycoplasmas.

1. Mycoplasmas usually cause diseases in insects, human beings and animals; however, phytoplasmas cause diseases in plants and in associated vectors.
2. Mycoplasma like organisms (MLOs) that are known to cause diseases in plants are called as phytoplasmas.
3. Phytoplasmas differ from mycoplasmas in that they are found inside the host cells. Most of the phytoplasmas cause yellowing or stunting of the host plants but few reduce growth of tissues.
4. Phytoplasmas are transmitted between plants by vectors such as plant hoppers and psyllids.
5. Phytoplasmas are associated with following abnormalties-

* Phytoplasmas cause gross changes in flower structure.
* They induce development of leaf like structures in plant inflorescences. Such abnormalities usually lead to the formation of phyllody.
* They induce leaf proliferation and witches brooms appearance in affected plants.

❍ Methods of detection

Phytoplasmas are obligate parasites in nature, having structural fragility. They are found in low numbers in infected plants. Thus, they can only be detected through an active effort employing highly specialized and specific tests. Such tests usually require skilled operator to perform and interpret results. Detection of phytoplasmas consist of two types of tests-

1. Direct culture with media- Direct culture requires the use of one or more complex nutritionally enriched media and carefully controlled environmental conditions. Even then, some strains are difficult to grow in culture without cells. Properly done, with appropriate positive and negative controls, direct culture testing offers the greatest security but is rather slow, usually requiring up to 28 days for completion.

2. Indirect tests- Indirect testing is done for measuring specific biochemical markers or other characteristics associated with phytoplasmas. There are many indirect tests of varying sensitivity and convenience. These tests include DNA fluorochrome staining, DNA probes, PCR, ELISA. Auto-radiography, immuno-fluorescenge and specific biochemical assays. Indirect tests are faster than direct culture methods; however, indirect tests are not yet so sensitive. Indirect tests usually offer two advantages over direct culture methods-

* Firstly, they can detect so-called non-cultivable phytoplasmal strains to which direct method can't be applied.
* Secondly, indirect methods are faster, usually taking only 1-5 days to complete.

DISTINGUISHING CHARACTERISTICS

❍ Molecular characteristics

Little information is available on the genetic architecture of the non-helical phytopathogenic mollicutes-the phytoplasmas. The genome size of several phytoplasmas have been determined that ranges from 530 to 1185 kb; however, very little is known about the genetic structure of phytoplasmas and genes involved in pathogenicity. Characteristically, G+C content of several phytoplasmas is at the lower end of the spectrum of different mollicutes. Phytoplasma genomes have been reported to contain rRNA genes, ribosomal protein genes, a tuf gene encoding the recognition factor and genes encoding a major membrane protein gene. Besides, the genome also contains an antigenic protein and nitro-reductase as reported. Extra-chromosomal DNA has been reported in some phytoplasmas; however, its role still remains speculative.

❍ Serological characteristics

1. The introduction of molecular methods for studying diseases incited by phytoplasmas has facilitated extraction of phytoplasmas from infected plant hosts and insect vectors.
2. Enriched extracts of phytoplasmas have been used as a source of immunogens to produce polyclonal or monoclonal antibodies against several phytoplasmas.
3. Production of monoclonals and polyclonals facilitated development of serological assays for pathogen detection and identification. Monoclonal antibodies have demonstrated promising results for serological detection and identification of phytoplasmas from broader range of host plants including woody perennials.
4. Monoclonals have also been found to be most suitable for differentiating very closely related strains.
5. It has been observed that phytoplasma enriched preparations may be utilized as a source of DNA for isolation and cloning. Cloned fragments of phytoplasma DNA have been widely employed as probes in dot hybridizations assays to detect and identify phytoplasmas. Southern hybridization in conjunction with restriction fragment length polymorphism (RFLP) analysis have enabled investigations of genetic relationships among phytoplasmas associated with similar hosts or with diseases with identical symptoms.
6. Serological techniques can also be used to identify protein antigens associated with phytoplasmas that may be important in how they function as pathogens.

❍ Structural characteristics and genomics

One of the major difficulties in working with phytoplasma is the inability to grow this organism in culture. All though phytoplasmas may retain their viability for several hours in phytoplasma-enriched extracts obtained from infected plants or insect vectors; however, genetic manipulation of these organisms may remain speculative as long as phytoplasmas are not cultured *in vitro*. Under such circumstances, due to their high sensitivity, polymerase chain reaction methods are well suited to the detection and identification of phytoplasmas. Only limited efforts have been made toward cloning and sequencing of Phytoplasma genes. However, it has been found that genomes of phytoplasmas consist of circular, 640 -1200 kb chromosome of low G+C content. Besides, phytoplasmas extra-chromosomal DNAs have revealed surprising sequence similarities with both plasmid of gram-positive bacteria and plant DNA viruses. Through the sequencing of ribosomal DNA, new phytoplasmas have been characterized. For example, phytoplasma known to induce a lethal disease in almond trees has been fully characterized by sequencing its 16 S rDNA. In addition to ribosomal sequences, tuf gene sequences have proved to provide relevant taxonomic information and have been used for better understanding of the taxonomic structure of *Aster yellows phytoplasma.*

❍ Phytoplasmas transmission

Phytoplasmas are obligate parasites in existence; therefore, they are completely dependent on their hosts for survival. They usually live in the phloem tissues of the host plants. Important peculiarities regarding transmission of phytoplasmas may be explained as under-

1. Phytoplasmas are known to move from diseased to healthy plants through insect vectors. In their insect vectors, phytoplasmas usually reproduce in the hemolymph before traveling to the salivary glands. They are then injected into the phloem of a host while the insect feeds upon them.
2. Phytoplasmas generally move from one locality to a new area by grafting, by planting infected cuttings, by dodders and by leaf hoppers. Leaf hoppers usually migrate from one place to the other annually, thus transmitting the phytoplasma disease from different localities and areas.
3. Transmission from infected to non infected hosts is also effected through dodder (*Cuscuta* species) that acts as a bridge between infected and non infected host plants.
4. Koch's postulates that consist of rules for proving the actual cause of a disease, has not yet been proved. It is because they are difficult to be cultivated on artificial media. However, Koch's postulates have been reported to be completed with a phytoplasma in poinsettia known to cause sought-after stunting and branch proliferation. Similarly, many phytoplasmas have been reported to be cultivatable; however, none have been repeatable. On account of this reason, transmission electron microscopy may be utilized to confirm PCR data relative to the success and mechanisms of transmission.
5. Although phytoplasmas are phloem limited and there is no direct connection with the developing embryo; however, it has been postulated that when phytoplasmas change the hormone balance in the plant, they are able to create direct vascular connection.
6. In addition to their importance in causing damage to crop plants, phytoplasmas are of interest because of their profound effects on morphology and physiology of their hosts. One group of phytoplasmas, referred to as the virescence agents, cause a wide range of symptoms which include phyllody (leaf-like flower petals), virescence (greening of normally pigmented floral organs),

proliferation (the development of shoots or flowers from adventitious meristems), stunting, stem elongation and seed sterility. Many of these host symptoms are similar to the responses that might be elicited by the exogenous application of plant growth substances.

7. One beet leafhopper transmitted phytoplasma has been demonstrated to induce flowering in plants grown under environmental conditions which do not permit non-inoculated control plants to flower (Golino, 1988). The nature of this host induction response (HIR) still remains to be determined.

❍ Phytoplasmas pathogenesis

As phytoplasmas can not be cultured under artificial conditions, therefore, they are difficult to be studied well. On account of this reason it is not clear how they induce diseases in plants. Keeping it in mind, a culturable plant pathogenic *Acholeplasma laidlawii* var. *granulum* known to be closely related with the phytoplasma has been selected as a model to investigate phytoplasmal pathogenicity. It has been observed that there exist two different forms of RNA polymerases (RNAPs) in this pathogen. One of it is not present in saprophytic types of *Acholeplasma laidlawii* or in other mycoplasmas not pathogenic to plants. It is thus supposed that the additional RNAP transcribes genes whose products are relevant for disease induction. Besides, there is also evidence that a fructose 1, 6-diphosphate-specific lectin is a product that plays a major role in pathogenicity. This lectin may mediate attachment of phytoplasmas to host membranes. Lectin seems to deregulate photosynthesis by binding of fructose 1,6-diphosphate. The depletion of this compound may cause uncontrolled synthesis of starch, leading to an enormous accumulation of this carbohydrate and the impairment of chloroplast function.

❍ Causation of diseases in plants

Phytoplasmas are well known to induce diseases in plants, causing considerable damage to the economic crop plants.

1. Aster yellows phytoplasmas have been reported to cause significant agronomic effects on a wide variety of crops including carrot, lettuce and barley. Similarly, they cause considerable damage to other crops like cucurbits, celery, onion and legumes. Besides, phytoplasmas have been found associated with slow decline of various shrubs and trees.
2. As most of the phytoplasmas have long incubation period, therefore, symptoms produced by them become evident after some years of infection. During such periods of disease appearance, the disease has already spread to many other trees of the orchards.
3. Disease symptoms vary between the species; however, the leaves show unusual yellowing or reddening and fall off prematurely leaving bare branches. The branches may be affected by die back from the tip, leading to the death of the plants. Once initial symptoms appear, plants seldom recover.
4. Diseases associated with the presence of phytoplasmas in phloem, typically exhibit an array of symptoms suggestive of profcund disturbances in the normal balance of plant hormones. Symptoms in such plants include sterility

of flowers, virescence (development of green flowers and loss of normal flower color), phyllody (development of floral parts into leafy structures), stunting and proliferation of axillary shoots.

5. Roots and crowns in affected plants are adversely affected.
6. Carbohydrate reserves are usually used for re-growth in the spring and after each cutting. Management practices such as cutting too frequently usually deplete carbohydrate reserves and lower stand persistence. Similarly, presence of phytoplasmas in the phloem of infected plants could affect the movement and available amount of carbohydrate reserves for the plant leading to reduced productivity and stand persistence.
7. The presence of phytoplasmas over several years in a field could also be partially responsible for the decline that often occurs as observed in alfalfa plantings over time.

❍ Host range of phytoplasmas

Phytoplasmas have been reported to cause severe diseases in food, fiber, industrial, vegetable, fruit trees and ornamental plants of economic importance. Interactions among phytoplasmas with their host plants and insect vectors play significant role in causation of diseases and their management. Biology and epidemiology of most of the phytoplasmas are not well understood. In addition to this distribution of these pathogens in the environment is clearly dependent on the movement and host selection of their insect vectors. Therefore, new vectors should be studies in relation to their movement in certain environment.

❍ Identification of phytoplasmas

There are different methods of identification of phytoplasmas. Some of the important methods may be summarized as under-

1. Preliminary identification can be made with staining methods. Two methods are well known that can be used to identify phytoplasmas. Such staining methods include DAPI method and Deines' staining method.
2. DAPI (4, 6-diamidino-2-phenylindole) is a nucleic acid-specific stain. It stains bacteria/phytoplasma present in the phloem of the infected plants; however, phytoplasmas that are stained by Dienes' stain usually metabolize and exhibit a blue colour. Healthy phloem remains free from such colouration.
3. There are some drawbacks in both of these methods of staining. Both of these stains are nonspecific. They lack specificity. However, Dienes' stain is more specific than DAPI.
4. Using microscopy, phytoplasmas can also be detected using scanning electron microscopy and more commonly the transmission electron microscopy.
5. Other detection methods include DNA probes, monoclonal and polyclonal antibodies and PCR.
6. There are currently 15 groups of phytoplasmas which have been distinguished by 16s rDNA RFLP analysis.
7. The use of the polymerase chain reaction (PCR) for amplification of ribosomal RNA and ribosomal protein gene sequences and the use of restriction fragment

length polymorphism (RFLP) and/ or sequence analysis of amplified DNAs are now widely used as standard methods for phytoplasmas identification.

❍ Phytoplasmas in cellular environments

Some of the most interesting aspects of the biology of phytoplasmas involve their limitation into phloem tissues of the infected plants and their transmission only by leafhoppers. They are never transmitted by any other insect vectors that are not phloem feeders. What limits these pathogens to remain in phloem, specifically to sieve cells is not well understood. Sites of phytoplasmas attachment with the insect vectors and interaction among host tissues, phytoplasmas and insect vectors are not yet well defined. In addition, molecular mechanisms found in leafhoppers but not in other insects including phloem feeding aphids are also important to be studied.

❍ Nomenclature and classification

Phytoplasmas have been placed under class- Mollicutes, order- Acholeplasmatales and family-Acholeplasmataceae. This family includes two genera *Acholeplasma* and *Phytoplasma* (plant yellows agents). Different groups of phytoplasmas may be summarized as under-

PHYTOPLASMA (PLANT YELLOWS AGENTS)

16 Sr 1 (Aster yellows group)

1. *Aconitum proliferation phytoplasma.*
2. *Alfalfa stunt phytoplasma.*
3. *Apricot chlorotic leafroll phytoplasma.*
4. *Aster yellows phytoplasma A.*
5. *Aster yellows phytoplasma B.*
6. *Aster yellows phytoplasma O.*
7. *Phaseolus vulgaris phytoplasma.*
8. *Blueberry stunt phytoplasma.*
9. *Candidatus phytoplasma japonicum.*
10. *Cherry little leaf phytoplasma.*
11. *Cirsium yellows phytoplasma.*
12. *Clover phyllody phytoplasma.*
13. *Cuban sugarcane yellow leaf phytoplasma.*
14. *Epilobium phyllody phytoplasma.*
15. *Gerbera jamesonii phytoplasma.*
16. *Ipomoea obscura witches broom phytoplasma.*
17. *Lactuca sativa witches'-broom phytoplasma.*
18. *Maize bushy stunt phytoplasma.*
19. *Marigold phyllody phytoplasma.*
20. *Mulberry dwarf phytoplasma.*
21. *Oat proliferation phytoplasma.*

22. *Onion yellows phytoplasma.*
23. *Paulownia witches'-broom phytoplasma.*
24. *Petunia flat stem phytoplasma.*
25. *Potato purple top phytoplasma.*
26. *Rose cv. Frisco phytoplasma.*
27. *Strawberry phylloid fruit phytoplasma.*
28. *Tomato big bud phytoplasma.*
29. *Valeriana yellows phytoplasma.*
30. *Phytoplasma sp. AY1.*
31. *Phytoplasma sp. DIV.*
32. *Phytoplasma sp. PY3.*

16Sr ll (Peanut WB group)

33. *Candidatus phytoplasma aurantifolia.*
34. *Faba bean phyllody phytoplasma.*
35. *Peanut witches'-broom phytoplasma.*
36. *Sweet potato witches'-broom phytoplasma.*

16Sr lll (X-disease group)

37. *Black locust witches'-broom phytoplasma.*
38. *Blueberry proliferation phytoplasma*
39. *Canadian peach X phytoplasma.*
40. *Chayote witches'-broom phytoplasma.*
41. *Choke cherry X phytoplasma.*
42. *Cirsium white leaf phytoplasma.*
43. *Clover yellow edge phytoplasma.*
44. *Dandelion virescence phytoplasma*
45. *Gaillardia phyllody phytoplasma.*
46. *Garlic decline phytoplasma.*
47. *Little peach phytoplasma.*
48. *Milkweed yellows phytoplasma.*
49. *Peach rosette phytoplasma.*
50. *Peach yellow leafroll phytoplasma.*
51. *Red suture phytoplasma.*
52. *Soybean veinal necrosis phytoplasma.*
53. *Strawberry leafy fruit phytoplasma.*
54. *Tsuwabuki witches'-broom phytoplasma.*
55. *Virginia grapevine yellows phytoplasmaVGYIII.*
56. *Walnut witches'-broom phytoplasma.*
57. *Western X phytoplasma*

16Sr IV (Coconut lethal yellows group)

58. *Carludovica palmata leaf yellowing phytoplasma.*

59. *Coconut lethal yellowing phytoplasma.*
60. *Texas Phoenix palm phytoplasma.*
61. *Yucatan coconut lethal decline phytoplasma.*
62. *Phytoplasma sp. LfY1-Guerrero.*
63. *Phytoplasma sp. LfY2(Alv2)-Guerrero.*
64. *Phytoplasma sp. LfY 4(MA3)-Oaxaca.*
65. *Phytoplasma sp. LfY 4(MA5)-Oaxaca.*
66. *Phytoplasma sp. LfY5(PE56)-Oaxaca.*
67. *Phytoplasma sp. LfY5(PE65)-Oaxaca.*

16Sr V (Elm yellows group)

68. *Alder yellows phytoplasma.*
69. *Candidatus phytoplasma ziziphi.*
70. *Cherry lethal yellows phytoplasma.*
71. *Elm yellows phytoplasma.*
72. *Flavescence doree phytoplasma.*
73. *Flavescence doree phytoplasma HD1.*
74. *Hemp dogbane yellows phytoplasma.*
75. *Jujube witches'-broom phytoplasma.*
76. *Nectarine yellows phytoplasma.*
77. *Peach yellows phytoplasma.*
78. *Rubus stunt phytoplasma.*
79. *Spartium witches'-broom phytoplasma.*
80. *Virginia creeper phytoplasma.*

16Sr VI (Clover proliferation group)

81. *Candidatus phytoplasma castaneae.*
82. *Centaurea solstitial is virescence phytoplasma.*
83. *Clover proliferation phytoplasma.*
84. *Potato witches'-broom phytoplasma.*

16Sr VII (Ash yellows group)

85. *Candidatus phytoplasma fraxini.*
86. *Erigeron witches'-broom phytoplasma.*

16Sr VIII (Loofah witches'-broom group)

87. *Loofah witches'-broom phytoplasma.*

16Sr IX (Pigeon pea witches'-broom group)

88. *Almond witches'-broom phytoplasma.*
89. *Candidatus Phytoplasma phoenicium.*
90. *Knautia arvensis phyllody phytoplasma.*
91. *Lactuca serriola phytoplasma.*
92. *Phaseolus lunatus phytoplasma.*
93. *Pigeon pea witches'-broom phytoplasma.*

16SrX (Apple proliferation group)

94. *Candidatus phytoplasma mali.*
95. *Candidatus phytoplasma prunorum.*
96. *Candidatus phytoplasma pyri.*
97. *Phytoplasma sp. 'ECA G32'.*

16SrXI (Rice yellow dwarf group)

98. *Rice yellow dwarf phytoplasma.*
99. *Sugarcane white leaf phytoplasma.*

16SrXII (Stolbur group)

100. *Buckland valley grapevine yellows phytoplasma.*
101. *Candidatus Phytoplasma australiense.*
102. *Lavender decline stolbur phytoplasma.*
103. *Papaya dieback phytoplasma.*
104. *Phormium yellow leaf phytoplasma.*
105. *Stolbur P3L phytoplasma.*
106. *Stolbur phytoplasma.*
107. *Stolbur SBR phytoplasma.*
108. *VK grapevine yellows phytoplasma.*

16Sr XIlI (Mexican periwinkle virescence group).

109. *Chinaberry yellows phytoplasma.*
110. *Mexican periwinkle virescence phytoplasma.*

16Sr XIV (Bermuda white leaf group)

111. *Bermuda grass white leaf phytoplasma.*
112. *Chinese Bermudagrass white leaf phytoplasma.*
113. *Date palm slow decline phytoplasma.*
114. *White tip die-back phytoplasma.*

16Sr XV (Hibiscus witches'-broom group)

115. *Candidatus phytoplasma brasiliense.*

❍ Unclassified phytoplasmas

1. Allocasuarina muelleriana' phytoplasma.
2. Fragaria multicipita phytoplasma.
3. Helichrysum bracteatum phytoplasma.
4. Momordica charantia phytoplasma.
5. Rehmannia glutinosa var. purpurea phytoplasma.
6. Vinca minor phytoplasma.
7. Alfalfa witches-broom phytoplasma.
8. Australian lucerne yellows phytoplasma.
9. Beet leafhopper transmitted virescence phytoplasma.
10. Bindweed yellows phytoplasma.

11. Black raspberry witches-broom phytoplasma.
12. Brinjal little leaf phytoplasma.
13. Cactus phytoplasma.
14. Martinez-SorianO-1999.
15. Cactus phytoplasma 'Martinez-Soriano 2001.
16. Cactus witches-broom phytoplasma.
17. Candidatus phytoplasma rhamni.
18. Carrot proliferation phytoplasma.
19. Cenchrus bunchy shoot phytoplasma.
20. Chinese pigeon pea witches-broom phytoplasma.
21. Chlorante-Aster yellows phytoplasma.
22. Cocky apple witches-broom phytoplasma.
23. Cosmos bippinatus phyllody phytoplasma.
24. Cuban Papaya phytoplasma.
25. Cynodon white leaf phytoplasma.
26. Elm phytoplasma 'Arlington Heights'.
27. Elm witches'-broom phytoplasma.
28. Ethiopian Gliricidia little leaf phytoplasma.
29. Florida Crotolaria witches'-broom phytoplasma.
30. Florida Pandanus decline phytoplasma.
31. Florida periwinkle virescence phytoplasma.
32. Florida periwinkle witches'-broom phytoplasma.
33. Florida pigeon pea witches'-broom phytoplasma.
34. Florida Rhynchosia little leaf phytoplasma.
35. Honduran Gliricidia little leaf phytoplasma.
36. Italian alfalfa witches-broom phytoplasma.
37. Kerala wilt disease phytoplasma.
38. Mexican coconut lethal decline phytoplasma.
39. Oenothera phytoplasma.
40. Oenothera phytoplasma 86-7.
41. Omani alfalfa witches'-broom phytoplasma.
42. Orange little leaf phytoplasma.
43. Palm lethal yellowing phytoplasma.
44. Periwinkle little leaf phytoplasma.
45. Petunia dwarf phytoplasma.
46. Picris echioides phyllody phytoplasma.
47. Picris echioides yellows phytoplasma.
48. Pigeon pea little leaf phytoplasma.
49. Poinsettia branch-inducing phytoplasma.
50. Protea spp. witches'-broom phytoplasma.

51. Prunus armeniaca phytoplasma.
52. Sorghum bunchy shoot phytoplasma.
53. Sorghum grassy shoot phytoplasma.
54. Sorghum grassy shoot phytoplasma variant I.
55. Sorghum grassy shoot phytoplasma variant II.
56. Spiraea stunt phytoplasma.
57. Strawberry green petal phytoplasma.
58. Strawberry lethal yellows phytoplasma.
59. Stylosanthes little leaf phytoplasma.
60. Sugarcane phytoplasma (uncharacterised).
61. Sugarcane phytoplasma type A.
62. Sugarcane phytoplasma type B.
63. Sugarcane phytoplasma type C.
64. Sugarcane phytoplasma type D.
65. Sugarcane phytoplasma type E.
66. Sugarcane phytoplasma type F.
67. Sugarcane phytoplasma type G.
68. Sugarcane phytoplasma type H.
69. Sugarcane phytoplasma type I.
70. Sugarcane phytoplasma type J.
71. Sugarcane Ramu stunt disease phytoplasma.
72. Sugarcane yellows phytoplasma type I.
73. Sunn-hemp phyllody phytoplasma.
74. Sunshine tree witches'-broom phytoplasma.
75. Sweet potato little leaf phytoplasma.
76. Vigna little leaf phytoplasma.
77. Weeping tea tree witches'-broom phytoplasma.

❍ Some other phytoplasma species

1. Phytoplasma sp. CWB.
2. Phytoplasma sp. Gph.
3. Phytoplasma sp. JWB-F.
4. Phytoplasma sp. JWB-G1.
5. Phytoplasma sp. JWB-G2.
6. Phytoplasma sp. JWB-Ko.
7. Phytoplasma sp. JWB-Ky.
8. Phytoplasma sp. pathovar mosaic-inducing.
9. Phytoplasma sp. PinP.
10. Phytoplasma sp. PY1.
11. Phytoplasma sp. PYCcwb.

12. Phytoplasma sp. SPLL-V4.
13. Phytoplasma sp. STRAWB1.
14. Phytoplasma sp. STRAWB2.
15. Phytoplasma sp. WDWB-K.

PHYTOPLASMA DISEASES IN PLANTS

❍ Aster yellows disease

Aster yellows disease is known to affect over 300 species of plants, including flowers, vegetables and weeds. Susceptible flowers include aster, chrysanthemum, cockscomb, coreopsis, cosmos, daisy, dianthus, echinacea (coneflower), gladiolus, marigold, petunia, and phlox. Susceptible vegetables include carrots, onions, potatoes, and tomatoes. Weeds like dandelions, plantain and thistle are also susceptible and can serve as a source of inoculum in home gardens.

Symptoms - Characteristic symptoms of the disease, usually varies from plant to plant. However, symptoms of aster yellows are more severe and appear more quickly during warm weather. The spread of aster yellows is worse in cool wet summers. Hot dry weather is not favorable for either the phytoplasma or the leafhopper. At low temperatures, plants may remain infected without symptom expression. The severity of the disease depends on the stage at which plants become infected and occurrence of the number of insect vectors that carry the organism. Characteristic symptoms of the disease may be observed as under-

1. Roots of the infected plants are bitter, stunted and deformed with characteristic tiny, hair-like roots developing all over the main root. Such plants may proliferate and produce secondary shoots, giving the plant a bushy appearance.
2. Yellowing of the upper parts of the plant along with yellowing of the foliage are the important characteristics of the disease. Carrots and marigolds can be severely affected by aster yellows. Leaves of infected carrots grow in tight bunches. The inner leaves are yellow and stunted; however, outer leaves usually turn rusty red to reddish purple. Leaves of infected marigolds usually remain small in morphology and yellow in colour.
3. Chlorosis and yellowing of the leaves may be observed while the veins of the infected plants remain characteristically green. Growth slows down and leaves may look smaller and more narrow than usual. Foliage is sometimes curled.
4. The symptoms of the disease will often differ depending upon what species is infected. For instance, carrot roots may be bitter and hairy while lettuce may show pink or tan spots and have twisted inner leaves.
5. Production of many spindled stems and/or flower stalks may be observed. Besides, conspicuous malformation of the flowers and flower parts including the petals may also be observed.
6. Diseased flowers are sterile and produce no seeds. Flowers often fail to develop colour, remain green and distorted. Flowers that are produced are often irregular, deformed and green.

Causal organism - *Aster yellows phytoplasma.*

Transmission- This phytoplasmal disease is transmitted by leaf hoppers. The six-spotted leafhopper is the main vector which transmits this phytoplasma.

Disease cycle - Aster yellows is primarily transmitted by insects called leafhoppers and through grafting. The phytoplasma survives during winter in perennial and biennial plants. In the spring, leafhoppers feed on infected plants and plant sap containing the phytoplasma is sucked into the leafhopper's body where multiplication of it takes place. Following an incubation period, the phytoplasma is transferred to healthy plants. When a leafhopper feeds on a plant infected with aster yellows it becomes infected with the phytoplasma and remains infected throughout its life. The phytoplasma multiplies and causes infection of the insect's salivary glands within one to three weeks. When the infected insects feed on healthy plants, they inject the phytoplasma containg sap into the plant phloem. Susceptible plants may exhibit symptoms in 10 to 40 days. As with many disease and pest problems, diagnosis is perhaps the most important factor in controlling aster yellows.

Management- Once a plant is infected with aster yellows, the disease becomes incurable. Early diagnosis and prompt removal of infected plants may help to reduce the spread of the disease. Controlling aster yellows is difficult. As long as infected leafhoppers are around, they can infect plants. A practical way to avoid having problems with this disease is to grow plants that are not susceptible to aster yellows. Verbena, salvia, nicotiana, geranium, cockscomb and impatiens are among the least susceptible plants. Vegetable growers may protect susceptible crops by using the mesh fabrics that keep leafhoppers and other insects away from the plants. Some growers put strips of aluminum foil between rows because bright reflections of sunlight confuse the leafhoppers. Remove weeds in lawn, garden and surrounding areas. Insecticides are generally not recommended for the control of leafhoppers in the home garden.

❍ Papaya bunchy top disease

Papaya bunchy top was first reported in Puerto Rico in 1931 It is now known to occur in most of the papaya growing areas especially Cuba southward to Trinidad. It is an important disease that causes considerable damage to the crop.

Symptoms - The disease is characterized by the appearance of faint mottling of the upper leaves. The laminae of infected leaves become chlorotic especially in interveinal areas and may exhibit marginal necrosis. Leaves and petioles show reduced growth and become rigid. Internodes become progressively shortened and petioles tend to assume a more horizontal position. Apical growth ultimately ceases with the shortening of internodes. As a result, bunchy top like appearance are seen. With the cessation of apical growth and decline of plant vigor, the oldest leaves progressively abscise, leaving fewer and stunted leaves at the top. Eventually, plants may be entirely killed; however, new shoots may sprout from the lower non affected portion of stems.

Causal organism - *Papaya bunchy top phytoplasma.*

Transmission- Two leafhoppers; namely, *Empoasca papayae* Oman and *Empoasca stevensi* Young are known to transmit papaya bunchy top agent. *Empoasca papayae* has most frequently been associated with the disease. *Empoasca papayae* has been reported as only leafhopper known to breed on papaya. *Empoasca stevensi* was originally described from specimens collected from papaya in Florida in 1940 but little is known about the ecology and distribution of this species.

Disease cycle - Single insect of both vector species is capable of transmitting bunchy top phytoplasma. Besides, it can also be transmitted by grafting. Symptoms usually begin to appear 30 to 45 days after inoculation. Phytoplasma as plant pathogen was observed to remain present in the phloem of infected plants using transmission electron microscopy. Infected plants treated with tetracycline-based antibiotics exhibited a remission of symptoms. Absence of latex flow from fresh puncture wounds in leaves, petioles, stems and fruits were considered to be diagnostic for bunchy top; however, a more recent study indicated that this technique is unreliable. The presence of phytoplasma in plants with foliar symptoms of bunchy top and normal latex flow was confirmed by electron microscopy. The DNA-binding fluorochrome, 4, 6-diamidino-2phenyl indole (DAPI), can be used to stain this phytoplasma in the phloem of numerous plant species, thus, making their presence detectable by epifluorescent microscopy. This technique has been used to detect phytoplasma in petiole and leaf vein tissue of papaya trees with bunchy top symptoms. The reliability of this method to diagnose bunchy top has not been established.

Management - Currently, the use of tolerant cultivars is the only practical means of control of bunchy top; however, it has limited application. Tolerant cultivars can only be grown commercially in locations with low disease pressure. Besides, application of insecticide to reduce the incidence of leafhopper vectors may be beneficial. Rouging of infected trees should also be done. Antibiotic therapy is an effective control measure from experimental standpoint but has not been applied commercially. Drenching the soil around infected plants with chlortetracycline or tetracycline hydrochloride and drenching combined with root dip treatments were both successful. The efficacy of foliar application or trunk injection has not been established.

❍ Phytoplasma X-disease in peaches

Phytoplasma X-disease has been diagnosed in several peach orchards worldwide. Once the disease is established in an area or orchard, it becomes difficult to manage it successfully. It becomes very destructive.

Symptoms - Characteristic symptoms of the disease on peach may be variable, depending upon the environment, variety and possibly other factors. However, once acquainted with general symptoms, it would not be difficult to diagnose the disease successfully. Characteristic symptoms are predominantly foliar but fruits may also be affected. This disease causes yellowing of leaves and curling upward. Characteristic red and water-soaked spots not limited by leaf veins may also be seebn frequently. The leaf disorder results in early defoliation of the oldest leaves, leaving a horse-tail appearance of young foliage at the end of affected terminal shoots. As a result of the disease, affected branches fall prematurely, starting at the base of the branch. Eventually, only a tuft of leaves remains at the tips of infected shoots. Fruit set on infected trees may appear normal at first; however, fruit on infected branches usually drop down prematurely.

Causal organism - *Peach X-disease phytoplasma*

Disease cycle - Peach X-disease often follows a 10-15- year cycle. The disease appears severely for 4 to 6 years and thereafter gradually disappears until the next cycle begins. Mixture of healthy and diseased branches on the same tree occurs primarily during the first and second years of infection. Two to three years after initial infection, most branches exhibit characteristic symptoms. The pathogen remains restricted into phloem and is transmitted by at least eight species of leafhoppers. They do not acquire the pathogen from diseased peaches because the population of the disease organism within diseased peach trees is so low that leafhoppers do not encounter the organisms while feeding. Leaf hoppers acquire the pathogen while sucking juices from the leaves. Wild chokecherry′is an important reservoir for the X-disease phytoplasma. A single infective insect therefore has the potential to infect numerous plants. Peach trees that become infected with X-disease are usually inoculated by leafhoppers during July and August and symptoms develop on the trees during the following year.

Control meausres – Remove infected trees near peach orchards and reduce the populations of leafhopper vectors for better management. Maintaining a vigorous insect control program from June through harvest with insecticides effective against leafhoppers should be useful in reducing spread of the disease.

❍ Strawberries leaf variegation or June yellows disease

Leaf variegation or June yellows in strawberries was first described as gold-striped and silver-striped as early as 1719. Various synonyms for the disorder are Blakemore yellows, spring yellows, chlorosis and non-infectious variegation.

Symptoms –Symptoms usually appear in the spring on new unfolding leaflets. Puckering and distortion may also be observed on leaves with a white streak type of variegation in early stages of the disease. Leaves of the infected plants become mottled, streaked or spotted with golden pale yellow-to-white and light green areas. A slight loss of plant vigor also accompanies the color change. Variegation has been observed only on the foliage and flowers but never on fruits. All runners and daughter plants produced by diseased plants are also variegated with no reversion to a normal green color. Affected plants never recover and usually die within two to three years.

Causual organism – *Strawberries leaf variegation phytoplasma.*

Disease cycle – No causal agent has been found associated with leaf variegation or June yellows. The disorder has not been transmitted by grafting or sap inoculation but can be transmitted sexually to seedlings of affected parents. The current theory is that leaf variegation is due to some entity within the strawberry host cells that acts like phytoplasma infection. Electron microscopy has not yet identified a virus or phytoplasma in diseased plants.

Control measures – Avoid propagation from variegated mother plants and never accept plants that show leaf variegation.

❍ Tomato yellow disease

Serious outbreak of tomato yellows have occured in southern British Columbia. After some years the disease became widespread throughout the Pacific coast region extending from British Columbia to Mexico.

Symptoms - Diseased plants are readily distinguishable in the field because they are rigid and have stiff brittle leaves that tend to roll inward along the midrib. Such leaves curve downward slightly and have a drooping but not wilting appearance. The veins are generally but not invariably purplish ; however, normal green leaves usually change to sulfur yellow in due course. As a result of the disease, the infected plant ceases to grow but fruits already formed do not enlarge. The pith dries out and the stem becomes hollow. Infected plants turn brown and die. Affected plants may recover somewhat but they never regain normal appearance. The small roots may become brown and decayed.

Causal organism - *Beet curly-top phytoplasma.*

Transmission - The disease is reported to be transmitted by beet leafhopper.

Management - In order to manage the disease, tomato crop should be grown separately from beets because the same phytoplasma is known as the causal agent of beet curly top. Besides, field sanitation should be maintained through good weed control.

❍ Purple-top disease of tomato

This disease is known to cause considerable damage to the crop.

Symptoms - Appearance of purplish tinge in the foliage is the most characteristic symptom of the disease. Such symptoms usually and particularly are apparent in the youngest leaves. Affected plants show an upright appearance because of slight hardening of the stem and leaf stalks. The leaves also show a tendency to roll slightly. Besides, considerable stunting of growth may also be observed.

Causal organism - *Aster yellows phytoplasma.*

Management - Purple-top disease is rarely serious enough to warrant specific control measures. Good weed control is always sound husbandry as it removes the sources of inoculum.

❍ Big bud disease of tomato

Symptoms - The characteristic symptoms of the disease are the malformation of fruit bearing shoots which look straight, thickened and dark green in morphology. Branching in affected plants is increased which gives the plant a witches' broom or rosette appearance. Calyx of the flower becomes enlarged, therefore they resemble like fruits. Fruits are dull coloured and hard. The flower buds stand erect, remain green and have sterile pollen.

The causal pathogen - *Tomato big bud phytoplasma.*

Disease cycle - The pathogen survives on its alternate host *Solanum nigrum.* It is known to be transmitted by the lead hoppers.

Management - Spraying of suitable insecticide for management of the insect vectors should be done. Diseased plants in the field should be root out and burnt immediately as soon as such plants are detected in the field.

❍ Yellows diseases of monarda and echinacea

Yellows diseases are the most important group of diseases spread by phytoplasmas. Phytoplasma causing the yellows diseases of Echinacea and monarda may be summarized as under.

Symptoms - Affected plants generally show leaf yellowing, reddening and stunting in the early stages of disease development. Yellowing symptoms are quite striking in appearance. Plants with yellows produce extremely numerous, small, branched axillary shoots coming from the stem nodes. It results into bunchy or witches'-broom appearance of the affected plants. In later stages of symptom development, infected flowers may change into vegetative leaf like structures, producing no seeds at all.Yellows can also reduce winter hardiness and kills affected plants.

Causal organism - *Yellows disease phytoplasma.*

Disease cycle - Phloem-feeding leafhoppers are responsible for transmission of this disease to healthy plants. Such leaf hoppers belong to Homoptera. These insects have a well-developed sensory system that enables them to reject unsuitable host plants without samping the sap. They usually transmit phytoplasma most efficiently to plants preferred for feeding. Leafhoppers feed on a variety of plants and can spread phytoplasma pathogens from wild to cultivated plants and *vice versa.* Infected biennial and perennial plants may allow phytoplasma to persist from one year to another in fields. Leafhoppers can survive through the winter as eggs and appear as early as May. The incidence of phyfoplasma diseases often depends upon the abundance and time of migration of leafhoppers from infested to healthy plants. Traditional field crops, such as alfalfa and potato may serve as symptomless carriers of phytoplasma pathogen. These plants also harbour adult leafhoppers which could transmit primary inoculum to adjacent plantings of specialty crops.

Management- An integrated strategy, focussing on both the pathogen and the vector must be followed for successful management of this phytoplasma disease in susceptible crops. Susceptible crops should not be planted close to the fields of forage legumes or other perennial crops affected by phytoplasma disease. Care should also be taken to control perennial weeds that may harbour phytoplasma and/or leafhoppers both in susceptible crops and in adjacent fields and around their margins. Suitable insecticides can be used to control leafhoppers in some situations. Besides, development of resistant cultivars is the most promising method of controlling phytoplasma diseases in plants.

❍ Potato purple-top wilt

This disease has been reported to occur in North America and is now known to occur in Europe and Asian countries. This disease has also been reported for the first time to occur in India where it causes considerableloss to the crop

Causal organism - *Potato purple-top wilt phytoplasm*a. It belongs to the aster yellows complex.

Symptoms - Apical leaves of the affected plants may appear pinched or curled, rolling inward and develop characteristic yellowish-purple pigments. Infected plants may lose their apical dominance and proliferation of the axillary buds may occur. As a result of the disease, plants may wilt and die prematurely. These plants commonly form hair sprouts. It has been suggested that primary symptom is purple top wilt and the haywire stage is due to secondary infection. Stunting, chlorosis and profuse axillary shoots with aerial tubers and swelling of nodes are also distinguishing symptoms of this disease. Some cultivars may develop only rolling but no colouration.

Disease cycle - Leafhopper - *Macrosteles fascifrons* and nymphs of *Alebroides nigroscutellatus (A. dravidanus)* have been found to be important vectors of this disease. Phytoplasma has been reported to be propagative in leafhopper - *Macrosteles fascifrons.* These vectors remain infective for life. Under natural conditions, potato purple-top wilt phytoplasma can be dispersed by its leafhopper vectors. Internationally, it could be carried in potato plants or in vector insects associated with them but such movement hardly occurs in practice. It should be stressed that aster yellows type phytoplasma are normally not tuber transmitted in potato. They are pleomorphic with a diameter up to 1000 nm. They occur mainly in the sieve tubes and can be seen there by electron microscopy or fluorescent detection methods. In India, nymphs of *Alebroides nigroscutellatus (A. dravidanus)* are better transmitters of the pathogen. The minimum acquisition access period is one hour and maximum transmission takes place with acquisition access period of three dyas. The phytoplasma needs 7 to 15 days of incubation period in the vector body as reported. One or a few infective vectors are required per plant for maximum transmission. Nymphs are more efficient than adults in transmitting the pathogen. Infected tubers seem to be the most important source of perennation and transmission.

Management- Manage the disease through control of vectors by use of suitable insecticide. Use of heathy seeds is also recommended.

❍ Grassy shoot disease of sugarcane

Grassy shoot, yellowing and white leaf (albinism) diseases of sugarcane is known to occur in India, Taiwan and Thailand. Grassy shoot was first noticed in India in 1919 in Maharashtra as a serious disease of sugarcane. It has been found in Andhra Pradesh, Tamil Nadu, Orissa, Bihar, Uttar Pradesh, Uttaranchal, Punjab and Rajasthan. Outside India, Grassy shoot is reported from Burma, Sri Lanka and Sudan.

Symptoms - The disease shows different types of symptoms at different stages of plant growth. Therefore, this disease has been variously described by different names like 'new chlorotic disease', 'albino disease', 'yellowing disease', 'bunchy disease' or 'leaf tuft' disease. Profuse tillering is the main symptom; therefore, name grassy shoot has been given to this disease. The most pronounced symptom is the grassy appearance of the affected stools. Shoots growing from diseased setts usually remain stunted and leaves are narrow and small like grasses. The canes are thin with short internodes that give the plant bunchy or grassy appearance to the clump. The leaves appear yellowish and in some cases may be entirely devoid of any pigment (white leaf or albinism). If many of the tillers are affected in this manner the entire stool characteristically dries. In secondary infection, leaves exhibit straight, long, white or light green or yellowish streaks. In systemically infected canes, the disease appears severely.

Causal organism - *Sugarcane grassy shoot phytoplasma.* The organism is present in the sieve tubes of the phloem as ovoid, spherical, or irregularly shaped bodies. The size of ovoid or spherical bodies is 300 to 400 nm in diameter and that of protruding filaments 30 to 50 nm in diameter. These cells are devoid of true cell wall and are bounded by a single triple layered membrane. They contain ribosomal granules and DNA strand.

Disease cycle- The grassy shoot phytoplasma perpetuates through diseased canes used for seed and spread through diseased sets and cane cutting knives (sap transmission). Ratooning of a diseased crop is an important source of perennation. Many aphids and a leafhopper have been reported to spread the pathogen from plant to plant in the field but only to a limited extent. The vectors are *Rhopalosiphum maidis (Aphis maidis), Aphis sacchari* and *Aphis indosacchari.* The minimum acquisition feed period is 34 seconds and inoculation feed period is 30 seconds. However, optimum acquisition feed period is 15 minutes. Transmission takes place in nonpersistent manner. Winged forms are more effective in spreading the disease in the standing crop. The disease has been transmitted from sugarcane to sorghum and from sorghum to sugarcane by using *Aphis sacchari (Melanaphis sacchari).* Sorghum is also a natural host of the phytoplasma.

Management - Healthy seed sets should be taken from a field where grassy shoot is not present even in traces. During the early stage of crop growth insect vectors can be controlled by weekly spraying of any suitable insecticide. Diseased clumps should be dug out and destroyed. Heat therapy has also been recommended. The sets should be kept in hot water at 50°C for two hours or in hot air at 54°C for eight hours. This treatment is feasible only for seed nurseries. Tetracycline antibiotics (250 ppm) applied to seed sets under negative pressure has been found to eliminate symptoms. Single bud sets can be treated with such antibiotics.

❍ Little leaf of eggplant

Little leaf of brinjal (*Solanum melongena*) is known to be found throughout India, Sri Lanka and probably in other neighbouring contries. In India, it was first reported from Coimbatore (Tamil Nadu). The disease has become a serious threat to the profitable cultivation of this vegetable crop in most of the states. When young plants are attacked they do not produce flowers and fruits, resulting in complete loss of the crop.

Symptoms - Characteristic symptoms of the disease are seen on whole plants. The main symptom is the production of very short leaves by the affected plant. The petioles are much reduced in size, therefore, the leaves appear sticking to the stem. Such leaves are narrow, soft, smooth and yellowish in colour. Newly formed leaves are also much reduced in size. The internodes of the stem are shortened and at the same time a large number of axillary buds are stimulated to grow into short branches with characteristic small leaves. This gives the whole plant a bushy appearance. As a result of the disease, such plants fail to form flowers. However, if flowers are formed they remain green. Fruiting is rare in most of the affected plants.

Causal organism - *Eggplant little leaf phytoplasma*

Disease cycle - In nature, Eggplant little leaf phytoplasma is transmitted by the vector *Cestius phycitis* or *Hishimonas phycitis.* The same phytoplasma also occurs on *Datura fastuosa and Vinca rosea.* Artificially, it is known to be transmitted to tomato, potato and tobacco. Probably, during the off-season of the brinjal crop the causal agent survives on weed hosts and from there it is transmitted to the main host by its insect vector.

Management- No effective control measures against the disease are known. However, antibiotic treatments with tetracyclines have been claimed to control the disease. In the absence of any definite control measure, eradication of weed hosts and diseased brinjal plants and control of insect vectors by insecticides are the only recommendations against the disease.

❍ Radish Phyllody

Symptoms- The disease is characterized by the symptoms that appear during flowering. All he floral parts are malformed in different ways. Sepals, petals and carpals of infected flowers of the plants exhibit characteristic phyllody appearance. Stamens are also malformed.

Causal pathogen- *Radish phyllody phytoplasma.*

Management- No specific control measures have been worked out so far.

❍ Sandal (*Santalum album L.*) spike disease

Sandal (*Santalurn album L.*) is an angiospermic semi-root parasite of many plant species which grows to the size of a tree. It is a perennial tree belonging to the f··nily Santalaceae. The heart wood of the tree is valuable owing to the presence of the fragrance oil and the wood is variably used. India has a monopoly in production and trade of sandal wood oil. Sandal (*Santalum album L.*) spike is a disease of great economic importance. Spike disease is the most destructive to this plant. It is a yellows type of disease with witches' broom effect. Trees of all ages and size are attacked and die within a few years of appearance of sysmptoms. The disease is most common in Karnataka but has also spread to parts of Tamil Nadu and Kerala.

Symptoms- Sandal (*Santalum album L.*) spike disease is characterized by the extreme reduction in size of leaves and internodes accompanied by stiffening of the leaves of the infected plants. Owing to the reduction in size of leaves and internodes, the whole shoot of the affected plant looks like 'spikes' inflorescence and the new shoots present the appearance of fine spike bearing four rows of fine bristles.

Generally two types of symptoms are produced. These are 'rosette spike' and 'pendulous spike'. The more common symptom is 'rosette spike', which is characterized by severe reduction in leaf size and shortening of the internodes. This results in crowding of leaves on the leaf bearing branches. The 'pendulous spike' is another characteristic symptom of this disease in which continuous apical growth of individual shoots without proportionate thickening of the shoot results in a drooping habit of the shoot.

Spiked plants do not bear flowers and fruits. Occasionally, phylloid or abortive flowers may develop in such plants. Spiked trees usually die with in 1-2 years, depending upon climatic conditions and age of the trees. Disease symptoms may appear initially on a new branch; however, other branches may remain healthy with flowers and fruits. *Vinca rosea* is the indicator plant of the pathogen.

Causal pathogen- *Sandal spike phytoplasma*. The pathogen has been reported to be present in phloem tissue of leaves, petioles, stems and roots. In cross section of the affected tissues, the pathogen appeared mostly as round bodies characteristic of phytoplasma, measuring 40-750 nm in diameter; however, some bodies were ovoid to ellipsoidal in shape as observed under Electron microscope. Typically, phytoplasmal bodies were devoid of cell walls and the cytoplasm was bound by a unit membrane, measuring 10-12 nm in thickness. The organism contained fibrillar network of DNA and ribosomal bodies. Presence of phytoplasmal pathogen with the host was not proved as per Koch's postulate due to lack of success in the *in vitro* cultivation and characterization of sandal spike *Phytoplasma*.

Transmission – The disease is known to be transmitted by insect vectors like *Moonia albimaculata* and *Jassus indicus.* Haustorial connections, grafting and dodder are other modes of transmission as reported.

Disease cycle – The spike disease is transmitted through root contacts and insect vectors. More than one species of leafhoppers seem to be involved in its transmission. These include *Nephotettix virescence* and *Moonia albimaculata*. The size of phytoplasma in the host ranges from 60 to 750 nm, the most commonly occuring form being ellipsoidal, measuring 180-220 × 250-300 nm in size. Some cells are elongated, measuring up to 750 × 150nm. The phytoplasma grows best at 30 to 38 °C as reported. Below and above this range the growth declines. The phytoplasma is reported to infect a large number of plant species such as *Eucalyptus grandis*, *Vinca resea*, *Zizyphus oenoplea*, *Dodonea viscose*, etc. The disease can be transmitted from *Vinca rosea* to sandal and *vice versa* through dodder.

Management – So far no specific measures for control of sandal spike disease have been developed. Like other plant diseases of phytoplasma etiology, sandal spike also show remission of symptoms after treatment with tetracycline. The systemic fungicide Benlate was also reported to bring about temporary remission of symptoms. Application of the antibiotic by the girdling method shows recovery of the trees 25 to 30 days after treatment with Terramycin alone or in combination with Benlate. However, these treatments result in only temporary relief for 50 to 150 days and then the disease reappears.

❍ Citrus greening disease

Citrus greening disease is a major cause of crop and tree loss in many parts of Asia and Africa. It is called by different names like yellow shoot (huang lung bin) in China ; likubin (decline) in Taiwan ; die back in India; leaf mottle in the Philippines; vein phloem degeneration in Indonesia and yellow branch, blotchy- mottle or greening in South Africa. Now it has became clear that all these were similar diseases. The name "greening" was widely adopted. In India, this is one of the most important and widely prevalent phytoplasmal diseases of citrus.

Symptoms – Symptoms can occur throughout the tree, especially if the infection occurs at or soon after propagation. If infection occurs later the symptoms and the causal organism are often partially confined. Infected trees or branches suffer heavy leaf drop followed by out-of-season flushing and blossoming with dieback occurring in severe cases. In general, leaf symptoms are of two types ; namely, the primary symptoms are characterized by yellowing of normal-sized leaves along the veins and sometimes by the development of a blotchy mottle. With secondary symptoms the leaves are small, upright, and show a variety of chlorotic patterns resembling those induced by zinc and iron deficiencies. Analysis of symptomatic leaves shows higher potassium content and lower calcium, mangnesium and zinc concentrations. Infected fruits remain small and have bitter taste, probably because of higher acidity and lowering of sugar. Many fruits usually fall prematurely while those that remain on the tree do not exhibit proper colouration. They remain green on the shaded side, hence the name greening has been given to this disease. Seeds in severely affected fruit are often abortive. Root systems are poorly developed with relatively few fibrous roots, possibly because of root starvation. New root growth is suppressed and the roots often start decaying form the rootlets.

Causal pathogen – *Citrus greening phytoplasma.*

Disease cycle – The pathogen is graft and psyllid vectors transmissible. Important vectors are *Trioza erytreae* and *Diaphorina citri.* Greening has been experimentally transmitted by doddar to periwinkle (*Catharanthus roseus*) in which it induced marked yellowing. As in its citrus hosts, African greening in periwinkle required temperatures 27 °C for symptom development, whereas the Asian form was more heat-tolerant. The dodder itself is a host for the greening pathogen as reported. Organism has been observed in the hemolymph and salivary glands of *Trioza erytreae.* Cytopathic studies have revealed the presence of pockets of necrotic phloem with characteristic abnormal cambial activity and starch accumulation in plasmids. Cytoplasmic membranes formed from invaginations of the plasmalemma, aberration of the cholorplast and mitochondrial collapse has also been observed. These changes indicate significant metabolic disturbances as a result of phytoplasmal infection.

Management- The production of greening-free trees is vital. Thermotherapy has been reported to be an effective measure for the management of this disease. Water saturated hot air treatment of graft wood at 48-58°C with no loss of tissue viability has been observed. Other attempts to eliminate Asian greening with heat have had varying degrees of success. In India, treatment of budwood at 47°C for 2 hours has been observed to reduce disease incidence to great extent. Treatment of infected young plants or seedlings budded with infected tissue at 38-40°C for three to four weeks also killed the pathogen. In South Africa, budwood from infected trees heated over hot water bath at 51°C for 1 hour, 49°C for 2 hours and 47°C for 4 hours have been found to eliminate the disease although some tissue viability was lost at the higher temperatures. Heat treatments have some application in the elimination of greening from horticulturally desirable trees, possibly in conjunction with shoot tip grafting. The association of prokaryotic organisms with greening prompted investigations into the use of antibiotics. In Philippines, antibiotics have been reported to suppress leaf symptoms with foliar spray of tetracycline hydrochloride and apparently eliminated greening. In India, immersion in a penicillin-carbendazin dip reportedly gave complete control of the disease. Spraynqs of agrimycin and carbendazin has also been reported. A derivative of tetracycline hydrochloride, N-pyrrolidinomethyl tetracycline (PMT) is more soluble in water, giving slightly better control of greening and causing no foliar phytotoxicity and minimal wood discoloration. As psylla are sap feeders, and so systemic insecticides are most effective. Weekly sprays of monocrotophos did not prevent infection, while high volume and mist blower applications destroy natural enemies of other citrus pests.

❍ Sesamum phyllody disease

This disease is quite common in sesamum growing areas. This disease was first reported as a graft transmissible disease in 1935.

Symptoms - Vein clearing of the leaves, phylloid flowers and stimulation of axillary buds are the characteristic symptoms of this disease. As a result of the disease, profused branching and reduction in leaf size may be observed. In affected plants, floral parts are transformed into green leaf like structures, causing complete sterility. Shortening of internodes are also observed.

Causal organism - *Sesamum phyllody phytoplasma.*

Disease cycle - This disease is graft transmissible and is also transmitted by leaf hopper- *Orosius albicinctus.* The incubation period of the pathogen in leafhoppers was found to be 15-63 days and 13-61 days in the host (Sesamum) depending upon the atmospheric conditions. Both male and female leaf hoppers were found to be equally infective. The disease could be transmitted through vectors or grafting to a number of plants of field crops, ornamentals and common weeds. Studies on the biology of the vectors showed that they can over winter at all the stages. They are also found to be present in nature throughout the year. The pathogen has a very wide host range. The important hosts are *Brassica campestris, Brassica rapa* and gram.

Management- The diseases are not important enough to merit any particular control measures. Late sowing of the crop may reduce the incidence of the disease..

❍ Elm yellows (Phloem necrosis)

Symptoms - Characteristic symptoms of elm yellows may be observed as yellowing and drooping of foliage of the affected plants followed by severe leaf drop and death of branches. Symptoms may appear at any time during the summer; however, characteristic symptoms most commonly occur in mid- to late summer. Susceptible trees usually exhibit symptoms over the entire tree with in few weeks but tolerant trees become stunted and may develop bunchy and prolific growth at the tips of branches or on the trunk. The inner bark tissues of infected trees often exhibit light brown discoloration in small streaks or flecks.

Causal organism - *Elm yellows phytoplasma.*

Disease cycle - The disease is believed to be spread by phloem-feeding insects as leafhoppers. The phytoplasma overwinters in infected tree roots and witches' brooms.

Management - The disease is not of major importance. No any control measure has yet been worked out

❍ Witches'-broom disease of bean

Although the disease is not of great importance; however, it is worth mentioning because it represents a different category of disease.

Symptoms - The disease is known to occur on beans and the characteristic symptoms may be observed as dwarfing of plants due to shortening of internodes. The infected plants produce extra shoots; therefore, they appear shooty and leafy. Petioles are borne at wide angles and flower peduncles are often elongated and wavy. The leaves may curl slightly and later become somewhat yellow in colour. As a result of the disease, pods setting are largely reduced. However, death of plants may not occur.

Causal organism - *Bean witches' broom phytoplasma.*

Disease cycle - Witches'broom phytoplasma may survive in perennial and biennial weeds and in eggs of infected leafhoppers in which they can propagate, passing through the eggs. Leafhoppers are the most important vectors that transmit the disease. Besides, the pathogen is also transmissible through grafting scions and by parasitic dodder plants.

Management - Control of leafhoppers by insecticides and removal of perennial and biennial weeds are important measures of disease management.

❍ Witches' broom diseases of red clover.

Symptoms - The disease is known to occur mainly in red clover. At first, a lot of small leaves usually appear from the center part of the plant. These leaves turn into reddish brown in colour. Original colour fades considerably. Infected plants gradually begin to rosette and wither.

Causal organism - *Red clover witches' broom phytoplasma.*

Disease cycle- The causal phytoplasma is known to survive on perennial and biennial weeds. The effective mode of transmission in nature is through leaf hoppers.

Management -For effective management, control of leafhoppers by the use of suitable insecticide and removal of perennial and biennial weeds are the key measures.

❍ Stunt disease of bushes

Symptoms - Characteristically, the disease causes stunting of bushes and reduction in size of leaves. Berries look smaller than normal. Leaf symptoms are the most characteristic to the disease diagnosis. Leaves of infected plants usually show downward cupping and yellowish margins. However, the normal green coloration of the leaves is usually retained along the midvein and lateral veins.

Causal organism - *Stunt disease phytoplasma.*

Disease cycle - Stunt disease of bushes is a serious disease caused by the phytoplasma. Almost all the cultivars are susceptible to the disease. Pathogen survives in infected bushes and is transmitted by the sharpnosed leafhopper- *Scaphytopius magdalensis.*

Management - Remove and burn infected bushes and replant disease-free stocks. The normal full-season insecticidal control program should be followed for blueberries to keep the leafhopper population under check.

❍ Prunus X disease

This disease is also known as Eastern peach X disease and Western peach X disease.

Symptoms - Symptoms of the disease usually appear six weeks after foliation. Characteristically, blotches develop across the leaf blades. Such blotches first appear as water-soaked which turn into red/yellow colouration in due course. Leaves of the infected plants may become chlorotic with upward rolled margins. Leaves become tattered as the blotches drop out. Affected leaves fall down prematurely leaving only small rosetted leaf tufts at the shoot tips. In early stage, symptoms remain limited to few branches and the disease progresses gradually. As a result of the disease, fruits may drop down soon after the appearance of symptoms. Undropped fruits produce shriveled seeds.

Causal organism - *Prunus X disease phytoplas*ma

Disease cycle- Leafhoppers are known to transmit the disease.

Management- The disease is not important enough to merit any particular control measurey.

❍ Peach yellows disease

Symptoms -The disease may be characterized by the leaves that are chlorotic, yellow and often rolled upward in appearance. Red spottings may also be observed when the leaves begin to droop. Severe infection may exhibit slender shoots with small, narrow, dwarfed and yellow leaves. Terminal dieback is common in one-year-old shoots. As a reslt of the disease, infected trees usually die with in 2 to 3 years following the appearance of symptoms. Fruits produced on infected plants are of poor quality and tend to reach maturity some three weeks earlier than normal.

Causal organism- *Peach yellows phytoplasma*

Disease cycle- The disease is known to be transmitted by leafhoppers.

Management- The diseases are not important enough to merit any particular control measure.

❍ Peach vein clearing disease

Symptoms - Mild chlorosis and partial rolling of the leaves may be observed as the characteristic symptoms of the disease. Vegetation is prolonged in autumn. In winter, bark became swollen and bud burst may be delayed from 6 to 8 days. The number of normal fruits is reduced; however, trees do not decline.

Causal organism - *Peach Vein clearing phytoplasma.*

Management - The diseases are not important enough to merit any particular control measure.

❍ Peach rosette disease

Symptoms - Characteristic symptoms usually develop quickly. The leaves usually reach to their normal size but become yellow and rolled inward. Veins of such leaves sometimes may appear red in colour followed by their defoliation. Internodes of new shoots are extremely short with leaves pressed into dense rosettes. Tufts of young leaves on the tips of bare shoots may also be seen as leaves on older parts of the trees have already fallen. As a result of the disease, blossoms rarely develop and the flowers do not set fruit on affected branches. Besides, most of the diseased trees may die within the first year of infection.

Causal organism - *Peach rosette phytoplasma.*

Management- The diseases are not important enough to merit any particular control measure.

❍ Peach red suture disease

Symptoms - Characteristic symptoms of the disease are generally attributed to a strain of *Peach yellows phytoplasma.* Fruits of affected trees mature and soften several days earlier than normal on their suture sides while their other sides remains green and hard. The suture side often becomes swollen and the flesh appears coarse and watery. Fruits may develop irregular colours. The suture side remains deeper red with purple areas at apex. Leaves of the affected plants usually exhibit yellowish-green or bronze colouration that can usually be observed after petal fall and before harvest. Foliages also develop characteristic coloration and two-year-old branches and buds may grow into spur-like outgrowths.

Causal organism - *Peach red suture disease phytoplasma.*

Management - The disease is not important enough to merit any particular control measure.'

❍ Little peach disease

Symptoms - Characteristic symptoms of the disease may be observed on the leaves of infected trees. Such leaves are distinctly greener than normal during the early part of the vegetation period. Proliferation on side branches and spurs of 2 to 3-year-old is also obserbed. Shoots are long and upright and branches of infected plants give the tree a bushy stature. Leaves are characteristically leathery and droop downwards. They may later become chloroitic. Symptoms first appear on one part of the tree and then spread to entire plant by the third year. Maturation of the small and malformed fruits is delayed. Flavor of affected fruits is advversly affected.

Causal organism - *Little peach disease phytoplasma.*

Management- The disease is not important enough to merit any particular control measure.

❍ Molieres disease

The disease has been reported to remain restricted in Southwestern France. It causes considerable damage to sweet cherry and European plum. All cherry cultivars and rootstocks appear susceptible; however, plum cultivars differ in susceptibility.

Symptoms - Initial symptoms of the disease usually appear as chlorotic leaves in summer. Small, deformed leaves, rosetting and poor lignification of young shoots as well as phloem and bark necrosis are found associated with the disease. In the following year, the trees bloom abundantly, though flowers are malformed and fruit setting remains poor. The few fruits if develop remain small. Fruits may drop prematurely. In new orchards, diseased trees are usually not observed until 3 to 7 years after planting.

Causal organism - *European stone fruit yellows phytoplasma.*

Management- The disease is not important enough to merit any particular control measure.

❍ Cherry decline disease

Symptoms. Characteristic symptoms may be observed in the form of leafy outgrowths or appearance of small protuberances along the midribs. Such symptoms usually appear on the lower surfaces of leaves. In some cases, only chlorotic areas are visible on the leaves. Additional symptoms may include narrow folded leaves, bud abortion, twig die back or terminal tufts of leaves. Fruits of black cherry may develop red spots with considerable yields decline. Necrotic symptoms may also appear on secondary roots. Besides, cankerous wounds and gummosis may be seen on branches of affected trees.

Causal organism. *Cherry decline disease phytoplasma.*

Management. The diseases are not important enough to merit any particular control measure.

❍ Cherry blossom anomaly disease

Symptoms. Leaf symptoms are similar to those of boron deficiency. Such leaves are elongated, narrow and curved inward. It may be accompanied by interveinal chlorosis. In older infections, leaves originate from terminal buds and form rosettes appearance at the tips of bare branches. Characteristically, white petals may exhibit varied amounts of green coloration starting from the midrib. Some petals appear leaf like and some flower buds look like leaf buds. However, yellow anthers may remain normal. Fruits developing from affected blossoms tend to remain pointed, having roughened skin.

Causal organism. *Cherry blossom anomaly phytoplasma.*

Management. The diseases are not important enough to merit any particular control measure.

❍ Cherry albino disease

Symptoms. The disease may be characterized by the leaves that roll inward and turn into golden bronze or olivebrown in colour. Colouring appears mostly along the main or secondary veins to form feathery patterns. Leaves produced from terminal buds in late summer usually form rosettes. Fruits from affected plants may remain small and fall down prematurely, assuming a light colour. In some cases, small white fruits may remain on the tree longer.

Causal organism. *Cherry albino disease phytoplasma.*

Management. The diseases are not important enough to merit any particular control measure.

❍ Apricot chlorotic leaf roll disease

Symptoms. Symptoms of this disease may vary in different susceptible young trees which become systematically infected. However, trees older than 5 years, may exhibit localized symptoms on the lower branches and spread to the crown. In either case, infected trees may not survive longer. Early bud opening and foliation are reliable symptoms. As a result of the disease, fruits remain undersized, sometimes bumpy and usually drop prematurely. The flesh of affected fruits may become brown in colour and spongy in texture near the pit. Necrosis may also develop in the bark which may become visible in transverse sections.

Causual organism. *European stone fruit chlorotic leaf roll phytoplasma.*

Management. The diseases are not important enough to merit any particular control measure.

❍ Some other phytoplasmal diseases

There are many other phytoplasmal diseases which are found associated with different plants. A partial list of some diseases may be summarized as under—

* *Witches' broom of Chinese jujube (Ziziphus jujuba* Mill.). This disease occurs most commonly in China and Korea. The causal agent has been confirmed to be a phytoplasma (Zhang *et al.* 1991, Zhu *et al.* 1988). The pathogen has been reported to be transmitted by a leaf hopper, *Hishimonoides chinensis.*
* *Marginal flavescence of potato disease.* This disease is prevalent in hills and the plateau area where cool weather prevails for a longer time during the crop season. The symptoms of marginal flavescence of potato disease include the appearance of chlorosis on the margins of upper leaves. Hairy root symptoms on tubers of 60 to 65 percent plants affected with this disease have been observed. The pathogen is leafhopper and graft transmitted. Five to 35 per cent tubers carry the pathogen and serve as a source of primary inoculum. Hot water treatment of tubers at 50°C for 10 to 15 minutes has been reported to eliminate the pathogen without adversely affecting the tubers (Sangar and Singh, 1985).
* *Withes broom of potato disease.* This disease causes extreme stunting of the plant and the production of numerous filamentous stems bearing simple leaves. The affected plants usually result in total loss of the plant produce because of very small tubers. The pathogen is leafhopper transmitted and perennates through tubers.

13

SPIROPLASMAS AND PLANT DISEASES

✉ ***Spiroplasma as mollicute, definition, general characteristics, distinguishing characteristics - biological properties, molecular properties, serological properties, taxonomy and classification, species, groups and strains of siroplasma, pathogenesis, transmission, symptoms, host range, some other peculiarities, plant diseases incited by spiroplasmas and RLO's.***

SPIROPLASMA AS PLANT PATHOGEN

Spiroplasmas differ significantly from viruses ; however, they produce symptoms identical to the plant viruses. In order to avoid confusion, it is desirable to know about spiroplasmas.

Spiroplasmas are wallless mollicutes that were discovered in 1972. Such microorganisms were observed to be helical in morphology and were envisioned by phase microscopy from sap of plants infected with corn stunt disease. In 1973, Davis and Worley, first coined the trivial term **'Spirop!asma'** for this helical, motile and filamentous mycoplasma-like organism that was found associated with corm (*Zea mays* L) stunt disease. A similar organism was further reported to be cultivated in certain laboratories of California and France. Of the unnamed spiroplasmas, only one (strain 277F) was readily cultivable. In 1975, two research groups achieved cultivation of the *Corn stunt spiroplasma*, but the cultured organism showed partial serological relationship with *Spiroplasma citri.* In 1975, cultivation of the *Corn stunt spiroplasma* in artificial media *in vitro* permitted conclusive evidence to be the causal agent of corn stunt disease.

After some time, a new spiroplasma genus *Spiroplasma kunkelii* was reported. By 1975, the close association of spiroplasmas with arthropod hosts was established. The causal spiroplasma was then reported to be able to cause pathology in some plant hosts also. However, in 1977 a link between spiroplasmas and arthropod disease was also established by Truman Clark's, working with a honeybee disease that had the ability to be lethal. When looking for the reservoir of these organisms, several different strains of spiroplasmas were detected on the surfaces of flowers. The first honeybee Spiroplasma- *Spiroplasma melliferum* and the first floral Spiroplasma-*Spiroplasma floricola* were described shortly thereafter.

Spiroplasmas are known to be present in the hemolymph of many insects and thus several million strains are known to occur. They can also cause diseases in plants, usually remaining associated with a insect vector. For example, a leafhopper carries a spiroplasma that infects orange trees. Morphologically, spiroplasmas are similar to the mycoplasmas as they do not have cell walls and have characteristic smallest genomes. Keeping in view important characteristics, Spiroplasma may be defined as under-

'Spiroplasmas may be defined as helical and filamentous mycoplasma-like organisms that exhibit characteristic chemotaxis, adherence to host cells, small size, high surface to volume ratio (for transfer of nutrients into the cell), cell wall-lessness, low G + C content of DNA (hypothesized to accumulate in host-dependent organisms), an evolutionary rate hypothesized to be higher than normal mutation rates and reduced biosynthetic capabilities that correlate well with life in host microhabitats that are transient, diverse and nutritionally rich'.

The spiroplasmas probably arose as gut symbionts in arthropods and later evolved to exploit emerging habitats within insects, ticks and animals. Radiation of the genus *Spiroplasma* (340 mya) coincides with the emergence of lineages of hemipteran (leafhopper) and insects that go through a complete metamorphosis.

❍ General Characteristics

Characterization of spiroplasmas requires the determination of morphological, biological and serological properties. Preliminary characterization of triply cloned *Spiroplasma* isolates involves microscopic observations of morphological characteristics. Darkfield microscopic observation allows for observation of motility and helicity. Electron microscopy reveals the lack of a cell wall and dimensions approximating 200 nm in width and a length ranging from 3-12 nm. General characteristics of *Spiroplasma* species may be summarized as under-

1. Spiroplasmas including phytoplasmas and rickettsia like organisms are considered to be causal agents of yellows diseases in plants. These organisms are filterable, therefore, were previously considered to be of virus origin.
2. Spiroplasmas are prokaryotic organisms and morphologically are identical with the members of order- Mycoplasmatales and Rickettsiales. Spiroplasmas have been placed in order- Mycoplasmatales.
3. Pleomorphic cells, varying in shape and helical in form, spiroplasmas lack true cell walls and are bounded by the triple layered membranes.
4. They are Gram positive in Gram reaction, requiring sterol for their growth.
5. They are attacked by viruses and like phytoplasmas they can be obtained

from infected plants and also from their insect vectors. Besides, they can be cultured on nutrient media.

6. Like bacteria they multiply by binary fission.
7. They are found confined to sieve tubes of phloem cells and are susceptible to tetracycline but not to penicillin.
8. They cause diseases like rice yellow dwarf, stubborn in citrus, stunt disease in corn and ornamental cactus.

Distinguishing Characteristics

❍ Biological properties

1. Spiroplasmas have the ability to be filtered through 220 nm pores membranes. They have ability to ferment glucose. They are resistant to 500 U of penicillin/ml.
2. They require cholesterol for growth. They are unable to hydrolyze urea. Variable characteristics include ability to hydrolyze arginine and optimal growth temperature. Despite all these different biological characteristics exhibited by Spiroplasmas, there is no single genus-specific property that distinguishes the Spiroplasmas from all other mollicutes.
3. Metabolically, some questions are still unanswered about *Spiroplasma* like nutritional uptake and energy metabolism, nutrient transport, DNA repair mechanisms, regulation of replication, transcription and translation.
4. Specific work is being continued through various experiments using genomic analysis which can give the answers how do mollicutes maintain cellular homeostasis; which genes are involved with pathogenesis; and how is the genome content organized.
5. All members of the genus *Spiroplasma* are obligately associated with insects (either as commensals, pathogens or mutualists) and may be one of the largest genera as a result of their diversification and co-evolution with their arthropod hosts. The Spiroplasmas display a combination of nutritional and microhabitat specializations and responses to ecological factors which are important determinants of diversity.
6. Spiroplasmas residing in arthropods are transmitted to plant surfaces by defecation and/or regurgitation of fluids on plant surfaces. They are introduced into the phloem by plant-sucking insects.
7. The majority of phylogenetic analyses conducted with members of the Mollicutes were based on the use of 16S rDNA sequence data. Using a large dataset and several of the available phylogenetic analysis programs, a very clear and consistent picture of *Spiroplasma* evolution has emerged, although there remain, some areas of low resolution which is thought to be due to recently diverged and, therefore, very closely related strains.
8. The phylogenetic analysis of the genus *Spiroplasma* was investigated using the 16S rDNA sequence analysis of 36 species, subgroups and strains. Several representatives from the genera Mycoplasma, Mesoplasma, Entomoplasma which were available on GenBank were combined with several single members from the genera *Ureaplasma, Phytoplasma, Acholeplasma, Anaeroplasma,*

Asteroplasma, Clostridium, Bacillus and *Escherichia* to establish a dataset to clearly provide outgroup support for the monophylly of the *Spiroplasma* clade and to show the close relationship between the Spiroplasmas and members of the Mycoplasma mycoides-Entomoplasma- Mesoplasma cluster.

9. Multiple phylogenetic analyses were performed on this dataset including neighbor joining, distance, maximum likelihood and parsimony analysis. These analyses make significant changes and greatly improve a preliminary UPGMA tree. The analysis revealed four main clusters that were monophyletic in all of the analyses. The representative tree indicated is that performed using Distance analysis.

❍ Molecular properties

G + C base composition, genome size and 16S rDNA sequence analysis are the basic molecular characteristics of Spiroplasmas. The only requirement for a new species description is the determination of G + C base composition (mol %). G + C base composition ranges from 24-31 % for Spiroplasmas and is performed using the melting temperature method. The genome size ranges from 940-2,240 kbp for *Spiroplasma* species.

❍ Serological properties

Currently the most important criterion in the characterization of new spiroplasma isolates is through the use of techniques to determine serological relatedness. The deformation test is universally used in *Spiroplasma* characterization. The deformation test screens new isolates against antisera to representatives of existing group strains. Isolates exhibiting a deformation test titer of greater than 1: 40 with established spiroplasma groups are considered candidates for subgroup status.

The metabolism inhibition (MI) test is usually the second serologic technique used. The MI test is more sensitive than the deformation test and is important in showing subgroup or serovar relationships. The growth inhibition and enzyme-linked immunosorbent assays are also occasionally used as a secondary serological assay after the deformation test has been performed.

TAXONOMY AND CLASSIFICATION

All available information provides a clear justification for understanding microbial host range and phylogeny when determining the evolutionary course of host-dependent microbes.

The use of comparative metabolism has also recently been explored as an additional means to determine the phylogenetic relationships among the different Mollicute genera. DNA sequence data alone may not definitively determine function. Many factors influence protein availability and function including: peptide folding (tertiary structure); peptide-peptide interactions (quarternary structure); substrate and cofactor concentrations and post translational modifications. These factors may cause the genotype and the phenotype to actually differ in an organism and must be considered when looking at the complex question of evolution.

Although microbiologists are more or less convinced that 16S rDNA sequencing yields reliable results, however, they are not prepared to base classifications solely on any single character. Rather, they prefer a total evidence or polyphasic approach that utilizes all the information available about a taxon. Polyphasic taxonomy utilizes different kinds of information (phenotypic, genotypic, and phylogenetic) and is essentially a consensus method that is coming into increased usage. Types of information used in bacterial polyphasic taxonomy include genotypic (rDNA-largely 16S-sequence homology, DNA-DNA hybridization, G+C content, DNA-based typing methods such as RFLP, plasmid analysis, codon usage, and PCR-based techniques) and phenotypic methods (morphological, physiological, and biochemical features) which may include cell wall composition, whole-cell protein analysis and serology. Many of these techniques have been applied in taxonomy of the Entomoplasmatales.

Spiroplasmas have been well documented in a wide range of hosts and as the causative agent of several plant and insect diseases. One major area of research is the continued identification and taxonomical characterization of new *Spiroplasma* species combined with a determination of phylogenetic relationships among the various Spiroplasma species and between the spiroplasmas and other members of the Mollicutes and Eubacteria.

Taxonomically, spiroplasmas are in the Domain Bacteria, Phylum Firmicutes, Class Mollicutes and Order Entomoplasmatales. The Order Entomoplasmatales is split into two families, one containing the Entomoplasmas and Mesoplasmas and the other containing the Spiroplasmas. Thus, *Spiroplasma* may be classified as under :

Class- Mollicutes

Order-Entomoplasmatales.

Family-Spiroplasmataceae.

Genus - *Spiroplasma* (type genus).

Table 13.1 Showing species, groups and strains of *Spiroplasma*

Species	Groups	Strains
Spiroplasma citri (type species)	Group I-1.	Type strain: R8A2
Spiroplasma melliferum	Group 1-2.	Type strain: BC-3
Spiroplasma kunkelii	Group 1-3.	Type strain: E275
Spiroplasma insolitum	Group 1~6.	Type strain: M55
Spiroplasma phoeniceum	Group 1-8.	Type strain: P40
Spiroplasma poulsonii	Group II.	Type strain: DW-1
Spiroplasma floricola	Group III.	Type strain: OBMG
Spiroplasma apis	Group IV.	Type strain: B31
Spiroplasma mirum	Group V.	Type strain: SMCA
Spiropiasma ixodetis	Group VI.	Type strain: Y32
Spiroplasma monobiae	Group VII.	Type strain: MQ-1
Spiroplasma syrphidicola	GroupVIII-1.	Type strain: EA-1
Spiroplasma chrysopicola	GroupVIII-2.	Type strain: DF-1
Spiroplasma clarkii	Group IX.	Type strain: CN-5
Spiroplasma culicicola	Group X.	Type strain: AES-1

Spiroplasma velocicrescens	Group XI.	Type strain: MQ-4
Spiroplasma diabroticae	Group XII	Type strain: DU-1
Spiroplasma saubaudiense	Group XIII.	Type strain: AR-1343
Spiroplasma corruscae	Group XIV	Type strain: EC-1
Spiroplasrna cantharicola	GroupXVI-1.	Type strain: CC-1
Spiroplasma turonicum	Group XVII.	Type strain: TAB4c
Spiroplasma litorale	Group XVIII.	Type strain: TN-1
Spiroplasma lampyridicola	Group XIX.	Type strain: PUP-1
Spiroplasma leptinotarsae	Group XX.	Type strain: LD-1
Spiroplasma taiwanense	Group XXII	Type strain: CT-1
Spiroplasma gladiatoris	Group XXIII.	Type strain: TG-1
Spiroplasma chinense	Group XXIV	Type strain: CCH
Spiroplasma diminutum	Group XXV	Type strain: CUAS-1
Spiroplasma alleghenense	Group XXVI.	Type strain: PLHS-1
Spiroplasma lineolae	Group XXVII.	Type strain: TALS-1
Spiroplasma platyhelix	Group XXVIII.	Type strain: PALS-1
Spiropla'sma montanense	Group XXXI.	Type strain: HYOS-1
Spiroplasma helicoides	Group XXXII.	Type strain: TABS-1
Spiroplasma tabanidicola	Group XXXIII.	Type strain: TAUS-1

Table 13.2 Showing genus-*Spiroplasma* species belonging to unnamed groups

Spiroplasma species	Group 1-4.	Type strain: 277 F
Spiroplasma species	Group 1-5	Type strain: LB-12
Spiroplasma species	Group 1-7.	Type strain: N525
Spiroplasma species	Group VIII-3.	Type strain: TAAS-1
Spiroplasma species	Group XV	Type strain: 1-25
Spiroplasma species	Group XVI-2.	Type strain: CB-1
Spiroplasma species	Group XVI-3.	Type strain: AR-1357
Spiroplasma species	Group XXI.	Type strain: W-115
Spiroplasma species	Group XXIX.	Type strain: TIUS-1
Spiroplasma species	Group XXX.	Type strain: BIUS-1
Spiroplasma species	Group XXXIV	Type strain: B1901

❍ Pathogenesis

Spiroplasmas established a vast array of interactions with plants and insects, ranging from epiphytic, symbiotic to pathogenic. Some important features of pathogenesis in *Spiroplasma* species may be summarized as under-

1. Spiroplasmas exhibit different types of interactions with their insect and plant hosts ranging from pathogenic to mutual relationships. Some *Spiroplasma* species do not replicate in insects and are found on flower

surfaces or insect intestines. However, some other *Spiroplasma* species replicate in insects, thereby causing diseases in insects.

2. Three *Spiroplasma* species are known to be transmitted to plants by leafhoppers and replicate in the phloem tissue of plants.
3. A fourth type of *Spiroplasma* species is transmitted to next generation insects through the embryo and kill the male progeny in the female insect. Such types of *Phytoplasma* species are called as sex ration organisms (SRO). At last, *Spiroplasma mirum* isolated from rabbit ticks is shown to infect rabbits when artificially injected ; however, the infection has never occurred in nature.
4. Though mollicutes are common as pathogens of plants, they are found even more frequently in insects and other arthropods. Some spiroplasmas cause disease in their arthropod hosts; however, most insects and mollicutes seem to share symbiotic or mutually non-detrimental co-existence. Such relationships between plant pathogens and the insects that serve as their vectors may reflect a long period of co-evolution of the two species.
5. The physical and physiological factors that determine whether a non phytopathogenic spiroplasma is able to penetrate the insect's intestine wall and colonize the hemolymph may also determine whether phytopathogenic mollicutes are transmissible by a certain insect.
6. The three plant pathogenic *Spiroplasma* species like *Spiroplasma kunkelii* (corn stunt spiroplasma or CSS), *Spiroplasma citri* (citrus stubborn spiroplasma), and *Spiroplasma phoeniceum* are transmitted by leafhoppers from plant to plant.
7. In insects, spiroplasmas are likely to adhere to receptors on the apical plasmalemma of the leafhopper gut and are absorbed by gut epithelial cells. After migrating through the cell, they are released into the space between the basal plasmalemma and the basal lamina and from there, move to the hemolymph where they circulate and replicate. Spiroplasmas move from the hemolymph into the salivary ducts and saliva through cell layers of the salivary glands. With the saliva, spiroplasmas are introduced into the phloem of plant by feeding leafhoppers. The latent period in the insect is at least two weeks.
8. In order to maintain themselves in their host organisms (regardless of strict or general specificity), spiroplasmas must have the ability to bind to the insect epithelial cells to avoid being flushed through the digestive tract. In many cases this is the extent of attachment. In order to become pathogenic, the spiroplasma must be able to invade into the hemolymph.

❍ Transmission

Transmission of spiroplasmas to plants occurs when leafhoppers feed from plant phloem. They are introduced into the phloem through insect saliva. In plants, spiroplasmas remain restricted to phloem tissues and systemically spread throughout the plant. Insect-transmitted plant-pathogenic spiroplasmas are not transmitted via plant seeds and are not transovarially transmitted to next-generation leafhoppers. Therefore, they cannot survive outside their hosts and are dependent upon transmission for survival and dispersal. However, the molecular and genetic mechanisms underlying the diverse interactions between plant pathogenic spiroplasmas and their plant or insect hosts remain unknown.

❍ Symptoms

Spiroplasmas cause severe symptoms, such as stunting, yellowing of leaves and yield losses in a variety of economically important crops.

❍ Host range

Most common hosts for spiroplasmas are the arthropods.

1. Spiroplasmas are found most commonly in the guts of insects as part of the normal gut flora but some pathogens can enter the hemocoel and other organs such as the salivary glands, ovaries and brain cells.
2. Initial isolation attempts of *Spiroplasma* species from their insect hosts may be difficult as many new isolates often require a transitional period with insect cell co-culture or preliminary anaerobic isolation prior to adaptation to artificial media under aerobic conditions.
3. Thus, spiroplasmas have predominantly been isolated from the six most evolutionarily advanced orders of insects although one *Spiroplasma* species strain PALS-1, was isolated from a dragon fly (*Pachydiplax longipennis*) which belongs to a more ancient order of insects (Odonata). However, since the dragon fly is predaceous on other insects, the isolate might have been transmitted during a feeding.
4. The six main orders of insects serving as *Spiroplasma* species hosts include:
   - Hymenoptera with spiroplasma isolates from honeybees, bees, and vespid wasps.
   - Coleoptera with spiroplasmas isolated from a variety of beetles including the green June beetle, soldier beetle, cucumber beetle, colorado potato beetle, scarabaeid beetle and firefly beetles.
   - Diptera with spiroplasmas isolated from syrphid flies, mosquitoes, tabanids, and fruit flies.
   - Lepidoptera with isolates from butterflies and moths (in both larval and adult stages).
   - Homoptera with spiroplasmas isolated from leafhoppers.
   - Hemiptera with isolates from the green leaf bug.
5. Although spiroplasmas are always associated with an insect or tick host at some point, several primary isolations have also been made from plants (both internally and from the surface).
6. Spiroplasmas were isolated from both the surfaces of flowers and the sap in the sieve tube elements of phloem.
7. As many insects feed primarily on nectar it has been suggested that the spiroplasmas found on flower surfaces were deposited there by feeding insects and thus serves as an excellent agent for transmission. Those isolates from the sieve tube elements were deposited there by plant sucking hemipterans e.g. leafhoppers.

SOME OTHER PECULIARITIES

1. Unusual sex-ratio disorders - A third type of pathogenic spiroplasma is transmitted to next generation insects through the embryo (transovarial transmission) and kills the male progeny in the female insect. This group of organisms is therefore referred to as sex ratio organisms (SROs).

2. Spiroplasma infections of animals - Only one *Spiroplasma* species *Spiroplasma mirum* strain SMCA (isolated from rabbit ticks), has been shown to infect animals. Early passage SMCA produced cataracts in suckling mice and rats when artificially infected in pathogenicity tests. The strain was also found to be pathogenic for 7 -day-old chick embryos. It is important to note that these pathologies have never been observed in nature.

3. Spiroplasmas and Jakob disease - Recent studies indicate a correlation between *Spiroplasma* infections and transmissible spongiform encephalopathies (TSE) in humans and animals.

4. Commensalistic relationships - Most spiroplasmas are currently classified as commensals in their arthropod hosts. These organisms attach to the epithelial cells of the host midgut and do not invade into the hemocoel or other tissues of the host insect.

5. Host interactions: mutualistic relationships- Although the majority of symbiotic relationships that exist between spiroplasmas and their hosts either fall into the category of pathogenic or commensalistic relationships. However, there is some evidence for the existence of mutualistic relationships as well. Plant-pathogenic mollicutes can be a mutually beneficial symbiont of leafhopper hosts. In efficient vector systems, infections with these mollicutes improve leafhopper fitness whereas in inefficient vector systems, infections result in virulent pathogenicity.

6. Detrimental effects -Differences in association can in part be explained ecologically. It has been observed that more ancient associations of spiroplasmas with their host organisms have less detrimental effects than relatively recent ones.

7. Serological tests - At least two serological tests are required to be performed to demonstrate the uniqueness of the candidate taxon. Growth inhibition was originally a technique of choice and was used for characterization of groups. This technique is based on the diffusion of specific antibody from a sensitivity disk placed on the surface of an agar plate that had been inoculated with the culture being tested.

PLANT DISEASES INCITED BY SPIROPLASMAS

❍ Corn stunt disease

The disease has been reported to be caused by *Spiroplasma* species that differs phenotypically from other bacteria by their minute size and lack of a cell wall. The disease is transmitted to a plant when the vector, the corn leafhopper (*Dalbulus maidis*), feeds from the plant phloem. The corn stunt pathogen is introduced into a healthy plant with the insect saliva. In the plant, the pathogen remains restricted to the phloem but spreads throughout the plant infecting all areas. *Corn stunt spiroplasma* was the first studied *Spiroplasma*. It was characterized by its helical shaped and being motile prokaryotic organism. This prokaryote lacks true cell wall and belongs to the genus *Spiroplasma*. *Corn stunt spiroplasma* cells measure about 0.15-0.2 micrometers in diameter and 2.0 to 15.0 micrometers in length. Sequencing of the approximately 1.6 Mb genome of *Spiroplasma kunkelii* was initiated in order to understand the genetic basis of spiroplasma interactions with their plant and leafhopper hosts. In total, 144712 nucleotides of non-redundant, high-quality *Spiroplasma kunkelii* genome sequence were obtained.

Symptoms- The infected plants remain stunted and leaves of the infected plants exhibit broad chlorotic strips. These strips acquire reddish-purple colour in due course. Internodes are reduced in length and infected plants bear numerous small ear shoots that are poorly filled.

Detection- The use of ELISA is a reliable means of detection for *Corn stunt spiroplasma.* This ELISA test system is based on a polyclonal antibody. The test is specific and relatively sensitive, producing a moderately strong reaction. *Corn stunt spiroplasma* can be detected easily in infected plant extract diluted at 1:270-810 strength.This *Corn stunt spiroplasma* test shows no cross-reaction with healthy maize tissue. Besides, no cross-reaction was found with other related corn pathogens including *Maize rayado fino virus* and *Maize bushy stunt phytoplasma.* It is suggested that the plant tissues should be ground thoroughly with suitable buffer in order to release maximum *Corn stunt spiroplasma* cells from the phloem.

Causal pathogen- *Corn stunt Spiroplasma / Spiroplasma kunkelii.*

Transmission - Corn leaf hoppers carry the disease from infected corn to healthy corn. The leafhoppers feed on an infected plant for several days before acquiring the spiroplasma. Two to three-week incubation period is required by the leafhopper to infect a healthy plant. Pathogen cannot survive outside its host and is dependent upon transmission for survival and dispersal.

Management - Resistance to corn stunt has been identified and is available in some hybrids. Vectors should also be kept under control.

❍ Rice yellow dwarf disease

This disease was first observed in Japan in 1910. Now it is widespread in many South-east Asian countries. In India, this disease has been reported from many parts of Orissa, Bihar, West Bengal, Andhra Pradesh and Delhi.

Symptoms - This disease is characterized by pronounced stunting and excessive tillering of plants with uniformly pale green to pale yellow chlorotic leaves. Early infected plants die prematurely while the late infected plants may survive but remain sterile. Sometimes they may bear a few poorly developed flowers and grains.

Causal organism - *Rice yellow dwarf Spiroplasma.*

Disease cycle - The disease is known to be transmitted by rice green hoppers - *Nephotettix species.* The causal organism of this disease has been found associated with the phloem cells of the infected leaf tissues.

Management - Attempts have been made in Japan to control the vectors of this disease by aerial application of insecticides over large areas. Seed dressing may be effective.

❍ Spiroplasma diseases of minor importance

Spiroplasmas cause many other diseases like stubborn in citrus and stunt diseases in ornamental cactus.

PATHOGEN CAUSING VIRUS LIKE DISEASES

Rickettsia-like organisams (RLOs) (Fastidious bacteria)

These organisms have been observed to be pathogenic and pathogenicity test have been proved in accordance with the Koch's postulates in many cases. In later years they have been renamed as rickettsia like bacteria or fastidious bacteria. These agents have been reported to cause diseases in plants including Pierce disease of grapevine, sugarcane ratoon stunting, citrus greening and almold leaf scorch.

❍ Distinguishing Characteristics

1. They have distinct cell wall like bacteria, being so small to be seen under electron microscope. Morphologically, they are rod shaped, coccoid or pleomorphic organisms having no flagella and most of these are gram negative in reaction. They resemble G-bacteria having outer layer in addition to the plasma membrane.
2. Rickettsia like bacteria also known as fastidious bacteria, differ from bacteria in respect that fastidious bacteria are obligate intracellular prokaryotic parasites in cells of hosts containing typical nuclei.
3. The phloem inhabiting fastidious bacteria responsible to cause citrus greening have not been grown in culture but the xylem inhabiting fastidious bacteria can be grown on complex nutrients media. On such media they usually grow slowly producing 1 to 2 mm colonies.
4. Rickettsia like bacteria (fastidious bacteria) differ from mycoplasmas in their posession of a cell wall which remain absent in mycoplasmas.
5. Rickettsia like organisms causing plant diseases are known to be transmitted by leaf hoppers. Multiplication of the pathogen in the body of the vectors has also been reported. Unlike phytoplasma (mycoplasma like organisms), they are susceptible to penicillin.
6. These organisms usually occur in xylem and phloem vessels and measure about 0.4 μm in diameter. Rickettsia like organisms causing diseases in plants resemble with typical rickettsia in shape and size and along with their inability to grow on artificial nutritent media.

❍ Ratoon stunting in Sugarcane

This disease is prevalent all over the world and is observed to cause considerable crop loss in most of the sugarcane growing areas. The losses in ratoon crops have been observed to be greater than in crops of first growing season.

Symptoms. (1) Infected plants grow slowly and remain stunted (2) Such plants have thinner and fewer stalks showing no any other chracteristic symptoms. (3) Infected plants often show characteristic pink discoloration just below the meristematic area of the infected plants. (4) Vascular bundles at the nodes of the infected plants may show discoloration and (5) Such vascular bundles appear to be plugged with gummy substances.

The causal pathogen. Fastidious bacterum—*Clavibactor xyli.* It is a fastidious xylem inhabiting bacterium which is coryneform in morphology, measuring about 0.3 — 0.5 × 1–4 μ*m* in size. It can be grown on specialized culture medium.

Diseases cycle. The pathogen perpetuates in infected sugarcane plants and in propagative materials such as seed cane. The disease is also known to be transmitted by infected cutting knives and equipments commonly used. New plants produced from infected canes usually develop the disease.

Management. (1) Use disease free cane and suspected canes should be heat treated before sowing. (2) Control the spread of disease by avoiding infected sugarcane germplasms. (3) Proper sanitation and use of resistant cultivars are the important measures to be followed.

14

VIRUS DISEASES OF FOOD CROPS

Virus diseases of wheat, Wheat streak mosaic potyvirus disease, wheat soil-borne mosaic tobamovirus disease, wheat American striate mosaic rhabdovirus, wheat European striate mosaic rhabdovirus disease, Wheat winter mosaic rhabdovirus disease, Wheat spindle streak mosaic potyvirus disease, wheat dwarf virus disease ; Barley yellow dwarf luteovirus disease, Barley yellow striate mosaic rhabdovirus disease, Table-showing other virus diseases of barley of minor importance ; Rice grassy stunt tenuivirus disease, Rice tungru or leaf yellowing disease, some other diseases of rice of minor importance ; Maize streak geminivirus disease, Key to some other important diseases of maize ; Virus diseases of sorghum, Table showing some other viral diseases of sorghum ; Different diseases of oat.

VIRUS DISEASES OF WHEAT (*Triticum aestivum*)

Wheat is an important crop standing first in acreage under cultivation and production in our country. It is an important source of nutrition throughout the world. Viruses are important among all pathogens responsible for reduction in production of this crop because they are difficult or usually impossible to control directly. Many of these viruses are known to occur throughout the world ; therefore, management of such viruses has become an indispensable factor for modern wheat production for betterment of the economy of the country.

Wheat yellow dwarf, wheat streak mosaic, wheat striate and wheat soil borne mosaic diseases are economically important.

❍ Wheat streak mosaic potyvirus disease

The disease is known to occur worldwide including Egypt, Asia, North America, Europe and in the Middle East, being one of the most important economic disease throughout the world.

Symptoms—(1) Primary symptoms of the disease are seen as changes in leaves and whole of the plants. (2) Appearance of chlorotic spots and streaks are usually seen on the leaves of the affected plant. (3) These streaks usually cover the entire leaf starting from the tips and margins of the leaf. (4) In due course, the leaves become chlorotic, gradually twist and dry out sometimes before the flowering of the plants. (5) The infected plants remain stunted and the number of sterile spike-lets increases by 26 to 58%. (6) Reduced chlorophyll contents are observed resulting in less plant photosynthetic activities which cause delayed growth.

The causal virus—*Wheat streak mosaic potyvirus.* The virus particles are filamentous, measuring about 700 × 15 nm in size. Infectivity of shorter particles are not yet proved. They consist of single stranded (+) RNA with a single molecule of 2800 kDa. Sedimentation coefficient is 165 S. Stability of the virus varies with the mode of preparation and storage temperature. Preparation moderately immunogenic. The virus is not related serologically with any known wheat virus. The virus is not known to be transmitted by mechanical means with the sap.

Disease cycle—The virus persists in infected wheat plants and is transmitted by the eriophyid mite. Following harvest, these vectors transmit the virus to the volunteer wheat plants where it remains infectious until the end of the season. From there, the virus is further transmitted to the winter wheat plants. Infected winter crop represents the source of further infection.

Transmission—Eriophyid mites including *Aceria tulipae* are natural vectors. Some other species of this mite has also been described in some areas. Mites are known to ingest the virus into its bodies only in the nymph stages and thereafter they become able to transmit both as nymphs and adults. Mites acquire the virus by feeding on diseased plants for about 15 minutes and they remain infective for about 9 days. The virus is not known to be transmitted transovarially to the next generation. Polyphagus mites are widespread and they colonize on different grasses including *Avena* species, *Hordeum* species, *Panicum* species and *Bromus* species. By moving from infected wheat plant, the mites resume feeding and infect these plants increasing source of infection.

Management—(1) Control the weed plants both as virus and mites hosts along with the destruction of volunteer wheat plants. (2) Resistant and tolerant wheat cultivars should be planted in high risk areas. (3) Chemical control of mites in wheat and weed plants should be done in case of severe infection. (4) Improved cultural operations should be done to increase vitality of the host. (5) Proeseler (1986a) has suggested breeding of cultivars of chromosome substitution from *Agropyron repens*.

❍ Wheat soil borne mosaic tobamovirus disease

The disease is known to occur in U.S., Europe and Japan.

Symptoms—(1) Chlorotic discoloration of leaf veins. (2) Excessive tillering. (3) Pronounced stunting and rosetting. (4) Under development of roots. (5) Poor development of inflorescences with few small grains.

The causal virus—*Wheat soil borne mosaic tobamovirus.* Virus particles are rigid rods in shape, vary in dimensions, ranging from 100–160 nm × 20 nm to 280–300 nm × 20 nm in size. Particles of 300 nm were found most infective. Particles contain two single stranded RNA classes. Sedimentation coefficient is 172 S and 211 S for 300 nm and 160 nm rods respectively. Thermal inactivation point is 60-65°C and dilution end point is 10^{-2} to 10^{-3} and *in vitro* longevity is 48-96 hours at 18-21°C. Virus preparation is strongly immunogenic.

Transmission—The virus is known to be transmitted by the fungus *Polymyxa graminis.* Infectivity is preserved in soil for more than 6 years in its resting spores. Zoospores released from resting spores function to infect epidermal cells and root hairs. Natural hosts are wheat, barley and rye. Other viral hosts are *Agropyron, Agrostis, Bromus, Dactylis* and *Panicum.*

Management—Grow resistant/tolerant cultivars.

❍ Wheat American striate mosaic rhabdovirus disease

The virus is known to occur in North America.

Symptoms—(1) Leaf striation is the general symptom accompanied by chlorosis that becomes intensive and necrotic in advance stages. (2) Growth delayed (3) Stunting (4) Grain crinkling and sterility of heads.

The causal virus—*Wheat American striate mosaic rhabdovirus.* Particles are bacilliform, measuring 250 × 75 nm in dimensions. Sedimentation coefficient is 875 S. Particles are composed of single stranded RNA. Thermal inactivation point is 55°C, dilution end point is 10^{-5} and longevity *in vitro* is 3 days at 4-10°C. The virus is weak immunogenic.

Disease cycle—The virus is preserved on infected biennial cereals and on some native grasses. Two Cicadellid leaf hoppers (Jassidae) namely *Endria inimical* and *Elymana virescens* serve as natural vectors. The virus is not seed transmitted.

Management—(1) Control leaf hoppers by suitable chemicals (2) Rogueing of infected plants. (3) Spatial isolation of susceptible plants in production fields (4) Grow resistant/tolerant cultivars.

❍ Wheat European striate mosaic rhabdovirus Disease

The disease was first reported in Europe and is known to occur in England, Germany and Spain.

Symptoms—Chlorotic striated spots occur on leaves causing complete leaflet desiccation.

The causal virus—*Wheat European striate mosaic rhabdovirus.* The virus particles are bacilliform. Natural virus hosts are *Triticum aestivum, Avena sativa, Hordeum vulgare, Bromus mollis, Lolium multiflorum* and *Phleum pretense.*

Disease Cycle—The virus perpetuates in natural host. Active virus vectors are leaf hoppers which include *Javesella pellucida* and some other species of this genus. The virus is not mechanical and seed transmissible.

Management—(1) Control virus vectors (2) Rogueing of infected plants and its natural hosts. (3) Growing of resistant/tolerant wheat cultivars.

OTHER VIRUS DISEASES OF WHEAT

❍ 1. Wheat spindle streak mosaic potyvirus disease

Disease is known to occur in North America, India and France. The disease causes considerable loss to the crop. Particles are filamentous, measuring 190 to 197 nm × 12.8 nm in size in leaf dip preparation and 3000 × 18 nm in thin sectioned wheat leaves. Thermal inactivation point is 50°C.

❍ 2. Wheat winter mosaic rhabdovirus disease

The disease is known to occur in Russia, Poland and Eastern Europe. The disease is characterized by excessive tillering resulting in dwarfing and rosetting appearance. The bacilliform virus particles measuring 260 × 60 nm are observed in infected plants. Leaf hopper-*Psammotettix alienus* is natural vector. The acquisition period of the vector is 13-27 days. Wheat, oat, barley and rye are natural hosts. Other hosts are *Agropyron cristatum, Avena byzantina, A. fatua, Calamagrostis* species, *Setaria glauca* and *Setaria viridis*.

❍ 3. Wheat dwarf virus disease

The diseases is known to occur in Russia and Eastern Europe. It is mechanically transmissible and is also transmitted by the leaf hopper-*Psammotettix alienus*. It transmits the virus in persistent manner. Characteristic symptoms are stunting, and delayed growth. Other cereals are potential hosts. Grow resistant/tolerant cultivars for management of the disease.

❍ 4. Wheat chlorotic streak

First discovered in the *Triticum durum* crop in Southern France. Particles are 355 × 55 nm *in situ* and 355 × 62 nm *in vitro*. Chlorotic streaksare screen mostly on emerging apical leaves followed by head mosaic and yellowing. Glumes remain short and grains get shriveled with reduction in weight. Cicadellid leaf hopper—*Laodelphax striatellus* transmits the virus in persistent manner. The virus is not transmitted by seed. Infected wheat and *Agropyron* plants are natural reservoirs for the virus.

❍ 5. Wheat yellow leaf closterovirus disease

The disease is known to occur in Japan. Virus particle are elongated, flexuous measuring 1600–1850 nm × 12 nm in size. Affected plants exhibit diffused chlorotic flecks followed by leaf tip yellowing and rapid plant death. Aphid *Rhopalosiphon maidis* transmits the virus in semi-persistent manner. No seed and mechanical transmission is known to occur. Wheat, barley, rye, oats are natural hosts. *Agropyron*, a native weed serves as reservoir of virus.

❍ 6. Barley stripe mosaic virus disease

Wheat, barley, oat, maize and numerous grasses are natural hosts of this virus. Distinguishing symptoms of the disease are mild stripe mosaic and necrosis followed by complete dwarfing. Reduction in yield and quality of seed are usually observed. The virus is readily seed and pollen transmissible. The virus is reported to survive 20 years in wheat and several years in barley seed. No any virus vector is known to transmit the virus. For management of the disease virus free healthy seeds should be grown.

❍ 7. Brome mosaic virus disease

The virus was isolated from awnless brome (*Bromus inermis*) plants and described as *Brome grass mosaic virus*. The disease is known to occur in African, North American and European countries. Natural hosts include wheat, barley, oat, maize and several grass species. Dicotyledonous plants are experimental hosts and *Chenopodium* species are indicator plants. Delayed growth, shortened spikes, elongated mosaic spots and stripes on leaves of infected plants are the important symptoms of this disease. The vectors include nematodes, beetles, mites and the rust fungus *Puccinia graminis* f.s. *trirtici*. The virus is also mechanically transmissible. For management of this disease, vector control and destruction of previous crop residues should be done.

❍ Diseases of minor importance

1. Agropyron mosaic virus disease- The virus was reported to cause systemic infection on different gramineous plants. This virus has been reported on wheat as a natural host in USA, Canada, New Zealand, Filand, Germany and some other Western countries. This virus was first reported on *Agropyron repens* and *Triticum* species. The indicator plant of the virus is *Chenopodium quinoa*. Mild to severe stunting of affected plants and reduction in yield are the important characteristics produced by the mild to severe strains of the causal virus.

2. Barley yellow dwarf virus disease- This virus has been reported to infect several wheat species including *Triticum aestivum, Triticum turgidum* var. *durum* and *Triticale,* causing considerable loss in yield. The virus causes symptoms such as yellowing, reddening and brittleness of leaves. Leaf discoloration usually begins from the leaf tips and leaves in severe cases may remain undersized. As a result of the disease, affected plants may mature late and growth of the plants may be stunted. The virus is transmitted by aphids. Important vectors include *Rhopalosiphon padi, Rhopalosiphon maidis, Metopolophium dirhodum, Macrosiphum avenae* and *Schizaphis graminum.*

3. Barley yellow striate mosaic virus disease- The virus has been reported to belong Rhabdovirus group, being identical to the *Wheat chlorotic streak virus.*

VIRUS DISEASES OF BARLEY *(Hordeum vulgare)*

Barley is an important food crop grown throughout the world. Virus diseases cause considerable loss to the crop. Barley stripe mosaic, barley yellow dwarf, barley yellow mosaic and yellow striate mosaic diseases are destructive whereas cereal tillering disease, cereal northern mosaic and cereal chlorotic mottle diseases are of minor importance. Economically important diseases of this important crop are being described in some detail.

❍ Barley stripe mosaic hordeivirus disease

The disease is worldwide in occurrence, chiefly observed in countries of North America, Asia, Australia, England, France and Germany, Former USSR, Denmark and many other countries. As a result of the disease quality and quantity of the produce are badly affected.

Symptoms- The disease is characterized by the several symptoms like striped mosaic and yellow or whitish chlorosis that usually appears near the base of the leaves in the beginning. In severe case of attack, chlorotic stripes are formed on the leaves, resulting in the chlorotic appearance of the affected plants. As a result of the disease, the growth of the plants is arrested, individual florets become sterile and anthers fail to open. Pollen formation is adversely affected causing the seeds to be shriveled and considerable reduction in yield.

Causal virus- *Barley stripe mosaic hordeivirus.* Virus particles consist of tripartite multi-component structure. Each particle usually contains RNA genome component and two to three genome components are necessary to incite infection. The dimensions of the viral particles vary from 108-175 X 22 nm depending on the method of sample preparation and measurement techniques used. Virus particles have been reported to contain as more as 96% protein and 3.7 to 4% RNA. The coat protein is 21 kDA and the molecular weights of the single stranded RNAs are 1400, 1170, 1040 and 930 kDA as reported. Thermal inactivation point of the virus ranges from 65 to 68 0C, dilution end point ranges from 5×10^{-2} to 1×10^{-4} and longevity *in vitro* is about one month. Different strains are known to occur on barley, wheat and oat plants that are called as yellow leaf, white leaf, dwarf and necrotic strains. Sample of the virus is highly immunogenic.

Transmission- The virus is known to be transmitted by seed and pollen of infected plants. It is easily transmissible by mechanical means also; however, vector transmission is not known. Gramineous plants are natural hosts; however, many dicotyledonous plants are also susceptible to the virus. Such plants include *Spinacia oleracea* (Chenopodiaceae), *Nicotiana tabacum* (Solanaceae) and many other with latent infection like *Gomphrena globosa* (Amaranthaceae) and *Primula malacoides* (Primulaceae). Local lesions appear on *Beta vulgaris, Chenopodium album, C. amaranticolor, C. ambrosiodes, C. gigateum, C. quinoa and C. hybridum.*

Management - Use of healthy seeds for sowing are recommended for management of the disease.

❍ Barley yellow dwarf luteovirus disease

The disease is known to be worldwide in occurrence especially reported from North America, Europe, Asia, Australia, Great Britain, France, Italy, Bulgaria, New Zealand and other European countries.

Symptoms—(1) Chlorosis of leaves and dwarfing of infected plants. (2) Leaf yeallowing is characterized by the golden yellow colour. (3) Yellowing first occur on leaf margins gradually spreading through the base resulting in coverage of whole leaflefts. (4) Infected leaves are erect, rather rigid and firm. (5) Plants show delayed growth, have a rosette like appearance and usually fail to develop grain heads. (6) Intensity of the disease symptoms usually depends on the stage of the plant infected.

The causal virus—*Barley yellow dwarf luteovirus.* Matthews (1982) described the virus related with luteovirus group. Virus particles are isometric in shape and vary in size from 20-30 nm. Sedimentation coefficient is 115-120 S. Thermal inactivation point in sap 65 to 70°C. The virion contains a single major protein of 23.5 kDa. Serologically, the virus preparation is readily immunogenic.

Disease cycle—The virus is preserved in nature on wild and perennial grasses which provide long term inoculum for infection and spread of the disease. Volunteer plants that grow in the fields also play important role in survival of the pathogen.

Transmission—More than 20 aphid species are known to transmit the disease. These vectors are primary vectors. Most abundant vectors are *Macrosiphum avenae, Rhopalosiphum maidis, R. padi* and *Schizaphis graminum*. The virus is not transmissible by sap of infected plants and seed. Experimentally the virus was transmitted from one infected plant to another healthy plant through *Cuscuta compestris.*

Management—(1) Control of aphids through chemical or biological methods should be done. (2) Destruction of wild and perennial grasses and volunteer plants which provide source of inoculum should be done. (3) Growing of resistant/tolerant cultivars should be preferred. (4) Suitable modification in cultural practices is also advised for management of the disease.

❍ Barley yellow mosaic potyvirus disease

This disease was first described from Japan. Besides, the disease has been reported from England, Germany, France, Belgium and China. The disease causes considerable loss to crop with reduction in yield estimated as high as 10-90 per cent.

Symptoms—(1) Small yellow spots and stripes first appear on the youngest leaves of the infected plants. (2) Usually third leaf of the infected plant is seen rolling causing erect habit and pointed appearance. (3) At low temperature below 5°C, the characteristic symptoms are sharp but with the increase in temperature plants develop normally. (4) Stunting of the infected plants with underdevelped roots are observed.

The causal virus—*Barley yellow mosaic potyvirus.* Virus particles are filamentous and are of two sizes viz., 275 × 13 nm and 550 × 13 nm. The virus contains two RNA species of 2800 and 1400 kDa and two proteins of 35 and 29 kDa (Huth 1988). Dilution end point is 10^{-2}, thermal inactivation point and longevity *in vitro* are not well known. The virus preparation is moderately immunogenic.

Disease cycle—The virus is soil borne. Viral particles that persist in the resting spores of the fungal vector are carried by the released zoospores which move actively in the soil. Disease development depends mainly on the vector. The activity of such vectors are controlled by the moisture content of the soil and its pH.

Transmission—The virus is probably transmitted by the fungus *Polymyxa graminis.*

Management—(1) Grow barley in non infested fields. (2) Suitable crop rotation and modification in cultural practices should be done. (3) Susceptible and high quality barley cultivars can be grown on heavy clay soils which is unfavourable for vector colonization. (4) Growing of resistant and tolerant cultivars should be preferred.

❍ Barley yellow striate mosaic rhabdovirus disease

This disease is known to occur in Italy and France.

Symptoms—Stunting, changeable striate mosaic symptoms, chlorotic striation and apical tip yellowing are important symptoms of the disease.

The causal virus—*Barley yellow striate mosaic rhabdovirus.* Virus particles are bacilliform with rounded ends, measuring 300–320 nm × 45 nm in size. The virus contains a single stranded RNA, a protein (currently not analyzed) and a lipid envelope. Thermal inactivation point is 50-60°C, dilution end point is 10^{-2} to 10^{-3} and longevity *in vitro* is 2-4 days at 5°C. Virus sample is moderately immunogenic.

Disease cycle—Virus is not transmitted by mechanical means and also not by seed. Plant hopper-*Laodelphax striatellus* is known to transmit the virus in persistent manner. The vector becomes able to acquire the virus after one hour of feeding. The latent period is about 5-29 days. The vector maintains infectivity for whole life and larvae of the viruliferous leafhoppers also become infective 2 weeks after hatching. More than 26 genera of *Langurus, Avena, Trisetum, Briza, Bromus, Dactylis, Poa, Hordeum, Lolium, Triticum, Secale, Phalaris, Sorghum, Zea, Panicum* and *Setaria* are known to be susceptible. No dicotyledonous plants are known to be susceptible.

Management—Chemical control of leaf hoppers may reduce the losses in areas of greater disease incidence.

❍ Barley as natural alternative host for some viruses

Barley has been observed and reported to serve as natural host for different viruses given bellow-

1. *Oat pseudo-rosette virus.*
2. *Wheat striate mosaic virus.*
3. *Wheat streak mosaic virus.*
4. *Wheat soil borne mosaic virus and*
5. *Wheat winter mosaic virus.*

VIRUS DISEASES OF BARLEY OF MINOR IMPORTANCE

1-Cereal tillering reovirus disease. This disease is known to occur in Northern Europe. It was first recognized on barley and oat by Lindsten *et. al.* (1973) in Sweden. The virus belongs to reovirus group. The disease is characterized by the excessive tillering, severe dwarfing with malformed and serrated margins of leaves. The virus is related serologically with *Maize rough dwarf virus*. It is known to be transmitted by the plant hopper-*Laodelphax stratellus.*

2. Cereal chlorotic mottle rhabdovirus disease. The virus being member of rhabdovirus is known to occur in Queensland, Australia and New South Wales. Characteristic symptoms include stunting of plant and chlorotic striping of leaves. Natural virus vestors are Jassid leafhoppers including *Nesoclutha pallida.*

3. Cereal northern mosaic virus disease. The disease is characterized by the appearance of light green stripes and spots on leaves and leaf sheaths. Affected plants may remain sterile and produce many tillers. It was first reported from Japan on barley and millets. Different species belonging to *Laodelphax, Delphacodes, Ukanodes* and *Muellerianella* are known to transmit the virus in persistent manner.

VIRUS DISEASES OF RICE (*Oryza sativa*)

Based on acreages under cultivation, rice stands second immediately following wheat but in production it stands first in the world. More than eleven virus species have been reported so far on rice causing considerable damage to the crop. The largest number of rice viruses have been described from Asian, African and American countries where the rice crop is grown most intensively and extensively.

❍ Rice grassy stunt tenuivirus disease

Rice is the only natural host of this virus which causes considerable loss to the crop in several Asian countries including India, Indonesia, Japan, Malaysia, Philippines, Taiwan and Thailand. Reduction in yield of plants infected during first month ranged from 70-100 per cent and in plants infected during second month 80% reduction in yield has been reported.

Symptoms—(1) The most distinguishing symptoms usually occur on seedlings early in the season. (2) Stunting of plants, excessive tillering and erect appearance of leaves are usually seen which are of variable size and shape. (40 Panicle formation may be impaired. (5) Yellowing and formation of brown panicles bearing abortive kernels are also observed when infections occur later in season.

The causal virus—*Rice grassy stunt tenuivirus.* The virus particles are filamentous and occasionally circular in morphology, measuring 950-1350 nm × 6-8 nm in size. The viral RNA consists of four segments and single protein species of 31 kDa. Two proteins have also been reported by some workers. Dilution end point varies with the method of preparation of sample such as in rice extract is 1×10^{-2} to 1×10^{-3} and in vector extract is 1×10^{-3} to 1×10^{-6}. Longevity *in vitro* is 12 hours at 24°C. Sample is strongly immunogenic in rabbits. Several strains are known to occur.

Disease cycle—Infected rice plants and plant hoppers as insect vectors serve as natural reservoirs for the virus.

Transmission—Plant hoppers namely, *Nilaparavata lugens, N. bakeri* and *N. muiri* are known to transmit the virus in persistent manner. Vector efficiency usually depends upon the environmental condition, rice variety, virus strain and development stage of the vector. The minimum acquisition feeding time is 1 hour for *Nilparvata lugens* and latent period is 3 to 28 days. Minimum time for successful inoculation being 9 minutes. The virus is not seed and mechanically transmissible.

Management—(1) Growing of resistant/tolerant cultivars should be preferred. In Indonesia, Philippines and Vietnam, a resistant gene has been isolated from *Oryza nivara* plants to derive such cultivars (Ling *et.al.,* 1970 ; Khush and Ling, 1974). (2) Chemical control of vectors has little importance especially in tropical areas where the crop is grown year-round.

❍ Rice tungru or leaf yellowing disease

The disease is widespread in the Philippines, Malaysia, Indonesia, India, Pakistan and Thailand. It ranks among economically important diseases of this crop.

Symptoms—(1) The young leaves of the infected plants are observed to be mottled with pale green to white spots. (2) The older leaves turn yellow to orange in colour starting from the tips and margins. (3) Plants remain stunted and bear poor panicles with empty glumes due to shortening of both the leaf sheaths, leaf blades and internodes. (4) Inter veinal chlorosis is marked in most cases.

The causal virus—*Rice tungru bacilliform virus* and *Rice tungru spherical virus.* This disease is caused by these two morphologically dissimilar viruses known as *Rice tungru bacilliform virus* (TRBV) having double stranded DNA genome and *Rice tungru spherical virus* (RTSV) having single stranded RNA genome.

Disease cycle—*Rice tungru spherical virus* consisting of single stranded RNA genome is transmitted independently by the leaf hopper—*Nephotettix virescens* while *Rice tungru bacilliform virus* is transmitted only when the vector first acquires *Rice tungru spherical virus.* Virus vector relationship is non-persistent and semi-persistent in nature.

Management—(1) Plants showing disease symptoms should be rooted out in the beginning and green stubbles should also be uprooted and burnt after harvest. (2) Vectors must be controlled by spraying of Dimecron-100 or any other suitable fungicide. (3) Before transplanting, seedlings should be dipped in Carbofuron-75 WP solution. To prepare the solution 25-30 g of Carbofuron-75 W P should be dissolved in 10 litres of water. (4) Grow tolerant varieties such as IR-20, Ratna, Jaya, Vijaya and IET 2507. (5) Avoid growing TN-I which is most susceptible.

SOME OTHER DISEASES OF RICE

❍ 1. Rice black-streaked dwarf reovirus disease

It is the most destructive disease occurring on maize, wheat and barley

Symptoms—The disease causes severe rice stunting and inflorescences are rarely formed on infected plants.

The causal virus—*Rice black-streaked dwarf reovirus.* The virus is composed of ds RNA genome divided into 10 segments. Virus sample is actively immunogenic. No data on strains are available.

Transmission—The disease is transmitted only by Cicadellid plant hoppers. No mechanical and no seed transmission have been demonstrated.

Management—Chemical control of vectors may help to reduce the extent of infection and spread of the disease.

❍ 2. Rice gall dwarf reovirus disease

The disease has been found to occur in Thailand, Malaysia and China.

Symptoms—*Oryza sativa* c.v. Taichung Native 1 is the diagnostic plant. The disease is characterized by the dwarfing of plants, delay in flowering and shriveled grain. Infected plants gradually turn dark green in colour with age. Whitish galls usually appear on lower surface of leaf being characteristic to the disease.

The causal virus—*Rice gall dwarf reovirus*. Virus particles are polyhedral, measuring 65 nm in diameter and consisting of double stranded RNA containing 12 segments with a total molecular weight of 16,900 kDa. Viral particles contain 7 kinds of proteins consisting of different molecular weights. Rice is the natural host of the virus.

Disease cycle—Natural hosts are wild rice (*Oryza nifipagon*), barley, wheat, rye, oats and Italian ryegrass. Leafhoppers but not plant hoppers are known to transmit the virus.

Management—Destroy natural hosts and control vectors.

❍ 3. Rice ragged stunt reovirus disease

The disease is known to occur in China, India, Japan, Malaysia, Philippines, Sri Lanka, Taiwan and Thailand.

Symptoms—The disease causes hypertrophy in parenchyma cells, resulting in enation formation on lower leaf surfaces and leaf sheaths. These enations are small protuberance resulting in appearance of ragged leaves. Natural hosts are rice plants including *Oryza sativa, O.latifoliand* and *O. nivara*. Infected plants remain dwarfed and increased branching are seen on internodes.

The causal virus—*Rice ragged stunt reovirus*. The genome consists of double stranded RNA containing of 8 segments with a total weight of 11,600 kDa. No strains are known to occur. The causal virus particles are polyhedral, measuring 50 nm in diameter.

Disease cycle—Rice brown plant hopper-*Nilaparvata lugens* is the only known vector which transmits the virus. It requires 3 hours for acquisition with latent period of 2-33 days and minimum inoculation period of 1 hour.

Management—Chemical control of vectors should be done to minimize the spread of disease and its incidence. Resistant/tolerant cultivars should be grown for better management.

❍ Rice stripe tenuivirus disease

This disease was first observed and described in Japan and there after was found to occur in countries of China, Korea, Taiwan and some other rice growing areas of the world. The disease causes considerable loss to the crop especially due to delayed emergence and maturity.

Symptoms- Chlorotic stripes usually appear in the beginning on the leaves of the affected plants. After some time, chlorosis of the entire leaves may take place. These chlorotic stripes gradually turn brown and become necrotic with the advancement of the disease. As a result of the disease, panicle formation is badly affected, causing considerable loss in yield.

Causal virus - *Rice stripe tenuivirus.* The virus consists of single stranded RNA genome consisting of four segments of different molecular weights, accounting 12% of the total viral weight. The virus capsid contains a single protein species of 32 kDA. The particles of the virus are filamentous in morphology. They are of indefinite length, measuring about 8 nm in diameter. Prticles usually sediment into three components-the middle (M) , the bottom (B) and the nB component. Only nB particle components are known to be infective. Sedimentation coefficients of the three virus sediments are 65 S (M), 80 S (B) and 98 S (Nb). Dilution end point of the virus in vector extracts has been reported to be 1×10^{-4} to 1×10^{-5}. Thermal inactivation end point of the virus sample is 50 to 55°C and longevity *in vitro* is 4 days at 4°C; however, longevity *in vitro* (LIV) in infected plant extract is 8 to 12 months at - 20°C. The virus sample is highly immunogenic in reaction.

Transmission- Natural hosts of the pathogen include rice, maize, wheat, oats, foxtail, millet and different wild grasses. Rice is the diagnostic plant of this virus. Natural hosts represent the sources of infection and transmission. Insect vectors include mainly *Laodelphax striatellus* as brown plant hopper that transmits the virus in persistent manner.

Management - Management of the insect vectors should be done by using suitable insecticide and tolerant/resistant varieties should be preferred for sowing.

❍ Virus diseases of minor importance

1. Rice hoja blanca tenuivirus disease - The disease is caused by *Rice hoja-blanca tenuivirus* and is wide spread in North and South America. The virus is characterized by the filamentous particles that are of indefinite length and 3-4 nm of diameter. The virus is composed of RNA genome that accounts about 12% of the total particle weight. The disease is not transmissible by mechanical means or by seeds of infected plants. Rice plant hopper - *Sagatodes orizicola* is known to transmit this virus in persistent manner.

2. Rice necrosis mosaic virus disease - This disease is mostly observed in Japan. The virus belongs to the potyvirus group consisting of particles, measuring 275 to 550 X13-14 nm in size. Thermal inactivation point of the virus sample in sap is 60 to 65°C, dilution end point is 5×10^{-3} to 1×10^{-4} and longevity *in vitro* is 7-14 days at room temperature. The virus sample is immunogenic in reaction. Soil fungus-*Polymyxa graminis* is the vector of this virus, transmitting it through its zoospores. Infected seed of infected plants also transmit the virus.

3. Rice yellowing rhabdovirus disease- The disease caused by *Rice yellowing rhabdovirus*, is known to occur in Taiwan, producing symptoms like yellowing, stunting and considerable reduction in number of tillering. Particles are bullet shaped, measuring 96X120 nm in size in leaf dip preparation. Sample is immunogenic in reaction. Rice green hopper-*Nephotettix apicalis* and *Nephotettix cincticeps* are vectors that transmit the virus in persistent manner. The virus is not transmissible by mechanical means or by seed.

❍ Rice as natural alternate hosts of different viruses

Rice has been observed and reported to serve as natural host for different viruses given below-

1. *Barley yellow dwarf luteovirus.*
2. *Maize dwarf mosaic virus.*
3. *Oat pseudo-rosette virus* and
4. *Ryegrass mosaic virus.*

VIRUS DISEASES OF MAIZE (*Zea mays*)

Maize is grown throughout the world especially in temperate zones and in tropical and subtropical areas. It ranks third in its distribution. More than 40 distinct viruses are known to cause diseases to this crop. Important diseases causing considerable damage to this crop may be summarized as under—

❍ Maize streak geminivirus disease

This disease is known to be world wide in distribution. It has been reported from African countries, southern Asian countries and India. However, the disease is not known to occur in European countries.

Symptoms—(1) Appearance of characteristic symptoms manifesting inter-veinal chlorotic streaks and narrow stripes along the leaf veins are observed. (2) Initial symptoms are round white spots formed at the base of the leaflets, which gradually elongate and appear as broken chlorotic streaks. (3) In severe cases, narrow chlorotic stripes usually cover the leaf surface. (4) Highly specific characteristic streaks are seen on susceptible maize, sugarcane and millets.

The causal virus— The disease is caused by *Maize streak geminivirus*, whose particles are isometric in shape usually occurring in pairs. The geminate particles are of 5-angular, measuring 30×20 nm and single particles are 6-angular measuring 20×20 nm in size. The nucleocapsids contain single stranded closed circular DNA molecules. Molecular weight of DNA is 710 kDa and protein molecular weight is 28 kDa. The Gemini particle sedimentation coefficient is 70 S to 76 S and 54 S for single particles. Thermal inactivation point of the virus is above 60°C and dilution end point is greater than 1/1000. The longevity of the virus at room temperature is not less than 24 hours. Serologically, the virus is moderate to highly immunogenic in reaction. Two strains—one strongly virulent and other mild are known to occur.

Disease cycle—Susceptible plant species which grow regularly and permanently provide source of inoculum every year.

Transmission—Five species of leaf hoppers including *Cicadulina storeyi, C. bipunctella zeae, C. latens* and *C. parazeae* are known as vectors of this disease. Vectors usually acquire the virus within 1 hour of feeding. Latent period in the hopper remains 6-12 hours at 30°C. All nymphs are active vectors and vectorship is maintained during molting. Once infected they remain viruliferous for life. Virus multiplication in leafhopper has also been reported. Virus is not transmitted by seed or by mechanical means. Sugarcane and millets are important hosts of the virus.

Management—

(1) Growing of susceptible plant species should be avoided for elimination and reduction of reservoirs of virus infections.

(2) Vector population in the field and nearby field should be reduced by judicious use of insecticides and destruction of reservoirs.

(3) Introduction of tolerant and resistant maize varieties should be done through breeding. Genes regulating resistance to this disease have been discovered.

❍ Maize dwarf mosaic potyvirus disease

This disease is known to occur in North and South America, Europe, Africa and Asia but not in Australia. Maize dwarf mosaic disease was first reported from North America and later in Europe. The disease induces delayed flowering affecting adversely the yield and quality of the produce.

Symptoms—

(1) The primary symptoms of the disease are seen as mosaic with various leaflet decolouration, stunting, sterility and premature death of the plants.

(2) Mosaic symptoms usually appear at the base of the youngest leaves when they remain in the leaf sheaths.

(3) Chlorotic streaks first appear at the base of these leaves and gradually spread along the leaflets parallel to the veins affecting all the leaves formed thereafter.

(4) Chlorotic yellow colour usually dominates in apical leaves and green colour remains present in the form of streaks, stripes and lines which are seen usually close to the veins.

Causal virus—*Maize dwarf mosaic potyvirus*. The causal virus particles are filamentous with an average size of 750×13 nm. The particles contain single stranded RNA with a molecular weight of ca. 3.32×10^6 Da as reported. The protein coat is composed of a single species of polypeptide with a native configuration molecular weight of 30.7 kDa.

Physio-chemical properties—Sedimentation coefficient of the particle is 176 ± 5S. Pin-wheel inclusion bodies are induced by this virus which helps in diagnosis of the disease. Thermal inactivation point of the virus is 55°C and dilution end point is 10^{-5}. *In vitro* longevity is 192 hours at 2 to 3°C. Serologically, the virus sample is moderately immunogenic. Antiserum has been successfully applied in ELISA, ISEM and electro-blot immunoassays. Several strains are known to occur in *Maize dwarf mosaic potyvirus* which infect maize, sugarcane and sorghum.

Disease cycle—In nature, the virus is known to survive over perennial and annual hosts chiefly Johnson grass (*Sorghum halepense*) as a perennial weed plant.

Transmission—Besides being rarely transmitted by seed in low percentage as observed by some virologists, the virus is mechanically transmissible through sap of infected plants. Different species of aphids are known to transmit the virus in a non-persistent manner. Important species are *Aphis craccivora, Macrosiphum avenae, Myzus persicae, Rhopalosiphon maidis, R. podi* and *Acyrthosiphon pisum. Macrosiphum festucae* has recently been recognized as new vector.

Management—(1) Elimination of weed hosts chiefly Johnson grass (*Sorghum halepense*) and foxtail (*Setaria* species) should be done to reduce the primary inoculum. (2) Use healthy seed to avoid the risk of infection source. (3) Rogueing should be done to eliminate the first infected plants in the crop especially in seed production. (4) Maize and sorghum production should be separated so as to avoid source of natural infection. (5) Vectors should be controled by judicious use of insecticide. (6) The coat protein gene of MDMV has been cloned, sequenced and inserted into maize germplasm, which may provide resistance against the disease (Anonymous, 1992).

❍ Maize chlorotic dwarf virus disease

The disease was first discovered in USA and is known to occur in Mexico, Ohio River valley and Pennsylvania.

Symptoms—Stunting of plants, discolouration of leaves, marginal chlorosis and development of chlorotic leaf stripe symptoms along with leaf yellowing and reddening are the characteristic symptoms of the disease.

The causal virus—*Maize chlorotic dwarf virus*. The virus particles are isometric measuring 30 nm in diameter. Molecular weight 8.8×10^6 Da. Sedimentation coefficient 83 ± 6 S. The nucleocapsids core consists of single stranded RNA of 3200 kDa with multipartite RNA genome. Serologically, virus sample is highly immunogenic. Immunofluorescence assay, micro immune agar gel diffusion, ELISA and ISEM are successfully applicable.

Disease cycle—The virus over winters in infected Johnson grass. Leaf hoppers including *Graminella nigrifrons* transmit the virus in to healthy plants. Johnson grass serves as source of primary inoculum. No mechanical and seed transmission are known to occur.

Management—(1) Eliminate the perennial virus hosts with its rhizomes. (2) Destroy vector population by judicious use of suitable insecticide. (3) Maize lines and hybrids displaying tolerant reaction should be grown in regions where this disease is known to cause considerable damage.

❍ Maize rough dwarf fijivirus disease

The disease in known to occur in Israel, Italy, Switzerland, Spain, France and Czechoslovakia. This virus was first described in 1949 in Northern Italy.

Symptoms—Characteristic leaf galls, vein thickening and vein enations occur on the lower surface of leaf. (2) These characteristic symptoms appear along leaf veins, on leaf sheaths and on roots of maize plants. (3) The virus causes atrophy of individual kernels and of the whole ear. (4) Shortening of internodes may be observed.

The causal virus—*Maize rough dwarf fijivirus*. Virus particles are isometric with double capsids and double stranded RNA. The virus contains RNA-dependent polymerase in sub-viral particles but not in the outer envelope. Capsid contains seven polypeptides and its genome is composed of 10 RNA segments. Characteristic A-spikes are located on the outer coat of the virus with internal B-spikes situated below each spike. The molecular weight of the genome is 18.9 kDa. Serologically moderately immunogenic. Thermal inactivation point is 55-60°C. Optimum pH for its preservation is 6.5.

Disease cycle—The virus persists in naturally infected plants belonging to grasses. Mechanical and seed transmissions have not been reported. The Delphacidae plant hopper (*Laodelphax striatellus*) is only known vector species responsible for natural transmission of the virus in persistent manner.

Management—(1) Alternate and naturally infected hosts should be destroyed. These plants include *Digitaria sanguinalis, Echinochloa crusgalli, Lolium multiflorum* and *Lolium perenne*. (2) Timely planting should be done. (3) Plant hoppers should be controlled with suitable insecticide.

❍ Maize mosaic rhabdovirus disease

The disease is found widely distributed in Hawaii, Cuba, Tanzania, Puerto Rico, Mauritius, and India. The disease is most destructive due to its widespread distribution and severe stunting of the plants.

Symptoms—(1) Appearance of yellow spots, leaf stripes and plant stunting. (2) Light green yellow spots usually appear on the leaves of infected plants. (3) These spots gradually develop to form mosaic mottling broken with stripes along and between the tiny leaf veins. (4) Internodes are reduced in length.

The causal virus—*Maize mosaic rhabdovirus*. Virus particles are bacilliform and bullet shaped. Particles dimensions on maize isolate were 140 × 63 nm. Particles consist of an outer envelope and the inner nucleocapsid. The nucleocapsid core consists of a single stranded non-infective negative sense (-) RNA. The nucleic core is surrounded by protein capsids whose synthesis is coded by the viral genome. Nucleocapsids contain the replicase (transcriptase) enzyme as its structural component which transcribes (-) RNA into (+) RNA, ensuring synthesis of viral protein.

Disease cycle—The virus survives on natural hosts. Natural hosts are maize, *Rottboellia exaltata* and *Setaria vulpiseta*. Experimental hosts are *Euchlena maxicana* and *Sorghum*.

Transmission—Transmission not by seed and not by mechanical means. Leaf hopper—*Peregrinus maidis* and its nymphs, both males and females, act as vectors which transmit the virus in persistent manner.

Management—(1) Destructon of infected plants as source of infection. (2) Reduction of vector population by use of insecticide. (3) Spatial isolation of susceptible plants in production area. (4) Planting of resistant maize cultivars should be given priority.

SOME OTHER DISEASES OF MAIZE OF MINOR IMPORTANCE

1. Maize white line mosaic virus disease—Particles are isometric, measuring 35 nm diameter, single stranded RNA, also in association with a satellite like virus. Wide spread in U.S., France, and Italy.

2. Maize chlorotic mottle machlomovirus disease—Particles isometric, 30 nm in diameter, single stranded RNA, wide spread in Peru, Argentina, Mexico and U.S.

3. Maize stripe tenuivirus disease—Particles filamentous, 3 nm in diameter, contain 5 species of ssRNA, widespread in Florida, Venezuela, Peru, Nigeria, Kenya and Mauritius.

4. Maize rayado fino marafivirus disease—Particles isometric, 31 nm in diameter, ssRNA. Wide spread in Central America, Mexico, Peru, Brazil, Colombia, and in Caribbean islands.

5. Maize leg fleck virus disease—First observed in California in 1952 and widespread in Bulgaria.

6. Sugarcane mosaic potyvirus disease—First described by Brandes (loc. Cit. Gordon *et al*, 1981).

7. Johnsongrass mosaic potyvirus disease—First described in Australia.

8. Sorghum mosaic potyvirus disease—Separated from sugarcane mosaic virus group (Shukla *et al*, 1989).

9. Barley yellow dwarf luteovirus disease—Reported from U.S.A. by Stoner, 1977.

10. Cereal chlorotic mottle virus disease—Belong to Rhabdovirus group with bacilliform particles of 240×65 nm.

11. Wheat streak mosaic virus disease—First discovered from sweet corn crop.

12. Brome mosaic virus disease—First discovered in maize from South Dakota (Stoner *et al* 1967).

13. Cucumber mosaic virus disease—First discovered from Florida.

VIRUS DISEASES OF SORGHUM (*Sorghum bicolor*)

This crop is also an important food crop grown through out the world in tropical and sub-tropical areas. In Asia, Africa, North and Central America, sorghum is consumed as human and animal food. This crop also provides several valuable raw materials for several processing industries. Numbers of viral diseases are known to cause considerable damage to this crop every year where this crop is grown extensively. Some important viral diseases may be summarized as under.

❍ Sorghum mosaic potyvirus disease

This disease is known to occur on sorghum and sugarcane. The disease has been reported from India, Japan, U.S. and Philippines. The disease causes considerable loss to sorghum and sugarcane crops.

Symptoms—(1) Appearance of yellow green short streaks which quickly turn reddish brown and become necrotic on the leaves. (2) Mosaic pattern are also seen on most of the sorghum cultivars. (3) Mild mottling and crinkling especially in sugarcane are seen which affect the leaves to get impaired. (4) Chlorotic and necrotic streaks coalesce forming broad reddish stripes seen frequently on the leaf surfaces.

The causal virus—*Sorghum mosaic potyvirus.* The virus particles are flexuous and filamentous in appearance, measuring about 750 nm in size. It contains single stranded RNA causing the adverse effect in the host cytoplasm as observed in the form of pinwheels and scrolls. Amorphous inclusions are also seen in the host cells.

Thermal inactivation point of the virus is 58°C, dilution end point is 1×10^{-2} to 1×10^{-4} and longevity *in vitro* at 20°C is 24 hours. The virus sample is moderately immunogenic and the antiserum may be used in micro- precipitation test, SDS-agar gel immuno-diffusion, ELISA, ISEM, Electro-blot- immunosorbent assay (EBIA) and Western Blots tests.

Disease cycle—Virus infectivity is preserved on sugarcane and no any other perennial plant is known except this.

Transmission—Plant aphids especially *Dactynotus ambrosiae* is known as highly efficient vector which transmits the virus probably in non-persistent manner.

Management—(1) Destruction of perennial hosts responsible for perpetuation of virus should be done. (2) judicious control of vectors by use of chemicals or by biological means should be done. (3) Development and growing of resistant/tolerant cultivars should be given preference.

Table 14.1 Some other virus diseases of sorghum with their characteristic features

S.No.	Name of virus disease	Characteristic features
1.	**Sorghum stunt mosaic virus disease.**	The disease has been reported as a new disease from California. Symptoms of the disease include chlorosis and streaking of the leaves accompanied with the severe stunting of the plant. Virus particles are bullet shaped as observed in infected plant tissue, measuring about 63 × 95 nm in size in leaf dip preparation. Leaf hopper-*Graminella sonora* is the main vector known to transmit the virus onto maize, sorghum and wheat plants. The virus is not mechanically transmissible with infected plant sap and no any other means of transmission except that of leaf hopper is known to occur.
2.	**Sorghum yellow banding virus disease**	Yellow banding is the characteristic symptom of this disease. The virus particles are isometric in morphology, measuring about 25 nm in diameter, containing a single species of single stranded RNA genome of 1500 kDa. Single capsid protein is of about 29 kDa MW. The virus infects Sudan grass (*Sorghum sudanense*) also.
3.	**Sorghum chlorotic spot virus disease**	Characteristic spots are usually seen on the leaves of the hosts which include some graminaceous and non-graminaceous plants. *Nicotiana benthamiana* is known as indicator plant of the virus. The virus belongs to the potyvirus group.
4.	**Maize dwarf mosaic virus disease**	The virus causing the disease occurs widely in all the sorghum production regions. Maize and sorghum are most important natural hosts of this pathogen.

OTHER DISEASES OF SORGHUM OF MINOR IMPORTANCE

Maize chlorotic dwarf virus, Maize chlorotic mottle virus, Maize mosaic virus, Maize streak virus, Maize stripe virus, Maize vein enation virus, Barley yellow dwarf virus, Barley yellow striate virus, Oat mosaic virus and *Oat pseudo-rosette virus* are known to cause diseases on sorghum inflicting characteristic symptoms and considerable losses.

VIRUS DISEASES OF OAT (*Avena sativa*)

Oat is the natural host of many viral diseases of considerable importance. In United States, Southern and Eastern Europe and many Asian and African countries, oat is grown having substantial acreages. Several virus diseases have been described. Some of the diseases are transmitted by plant hoppers while others are soil- borne or mechanically transmissible by sap inoculation.

❍ Oat sterile dwarf reovirus disease

This disease is known to occur in European countries including Poland, Great Britain, Germany, Finland, Norway and Sweden. Losses as high as 70 to 100% have been reported from different parts of their occurrence.

Symptoms—(1) Appearance of dark green to yellow striated spots along with the reduced size of the leaves are usually observed. (2) Small enations may appear on lower surface of the leaf. (3) After some days the entire leaves turn yellow, red and partially violet red in colour. (4) Affected plants remain stunted giving rise a rosette like appearance and (5) Flowers are found sterile in most cases.

The causal virus—*Oat Sterile dwarf reovirus.* Virus particles are isometric in shape, measuring 65 to 70 nm in diameter. The virus consists of double stranded RNA divided into 10 segments with total molecular weight of 18,400 kDa. The virus is known to be serologically related with *Lolium enation virus* and *Arrhenatherum blue dwarf virus*. It belongs to reovirus group.

Disease cycle—The virus overwinters in its perennial hosts especially *Lolium perenne* from which it is transmitted year after year.

Transmission—Plant hoppers including *Javesella pellucida, J. discolor, J. dubia* and *Dicranotropis hamata* are important vectors transmitting virus in persistent manner. They have shortest acquisition feeding period of 30 to 60 minutes with latent period of 3 to 4 weeks. These vectors remain viruliferous whole of their life after they acquire the virus. The virus is neither transmitted by plant sap and nor through seed.

Management—(1) Elimination and destruction of spontaneous virus hosts should be done. (2) Control of vector population through chemical or biological means immediately prior to the occurrence of dense population should be done for better management of the disease. (3) Growing resistant/tolerant cultivars should be given preference.

❍ Oat blue dwarf virus disease

The disease is known to occur chiefly in North America and Europe infecting both monocotyledonous and dicotyledonous plants. Suitable diagnostic plants of this virus are oats, common flax (*Lignum usitatissimum*), common chickweed (*Stellaria media*) and some other plants. The virus causes damage to the crop through dwarfing of plants and floret sterility.

Symptoms—(1) Appearance of bluish-green coloration on infected leaves under field conditions. (2) Enations on leaf veins and stem are usually seen. (3) Necrosis of the leaves and floral sterility are the characteristic symptoms of the disease. (4) Infected oat plants remain stunted and trend toward excessive tillering. (5) Infected flax may show malformed and crinkled appearance of leaves.

The causal virus—*Oat blue dwarf virus.* Virus particles are isometric in morphology, measuring 28 to 30 nm in diameter and consisting of single stranded RNA genome. Sedimentation coefficient of the virus is 119 S. Dilution end point of infected barley extract tested with the aid of leaf hopper vector is 1/256 to 1/512. Longevity of the virus sample *in vitro* is 10 minutes at 60°C and 16 days at 24°C.

Disease cycle—Infected plants are the main source of primary inoculum. Cicadellid leaf hopers are known vectors transmitting the virus in persistent manner. These vectors include *Macrosteles fascifrons* in North America and *M. laevis* in Europe. Vectors acquire the virus from the infected plants in 15 minutes and transmit it to healthy plants after 7 days of inoculation. Vectors are known to remain viruliferous for more than 2 months as reported. The virus is neither mechanically transmissible through infected plant sap nor through the oat seed.

Management—(1) Control of vectors through judicious use of suitable chemical and (2) Growing more tolerant/resistant oat cultivars may help in reducing the loss caused by this virus.

SOME OTHER ECONOMIC DISEASES OF OAT

❍ Oat pseudo-rosette virus disease

The disease is known to occur in Siberia and Japan. It is characterized by the appearance of shoot proliferation with the formation of many tillers giving the plant a tufted appearance. Some times leaves become reddish to brown and more rigid. Virus particles are bacilliform in appearance, measuring 167 ±20 × 57 nm in size. Smith (1972) reported two types of particles *viz.,* bacilliform of 60 nm diameter and rod shaped of 500–600 × 40 nm in size. No information on biophysical and biochemical properties is available so far. The virus over winters in its vectors. Infected perennial grasses like *Agropyron repens, Bromus inermus, Echinochloa crusgalli* and *Setaria viridis* are important source of virus perpetuation. Plant hoppers like *Laodelphax striatellus* is known to transmit this virus in persistent manner. These vectors acquire the virus within 6 hours. Latent period is approximately 6 days, after which healthy plants can be inoculated within 5 to 10 minutes of feeding. The virus is neither sap transmissible nor seed transmissible.

❍ Oat mosaic virus disease

The disease is wide spread in United States, New Zealand, England and some other countries of the world. It causes losses to the crop as high as 25% to 50%. The disease is characterized by the appearance of leaf mottling. Majority of infected plants of susceptible cultivars remain sterile. Virus particles are rod shaped, measuring 600 to 750 nm × 12 to 14 nm in size. The thermal inactivation point is 44 to 46°C, dilution end point is 1×10^{-2} to 1×10^{-3} and longevity *in vitro* is 24 to 48 hours at 20°C. The virus is soil borne. Fungal vector *Polymyxa graminis* is known to transmit the virus through its zoospores. Selection of non-contaminated soils and growing of resistant/tolerant cultivars are protective measures to be followed.

DISEASES OF OAT OF MINOR IMPORTANCE

Besides above diseases of economic importance, many diseases of minor importance have also been reported from different parts of the world. Such diseases are oat soil-borne stripe disease, oat striate mosaic disease and oat necrotic mottle disease. Some other virus diseases occurring on oat are barley yellow dwarf virus disease, barley yellow striate mosaic disease, cereal tillering disease, maize rough dwarf disease, cereal northern mosaic disease and wheat winter mosaic disease.

VIRUS DISEASES OF RYE (*Secale cereale*)

Rye is susceptible to many virus diseases but no one has described this host as main host of any virus. Thus, the rye is an alternative host of many viruses whose main hosts are cereals like rice, wheat, maize, barley, sugarcane and many other grasses. This crop is grown world wide chiefly in Europe, former U.S.S.R. and Asia. Rye is used for human as well as animal nutrition.

DISEASES OF RYE OF MINOR IMPORTANCE

Maize streak virus disease, wheat American striate mosaic disease, wheat soil borne mosaic, wheat dwarf virus disease, wheat streak mosaic, wheat winter mosaic, wheat yellow leaf disease, barley stripe mosaic, barley yellow dwarf, barley yellow striate mosaic, oat blue dwarf, oat pseudo-rosette, oat sterile dwarf, cereal chlorotic mottle, cereal tillering disease, northern cereal mosaic, rice dwarf disease, rice gall dwarf, rice hoja blanca, rice ragged stunt, agropyron mosaic, brome mosaic, cocks foot mild mosaic, cocks foot mottle, lolium mottle, phleum mottle, cucumber mosaic and rye stripe etc.

15

VIRUS DISEASES OF VEGETABLES

Diseases of tomato—mosaic, bushy stunt, aspermy, black ring, golden ring spot, spotted wilt, top necrosis, yellow dwarf, yellow leaf curl, yellow top and yellow net disease ; Egg plant diseases—mosaic and mottled dwarf ; Diseases of pepper—mottle, mild mottle ; Disease of cabbage—black ring ; Disease of cauliflower—mosaic ; Diseases of radish, turnip and lily; Diseases of cucumber—mosaic, green mottle, leaf spot and necrosis; Table showing diseases of melon, water melon and squash ; Diseases of bean-yellow mosaic and table showing different diseases of bean; Diseases of broad bean-wilt, mottle and table showing important diseases of broad bean ; Diseases of pea-early browning, carnation mosaic and streak ; Diseases of cow pea, carrot, celery, parsnip, artichoke, lettuce and spinach.

Vegetables include roots, bulbs, stems, leaves, fruits, inflorescences and un-ripped seeds of different annual and perennial herbaceous plants belonging to more than ten families. Depending on the plant species different parts of the plants are consumed as the human food. Vegetables are rich in nutrients providing main caloric needs of carbohydrates, proteins, oils, minerals and essential vitamins. Besides all above, they also contain specific organic acids, ethereal oils and many other essential constituents. A large number of viruses cause diseases of various descriptions inflicting severe loss to a number of economically important vegetable crops. They usually limit the production of these crops potentially and need the use of economic practices for successful cultivation of vegetables.

VIRUS DISEASES OF SOLANACEOUS VEGETABLES

Solanaceous vegetable which includes chiefly tomato, pepper and egg plant are susceptible to many virus diseases of economic importance. Economically important diseases of these crops are being described as under :

VIRUS DISEASES OF TOMATO (*Lycopesicon* species)

Tomato is an important fruit used as vegetables through out the world. It is rich in minerals and vitamins necessary for good health and well being. Important diseases are incited by *Tomato mosaic tobamovirus, Tomato bushy stunt tombusvirus, Tomato spotted wilt virus, Tomato ring spot nepovirus*, *Tomato black ring nepovirus* and *Yellow leaf curl virus.*

❍ Tomato mosaic tobamovirus disease

This disease is widespread in distribution and is known to occur wherever tomato is grown. The disease reduces plant vigor and yield by 3 to 25%.

Symptoms

1. Appearance of pale and dark green mosaic pattern on the leaves of infected plant.
2. Young leaves are malformed, some times stunted and may become fern-shaped.
3. Necrosis of leaves, stems, petiole and some times fruits may be seen.
4. Necrosis is more severe in mixed infection.
5. Infected plants may remain stunted.

The causal virus—*Tomato mosaic tobamovirus.* Virus particles are rigid rods of 300×18 nm. They contain single stranded RNA of 2000 kDa and a coat protein of a single polypeptide of 21 kDa. Thermal inactivation point of the sap is 80 to 90 C°. Dilution end point is 1×10^{-5} to 1×10^{-6} and the longevity *in vitro* is several months at 24°C. Serologically particle are actively immunogenic.

The disease cycle—Infected seeds and plants are important sources of inoculum in nature. Infected seeds usually transmit the virus year after year ensuring a permanent disease cycle. Further spread of disease takes place through mechanical means especially during transplanting by handling and cultural operations.

Management—(1) Clean and healthy seeds should be sown. Before sowing, seeds should be disinfected by soaking in 10% (w/v) trisodium phosphate ($Na_3\ PO_4$) solution for 20 minutes to eliminate external seed infections. (2) Management of the disease through cross protection and (3) Use of resistant/tolerant cultivars should be preferred for economic management of the disease.

❍ Tomato bushy stunt tombusvirus disease

The disease is known to occur in Europe, Africa, South and North America and some other countries of the world. The virus infects a number of plants both herbaceous and woody plants. Several vegetables such as pepper, spinach, artichoke and melon ; flowering plants such as carnation, petunia and tulip ; weeds such as *Chenopodium album, Plantago major* and *Stellaria media*, and woody plants such as apple, cherry, plum and grapevine are known hosts of this virus.

Symptoms—(1) Bushy appearance of the infected plants, resulting from secondary shoots which are formed following apical meristem necrosis. (2) Yellow or violet-red spots and mosaic like symptoms appear on the leaves of the infected plants. (3) Older leaves become chlorotic, curl up and ultimately fall off. (4) Infection of young plants causes a decline and wilt due to basal stem necrosis. (5) Infected plants bear fruits which are seedless and such fruits display bleaching plus ring like spots.

The causal virus—*Tomato bushy stunt tombusvirus.* Virus particles are isometric and 30 nm in diameter. Particles consist of single stranded RNA of 1500 kDa. Four different polypeptides are known to occur in the coat protein. Dilution end point is 1×10^{-2} to 1×10^{-6}. Longevity of the pathogen *in vitro* is 4 to 5 weekș at 20°C. The virus comprises several strains. Sample is actively immunogenic.

Disease cycle—The virus seems to be soil borne in nature. It is not known to be transmitted by seed. Infected woody plants represent perennial source of perpetuation from which the virus is carried on through propagation.

Management—(1) Young infected plants should be rogued out quickly from the site. (2) Soil should be disinfected on smaller acreage.. (3) Suitable crop rotation should be followed and (4) Only virus free seed materials should be used.

❍ Tomato aspermy cucumovirus diseases

The disease is known to occur worldwide. Tomato, chrysanthemum and tobacco are well known natural hosts.

Symptoms—The disease is characterized by the bushy appearance of the tomato plant. Apical meristem are usually killed in this disease, resulting in stimulation of secondary branching which give rise bushy appearance of the infected plants.

The causal virus—*Tomato aspermy cucumovirus.* Virus particles are isometric in morphology, measuring about 30 nm in diameter.

Disease cycle—Chrysanthemum is a perennial host on which virus perpetuates and different species of aphids transmit the virus in non-presistent manner.

Management—Heat treatment of chrysanthemum meristem has been found to be effective to certain extent. Control of aphids should be done properly well in time.

❍ Tomato black ring nepovirus disease

The virus is known to infect more than 270 species of both monocots and dicots which include cultivated and wild species.

Symptoms—The disease if characterized by the appearance of black nectotic rings on all parts of the infected plants.

The causal virus—*Tomato black ring nepovirus.* The virus perpetuates in the root of herbaceous and woody host plants.

Transmission—They are usually transmitted by nematodes— *Longidorus elongatus* and *L attenuatus* which are known vectors. The virus is seed transmissible also.

Management—Use of virus free seed material, control of nematode vectors and cultivation of resistant/tolerant cultivars are important measures for the management of the disease.

❍ Tomato golden mosaic geminivirus disease

The disease is known to occur in Brazil, Africa and many Asian countries.

Symptoms—The disease is characterzied by the appearance of yellow blightening, stunting and deformation of leaves and stems

The causal virus—*Tomato golden mosaic geminivirus*. The virus particles are geminate (twins) measuring 25 × 13 nm in diameter. Particles consist of single stranded circular DNA composed of separate segments A and B of 840 kDa. The coat protein is a single polypeptide of 28.5 kDa.

Transmission—The whitefly—*Bemisia tabaci* is the only known natural vector. Mechanical transmission is also possible.

Management—Control whiteflies by using suitable insecticide.

❍ Tomato ringspot nepovirus disease

The diseases is more prevalent in U.S., Europe, former U.S.S.R. and Japan. Natural hosts include economically important woody plants like apple, apricot, cherry, respberry and grapevine etc.

Symptoms—Characteristic symptoms are local necrotic ring spots, necrosis of some parts and systemic mottling.

The causal virus—*Tomato ringspot nepovirus*. The virus particles are isometric, measuring 28 nm in diameter. Virus genome contains two RNA species (bipartite). The single standed RNA of one species is 2800 kDa and of the other is 2400 kDa. The thermal inactivation point of the crude sap is 58°C and LIV is several months at —20°C. Virus sample is strongly immunogenic. Several strains are known to occur.

Disease cycle—Many woody, ornamentals and vegetatively propagated flowering plants are important sources of virus perpetuation. Virus vectors are nematodes—*Xiphinema* species.

Management—For management of the phyto-crop, virus free materials should be used in nematode free field and sanitary precautions should be taken for production of seeds to be used for sowing.

❍ Tomato spotted wilt virus disease

The disease has been recorded from both temperate and subtropical regions of the world.

Symptoms—Initial symptoms are vein swelling and appearance of necrotic ring spots on young leaves of the infected plants. The leaves twist upward or downward and become brittle. Stems also twist, shorten and in due course shoots are converted in to bushy appearance. Suitable diagnostic plants are *Petunia hybrida* producing local necrotic spots without systemic infection and *Lycopersicon lycopersicum* in which inoculated leaves remain symptomless and bronze patching are seen on leaves.

The causal virus—*Tomato spotted wilt virus*. Virus particles are isometric, 85 nm in diameter. The virus is composed of three genomic RNAs. TIP is 40—46°C, DEP is 2×10^{-2} to 1×10^{-3} and LIV is 2—5 hours at 24°C.

Host-range—Tomato, pepper, potato and eggplants are main hosts among vegetables. Other susceptible hots include *Lactuca sativa, Phaseolus vulgaris, Pisum sativum, Vicia fabae, Nicotiana tabacum* and *Vigna sincensis*. Different species of flowers such as *Petunia, Begonia, Chrysanthemum, Dahilia* and *Zinnia* are also susceptible hosts.

Transmission—Thrips species are natural virus vectors. The insect acquires virus in their larval stage and transmit it only in the adult stage. The acquisition by larvae requires feeding on infected plants for about 10 minutes with incubation period of about 10 to 23 days. The virus is not known to be transmitted transovarially to the offspring.

Management—Chemical control should be done to prevent excessive insect multiplication. Tomato and pepper seedlings should be prepared in seprarate seed beds isolated from tobacco seedlings to avoid initial infection potential. Besides these, other susceptible plants including weeds should be destroyed for successful management of this disease.

Fig. 15.1 Showing wilt symptoms on tomato fruit incited by *Tomato Spotted wilt virus.*

❍ Tomato top necrosis virus disease

The virus tentatively placed under nepovirus group consists of three isometric particles (T, M and B) with different sedimentation coefficients of 52 S (T), 102 S (M) and 126 S (B) respectively. No insect vector responsible for transmission of the virus is known so far.

❍ Tomato yellow dwarf virus disease

The virus with geminate particles belongs to geminivirus group. The whitefly —*Bemisia tabaci* is the main vector of this virus. The virus is known to cause considerable damage to the crop in different countries.

❍ Tomato yellow leaf curl virus disease

The disease is moe prevalent in Israel, Tunisia, Africa, India, Mexico, Venezuela and Europe.

Host-range—Tomato (*Lycopersicon lycopersicum* and *L. esculentum*), *Datura stramonium* and *Malva* species are natural virus hosts.

Symptoms—Infected tomato plants are small, malformed, curled upward and severely chlorotic.

Transmission—The whitefly -*Bemisia tabaci* is the principle vector that transmits the virus in persistent and circulative manner.

Management—Chemical control of vector, use of resistant/tolerant cultivars and suitable cultural practices are important measures for the management of the disease.

❍ Tomato yellow top virus disease

The virus is possible member of luteovirus group produces chlorotic and yellow apical colouration on the infected plant. The virus is known to be transmitted by the aphid—*Macrosiphum euphorbiae*.

❍ Tomato yellow net virus disease

The virus usually causes yellow net smptoms on the infected tomato plants and belongs probably to luteovirus group. The aphid—*Myzus persicae* is the only known vector of this virus.

❍ Tomato as natural alternate hosts of different viruses

Tomato has been observed and reported to serve as natural host for different viruses given bellow-

1. *Alfalfa mosaic virus.*
2. *Cucumber mosaic virus.*
3. *Tobacco mosaic virus.*
4. *Potato virus X.*
5. *Potato virus Y.*
6. *Broad bean wilt fabavirus.*
7. *Beet curly top (possible) geminivirus.*
8. *Tobacco leafcurl Geminivirus.*
9. *Tobacco streak ilarvirus.*

VIRUS DISEASES OF EGG PLANT
(*Solanum melongena*)

Diseases incited by *Egg-plant mosaic tymovirus* and *Eggplant mottled dwarf rhabdovirus* cause considerable loss to the crop and are economically important. *Cucumber mosaic virus, Tobacco mosaic virus* and *Tomato spotted wilt virus* are also known to occur on egg-plants.

❍ Egg-plant mosaic tymovirus disease

This disease is wide spread in West Indies, Colombia, Peru and many other countries of the world. More than 30 plant species mostly belonging to solanaceae and chenopodiaceae are susceptible to this virus. Natural hosts are eggplant, tomato, potato, *Chenopoditum amaranticolor, C. quinosa, Cucumis sativus, Datura stramonium, Nicotiana* species and *Petunia hybrida.*

Symptoms—(1) Characteristic symptoms are the presence of mosaic and mottle pattern on the leaves of infected plants. (2) Other plants such as *Chenopodium* species produce systemic symptoms and (3) Latent local lesions are observed on *Cucumis sativus.*

The causal virus—*Egg-plant mosaic tymovirus.* Virus particles are isometric, measuring 30 nm in diameter. The single stranded RNA is 2500 or 2000 kDa depending on the method of preparation. The coat protein is composed of single species of 20.5 kDa. The thermal inactivation point is 90°C and dilution end point is 1×10^{-7}. Longevity *in vitro* is 7 days at 24°C. Virus sample is strongly immunogenic. Strains are known to occur.

Disease cycle—The disease is known to be preserved through seed and secondary spread takes place through mechanical inoculation by sap. The flea-beetle-*Epitrix* species is the natural vector which transmits the virus from the infected plant to healthy plants situated in nearby and some more distant areas.

Management—Chemical control of vectors and avoidance of mechanical sap transmission should be practiced for reducing the damage.

❍ Egg-plant mottled dwarf rhabdovirus disease

This disease is known to occur in Spain and Southern Italy, causing severe stunting of plants. Only 1 to 20% plants are infected therefore, it does not cause much damage to the crop.

Symptoms—(1) Appearance of mosaic mottle on the leaves of infected plants are seen. (2) Leaf roll symptoms are also observed usually accompanied with the mosaic mottling and (3) Infected plants remain stunted and sterile, resulting in no fruiting at all.

The causal virus—*Eggplant mottled dwarf rhabdovirus.* Virus particles are bacilliform, measuring about 220×60 nm in diameter. Presence of lipids in the outer envelope has also been observed. The thermal inactivation point of the virus is 54°C and dilution end point is 1×10^{-3} to 1×10^{-4}. Longevity *in vitro* has been boserved to be 30 to 44 hours at 4°C.

Disease cycle—The virus is known to be transmitted through infective plant sap. Natural vectors have not yet been identified so far. Egg plants and many of their susceptible cultivars are the sources of virus perpetuation. Experimental virus hosts are *Nicotiana tabacum* and *N. glutinosa* on which local spots are seen on inoculated leaves followed by sytemic vein yellowing.

Management—Use of healthy seeds and elimination of infected source plants from the production fields are suitable control measures.

❍ Eggplant as natural host of different Viruses

Eggplant has been observed and reported to serve as natural host for different viruses as given bellow-

1. *Alfalfa mosaic virus*- It causes yellow mosaic with characteristic yellow to white spots over the leaf surfaces of the affected plants.
2. *Cucumber mosaic virus*- It causes specific mosaic on eggplant.
3. *Tobacco mosaic virus*- The virus is known to incite mosaic symptoms and causes considerable loss to the crop.
4. *Tomato spotted wilt virus*- This virus occurs on eggplant and is transmissible to other plants by thrips as vectors.

VIRUS DISEASES OF PEPPER (*Capsicum annuum*)

❍ Pepper mild mottle tobamovirus disease

The disease is known to occur in different countries including North America, Australia, Japan, Denmark, Iceland, England, France, Greece, Italy, Netherlands and Spain. The virus causes severe infection both in sweet pepper and hot peppers.

Symptoms—

1. Mild leaf chlorosis and reduced growth of infected plants at early stages are usually observed in the fields and glass houses.
2. Infected fruits remain small and malformed showing characteristic necrotic depresed zone on the surface (Fig. 15.2).
2. All plants in a field may get infected resulting in complete loss of the crop.

The causal virus—*Pepper mild mottle tobamovirus*. Virus particles are rod shaped in morphology, usually measuring about 312 × 18 nm in size. The coat protein consists of 158 amino acids residues and virus sample is actively immunogenic.

Disease cycle—The virus perpetuates on infected especially on the outer coat of the seed. The virus is transmitted mechanically during cultivation. Transmission by vectors or other means is not known. Diagnostic plants are *Datura stramonium, Chenopodium amaranticolor* and C. *quinoa*

Management—

1. Use only healthy disease-free seeds for production.
2. All contacts between hands or tools and disease plants should be avoided.
3. Soaking of seeds in 4.2% calcium hypochloride for 15 minutes or 10% trisodium phosphate for 30 minutes has been found to eliminate the virus from the seed coat surfaces.

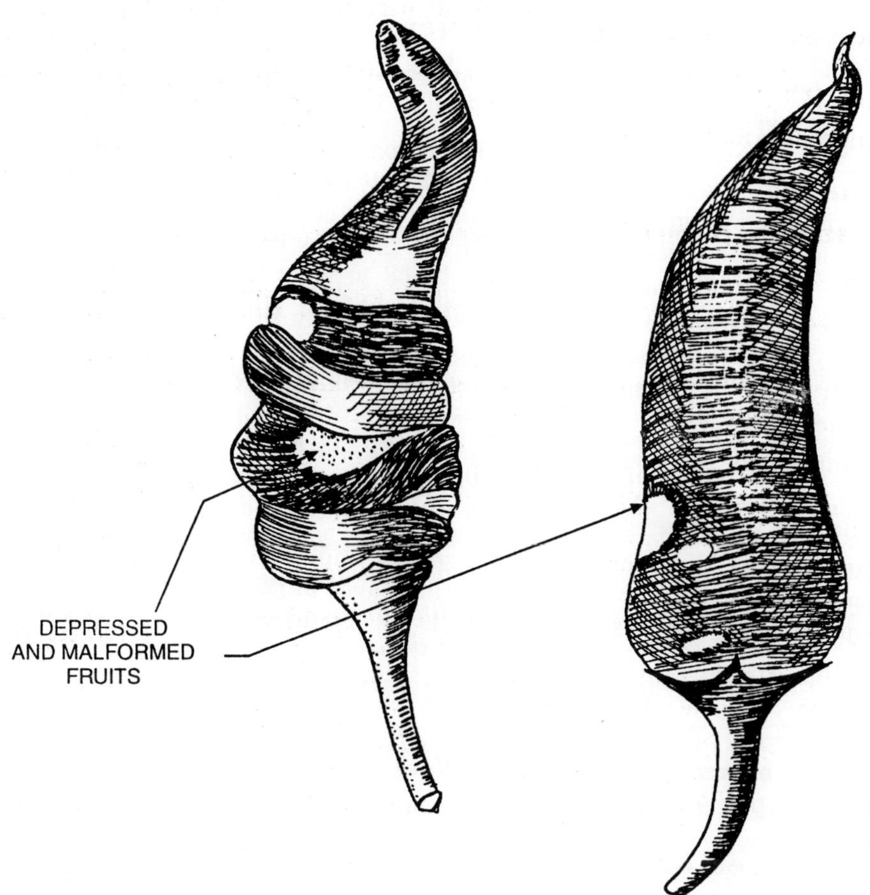

Fig. 15.2 Showing fruit of pepper infected from *Pepper mild mottle tobamovirus*

❍ Pepper mottle potyvirus disease

The disease is well known to occur in many countries including Florida, New Mexico, Texas, Arizona and California.

Symptoms—Necrotic lesions followed by systemic necrosis and death of the plants are characteristic symptoms of the disease.

The causal virus—*Pepper mottle potyvirus.* The virus particles are flexuous filamentous particles, measuring about 737 nm in lenght. Serologically, the virus sample is actively immunogenic.

Transmission—Several aphid species including *Myzus persicae* transmit the virus in non-persistent manner. Both nymphs and adults are eqully capable to transmit the virus successfully. The virus is also transmissible mechanically through sap during handling and cultivation.

Management—For management of the disease, healthy seedlings should be insured for production and special measures should be taken to avoid mechanical inoculation. Chemical control of aphids should be done to manage vector transmission.

❍ Pepper as natural host of different viruses

Pepper has been observed and reported to serve as natural host for different viruses as given bellow-

1. *Alfalfa mosaic virus.* Irregular shaped spots usually occur on the leaves. These spots enlarge and spread from the leaf base toward the tip. Infection is known to occur through seeds from the infected plants. Use only healthy and virus free seed and rogue out all the infected plantlets from the nursery. Control aphid vectors by chemicals for management.

2. *Cucumber mosaic virus-* The disease incited by this virus is characterized by visible, irregular and circular yellow spots on the leaves. Flower malformation and pollen sterility may be found, resulting in the formation of dwarfed and malformed fruits with necrotic spots.

3. *Potato virus X* - Symptoms may be observed as necrotic, chlorotic or mixed type lesions on the leaves and stems. Systemic infection may not occur. The disease is aphid and sap transmissible in nature.

4. *Potato virus Y-* It causes mosaic, mottle and crinkle like symptoms of apical leaves with characteristic vein banding on the leaves of the affected plants. No typical fruit symptoms may be observed. Control of aphid vectors is essential for crop protection.

5. *Tobacco leaf curl virus-* It causes curling, yellowing and puckering of pepper leaves.

6. *Tobacco mosaic virus-* It produces mosaic symptoms and causes severe damage to the pepper crop.

❍ Some viruses on pepper from other hosts

1. *Tomato bushy stunt virus.*
2. *Tomato spotted wilt virus.*
3. *Broad bean wilt virus.*
4. *Pepper golden mosaic Geminivirus.*
5. *Bean golden mosaic virus.*
6. *Squash yellow leaf curl Geminivirus.*
7. *Tomato yellow leaf curl Geminivirus.*

❍ Other diseases of pepper of minor importance

Pepper veinal motle potyvirus disease, Alfalfa mosaic virus disease and Cucumber mosaic virus disease are also known to occur on pepper in different countries of the world. Some potato and tobacco virus diseases are also observed to occur on pepper.

VIRUS DISEASES OF CRUCIFEROUS VEGETABLES

Plants belonging to *Brassica* species are common hosts of several viruses that cause considerable damage to these crops. Cabbage black ring spot, cauliflower mosaic and radish mosaic are economically important virus diseases.

VIRUS DISEASE OF CABBAGE (*Brassica oleracea* var. *capitata*)

Cabbage is an important cruciferous vegetable crop. It suffers from black ring spot disease which is known to be a destructive disease of the crop.

❍ Cabbage black ring spot virus disease (Syn. *Turnip mosaic potyvirus*)

The disease is widespread in distribution. It has been reported from temperate zones of America, Europe, Asia, Africa and Yugoslavia.

Symptoms—(1) The most common symptoms of the disease are the presence of chlorotic spots between the veins. (2) Some times these spots are bounded by small veins and have an angular appearance. (3) On red cabbage, the spots are usually green on reddish leaf background. (4) Slight mottling and chlorosis of older leaves may be seen. (5) Circular chlorotic spots with green centers are observed usually accompanied with diffused coloration in leaves.

The causal virus—*Cabbage black ring spot virus*. Syn. *Turnip mosaic potyvirus*. Particles of *Tulip mosaic potyvirus* are filamentous, measuring about 750×12 nm in size. Thermal inactivation point is 62°C, dilution end point is 1×10^{-3} to 1×10^{-4} and longevity *in vitro* is 3 to 4 days at 20°C.

Disease cycle—The virus perpetuates in several cultivated plants and weeds. Out of more than 40 aphid species, *Myzus persicae* and *Brvicoryne brassicae* are the most common aphids known to transmit this virus in non-persistent manner. The virus is also easily transmissible by the infected sap. No seed transmission is known to occur. Natural hosts of this virus are different species of *Brassica*. Besides this, the virus also infects lettuce, oilseed rape, poppy, wall flower and several species of weeds.

Management—(1) Source of infection should be reduced by the destruction of plant residues, particularly folllowing cabbage harvest. (2) Use of suitable chemicals to control vectors and weeds are useful measures. (3) Individual plant species should be grown separately because mixed plant population usually increases source of infection. (4) Tolerant or resistant cabbage and other *Brassica* cultivars should be used in production. (5) New plantations should be developed from virus free stocks and through meristem tip culture.

VIRUS DISEASES OF CAULIFLOWER (*Brassica oleracea* var. *botrytis*)

Although many viruses are reported on cauliflower but only one virus disease is known to be economically important.

❍ Cauliflower mosaic caulimovirus disease

The cauliflower mosaic caulimovirus disease is widely distributed in the U.S., New Zealand and several other European countries and in temperate regions of the world wherever cauliflower is grown extensively. The causal agent of the disease is the type member of the family Caulimoviridae which consists of double stranded DNA.

The virus has played important role in genetic engineering of plants because its genome is the source for the 35 S promoter. This promoter is capable of directing a high level of transcription in most types of plant tissues.

Symptoms—(1) Appearance of mild vein chlorosis starting from the leaf base towards the outer edges. (2) Pronounced vein yellowing and entire leaf chlorosis develop after some time (3) Whitish spots first appear on leaf blades which gradually become necrotic and dark coloured. (4) These symptoms may disappear above 25°C making it difficult to distinguish diseased from healthy plants. (5) The virus induces the formation of amorphous inclusion bodies within infected cells that can be visualized with light microscope in stripes of epidermal tissue after staining with phloxine B. (6) The inclusion bodies are not bound by the membrane and can range in diameter from 5 to 20 nm and may occur in all types of plant cells. The inclusions contain most of the virions found in the cell and the virions are embedded in a matrix that consists of several other cauliflower mosaic virus proteins.

The causal virus—*Cauliflower mosaic caulimovirus*. The virus particles are isometric, measuring 50 nm in diameter of 22800 kDa. The coat protein is composed of single polypeptide with high lysine and argentine. The virus genome consists of double stranded DNA of about 5000 kDa. It is circular with at least 6 ORFs. Biophysical properties include thermal inactivation point of 75 to 80°C, dilution end point of 1×10^{-3} and longevity *in vitro* for 5 to 7 days at 20°C. Serologically, the virus is moderately immunogenic. The virus is well characterised at molecular level. Its nucleic acid is composed of circular, double stranded DNA approximately 8000 base pairs in length. The nucleic acid of several strains of this virus has been completely sequenced and this information has revealed that the viral genome consists of 6 genes. In addition to the aphid transmission factor and capsid protein, the viral DNA encodes a cell to cell movement protein, a DNA binding protein, a reverse transcriptase and a multifunctional protein that is required for proper expression of other viral genes. The replication strategy of the virus differs from that of most of the other plant viruses. This virus produces a terminally redundant RNA, the 35 S RNA, which serves as a template for reverse transcription to dsDNA. The reverse transcription process is thought to occur within the cauliflower mosaic virus virion.

Disease cycle—Infected seed stock plants such as cabbage, cauliflower and some others serve as a reservoir to allow transmission of the virus year after year. The virus is easily transmissible with infective plant sap. The virus initiats infections in its hosts after mechanical inoculation or through aphid transmission. In nature the virus is also transmitted by more then 27 aphid species. A number of susceptible hosts exist among cruciferous plants.

Management—(a) Avoid growing susceptible annuals and perennials with this crop. (2) Control aphids by using suitable insecticide. (3) All the susceptible weeds should be destroyed and all residues of the previous crop must be eliminated. (4) Virus free plants can br obtained from inflorescence tissue through meristem tip culture. Some effort has been directed toward creating transgenic cauliflower plants resistant to this virus infection. Transgenic canola and cauliflower plants that express either the capsid gene or an antisense construct of gene VI have been created and are being evaluated for their ability to resist infection from this virus.

❍ Broccoli necrotic yellows rhabdovirus disease

The disease was first reported from Great Britain and is known to occur in Australia and North America in severe form.

Symptoms—It infects to cauliflower, headed broccoli and brussels sprouts and manifests mosaic and yellow leaf mottling symptoms followed by tissue necrosis of the leaves.

The causal virus—*Broccoli necrotic yellows rhabdovirus.* Virus particles are bacilliform, measuring 675×75 nm or bullet shaped, measuring, 266×66 nm in sizes depending on method of preparation. Sedimentation coefficient has been reported to be 874 ± 4 S. Biophysical properties include thermal inactivation point to be 50°C in *Datura* species and dilution end point of 1×10^{-3} to 1×10^{-4} with the longevity *in vitro* for 24 hours at 23°C.

Disease cycle—Infected virus host plants including cauliflower, headed broccoli and brussels sprouts grown continuously represent natural virus reservoirs. Aphid—*Brevicoryne brassicae* in which virus particles have been observed, transmit the virus successfully.

Management—Control of vector and use of resistant cultivars can reduce the loss imposed by the virus.

DISEASES OF RADISH, TURNIP AND LILY

Table 15.1 Showing virus diseases of radish (*Raphanus sativus*), Turnip (*Brassica rapa*) and lily (*Allium* species).

Name of diseases	Distinguishing characteristics
1. Radish mosaic comovirus disease	The disease was reported from California and is known to occur in Japan, Hungary, Austria, Germany and former Yugoslavia. Characteristic symptoms are appearance of small, circular and regular chlorotic spots on the leaves of infected plants. The virus particles are isometric, measuring about 30 nm in diameter. Thermal inactivation point of the virus is 65 to 70°C, dilution end point is 15×10^{-3} and longevity *in vitro* is 2 to 3 weeks at 20°C. Most crucifers including radish, cabbage, cauliflower, brussels sprouts, turnip, and experimental hosts such as species of *Chenopodium* are susceptible plants. The virus is preserved on the natural hosts and is transmitted by the beetles namely, *Epitrix hirtipennis* and *Phyllotreta cruciferae* and some of its other species. The virus is also transmissible thorough infected plant sap but not transmissible through seed. Chemical control of beetles, use of resistant/tolerant cultivars and destruction of virus reservoirs are the important measures to be followed for the management of the disease.

Name of diseases	Distinguishing characteristics
2. Radish yellow edge virus disease (The crop also serves as alternate host of *Beet western yellows virus* and *cucumber mosaic virus).*	The disease is widespread in Japan, Australia, China, England, Italy and U.S. of America. Radish is the only natural host of the virus. Infected plants manifest symptoms of leaf edge yellowing but some infected plants in Japan remained symptomless. The virus particles are isometric in morphology, measuring about 30 nm in diameter. It contains double stranded RNA which readily distinguishes it from other viruses. The virus perpetuates in infected seeds. It is not known to be transmitted through sap and no any vector is known so far in nature.
3. Turnip crinkle tombusvirus disease	The disease is known to occur severely in Scotland, England and former Yugoslavia. On leaves mottling symptoms usually appear in the beginning and in advanced cases crinkling and distortion of leaves are observed. Virus particles are isometric in shape, measuring about 28 nm in size. It probably consists of single stranded RNA of 1400 kDa. Thermal inactivation point is 90 to 95°C, dilution end point is 1×10^{-6} and longevity *in vitro* is 6 weeks at 20°C. Infected turnip plants and other *Brassica* species are important source of inoculum. Both larvae and adults of flea beetles chiefly 8 species of *Phyllotreta* and two species of *Psylliodes* are known to be active vectors of the virus. *Chenopodium amaranticolor, C. quinoa* and *Datura stramonium* are diagnostic hosts.
4. Turnip mosaic virus disease	Already described as cabbage black ring spot virus disease.
5. Tulip rosette mosaic (probable) sobemovirus disease	This disease is very popular in Scotland and Switzerland infecting crucifiers and some other plants belonging to compositae and solanaceae families. The virus causes necrosis on petioles and veins followed by leaf twisting and rosetting. The virus particles are isometric in morphology, measuring 28 nm in diameter. Biophysical properties include thermal inactivation point of 85 to 95 C°, dilution end point of 1×10^{-5} to $1 \times .10^{-6}$ and longevity *in vitro* over 30 days at 20 C°.
6. Tulip yellow mosaic tymovirus disease	The disease was first reported from Europe. Characteristic symptoms appear as vein chlorosis in young leaves followed by the development of pale yellow spots. The virus particles are isometric, measuring about 28 nm in diameter. Three particle components have been

Name of diseases	Distinguishing characteristics
	recognized from centrifugation preparations, which are top component (T) as non infective and two types of bottom components both being infective. 'The non infective particles contain sub- genome RNA (Matthews), 1980). The thermal inactivation point of the virus sample is 70 to 75 C°, dilution end point is 1×10^{-4} to 1×10^{-6} and longevity *in vitro* is 7 days at 24 C°. The virus perpetuates in its hosts. The important vectors of this disease are flea beetles namely, *Phyllotreta alta,* *P. cruciferae nemorum* and *P. undulate*. The virus is easily transmissible through infective plant sap but not through seeds. For management of the disease, infected plants serving as reservoir of the virus should be destroyed and vectors must be controlled by use of suitable insecticide. Besides these measures, growing of resistant/tolerant cultivars should be perferred.
7. Onion yellow dwarf potyvirus disease (*Tomato spotted wilt virus* is also known to occur on onion causing damage in onion seed production).	The disease is world wide in distribution wherever onion, shallot and leek are grown. The disease causes considerable damage to the crop since infected plants neither produce flowers nor they bear seeds. Infected leaves become chlorotic, partially flattened and crinkled, resulting in wilting of leaves. Virus particles are elongated having different length, measuring 750–775 × 14–16 nm in size. Biophysical properties include thermal inactivation point to be 60-65 C°, dilution end point to be 1×10^{-2} to 1×10^{-4} and longevity *in vitro* to be 2 to 3 days at room temperature. Natural hosts include onion, shallot, garlic and leek. The virus perpetuates in infected onion bulbs and in the bulbs for onion seed plants. Infected wild and ornamental *Allium* species are also natural source of infection. More than 60 aphid species including *Acrythosiphon pisum, Aphis craccivora, Aphis fabae, Rhopalosiphum* and *Myzus* species are known to transmit the virus in non-persistent manner. The virus is also transmissible through sap but not through seed. For management of the disease, the infected plants should be rogued and destroyed. All discarded bulbs and commercial onion residues should also be destroyed because they serve as potential virus reservoir for further infection. Chemical control of aphids should be done to prevent infection in growing onion bulbs and seed bulbs.

Name of diseases	Distinguishing characteristics
8. Leek yellow stripe potyvirus disease (*Tomato black ring virus* is also known to infect leek which is transmitted by *Longidorus atteneatus* and *L. elongatus* nematode vectors).	The disease is common wherever this perennial crop is grown extensively. The disease is characterized by the appearance of chlorotic spots on the infected leaves close to the leaf base and gradually spread toward the tip. The virus particles are flexuous measuring 815 to 820 nm in length. It has a coat protein of 34 kDa. Biophysical properties include thermal inactivation point of 50-60C°, dilution end point-1×10^{-2} to 1×10^{-3} and longevity *in vitro* for 3-4 days. The sample is strongly immunogenic. Leek, shallot and onion are natural virus hosts. Experimental hosts are *Chenopodium amaranticolor, C. album* and *C. quinoa*. On inoculation, local chlorotic and necrotic spots are observed, making them suitable for diagnosis and assay investigation. The virus is usually transmitted by *Aphis fabae* and *Myzus persicae* in non-persistent manner. virus transmission also occurs through infective plant sap but not through seed. The main preventive measures are to produce healthy seedlings and provide adequate isolation from over wintered onion crop to avoid source of infection. All plants showing symptoms should be rogued during summer and all plant residues should be destroyed following harvest. Chemical control of aphid vectors for seedling production is also recommended.
9. Garlic mosaic (possible) potyvirus disease (Garlic latent virus disease is also a minor disease which induces symptomless systemic infection on garlic and is known to be transmitted by mechanical means into onion and leek).	It ranks among common garlic diseases and occurs wherever this crop is cultivated through out the world. It causes general chlorosis thereby reducing growth and vitality. Individual bulb remains under developed. The virus particles are elongated, measuring 640×14 nm in size. Biophysical properties include thermal inactivation point of 70C° and dilution end point to be 1×10^{-4}. Garlic is the primary natural host of the virus. Experimental hosts are *Allium galanthum, A. hymnorrhizum, A. longicuspis, A. proliferum* and *A. rotundum*. Disease symptoms usually appear on first leaves as pale chlorotic narrow stripes and streaks. These spots gradually spread from the leaf base toward the tip and merge together causing general leaf chlorosis. The pathogen perpetuates in infected bulbs which are used for garlic propagation. The virus is sap transmissible and no natural vector is known as yet. The production and use of healthy seed bulbs is the primary and possibly the suitable measure for management of the disease. The use of meristem tip culture and thermotherapy have also been found to be successful for obtaining virus free bulbs.

❍ Lily vegetables as natural host of different viruses

Lily vegetables has been observed and reported to serve as natural host for different viruses as given bellow-

1. *Tomato spotted wilt virus* in onion- It causes considerable loss to the onion crop by infecting flower stems. It produces pale green and depresses yellow coloured spots. Tissues within the spots become necrotic. As a result of the disease, infected onion plants may not bear seeds at all.

2. *Tomato black ring virus* in leek-It causes natural infection in leek. It has been reported to be transmitted by nematodes- *Longidorus atteneatus and Longidorus elongatus.*

3. *Garlic latent virus* in garlic - The virus belongs to carlavirus group and causes symptomless systemic infection. The virus is mechanically transmissible into onion and leek as reported.

VIRUS DISEASE OF OKRA (*Abelmoschus esculentus*)

❍ Yellow vein mosaic of okra

Okra usually called as Bhindi in Hindi suffers from yellow vein mosaic disease which is much destructive in India, Pakistan and Bangladesh. This disease was first reported by Kulkarni during the year 1924 and has been studied in detail by different workers. The extent of loss due to this disease has been estimated to be as high as 85 to 96% when the crop was found infected during early stage of growth.

Symptoms—(1) Vein clearing and veinal chlorosis of leaves of infected plants are the most distinguishing characteristics of the disease. (2) Yellow network of veins is very conspicuous along with thickening of veins and veinlets. (3) In case of severe infection, chlorosis may extend to the inter veinal areas, resulting in complete yellowing of leaves. (4) Fruits if develop, they are smaller in size, yellowish green in colour and are malformed in appearance.

The causal virus—*Yellow vein mosaic virus* of okra. The virus is not sap transmissible but under artificial conditions, it could be transmitted by grafting.

Disease cycle—Several weed hosts and roadside plants including *Croton sparsiflora, Malvastrum tricuspidatum* and *Ageratum* species are known to harbour the virus assisting in perpetuation of the disease. The virus is transmitted by the insect vectors including white fly-*Bemisia tabaci.* Presence of leaf hopper—*Empoasca devastans* in the infected field is also suspected to be the transmitting vector of the virus.

Management—(1) Spray suitable insecticide starting from the 7-10 days of germination so as manage insect vectors. Sprayings (4 to 6) of the mixture of dimecron and nuvan@ 1ml each i.e. 2ml/3 liters of water should be done at 15 days intervals. Other insecticide like metasystox or rogor can also be used. (2) Destruction of weed and wild hosts should be done so as to avoid perpetuation of the virus. (3) Use of resistant/tolerant cultivars is recommended for the management of the disease in large scale cultivation.

VIRUS DISEASES OF CUCURBITACEOUS VEGETABLES

Cucurbits include cucumber (*Cucumis sativus*), melon (*Cucumis melo*), water melon (*Citrullus lanatus*), squash (*Cucurbita maxima*) and pumpkin (*C. pepo*). All these plants serve as main or alternate hosts of cucumber mosaic, cucumber leaf spot and cucumber necrosis viruses. Some important virus diseases are being described in some more detail.

❍ Cucumber mosaic cucumovirus disease

Cucumber mosaic virus is one of the most wide spread virus disease especially in temperate areas where conditions are suitable for the development of aphids which are the primary vectors of this disease.

Symptoms—(1) All parts especially leaves and fruits are usually infected. (2) Leaves are observed showing symptoms of yellow mosaic. (3) On young leaves, small green yellow spots, edged with small veins are seen which appear slightly transparent. (4) Infected leaf blades are distorted and plants remain stunted. (5) Less flowers and fruits are produced. (6) Wart-like protuberances are observed late in the season on fruits, resulting in distortion of fruits.

The causal virus—*Cucumber mosaic cucumovirus.* It usually consists of three types of isometric particles each measuring 28 nm in size. The virus contains single stranded RNA genome. Four RNA species are RNA-1 (1270 kDa), RNA-2 (1130 kDa), RNA-3 (820 kDa) and RNA-4 (350 kDa). These all are encapsidated as RNA-1 and RNA-2 separately and RNA-3 and RNA-4 together in one particle as reported. RNA-1, RNA-2 and RNA-3 are infective whereas RNA-4 contains the gene for the coat protein. Some CMV isolates contain a small single stranded RNA (10 kDa) known as a satellite and it depends completely on CMV for its replication. This satellite RNA is believed to be associated with special symptom expression. Nearly 70 strains of this virus are known. It has a thermal inactivation point of 70 C°, dilution end point 1×10^{-4} and longevity *in vitro* at 24 C° for several hours to several days. The virus is poorly immunogenic.

Disease cycle—Numerous alternate annual and perennial plants are natural hosts, including pepper, tomato, tobacco, alfalfa and red clover etc. Cucumber and melon are severely infected from this disease.

Transmission—The virus is easily transmissible through sap, through more than 10 species of *Cuscuta* but not transmissible through cucumber seed. It is seed transmissible in more than 20 species including tomato, pumpkins, beans, blue lupins and cowpea. In nature the virus is readily transmitted by different species of Aphids which include *Myzus persicae, Aphis gossypii, A. craccivora* and *A. fabae*. All the vectors acquire the virus with in 5 to 10 seconds and remain capable of transmission for two hours.

Management—(1) Cucumber mosaic infected plants situated indoor should be rogued immediately upon detection. (2) Control of aphid vectors by chemical application successfully reduces disease incidence in indoor production. (3) Weeds related to cucurbits should be destroyed. (4) Cucumber, Datura and begonia bulbs can be made virus free by subjecting CMV infected plants to heat therapy.

❍ Cucumber green mottle mosaic tobamovirus disease

The disease is widespread in Europe and Asia including India and Japan. It causes considerable damage to indoor cucumber production and loss in yield has been estimated to be as high as 30%. Besides, quality of fruits is reduced considerably.

Symptoms—(1) Mild vein clearing and wrinkling develop into pale to dark green mosaic on the leaves of the infected plants, (2) Leaves are reduced in size and are observed to be malformed, (3) Some strains of this virus produces pale yellow to white line, ring or star shaped spots, (4) Infected fruits seldom produce any remarkable symptoms.

The causal virus—*Cucumber green mottle mosaic tobamovirus.*

Disease cycle—Infective seeds of cucumber, melon and bottle gourd (*Lagenaria siceraria*) play important role in virus perpetuation. The virus is transmitted with infective plant sap by contact. Infective plant parts in the soil may also represent source of infection. No insect transmission is known to occur.

Management—(1) Virus free seed should be transplanted and seed of unknown origin should be disinfected by heat treatment for 3 days at 70 C° or by soaking in a 15% solution of trisodium phosphate for 3 days. (2) All tools should be disinfected and workers should be advised to disinfect their hands by washing at regular interval with soap or detergent. (3) Virus infected plants should be rogued immediately.

SOME OTHER DISEASES OF MINOR IMPORTANCE

❍ Cucumber leaf spot (Possible) tombusvirus disease

This disease is known to occur in Germany, Greece, Great Britain and Jordan. Pale green to yellowish irregular spots with necrotic centers are usually observed on infected cucumber leaves. Cucumber is only host of this virus. Virus particles are isometric, measuring 28 nm in diameter. The type strain contains a single stranded RNA of 1650 kDa and a single polypeptide coat protein of 44 kDa. Thermal inactivation point of the virus sample is 80 to 85 C°, dilution end point is 1×10^{-6} to 1×10^{-7} and longevity *in vitro* at 22 C° is about 20 days. *Celosia argentea* and *Chenopodium quinoa* are known experimental hosts. This virus perpetuates in cucumber plants continuously grown in field and glass house. The virus is transmitted through seed, soil and infective plant sap. No insect vector is known to occur. Planting of healthy seeds and disinfection of soil are the main protective measures.

❍ Cucumber necrosis (Possible) necrovirus disease

The disease was first discovered from Canada. It causes necrotic spots, pronounced leaf malformation and dwarfing of plants. Experimental hosts are species of families Amaranthaceae, Chenopodiaceae, Compositae, Leguminosae and Solanaceae. The virus particles are isometric, measuring 31 nm in diameter of 8600 kDa. The thermal inactivation point is 75-80C° and dilution end point was observed as 1×10^{-4} to 1×10^{-5}. Its longevity *in vitro* is about 30 days at 24 C°. The virus is preserved in infected plant parts in soil and is transmitted by the zoospores of the fungus *Olpidium cucurbitacearum*. Uncontaminated soil is the important measure for the protection of this disease.

CUCUMBER AS NATURAL ALTERNATE HOST

Cucumber has been observed and reported to serve as natural host for different viruses as given bellow-

1. *Tobacco necrosis virus*- The virus has been reported to cause grey brown spots on the leaves of infected plants. Pale sunken spots surrounded by moist dark green edges may be seen on fruits. The virus is preserved in infected plant parts in the soil and is transmitted by the fungus- *Olpidium brassicae.*

2. *Tobacco ring spot virus*- It causes a disease of minor importance, causing characteristic ring spot symptoms on leaves of the affected plants.

3. *Arabis mosaic virus*- The virus causes yellowing followed by leaf necrosis of the affected plants. Dwarfing of the plants may also be observed. As a result of the disease, there may be no fruit formation.

4. *Tomato black ring virus*- This virus has been observed in cucumber field contaminated with nematode vector of the virus.

5. *Hop stunt viroids*- The viroid causes the cucumber to become pale as reported from the some glass houses of Netherlands. The disease may be characterized by the pale green lesions on the fruits of the infected plants. Leaves of the diseased plants usually exhibit small, bluish and wrinkled symptoms with characteristic downward turned tips. Shortening of internodes usually cause bushy appearance of the plants. Infective plant sap is the chief mode of transmission.

Besides above, some other viruses have been reported to survive on cucumber as the potential natural host. Such viruses are *Beet curly top virus, Beet pseudo yellows virus, Melon necrotic spot virus, Watermelon mosaic potyvirus, Zucchini yellow mosaic potyvirus* and *Zucchini yellow fleck virus.*

DISEASES OF MELON, WATER MELON, SQUASH AND COURGETTE

Table 15.2 **Showing different important diseases of melon (*Cucumis melo*), water melon (*Citrullus vulgaris*), Squash (*Cucurbita maxima*) and Courgette (*Cucurbita pepo*).**

Name of the disease	Characteristics features
1. Melon necrotic spot virus disease	The disease is common is melon and cucumber crops world wide and causes reduction in yield. Melon and cucumber are natural hosts manifesting disease symptoms as necrotic lesions and spots on leaves and stems. Diagnostic plants are *Cucumis melo* and *Citrullus lanatus*. The virus particles are isometric, measuring about 30 nm in diameter. The virus consists of single stranded RNA genome and the coat protein consists of single polypeptide of 46 kDa. The biophysical properties include thermal inactivation point of 60 C°, dilution end point as

Name of the disease	Characteristics features
	1×10^{-4} to 1×10^{-5} and longevity *in vitro* from 9 to 32 days at 4 C°. The virus sample is serologically strongly immunogenic. The virus is preserved in soil and known to be transmitted by infective plant sap and zoospores of the fugus *Olpidium radicale*. For management of the disease (1) Growing of plants and production of healthy seed in uncontaminated soil are advised and (2) Transmission and spread through mechanical means should be avoided.
2. Watermelon mosaic potyvirus-2 disease	The disease is known to be present in cucurbit production areas of the world. It causes considerable damage to watermelon and other susceptible cucurbits. First of all, mild chlorosis followed by mosaic and distortion of leaves are observed on the leaves of the infected plant. In advance stage, green bubbles like protuberances are observed on chlorotic inter-veinal leaf parts. The virus is filamentous in morphology, measuring approximately 760 nm in length. Thermal inactivation point is 60 to 65 C° and dilution end point differing from 1×10^{-2} to 1×10^{-4} according to the isolates. Longevity of the virus sample *in vitro* was observed to be 10 to 20 days at 18 to 24 C°. Watermelon, melon, courgette, pumpkin, beans, peas and squash are important natural hosts. Diagnostic plants are *Chenopodium amaranticolor* and *Lavatera trimestris*. More than 38 aphid species including *Aphis citricola, A. craccivora, A. gossypii, Macrosiphum euphorbiae* and *Myzus persicae* are important vectors that transit the virus successfully. Virus transmission through seed has not been reported. For management of the disease (1) Susceptible plants should be grown on isolated fields less favourable for aphid development. (2) Weeds should be destroyed and chemical control of aphids should be done timely. (3) Resistant/tolerant cultivars should be evolved and grown.
3. Squash mosaic comovirus disease	The disease is known to occur in different countries of the world. In nature, the disease causes distinguishing symptoms on squash, cucumber, courgette, pumpkin, melon and watermelon. Infected plants show symptoms or may remain symptomless. Characteristic symptoms include appearance of mosaic, blister mottle, ring pattern, enation and leaf deformations. In case of severe infection, the fruits are deformed and less produced. The virus consists of three isometric particles (T, M and B) of 30 nm in diameter. Thermal inactivation point is 70 to 80 C° and dilution end point is 1×10^{-4} to 1×10^{-6}. Longevity

Name of the disease	Characteristics features
	of the virus *in vitro* is 4 weeks at 20 C°. The virus is strongly immunogenic. The virus is seed borne in nature and is transmitted in nature by beetles. Transmission through infective plants sap is also known to occur. Use of healthy seeds produced under phyto-sanitary conditions should be used for production. Chemical control of vectors is also an effective measure of be adopted.

SOME OTHER DISEASES RECORDED ON THESE PLANTS

1. *Zucchini yellow mosaic potyvirus*—Filamentous particles, measuring about 750 nm consisting of single stranded RNA. The virus is transmitted by aphids.

2. *Zucchini yellow fleck virus*--Characterized by the appearance of yellow spots on leaves which coalesce to form general yellowing of whole leaf. Usually transmitted by aphids in non-persistent manner.

3. *Squash leaf curl geminivirus*—It causes considerable loss to the crop by producing leaf curl symptoms.

❍ Melon, squash and water melon as alternate hosts

Melon, squash and water melon have been observed and reported to serve as natural host for different viruses as given bellow-

Melon, squash and water melon are known as the alternate hosts of different viruses. Such viruses include *Cucumber mosaic virus* and *Cucumber green mottle mosaic tobamovirus*. Besides, *Papaya ring spot virus* may be found on courgette, melon and water melon. Similarly, *Arabis mosaic nepovirus* and *Tomato black ring nepovirus* are known to occur on courgette and *Tobacco necrosis virus* on melon. These viruses may exhibit characteristic symptoms on respective plants under suitable conditions in presence of suitable vectors.

VIRUS DISEASES OF LEGUME VEGETABLES

Legumes are widely cultivated through out the world, owing to their constituents they contain. They are rich in protein and oils representing important part of our diet. More than 40 different viruses are known to occur on different legume vegetables including bean (*Phaseolus vulgaris*), pea (*Pisum sativum*), broad bean (*Vicia faba*) and cowpea (*Vigna* species). These plants are natural primary hosts for some viruses and alternate natural hosts for remaining of the viruses occurring on these plants.

VIRUS DISEASES OF BEAN (*Phaseolus vulgaris*)

❍ Bean common mosaic potyvirus disease

This disease is one of the most damaging diseases of this crop. High losses in bean yields have been observed when crop densities favour the occurrence and spread of natural infections.

Symptoms—(1) Mild to severe mosaic, vein banding, leaf malformation and curling of leaves are usually observed as characteristic symptoms of the disease. (2) Slight narrowing of systemically infected leaves is also observed. (3) Pods also exhibit symptoms of mosaic and malformation. (4) Some strains under certain conditions cause systemic necrosis that spreads in to various plant parts leading to black root syndrome and plant death.

The causal virus—*Bean common mosaic potyvirus.* The virus particles are filamentous in morphology, measuring about 750 × 12 – 15 nm in size. The virus consists of one coat protein polypeptide of 32-35 kDa and single stranded RNA genome of 3500 kDa. Thermal inactivation point of the virus has been observed to be 60 C° with dilution end point of 1×10^{-3} to 1×10^{-4} and longevity *in vitro* for 1 to 4 days at 24C°. The virus contains several strains that vary in host susceptibility and symptoms.

Disease cycle—The disease is seed borne in nature. Natural hosts are *Phaseolus* species, *Lupinus luteus* and wild legumes like *Rhynchosia minima*. Experimental hosts are *Cicer aretinum, Glycine max, Trifolium incarnation* and *Vicia faba*. Non-leguminous hosts include *Nicotiana clevelandii* and *N. benthamiana*.

Transmission—Several aphid species including *Acyrthosiphon pisum, Aphis fabae* and *Myzus persicae* transmit the virus is non-persistent manner in the nature. Some other species of the aphids such as *Aphis gossypii, A. medicaginis* and *Macrosiphum pisi* have recently been reported.

Management—(1) Only healthy seeds should be sown since seeds represent most important source of natural infection. (2) Plants for seed production should be grown in isolation from other susceptible legume crops and under conditions least favourable for aphid development. (3) Each infected plant should be rogued immediately from such crop upon detection. (4) Chemical control of the aphids for seed crop is also recommended.

❍ Bean yellow mosaic potyvirus disease

Syn.- *Pea* (common) *mosaic virus*

The disease is common in occurrence through out the world where legumes are grown abundantly. The virus causes economic damage to susceptible beans that react with bud necrosis leading to the death of the plant.

Symptoms—(1) Appearance of mosaic spots on the leaves. (2) Mosaic spots are bright yellow in colour. (3) The entire surface of the infected leaves becomes wrinkled. (4) Leaflets that emerge and develop from infected plants show significant alterations in shape and size. (5) Early infected plants grow slowly, often resulting in loss of grain and pod yield.

The causal virus—*Bean yellow mosaic potyvirus*. The virus consists of filamentous particles, measuring about 750 × 15 nm in size. It has a sedimentation coefficient of 140 to 144 S with major coat protein subunit of 33 kDa and a minor one of 28 kDa. The thermal inactivation point of the virus is 55 to 60 C°, dilution end point is 1×10^{-3} to 1×10^{-4} and longevity *in vitro* is 1 to 7 days. The virus is known to comprise several strains.

Disease cycle—The virus is preserved and transmitted from year to year in its numerous perennial hosts of legumes and some flowers and weeds. The disease has been observed to occur in high percentage in beans growing near the gladiolus.

Fig. 15.3. Showing mosaic Symptoms on bean leaves infected from *Bean yellow mosaic virus.*

Transmission—In nature more than 20 aphid species including *Acyrthosiphon pisum, Macrosiphum euforbiae, Myzus persicae* and *Aphis fabae* are known to transmit this virus in non- persistent manner. This virus is not transmitted through bean seed but is seed transmitted through *Vicia fabae, Melilotus alba* and *Lupinus luteus.* The virus is also easily transmissible through infective plant sap, so mechanical transmission may be important in virus spread among plants grown in dense population.

Management—(1) Beans should be grown isolated from perennial virus hosts. (2) Weeds and other known hosts should be destroyed. (3) Control of aphids by use of suitable chemicals is beneficial to prevent early infection. (4) Virus free plants obtained from thermotherapy or meristem-tip culture are particularly important.

SOME OTHER DISEASES OF BEAN

Table 15.3. Showing different diseases of bean found frequently in different parts of the world.

Name of the diseases	Distinguishing Characteristics
1. Bean leaf roll luteovirus disease	The disease is known to occur in several countries including America, Europe, India, The Middle East and North Africa. The characteristic symptoms are usually

Name of the disease	
	observed on French bean, chickpea, cowpea, and lentil plants, The diagnostic symptoms are chlorosis and downward leaf roll. Inter-veinal yellowing, upward leaf roll and reduced pod setting are also observed in severaly infected plants. The causal virus particles are isometric in morphology, measuring about 27 nm in diameter. The virus consists of a single polypeptide coat protein of 35 kDa and single stranded RNA genome of 2400 kDa. Virus samples are good immunogenic. Perennial alfalfa and white clover are systemically infected hosts and are important in disease cycle. Aphids transmit the virus in non-persistent manner. *Acyrthosiphon pisum* is the principal vector of this virus. For management of this disease, susceptible vegetable legumes should not be grown near alfalfa crops which represent the primary natural source of infection. Chemical control of vectors is useful in crops isolated from severe focal points of infection.
2. Bean southern mosaic sobemovirus disease	The disease occurs widely in warm temperate and tropical regions of America, Africa, Brazil, India and France. Economically important hosts are restricted to the members of family Leguminosae chiefly bean, cowpea, green gram and soybean. There are general mosaic symptoms, mottling and puckering of leaves of infected plants. Veinal necrosis, defoliation and dark green blotched spots on pods are also seen. Virus particles are isometric, measuring about 30 nm in diameter. The single polypeptide coat protein is 28 kDa. and single stranded RNA is 1400 kDa. Biophysical properties include thermal inactivation point to be 90 to 95 C°, dilution end point of 1×10^{-5} to 1×10^{-8} and longevity *in vitro* for 20 to 165 days at 22 C°. Well known strains are B, G and M. The virus is good immunogenic. The virus is mechanically transmissible through sap and some strains are seed transmissible. The virus spread in the field through beetles chiefly *Ceratoma trifurcate, Epilachna varivestis* and *Ootheca mutabilis* have also been observed. Chemical control of vectors is of little importance to check initial infection. Use of healthy and resistant/tolerant cultivars is useful in management of the disease.
3. Bean golden mosaic geminivirus disease	The virus first discovered in Brazil (1965), was reported later from tropical and sub-tropical America and many other countries. The disease is characterized by the appearance of irregular spots followed by vein chlorosis

Name of the disease	
	and finally appearance of over all golden mosaic on the leaves. Growth of infected plants is slow and fewer pods are formed on the infected plants. The virus particles are about 19 nm in diameter that occurs in pairs. The coat protein subunit is 31 kDa and RNA is 750 kDa. Bean golden mosaic virus is the first plant virus reported to have single stranded RNA. Thermal inactivation point of the virus is 50 to 55 C°, dilution end point is 1×10^{-2} to 1×10^{-3} and longevity *in vitro* is 48 to 70 hours at room temperature. BGMV is weekly immunogenic. Whitefly- *Bemisia tabaci*, both male and female transmits the virus in nature. The vector acquires the virus and transmits it within 6 minutes. Experimentally, the virus is also sap transmissible.
4. Bean mild mosaic comovirus disease	The virus particles are isometric in morphology, measuring about 20 nm in diameter. It is composed of single stranded RNA. Thermal inactivation point of the virus is 84 C° and dilution end point is 1×10^{-8}. The longevity of the virus *in vitro* is 6 weeks at 20 C°. It infects in nature various *Phaseolus* species and *Glycine max* causing mild mosaic and sometimes remains symptomless. Several beetles serve as vectors of the virus. The virus is also transmissible through infective plant sap.
5. Bean pod mottle comovirus disease	The virus produces severe systemic mottle and chlorosis in bean leaves. Severe systemic mottle occurs on leaves, pods and seed coat of soybean. The virus consists of isometric particles, measuring 30 nm in diameter. The single stranded RNA components M and B both are required for infection. Thermal inactivation point of the virus is 70 to 75 C°, dilution end point is 1×10^{-4} to 1×10^{-5} and longevity of the virus *in vitro* is 62 to 93 days at 18 C°. The bean leaf beetles (*Ceratoma trifurcate, Diabrotica balteata* and *D. undecimpunctata* etc.) are known to transmit the virus in nature. The virus is also transmissible through infective plant sap.
6. Bean rugose mosaic comovirus disease	This disease is common in occurrence in Central America and many other countries. Severe mosaic, puckering and malformation are observed on leaves and pods of the infected plant. *Bean rugose comovirus* has isometric particles of about 28 nm in diameter. The coat protein consists of polypeptides of 38 and 22 kDa. The single stranded RNAs are of 2300 and 1400 kDa. Thermal inactivation point of the virus is 65 to 70 C°, dilution

Name of the disease	
	end point is 1×10^{-4} to 1×10^{-5} and longevity *in vitro* is 2 to 4 days at 22 C°. Severe and mild strains are serologically identical or closely related. The virus is transmitted by Chrysomelidae beetles which are natural vectors. The virus is also known to be transmitted by infective plant sap.
7. Bean summer death geminivirus disease	The virus was first described from Australia on bean (*Phaseolus vulgaris*). Leafhopper (*Orosius argentatus*) was reported as natural vector.

BEAN AS ALTERNATIVE HOST

Bean has been observed and reported to serve as natural host for different viruses as given bellow-

1. *Alfalfa mosaic virus*- It induces lemon yellow spots of different shapes and size on bean leaves of affected plants.

2. *Cucumber mosaic cucumovirus*- It causes symptoms like leaf curling and chlorotic striping along the veins of the leaves of the infected plants.

3. *Tomato black ring nepovirus*- The virus incites yellow, brown and ring shaped necrotic lesions on he leaves of the affected plants.

4. *Tomato necrosis necrovirus*- It causes reddish brown necrosis on bean leaves. As a result of necrosis of leaf, petioles and stalks, plants may die prematurely.

5. *Pea green mottle virus*- It produces symptoms on bean leaves that are translucent with characteristic pale coloured ring spots.

6. *Artichoke yellow ring spot nepovirus* - It produces bright yellow blotches, ringspots and line pattern on the leaves.

7. *Peanut stunt cucumovirus* - It causes shortening of the petioles, reduction in leaflets size, chlorosis and malformation of the affected plants.

8. *Tomato spotted wilt virus*- It causes vein swelling and necrotic ring spots on young leaves of the affected plants. Bushy appearance of the plants may be seen in some cases.

DISEASES OF BROAD BEAN (*Vicia faba*)

Diseases incited by *Broad bean mottle bromovirus, Broad bean wilt* (possible) *comovirus* and *Broad bean true mosaic comovirus* are economically important, as they cause considerable damage to this crop.

❍ Broad bean wilt (possible) comovirus disease

The disease is known to occur in U.S.A., Japan, Australia, Africa and Europe. This virus consists of several strains described from different hosts.

Symptoms—(1)Scattered chlorotic spots and vein clearing are observed on the leaves as initial symptoms of this disease. (2) Infected plants remain stunted. (3) With the development of the disease, necrosis affects apical leaves. (4) Leaves and flowers fall off and plants wilt and die, causing reduction in yield. (5) General wilting symptom is found associated with the defoliation and flower loss in infected plants. (6) Loss in yield has been observed to be directly correlated with the number of infected plants.

The causal virus—*Broad bean wilt* (possible) *comovirus*. The virus particles are isometric in morphology, measuring about 25 nm in diameter. It consists of three components : empty protein shells without RNA (T) and two with RNA labeled (M and B). Sedimentation coefficients are 63 S (T), 100 S (M) and 126 S (B). Single stranded RNA (probably) accounts for 0, 22 and 33% of each particle weight respectively. Thermal inactivation point of the virus is 58 C° to 70 C°, dilution end point is 1×10^{-4} to 1×10^{-6} and longevity *in vitro* is 2 to 9 days at 21C°. The virus is strongly immunogenic.

Disease cycle—The virus is known to perpetuate in numerous perennial hosts which serve as reservoirs for transmission year after year. Broad bean and pea are the most important natural hosts. It also occurs on red clover, pepper, carrot, lettuce and spinach.

Transmission—More than 20 aphid species chiefly *Myzus persicae, Aphis craccivora* and *Macrosiphum euphorbiae* are well known to transmit this virus in non-persistent manner. The disease is also transmissible through infective plant sap but not through seed of broad bean and nasturtium.

Management—(1) Broad bean must be grown isolated from perennial hosts. (2) Control aphid vectors to protect the broad bean crop. (3) Inbred lines may be used as resistant parents in breeding programs.

❍ Broad bean mottle bromovirus disease

The disease is wide spread in England, Portugal and Sudan. It is restricted in areas where broad bean is grown extensively.

Symptoms—(1) First inoculated leaves may remain symptomless for some time. (2) Vein clearing accompanied by mottle mosaic symptoms may be observed on the apical leaves. (3) Most of the cultivars of broad bean have been observed to be susceptible. (4) *Chenopodium amaranticolor* with chlorotic local lesions and *Nicotiana clevelandii* with mild systemic mosaic and some other plants are diagnostic plants.

The causal virus—*Broad bean mottle bromovirus*. The virus consists of isometric particles, measuring about 26 nm to 29.4 nm in diameter. Virus particles contain 4 single stranded RNA molecules of 1100 (RNA), 1030 (RNA), 900 (RNA) and 360 (RNA) kDa respectively. The thermal inactivation point is 95 C°, dilution end point is greater than 1×10^{-3} and longevity *in vitro* is more than 20 days at 15C°.

Disease cycle and transmission—The disease is easily transmitted by infective plant sap. Vectors responsible for transmission include *Acalymma tricitrate* (striped cucumber beetle), *Collapses fluvial* (grape colaspis), *Diabrotica undecimpunctata* (spotted cucumber beetle) and *Sitona lineata* (pea leaf weevil). Transmission through French bean and broad bean is not confirmed.

Management—Use of suitable insecticide to keep insect vectors under control and destruction of perennial suspected hosts are the measures to be followed for management of the disease.

Table 15.4 Some other virus diseases of broad bean found most frequently in different parts of the world.

Name of diseases	Distinguishing characteristics
1. Broad bean true mosaic comovirus disease	The disease is limited in distribution and occurs chiefly sporadically in Africa and Europe. Variable mosaic pattern may be observed on broad bean leaves. Curling of small leaves with malformation and reduction of internodes are usually observed which causes losses of grains from 30 to 76%. The virus particles are isometric, measuring about 25 nm in diameter. Thermal inactivation point of the virus is 65-75°C. Dilution end point is 1×10^{-4} and longevity *in vitro* is 7 days at 24 C°. The disease is seed transmitted. Broad bean and pea are natural hosts. Weevils are suspected to be the important vectors of the disease. Production of healthy seeds and its use is the important way to prevent infection and occurrence. Control of vectors in time may help to minimize the disease to greater extent.
2. Broad bean necrosis tobamovirus disease	The virus was first discovered in Japan. Broad bean is only the natural host known so far. Necrotic local lesions, necrotic spots and veinal necrosis of leaves and streaks on stems and petioles are the characteristic symptoms of the disease. The virus contains rod shaped particles, measuring $150–250 \times 25$ nm in size. Thermal inactivation point of the virus is 55 to 60 C°, dilution end point is 1×10^{-3} to 1×10^{-4} and longevity of the virus *in vitro* is 8 days at 20 C°. The sample is moderately immunogenic. The disease is known as soil borne. No vector is reported. It is also transmitted by infective sap through mechanical means.
3. Broad bean stain comovirus disease	The disease is common in Europe, North Africa and Australia. It infects broad bean (*Vicia faba*). Other legume hosts include *Phaseolus vulgaris* (French bean), *Pisum sativum* (pea) and *Trifolium incarnation* (crimson clover). Chlorotic mottle, mosaic of leaves and discolored leaves are the important characteristic of the disease. The virus particles are isometric in morphology, measuring about 25 nm in diameter. Centrifugation separates three particles of equal size with sedimentation coefficients of 60, 100 and 127 S. The single stranded RNA is usually present in the two heavier particles. The thermal inactivation point is 60 to 65 C°, dilution end point is 1×10^{-5} and longevity *in vitro* is 31 days at 4 C°. It is moderately immunogenic. Virus infected seed is the main source of perpetuation. No any vector has been

Name of diseases	Distinguishing characteristics
	established. Use of virus free seed is main and primary preventive measure.
4. Broad bean mild mosaic virus disease	Infected plants exhibit symptoms of mild mosaic and partial necrosis producing discolored and malformed seeds. The virus measures about 25 nm in diameter. The virus is transmissible through seed and mechanical sap inoculation. *Chenopodium quinoa* is diagnostic plant producing local lesion and mosaic.

❍ Broad bean as natural alternative host of some viruses

Broad bean has been observed and reported to serve as natural host for different viruses as given bellow :

1. *Alfalfa mosaic virus.*
2. *Bean leaf roll luteovirus* (Syn. *Pea leaf roll virus*).
3. *Bean yellow mosaic potyvirus* (Strain- *Pea common mosaic virus*).
4. *Cucumber mosaic cucumovirus.*
5. *Pea enation mosaic virus.*
6. *Pea seed-borne mosaic potyvirus.*
7. *Artichoke yellow ring spot virus.*
8. *Pea early browning tobravirus.*

VIRUS DISEASES OF PEA (*Pisum sativum*)

Different viral diseases namely, pea common mosaic virus disease (**Syn.** bean yellow mosaic virus disease), pea early browning tobravirus disease, pea enation mosaic virus disease, pea seed borne mosaic potyvirus disease and pea streak carlavirus disease are economically important diseases of this crop.

❍ Pea early browning tobravirus disease

The disease is mostly observed in Holland, England and Morocco. In addition to pea, other natural hosts such as alfalfa, French bean and broad bean are also infected from this disease.

Symptoms—(1) Necrosis of whole plants may be seen which causes the death of entire shoots. (2) First of all, necrosis occurs in the stipules and leaflets followed by appearance of necrotic areas on pods. (3) Symptoms on other plants are observed as leaf chlorosis and distortion in alfalfa, mosaic and malformation in French bean and mild mosaic in broad bean.

The causal virus—*Pea early browning tobravirus*. The virus particles appear as rigid rods about 22 nm wide with 105 to 215 nm in length. The molecular weight of the coat protein is 24 kDa, the single stranded RNA is 1300 kDa for shorter particles and 2500 kDa for longer particles. Only long particles are infective but both the particles are essential for replication in the host. Thermal inactivation point in *Nicotiana clevelandii* sap is 74 to 78 C° and dilution end point of the sap is 1×10^{-5}. Longevity of the virus has been observed to be one year. The virus sample is moderately immunogenic. Different strains are known to occur namely, Dutch strain, British strain and Italian No. 6 strain. Diagnostic plants are *Chenopodium amaranticolor* and *Nicotiana clevelandii.*

Disease cycle and transmission—The virus is preserved in its perennial host—alfalfa in nature. Nematodes such as *Trichodorus teres* and *T. pachydrmus* in Netherlands and *Trychodorus anemones, T. primitivus* and *T. viruliferous* in England have been observed as natural vectors. The disease is also known to be transmitted through seed and sap inoculation.

Management—(1) Soil uncontaminated with the nematodes should be used for pea production. (2) Disinfection of field against nematodes should be done. (3) Resistant/tolerant cultivars of pea should be grown keeping in view the risk of arising of strains.

❍ Pea enation mosaic virus (Type) disease

The virus was first discovered in New York and is considered as an economically important disease in northern temperate regions of the world. The disease has also been observed in the warmer areas of Silicily and Iran. In Europe, the disease has been reported to cause yield loss via rolling and occasional necrosis of leaves. Garden and field pea, broad bean and sweet pea (*Lathyrus odoratus*) are natural hosts of this virus.

Symptoms—(1) Initial symptoms on leaves are seen as mosaic and mottling. (2) Leaves of infected plants usually curl and internodes are reduced in length. (3) The initial chlorotic spots on leaves become white and poorly translucent. (4) The infected plants look bushy in appearance. (5) Over growth, protuberances and enations from near veins on the lower leaf surface and cell proliferation are the characteristic symptoms of the disease. (5) Infection prior to pod formation results in twisting of pods and formation of chlorotic and smaller seeds.

The causal virus—*Pea enation mosaic virus* (Type). The virus particles are isometric in shape, measuring about 28 nm in diameter. Particles consist of two sedimenting components—the top and the bottom. They are 43800 kDa (T) and 55700 kDa (B) with sedimentation coefficient of 99 S and 112 S respectively. The single stranded RNA is bipartite, with RNA-1 in the B component of 1700 kDa and RNA-2 in the T component of 1300 kDa. RNA-1 code for the major polypeptide coat protein of 22 kDa. A mixture of both components are necessary for infection. The thermal inactivation point of the virus is 56 to 58 C° and dilution end point is 1×10^{-3} to 1×10^{-4}. Longevity of the virus *in vitro* has been reported to be 4 days at 20 C°.

Disease cycle—The perennial alfalfa (*Medicago sativa*) and subterranean clover (*Trifolium subterraneum*) are the main reservoir for the pathogen. Diagnostic plants are *Chenopodium album, C. amaranticolor* and *C. quinoa.*

Transmission—The aphid vector—*Acyrthosiphon pisum* is the important vector responsible for transmission of the virus in circulative and semi-persistent manner. Nymphs more actively acquire the virus in 15 minutes whereas adults acquire the virus in 1 to 2 hours. Infectivity is retained up to molts for 30 days but does not pass on to the offspring. The virus is sap transmissible. The virus is not transmitted through pea seed but known to be transmissible through seed of broad bean.

Management—(1) Pea and broad bean should not be grown neither with each other nor near perennial reservoir hosts of the virus. (2) Only healthy broad bean seeds should be grown. (3) Chemical control of aphids should be done if so desired. (4) Resistant/tolerant cultivars should be used in high risk production areas.

❍ Pea seed-borne mosaic potyvirus disease

The disease is of world wide distribution that might be due to the international exchange of pea seed germplasm. The disease is known to infect more than 47 species belonging to 12 dicots families.

Symptoms—(1) A translucent clearing occurs on leaf veins of infected plants. (2) Leaflets roll downward, shoots curl, internodes shortened and plants are rosetted. (3) Early infections reduce flowers and pods formation. (4) Leaf margins are rolled and leaflets are distorted in broad bean as disease manifestation.

The causal virus—*Pea seed—borne mosaic potyvirus*. The virus particles are filamentous in morphology, measuring about 770×12 nm in diameter. They have a sedimentation coefficient of 154 S. The coat protein subunit is 34 kDa. It consists of single stranded RNA, accounting for about 5.3% of the particle weight. Thermal inactivation point of the virus is 55C°, dilution end point is 1×10^{-3} to 1×10^{-4} and longevity *in vitro* is 24 to 96 hours at room temperature. The virus sample is moderately immunogenic.

Disease cycle—The virus is preserved in seeds and it is transmitted through infected seed. Alfalfa is its natural potential host and a permanent source of infection.

Transmission—About 10 aphid species including *Acyrthosiphon pisum, Macrosiphum euforbiae, Myzus persicae* and *Rhopalosiphum padi* are known to transmit the virus in non-persistent manner.

Management—(1) Use only healthy seeds. (2) First infected plants should be rogued immediately from the field. (3) Natural potential hosts should be destroyed immediately.

❍ Pea streak carlavirus disease

The disease is most common in occurrence on pea in North America, on clovers in Canada and on sweet clover in West Germany. Pea and clover are natural hosts. Experimental hosts are *Chenopodium amranticolor* and *Gamphrena globosa* that react with necrotic local lesions.

Symptoms—(1) Appearance of necrotic streaks on leaves and stripes on stem, petioles and leaves. (2) Vein necrosis is also observed. (3) Pods are spotted, malformed and seedless. (4) The leaves and apices of infected plants wilt and die. (5) Infected red clover remains symptomless.

The causal virus—*Pea streak carlavirus*. The virus particles are filamentous in morphology, measuring about 620×12 nm in size. It consists of single stranded RNA which accounts about 5.4% of the particle weight. Thermal inactivation point of the virus is 78 to 80 C° with dilution end point of 1×10^{-6} to 1×10^{-7}. Longevity of the virus *in vitro* has been reported to be 2-7 days at room temperature. Few strains have longevity *in vitro* for 50 to 70 days. The virus is related to red clover mosaic and sample is strongly immunogenic.

Disease cycle—The virus is preserved in annual and perennial plants.

Transmission—It is transmitted by the aphids chiefly *Acyrthosiphon pisum* in non-persistent manner. Transmission through infected plant sap is possible but is of little importance in nature.

Management—Chemical control of aphids and use of resistant pea cultivars may be useful to reduce the infection.

PARTIAL LIST OF OTHER VIRUS DISEASES OF PEA OF MINOR IMPORTANCE

(1) **Pea mild mosaic comovirus disease**—Characterized by the appearance of vein clearing followed by vein etching and necrosis.

(2) **Pea** (*Pisum*) **rhabdovirus disease**—Transmissible through mechanical means. No any vector is known.

(3) **Pea stunt virus disease**—It causes stunting of the infected plants.

PEA AS ALTERNATE HOSTS OF SOME VIRUSES

Pea has been observed and reported to serve as natural host for different viruses as given bellow-

1. *Alfalfa mosaic virus*- In Europe, it is most common in occurrence. It causes characteristic mild mosaic symptoms with translucent veins and diffused green yellowing of tender parts of the affected pea cultivars. Infected plants may grow slowly, resulting in the formation of malformed pods and reduction in yield.

2. *Cucumber mosaic cucumovirus*- It produces chlorotic mosaic and necrotic spots on pea leaves. Infected plants may remain stunted.

3. *Tobacco necrosis necrovirus*- This virus has been reported to be found associated with the roots of the affected pea crops.

4. *Tomato spotted wilt virus*- It causes purple to brown leaf petiole and stem discoloration in the affected plants. Infected plants may also exhibit leaflet spotting, vein necrosis and concentric ring spots on the pods.

5. *Beet mosaic virus*- It produces characteristic dark, necrotic stripes on stems and petioles with diffused clearing and wilting of leaflets.

6. *Broad been mild mosaic virus*- It causes curling of leaves, shortening of internodes and plant stunting. Seeds are malformed and discoloured.

7. *Broad bean stain comovirus*- Characteristically, leaves of the infected plants remain small, crinkled and mottled. Affected plants are observed to be stunted.

8. *Broad bean true mosaic virus*-The virus produces symptoms like vein clearing, chlorosis, diffused spotting and discoloration on leaves of the affected plants.

9. *Broad bean wilt virus*-It produces translucent chlorosis and mosaic like symptoms on the leaves of the affected plants. Shortening of internodes causes dwarfing of the affected plants. As a result of the disease pod formation and yield are adversely affected.

10. *Bean leaf roll virus*-Characteristic clearing between lateral veins at the leaf margins may be easily observed on the affected plants. Diffused green colouration spreads gradually along the veins, resulting in the upward rolling of the leaves of such plants.

11. *Bean yellow mosaic potyvirus* (Strain-*Pea common mosaic virus)*-It produces yellowing along the veins with characteristic yellowish network on the leaves of the affected plants.

12. *Red clover mottle comovirus*- It remains symptomless; however, produces diffused chlorotic mottle in differential host-Pisum jomardi.

13. *Red clover vein mosaic carlavirus*- The virus produces shortening of internodes, causing rosette appearance of the affected plants. Violet streaked spots may be observed on the stems. and petioles.

14. *Tobacco black ring nepovirus*- It produces yellowing and dark brown ring spots on the leaves of the affected plants. In severe cases, necrosis of leaves, veins and stems may take place, causing stunting of the affected plants.

VIRUS DISEASES OF COWPEA (*Vigna* species)

Diseases incited by *Cowpea mosaic comovirus*, *Cowpea severe mosaic comovirus*, *Cowpea chlorotic mottle bromovirus* and *Cowpea aphid-borne mosaic potyvirus* are economically important as they cause considerable damage to the crop every year in different cowpea growing areas of the world.

❍ Cowpea severe mosaic comovirus disease

This disease is well known to cause considerable loss in U.S., Cuba, Netherlands, Nigeria and some other countries of the world. Loss in yield has been reported to be as high as 95%.

Symptoms—(1) Appearance of faint diffused mosaic followed by systemic mosaic on leaflets. (2) Leaves may be malformed having yellow mosaic appearance. (3) Stopping of plant growth and reduction in number of flowers usually cause reduction in yield. (4) *Chenopodium amaranticolor* and *Phaseolus vulgaris* are diagnostic hosts. They produce necrotic lesions and local lesions respectively on these plants.

The causal virus—*Cowpea mosaic comovirus*. The virus particles are isometric in morphology. They consist of three equal size particles—T (RNA-free) whereas M and B contain RNAs. These particles have sedimentation cofficients of 58 S (T), 95 S (M) and 115 S (B) having molecular weights of 3800 (T), 5150 (M) and 5870 (B) kDa respectively. Both M and B particles are essential for causing infection. Biophysical properties include thermal inactivation point as 55 to 65 C°, dilution end point as

1×10^{-4} to 1×10^{-6} and longevity *in vitro* for 4 to 10 days at room temperature. Strains are known to occur.

Disease cycle—*Vigna* species is the primary natural host. Perennial legumes and infected seeds represent continuous source of infection. Pigeon pea (*Cajanus cajan*) is suspected to be important host. Seed transmission is reported.

Transmission—Several Chrysomelidae beetle species in different geographical areas are known as vectors of the virus. Two thrips and two grass hopper species have also been reported as vectors. The virus is also transmissible through infective plant sap.

Management—Elimination of perennial hosts and virus free seed production are useful plant protection measures to be followed for management of the disease.

❍ Cowpea aphid-born mosaic potyvirus disease

The disease is known to occur where cowpea is grown especially in Africa, Asia, U.S. and Europe. Natural hosts include *Vigna sinensis, V. unguiculata* and *Gladiolus* species. It experimentally infects both legumes and non-legumes.

Symptoms—(1) Appearance of yellowish vein clearing on leaves of infected cowpea plants. (2) Vein clearing is followed by the appearance of mosaic symptoms of varying degrees according to the susceptibility of the cultivars. (3) Finally dark green vein banding, inter-veinal necrosis and leaf malformation are observed. (4) Stunting of the plants may be frequently observed.

The causal virus—*Cowpea aphid-born mosaic potyvirus*. The virus particles are filamentous in morphology, measuring about 750 nm in size, having sedimentation coefficient of 150 S. The coat protein subunits are of 34-35 kDa. The thermal inactivation point is 57 to 60 C°, dilution end point is 1×10^{-3} to 1×10^{-4} and longevity of the virus *in vitro* is 1 to 3 days at 20 C°. The virus is moderately to strongly immunogenic. It is closely related to several legume potyviruses. Virus strains have been classified on the basis of the symptoms, hosts and place of origin. European (type) strain, African (neo type) strain, African mild strain and African vein banding strain are common in occurrence.

Disease cycle—The virus is transmitted year after year through cowpea seed from infected plants. The extent of transmission depends on susceptibility of the cultivars and strains.

Transmission—Several aphid species especially *Aphis craccivora, A. fabae* and *A. gossypii* serve as vectors to transmit this virus in non-persistent manner. Mechanical transmission with infective plant sap is possible.

Management—(1) Use of virus free seed. (2) Chemical control of vectors with suitable insecticide and (3) Earlier planting to encourage adequate plant growth before aphids move to the crop are effective measures for the management of the disease.

❍ Cowpea mosaic comovirus disease

The disease is common in occurrence where the cowpea is grown extensively. It occurs chiefly on cowpea (*Vigna unguiculata*) and soybean (*Glycine max*). Other natural hosts are *Phaseolus lathyroides* and perennial plant—*Desmodium canescens*. *Chenopodium amaranticolor* is suitable diagnostic plant reacting only with necrotic local lesions on inoculated leaves.

Symptoms—(1) Inoculated leaves become necrotic. (2) Vein clearing and chlorotic mottling on leaflets are observed as systemic symptoms and (3) In advance cases light and dark green mosaic areas are followed by the distortion of the leaves.

The causal virus—*Cowpea mosaic comovirus*. The virus consists of isometric particles, measuring about 25 nm in diameter. On centrifugation, they sediment into three bands of morphologically/serologically identical particles. The top one contains no RNA whereas particles of middle and bottom contain RNA. Their sedimentation coefficients are 58 S (T), 95 S (M) and 115 S (B) respectively. The two RNA species of different molecular weights by analogy occur separately in the M and B components. Both M and B particles are essential for infection. Thermal inactivation point of the virus is 65 to 75 C°, dilution end point is 1×10^{-4} to 1×10^{-5} and longevity *in vitro* is 1 to 5 days at 23 to 24 C°. The virus is strongly immunogenic, producing antiserum of high titre.

Disease cycle—Perennial legume hosts and infected seeds are the natural source of infection. Perennial hosts represent primary inoculum.

Transmission—Leaf feeding beetles chiefly *Ceratoma ruficornis* and *C. trifurcata* transmit the virus from primary host to the field. The virus is also mechanically transmissible by infected plant sap.

Management—(1) Rogueing of perennial hosts especially weeds as primary source of infection. (2) Isolation of the cultivated crop from infected hosts. (3) Use of healthy and disease free seed is important. (4) Chemical control of vectors should be given priority.

COWPEA DISEASES OF MINOR IMPORTANCE

Table 15.5 Showing other virus diseases of cowpea of minor importance.

Name of diseases	Distinguishing characteristics
1. Cowpea chlorotic mottle bromovirus disease	The disease was reported from Southern U.S. and Central America. Appearance of mosaic and leaf mottle are the main symptoms of the disease. Occasionally, local lesions and vein necrosis may be observed. The virus has been isolated from natural legume hosts such as bean (*Phaseolus vulgaris*), cowpea (*Vigna unguiculata*), soybean (*Glycine max*) and *Desmodium laevigatum*. Diagnostic plants are *Chenopodium album* and *C. hybriddum*. They produce local lesions. The virus consists of isometric particles, measuring 25 nm in diameter. Its purified preparations consist of three particles of equal size with same sedimentation coefficient. Each particle contains four RNA genomes of 1100 (RNA), 1000 (RNA),

Name of diseases	Distinguishing characteristics
	700 (RNA) and 300 (RNA) kDa respectively. The coat protein subunits are of 19.4 kDa. Its multi component structure makes it easier to study genetics and molecular biology. The thermal inactivation point of the virus is 67 to 76 C°, dilution end point is 1×10^{-4} to 1×10^{-5} and longevity of the virus *in vitro* is up to 44 days. It is moderately immunogenic. The virus is usually transmitted by different species of beetles. These include *Ceratoma ruficornis, C. trifurcate* (bean leaf beetle), *Diabrotica balteata* (banded cucumber beetle) and *D. undecimpunctata* (spotted cucumber beetle). Chemical control of vectors and any other measure to reduce the vector population are useful in crop protection. Source of resistance should be searched and used for cultivation.
2. Black eye cowpea mosaic potyvirus disease	The disease occurs wherever cowpea is grown. The disease is identified by the appearance of mosaic symptoms on cowpea leaves. Cowpea (*Vigna unguiculata* subspecies *sesquipedalis*), *Crotolaria spectabillis* and *Desmodium* species are natural hosts. The virus consists of filamentous particles, measuring 750 nm in size. The coat protein subunit is 34 to 35 kDa. and single-stranded RNA is 2900 kDa. Thermal inactivation point of the virus is 60-65 C°, dilution end point is 1×10^{-3} to 1×10^{-5} and longevity *in vitro* is 1 to 2 days. *Chenopodium amaranticolor* and *C. quinoa* produce local lesions and are suitable diagnostic hosts. Infected seed represents primary source of inoculum. Many aphids including *Aphis craccivora* and *Myzus persicae* transmit the virus in non-persistent manner. The use of healthy virus free seed is the main prerequisite to eliminate source of infection.
3. Cowpea mild mottle carlavirus disease	The disease is known to occur in Eastern Ghana and India in ground nut. The natural hosts of the virus are cowpea and soybean. Cowpea exhibit symptoms of infection as mild leaf mottle and sometimes systemic chlorosis and necrosis. The causal virus has filamentous particles of 650×13 nm, consisting of a coat protein polypeptide of 32 kDa and an RNA that accounts for 5% of the particle weight. The experimental hosts are mostly legumes, but they also include some non-legumes. Necrotic local lesions without systemic infection occur in inoculated leaves of *Beta vulgaris*. It can be transmitted mechanically. Whitefly vectors have been reported. The disease is seed transmissible also. Virus free seed is essential for sowing new crop.

Name of diseases	Distinguishing characteristics
4. Cowpea mottle virus disease	The disease has been reported to occur severely in Nigeria. The characteristic symptoms of the disease include yellow mosaic, leaf distortion, witches broom symptoms and green mottling. The virus consists of isometric particles, measuring about 30 nm in diameter. It constitutes a single component of 122 S with coat protein subunit of 44.5 kDa. and a single stranded RNA of 1400 kDa. that accounts for about 20% of the particle. The virus is known to be transmitted through cowpea, Bambarra ground nut and French bean seed. The virus is mechanically transmissible through infected plant sap. Vectors transmitting the virus include beetles like *Ootheca mutabilis* and *Paralupero-deslineata*. Planting of healthy, virus free seed is the most important plant protection measure to be adopted.
5. Black gram mottle virus disease.	The disease is well known in India and Thailand. Black gram is the natural host of this disease which is seed transmitted with 8% incidence. Only legumes are experimental hosts. The virus consists of isometric particles, measuring about 28 nm in diameter, having a sedimentation coefficient of 122 S. Its protein coat is a single species of 38.2 kDa and its single stranded RNA accounts for 20% of the particle weight. Local lesions without systemic infection result in inoculated leaves of *Cyamopsis tetragonoloba*. The virus is sap transmissible and is known to be transmitted in nature by leaf beetle-*Ceratoma trifurcate* and the Mexican beetle-*Epilachna varivestis*.
6. Mung bean yellow mosaic geminivirus disease.	The disease being very much destructive in nature, is most common in Asia. Its natural hosts include Mung bean and black gram. Characteristic symptoms include appearance of yellow specks on the lamina with thin upward curled pods in mung bean and symptoms like yellow mottle and necrotic mottle in black gram. The virus has paired-isometric particles of 30 × 18 nm. Its coat protein is, a 27.5 kDa polypeptide. Its DNA is circular, single stranded and 800 kDa. It accounts for 20% of the particle weight. The virus is mechanically transmissible by infected plant sap. The virus is also transmitted by whiteflies chiefly *Bemisia tabaci.* which transmits the virus in non-persistent manner. Adult females are more efficient than males. The disease is not seed transmissible in nature.

COWPEA AS NATURAL ALTERNATIVE HOST FOR SOME OTHER VIRUSES

Cowpea has been observed and reported to serve as natural host for other viruses as given bellow :

1. *Alfalfa mosaic virus.*
2. *Bean yellow mosaic potyvirus.*
3. *Bean summer mosaic virus.*
4. *Cucumber mosaic virus.*
5. *Tobacco streak ilarvirus.*
6. *Tobacco ring spot virus.*
7. *Tomato spotted wilt virus.*

VIRUS DISEASES OF UMBELLIFEROUS VEGETABLES

The important umbelliferous vegetables include carrot (*Daucus carota*), celery (*Apium graveolens*), parsnip (*Pastinaca sativa*) and parsley (*Petroselinum crispum*). These are the biennial root crops and are important source of nutrition in human diet. They are rich in vitamins and minerals. Parsnip and parsley are valuable as aromatic spices. Numerous virus diseases are known to cause considerable damage to these crops as described below.

VIRUS DISEASES OF CARROT (*Daucus carota*)

❍ Carrot mottle virus disease

This disease is wide spread in New Zealand, Japan, U.S., Australia and Europe. The disease causes substantial reduction in growth and significant loss in yield.

Symptoms—(1) Infected leaves turn yellow-green and curl veil-like in appearance. (2) The petioles become erect. (3) The virus occurs usually with carrot red leaf virus causing mixed infection. (4) Such mixed infection causes variable leaf mottle and plant dwarfing being identified as carrot mottle dwarf disease. (5) Such mixed infections also occur in parsley.

The causal virus—*Carrot mottle virus.* The virus particles are isometric, measuring about 52 nm in diameter with sedimentation coefficient of 270 S. It has a single stranded RNA. Thermal inactivation point of the virus is 67.5 to 70 C°, dilution end point is 1×10^{-3} and longevity of the virus *in vitro* is 9 to 24 hours at 24 C°. The virus is immunogenically active.

Disease cycle—The virus survives in biennial umbelliferous plants.

Transmission—The virus is transmissible through infective plant sap but no transmission from seed obtained from infected plant is known to occur. The carrot-willow aphid (*Cavariella aegopodii*) functions as vector and ensures further transmission of the virus from infected plants to healthy plants. It is believed that the vector transmits the virus when its helper—the *Carrot red leaf virus* is found present. *Brachycolus heraclei* is the aphid vector known to occur in Japan.

Management—All residual plants and umbelliferous weeds representing sources of infection and serving as hosts of vectors should be destroyed. Tolerant cultivars should be grown.

❍ Carrot red leaf (Possible) luteovirus disease

The complex has been reported from New Zealand, Canada, Europe, Japan and Australia. Natural hosts include wild carrot, parsley, cow parsley and *Heracleum sphondylium*.

Symptoms—The virus causes reddening and yellowing of carrot leaves along with the stunting of plants. Mottle dwarf symptoms may also be observed. The virus seems to remain confined to the phloem tissue of the host.

The causal virus—*Carrot red leaf* (possible) *luteovirus*. The virus has isometric particles of 25 nm diameter with a sedimentation coefficient of 104 S. The coat protein is 25 kDa. and the single stranded RNA is 1800 kDa. It accounts for 28% of the particle weight. The *Carrot red leaf virus* is helper to *Carrot mottle virus* both in transmission and multiplication. The virus is immunogenically active.

Transmission—The disease is neither transmissible through seed nor through mechanical inoculation. The carrot-willow aphid (*Cavariella aegopodii*) is the chief vector that transmits the virus in persistent and circulative manner. The minimum period for acquisition is 30 minutes with 2 minutes time for inoculation.

Management—All measures suggested for management of *Carrot mottle virus* may be used to manage this disease.

❍ Carrot thin leaf potyvirus disease

The disease is known to occur chiefly in semi-desert irrigated zones of North Western U.S.A.

Symptoms—Twisting and narrowing of leaves are the important characteristic of the disease.

The causal virus—*Carrot thin leaf potyvirus*. The virus particles are filamentous, measuring 736×11 nm in size. Thermal inactivation point of the virus is 50-55 C°, dilution end point is 1×10^{-5} and longevity *in vitro* is 2 days at 22 C°.

Disease cycle—Infected carrot roots remaining in the field after harvest represent the major source of inoculum. Cultivated and wild carrots and weed hemlock (*Conium maculatum*) are natural hosts. Experimentally it infects different species belonging to families— Chenopodiaceae, Solanaceae and Umbelliferaceae.

Transmission—The aphid vector chiefly *Myzus persicae* and *Cavariella aegopodii* transmit the disease in non- persistent manner. It is mechanically transmissible with infective plant sap but not transmissible through seed.

Management—For management, field sanitation and control of vectors are essential measures.

SOME OTHER VIRUS DISEASES OF MINOR IMPORTANCE

(1) Carrot latent rhabdoviruse disease—The disease is wide spread in Japan. It is not transmitted with infective plant sap. *Semiaphis heraclei* is known as vector.

(2) Carrot yellow leaf closterovirus disease—The disease is identified by the symptoms produced as yellow discoloration on the leaves. The virus has flexuous particles, measuring 1600 × 12 nm in size.

(3) Carrot mosaic (possible) **potyvirus disease**—The disease is most common in U.K. and Europe. It causes spots with unclearly defined margins. Slight malformation in infected leaves may be seen. *Chenopodium quinoa* and *C. gigantean* are well known diagnostic plants. Aphids chiefly *Myzus persicae* and *Cavariella aegopodii* are important vectors that transmit the virus in non-persistent manner.

CARROT AS ALTERNATE HOST OF SOME VIRUSES

The carrot serves as natural hosts of many viruses including *Alfalfa mosaic virus, Artichoke mosaic virus, Cucumber mosaic virus* and *Broad bean mottle virus.*

VIRUS DISEASES OF CELERY (*Apium graveolens*)

○ Celery mosaic potyvirus disease

The disease is known to cause considerable damage up to 50% to the crop in some American and European countries.

Symptoms—(1) Appearance of mosaic symptoms on the leaves of infected plants. (2) Infected plants grow slowly and leaves are malformed. (3) Chlorotic lesions particularly on young leaves may be observed.

The causal virus—*Celery mosaic potyvirus.* The virus consists of filamentous particles, measuring about 760 × 12–15 nm in size. Thermal inactivation point of the virus is 55-60 C°, the dilution end point is 1×10^{-2} to 1×10^{-3} and longevity *in vitro* is 6 days at 24 C°. Some strains of the virus have strong immunogenicity.

Disease cycle—The virus is preserved in its biennial winter hosts. Natural hosts are celery, carrot (*Daucus carota*), parsnip (*Pastinaca sativa*), parsley (*Petroselinum crispum*), dill (*Anethum graveolens*), caraway (*Carum carvi*) and hemlock (*Conium maculatum*). *Chenopodium amaranticolor* and *C. quinoa* which react with chlorotic and necrotic local lesions are diagnostic plants.

Transmission—More than 26 aphid species including *Acyrthosiphon pisum, Aphis apigraveolens, A. fabae, Cavariella aegopodii, C. pestinacae* and *Myzus persicae* are known to transmit the virus in non-persistent manner. The virus is sap transmissible but not through the seeds obtained from infected plants.

Management—(1) New celery crop should be kept isolated from other susceptible biennial natural hosts of the virus. (2) All natural host plants should be destroyed. (3) Control of aphids should be done to reduce the risks of virus transmission and spread.

SOME OTHER VIRUSES OF CELERY

1. *Celery ring spot virus-* It produces pale green yellow ring spots on the leaves of affected plants. The disease is most common in occurrence in Western European countries.

2. *Celery latent virus-* This virus produces no visible symptoms of the disease and is transmitted through seed of celery as reported. The virus particles have been reported to be filamentous in morphology, measuring 885 nm in length.

3. *Celery yellow spot luteovirus-* This virus has been reported from some European countries and U.S. A.. Characteristic whitish spots have been reported to be observed on the leaves of the affected plants.

4. *Celery yellow net virus-* Reported from Western Europe, this virus produces pale yellow spots, line pattern along the veins, diffused colouration and malformation of leaves of the affected plants.

CELERY AS NATURAL ALTERNATE HOST

A large number of economically important viruses are known to occur naturally cereal crops. Some most common reported viruses may be summarized as under-

1. *Alfalfa mosaic virus.*
2. *Artichoke mosaic virus.*
3. *Cucumber mosaic virus.*
4. *Strawberry latent ring spot virus.*
5. *Tomato aspermy cucumovirus.*
6. *Tomato black ring nepovirus.*

VIRUS DISEASES OF PARSNIP (*Pastinaca sativa*)

○ Parsnip mosaic potyvirus disease

The virus was first reported from England and is known to occur in some other countries also. Some virologists suggest that it may be a strain of *Celery mosaic virus.*

Symptoms—It causes mild mosaic symptoms which disappear later in season. The virus also infects plants related to families—Umbellifereae, Amaranthaceae, Chenopodiaceae and Scrophulariaceae. *Chenopodium amaranticolor* and *C. quinoa* are diagnostic plants.

The causal virus—*Parsnip mosaic potyvirus.* The virus particles are filamentous in morphology, measuring about 730 × 14 nm in size. They have sedimentation coefficient of 149 S. The thermal inactivation point of the virus is 55 to 58 C°, dilution end point is 1×10^{-3} to 1×10^{-4} and longevity of the virus *in vitro* is 7 to 10 days at 18 C°.

Disease cycle—The virus is known to be transmitted by infective plant sap and by aphids chiefly *Cavariella aegopodii, C. theobaldi* and *Myzus persicae.*

Management—Eradication of different suspected host plants and control of vectors are important plant protection measures to be followed.

○ Parsnip yellow fleck virus disease

The disease was first reported from England and Germany. Now the disease is probably wide spread.

Symptoms—General chlorosis along with longer and smaller veins may be observed on the leaves of the infected plants, resulting in net like appearance of the leaves. Early infected plants give rise to rosette like appearance.

The causal virus—*Parsnip yellow fleck virus*. The virus particles are isometric in shape, measuring about 30 nm in size with sedimentation coefficient of 148S. The virus is composed of single stranded RNA genome of 3700 kDa. Thermal inactivation point is 57-65 C°, dilution end point is 1×10^{-3} to 1×10^{-4} and longevity of the virus *in vitro* is 4-7 days at room temperature.

Disease cycle—Parsnip and chervil (*Anthriscus*) are natural hosts of the virus.

Transmission—The virus is mechanically transmissible with infective plant sap. The aphid-*Cavariella aegopodii* is known to transmit the virus semi-persistently in circulative manner. This transmission occurs simultaneously with the transmission of *Anthricus yellows helper virus* which is 22 nm in diameter and causes yellows on chervil plants.

Management—Destruction of source of infection and control of vectors are the important protective measures.

PARSNIP AS NATURAL ALTERNATE HOST

Parsnip has been observed and reported to serve as natural alternative host for some viruses as given bellow-

1. *Cucumber mosaic virus.*
2. *Parsnip mosaic potyvirus.* (Strain-*Carrot mottle virus).*
3. *Tomato black ring nepovirus.*

VIRUS DISEASES OF PARSLEY (*Petroselinum crispum*)

More than 10 viruses have been described to infect parsley as their natural host. Among these *Parsley latent virus* and *Parsley virus* 5 are important.

Parsley is also known as alternate host of many viruses as they cause symptoms of different kinds and descriptions. *Carrot mottle virus* incites parsley *symptomless* infection, *Celery mosaic potyvirus* produces parsley mosaic symptoms, *Alfalfa mosaic virus* causes parsley yellow mottle symptoms and *Cucumber mosaic virus* causes irregular yellow mottling.

VIRUS DISEASES OF COMPOSITAE VEGETABLES

VIRUS DISEASES OF ARTICHOKE (*Cynara scolymus*)

Many viruses are known to cause considerable damage to the crop. The important diseases are incited by *Artichoke yellow ring spot nepovirus, Artichoke vein banding (tentative) nepovirus* and *Artichoke Italian latent nepovirus*. Diseases of minor importance are incited by *Artichoke curly dwarf virus, Artichoke latent nepovirus, Artichoke mosaic disease virus* and *Artichoke mottled crinkle tombusvirus*.

❍ Artichoke yellow ringspot nepovirus disease

The virus infects a numbr of weeds and shrubs causing yellow discolouration of leaves. *Gomphrena globosa* and *Chenopodium quinoa* are experimental hosts that react with local lesions and systemic infection can serve as assay hosts.

Symptom—Artichoke and cardoon are natural host of this virus. They exhibit bright yellow blotches, ring spot and line patterns on leaves.

The causal virus—*Artichoke yellow ringspot nepovirus*. The virus consists of isometric particles of three types-the first one RNA free and remaining two containing single stranded RNA that are infective only when mixed together. Particles usually measure about 30 nm in diameter. The coat protein is single polypeptide of 53 kDa. Biophysical properties include thermal inactivation point of 60 C°, dilution end point of 1×10^{-3} to 1×10^{-4} and longevity *in vitro* at 22 C° for 48 to 72 hours.

Disease cycle—The virus is transmitted through seed and pollen of the infected plants. The disease is also transmitted through infective plant sap and vegetative propagation. No vector transmission is known to occur.

Management—Healthy seed material should be used.

❍ Artichoke vein banding (Tentative) nepovirus disease

The disease is known to originate from Turkey and occurs chiefly in artichoke growing regions of southern and central Italy. *Chenopodium amaranticolor* and *C. quinoa* are well known local lesion diagnostic hosts.

Symptoms—Artichoke is only natural host of this virus. It causes chlorotic discolouration on leaves of infected plants.

The causal virus—*Artichoke vein banding nepovirus*. The virus particles are isometric, measuring about 30 nm in diameter. It consists of three particles—one RNA free (T) and remaining two (M) and (B) containing RNA. Sedimentation coefficients are 56 S (T), 92 S (M) and 124 S (B). The mixture of M and B particles is infective. Protein preparations consist of three polypeptide of 22, 24 and 27 kDa. One additional polypeptide has also been observed.

Disease cycle—The disease is easily transmitted by infective plant sap. No other mode of transmission is known.

Management—No work on management has been done so far. However, precaution to avoid mechanical transmission should be taken.

❍ Artichoke Italian latent nepovirus disease

The disease is reported to be widespread in Bulgaria, Greece and Italy and is known to occur on artichoke and cultivated species of chicory, gladiolus, grapevine, lettuce and pelargonium. Several weeds are also reservoir of the virus. They are *Crespis neglecta, Lactuca virosa* and *Lamium* species.

Symptoms—More than 60 species are known to be experimentally infected with this virus. General leaf yellowing and stunting of plants are the distinguishing characteristics of the disease. However, most cvs. may remain symptom less. *Gomphrena globosa* and *Nicotiana tabacum* are important diagnostic hosts. They produce necrotic white local lesions and chlorotic necrotic ring spots with line pattern as their symptoms respectively on inoculation.

The causal virus—*Artichoke Italian latent nepovirus*. The isometric particles of the virus are about 30 nm in diameter. The virus consists of three different components—the top (T) which is RNA free and remaining two the middle (M) and the bottom (B) are found with RNA. Only the mixture of M and B particles is capable to cause infection. The coat protein composition is single polypeptide of 54 kDa. The thermal inactivation point is 55 to 60 C°, dilution end point is 1×10^{-2} to 1×10^{-5} and longevity *in vitro* is 3 to 14 days at 4 C°. Serologically the virus has good immunogenicity.

Disease cycle—The virus is preserved in the soil and is transmitted by the nematodes chiefly *Longidorus apulus* and *L. fasciatus*. The virus is also transmitted by infective plant sap.

Management—Planting the crop in nematode—free soils and suitable cultural practices with precaution to avoid mechanical virus transmission are the important protective measures for management of the disease.

Table 15.6 **Showing some other diseases of artichoke of minor importance.**

Name of diseases	Distinguishing characteristics
1. Artichoke curly dwarf virus disease	Curling of leaves, necrotic pockets in shoots, veinal necrosis in young leaves and stunting of plants with shortened internodes are important characteristics of the disease. The virus is probably potyvirus and has flexuous rod like particles, measuring 582×15 nm in size. Thermal inactivation point is 55-60 C°, dilution end point is 1×10^{-3} to 1×10^{-4} and longevity *in vitro* is 2 to 3 days. *Zinnia* species produce local lesion at 13-18 C°. The virus is mechanically transmitted by infective plant sap.
2. Artichoke latent nepovirus disease	The disease is known to occur in Mediterranean countries including California and Brazil. Some cvs. remain symptomless while others manifest symptoms like stunting and mottling. The virus is transmitted by aphids non-persistently. Also transmissible by propagating materials but not through seed from infected plants. Healthy plants can be obtained by meristem-tip culture.
3. Artichoke mottled crinkle tombusvirus disease	This disease was reported from Greece, Italy, Tunisia and Morocco. Crinkle, chlorotic blotches, leaf malformation and smaller and fewer flower heads are the important characteristics of the disease. Some

Name of diseases	Distinguishing characteristics
	cultivars may be observed without any significant symptom. *Datura stramonium* is suitable assay host as it produces chlorotic and necrotic local lesions. The virus is mechanically transmissible and also transmitted by propagating materials. Potential vector of the virus is not yet known.
4. Artichoke mosaic virus disease	The virus has not yet been defined etiologically. It is mechanically transmissible and in addition to mosaic, it produces bright yellow spots with blotches of irregular shape on the leaves of the infected plant.

ARTICHOKE AS NATURAL ALTERNATE HOST

Artichoke has been reported o serve as natural alternative host for many viruses. Some reported viruses are as under-

1. *Bean yellow mosaic virus.*
2. *Tomato bushy stunt virus.*
3. *Tobacco streak ilarvirus.*

VIRUS DISEASES OF LETTUCE
(*Lactuca sativa*)

○ Lettuce necrotic yellows rhabdovirus disease

The disease has been reported to cause considerable damage to this crop in Australia and New Zealand. Lettuce is the only economically important natural host of this virus.

Symptoms—Inter-veinal chlorosis, faint coloured mosaic and downward curling are the important characteristic symptoms of the disease.

The causal virus—*Letture necrotic yellows rhabdovirus.* The virus particles are bacilliform in morphology. They usually measure 227 × 66 nm in size with a sedimentation coefficient of 940 S. The RNA genome has an outer envelope covered with uniformly arranged projections. Thermal inactivation point of the virus is 52 C°, dilution end point is 1×10^{-2} and longevity *in vitro* is 8-24 hours at room temperature.

Disease cycle—Infected weeds and lettuce grown continuously at the same land in field and indoors represent primary source of infection. Sow thistle (*Sonchus oleraceus*), dune thistle (*Embergeria megalocarpa*) and the weed-*Reinchardia tingitana* represent as natural hosts for infection.

Transmission—The aphids-*Hyperomyzus lactucae* and *H. carduellinus* are important known vectors of the virus. The virus is also mechanically transmissible. *Datura stramonium* and *Nicotiana glutinosa* are suitable diagnostic plants.

Management—Destruction of virus source plants should be done and vectors should be managed by application of suitable insecticide.

❍ Lettuce mosaic potyvirus disease

The disease is known to occur worldwide where the lettuce crop is grown. It is a damaging disease as it causes yield loss as high as 50%. If early infection occurs, the plants remain dwarfed with heads half of the size of the healthy ones.

Symptoms—(1) Vein clearing is the primary symptom observed on the leaves of the infected plants. (2) Appearance of pale and dark green mosaic. (3) Striped mosaic symptoms along and around the veins. (4) Early infection prevents formation of heads and rosette like appearance is usually observed.

The causal virus—*Lettuce mosaic potyvirus.* The virus particles are filamentous, measuring about 750 × 13 nm in size. The virus consists of single component with a sedimentation coefficient of 143 S. The single stranded RNA is 3000 kDa. and the coat protein is a single polypeptide of 33 kDa. The thermal inactivation point is 5 to 60 C°, dilution end point is 1×10^{-1} to 1×10^{-2} and longevity of the virus *in vitro* is 1 to 2 days. Serologically, the virus sample is moderately immunogenic. *Chenopodium amaranticolor* and *C. quinoa* with local lesions on inoculated leaves are suitable diagnostic plants.

Disease cycle—The virus is transmitted through seed of lettuce, grinsel (*Senecio vulgaris*) and wild lettuce (*Lactuca serriola*). It has also been reported to be transmitted through pollen and ovules of the infected plants. Biennial hosts are important source for preservation and transmission of the virus. Economically important natural hosts are lettuce, spinach and pea. *Chenopodium album, C. morale, Lamium amplexicaule, Senecio vulgaris, Sonchus asper* and *Stellaria media* are common weeds which are infected by this virus.

Transmission—The virus is known to be transmitted by more than 15 species of aphids. *Myzus persicae* which colonizes lettuce plants readily in the growing season is considered primary vector is some countries. Other vectors are *Macrosiphum euphorbiae* and *Pemphigus bursarius.*

Management—(1) Use of healthy and virus free seed is important to manage the disease. (2) Aphids should be closely monitored and systematically sprayed with suitable insecticide. (3) All infected plants should be rogued out immediately. (4) Plants residues should be destroyed after harvesting.

SOME OTHER DISEASES OF LETTUCE

❍ Lettuce big vein virus disease

This disease is common in occurrence in Europe and North America. The disease occurs on lettuce crops manifesting characteristic symptoms of swollen leaf veins much larger than normal especially prominent on the midribs. Chlorotic stripes usually accompany and appear near the veins. The midrib is shortened, causing crumple and distortion of leaf blade. Leaf blades are also found swollen, brittle which break easily. The elongated virus particles usually measure 350 × 18 nm in size. Cool weather during active plant growth usually favours the development of the disease. The disease is known to be soil borne and zoospores of *Olpidium brassicae* are known as active vectors of the disease. Control of vector through soil disinfection is the important preventive measure of the disease.

Fig. 15.4. Lettuce big vein symptoms on lettuce leaves incited by *Lettuce big vein virus*

❍ Letture necrosis virus disease

The disease was first discovered from England and is known to occur in other parts of the world also. Early infection causes leaf necrosis and death. Distinguishing characteristics are appearance of bronze necrosis along leaf veins, forming a net like

Fig. 15.5. Showing *Tobacco rattle virus* symptoms in lettuce leaf

pattern on some leaf parts. Ring spots of irregular shape and size may also be observed in interveinal tissues. The disease is transmitted in nature by aphids-*Aulacorthum solani, Myzus ascalonicus* and *M. ornatus*. It is seldom transmitted through mechanical means. Control of aphids and destruction of natural host such as dandelion (*Taraxacum officinale*) in and around the lettuce crop are important protective measures.

❍ Lettuce infectious yellows closterovirus disease

Very little information is available on the virus. It is known to be transmitted by *Bemisia tabaci*.

LETTUCE AS NATURAL ALTERNATIVE HOST

Some important viruses known to occur on lettuce produce symptoms of different descriptions as given below-

1. *Arabis mosaic nepovirus*- It produces characteristic dwarfing of infected plants and chlorotic lesions on the leaves.
2. *Alfalfa mosaic virus*- Characteristic lesions include vein clearing and mottling of the leaves of the affected plants.
3. *Beet western yellows luteovirus*-Characteristic interveinal yellowing and dark brown marginal leaf necrosis may be observed as the characteristic symptoms of the disease.
4. *Cucumber mosaic cucumovirus*-Chlorosis along the veins and stunting of affected plants may be observed as characteristic symptoms. Besides, mosaic and necrotic changes are also found on the affected plants.
5. *Tobacco necrosis necrovirus*- Transmitted by the zoospores of fungus- Olpidium brassicae. This virus produces root and leaf vein necrosis on the affected plants.
6. *Tobacco rattle tobravirus*- It causes leaf curling, malformation and slowness in growth. Nematode vectors play important role in epidemiology.

❍ Some other viruses of minor importance

1. *Artichoke Italian latent nepovirus.*
2. *Beet pseudo yellows closterovirus.*
3. *Beet yellow stunt closterovirus.*
4. *Broad bean wilt fabavirus.*
5. *Tobacco streak ilarvirus.*
6. *Sowthistle yellow vein nucleo rhabdovirus.*
7. *Tobacco ring spot virus.*
8. *Tomato black ring virus.*
9. *Turnip mosaic potyvirus.*

VIRUS DISEASES OF CHENOPODACEOUS VEGETABLES

VIRUS DISEASES OF SPINACH (*Spinacia oleracea*)

This crop is susceptible to many virus diseases including spinach latent virus disease which causes considerable damage to this crop as described below. Spinach also serves as alternate host of many viruses.

○ Spinach latent (possible) ilarvirus disease

The disease has been described in Holland and Yugoslavia. Spinach is only known natural host of this disease.

Symptoms—The diseased plants may remain symptomless or may exhibit transient symptoms.

The causal virus—*Spinach latent* (possible) *ilarvirus*. The virus particles are quasi-isometric and 27 nm in diameter. Sedimentation consists of three components with sedimentation coefficients of 87 S, 98 S and 103 S. The virus contains 5 single stranded RNA species of 1300 (RNA-1), 1180 (RNA-2), 910 (RNA-3), 350 (RNA-4), and 270 (RNA-5) kDa respectively and a single polypeptide coat protein of 28 kDa. The thermal inactivation point is 60 to 65 C°, dilution end point is 1×10^{-3} to 1×10^{-4} and longevity of the virus *in vitro* is 6 to 8 days at 24 C°. The virus is immunogenically week.

Disease cycle—Spinach seed is the primary source of infection. It is also transmissible with infective plant sap but no any other mode of transmission is known.

Management—For management healthy disease free seed should be grown.

SPINACH AS NATURAL ALTERNATE HOST

Spinach serves as natural alternate host for many viruses. Some important reported viruses as under-

1. *Beet mosaic virus.*
2. *Beet yellows virus.*
3. *Beet curly top Geminivirus.*
4. *Beet mild yellowing luteovirus.*
5. *Beet necrotic yellow vein tobamovirus.*
6. *Beet western yellows luteovirus.*
7. *Cucumber mosaic cucumovirus.*
8. *Lettuce mosaic potyvirus.*

16

VIRUS DISEASES OF INDUSTRIAL PLANTS

✉ ***Virus diseases of sugarcane—mosaic, fiji disease; Diseases of sunflower-mosaic; Diseases of soybean-mosaic, dwarf virus disease and mottle virus disease; Diseases of sugarbeet-curly top, mosaic, necrotic yellow vein, beet yellows and beet western yellows; Diseases of potato-leaf curl,. Poty virus X., aucuba mosaic and other diseases; Diseases of tobacco-mosaic and etch disease; Diseases of hop-mosaic, latent virus disease, chlorotic, mosaic, yellow net disease; Diseases of peanut-bud necrosis, clump virus and some other diseases of peanut; Diseases of cotton.***

Potato, tobacco, sugarcane, sugar beet, soybean, peanut and hop are important industrial plants. These plants are cultivated and processed into value aided food and food byproducts. Majority of these plants are important for international trade. Many of the industrial plants are natural hosts for many viruses. Important virus diseases causing considerable damage to such crops are being summarized as under.

VIRUS DISEASES OF SUGARCANE (*Saccharum officinarum*)

Sugarcane is a perennial plant belonging to the Graminae family. It accounts about 68% of the world sugar production. It also provides raw material for the production of rum, molasses and denatured alcohol. This vegetatively propagated perennial plant is infected by a number of viruses which cause considerable damage to this economic crop.

❍ Sugarcane mosaic potyvirus disease

The disease was first recorded from Jawa in 1890 and now is known to occur everywhere the crop is grown. It is the most damaging disease of this crop.

Symptoms. Appearance of mosaic pattern as the main symptom of the disease is observed on the leaves of the infected plants. Such symptoms are also accompanied with yellow striping or necrosis. Development of the infected plants is markedly affected and the yield is significantly reduced.

The causal virus. *Sugarcane mosaic potyvirus*. Virus particles are flexuous rods in morphology, measuring about 750×13 nm in size. It contains single stranded RNA of 3000 kDa, constituting 5% of the viral particle. Coat protein consists of single polypeptide of 35 kDa. The sedimentation coefficient of MB strain is 176 ± 5S. Thermal inactivation point of the virus is 50-55°C, dilution end point is 1×10^{-2} to 1×10^{-3} and longevity *in vitro* is 1 day at 20°C. Virus is serologically moderately immunogenic. Diagnosis through ISEM, ELISA and electro-blot immunossay (EBIA) has been found to be practicable.

Disease cycle. The virus is preserved in numerous perennial graminae host species especially sugarcane. Aphid species such as *Dactynotus ambrosiae, Hysteroneura setariae, Rhopalosiphum maidis* and *Toxoptera graminis* are active natural vectors transmitting the virus in non-persistent manner. The virus is also transmissible through infective plant sap but no any other mode of transmission is known.

Management. (1) Weed host plants should be destroyed in and near sugarcane fields. (2) Control of aphids with suitable insecticide is essential to check the spread of the disease. (3) Spatial isolation of sugarcane from susceptible hosts should be done. (4) The disease can be eliminated from mosaic infected ratoons by thermotherapy and meristem tip culture. (5) Use of cultivars resistant/tolerant to the disease is the most suitable control measure.

❍ Fiji reovirus disease

This disease was first discovered in Fiji islands where it caused severe losses to the crop until resistant cultivars were developed. The disease is not known to occur in different countries especially New Guinea, New Britain, Australia, Madagascar and New Hebrides.

Symptoms. (1) Elongated galls usually develop along the veins on the underside of sugarcane leaves of infected plants. (2) These galls formed due to cell proliferation in vascular bundles contain two types of abnormal cells. (3) These abnormal cells are lignified gall xylem and non-lignified gall phloem cells. (4) Infected sugarcane plants usually remain stunted and dwarfed resulting in bushy appearance of the infected plants.

The causal virus. *Fiji disease reovirus.* The virus particles are polyhedral in morphology and are 70 nm in diameter with double stranded RNA. RNA consists of 10 individual segments varying from 1100 to 2900 kDa. with total molecular weight of 20,000 kDa. No much information is available on biophysical and serological properties of this virus.

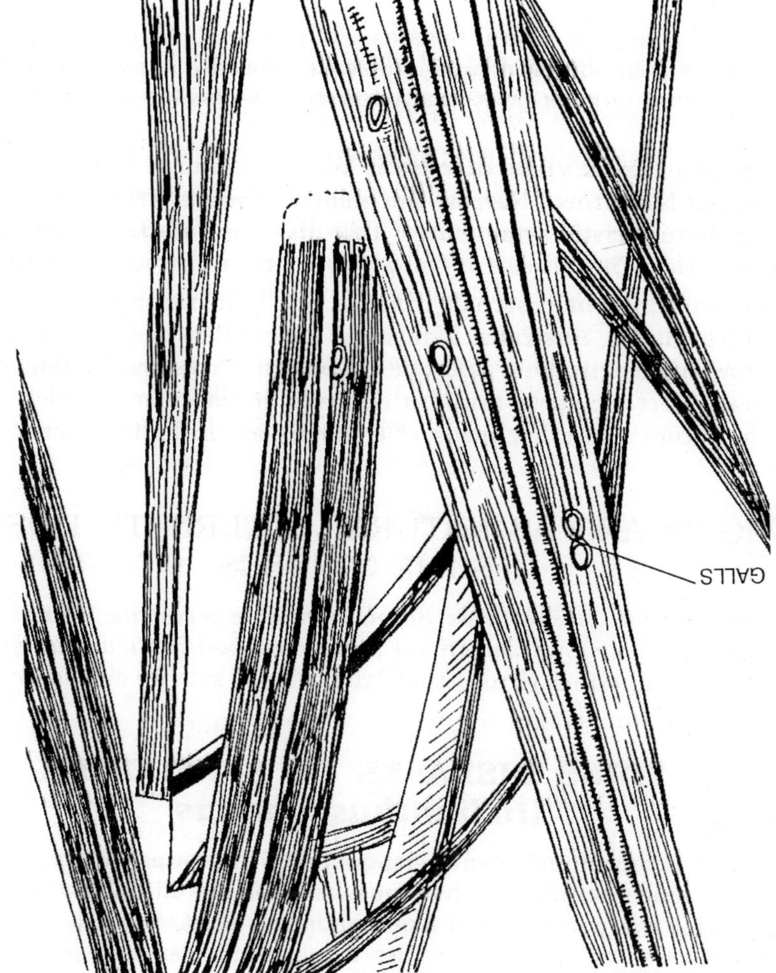

Fig. 16.1 Sugarcane leaves showing symptoms inicited by *Sugarcane fiji virus*

Disease cycle. The virus is known to be preserved in perennial sugarcane. The virus is transmitted by infected planting materials through the transport in different sugarcane growing areas. Plant hoppers such as *Pekinsiella saccharicida, P. vitiensis* and *P. vastatrix* are known to transmit the virus in persistent manner. Infected leaf hoppers are life long vectors.

Management. Selection of virus free planting materials and control of vectors are important measures for the management of the disease. However, the most important preventive measure is to develop cultivars resistant/tolerant to this disease.

SOME OTHER DISEASES OF SUGARCANE

Several virus and virus like diseases have also been described on sugarcane. Important diseases such as sugarcane serch disease, streak virus disease and chlorotic streak disease are known well in occurrence.

Sugarcane serch disease is well known to occur in Philippines, Formosa, South Africa, Java and India. The disease is characterized by the severe stunting of the plants and development of lateral buds as leafly shoots. Abnormal formation of aerial roots on nodes is also observed in this disease. Besides these, reddening of vascular bundles by coloured gum is most characteristic. No vector of the virus is known by now.

Sugarcane streak virus disease is known to remain restricted to South Africa, Egypt, India and Mauritius. Narrow and elongated white streaks are usually observed on leaves as characteristic symptoms of this disease. Infected plants remain stunted with reduced yield. The disease is known to be transmitted by *Cicadulina mbila*.

Sugarcane chlorotic streak disease has been reported to cause considerable damage in Java, Hawai, Australia, Mauritius, Puerto Rico and Louisiana. Appearances of long, narrow and longitudinal chlorotic streaks on leaves are the important symptoms of the disease. Necrotic spots are also observed in vascular bundles. The disease is soil borne in nature and other mode of transmission including vector species are not known.

SUGARCANE AS NATURAL ALTERNATE HOST OF SOME VIRUSES

Sugarcane striate mosaic virus, *Sorghum mosaic potyvirus*, *Peanut clump furvirus*, *Maize dwarf mosaic potyvirus*, *Sugarcane bacilliform bandnavirus* and *Sugarcane yellow leaf luteovirus* are important viruses that are known to survive on sugarcane as alternate host.

VIRUS DISEASES OF SUNFLOWER (*Helianthus annuus*)

Sunflower is an annual plant belonging to Compositae family. Its seed contains natural raw oil much suitable for human nutrition. Its oil is also used for margarine and as industrial raw material for manufacturing paint, varnish and stearine which is used in production of candles. Besides these, sunflower also serves as animal feed as silage or as green fodder. Important virus diseases of sunflower may be summarized as under.

❍ Sunflower mosaic virus disease

This disease is known to be most destructive and widespread in different countries of the world. It occurs chiefly in Africa-Kenya; Mauritius and Uganda; South America-Argentina and Brazil; South America-Florida, Maryland and Texas; Europe; Former Soviet Union and Asia including India.

Symptoms. In India, mosaic pattern on leaves are usually observed as characteristic symptoms of the disease. In severe cases, ring spots and chlorotic lesions are also observed. These lesions usally coalesce with each other, covering a large part of the leaves. The virus causes systemic infection in sunflower. Mosaic pattern on leaves are usually composed of circular spots. Leaf deformation, reduced plant rooting and pollen sterility may also be observed in most cases of disease severity. *Chenopodium amaranticolor* is the diagnostic host and produces chlorotic local lesions on leaves.

The causal virus. *Sunflower mosaic virus*. Thermal inactivation point of the virus is 46-48°C, dilution end point is 5×10^{-3} to 5×10^{-4} and longevity of the virus *in vitro* is 2 to 3 days at 25°C.

Disease cycle. The disease is thought to be a complex disease and the important virus is known to be transmitted by infective plant sap, grafting and seed from infected plants. The vector- *Bemisia tabaci* is important to transmit the virus in persistent manner as it retains infective for more than 8 days.

OTHER VIRUS DISEASES OF SUNFLOWER

Different virus diseases on sunflower have also been reported. A partial list of these disease are being summarized as under :

(1) Rugose mosaic. Characterized by the leaf crinkling and rugosity. Leaf margins may roll downward whereas upper leaves exhibit severe mottling.

(2) Yellowing mosaic. Young infected leaves are malformed with characteristic dwarfing of plants.

SUNFLOWER AS NATURAL HOST OF SOME OTHER VIRUSES

Turnip mosaic potyvirus, Tomato spotted wilt tospovirus, Tobacco ring spot nepovirus, Tobacco streak ilarvirus, Tobacco rattle tobravirus, Cucumber mosaic cucumovirus and *Beet western yellows luteovirus* are important viruses that usually survive on sunflower.

VIRUS DISEASES OF SOYBEAN (*Glycine max.*)

Soybean is an annual plant which belongs to Leguminosae family. It contains both protein and oil for human nutrition. As food, soybean is used in various forms such as milk, butter, cheese and meat substitutes. Its protein provides raw materials for the processing industry in production of artificial rubber, plastic, paint and varnish. Besides, soybean is used as green fodder for animal nutrition. The symbiotic soybean *Rhizobium* species nodulation process enhances soil fertility by fixing nitrogen.

Soybean is susceptible to infection by several viruses that usually cause considerable damage to the crop, resulting in reduction in yield and product quality. Some economically important diseases incited by viruses may be summarized as under :

❍ Soybean mosaic potyvirus disease

The disease is economically important because it causes reduction in yield and soil fertility. It reduces soil fertility because it decreases the formation of nodules as roots are fewer, smaller and lighter. As a result, the nitrogen fixing activity of nodules of *Rhizobium* species is reduced considerably.

Symptoms. (1) Systemic vein clearing usually in youngest leaves are the characteristic symptoms of the disease. (2) With the severity of the disease, leaves curl gradually, leaf margins twist downward and leaf blades are observed to be smaller and brittle. (3) Infected plants remain stunted and progressive necrosis may occur in some cultivars. (4) Fewer pods are formed and sometimes such pods are deformed and seedless. (5) Necrotic local lesions occur in experimentally infected bean plants. (6) *Chenopodium quinoa* and *C. album* are suitable assay plants.

The causal virus. *Soybean mosaic potyvirus.* The virus particles are flexuous rods in appearance, measuring about 750 × 15 nm in size. Particles may vary from 300 to 900 nm in length. The single stranded RNA is of 3250 kDa. which accounts for 5.3% of the particle weight. The thermal inactivation point of the virus is 55 to 70°C and the virus in sap is known to remain infective for more than 2 to 5 days at 25 to 33°C. It is quite immunogenic.

Disease cycle. The infectivity of the virus is preserved in soybean seed. Seed harvested from infected plants is important source of disease perpetuation. The virus particles are known to occur equally both in seed coat and in the embryo.

Transmission. The virus is mechanically transmissible easily by infective sap but it does not play an important role in epidemiology. Aphids are known to transmit the virus in non-persistent manner. Some important species of the aphids that are responsible to transmit the virus are *Acyrthosiphon pisum, Aphis craccivora, A. fabae, Myzus persicae, Rhopalosiphum maidis* and *R. padi.*

Management. Healthy/virus free seeds should be used for production of the crop. Soybean seed crop should be isolated from other production fields. Infected plants if seen in the field should be spotted and rogued immediately. Control of aphids by judicious use of chemical has also been recommended.

❍ Soybean dwarf luteovirus disease

The disease is widespread in many countries including Japan where it causes considerable damage to the crop every year.

Symptoms. Two strains are important to cause different types of symptoms. The dwarfing strain causes stunting of the plant, shortening of internodes and downward leaf curling. The yellowing strain causes yellowing of leaves between the veins and sometimes infected leaves become brittle in appearance.

The causal virus. *Soybean dwarf luteovirus.* The virus particles are isometric in morphology, measuring about 25 nm in diameter. Thermal inactivation point of the virus is 45 to 50°C, dilution end point is 0.5 and longevity *in vitro* is 20 days at 15°C and 4 months at 4°C. It is strongly immunogenic.

Disease cycle. The virus perpetuates permanently in perennial hosts which include *Trifolium pratense* and *T. repens.*

Transmission. The virus is not mechanically transmissible. It is not transmitted by the seed also. The vector-*Aulacorthum solani* is known to transmit this virus in persistent manner.

Management. Use of resistant/tolerant cultivars and control of vectors are the important measures to be followed for the management of this disease.

❍ Soybean chlorotic mottle caulimovirus disease

The disease is usually restricted in Japan and soybean is the only natural host of this virus.

Symptoms. Vein clearing and chlorosis are observed on young leaves which develop into mottling. The infected plants are usually observed to remain stunted.

The causal virus. *Soybean chlorotic mottle caulimovirus.* The virus particles are isometric in morphology, consisting of double straded DNA of 5450 kDa. No information is available about the chemistry of coat protein. Thermal inactivation point of the virus is 85 to 90°C, the dilution end point is 1×10^{-3} to 1×10^{-4} and longevity of the virus *in vitro* is 1 to 3 days at 20°C. The sample is moderately immunogenic. No any strain has been identified.

Disease cycle. The virus is transmissible through infective plant sap. No seed transmission has been observed. Transmission through vector is not known to exist. This virus has been mechanically transmitted to some other hosts also. Such hosts include *Dolichos lablab, Phaseolus vulgaris* and *Vigna unguiculata.*

❍ Soybean yellow mosaic disease

The disease is widespread in different countries including India. It causes considerable damage to the crop every year.

Symptoms. (1) The leaves of the affected plants show bright yellow spots and sometimes diffused patches. (2) These patches increase in size gradually, resulting in bright yellow colouration of the entire lamina. (3) The leaflets of the affected plants become narrower and reduced in size. (4) Lesser number of pods may be formed in the infected plants. (5) Such pods bear very few grains and sometimes no grains are formed at all.

The causal virus. *Mung bean yellow mosaic geminivirus.* Virus particles are geminate usually occurring in pairs. Virus particles measure about 18-20 nm in size. The genome of the virus is single stranded DNA.

Disease cycle. The virus perpetuates on host plants mainly green gram, black gram, cowpea and French bean. It is known to be transmitted by the white flies chiefly *Bemisia tabaci.*

Management. (1) Roguing of infected plants from the field should be done regularly in the beginning. (2) Spraying of any suitable insecticide such as Metasystox or Endosulfan @ 1 or 2ml/liter of water may be done at the interval of 15 days for the management of the whiteflies in order to check the spread of the disease. (3) Resistant varieties like alankar and shilajeet should be grown.

SOYBEAN AS ALTERNATE NATURAL HOST FOR SOME OTHER VIRUSES

About 111 viruses including their strains are known to infect soybean in nature and under experimental conditions. Mixed infection in soybean incited by several viruses are more damaging than the individual infections.

Important viruses that are known to cause infections to soybean. Soybean is alternate host of *Alfalfa mosaic virus, Cucumber mosaic virus, Peanut mottle potyvirus, Cowpea chlorotic mottle bromovirus, Pea mosaic virus* and *Pea streak carlavirus* etc.. These viruses cause different kinds of symptoms.

VIRUS DISEASES OF SUGARBEET
(*Beta vulgaris*)

Sugar beet viruses may be divided in to two major groups (1) Most intensely investigated virus diseases are sugar beet mosaic and beet yellows virus disease. (2) Other virus diseases of minor importance are beet mild yellowing, beet western yellows and beet necrotic yellow vein disease. Different virus diseases of this crop are summarized as under.

❍ Beet curly top (Possible) geminivirus disease

This disease is widespread in arid and semi-arid Western parts of North and South America, Iran, India, Pakistan and many other Asian and European countries.

Symptoms. (1) The most important characteristic symptoms are observed as vein clearning during the period of growth of the infected plant. (2) Leaves of the infected plant, usually twist upward and inward with general dwarfing and yellowing. (3) Wart-like formations may develop on the veins of the lower leaf surface. (4) Exudates emanate from the phloem on larger leaf veins and petioles. (5) The virus remains limited to the phloem tissues and necrosis of phloem as dark concentric circles may be evident in cross-section of roots. (6) Diagnostic plants are sugar beet, cucumber and French bean.

The causal virus. *Beet curly top* (possible) *geminivirus*. The particles are isometric in morphology, measuring about 20 nm in diameter. The virus particles occur singly or geminate. Sedimentation coefficients which include both types of particles are 55 S and 86 S respectively. The virus contains single stranded DNA with no information about its protein. Both single and double-component viral particles are infective. The thermal inactivation point of the virus is 80°C, dilution end point of the virus is 1×10^{-3} and longevity *in vitro* is 8 days at 24°C. It is strongly immunogenic. Several strains are known to exist in nature.

Disease cycle. The virus survives in perennial hosts. Leafhoppers chiefly *Circulifer tenellus* (U.S.), C. *apacipennis* (Iran) and *Agallia albidulla* (India) are known vectors that transmit the virus in non-persistent manner.

Natural hosts. In addition to sugar beet, natural hosts include spinach, tomato, potato, cucumber, tobacco, bean, flax, clover, parsley and many ornamental and woody plants.

Management. Chemical control of vectors, early sowing of sugarbeet seed and use of resistant sugarbeet cultivars are suitable control measures for the management of the disease.

❍ Sugar beet mosaic potyvirus disease

The disease is known to occur every where the sugar beet is grown, especially in temperate zones. It reduces industrial sugar beet yield up to 30% and beet seed crops infected in the first year may result in 50% lower seed yield.

Symptoms. (1) Appearance of numerous small yellow spots and blotches on one or several central leaves. (2) A light mosaic and mottle occur on young leaves as the disease advances in severity. (3) Leaflets with initial symptoms are found reduced in size with curling and rolling of leaf margins and leaf tip necrosis. (4) In contrast to beet yellows, no phloem necrosis or starch accumulation occurs in leaves infected by this disease.

The causal virus. *Beet mosaic potyvirus.* The virus particles usually measure about 730 × 13 nm in size. Thermal inactivation point is 55-60°C, dilution end point is 4×10^{-4} and longevity *in vitro* is 24-48 hours at 20°C. The virus is moderately immunogenic and serologically related to *Bean yellow mosaic virus* and *Potato virus Y*.

Disease cycle. For year to year spread, the virus is maintained in natural hosts including biennial seed crops and winter spinach. More than 24 aphid species chiefly *Myzus persicae* and *Aphis fabae* are important vectors, responsible for spread of the disease in non-persistent manner. The aphids acquire the virus in 6 to 10 seconds and can transmit it to the healthy plants in 5 to 10 seconds. Winged forms of aphids are more active in transmission of the virus. The virus is also transmissible through infective plant sap but not transmissible through seed obtained from infected plants.

Host-range. Natural hosts include all cultivated sugar beet cultivars. Other hosts includes *Beta vulgaris* sub sp. *maritime, Amaranthus retroflexus, Campanula ranunculoides, Chenopodium album, Delphinum consolida, Melilotus officinalis, Papaver somniferum, Spinacia oleracea, Stellaria media, Trifolium incarnation* and *T. repens.* About 100 species in 26 dicots families have been observed to be infected by artificial inoculation. *Amaranthus retroflexus, A. caudatus, Chenopodium quinoa* and *Gomphrena globosa* are suitable assay plants that react to infection by producing local spots.

Management. Ample separation between industrial and sugarbeet seed crops, suitable chemical control of vectors and elimination of plants known to harbor the virus are important measures to be followed for management of the disease.

❍ Beet necrotic yellow vein tobamovirus disease

The disease was first reported from Italy in 1954 and 1957. Now the disease is known to occur in Japan, France, Germany, China, U.S. and former U.S.S.R. It is very widespread disease known to cause considerable damage to the crop year after year.

Symptoms. (1) Appearance of yellow and roundish patches in the field, usually occurring in small depressions in which the water remains present following heavy rains. (2) During the development of the disease, these yellow patches merge making easy detection of infected spots. (3) With the advancement of the symptoms vein clearing, yellowing and necrosis occur on leaves of the infected plants. (4) Infections later in the season result in slight colour changes, making difficult detection. (5) Other characteristic symptoms are elongation of leaf petioles and narrowing of leaf blades. (6) In the roots, malformations are observed as hairy roots, dwarf roots or narrowed roots. (7) Hairy roots develop from the over-development of numerous hairs. (8) Dark coloured vascular bundles may be observed in cross and longitudinal sections of diseased roots, resulting from necrosis of infected cells.

The causal virus. *Beet necrotic yellow vein tobamovirus.* The virus is rod shaped in morphology. Multi component particles are characterized. The virus particles have a single coat protein of 21 kDa. and four species of single stranded RNA of 2300, 1800, 700 and 600 kDa. respectively. Thermal inactivation point of the virus is 65-70°C, dilution end point is 1×10^{-4} and longevity *in vitro* is 5-6 days at 20°C. Virus sample is moderately immunogenic.

Disease cycle. The virus is soil borne in nature. In the soil it is transmitted by the fungus-*Polymyxa betae* as the vector.

Management. Sugar beet crop should not be grown on contaminated soils. Fields with water drainage problem should not be selected for its production. Deep tillage should be done as a normal cultural practice. In addition to these, early sowing and better soil aeration are important measures.

❍ Beet yellows closterovirus disease

The disease is widespread where the crop is grown in Europe, Asia, North and South America, Africa and Australia. Damage caused by the virus is due to the reductions of root and green matter yield alongwith total sugar content.

Symptoms. (1) Beet yellows symptoms are first observed on older leaves and initial yellows symptoms occur at apical and external portions of the leaf blade which spread toward the leaf base. (2) Chlorosis of certain leaf parts varies from pale, greenish yellow to orange or even red. (3) Severely infected plants become yellow, dry out and rustle when touched. (4) Brittle leaf blades split into small fragments and crack when bent. (5) Sugar content decreases in phloem cells.

The causal virus. *Beet yellows closterovirus*. The virus particles are flexuous filaments, measuring about 1250×10 nm in size. The virus is composed of a single stranded RNA of 4150 kDa. that accounts about 5% of the total particle weight. It consists of a single polypeptide coat protein of 23 kDa. Thermal inactivation point is 50-55°C, dilution end point is 1×10^{-4} and longevity *in vitro* is 1 day at 24°C. Although immunogenic but antiserum has low titre.

Disease cycle. The virus survives in natural hosts including sugar beet seed plants and some other biennials. Aphids chiefly *Myzus persicae* is known to be the important vector of this virus which transmits the virus in non-persistent manner. Under experimental conditions, the virus can be transmitted through infective plant sap. *Cuscuta* is also known to transmit the virus but seed transmission has not been confirmed.

Management. (1) Seed crop which is known to harbor the virus should be grown in adequate isolation. It should also be separated from susceptible crop of fodder beet, garden beet and spinach. (2) Chemical control of aphids both in the commercial and seed sugar beet crop should be done. (3) Losses can be reduced by early sowing of commercial beet. (4) The root top dressing instead of foliar top dressing of fertilizer has been observed to increase the yield. (5) Tolerant sugar beet cultivars should be grown.

❍ Beet western yellows luteovirus disease

The disease has been recorded in different countries including Asia, North America and Europe. Significant losses in yield and inequality of the produce are recorded due to this disease.

Symptoms. The virus causes most severe symptoms on sugar beet and lettuce, although it infects a number of hosts. (1) Leaf yellowing is the characteristic symptom of the disease. (2) Yellows symptoms first appear as mild chlorotic spots between the veins followed by marked yellowing of all inter veinal tissues. (3) These symptoms develop in acropetal order from lower towards apical leaves. (4) Symptoms seldom occur on the youngest leaves.

The causal virus. *Beet western yellows luteovirus*. The causal virus is isometric, measuring about 26 nm in diameter. It has single stranded RNA species of 1900 kDa. However, two RNA species have also been suggested in the particles of other isolate. The virus has strong immunogenicity and is phloem restricted. Its concentration is very low in the infected plant.

Disease cycle. The virus survives on infected weeds such as *Capsella bursa-pastoris* and *Senecio vulgaris* and in winter rape.

Transmission. More than 8 aphid vectors chiefly *Myzus persicae* is the important vector of this virus which transmits it in non-persistent manner. It is not mechanically transmitted by infective plant sap, but is transmissible through seed at only very low levels.

Management. For management of this disease elimination of all plants especially owerwintering ones should be done. Chemical control of vectors with suitable insecticide may be done. Biological control measures and growing of tolerant or resistant sugar beet cultivars should be preferred.

SOME OTHER VIRUS DISEASES OF BEET

Beet leaf curl rhabdovirus. *Beta vulgaris* (sugar and fodder beet) and *Spinacea oleracea* are the main natural hosts of the virus. The typical symptoms produced by this virus are vein clearing on young leaves that later curl inward causing bushy and stunted appearance of the infected plants. The virus particles are bacilliform in morphology, measuring about 225 × 80 nm in size. The chemical structure of the virus is not well known. Thermal inactivation point of the virus is 54-58°C, dilution end point is 1×110^{-4} to 1×10^{-5} and longevity *in vitro* is 24 hours at 25°C. The bug-*Piesma quadratum* is known to transmit this virus in non-persistent manner. The virus multiplies in its vector and then can transmit it for life. The virus is not transmitted by infective plant sap and no any other mode of transmission is known so far.

Beet mild yellowing luteovirus. The disease is known to be wide spread in northern, western and central Europe and some other parts of the world. *Beta vulgaris* and *Spinacea oleracea* are economically important natural hosts of the virus. Some weed hosts such as *Capsella bursa-pastoris, Lamium amplexicaule, Plantago* species, *Senecio vulgare* and *Stellaria media* are also important in the disease cycle of this virus. Occurrence of orange yellow symptoms on intermediate sugar beet leaves are the characteristic symptoms of the disease. The causal virus consists of isometric particles, measuring about 28 nm in diameter.

Beet pseudo yellows virus. This virus is known to cause disease of considerable importance and occurs usually in North and South America, Western and Soutehrn Europe and Australia. Characteristic symptoms are interveinal yellowing, swelling and brittleness of the infected sugar beet leaves and stunting of the infected plants. The whitefly-*Trialeurodes vaporatiorum* is known to transmit this virus in nature and no other mode of transmission is known.

Beet yellow net virus. This virus incites net like appearance and chlorotic spots on the only natural host of sugar beet leaves. *Myzus perisicae* and *Aphis fabae* are known as vectors of the virus transmitting it in persistent manner. The virus particles are straight rod, measuring about 300 × 32 nm in size.

Beet yellow stunt closterovirus. It is known to cause considerable damage to different hosts such as red beet, mangold, spinach and many other species belonging to 11 different families. The virus particles are filamentous in morphology, measuring about 1250 × 12 nm in size. It produces leaf mottling, yellowing, severe twisting and epinasty of intermediate leaves. *Chenopodium capitatum, Claytonia perfoliata, Lactuca sativa, Senecio vulgaris* and *Sonchus oleraceus* are important assay plants.

Cucumber mosaic cucumovirus. Infected leaves are twisted downward with pronounced vein clearing and yellow green bronze colouration. Infected seed crops give reduced seed yield.

Tobacco rattle tobravirus. It causes red yellow ring spots on leaves of the infected plants. The virus is transmitted by mechanical means with infected plant sap and also by the nematode-*Trichodorus pachydermis.*

Tomato black ring nepovirus. It produces irregular ring spots on the leaves of the infected plants and some times remain symptom-less. It is transmitted by infected sugar beet seed and by pollen.

VIRUS DISEASES OF POTATO
(*Solanum tuberosum*)

Potato is an important food used as vegetable. It is an important raw material for the chemical and food industries. Potato is a herbaceous plant, on which symptoms of different viruses have been fully determined. Discovery of the first potato virus disease marked the beginning of research and since then, world wide potato research has identified more than 33 viruses/phytoplasma diseases. The losses caused by the potato viruses are not only confined to the year when infection takes place but continue to affect the crop as long as the diseased tubers are used as seed. Economically important diseases of potato incited by different viruses may be summarized as under :

❍ Potato leaf roll luteovirus disease

The disease is known to occur every where the potato crop is grown. The incidence of the disease has been estimated as high as 60-70% and annual loss of about 20 million tones of tubers worldwide.

Symptoms. (1) Primary symptoms occur on plants grown from healthy tubers and infected during the vegetation period. Such symptoms are more pronounced on apical leaves which are erect in appearance and look light green in colour. The leaf base usually turns blue-violet or reddish in colour. (2) Leaflets of infected plant twist upward markedly. (3) In some strains upper leaves are erect and chlorotic and in some others lower leaves roll upward with necrotic patches appearing along the leaf margins with the advancement of disease. (4) Virulent strains cause discolouration and severe leaf roll and plant stunting. (5) Phloem necrosis occurs in stems and tubers of infected plants. (6) Net-like tissue necrosis occurs in some susceptible cultivars. (7) Infected plants produce small tubers worthless for consumption and for marketing due to deterioration in quality.

The causal virus. *Potato leaf roll luteovirus*. The virus particles are isometric in morphology, measuring about 24 nm in diameter. The virus is known to remain restricted in the phloem tissue. The virus consists of single stranded RNA to which a small genome-linked protein of 7 kDa. and a single coat protein of 26 kda. are bonded. Thermal inactivation point of the virus is 70-80°C, dilution end point is 1×10^{-4} and longevity *in vitro* is 5 to 10 days at 2°C.

Disease cycle. Infected tubers are the main source of virus inoculum, which is preserved and transmitted from generation to generation.

Transmission. The virus is transmitted through aphids, including *Myzus persicae, M. assalonicus, M. ornatus, Macrosiphum euphorbiae, Brachycaudus helichrysi* and *Phorodon humuli*. Aphids that transmit the virus in persistent manner require 48 to 72 hours to transmit the virus. The aphids are known to acquire the virus in 12 to 14 hours which takes 12 to 24 hours to move through intestinal canal to the salivary glands and into the mouth apparatus. No information is available about the multiplication of the virus in aphids.

Management . (1) Use healthy seed material for planting. (2) Control aphids by spraying suitable insecticide. (3) To prevent subsequent infection, protection of the crop from aphids is necessary. (4) In case of severe incidence, destruction of infected parts above the ground level either mechanically or by defoliation at the beginning of the first aphid flight should be done. It eliminates source of inoculum for further infection.

❍ Potato protexvirus X disease

The disease is known to occur world wide where the crop is grown regularly. It causes mild disease and is less damaging. Yield reduction ranging from 10 to 20% has been reported. Mixed infection with *Potato potyvirus A* and *Potato potyvirus Y* are more damaging.

Symptoms. (1) The mild mosaic is the general symptom clearly visible on young plants at the beginning of infection. (2) As the season progresses due to increasing temperature, the mosaic symptom becomes less apparent. (3) In some cultivars, mosaic becomes more severe with increased temperature. (4) Leaflets are malformed. (4) Plant tip necrosis may be observed in some rare cases. (5) Cloudy weather and temperatures of 16 to 20°C usually favours the symptom development.

The causal virus. *Potato potexvirus X* (Type). The particles of the virus are flexuous rods, measuring about 515×13 nm in size with sedimentation coefficient of

117 S. The virus consists of single stranded RNA of 2100 kDa. which accounts 6% of the particle weight. The coat protein capsid consists of 1400 protein subunits each of 27 kDa. Thermal inactivation point of the virus is 68-76°C, dilution end point is 1×10^{-5} to 1×10^{-6} and longevity of the virus *in vitro* is several weeks at 20°C. It is strongly immunogenic.

The disease cycle. The diseased tubers are the primary source of perpetuation and disease spread. It is also transmissible through contact between infected and healthy plants where plant population is dense. Soil transmission through the zoospores of the fungus *Synchytrium endobioticum* has also been reported in very rare cases. There is also report that the soil transmission through the fungus-*Spongospora subterranean* is also possible.

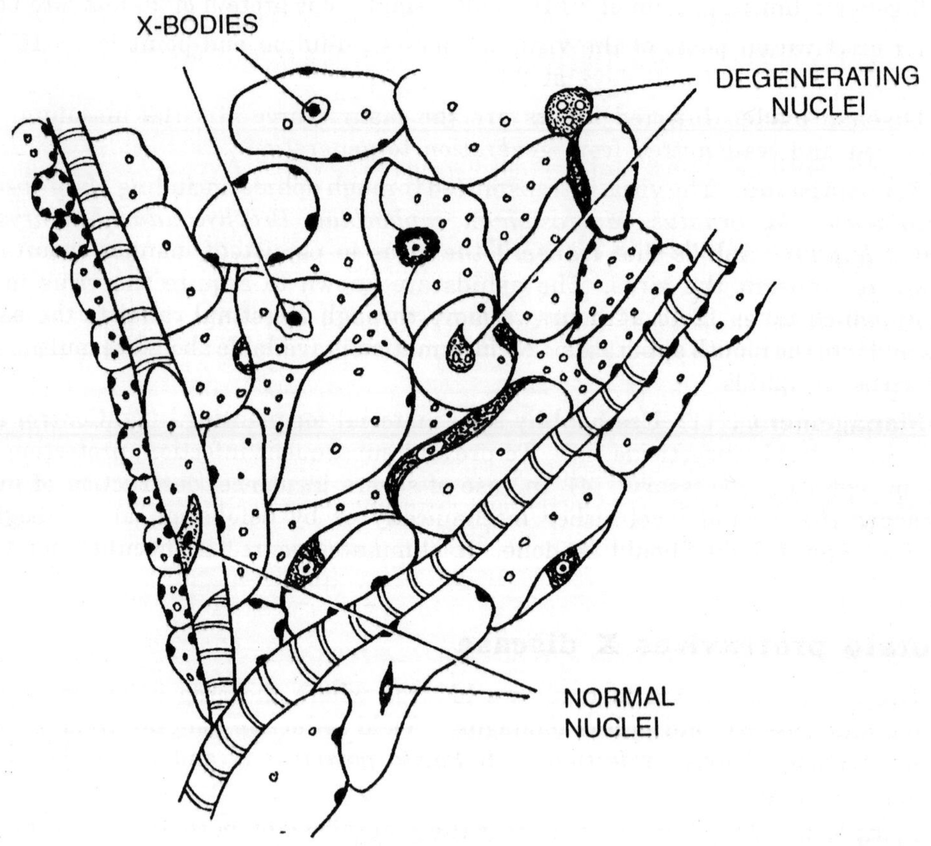

Fig. 16.2 X-bodies in *Potato Virus X* infected leaf section.

Management. (1) Only virus free seed tubers should be used for planting. Any tuber suspected to be infected with the above stated fungus should be rejected. (2) Soil used for production should be free from residual tubers and resting spores of the vectors. A long duration crop rotation may be an important measure in this respect. (3) Chemical sterilization of tools with formaldehyde should be done.

❍ Potato aucuba mosaic (Possible) potexvirus disease

The disease usually occurs sporadically in all the potato growing areas of the world. It causes considerable loss during storage at high temperature. Potato is the only natural host of this virus.

Symptoms. (1) Appearance of mild and light-yellow spots on lower and middle leaves of the infected plants are seen. (2) Leaflet malformation and tip necrosis may be observed in some susceptible cultivars. (3) Occurence of bronze coloured necrotic spots especially on lower leaves may be observed as characteristic symptoms. (4) The potato pseudo-aucuba disease has similar symptoms on potato leaves.

The causal virus. *Potato acucuba mosaic* (possible) *potexvirus.* The virus particles are elongated, measuring about 580 × 11 nm in size. Virus particles sedimentation coefficient is 130 S. Its RNA consists of 5% of the particle weight and coat protein units are 26 kDa. The virus has strong immunogenicity. *Datura metel, D. tatula, Hyoscyamus niger, Nicotiana clevelandii, Solanum melangena, Amaranthus retroflexus* and pepper are diagnostic hosts.

Disease cycle. The virus perpetuates in infected potato tubers and is transmitted through aphids. *Myzus persicae* and *Aphis nasturtii* are important vectors. Aphid transmission to potato is assisted by other helper viruses in infected plant sap.

Management. (1) Use healthy tubers for planting. (2) Infected plants should be rogued out from the field. (3) Tubers with characteristic necrotic spots should be discarded immediately. (4) General preventive measures effective to control potato virus diseases are recommended to be followed.

❍ Potato carlavirus M disease

The disease is most popular in different parts of the world especially Europe and North America. The virus particles are elongated, measuring about 650 × 12 nm in size. The thermal inactivation and point of the virus is 65 to 71°C, dilution end points is 1×10^{-2} to 1×10^{-3} and longevity *in vitro* is several days at 20°C. It is good immunogenic. Symptoms of the disease include the appearance of mosaic, leaf roll, interveinal leaf mosaic and abnormal leaf crinkle. The virus is preserved in and transmitted by potato tubers. Aphids usually transmit this virus in non-persistent manner. Important aphid species is *Myzus persicae.* Which is the most efficient vector. The less active vectors are *Aphis frangulae, A. nasturtii, Aulacorthum solani* and *Macrosiphum euphoribae.* Virus free plants should be planted. Such plants can be obtained by thermotherapy and meristem-tip culture.

❍ Potato carlavirus S disease

The disease is most wideiy found in all potato growing areas of the world. It causes minor loss to the crop. The virus particles are elongated, usually measuring about 650 × 1 nm in size. Thermal inactivation point of the virus is 55-60°C, dilution end point is 1×10^{-2} to 1×10^{-3} and longevity *in vitro* is 3 to 4 days at 20°C. The virus is strongly immunogenic. Infected potato tubers represent the main source of infection. In nature the virus is transmissible mechanically through infective plant sap. Aphids usually transmit the virus non-persistently. *Aphis nasturii* is the most efficient vector among several species. For management of this disease, use of virus free seed and control of vectors through suitable insecticide should be practised.

❍ Potato potyvirus Y (Type) disease

The virus is known to be one of the most damaging viruses throughout the world. Tuber yield in infected plants may be reduced to as low as 33 to 70%.

Symptoms. The disease induces severe symptoms which include crinkling, rugosity, necrosis and leaf dropping. Secondary symptoms are dwarfing of plants, wrinkling and brittleness of leaves.

The causal virus. *Potato potyvirus Y* (type). The virus particles are filamentous in morphology, measuring about 730 × 1 nm in size with sedimentation coefficient of 145 S. Particles contain single stranded RNA that accounts for 6% of the particles weight with coat protein unit of 34 kDa. Thermal inactivation point is 50-62°C, dilution end point is 1×10^{-2} to 1×10^{-6} and the longevity *in vitro* is 7 to 50 days at 22°C. *Potato potyvirus Y* is strongly immunogenic. Several strains are known to occur.

Disease cycle. Potato tubers, the vegetative reproductive organs represent the primary source of infection. In nature, PVY is transmitted by plant aphids such as *Myzus persicae, Aphis nasturtii, Aphis frangulae* and *Macrosiphum euphrobiae.* The virus is mechanically transmissible also and can spread mechanically by contact. Following 2-7 hours of starvation period, aphids acquire PVY in 0.5 to 5 minutes and remain infective for 1 minute to 24 hours. Aphid transmitted PVY and other potyviruses are mediated by a helper component which is a virus coded protein.

Management. Clonally selection of potato based on isolation of symptomless tubers is the primary recommendation for control. Such tubers are primarily used as planting material for reproduction and production of commercial tubers.

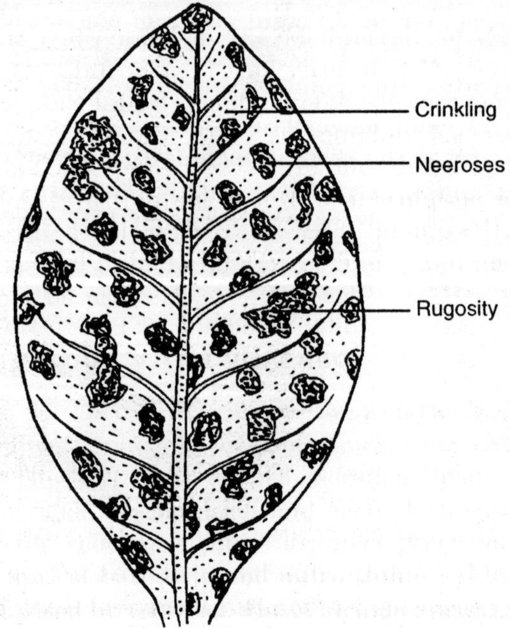

Fig. 16.3 Primary lesions incited by *Potato Virus* Y on tobacco leaf

Fig. 16.4 Symptoms of *Potato Virus* Y on potato

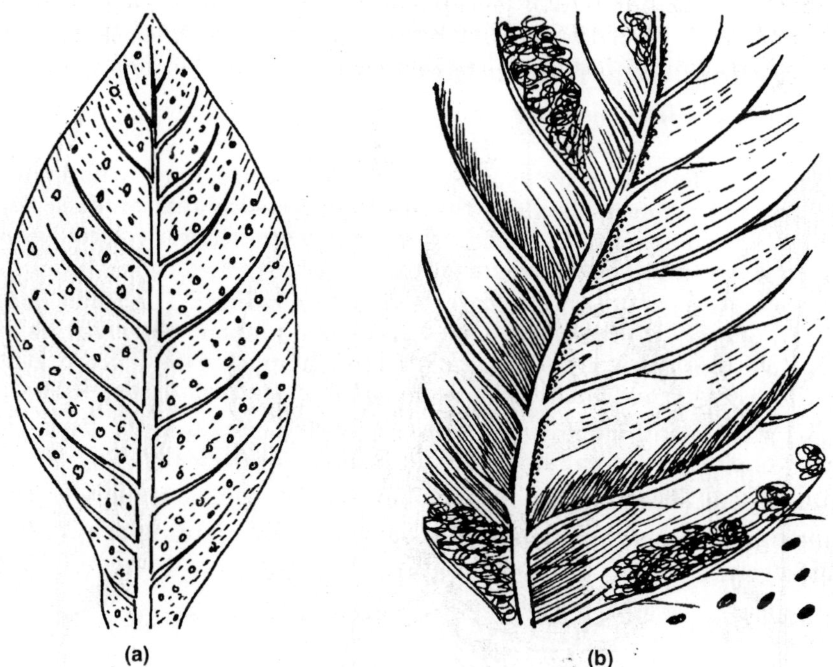

Fig. 16.5 Characteristic symptons of (*a*) *Potato virus* Y infected and (*b*) *Potato virus* X infected leaves of tobacco.

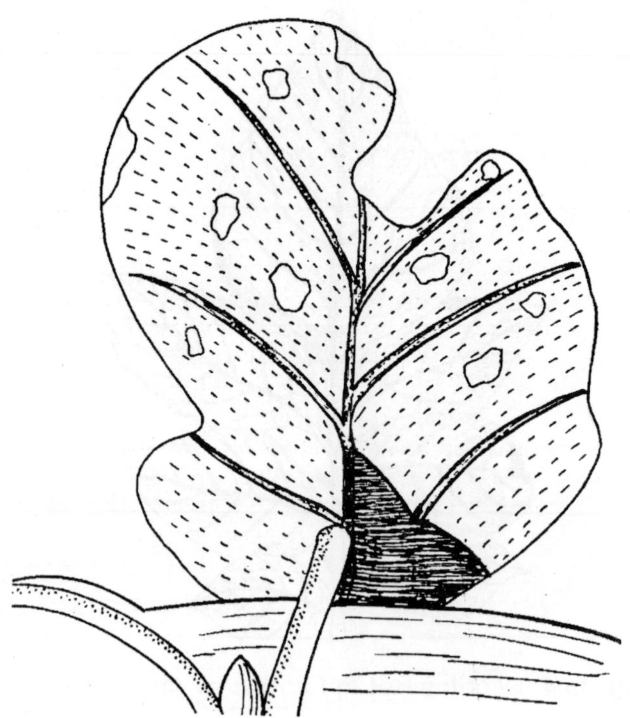

Fig. 16.6 Leaf of tobacco showing toxic effect of *Myzus pseudosolani*

❍ Potato yellow dwarf rhabdovirus disease

The disease was first discovered in U.S.A. Now it is known to occur in different countries.

Symptoms. Characteristic symptoms of the disease may usually be observed as leaf chlorosis and pit necrosis along the stem. Infected plants produce fewer tubers with less germination potential. *Nicotiana rustica* with chlorotic local lesion, mottle and leaf chlorosis is suitable diagnostic plant.

The causal virus. *Potato yellow dwarf rhabdovirus*. The virus particles are bacilliform or bullet shaped in morphology, measuring about 380×75 nm in size. It is single particle type with a sedimentation coefficient of 810- 950 S. It has single stranded RNA. The thermal inactivation point in *Nicrotiana rustica* sap is 50°C. Dilution end point is 1×10^{-3} and longevity *in vitro* at 23-27°C is 2.5 to 12 hours. The virus is moderately immunogenic and is easily detectable serologically.

Disease cycle. Diseased tubers play important role in perpetuation of the disease.

Management. Healthy virus free seed tubers for planting should be used and crop should be grown as far away as possible from potential source of infection.

POTATO AS NATURAL ALTERNATE HOST FOR SOME VIRUSES

More than 10 viruses have been reported on potato as their natural hosts. The important viruses are :

(1) Tobacco viruses such as *Tobacco mosaic virus, Tobacco necrosis virus* and *Tobacco rattle virus.*
(2) Tomato viruses such as *Tomato spotted wilt virus.*
(3) Other viruses such as *Alfalfa mosaic virus, Carnation latent virus* and *Cucumber mosaic virus.*

VIRUS DISEASES OF TOBACCO (*Nicotiana tabacum*)

Tobacco is an important industrial crop consumed for chewing and smoking purposes. Besides, tobacco is used in industries and as fertilizers. It is of great importance in the historical development of plant virology because it is both the natural and experimental host for many plant viruses. The Royal Society of Edinburgh, Scotland held a special Centenary Symposium in 1998 to celebrate the discovery of TMV and to review its impact it has on the science of plant virology. At present, in modern plant virology tobacco plant has been used to transfer desired genes via gentic engineering. The virus gene that determines the code for virus capsid protein synthesis was first introduced in to tobacco cells with the aid of *Agrobacterium tumefaciens* Ti-plasmids. Such plants, with the introduction of 'foreign TMV coat protein genetic material' are now reproducing that gene in them is labelled transgenic plants.

Protein in transgenic plants, whose synthesis is coded by foreign introduced virus genes, increases the resistance of these plants to the virus. Sutic and Sinclair 1991 observed that such transgenic tobacco plants resist infection by *Alfalfa mosaic virus, Cucumber mosaic virus* and *Potato virus X.*

Viruses described on tobacco differ in their morphological characteristics, host range, mode of perpetuation and transmission in nature. Important viral disease of tobacco may be summarized as under :

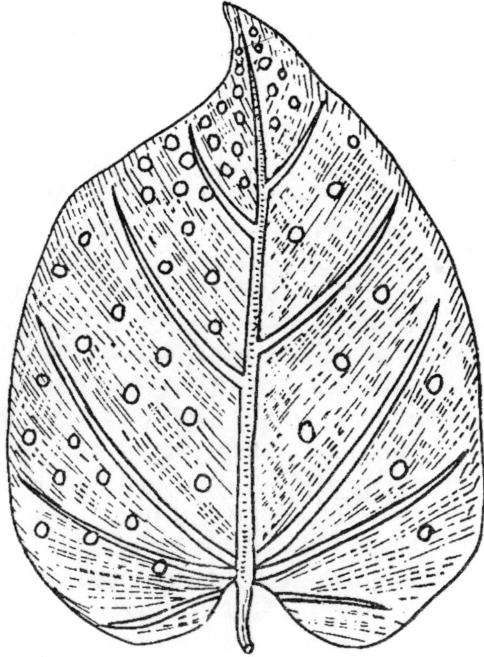

Fig. 16.7 Local lesion of *Tobacco mosaic virus* on leaf of *Nicotiana glutinosa.*

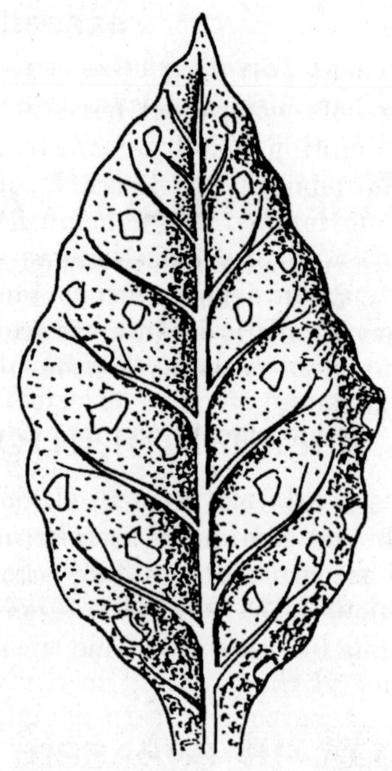

Fig. 16.8 Tobacco mosaic symptons

Tobacco mosaic tobamovirus, Tobacco etch potyvirus, Tobacco vein mottling potyvirus, Tobacco leaf roll geminivirus, Tobacco yellow dwarf geminivirus, Tobacco necrotic dwarf luteovirus, Tobacco rattle tobravirus, Tobacco ring spot nepovirus, Tobacco necrosis virus, Tobacco stunt virus and *Tobacco streak ilarvirus* are economically important as they causes different diseases.

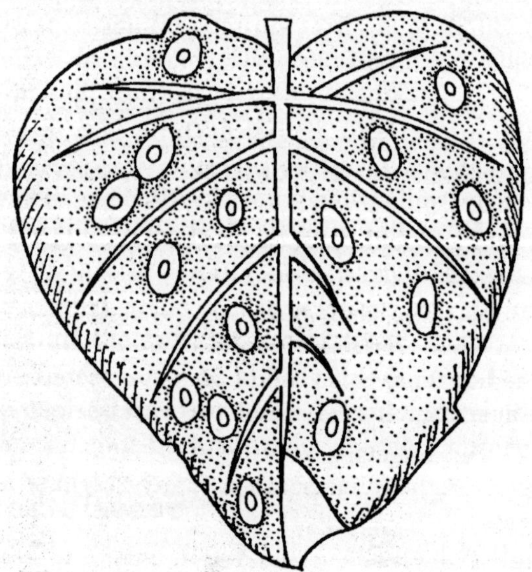

Fig. 16.9 Lesions of *Tomato spotted wilt virus* on *Nicotiana glutinosa* leaf after inoculation

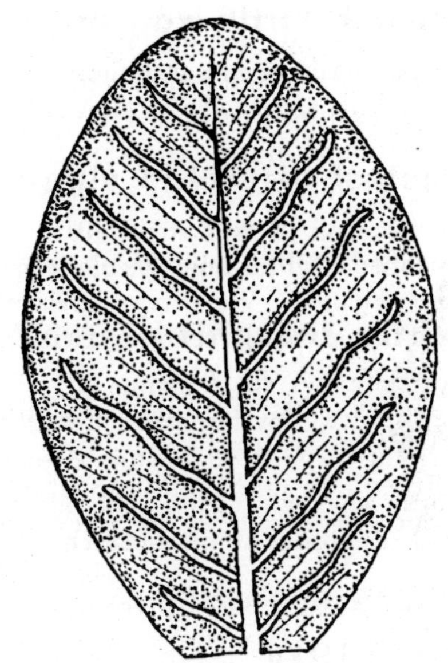

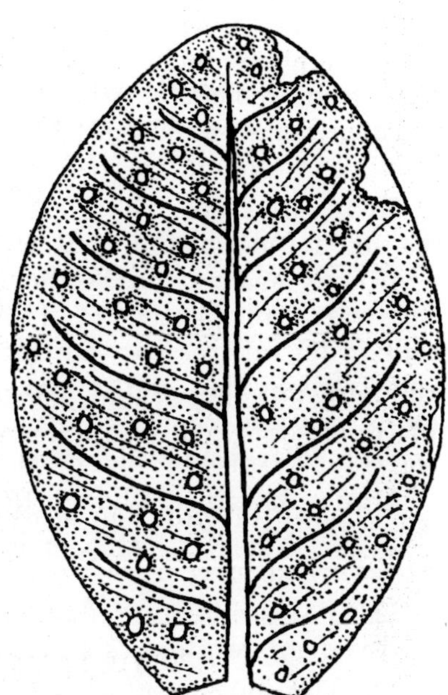

Fig. 16.10 Local lesion seen in tobacco leaf after inoculation.

❍ Tobacco mosaic tobamovirus disease

The disease is wide spread in occurrence and is well known in countries where tobacco is grown. As high as 55% reduction in produce, has been observed in different countries of the world. The quality of the produce is also reduced considerably making the produce sub-standard in the market. Quality reduction involves a decrease of soluble carbohydrates, starch and polyphenol content. Such reductions are reflected in lower content of nicotine, nitrogen and protein nitrogen, resulting in an increase in protein content. Increased protein content greatly influences tobacco quality deteriorating poor smoking quality by producing throat irritant acid taste.

Symptoms. (1) Leaves of infected plants show mild clearing of veins. (2) Clearly visible mottle and mosaic occur in younger leaves later in the season. (3) Golden yellow mosaic or light green spots are seen on *Nicotiana sylvestris* cv. *otlja* and tissue necrosis occurs within these spots in some other cultivars. (4) Wrinkling, crinkling, twisting of margins and narrowing of leaflets are also observed. (5) There are marked reduction in growth and substantial reduction in yield.

The causal virus. The virus particles are rod shaped in morphology, measuring about 300×18 nm in size. Particles contain single-stranded RNA composed of 6300 nucleotides. The capsid consists of 2130 identical protein subunits, each 17.5 kDa. TMV is one of the most stable viruses. Thermal inactivation point is above 90°C, dilution end point is 1×10^{-6} and longevity *in vitro* is several months to 5 years at 24°C with preservatives. It is strongly immunogenic. Many strains have been described based on biological virulence.

Disease cycle. The virus is preserved in nature in herbaceous and woody plants. Vegetables including tomato, potato and pepper grown indoors usually transmit the virus from crop to crop. The virus has wide host range and more than 550 species of flowering plants including 60 natural and many other experimental hosts are known. Natural hosts include several species of tobacco, tomato, potato, wild apple, plum and grapevine. Some strains of TMV also infect fungal species like *Erysiphe graminis, E. polygoni, Phyllactinia corylea* and *Sphacrotheca lanestris* and many other species.

Transmission. The virus may remain infective in the roots or organic matter of the soil for more than 2 years if such soil is not exposed to freezing and drying. The virus is easily transmitted by smoke through contact with susceptible plants. Mechanical transmission of TMV is unique among viruses. Weeding, uprooting, transplanting, inflorescence cutting and periodical harvesting usually create environment for the transmission of the virus from the source to the healthy plants. No insect vector is possibly known to exist, however, grass hoppers, butterfly and caterpillars are known to transmit the virus through mechanical means by contact.

Management. Although this disease is very difficult to manage because of the marked ability of the virus. Experimental results have suggested some preventive measures which may be summarized as under :

(1) For seedling production, planting of only clean and healthy seed, free of plant-residues, should be done.

(2) Use uncontaminated soils for seed production.

(3) Disinfect all soils of unknown origin prior to sowing and produce only tobacco seedlings in flower beds. Do not use same flower beds for tomato and pepper seedlings.

(4) All workers should disinfect their hands at regular intervals. Restrict smoking by workers.

(5) All infected and suspected plants should be removed from the vicinity of the nurseries.

(6) Grow tobacco in three-year crop roation with maize and wheat, avoiding tomato and pepper crops.

(7) Infection by mechanical inoculation can be reduced in limited area by spraying plants with skim milk or butter-milk. Leaves from healthy plants should be harvested first and then those from infected plants.

❍ Tobacco etch potyvirus disease

The disease is wide spread in U.S., Canada, Mexico, Pueroto Rico, Venezuela and South Eastern Europe. It infects natural cultivated hosts such as tomato, tobacco and pepper along with a number of susceptible weeds.

Symptoms. (1) Characteristic symptoms are usually more evident at the time of flowering. (2) Initial symptoms include vein clearing which is accompanied by the appearance of chlorotic mosaic and necrotic ethching on the leaves of the infected plants. (3) In older leaves, necrosis and yellowing are observed along the veins and (4) Infected plants may remain stunted.

The causal virus. *Tobacco itch potyvirus.* Virus particles are flexuous filaments in morphology. They usually measure 730 × 12-13 nm in size with sedimentation coefficient of 154 S. They are composed of single stranded RNA of 3200 kDa. which accounts about 5% of the particle weight. The capsid protein consists of subuits of

30 to 32 kDa. Thermal inactivation point is 55°C, the dilution end point is 1×10^{-4} and longevity *in vitro* is 5-10 days at 20°C. The virus is known to be serologically related with *Potato virus A, Potato virus Y* and *Henbane mosaic virus.* Both severe and mild strains are known to exist based on virulence.

Disease cycle. The virus survives on both cultivated natural hosts and susceptible weeds. Natural hosts include *Nicotiana tabacum, Capsicum annum, Linaria canadensis, Lycopersicon lycopersicum, Physalis angulata, Solanum nigrum, Solanum acuelatissimum* and several weed species including *Datura stramonium, Cassia obtusifolia* and *Cirsium vulgare.* Diagnostic plants include *Nicotiana tabacum, Datura stramonium* and *Cassia obtusifolia* On *Nicotiana tabacum* chlorotic spots and necrotic rings may be observed on inoculated plant leaves. Vein clearing and necrotic etching are usually observed as a result of systemic infection. *Datura stramonium,* the first known natural host of this virus, produces diagnostic symptoms like leaf mottling, distortion of leaves and vein banding. *Cassia obtusifolia* produces necrotic local lesions and systemic infection exhibits chlorosis, necrosis and stunting of infected leaves.

Transmission. Transmission of the virus through infected plant sap is important in transmission of the disease. Several cultural operations allow contact of the machinery with the diseased plants which help in the spread of the disease. Several aphid species including *Myzus persicae, Macrosiphum euphorbiae* and *Aphis fabae* usually transmit the virus in non-persistent manner. This virus is also transmissible by dodder—*Cuscuta* species. The virus is not reported to be transmitted through seed.

Management. (1) Hands, clothing, implements and tools used in cultivation should be disinfected at regular intervals during cultivation. (2) Isolation of the crop from susceptible plants and weeds is recommended to reduce the infection. (3) Control of weeds through herbicides and control of aphid vectors by use of suitable insecticide should be done.

❍ Tobacco ring spot nepovirus disease

The virus has been found to occur on different hosts and is world wide in distribution. It occurs in Africa, Asia, Japan, North America, Canada and Europe. It causes serious damage in India as reported.

Symptoms- The virus causes characteristic ring spots which gradually become larger forming wavy necrotic zones along the midribs of the leaves. Isolated ring spots may be characterized by the inter-veinal necrosis of tissues. Infected plants usually remain stunted and grow slowly with characteristic poor quality leaves. Symptoms may disappear with time and new growth may exhibit no symptoms at all.

The causal virus- Tobacco ring spot nepovirus. Virus particles are isometric in morphology, measuring 28 nm in diameter. They consist of three components; viz, top (T), middle (M) and bottom (B) based on their sedimentation rates in density gradient columns. The sedimentation coefficients are 53 S, 91 S and 126 S respectively. Some isolates of the virus contain satellites of RNA that produce additional pair of particles. TIP of the virus in infective sap is 60 to 65°C, DEP is 1×10^{-3} to 1×10^{-4} and LIV is 1 to 2 weeks at 24°C.

Transmission - The virus retains infectivity in many herbaceous and woody hosts. *Xiphinema americanum* nematode serves as a vector by feeding first on tobacco ring spot infected roots after which they remain infective for 24 hours. Some other vectors reported include nymphs of *Thrips tabaci* that transmits this virus to soybean. Besides, many other vectors like spider mite, grass hopper, flea beetle and some aphids are also responsible for transmission.

Management- Elimination of sources of the virus especially the infected perennial plants should be done. Only nematode free soil should be used for the cultivation of the tobacco.

❍ Tobacco necrosis virus disease

The disease is known to occur wherever tobacco is cultivated, owing to its large number of susceptible hosts.

Symptoms- The virus usually affects the roots of susceptible plants in the beginning and there after moves systemically. Infected tobacco plants exhibit necrotic spots on the leaf midrib followed by mosaic and mottling with characteristic grey mosaic leaf pattern along larger leaf veins. As a result of infection, young leaves die frequently.

Causal virus- The virus consists of isometric particles, measuring 28 nm in diameter. Single stranded RNA genome accounts for 18-21% of the weight of the viral particle. The molecular weight of the virus particle is 6300 to 7600 kDa and of the protein coat subunit is 30 to 33 kDa as reported. This virus is usually found associated with a satellite virus. Satellite virus particles are isometric, measuing 17 nm in diameter and is composed of an RNA of some 400 kDa and coat protein subunits of 22 kDa. *Tobacco necrosis virus* replicates independently in cells of the host plants. However, the satellite virus particles replicate only in presence of *Tobacco necrosis virus*. Thus, the satellite virus RNA is dependent on the *Tobacco necrosis virus* RNA. Satellite virus is capable of synthesizing only its coat protein. Several strains are known to occur.

Transmission- Zoospores of *Olpidium brassicae* is known to transmit this virus. It is also transmissible mechanically; however, other modes of transmission are not known.

Management- Suitable crop rotation and use of resistant varieties are recommended. Soil sanitation prior to sowing and soil aeration and moisture regulation are also necessary for better management of the disease.

SOME OTHER DISEASES OF TOBACCO

Table 16.1 **Showing some other important diseases of tobacco with their causal virus, symptoms and mode of transmission.**

Diseases and their distribution	Causal virus	Symptoms	Transmission
1. Tobacco vein mottling poty virus disease. It was reported from South-eastern U.S. and is limited in distribution.	*Tobacco vein mottling potyvirus* Virus particles are flexuous, measuring 13× 765 nm in size, consisting of single	Characteristic spots and necrosis in the veins and leaves are seen on the leaves of the affected plants. The virus also infects tomato.	The virus is transmissible by infective plant sap and by aphids. Certain aphid species including *Myzus persicae,*

Diseases and their distribution	Causal virus	Symptoms	Transmission
	stranded RNA genome of 3200 kDa.TIP is 60-70°C, DEP is 1X 10 -2 to 1 X 10-3. LIV is 48 hours at 22-25°C.		*Macrosiphum euphorbiae, Aphis gossypi, Rhopalosiphum maidis* and *R. padi* are common vectors. For management, spraying of suitable insecticide should be done to reduce vector transmission.
2. Tobacco necrotic dwarf luteovirus disease. The disease has been reported from Japan on Tobacco, spinach and *Capsella bursa-pastoris.*	*Tobacco necrotic dwarf luteovirus.* The virus consists of isometric virus particles, measuring 25 nm in diameter. The particles consist of single stranded RNA genome of 2000 kDa and a capsid consisting of 25.7 kDa coat protein subunit. TIP is 80°C and LIV is over 6 months at 4°C. Sample is strongly immunogenic.	The virus causes early yellowing of lower and middle leaves of the affected plants. As a result of the disease, affected plants may remain stunted. The virus remains limited in phloem and may cause phloem necrosis and vein yellowing.	Natural hosts represent permanent sources of infection in nature. It overwinters in winter providing infective virus for new spring crop. *Myzus persicae* is the main vector known to transmit the virus.
3. Tobacco yellow dwarf Geminivirus disease. The disease is wide spread in Australia.	*Tobacco yellow dwarf Geminivirus.* Particles are geminate, measuring 20X35 nm in size. They have sedimentation coefficient of 76 S . The virus consists of single stranded DNA genome. The coat protein subunit has been reported to be 27.5 kDa. TIP is	Characteristic symptoms of the disease include severe tobacco stunting and phloem cells necrosis. *Nicotiana tabacum* and *Phaseolus vulgaris* are economically important natural hosts of the pathogen. However, the virus has been	Leaf hoppers including *Orosius argentatus* are known to transmit the virus in persistent manner. No other mode of transmission is known.

Diseases and their distribution	Causal virus	Symptoms	Transmission
	50-60°C, DIP is 1/50 to 1/500 and LIV is 26 days at 40°C. Virus samples are serologically moderately immunogenic.	transmitted experimentally to more than 30 plant species belonging to dicotyledonous families.	
4. **Tobacco leaf curl Geminivirus disease.** The disease is wide spread in both tropical and subtropical areas of Japan and Europe.	*Tobacco leaf curl Geminivirus.* The virus consists of geminate particles in morphology, measuring 15-20 nm X 25-30 nm in size. Particles have circular single stranded DNA genome. Individual virus isolates have been reported to differ significantly.	Infected plants have been reported to remain stunted with characteristic twisted stems and small, curled and rolled leaves. Enations also occur along the veins on lower leaf surfaces. The virus remains restricted in phloem of the infected plants.	The virus has been reported to be preserved in *Lonicera japonica* which represents as a potential reservoir. Whitefly *-Bemisia tabaci* is known as the primary vector that transmits the virus in persistent manner.
5. **Tobacco rattle tobravirus disease.** Wide spread in distribution especially in North and South America, Europe and Japan.	*Tobacco rattle tobravirus.* The virus with single stranded RNA genome consists of particles of two different sizes. They are known as long and short particles. In this way long particles measure 180-200 X 22 nm in size and short particles measure 50-110 X22 nm in size. Sedimentation coefficients are 300 S and 155-243 S respectively. TIP in *Nicotiana clevelandii* sap is 80 to 85°C, DIP is	Large grey spots that turn into dark necrotic zones are the characteristic symptoms of the disease. Systemic infection results in the formation of necrotic spots along the leaf veins may also be observed.It causes mosaic and mottle on stems and corky ring spots on potato tubers. *Nicotiana tabacum* and *Cucumis sativus* support systemic infection; therefore, they are suitable for transmission studies.	The virus is known to survive in numerous biennial and perennial hosts. Larvae and adults of plant parasitic nematodes belonging to *Trichodorus* and some other genera have been reported to transmit this disease.

Diseases and their distribution	Causal virus	Symptoms	Transmission
	1×10^{-3} to 1×10^{-4} and LIV is 6 weeks at 20°C. Virus samples are weekly immunogenic.	*Chenopodium amranticolor* and *Phaseolus vulgaris* exhibits local spots with out systemic infection, are suitable assay plants.	
6. Tobacco stunt virus disease. This disease was first reported from Japan.	*Tobacco stunt virus.* The virus consists of rod shaped particles, measuring 300-340 X 18 nm in size. The genome of virus particles are composed of double stranded RNA and single species of 48 kDa protein. TIP of the virus in tobacco sap is 40 to 50°C and DEP is 1×10^{-3} to 1×10^{-4}.	Important symptoms include vein clearing followed by vein necrosis, ring like pattern,mosaic mottling and stunting of plants. The virus has been reported to be preserved in resting spores of *Olpidium brassicae* which represents permanent soil source of infection.	Suitable crop rotation, non contaminated soils and avoidance of vectors are important measures for management of the disease.
7. Tobacco streak ilarvirus disease. The disease is wide spread in Europe, America, Japan and New Zealand.	*Tobacco streak ilarvirus.* Virus particles are isometric in morphology, consisting of particles of three sizes. It consists of single stranded RNA genome. Four types of RNA are required for successful infection. TIP is 53-64°C, DIP varies from 1/30 to 1/ 15625 and LIV is 36 hours in diluted tobacco sap.	Necrotic ring symptoms may appear in inoculated leaves of *Nicotiana tabacum* var *xanthi*. Characteristic necrotic lines may appear rapidly along small veins of newly emerging leaves, resulting in the death of the plants in due course.	The virus is known to infect perennial hosts. *Thrips tabacior* and *Frankiliniella* species are known as vectors. Use seeds from healthy plants, use virus free seedlings and control of vectors are important for the management of the disease.

❍ Tobacco as natural alternative host for other viruses

Tobacco distortion luteuvirus and *Tobacco yellow net luteovirus* are important viruses known to cause diseases of economic importance. These two diseases are transmitted by different species of aphids. Besides these, many other viruses are also known to occur on tobacco causing characteristic symptoms. A partial list of such viruses may be summarized as under-

1. *Alfalfa mosaic virus.*
2. *Beet curly top geminivirus.*
3. *Cucumber mosaic cucumovirus.*
4. *Potato potyvirus X.*
5. *Potato potyvirus Y*
6. *Tomato ringspot nepovirus.*
7. *Tomato spotted wilt virus*

VIRUS DISEASES OF HOP (*Humulus lupulus*)

Hop is a perennial plant belonging to the family Cannabinaceae. It is grown for floral cones used extensively in the production of beer and pharmaceutical items in the pharmaceutical industry. It is grown worldwide chiefly in Europe and former Soviet Union that are the largest producers. Hop is the primary and alternate host for many viruses of great economic importance. Important diseases are as under :

❍ Hop mosaic carlavirus disease

The disease is known to occur worldwide and has been described in Europe, North America and Tasmania. The disease may cause losses in yield as high as 40% to 70%.

Symptoms. (1) Initial symptoms are vein clearing of leaves with pale green to yellow spots near the leaf veins of the infected plants. (2) Leaf margins twist downward. (3) Leaves become yellow green, brittle and distorted. (4) Internodes are shortened and plants become bushy in appearance. (5) Twisted and poor quality floral cones are formed. (6) The roots of the infected plants usually decline, resulting in early death of the infected plants.

The Causal Virus. *Hop mosaic carlavirus.*

Transmission. The virus is known to be transmitted through aphids chiefly *Macrosiphum euphorbiae, Myzus persicae* and *Phorodon humuli* in non-persistent manner. The virus perpetuates in its host.

Management. (1) Use of virus free planting stocks for establishment of the and plantation (2) Rogueing of infected plants from the newly established plantations. (3) Control of vectors to avoid further spread of the disease and (4) Growing of resistant/tolerant cvs. may be recommended as precautionary measures for the management of the disease.

❍ Hop latent carlavirus disease

This disease is widespread in distribution chiefly in Europe, U.S. and Australia.

Symptoms. Infected plants may remain symptomless and thus these plants are dangerous source of disease spread. Suitable assay plants are *Phaseolus vulgaris, Chenopodium murale* and *Humulus lupulus*. These plants are used for diagnosis.

The causal virus. *Hop latent carlavirus*. The virus consists of filamentous particles, measuring about 675×14 nm in size and having single stranded RNA of 2900 kDa. The thermal inactivation point of the virus is 70 to 75°C, dilution end point is 1×10^{-2} to 1×10^{-3} and longevity of the virus *in vitro* is 25 days. The virus sample is moderately immunogenic.

Disease cycle. The virus is preserved in its potential hop host and is transmitted to the new established hop gardens.

Transmission. The virus is known to be transmitted by the aphid-*Phorodon humuli* in non-persistent manner. It is also transmissible through infective plant sap by mechanical inoculation.

Management. All measures as suggested for hop mosaic carlavirus disease should be followed.

❍ Hop American latent carlavirus disease

The disease is well known in occurrence in many U.S. hop gardens where it causes considerable loss to the plants. Appearance of ring and line pattern on leaves of the seedlings are the characteristic symptoms of the disease. The causal virus-*Hop American latent carlavirus*, consists of filamentous particles which are 680×16 nm in measurement. It contains single stranded RNA of 3000 kDa. which accounts 5 to 7% of the particle weight. It contains a coat protein of 32.7 kDa. The virus is preserved permanently in infected hop plants and retained in planting stocks. The virus is sap transmissible and is also transmitted by the vector-*Phorodon humuli* in non-persistent manner. Measures to manage the disease are similar to those as described for management of hop latent carlavirus.

❍ Hop chlorotic disease

The disease is known to cause damage in many of the European countries. The causal virus is *Hop chlorotic virus*. Pale or green yellow spots on primary leaves of infected hop plants are usually observed as characteristic symptoms of the disease. Chlorotic stripes, inter-veinal necrosis and toothed leaf margins are also characteristic symptoms of the disease. Infected plants may remain stunted and there may be poor development of inflorescences. The virus is known to be transmitted through infective plant sap and seed obtained from infected plants. However, no insect vector is known so far that transmits the virus and spreads the disease. All prevention measures as described above are useful to be followed for management of this disease.

Fig. 16.11 Chlorotic symptoms on leaves of hop

❍ Hop mosaic chlorosis virus disease

The disease has been studied well in Eastern Europe where this disease is wide spread in occurrence. Appearance of chlorotic lesions on the inter-veinal tissues of infected plants are the characteristic symptoms of the disease. *Chenopodium album* which produces pale spots as local lesion is an important assay plant. The causal virus-*Hop mosaic chlorosis virus* consists of particles measuring 680×18–20 nm in size. Thermal inactivation point of the virus is 43°C, dilution end point is 2.5×10^{-2} and longevity *in vitro* is 15 hours at 24°C. Infected hop plants are the important source of disease perpetuation. In nature, the disease is transmitted by the aphid vector chiefly *Phorodon humuli* in non-persistent manner. Mechanical transmission by infected plant sap is also well known.

❍ Hop yellow net virus disease

The causal virus-*Hop yellow net virus* is known to cause symptoms like yellowing of veins in the third row whereas veins of first and second rows remain green as usual. Plant growth is not affected by the disease. The viral nature of the disease has been reported. Physical and chemical properties of the virus have not yet been studied. Virus is graft transmissible. Planting of healthy planting materials for the establishment of new gardens and rouging of infected plants are the important measures for the management of the disease.

HOP AS NATURAL ALTERNATE HOST OF DIFFERENT VIRUSES

Many viruses are known to harbor on hop and incite symptoms of different descriptions on it. Some important viruses are as under :

❍ *Arabis mosaic nepovirus*

It is a damaging agent in Europe. Infected plants grow more slowly, intenodes are shorter and bushy appearance are important characteristics of the disease. It is transmitted from plant to plant mechanically by grafting and by *Xiphinema diversicaudatum* (nematode) in the soil. Nematode management in the soil and rogueing weeds in hop gardens are important measures to manage the disease.

❍ *Apple mosaic ilarvirus*

Two strains of this virus namely, hop A and hop C are known to occur frequently in nature and are symptomless. Under suitable conditions, the causal virus-*Apple mosaic ilarvirus* may initiate appearance of chlorotic and necrotic line mosaic pattern on leaves of the infected plants.

❍ *Prunus necrotic ringspot ilarvirus*

The virus is known to infect many species of *Prunus* and causes rose mosaic symptoms. Other symptoms produced by the virus are appearance of ring and band pattern mosaic along with necrotic crinkle mosaic on the leaves of the infected plants. General preventive measures should be adopted to manage this disease.

❍ *Tobacco necrosis necrovirus*

The virus is known to be preserved in and transmitted by the zoospores of *Olpidium brassicae* in the soil.

VIRUS DISEASES OF PEANUT (*Arachis hypogaea*)

A number of plant viruses are known to infect this valuable crop. A partial list of economically important viruses may be summarized as under :

Cowpea chlorotic mottle virus, Peanut stunt virus, Sun flower yellow blotch virus, Cowpea mild mottle virus, Peanut clump virus, Groundnut crinkle virus, Indian peanut clump virus, Groundnut rosette assistor, Peanut chlorotic streak virus, Ground nut yellow mosaic virus (Bean golden yellow mosaic virus), Groundnut veinal chlorosis, Groundnut chlorotic spotting virus, Cucumber mosaic virus, Tobacco streak virus, Bean yellow mosaic virus, Groundnut eye spot, Passion fruit woodiness virus, Peanut green mosaic virus, Peanut bud necrosis virus, Peanut yellow spot virus, Tomato spotted will virus, Groundnut yellow mottle virus and *Groundnut rosette virus.*

Important diseases of this crop are being described below in some detail.

❍ Peanut bud necrosis tospovirus disease

The disease is known to occur in different countries. It is distributed in occurrence in America, Africa and Australia whereas it appears to be widely distributed in Asia including India.

Symptoms. (1) Initial symptoms of the disease appear as chlorotic spots or mild mottle on peanut. (2) Necrotic, chlorotic rings and streaks develop in due course. (3) Necrosis of terminal buds is usually observed when temperature goes above 30°C. (4) Infected plants may die due to spread of the necrosis to whole of the plants. (5) Stunting and proliferation of axillary shoots are also observed. (6) Early infected plants are stunted and seeds formed are small and shrivelled. (7) Late infected plants can produce seeds of normal size but seed coats are often mottled and cracked.

Diagnostic hosts are cowpea on which both the *Peanut bud necrosis virus* and *Tomato spotted wilt virus* produce concentric, necrotic and chlorotic lesions. On *Petunia hybrida* necrotic lesions are produced.

The causal virus. *Peanut bud necrosis virus*. Virus particles are spherical, measuring 80 to 100 nm in size and surrounded by a glycoprotein-rich lipid membrane. They usually encapsulate three species of RNA *i.e.* small, medium and large. The complete nucleotide sequence of all the three RNA species has been published. Small, medium and large-RNAs of *Peanut bud necrosis virus* contain 3057, 4801 and 8911 nucleotides respectively. The large RNA is of negative polarity, whereas M-and S are of different character. Purified virus particles are not infective. *Peanut bud necrosis virus* has a low thermal inactivation point (45 C° for 10 minutes). Longevity *in vitro* is 5 hours at room temperature.

Fig. 16.12 Showing chlorosis, line pattern and leaf distortion of peanut leaves incited by *Peanut bud necrosis virus*

Nucleotide sequence of S-and M-RNA, deduced amino acid sequence of the nucleocapsid protein gene, host range and species of thrips vector are used to differentiate *Peanut bud necrosis virus* and *Tomato spotted wilt virus.*

Disease cycle. *Tomato spotted wilt virus* is transmitted by two species of thrips namely, *Franlliniella occidentalis* and *F. fusca*. *Peanut bud necrosis virus* is transmitted by *Thrips palmi.*

Management. Cultural practices such as date of planting, maintenance of optimum plant poluation (approximately 200,000, to 300,000 per hectare), vigorous crop growth and intercropping with fast growing cereal crops have been found to reduce the incidence of the disease. Good sources of field resistance against both *Peanut bud necrosis virus* and *Tomato spotted wilt virus* have been found. Genes governing resistance have been transferred to some widely grown peanut cultivars.

❍ Peanut clump virus disease

The virus is well known to occur in different southern Asian and Western African countries chiefly, India, Pakistan, Niger republic, Gambia and Senegal. The disease causes losses as high as 38 million dollars at global scale.

Symptoms. (1) Infected plants are seen stunted and dark green in the field. (2) They are seen in patches. (3) Mottling mosaic and chlorotic rings are usually observed on young quadrifoliates. (4) Early infected plants are severely stunted and such plants seldom produce well developed pods. (5) The virus has wide host range and they usually infect both mono-and dicotyledonous plants including wheat, barley, maize, sorghum, pearl millet, peanut and pigeon pea.

The causal virus. *Peanut clump virus.* The genus *Peclus* contains *Peanut clump virus*, which causes peanut clump disease in Western Africa. Indian *Peanut clump virus* causes clump diseae in the Indian subcontinent. These two viruses differ in their symptoms they produce. The *Indian peanut clump virus* isolates can be identified by the symptoms produced in *Canavalia ensiformis, Nicotiana clevelandii* and *N. benthamiana.* Isolates produce differnt symptoms in *Chenopodium amaranticolor*. These two viruses contain two rod shaped particles, measuring 245 nm and 190 nm respectively in length having about 21 nm diameter.

Disease cycle. Peanut clump disease is soil borne. Both the viruses are transmitted by the fungus *Polymyxa* species. Only monocotyledonous hosts are suitable for multiplication of the fungus. Seeds of wheat, corn, millets and rhizomatous grasses such as *Cynodon dactylon* are likely to contribute the establishment of this disease in the soils inhabiting *Polymyxa* species. Both the viruses are also transmitted by mechanical sap inoculation. The viruses remain present in the sap but are very difficult to be transmitted mechanically.

Management. Early planting, trap cropping with pearl millet and avoidance of crop rotation with highly susceptible cereal hosts such as maize and wheat have been found to be very effective in minimizing the disease incidence. Soil solorization has also been found effective.

❍ Groundnut rosette disease

Occurrence of the disease in India, Argentina, Philippines and Indonesia is not so common as observed in African countries. The disease is economically important especially in southern Africa.

Symptoms. (1) Chlorotic rosette appears on young leaflets alongwith mild chlorosis interspersed with a few green islands. (2) Leaflets produced subsequently remain yellow with green veins. (3) Early infected plants produce chlorotic, curled and distorted leaflets. (4) Plants infected may remain stunted and such plants look darker than healthy plants. (5) Usually symptoms of mosaic rosette resemble with those of chlorotic rosette.

The causal virus. *Groundnut rosette virus* and *Groundnut rosette assister virus*. Groundnut rosette disease is caused by a complex of two viruses and a satelite RNA. The one of the two viruses is usually referred as *Groundnut rosette virus*, which is mechanically transmissible umbravirus and is coat protein deficient. The other virus is *Groundnut rosette assistor luteovirus. Groundnut rosette virus*-RNA contains 4019 nucleotides and contains 4 large ORFs. The *Groundnut rosette virus* is dependent on *Groundnut rosette assistor leteovirus* for aphid transmission. The satellite plays important role in *Groundnut rosette assistor luteovirus*-dependent aphid transmission of *Groundnut rosette virus*. Infected plants, manifesting usual symptoms generally contain all three virus components.

Disease cycle. Groundnut plants usually infected with the virus, is the main and initial source of virus infection. The disease is transmitted by the aphid-*Aphis craccivora* in a semi-persistent or circulative manner.

Management. (1) Cultural practices such as early planting, planting at high density and maintenance of plant population should be adopted. (2) Early maturing and rosette resistant peanut genotypes should be utilized to produce resistant cultivars. (3) Coat protein gene of groundnut rosette assistor luteovirus has been sequenced, therefore, resistant Groundnut cultivars should be developed.

SOME OTHER DISEASES OF PEANUT

❍ Peanut mottle potyvirus disease

The disease is of global importance because it is known to occur in most of the peanut growing countries of the world.

Symptoms. Mild mottle and sometimes mosaic with dark green and irregular discoloured islands are usually observed on young leaflets. Characteristic interveinal depressions with upward rolling of leaf edges also appear. Diseased plants may remain stunted. *Phaseolus vulgaris* is diagnostic host of this virus.

The causal virus. *Peanut mottle potyvirus.* The virus particles are flexuous rods, measuring about 750×12 nm in size and containing a single stranded RNA. Molecular weight of coat protein is 32 to 36 kDa. The coat protein gene has been found to contain 1247 nucleotides. The thermal inactivation point of the virus is 55 to 65°C and longevity *in vitro* is 1 to 2 days at room temperature.

Transmission. The virus is readily transmitted by mechanical sap inoculation and by several species of aphid in non-persistent manner. The virus is also seed transmissible. Infected seed is the primary source of inoculum.

Management. Planting of virus free seed is important.

❍ Peanut stripe potyvirus disease

The disease was first reported from U.S.A. in 1983. Now the disease is well known to occur in China, India and many other countries of Southern and Eastern Asia.

Symptoms. Appearance of discontinuous dark green stripes along the lateral veins of young leaflets are seen. Irregular green blotches on young leaflets may also be observed to persist for longer time. The disease may cause stunting of plants and yield reduction upto 60%.

The causal virus. *Peanut stripe potyvirus.*

Natural hosts. Natural hosts are *Centrosema pubescens, C. macrocarpum, Calopogonium coeruleum, Crotaloria striata, Desmodium siliquasum* and *Pueraria phaseoloides.* It does not produce local lesion on *Phaseolous vulgaris*, therefore, it can be differentiated from *Peanut mottle virus.*

Disease cycle. The virus perpetuates through infected seed. It is mechanically transmissible from infected plant sap inoculation and also through aphids in non-persistent manner.

Management. Planting virus free seed has been observed to reduce the incidence of the disease. Since *Peanut stripe potyvirus* has been sequenced, therefore, resistant genes are expected to be utilized in developing transgenic peanuts.

❍ Peanut stunt cucumovirus disease

The disease has been reported from U.S., China and Sudan and is of minor importance.

Symptoms. It causes severe stunting of entire plant or some of its branches. Characteristic symptoms are shortening of the petiole, reduction in leaflet size, chlorosis and malformation. Very few pods are produced in early infected plants.

The causal virus. *Peanut stunt cucumovirus.* The virus particles are 25-30 nm in diameter consisting of 4 single stranded RNAs (ca. 3300, 3000, 2200 and 1000 nucleotides). The fourth RNA is sub genomic and coats for the coat protein gene. The virus is seed transmissible and is also transmitted by *Aphis craccivora, A. spiraecola* and *Myzus persicae.*

Disease cycle. The virus survives on white clover, providing the primary source of inoculum.

Management. For management of the disease, peanuts should not be planted in fields located near leguminous hosts.

❍ Cucumber mosaic cucumovirus disease

The disease has been reported on this crop from China and is referred to as peanut yellow mosaic which is now recognized as economically important.

Symptoms. Initial symptoms are appearance of chlorotic spots and upward rolling of young leaflets. Leaflets are sometimes deformed and plants are slightly stunted.

Causal virus. *Cucumber mosaic cucumovirus.*

Transmission. The virus is transmitted by sap inoculation and by the aphids.

Management. Cultural measures such as mulching with transparent plastic sheets and removal of diseased seedlings at early stages of plant growth are advised for reducing incidence of the disease.

❍ Cowpea mild mottle carlavirus disease

The disease is widely distributed in different countries of Asia and Africa.

Symptoms. Characteristic symptoms include appearance of vein clearing followed by downward rolling of the edges of leaflets and vein banding.

The causal virus. *Cowpea mild mottle carlavirus.* Physiochemical properties of the virus usually resemble with carlaviruses. Particles are rod shaped, measuring about 650 × 15 nm in size. They consist of a coat protein of 31 to 33 kDa. and a single stranded RNA of 2500 kDa. The genome contains 11.7 k open reading frame at the 3′ terminus containing a zinc-finger motif characteristic to carlavirus. Thermal inactivation point is 75 to 80°C.

Natural hosts. Cowpea and soybean are susceptibe and are preferred hosts for efficient vector-*Bemisia tabaci.*

Management. For management of the disease, sowing of peanuts near cowpea and soybean fields and intercropping peanut with these susceptible hosts should be avoided.

❍ Peanut chlorotic streak caulimovirus disease

This disease is widely distributed in different parts of Asia especially in India. In our country it is known to occur both in North and South India.

Symptoms- Characteristic symptoms of the disease are observed as reduction in size of the leaflets and appearance of chlorotic streaks on such leaflets. Infected plants may remain stunted in most cases.

Causal virus- *Peanut chlorotic streak caulimovirus.* Particles are icosahedrical in morphology, measuring about 50 nm in diameter. Particles usually consist of double stranded DNA of 8174 base pairs. The genome has been reported to encode eight major reading frames.

Transmission- This virus is easily transmitted by mechanical sap inoculation. The disease is known to affect plants belonging to the families Leguminosae and Solanaceae.

Management- Manage the disease through use of resistant/tolerant varieties. No any other specific control measure has been worked out.

SOME OTHER DISEASES OF MINOR IMPORTANCE

Cowpea chlorotic mottle virus, Groundnut crinkle virus, Bean yellow mosaic virus, Passion fruit woodiness virus, Tobacco streak virus and *Sunflower yellow blotch virus* are also known to incite diseases on this crop. These diseases are of minor importance.

VIRUS DISEASES OF COTTON

Cotton (*Gossypium* species) is an economically important industrial crop. It is known to be infected by a number of virus diseases that cause considerable damages to the crop by reducing the yield and quality of the produce. Some most common and economically important virus diseases of the crop may be summarized as under :

❍ Cotton leaf curl geminivirus disease

The disease was first reported on *Gossypium barbadense* from Nigeria in 1912 and is known to occur on *Abelmoschus esculentus* and *Corchorus fasienlaris* also. It is a major disease of cotton in Asia and Africa. In Asia, it has been reported from Pakistan and Western India inciting severe disease symptoms characteristic to this disease. Severe epidemics of cotton leaf curl disease have occurred in Pakistan in the past few years with yield losses as high as 100% in fields where infection occurred early in growing season.

Symptoms. (1) The infected plants remain stunted and their leaves show distinct upward and downwards curling. (2) The curling occurs due to increase in inter-veinal tissues. (3) At the later stage, all the diseased leaves develop enations which become prominent. (4) Chlorosis, thickening and malformation of veins, petioles and leaves are commonly observed.

The causal virus. *Cotton leaf curl geminivirus.* The virus belongs to the subgroup of geminivirus. Analysis of nucleic acid sequences has indicated that *Cotton leaf curl geminivirus* is closely related to *Tomato yellow leaf curl virus, Cassava latent virus* and *Indian cassava mosaic virus.*

Disease cycle. Chilli pepper often overlaps the cotton crop and might serve as an important inoculum for the disease development. Okra crop is also considered to be the important source of inoculum. Chilli pepper has been shown to contain begomoviruses and a distinct DNA has been isolated but there is no report of cotton leaf curl affecting chilli pepper. The disease is known to be transmitted by whitefly vector-*Bemisia tabaci.*

Management. (1) Growing of okra crop in and around the cotton field should be discouraged. (2) Intercropping with wild species of *Solanum* should be followed. (3) Whitefly vector-*Bemisia tabaci* should be managed by growing whitefly resistant varieties or by judicious use of any suitable insecticide. Methyle-o-demeton, triazophos and neem preparations have been found effective to control the whitefly through its application. (4) Affected plants should be rogued out.

❍ Cotton leaf crumple geminivirus disease

This disease is known to occur in Arizona, California and Mexico.

Symptoms. The characteristic symptoms of the cotton leaf crumple disease are distinguishable from cotton leaf curl disease. In cotton leaf crumple disease, infected leaves curl downward and are accompanied by interveinal hypertrophy and foliar mosaic.

The causal virus. *Cotton leaf crumple geminivirus.* Both *Cotton leaf curl geminivirus* and *Cotton leaf crumple geminivirus* infect dicotyledonous plants and are whitefly transmitted. However, little information is available on relationship of these two viruses with each other and with other subgroup of geminiviruses. Polymerase chain reaction amplified DNA fragments from both *Cotton leaf curl geminivirus* and

Cotton leaf crumple geminivirus indicated that *Cotton leaf crumple geminivirus* is more closely related with *Potato yellow mosaic virus, Bean dwarf mosaic virus* and *Bean golden mosaic virus.*

Disease Cycle. Not much information is available so far on disease cycle of this disease.

Management. (1) Whitefly vector-*Bemisia tabaci* should be managed by growing whitefly resistant varieties or by judicious use of suitable insecticide. Methyle-o-demeton, Acephate, Triazophos and Neem preparations have been found effective to control the whitefly through its application. (2) Affected plants should be rogued out.

❍ Stenosis or cotton small leaf virus disease

Symptoms. (1) The disease is characterized by the extreme stunting of the aerial portions of cotton. (2) The size of the leaves is drastically reduced along with its distortion to greater extent. (3) Besides, the leaves of the infected plants are variously lobed. (4) Very few flowers are produced which are very small with aborted ovaries, resulting in no production of bolls. Some times only one or few branches of the plant may show characteristic symptoms.

The causal virus. This disease is caused by *Cotton small leaf virus.*

Management. No work on disease cycle, mode of perpetuation and management has been worked out.

GRAPEVINE DISEASES (*Vitis* species)

Grapevine as an ancient food plant for several people is nutritious for human. It is used as an industrial raw material for developing new food products, juices and beverages. This crop is naturally affected by more than 20 viruses that cause considerable damage to this crop. Some most common and economically important diseases may be summarized as under-

❍ Grapevine fan leaf disease

This disease is very common in occurrence and wide spread where grapevine is grown. The disease is known to affect growth of the plants adversely, causing reduced fruit yield and quality.

Symptoms- The pathogen produces variable symptoms of the disease, depending on the virus strain and age of the plant at which it is infected. Alteration in the colour of the leaves may be observed. Such discolouration usually includes variable chlorotic, yellowing and mosaic pattern of different shapes. Colour change of the leaves is observed as primary symptom immediately after the infection. As a result of the disease, uneven growth of leaf blades may also be observed with characteristic distorted appearance. Irregular petiolar sinuses cause the parsley like appearance of leaves or the complete absence of petiolar sinuses. Primary leaf veins are swollen and gathered, giving the leaves a appearance of open fan. Besides, infected shoots have shortened internodes and branches are reduced in number and size.

Causal virus - *Grapevine fan leaf nepovirus.* The virus particles are isometric in morphology, measuring about 30 nm in diameter. Three components in purified preparation with sedimentation coefficients of 50 S (T), 86 S (M) and 120 S (B) respectively have been reported. They exhibit that T contains no RNA, M contains one 1400 kDa RNA 2 molecules and B contains one 2400 kDa RNA 1 or two RNA 2 molecules. RNA 1 directs the synthesis of a polypeptide involved in the composition of two proteins, one of which is the coat protein as reported. TIP of the virus in infective sap of herbaceous plants is 60-65°C, DEP is 1×10^{-3} to 1×10^{-4} and LIV is 15-30 days at 20°C.

Disease cycle- Systemically infected canes are important sources of this virus for further infection. The virus has been reported to remain infective for more than one year in infected plant parts in the soil. Besides, infected cuttings and stocks or scions play important role in perpetuation.

Transmission- The virus is known to infect only grapevine plants in nature. The virus is also naturally infected by nematode-*Xiphinema index* and *Xiphinema italiae* in soil. The virus is transmitted by seed of experimental *Chenopodium amaranticolor, Chenopodium quinoa* and soybean hosts. Transmission through grapevine seed is not well established. However, mechanical transmission through sap of infected herbaceous hosts and graft transmissible nature of the virus are of only experimental importance.

Management- Use of virus free planting stocks and selection of nematode and grapevine residues free soil are important measures for the management of the disease.

❍ Some other diseases of economic importance

1. *Grapevine Bulgarian latent nepovirus*-Virus particles are isometric in morphology, measuring 28-30 nm in diameter. Purified preparations consists of biocomponent particle -one an empty protein devoid of RNA (T) and the other as nucleoprotein. TIP ranges from 65 to 70°C, DEP ranges from 1×10^{-5} to 1×10^{-6} and LIV ranges from 15-20 days. The virus is graft transmissible and mechanically transmissible with the aid of purified preparation into seedlings and root cuttings. Nematode transmission has not been confirmed.

2. *Grapevine chrome mosaic nepovirus*- Virus particles are isometric in morphology, measuring 30 nm in diameter. It sediments as two equal size components containg single stranded RNA genome. TIP in bean sap is 60-62°C, DEP is 1×10^{-3} to 1×10^{-4} and longevity *in vitro* is one week at 22°C. The virus is naturally seed borne in nature and is both mechanically and graft transmissible. Transmission by *Xiphinema* species has also been reported experimentally.

3. *Grapevine viroids disease* - This viroids causes economic disease or latent infection in the plant. Viroids were recently discovered in grapevine in Australia, Europe, Israel and United States. Viroids have been reported to be wide spread among all cultivars and root stocks in all vine growing areas. Most important viroids known cause severe damage to the grapevine are *Hop stunt viroid, Citrus exocortis viroid, yellow speckle viroid* and two other grapevine viroids. Viroids occur as single or mixed infections.

❍ Grapevine as natural alternative host

Following viruses have been reported to affect grapevine. A partial list of such viruses may be summarized as under-

1. *Arabis mosaic potyvirus-*
2. *Alfalfa mosaic virus.*
3. *Tomato black ring nepovirus.*
4. *Tomato ringspot nepovirus.*
5. *Tomato bushy stunt virus.*
6. *Tobacco ring spot nepovirus.*
7. *Tobacco mosaic virus.*
8. *Tobacco necrosis virus.*
9. *Strawberry latent ringspot nepovirus.*
10. *Sowbane mosaic virus.*
11. *Raspberry ring spot nepovirus.*
12. *Peach rosette mosaic nepovirus.*
13. *Artichoke Italian latent nepovirus.*

❍ Some other diseases of minor importance

1. Grapevine asteroid mosaic disease.
2. Grapevine corky bark disease.
3. Grapevine fleck disease.
4. Grapevine leaf roll disease.
5. Grapevine stem pitting disease.
6. Grapevine yellow speckle disease.

17

VIRUS DISEASES OF FRUITS

Disease of citrus-citrus tristeza, variegation, exocortis and other diseases; Papaya-mosaic and ring spot; Apple-mosaic, chlorotic leaf spot, rough skin and some other diseases; Pear-bud drop, necrotic spot and other diseases; Quince-stunt, ring pattern, sooty ring spot and some other diseases; Peach-rosette mosaic, enation, line pattern and other diseases; Banana-bunchy top and bract mosaic; Plum-plum pox, dwarfing, necrotic ring spot and other diseases; Apricot- chlorotic leaf spot, necrosis, ring spot and other diseases; Sweet cherry-leaf roll, rasp leaf and other diseases; Sour cherry-necrotic ring spot and other diseases; Almond-necrotic ring spot and other diseases; Walnut-line pattern and other diseases; Fig diseases; Olive diseases; Strawberry- crinkle, mottle and other diseases; Raspberry-vein chlorosis, ring spot and other diseases; Black berry-necrosis and other diseases; Goose berry- ring spot, vein banding and other diseases; Different diseases of black currant, red currant and blue berry.

Fruits are important source of human nutrition. Although adapted to different ecological conditions, fruits are mostly grown in temperate and sub-tropical climatic regions of the world. Temperate and sub-tropical fruits are **pome fruits** (apple and pear), **stone fruits** (apricot, cherry, peach and plum), **shell fruits** (walnut, chestnut and hazelnut) and **small fruits** (strawberry, raspberry, gooseberry and blueberry). The fruit tree species grown in tropical regions are called as **tropical plants** which include chiefly banana, citrus and papaya.

Fruits represent natural source of nutrition and contain carbohydrate, protein, minerals, lipids, vitamins, enzymes, aromatic compounds, organic acids and glycosides in considerable amount. Due to their complex and heterogenous composition, rich in nutrients, minerals and vitamins, fruits represent a valuable raw material for the food and soft drink industries.

Important discoveries relating to fruit tree virus disease identification began after 1930 by the advancement in methodology used in plant virology. Fruit tree viruses are usually transmitted with vegetative propagation, infected seed and pollen and by different insect vectors. Important diseases of fruits may be summarized as under :

VIRUS DISEASES OF CITRUS (*Citrus* species)

❍ Citrus tristeza closterovirus disease

The disease is widespread and is known to occur wherever citrus is grown. *Citrus tristeza virus* belongs to genus *Closterovirus* of family Closteroviridae.

Symptoms. Typical tristeza symptoms appear usually in sweet orange and other citrus species grafted onto sour orange root stocks. Characteristic overgrowth (pathological meristemization) and honey comb pitting just below the union occur in the bud union points. The meristematic (callus) tissue becomes necrotic, sieve tubes clog and woody ray cells grow slowly. As a result of rootlets desiccation, water and nutrition supply to the infected plants is impaired. Other symptoms include reduced plant growth, decreased development of branches and deformed fruit setting. In grapefruit, sour orange and lemon, seedlings represent special disease symptoms resulting in slow growth and yellowing of leaves of the seedlings.

Diagnostic plants are *Citrus aurantifolia* (seedlings with vein clearing) and *C. sinensis* (quick decline at the graft union). Recently *Nicotiana benthamiana* has been reported as experimental host.

Several diagnostic laboratory methods are used effectively for quick virus detection. These methods include Sodium dodecylsulphate (SDS) Immunodiffusion, ISEM, ELISA, Radio-immunoassay (RIA), double-stranded RNA profiles and nucleic acid hybridization with cloned cDNA.

The causal virus. *Citrus tristeza closterovirus*. Particles are flexuous, about 2000×11 nm in size and contain a non-segmented positive sense single stranded RNA genome. The first *Citrus tristeza closterovirus* genome to be entirely sequenced was the Florida decline isolate T-36. The isolate had 19,296 nucleotides and contained 12 possible open reading frames (ORFs) encoding 17 proteins. The virus is mostly confined to the phloem tissue. Inclusion bodies are formed in the phloem tissue. Inclusion bodies upon staining may be used for diagnosis by light microscope.

Host range. It infects nearly all the citrus species including sweet orange,lemon, mandarin and grapefruit.

Disease cycle. The virus is preserved in infected citrus trees which represent a perennial source of infection. Tropical citrus aphids-*Toxoptera citricida, Aphis gossypii* and *A. citricola* are the important vectors that transmit the virus in semi-persistent manner. The virus *Citrus tristeza closterovirus* is not transmitted by the seed and plant sap obtained from the infected plants. The virus has also been reported to be transmitted by two species of dodder-*Cuscuta subinculsa* and *C. americana*. Long distance movement of the virus is mostly by movement of infected plant material.

Management. Removal of infected trees and re-planting with resistant root stocks/scions are important measures for the management of the disease. Some other species such as *Citrus aurantium, C. aurantifolia, C. excelsa, C. jambhiri, C. limonia, C. macrophylla, C. medica, C. mitis, C. pennivsesiculata* and *C. reshni,* trifoliate orange (*Poncitrus trifoliate*), sweet lime *(C. limetta), C. volkameriana* and *Severenia buxifolia* are resistant to this disease.

❍ Citrus variegation ilarvirus disease

The disease is known to occur in all the important citrus growing areas of the world but is economically important where severe strain of the virus exist and cause severe loss to the plants.

Symptoms. The virus infects only citrus species and produces chlorotic spots and crinkle on leaves. Warping and pocketing of leaves with severe distortions and variegation may be observed in infected plants. As a result of the severity of the disease, the fruits are found to remain deformed.

The causal virus. *Citrus variegation ilarvirus* is known as causal agent of the disease. It consists of isometric particles, measuring about 30 nm in diameter. Multi-component structure of the virus contains particles of different sizes. The zones of fasted sedimentation usually contain particles of 28, 31 and 33 nm in diameter. Individual particles are not infective and a mixture of all three of the largest particles, have been found to remain infective. Thermal inactivation point of the virus is 55 to 60°C and longevity of the virus *in vitro* is 8 hours at 20 to 22°C.

Disease cycle. The virus perpetuates in infected plants and is transmitted in nature by infected planting material. The virus is also mechanically transmissible through infected plant sap. No any insect vector has been reported so far.

Management. Only healthy virus free planting material obtained by thermotherapy, nuclear embryology or shoot tip grafting should be used for establishment of the new orchard.

SOME OTHER DISEASES OF CITRUS

❍ Satsuma dwarf virus disease

The disease is widespread in Satsuma orange in Japan, Turkey, former Yugoslavia and former U.S.S.R. The virus causes stunting of stems, leaves, shoots and fruits, leading to severe loss in yield and quality of the produce. Leaf and fruit deformations are the characteristic symptoms of the disease. The causal virus-*Satsuma dwarf virus* is isometric in morphology, measuring about 26 nm in diameter. Three components chiefly top (T), middle (M) and bottom (B) have sedimentation coefficients of 119 S (M) and 129 S(B). Particles T probably contain no RNA whereas particles M and particles B are infective as they contain RNA. The RNA is usually single stranded and accounts for about 33% M and 37% B particle weight. Thermal inactivation point is 50 to 55°C and dilution end point is 1.2 to 2.5×10^{-3}. Longevity of the virus *in vitro* is 8 to 12 days at 24°C. The virus perpetuates in natural hosts and is transmitted and spread through infected planting material. Insect vector transmission is not known.

CITRUS DISEASES ASSUMED TO BE CAUSED BY VIRUSES

❍ Citrus cachexia-xyloporosis disease

The disease is most widespread in Mediterranean countries and is assumed to be caused by the virus. Characteristic symptoms are bark pegging and pitting on stems. Pegs formed on the bark usually project into the pits. These pegs which penetrate into the cambium, crush the cells in the phloem regions and gum is deposited in the rings of the xylem. The causal agent spreads through the planting material. It is also transmitted mechanically by pruning knives.

❍ Citrus concave gum disease/citrus blind pocket disease

Characteristic symptoms of the disease are concavities occurring on stems and branches of infected trees of citrus. These concavities may be large and wide. In some cultivars concavities may be accompanied by the formation of gum deposits. Narrow, pronounced and depressed concavities with adjoining vertical sides usually give the appearance of blind pocket disease. Individual or combined symptoms of vein flecking and oak-leaf patterns may occur on young leaves. The causal agent spreds with infected planting material.

❍ Citrus cristacortis disease

The disease is not economically important because it does not cause considerable loss to the crop. Susceptible hosts are grapefruit, mandarin, rough lemon, sour orange, sweet lime, sweet orange, tangelos and tangers. Symptomless hosts are bergamot, citruses, citrons, lemons and acid limes. Stem pitting with pegs on the bark may occur in the woody parts of diseased plant. The causal agent is transmitted with infected planting material. It can also be transmitted experimentally by pollen but not in the nature.

❍ Citrus gummy bark disease

The characteristic symptoms of the disease are the formation of gum on the bark near the bud union point along with discolouration of the affected plants. Affected barks become detached and fall off above the union line. The disease is graft transmitted by bud propagation. Healthy planting material is the important measure for the establishment of the new orchard.

❍ Citrus psorosis disease

Scaly barks on trunks and limbs are the characteristic symptoms of the disease. The disease usually spreads through bud propagation. The use of virus-free healthy buds represent primary measure of disease control. Transmission of causal agent may be done experimentally by inoculation with the use of infected bark.

❍ Citrus ringspot disease

In most countries it causes damage to the plants usually in mixed infection with severe scaly bark disease. In older leaves, yellow blotches, chlorotic vein banding and chlorotic rings may be observed as characteristic symptoms of the disease. Local necrotic and chlorotic lesions occur on inoculated herbaceous indicator plant-*Chenopodium quinoa* leaves. In nature, the disease spreads with infected propogative material. Mechanical transmission into herbaceous plants may also occur experimentally.

❍ Citrus vein enation disease and citrus woody gall disease

Characteristic symptoms of the disease include appearance of irregular tumors along the leaf veins on the lateral surface of the leaves with corresponding depressions on the upper surface. The enation and gall symptoms have also been observed in rough lemon and Mexican lime.

In nature, the causal agent is transmitted with infected propogative material. Aphid-*Myzus persicae, Toxoptera citricidus* and *Aphis gossypii* are known to transmit the causal agent. It is also graft and dodder transmitted experimentally. The use of healthy bud wood and tolerant root stocks represent the primary measure of disease management.

VIRUS DISEASES OF PAPAYA
(*Caprica papaya*)

❍ Papaya mosaic potexvirus disease

The disease was first reported in Florida and Venezuela in 1971 and is of minor importance. Papaya is the only natural host of the virus.

Symptoms. The virus causes mosaic and retarded growth of leaves. It is known to be transmitted experimentally to 17 species of 9 dicots families. Diagnostic hosts are *Cassia occidentalis, Chenopodium amaranticolor* and *C. globosa*.

The casual virus. *Papaya mosaic potexvirus.* Particles are filamentous in morphology, measuring about 530 nm in size. The single stranded RNA of 220 kDa accounts for 7% of the particle weight. The capsid is composed of homologous coat protein subunits of 19 kDa. The virus is stable enough and thermal inactivation point in papaya sap is 73 to 76°C. Dilution end point is 1×10^{-4} and longevity *in vitro* is about 6 months at 24°C.

Host range. Susceptible hosts include *Cassia accidentalis, Antirrhinum mazus, Chenopodium amaranticolor, C. quinoa, Cucumis sativus, Glycine max, Gomphrema globosa, Nicotiana benthamiana, Phaseolus vulgaris, Vigna sinensis, Vinca rosea* and *Zinnia elegans*.

Disease cycle. The disease is known to be transmitted with infective plant sap. No any other mode of transmission is known.

❍ Papaya ring spot potyvirus disease

The disease is widespread where papaya and cucumber are grown. The disease has been reported from Africa, India, South Africa, Taiwan, Mexico, Middle East countries, U.S. and South America.

Symptoms. The virus usually infects papaya and cucurbits and can infect many plants especially dicots belonging to Caricaceae, Chenopodiaceae and Cucurbitaceae families. Characteristic symptoms of the disease include appearance of leaf mottle, distortion and ring spots on the surface of the leaves. Cucurbit plants infected with this virus usually manifest chlorotic mottle with fruit and leaf malformation, resulting in reduction in quality and yield of infected plants.

The causal virus. *Papaya ring spot potyvirus*. The virus is a filamentous particle, measuring about 780 × 12 nm in size with single standed RNA and coat protein subunits of 36 kDa. The virus consists of two strains and one of the strains infects both the papaya and the second strain(Wm MV1-water melon mosaic virus-1) infects only water melon and cucurbits. Both the strains differ in symptomological reactions in individual hosts. Both the strains differ in biophysical properties also. Thermal inactivation point of the virus in papaya sap is 54 to 56 C°, dilution end point is $1 \times 10^{--3}$ and longevity *in vitro* is 8 hours at 24°C. Thermal inactivation point of watermelon mosaic virus 1 in squash sap is 60°C, dilution end point is 5×10^{-4} and longevity *in vitro* is 40 to 60 days at room temperature.

Disease cycle. Virus papaya strain is preserved in infected perennial plants and virus watermelon strain is preserved in continuously grown different cucurbit species. In the field both the strains are transmitted by different aphid species including *Myzus persicae, Aphis gossypii, A. craccivora, Aulacorthum solani* and *Macrosiphum euphorbiae*. Both the strains of the virus are also transmissible experimentally through infective plant sap. No seed transmission has been reported in any of the strains.

Management. Papaya has been engineered for resistance against the virus by cloning the coat protein gene into papaya. Destruction of affected plants should be undertaken. Spraying of suitable insecticide should be done to check the spread of the disease.

❍ Papaya leaf curl disease

Papaya leaf curl is not much common in occurrence in most of the areas, however, in some other papaya growing areas, considerable loss to the crop has been reported by the growers. Host range of the virus includes papaya, tomato, tobacco, zinnia, hollyhock, *Althea* and many other plant species.

Symptoms. (1) The characteristic symptoms of the disease include severe curling, crinkling and distortion accompanied by vein clearing and reduction in size of the leaves of the infected plants. (2) Leaves of infected plants become leathery and brittle. (3) Inter-veinal areas of the leaves are raised due to hypertrophy in cells, producing rugocity. (4) The curled leaves have thickened veins and petioles are twisted in zig-zag mater. (5) Sometimes all the leaves at the top of the plant may produce these characteristic symptoms. (6) Infected plants may remain stunted and in advanced stage of disease development, defoliatin may take place. (7) Disease plants fail to bear flowers and fruits.

The causal virus. *Papaya leaf curl geminivirus*. The virus is similar to the

Tobacco leaf curl virus. The virus can be easily transmitted from papaya to tobacco and tomato. *Tobacco leaf curl virus* can produce this disease in papaya when inoculated on it. On the basis of these characteristic it has been suggested that papaya leaf curl is caused by *Tobacco leaf curl geminivirus.*

Diseae cycle. The virus is preserved in the diseased host plant and is known to be transmitted by the whitefly-*Bemisia tabaci.* The diseased papaya plants never recover. The virus is not mechanically transmissible. In tomato, dodder transmission has also been reported.

Management. (1) Diseased papaya plants should be destroyed immediatly as soon as it is spotted in the orchard. (2) Management of the white fly vector should be done. Effect of granular insecticides on the incidence of leaf curl in tomato has been reported. Sprays of any suitable insecticide should be done time to time to keep the population of whitefly under control. (3) None of the resistant varieties are known so far.

PAPAYA AS ALTERNATE HOST OF DIFFERENT VIRUSES

Papaya is alternate host of some viruses including *Tobacco ring spot virus, Tomato spotted wilt virus* and one or more rhabdoviruses. All these viruses are easily distinguishable from papaya mosaic and papaya ring spot diseases.

VIRUS DISEASES OF POME FRUITS

Apple and pear are important fruits described under pome. More than 30 viruses are known to cause diseases in apple and pear. Some important virus diseases are described below :—

❍ Apple mosaic ilarvirus disease

The disease is known to occur everywhere the apple is grown in the world. It causes economic damage to susceptible cultivars, reducing growth by 50% and yield by 30%.

Symptoms. (1) Mosaic symptoms occur as light yellow sharp bordered spots on the leaves of the infected plants. (2) Chlorotic veins are usually observed on leaves. (3) With the advancement of the disease, the spots turn dark brown in colour, resulting in the defoliation of diseased leaves. Diagnostic hosts are *Cucumis sativus, Tournier fournier, Vinca rosea, Cyamopsis tetragonoloba* and *Phaseolus vulgaris.* These hosts produce diagnostic lesions such as chlorotic spots on cotyledons. In leaves, light yellow mosaic, chlorotic ring spots and line pattern are observed on leaves. Besides, necrotic spots and dark local spots may also be found.

The causal virus. *Apple mosaic ilarvirus.* The virus consists of isometric particles of about 26 to 29 nm in diameter. The partcles of the virus are quite unstable in extracted plant sep but in buffer infectivity can be maintained for few hours. Thermal inactivation point is 54°C and dilution end point is 2×10^{-3} It has moderate immunogenicity.

Disease cycle. In nature the virus is transmitted most frequently with infected root stocks or buds and scions taken from infected trees during grafting.

Transmission. The virus is transmissible through mechanical inoculation in herbaceous hosts. Other mode of transmission in nature is not known. More than 65 species belonging to 19 families are known as hosts of this virus. Some of the natural hosts are *Prunus amygdalus, P. domestica, P. triloba, P. virginiana, Rosa* species, *Betula alleghaniensis, B. papayrifera, Coryllus avellana* and *Humulus lupulus*.

Management. (1) Only healthy propagating materials should be used for establishment of the new apple plantation. (2) All infected plants should be eliminated from nurseries. (3) Young dense population of plants in the nurseries should be avoided. (4) Healthy materials for reproduction can be obtained through thermotherapy treatment by exposing infected plants to dry heat at 37°C for 3 to 4 weeks.

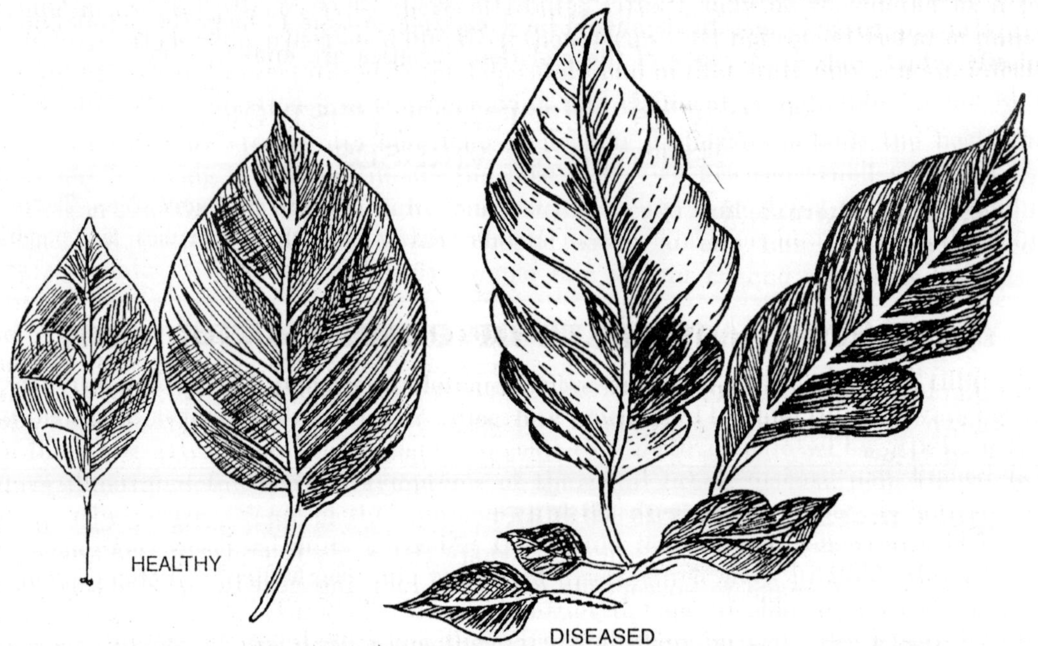

Fig. 17.1 Infected leaves of apple incited by *Apple mosaic virus*

❍ Apple chlorotic leaf spot closterovirus disease

The disease is worldwide in distribution and is known to cause considerable damage to different hosts including pome fruits, stone fruits and some woody and wild ornamentals belonging to Rosaceae family.

Symptoms. (1) The virus is usually found to remain latent and can be detected by specific symptoms produced on several indicators. (2) Diffused chlorotic mosaic may be observed on leaves of infected *Malus platycarpa* which gradually become roundish spots. (3) On the Russian apple clone R. 12740-7 A, leaf crinkling and chlorotic spots varying in size are usually observed as important symptoms of the disease. Indicator plants include *Chenopodium amaranticolor* and *C. quinoa* with local lesions and systemic spots. Different other indicator plants are *Prunus persicae, P.tomentosa, cydonia vulgaris* and *Pyronia veitchii*.

The causal virus. *Apple chlorotic leaf spot closterovirus.* The virus consists of filamentous particles, measuring about 600-740 × 12 nm in size. The sedimentation coefficient is 96 S with no accessory virus particles known. The single stranded RNA of 7555 nucleotides is 2200-2400 kDa. or 2500 kDa. and single polypeptide coat protein is 23.5 kDa. Thermal inactivation point is 52-55 °C, dilution end point is 1×10^{-4} and longevity *in vitro* is 1 day. The virus is moderately antigenic. The virus consists of different strains.

Disease cycle. The virus is preserved permanently in infected fruit trees, ornamentals and wild woody hosts. Infected apple rootstocks usually play the key role in dissemination of the virus. Field spread of the disease has been observed but mode of transmission is unknown.

Management. Virus-free propagating materials should be used to establish orchards. Such materials can be obtained through heat therapy by exposing young plants and plant parts to the temperature of 37 to 38 C°. Virus can be eliminated from mother stocks by meristem culture method also. Shoot-tip grafting has been observed to be most successful.

❍ Apple green crinkle disease

Apple green crinkle fruit disease is among the important diseases of the apple. It has been described in North and South America, Asia, New Zealand and Europe.

Symptoms. (1) After flowering, a depression on young fruits, measuring about 2 cm. in diameter may be seen. (2) Such depressions may later become wart like in appearance. (3) As the infected fruits mature, uneven growth and swellings from irregular crinkles usually develop on the surface. (4) Sometimes crinkle tissues split and the vascular bundles under the skin become irregular and greenish. (5) Fruits may remain undersized and are severely distorted.

The causal virus. *Apple green crinkle virus.*

Disease cycle. The virus is transmitted with infected planting material during grafting. Natural spread occurs in the field but mode of transmission is unknown.

Management. Use of healthy planting material is the main measure for control of this disease.

❍ Apple stem grooving disease

The disease is known to occur in different countries including North America, Australia, Asia, South America and New Zealand.

Symptoms. (1) Infected commercial rootstocks and cultivars usually display no visible symptoms. (2) It produces symptoms only on indicator plants. *Malus syvestris* cv. Verginia Crab is the most susceptible indicator. (3) Specific symptoms include sunken areas and longitudinal grooves visible when the bark is peeled off the trunk. (4) Elongated grooves and sunken areas are covered with marginal furrows.

The causal virus. *Apple stem grooving virus.* The virus is filamentous in morphology, measuring 600 to 700 × 12 nm in size. It contains a single coat protein of 27 kDa. Sedimentation coefficient of the virus is 112 S. Thermal inactivation point of the virus is 60 to 63°C, dilution end point is 1×10^{-4} and longevity *in vitro* is 2 days at 20°C. It is moderately immunogenic. ELISA and ISEM methods may be used for mass scale virus testing.

Disease cycle. Infected stocks usually represent the greatest source of disease perpetuation and its spread. Besides mechanical transmission, it is graft and seed transmissible also. Spread of disease in nature is seen but mode of its spread is not known.

Management. It has been suggested that mother stocks can be cured by incubating infected plantlets to 37°C for weeks. Other measures are similar to other viral diseases of apple.

❍ Apple rough skin disease

This disease is known to occur most frequently in India, North America and several other European countries. The causal virus is *Apple rough skin disease virus*. Symptoms of the disease usually occur on the fruits of apple—*Malus sylvestris*, the only natural host. Characteristic symptoms manifesting brown-corky patches are usually observed on the fruit skin. The superficial corky patch-affected tissues split resulting in development of rough surface of the fruit. Severely affected fruits grow slowly. Symptoms usually appear first on fruits born on one branch, then spread gradually through the entire crown, more so in wet and cloudy seasons. Under dry, warm and sunny conditions, such symptoms may not appear. The causal virus is transmitted with infected vegetative parts used for grafting. The natural mode of infection is unknown. The use of healthy planting materials is must for management of the disease.

❍ Apple tulare mosaic ilarvirus disease

The disease was first discovered in apple in Tulare county, California. The disease is of minor importance. The causal virus is *Apple Tulare mosaic ilarvirus*. The virus consists of isometric particles, measuring about 33 nm in diameter. Particles are of two types with sedimentation coefficients of 85 S and 91 S. Only 91 S particles are infective. Particles are unstable in infective plant sap but may remain stable in buffer. Thermal inactivation point is 60 to 62°C. The virus sample is moderately immunogenic. Apple-*Malus pumila* and hazelnut-*Corylus avellana* are natural hosts for this disease. The virus is transmissible experimentally to different hosts such as *Chaenomeles joponica*, *Crateagus chlrosarca*, *Cydonia oblonga*, *Pyrus communis*, *Sorbus* species, *Nicotiana tobacum*, *Phaseolus vulgaris*, *Chenopodium foetidum*, *Gomphrena globosa*, *Helianthus annuus* and *Vicia fabae*. The virus is transmitted mechanically by infective plant sap into herbaceous plants and experimentally into woody plants by grafting. It is also transmissible through dodder-*Cuscuta subinclusa* and *C. compestris*. Other mode of transmission is unknown.

❍ Apple leaf pucker disease

The disease has been found in several countries. Apple leaf pucker is caused either by different strains or by several viruses. Vivid yellow or green spots, vein chlorosis, ring spots and line patterns on leaves usually pronounced in cold weather are observed in infected plants. Leaf and fruit symptoms vary and are characteristic for individual apples. Therefore, different names such as apple russet, ring disease and apple blotch disease have been used to this disease. The virus is known to be transmitted with infected buds and vegetative rootstocks during grafting. No other mode of transmission is known. Pathogen free planting materials should be used to manage the disease successfully.

SOME OTHER KNOWN DISEASES OF APPLE

❍ Apple stem pitting disease

The disease is presumed to be caused by the virus. Many studies suggest that the causal agent of this disease and of spy epinsaty and decline, quince sooty ring spot, pear stony pit and pear vein yellows are same.

❍ Apple platycarpa scaly bark disease
(Syn. Apple platycarpa dwarf disease)

The disease has been described in diferent countries including U.S., Canada, Australia, Israel, Japan, New Zealand and South Africa. Symptoms of this disease occur in apple-*Malus platycarpa* trees as rough and scabby bark on young trees, usually accompanied by swelling. Secondary fungal infections manifesting fissures, usually complicate the diagnosis of the disease. Dwarfing of the infected plants may also be observed. The causal agent of the disease is transmitted by grafting, infected buds and rootstocks from diseased mother stocks. The use of healthy seed stocks is the only known measure to manage the disease.

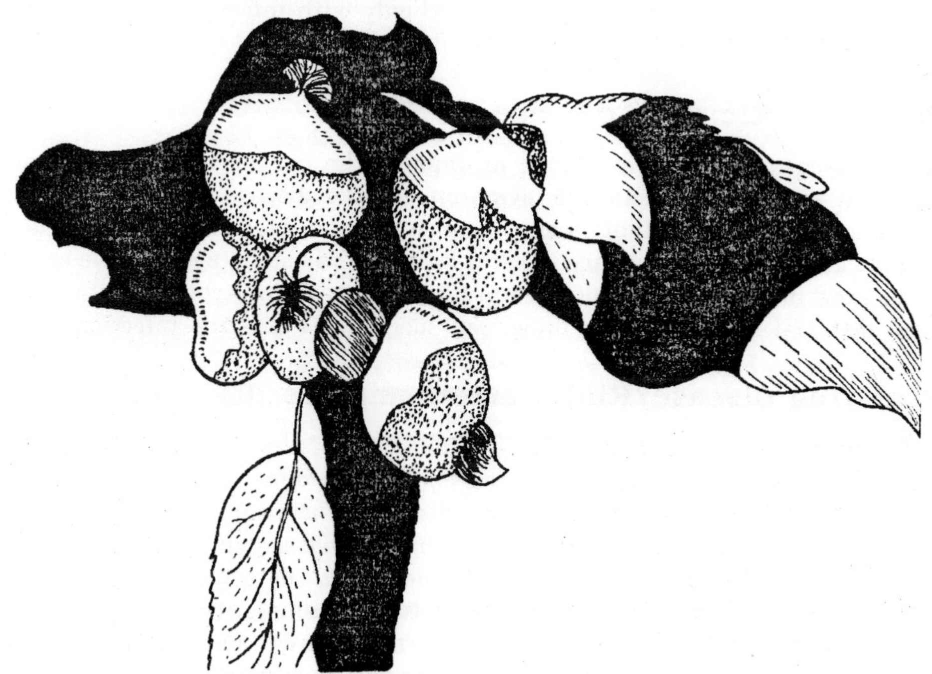

Fig. 17.2. Showing apple injured by Apple aphid

APPLE AS ALTERNATE HOSTS

Many viruses are known to cause diseases of different descriptions on other hosts. They usually occur on apple also. Some of the important viruses may be listed as under:

Cherry rasp leaf virus, Carnation ringspot virus, Tomato ring spot virus, Tomato bushy stunt virus, Tobacco ring spot virus, Tobacco necrosis virus, Tobacco mosaic virus and *Sowbane mosaic virus.*

VIRUS DISEASES OF PEAR (*Pyrus Communis*)

More than 15 virus and virus like diseases have been described in pear but causal agents of some of them are ill defined. Some important diseases are as below :—

❍ Pear bud drop disease

The disease was first described as a new disease in France during 1965. The causal agent, still ill defined and is presumed as virus, is based on budding/grafting transmission and symptoms produced by it. Characteristic symptoms usually occur on leaves and buds. Leaves of the infected plants curl downward and display characteristic epinasty. Bud drop occurs due to tissue necrosis at the bud base. Leaf buds formed during the previous year, usually open at the initiation of the vegetation period. The causal agent is graft transmitted only with infected buds and other plant parts during the grafting-propagation period.

❍ Pear necrotic spot disease

The disease was first described in Japan. The causal agent and its properties are not well known. Characteristic symptoms of the disease usually occur on leaves as numerous chlorotic spots that quickly changes to red or black in colour. *Pyrus serotina* and *P communis* f. sp. *sativus* are natural hosts of the causal agent. The causal agent has been experimentally transmitted into Chinese pear and hybrid seedlings. Healthy planting material represents the important measure to prevent infection.

❍ Pear ring disease/Ring pattern mosaic disease

The disease is widespread in U.S., Canada, Asia, New Zealand and South Africa. The causal agent in presumed to be the *Apple chlorotic leafspot virus* belonging to closterovirus. This disease has also been described as pear green spot, pear mosaic and pear ring spot mosaic disease. In this disease, many pear cvs. remain symptomless. Symptoms occur on leaves and fruits on some susceptible cultivars. Symptoms that occur in young leaves upon bud opening include mosaic, green ring mosaic and mosaic ring spot. Leaves midrib grow slowly, bend and result in a curled appearance. Infected pear parent trees and quince clones used as vegetative root stocks for pear represent chief sources of infection. Grafting of infected plant parts usually represent means of disease spread. The virus is mechanically transmissible as observed experimentally. For management of the disease use of virus free healthy stocks are recommended.

❍ Pear stony pit disease/pear vein yellows disease

Pear stony pit and pear vein yellows were previously described as two different diseases ; however, they are now presumed to be caused by the same virus. This disease has also been named as red mottle disease and the same causal agent probably causes apple spy epinasty and decline, apple stem pitting and quince sooty ring spot diseases. The symptoms of the disease on fruits of susceptible pear cultivars occur early in the season. Individual parenchyma cells become lignified which causes uneven and irregularly deformed fruit development. Vein yellows usually occur along the secondary and smaller leaf veins in several pear cultivars in parts or on entire leaves. Some times, red mottling, cracks and necrosis of barks may also be observed. Pear (*Pyrus communis*) and quince (*Cydonia oblonga*) are natural hosts of the virus. Causal agent may be transmitted experimentally to *Pyrus betulaefolia*, *P. callryana*, *P. ussuriensis* and *Pyronia veitchii*. Since the causal agent is transmitted only through infected plant parts, the use of healthy stocks represent the important plant protection measure.

❍ Pear freckle pit disease

The disease produces numerous dark green sunken pits beneath which dark green strands are formed. During disease development, pits become pale green and the strands become darker. Pits are more abundant near the calyx and the peduncle. The disease is known to be transmitted by infected planting material and that should be avoided to use for planting in order to manage the disease.

PEAR AS ALTERNATE HOST

Pear is known to be the alternate host of different viruses such as *Apple stem grooving virus, Carnation ringspot virus*, and *Tobacco mosaic virus*.

VIRUS DISEASES OF QUINCE
(*Cydonia oblonga*)

No virus has been reported to quince as primary host but several viruses and virus like diseases are identical to those observed in apple and pear. Important diseases of quince may be summarized as under :

❍ Quince stunt disease

Apple chlorotic leafspot virus causes typical stunting in quince (*Cydonia oblonga*). It occurs naturally in quince and pear (*Pyrus communis*). Susceptible plants exhibit irregular shaped yellow spots and curling in leaves. Shoots grow slowly and die in severe cases. The use of healthy parent plants is the suitable measure to manage the disease. Virus free quince planting materials may be obtained by incubating it for 11 days at 37°C.

❍ Quince ring pattern mosaic

Apple chlorotic leaf spot virus causes ring pattern mosaic. Symptoms are usually evident in some susceptible cultivars, however, in most cultivars, infected plants remain symptomless. Pale green and yellow ring and line patterns usually occur on the leaves of the test plants of quince, apple, pear and some other rosaceous host plants.

❍ Quince sooty ringspot disease

The disease has been reported in U.S., Australia, New Zealand, South Africa and Europe to occur frequently on quince. Natural hosts include apple and pear besides quince in which the disease has been described under separate names. The characteristic symptoms of the disease may be observed as necrosis along smaller leaf veins. Reddening of the leaf cuticle around the veins and appearance of the pale yellow spots on the leaves usually look like sooty mold may also be observed. As the causal agent is transmitted by infected planting material, therefore, healthy parent plants for production may be the main control measure. Healthy planting material can be obtained by incubating infected young plants at 36°C for three weeks.

❍ Quince fruit deformation disease

Quince is natural host of this disease which is well known to occur in Europe. The disease is of minor importance. Infected fruits have uneven growth with crinkling and depressions of different shapes and sizes. The skin in the depressions is usually greenish to brown in appearance. Diffused pale green spots and deformations on leaves may also be observed.

VIRUS DISEASES OF PEACH (*Prumus persica*)

A number of diseases are known to be caused by viruses. Important diseases incited by viruses are peach rosette mosaic, peach enation disease, peach line pattern and leaf curl virus disease. Viroids also cause diseases in peach. Economically important disease incited by viroid is peach latent viroid disease.

❍ Peach rosette mosaic nepovirus disease

The disease is known to occur in U.S. and Europe where it causes considerable damage to the crop every year.

Symptoms. (1) The growth of early leaves has been observed to remain slow and sometimes they reach only one third of the normal length. (2) Leaf blades are wrinkled and scattered chlorotic spots are usually observed on it. (3) Leaves formed later stage remain smaller in size but remain without spots. (4) Internodes and ots are shortened. (5) Other alterations are observed as delayed foliation, chlorotic mottle, deformed leaves and rosette like shoots and crowns. (6) Susceptible indicator hosts are *Chenopodium amaranticolor* (mild local lesion spots) and *C. quinoa* (mild local chlorotic spots). (7) *Nicotiana glutinosa, Petunia hybrida*-and tomato are systemic hosts of this virus.

The causal virus. *Peach rosette mosaic nepovirus*. The virus consists of isometric particles, measuring about 24 to 31 nm in diameter. Purified particles are of three types- top (T), middle (M) and bottom (B) with sedimentation coefficients of 52, 115 and 134 S respectively. T contains no RNA and is non-infective, while M and B particles are infective containing single stranded RNA of 2200 kDa. and 2500 kDa respectively. Thermal inactivation point is 58 to 68°C, dilution end point is 1×10^{-3} to 1×10^{-5} and longevity *in vitro* is 15 to 25 days at 20°C. The virus is moderately immunogenic.

Disease cycle. The virus is preserved in peach and grape. Grafting is the important mode of transmission. In the soil, it can be infected from diseased to healthy plants by the nematode-*Xiphinema americanum*. The nematode can transmit the virus from herbaceous to the woody plants. Mechanical transmission of the virus is limited to be the experimental only.

Management. (1) The use of healthy virus free planting materials for establishment of new peach and grapevine plantations is the primary preventive measure. (2) All potential sources of infection should be eliminated from young plantations. (3) Soil must be disinfected to control nematodes.

❍ Peach enation virus disease

The disease is widespred in Japan and *Prunus persicae* is the only natural host of this virus. The disease is characterized by the presence of small enations along the main veins, usually followed by leaf distortion and shortening of shoot internodes. The virus particles are isometric in morphology, measuring about 33 nm in diameter. Thermal inactivation point of the virus is 50 to 60°C, dilution end point is 1×10^{-3} to 1×10^{-4} and longevity of the virus is 30 to 40 days at room temperature. The causal virus-*Peach enation virus* has been transmitted experimentally into *Prunus persicae* seedlings and several herbaceous hosts including *Chenopodium amranticolor, C. quinoa, C. album, C. globosa, Nicotiana tabacum* and *Petunia hybrida*. Infected planting materials should be avoided for the management of the disease.

❍ Peach line pattern and leaf curl disease

This virus was first reported from Hungary in 1983. *Prunus persicae* and *P. avium* are known as natural hosts of this disease. The characteristic symptoms of the disease are appearance of yellow green discoloration followed by irregular growth and deformity in leaves. The virus has been experimentally transmitted to many woody plants including *Prunus armeniaca, P. domestica* and *P. cerasus*. Many herbaceous plants like *Chenopodium amaranticolor, C. quinoa. C. sativus* and *Nicotiana clevelandii* are experimental hosts.

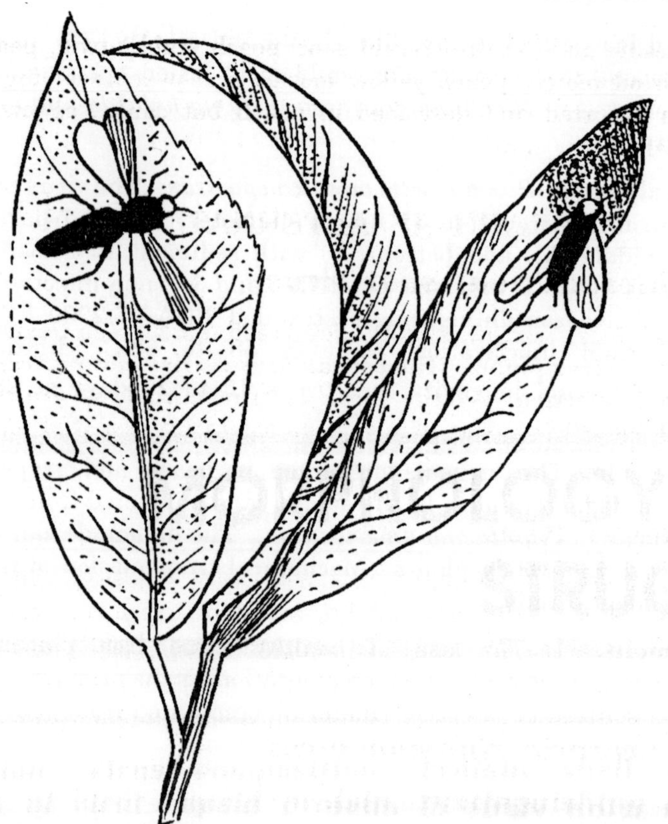

Fig. 17.3 Peach borer which play roll in transmission of peach virus

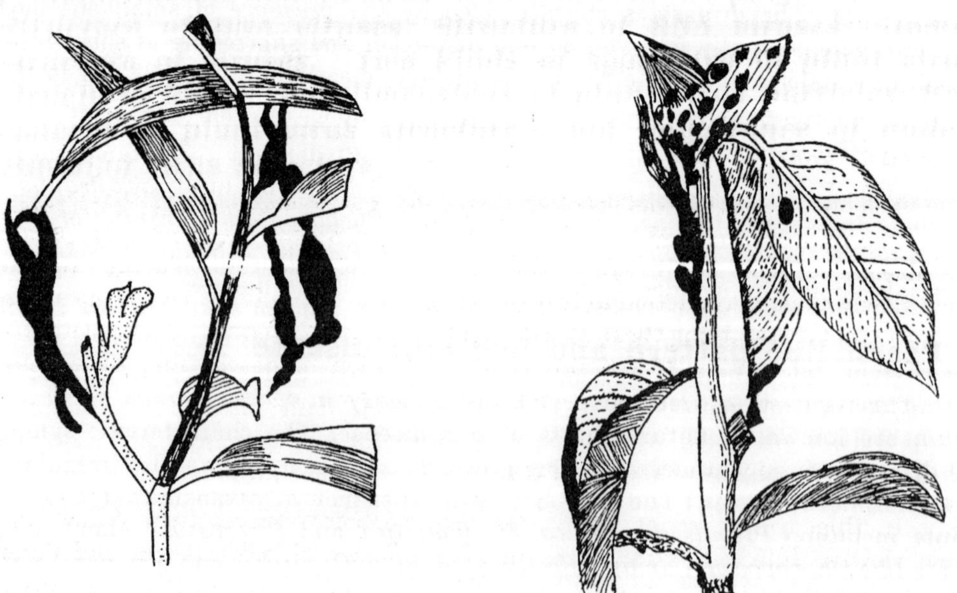

Fig. 17.4 Injury on peach twig caused by larvae of peach moth

Peach mosaic and peach asteroid spot, peach stubby twig, peach bark and wood grooving, peach oil blotch, peach yellow mosaic and peach seedling chlorosis diseases have also been reported and described in peach but causal agents of these diseases are not well defined by now.

PEACH AS ALTERNATE HOST

❍ *Apple chlorotic leaf spot virus*

The virus causes narrow, slightly depressed, dark green flexuous lines and spots on leaves of the infected plants. The causal virus-*Apple chlorotic leaf spot virus* usually occurs as mixed infection. As the virus is transmitted by grafting, therefore, the production and use of virus-free planting materials are essential for successful control of the disease.

❍ *Prune dwarf virus*

The causal virus is known to cause peach stunting with shortened shoot internodes. Leaves of the infected plants are dark green and erect which are most obvious in spring season. Delaying in growth and reduction in yield are usually observed.

❍ *Prunus necrotic ringspot virus*

The disease is widespread in peach and other fruit species. The disease caused by the virus, usually develops in two different stages, namely, acute stage and chronic stage. Acute stage symptoms are more severe and are characterized by delayed bud opening and death of flowers and leaf buds. Branches of the previous year are usually killed and canker symptoms appear at the nodes. Recovery of the disease may occur at chronic stage.

❍ *Plum pox virus*

The virus causes the most economically damaging peach disease, resulting in fruit drop and marked reduction in the quality of fruits. The important symptoms of the disease occur as bud break in the spring season and vein clearing. Infected veins grow slowly causing reduction in leaf shape and size. Sometimes ring spots and irregular chlorotic spots resembling those caused on plum leaves also occur. All measures including selection of tolerant cultivars and spatial isolation of peach from plum and apricot orchards are necessary to reduce the risk of disease spread.

❍ *Tomato black ring virus*

In this disease shoot internodes are shortened, leaves turn yellow and plants grow slowly. Infected young trees usually produce chlorotic spots and deformation. Appearance of bare twigs, rosetted growth and setting of few fruits are usually observed in infected plants.

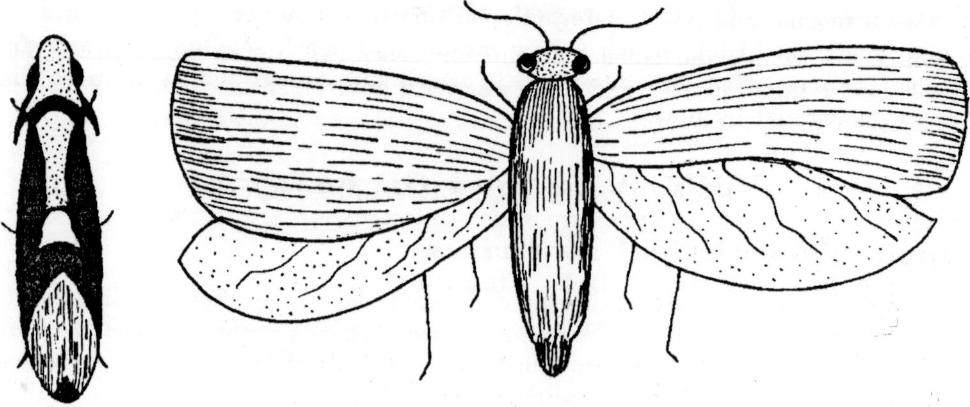

(a) Fruit moth wings folded (b) Wing spread

Fig. 17.5 Fruit moth that causes injury to peach.

Fig. 17.6 Peach leaf showing ring spot incited by *Tomato ring spot virus.*

❍ *Tomato ring spot virus*

Strains of *Tomato ring spot virus* cause stem pitting in peach. Leaves of infected trees remain smaller and yellow to radish in colour. Such leaves usually fall prematurely.

❍ *Strawberry latent ringspot virus*

Symptoms in infected trees are mild to severe in nature. As a result of this disease, leaves remain shorter and narrower with shorter shoot growth. Flowering is also delayed in most cases and only few and distorted fruits are formed.

VIRUS DISEASES OF BANANA (*Musa paradisiaca*)

❍ Banana bunchy top virus disease

The disease is known to occur in most of the banana growing regions through out the world, incuding Australia, Asia, Pacific Islands and Africa. The virus causes complete destruction of plantations, if not controlled.

Symptoms. (1) Irregular dark green streaks develop along the leaf veins. (2) The leaves in the apical plant part are bunched as rosettes. (3) Infected plants grow slowly and fail to produce fruits.

The causal virus. *Banana bunchy top virus.* It consists of isometric particles, measuring about 30 nm in diameter. It has a single stranded DNA with a multi-component genome and 6 of which have been cloned and sequenced. *Banana bunchy top virus* contains two important strains based on sequence analysis.

Disease cycle. The virus is preserved permanently in infected perennial banana and is transmitted naturally with infected suckers used as planting material. The virus is aphid transmissble also. The aphid-*Pentalonia nigronevosa* is known to transmit the virus in non-persistent manner.

Management. (1) Virus free suckers should be used to establish new orchard. (2) Aphid vectors should be managed by using suitable insecticide. (3) Infected trees should be destroyed immediately upon detection. (4) Quarantine regulatory measures should be strictly followed to avoid introduction of virus infected planting materials into new areas.

❍ Banana bract mosaic potyvirus disease

The disease was first reported in 1979 from Philippines. Similar disease with characteristic symptoms has also been observed in Tamil Nadu regions of India. The virus causes apparent losses in yield with smaller and fewer fruits per plant.

Symptoms. (1) Appearance of broad green or brown spindle streaks and discontinuous stripes distributed irregularly along the petioles are the characteristic symptoms of the disease. (2) Mosaic streaks on the leaf blade may or may not be observed. (3) Dark purple streaks on bracts of inflorescences and the fruit bunch are also observed.

The causal virus. *Banana bract mosaic potyvirus.* It looks like a flexuous rod, measuring 660 to 760 × 12 nm in size. Partially purified virus particles consist of positive-sense single stranded RNA. The virus usually occurs in low concentration in the banana plant. The coat protein is a single poly peptide of about 36 kDa. A partial sequence of the amino acids has been determined for the coat protein. Further progress is being made in sequencing and cloning of several genes of the virus.

Disease cycle. The virus has been experimentally transmitted by two aphid species-*Rhopalosiphum maidis* and *Aphis gossypii* in non-persistent manner.

Management. The management of the disease is difficult due to the systemic infection of all shoots and vegetative propagation system. Application of biotechnology incorporating viral resistance through coat protein gene of this virus may be useful for the management of the disease in future.

VIRUS DISEASES OF PLUM

❍ Plum pox potyvirus disease

The disease is known to be widespread in Sweden, Switzerland, Poland, Austria, Albania, Belgium, former Czehoslovakia, France, Germany, Great Britain, Greece and Italy.

Symptoms. (1) The causal virus produces symptoms on both the leaves and fruits of plum, apricot, peach and myrobalan plum. (2) Symptoms of the disease on the susceptible hosts may be observed as vein clearing and chlorotic patterns on the leaves bordering main and secondary veins. (3) Early symptoms include appearance of pale green areas and oily patches irregularly distributed on the leaves. (4) Early fruit symptoms may be observed as irregular blue and shallow depressions on the skin. (5) Deep irregular grooves, rings and characteristic lines usually develop on the surface of ripened fruits.

The causal virus. *Plum pox potyvirus.* It consists of filamentous particles of 720×18 nm in size while some isolates vary from 660 to 770 and 700 to 800 nm in length. The single stranded RNA is 3500 kDa. that accounts for 7% of the particle weight. Protein capsid usually consists of three polypetides of 43.5, 29 and 27 kDa. Thermal inactivation point is 52 to 58°C, dilution end point is 1×10^{-3} to 1×10^{-5} and longevity *in vitro* is 24 to 50 hours at 20°C. Some strains of the virus have been described.

Host range. The virus infects numerous hosts such as many *Prunus* species including *P. amygdalis, P. armeniaca. P. brigantine, P. curdica, P. domestica* and *P. holoserica* etc. New herbaceous hosts such as opium poppy (*Papaver somniferum*) and chick weed *(Stellaria media)* have recently been discovered. Other herbaceous hosts worth mentioning include *Lamium album, L. purpureum, Melilotus albus, Vicia sativa, V. cracca, Ranunculus arvensis, Nicotiana acuminate, N. bigelowii, N. excelsior* and *N. megalosiphon.*

Disease cycle. The virus is preserved in natural *Prunus* hosts and plum which are important sources of perpetuation. Aphids usually transmit the virus in non-persistent manner. *Brachycaudus helichrysi* is an important aphid vector.

Management. The causal virus can be eliminated from young infected plants by incubation at 37 to 38°C for two months. Plants resulting from grafting of terminal buds of thermotherapy-derived plantlets onto virus free rootstocks may be used successfully as healthy planting material. Control of aphids is indispensable for the production of young nurseries and establishment of plum plantations.

Fig. 17.7 Plum leaf infected from *Plum pox virus.*

❍ Prune dwarf (Possible) ilarvirus disease

The disease is one the most damaging diseases of the plum. It reduces the yield and the quality of the produce.

Symptoms. (1) The disease is characterized by the reduction of the leaf size with characteristic narrowing. (2) Infected leaves are wrinkled, usually on midribs with diffused mottling. (3) The surface of the leaves usually become compacted and leathery in appearance. (4) Shoot internodes are observed to remain short but some branches maintain normal appearance. (5) Many flowers of the infected trees are observed to have stunted and deformed styles with elongated and irregular calyx. Strains differ symptomatologically from the type.

The causal virus. The virus is *Prune dwarf ilarvirus.* It consists of quasi-isometric particles, measuring 19 to 20 nm and bacilliform particles measuring 73×20 nm in sizes. The multi-component virus has 6 particle types with sedimentation coefficients of 75, 81, 85, 99 and 113 S. The virus contains 14% RNA and has 24 kDa. protein. Thermal inactivation point of the virus in chemically stabilized sap is 45 to 54°C. It has moderate immunogenicity.

Host plants. Important natural hosts are plum *(Prunus domestica),* Cherry *(P. avium),* sour cherry *(P. cerasus),* apricot *(P. armeniaaca)* myrobalan plum *(P. cerasifera)* and rock cherry *(P. mahaleb).* It has both woody and herbaceous indicator hosts.

Disease cycle. The virus is preserved in many wide spread perennial hosts. It is usually transmitted by grafting (buds/scions) particularly during production of planting materials. In nature it spreads through infected pollen particularly in cherry plantations. It is also transmitted mechanically with infective plant sap from succulent parts of woody plants into herbaceous hosts.

Management. The use of virus free planting materials is the important measure for the management of the disease.

❍ Prunus necrotic ringspot ilarvirus disease

The disease is caused by one of the most widely distributed viruses in *Prunus* and *Rosa* species frequently observed in temperate regions of the world. The first occurrence of a ringspot disease, possibly incited by *Prunus necrotic ringspot virus* was reported in plum and peach and later in sweet and sour cherry as reported by different workers.

Symptoms. (1) In susceptible plum cultivars, the symptoms of ring spots and lines are usually observed to be surrounded by dark necrotic tissues. (2) These symptoms are seen on first emerging leaves especially in spring season. (3) In due course, the necrotic tissues tatter and fall out, leaving irregular characteristic shot holes. (4) Symptoms may fade or fail to appear in leaves emerged later in season, which is assumed to be latent during chronic stage.

The causal virus. The virus-*Prunus necrotic ringspot ilarvirus*. It is isometric in morphology, measuring 23 nm in diameter. It is composed of multi-components with sedimentation coefficients of 72, 90 and 95 S, having some bacilliform particles. The virus contains 16% RNA and a major polypeptide coat protein of 25 kDa. Virus particles have some smaller components. The virus is unstable in undiluted plant sap but remains infective in buffer solution. Thermal inactivation point is 55 to 60°C and dilution end point is 5×10^{-1}. The virus is serologically related to Danish plum line pattern disease and distantly related with *Apple mosaic virus* and *Rose mosaic virus*.

Host range. The virus has many natural and experimental hosts. Natural hosts include nearly all cultivated fruit trees. Among hosts, sweet cherry, sour cherry, plum, peach, nectarine (*Prunus persica* cv *nectarine*), apricot, myrobalam, rock cherry, European bird cherry, black cherry, apple and several rose species are important natural hosts. Diagnostic hosts are *Cucumis sativus* producing chlorotic primary spots on cotyledons and necrosis or mosaic on leaves. *Prunus serrulata* cv. Shirofugen produces necrosis in bud grafts and *Momordica balsamina* produces necrotic primary spots on leaves and sometimes causes systemic infection.

Disease cycle. (1) Infected parent trees from which buds and scions are grafted onto infected vegetative rootstocks and (2) planting materials with latent infection are the important sources of infection and disease perpetuation. The *Vasates fockeui* mite and *Longidorus macrosoma* nematode are potential vectors of the virus. It is also transmitted by infective plant sap experimentally.

Management. (1) Use of virus free planting materials for establishment of the plantations is the important measure to be followed. (2) Infected plants as the potential source of infection should be eliminated immediately from the new plantation. (3)

Healthy planting materials can be obtained by exposing the tips of young plants to 38°C for 24 to 32 days and after that these should be grafted onto healthy rootstocks.

❍ Plum line pattern virus disease

Plum line pattern viruses are known to cause different kinds of symptoms on plum. *Plum American line pattern virus* and *Plum European line pattern virus* are two important viruses known to cause line pattern disease. These viruses cause considerable losses to the plant every year. *Plum American line pattern virus* is assumed to be the member of ilarvirus group.

Symptoms on leaves are observed as lines, striated spots and oak like mosaic with characteristic small rings and striped chlorosis along the veins. The virus is quasi-isometric with 4 particle types, measuring, 26 (T), 28 (M), 31 (B) and 33 (B_2) nm in diameters. The presumed ssRNA accounts for 17% of viral particle weight. All the 4 types are known to be infective. Natural host of the virus includes all *Prunus* species.

Plum European line pattern viruses incude *Apple mosaic virus* and *Prunus necrotic ringspot virus*. They usually cause line pattern symptoms on different tissues. Characteristic symptoms in infected plum include leaf line and oak line pattern associated with chlorotic lines.

PLUM AS NATURAL ALTERNATE HOST

A large number of viruses are known to occur on plum. The plum is alternate host of different viruses including *Apple chlorotic leafspot virus, Tomato ringspot virus, Raspberry ringspot virus, Strawberry latent virus* and many other latent viruses. Due to limited or no spread, these latent viruses are of little economic importance.

PLUM DISEASES OF UNKNOWN ETIOLOGY

Like other plants, a few diseases caused by unknown pathogens have also been described in plum. They are usually transmitted through vegetative plant parts by grafting, budding and chip budding. These diseases are Plum fruit crinkle and peach leaf necrosis.

VIRUS DISEASES OF APRICOT (*Prunus armeniaca*)

Apricot usually serves as alternate hosts for different virus diseases and no virus has been described in apricot as its primary host. Apricot is known to be the first transgenic rosaceous fruit to receive the coat protein gene of *Plum pox potyvirus* via genetic engineering technology.

APRICOT AS ALTERNATE HOST

❍ Apple chlorotic leaf spot virus disease

The causal virus-*Apple chlorotic leaf spot virus* is latent in apricot. In susceptible cultivars the virus causes shortening of internodes of shoots, resulting in leaves compacted into rosette. Bud death and gummosis also occur in susceptible cultivars and clones when a virus infected partner is used for grafting. The virus is graft transmissible and no other mode of transmission is known. Therefore, production and use of virus free materials for establishment of new plantations are effective and successful control measures.

❍ Prune dwarf virus disease

This disease is incited by *Prune dwarf virus* and is known to occur in most apricot crops. It usually occurs as mixed infection with one or more viruses. Necrotic spots usually occur on infected apricot leaves with gummosis on smaller branches. These leaves may become yellow in later stage and as a result of the severity of the disease, fruits drop before ripening. Diseased branches gradually die. Causal agent of apricot gummosis is both graft and seed transmissible. Virus has also been detected in pollen grains of the apricot.

❍ Prunus necrotic ringspot nepovirus disease

Two different types of symptoms are known to occur in leaves of infected apricot which are incited by two different strains of the virus. These are apricot line pattern disease and apricot ring spot disease. Line pattern is characterized by pale yellow or yellow green bands, spots and ring spots on new leaves. Apricot ring spot is characterized by gum flow on stems and branches with unusual fruit disorders. The causal virus- *Prunus necrotic ringspot nepovirus* is mostly graft transmitted. Transmission through pollen and seed of stone fruits are also reported.

❍ Plum pox potyvirus disease

The disease is widespread in the Mediterranean where rosaceous stone fruits are grown extensively. Infection of this virus usually occurs in regions where plum and peach are also grown. Initial symptoms of the disease mostly occur on newly emerging apricot leaves with pale chlorotic areas surrounding leaf veins which later merge into bands along the veins. More than 62% virus inoculated apricot seedlings display plum pox symptoms on leaves within one month of inoculation and thus it may be used as indicator plant for rapid detection. In order to manage the disease special attention should be paid for spatial isolation of apricot from plum and peach. Tolerant/resistant cultivars should only be used.

❍ Tomato ring spot virus disease

Stem pitting in apricot is caused by a strain of *Tomato ring spot virus*. Characteristic symptoms include lower trunk thickening, usually accompanied by length wise bark cracks. The bark is thickened, becomes spongy and sporadically necrotic. The virus may also cause discoloration and early decline of leaves. Mixed infection of *Strawberry latent ring spot virus* plus *Cucumber green mottle mosaic virus* has been found to cause the apricot bare twig and unfruitfulness. There are some diseases which are assumed to be caused by viruses. These include apricot ring pox disease and apricot asteriod spot disease.

VIRUS DISEASE OF SWEET CHERRY
(*Prunus avium*)

Cherry leaf roll and cherry rasp leaf are two important diseases of cherry. Besides these diseases, a number of viruses are known to occur on cherry as it is alternate host of many viruses.

❍ Cherry leaf roll nepovirus disease

The disease has been observed to occur in different countries of the world. The disease is widespread in North America, Europe, Turkey, former U.S.S.R. and New Zealand. The causal agent—*Cherry leaf roll nepovirus* causes tree decline usually 5 years after the appearance of first symptoms.

Symptoms. (1) Causal virus produces similar symptoms in sweet and sour cherry. (2) Infected trees grow slowly and leaves are compacted in to rosette. (3) Leaf margins twist and colour of the leaves usually changes. (4) Cracks and gum flows appear on infected susceptible trees. (5) In mixed infection usually with *Prunus necrotic ringspot nepovirus*, bud necrosis occurs after bud opening, Indicator hosts are *Chenopodium murale, C. quinoa, Cucumis sativus* and *Nicotiana tabacum*.

The causal virus. *Cherry leaf roll nepovirus.* The virus is observed as isometric particles, measuring about 28 nm in diameter. It consists of three types of particles—The top component (T) is RNA free and two other medium (M) and bottom (B) are nucleoprotein components with sedimentation coefficients of 52 S (T), 155 S (M) and 128 S (B). Molecular weights of different components are 3240 kDa (T), 5530 kDa. (M) and 6060(B). The single-stranded RNA consists of two genomic species RNA-1 and RNA-2 separately located in B and M particles of 2400 kDa (RNA-1) and 210 kDa.(RNA-2). Both M and B particles are not infective and all the three particles are essential for infectivity.

Fig. 17.8 Symptoms on cherry leaves infected with *Cherry rusty mottle virus.*

Fig. 17.9 Sweet cherry leaf showing enations on leaf incited by *Prunus necrotic ring spot virus.*

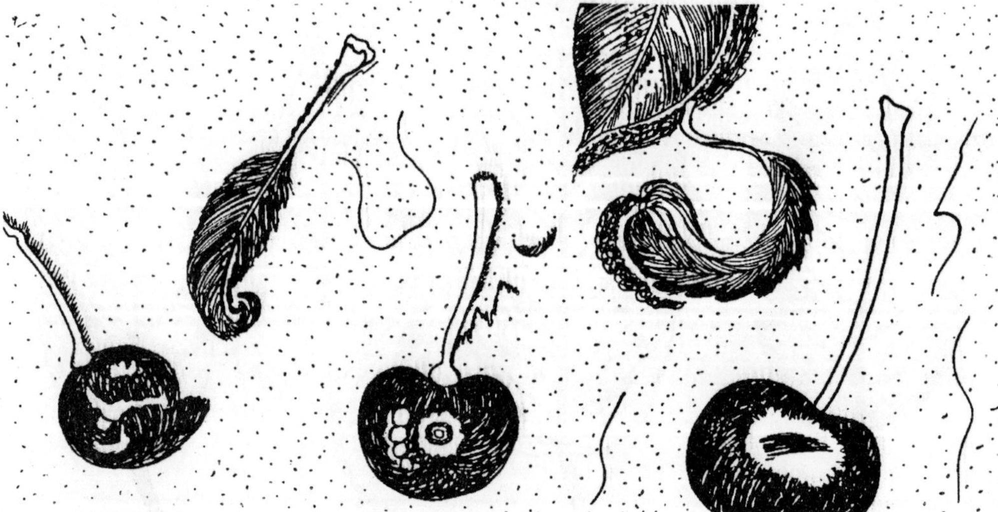

Fig. 17.10 Deformed leaves and necrotic sweet cherry fruits incited by *Tomato bushy stunt virus.*

Disease cycle. The causal virus is preserved permanently in its natural hosts. It is graft transmissible by buds and scion. The disease is also known to spread through vegetative planting materials if the mother plants were infected. Some strains like Walnut strains may also spread in the orchards via pollen from infected trees. Sweet cherry and sour cherry (*Prunus cerasus*) are important natural hosts. Other hosts are species of *Betula, Cornus, Juglans, Ligustrum, Olea, Ptelea, Rhem* and *Ulmus*.

Management. Use of healthy planting material represents the primary measure for virus control in sweet cherry, sour cherry and other woody hosts. Infected trees should also be eliminated from the new plantations so as to avoid pollen transmission.

❍ Cherry rasp leaf disease

The disease is known to be incited by *Cherry rasp leaf* (probable) *nepovirus*. The virus causes rasp like enations characteristics to the disease on the under side of cherry leaves. Cherry American rasp leaf and cherry European rasp leaf diseases are most common in occurrence. Besides these two diseases, cherry epirus virus disease has also been described in Greece.

SWEET CHERRY AS ALTERNATE HOST

Sweet cherry has been reported to be alternate hosts of different viruses. Some of the common viruses occurring on sweet cherry are being summarized as under:

Prune dwarf virus, *Prunus necrotic ringspot virus*, *Tomato bushy stunt virus*, *Tomato ring spot virus* and *Apple chlorotic leafspot virus* are most common viruses known to be found on sweet cherry which serves as alternate host.

Cherry rusty mottle disease, cherry green ring mottle disease, cherry little cherry disease, cherry twisted leaf disease, cherry leaf mottle disease, cherry spur cherry disease and cherry black canker disease are some of the important diseases which cause losses of considerable importance and are assumed to be caused by viruses.

VIRUS DISEASES OF SOUR CHERRY
(*Prunus cerasus*)

❍ Prunus necrotic ringspot virus disease

The virus-*Prunus necrotic ringspot virus* is geneally widespread in stone fruits and has many strains that cause symptoms of different descriptions on different plant species. Darkening and desiccation of flowers and leaf buds on the branches of the infected plants are observed. Pale-green and brown necrotic ringspots which break later in the season may be seen in older leaves. Leaves of the infected plants showing characteristic spots exhibit shot holes appearance. In severe cases, the infected plants may die. The virus is transmitted by sweet and sour cherry pollen and seed. The use of virus free planting materials for the establishments of orchards is the primary measure of management. Virus free condition of mother trees for scion production should be inspected regularly and all flower buds should be removed to avoid pollen transmission. rootstock seedlings should be produced only from healthy seed and infected trees that represent important sources of the virus perpetuation should be eliminated from the young orchards.

○ Prune dwarf virus disease

Prunus dwarf virus infects several fruit tree species of *Prunus,* sweet and sour cherry. Infected shoots of the infected trees grow slowly and only a few leaves and flower buds are formed on terminal shoots. Pollen germination ability is reduced, leading to poor pollination and flowering. It results in considerable reduction of the yield. The virus is graft transmissible with infected plant material. Pollens from infected plants are important in natural virus transmission into sour cherry seed. Healthy planting material is the primary measure of the disease management. Virus free scions and rootstocks are essential to reduce the spread of the disease. Besides these, virus free mother trees should be used for seed production.

OTHER DISEASES

Sour cherry green ring mottle disease has also been reported which is assumed to be caused by the virus. Characteristic symptoms include green ring mottle and vein spots on the leaves of the infected plants. Measures for the management are similar as for sweet cherry. Besides these, American rusty mottle, sour cherry line pattern, sour cherry pink fruit, sour cherry bark splitting and sour cherry gummosis are some common diseases.

VIURS DISEASES OF ALMOND (*Prunus communis*)

Prunus necrotic ringspot virus, Prune dwarf virus, Plum pox virus, Apple chlorotic leaf spot virus and *Tomato ring spot virus* are known to occur in almond, causing diseases of significant importance.

○ Prunus necrotic ringspot virus disease

The causal agent-*Prunus necrotic ringspot virus* is probably the most widespread and the most damaging virus in almond. Different strains of the virus cause almond calico, almond line pattern and almond necrotic disease.

Almond calico disease was first observed in U.S. in 1939. The disease is characterized by the appearance of chlorotic spots on the leaves of infected plants. These spots usually merge with each other forming pale yellow with white areas especially evident in early spring. Lateral shoot buds usually fail to develop in severe cases.

Almond line pattern disease is usually caused by this virus alone or sometimes is found in complexes with other viruses. The disease may be observed sporadically or sometimes may occur in all the trees of the orchard.

Almond necrotic ringspot disease is known to occur to U.S., South Africa and Mediterranean countries. The disease is characterized by the nectrotic ringspots on leaves. In the sock stage, bud and bark necrosis are also observed.

○ Prune dwarf virus disease

The disease is caused by *Prune dwarf virus.* Almond is the natural host of the virus. In most cases the virus does not produce visible symptoms and remain latent.

❍ Plum pox virus disease

Almond has been observed to be infected experimentally. It may be an occasional natural host of the virus and produces symptoms characteristics to the disease.

❍ Apple chlorotic leafspot virus disease

This virus has been observed in almond. No detailed information on incidence of the disease along with the extent of damage is available.

❍ Tomato ringspot virus disease

The causal virus-*Tomato ringspot virus* causes yellow bud mosaic and stem pitting in almond. Almond yellow bud mosaic is identical in symptoms to symptoms produced in peach caused by this virus.

Besides these diseases, almond bud failure disease and almond mosaic disease are also observed in almond. Causal agents and etiology of these diseases are not well known.

VIRUS DISEASES OF WALNUT (*Juglans regia*)

Cherry leaf roll virus, inciting an economically important disease was first observed in southern Italy in 1976. In United States, the virus was isolated and identified to cause black line disease. This disease reduces walnut growth and yield considerably. The virus also causes leaf patterns and blackline at the graft union points. Leaf patterns include yellow mosaic and ring spots which are considered as separate disease by some workers. The virus is known to be graft transmissible when scions from infected trees are used. The virus is also transmitted by pollen and seed. Virus free planting materials- both scions and walnut seedlings should be used for establishment of the new orchards. Infected trees that provide sources of infected pollen should be eliminated immediately. Seed infection may be reduced by storing seed at 4 to 5°C prior to germination.

❍ Walnut line pattern disease

The disease is of minor importance and is characterized by the presence of pale green or yellow spots with characteristic broad lines and stripes usually spread around and along the leaf veins. The virus is graft transmissible, therefore, healthy seedlings should be used to establish new orchards.

❍ Walnut mosaic disease

It is an important disease as it causes considerable damage to the infected plants. Characteristic symptoms are observed as small, usually roundish dark green or yellow green spots on the leaves of the infected trees. Cell necrosis also occurs within the mosaic spots, resulting in distortion of leaves. Small irregular groove-like depressions have also been observed on the fruits shells. The disease is graft transmissible. Use of healthy seedlings is the important measure for the management of the disease.

VIRUS DISEASES OF FIG (*Ficus carica*)

❍ Fig mosaic disease

It is widespread and most common disease of fig. It is known to occur in North America, Australia, Africa, Asia and Europe.

Symptoms. (1) Chlorotic fleck and veinal chlorosis on the leaves are usually observed as characteristic symptoms. (2) Tissue necrosis may also be observed on flecks starting from the centre. (3) Veinal chlorosis affects tissues along and around the veins. (4) The disease usually affects at least 16 *Ficus* species including *Ficus altissima, F. carica, F. krishna* and *F. tsida*.

The causal virus. *Fig mosaic virus.* The causal agent of the disease is not well defined. In parenchyma cells of diseased fig leaves, broad polymorphous particles were discovered with the aid of electron microscope. Isometric particles measure about 120 to 150 nm in diameter. Elongated particles measure about 200 nm in length. Primary symptoms of the disease are observed on leaves.

Fig. 17.11. Showing mosaic symptoms on fig leaves incited by *Fig mosaic virus.*

Disease cycle. The causal agent is permanently preserved in infected fig trees and spread naturally with infected cuttings and suckers by which fig is propagated. It is graft transmissible. *Aceria ficus* mite is known to contribute the spread of the virus in the field.

Management. The disease is found present everywhere, therefore, it is difficult to select healthy stock. Thermotherapy also has not yielded satisfactory result. Recent research suggests possible success soon in the production of healthy fig. stocks.

VIRUS DISEASES OF OLIVE
(*Olea europea*)

❍ Olive latent ringspot nepovirus disease

This virus disease was reported from central Italy in 1985. The virus infected olive trees are symptomless. Experimentally infected *Chenopodium quinoa* expresses symptoms of local lesions and systemic mosaic suitable for disease diagnosis. *Chenopodium amaranticolor* and *Gomphrema globosa* are also diagnostic. The virus particles are isometric in morphology, measuring about 28 nm in diameter. Purified preparation usually consists of three types of particles-T, M and B with sedimentation coefficients of 52 S (T), 97 S (M) and 132 S (B). The single stranded RNA consists of species RNA-1 from particle B and RNA-2 from both particles. Both RNA species are necessary to cause infection. Thermal inactivation point in *Chenopodium quinoa* sap is 60°C, dilution end point is 1×10^{-3} and longevity *in vitro* is 15 days at 20°C. No strain has been reported. The virus is transmitted mechanically by sap. The virus being latent in nature is preserved in infected olive trees. It is transmitted with propogative materials. No other mode of transmission is reported.

❍ Olive latent viruses 1 and 2

Two species of latent viruses have been isolated from symptom less olive trees. *Olive latent virus-1* consists of isometric particles and *Olive latent virus-2* particles are quasi-spherical to bacilliform in morphology. Both the viruses are transmitted mechanically with infective plant sap.

Olive is alternate hosts of many viruses, such as *Arabis mosaic virus, Cherry leaf roll virus* and *Cucumber mosaic virus.* All are transmitted with infective plant sap.

VIRUS DISEASES OF STRAWBERRY
(*Fragaria chiloensis*)

❍ Strawberry crinkle rhabdovirus disease

The disease has been observed in different countries including North and South America, Europe, New Zealand and Australia in moderate to severe form. It usually causes considreable damage to the strawberry plants every year.

Symptoms. Several strains have been described based on symptom severity in host plants. Virulent strain of the virus causes variable symptoms on susceptible host. In susceptible cultivars, the symptoms of the disease are observed on the leaves as small scattered dotted spots which develop into large chlorotic spots in advanced cases of the disease severity. The leaf tissues with in these spots frequently become necrotic. In severe attack, the leaf blades become smaller with irregular shapes and uneven margins.

The causal virus. *Strawberry crinkle rhabdovirus.* It is a bacilliform virus, features usually enveloped particles, measuring 190 to 280 × 59 ± 5 nm in size. Different strains are known. Out of that two strains viz.,severe strain causes characteristic symptoms described above and mild strain results no symptoms on strawberry. Biophysical and biochemical properties of the causal virus have not been studied well.

Disease cycle. The virus is preserved in systemically infected strawberry plants. It spreads by infected runners as vegetatively propagated plant parts. Aphid vectors chiefly *Chaetosiphon fragaefolii* and *C. jacobi* are known to transmit this virus in persistent manner. *Chaetosiphon fragaefolii* acquires the virus and transmits it within 24 hours. Latent period of the virus in the vector has been reported to be about 2 weeks. It multiplies in vector-*C. jacobi.* The virus is also known to be transmitted by grafting which is generally used for indexing strawberry plants. The virus was transferred experimentally by needle inoculation from aphid to aphid and by injection with aphid vector extract to non-vector bean aphid-*Megoura viciae.* It has not been reported to be transmitted mechanically by sap inoculation.

Management. The use of virus free runners is the main prevention measure in the establishment of strawberry plantation. Rogueing of infected plants from the plantations and management of aphids are also important so as to prevent the spread of the virus. Other measures include isolation of the plantation from potential sources of infection and virus free planting materials should be obtained through heat therapy and by meristem culture.

❍ Strawberry mottle virus disease

The disease is widespread with high incidence, which reduces yield of the produce by 25 to 30%. When the disease occurs with other viruses as complex, the yield is reduced even more.

Symptoms. All commercial strawberry cultivars infected with this virus, although symptomless, have reduced vigour and yield. Different strains of the virus may produce various symptoms in *Fragaria vesca* indicator plant. Such symptoms include mild mottle to severe degeneration with characteristic mottle, downward leaf curl, vein chlorosis, shortened leaf petioles, leaf deformation and crown proliferation. *Chenopodium quinoa* and *Physalis floridana* as indicator plants react with systemic symptoms of infection.

The causal virus. *Strawberry mottle virus.* Isometric virus particles, measuring about 20 nm in diameter from ultra-thin sections of infected strawberry and *Chenopodium quinoa* leaves have been detected. Biophysical and biochemical properties of the virus have not been studied in detail.

Disease cycle. The virus is preserved in systemically infected propogative plant material. The virus is mechanically transmitted by infective plant sap, by dodder-*Cuscuta groncvii, C. subinclusa* and also by insect vectors. Aphids are known to transmit the virus in semi- persistent manner. Important vectors are *Chaetosiphon fragaefolii, C. thomasi, C. jacobi* and *C. minor.* Besides these, *Acyrthosiphon pelargonii* var. *rogersii,*

A. porosum, Aphis gossypii, Chaetosiphon tetrarhodus, Myzaphis rasarum, Myzus ascalonicus and *M. ornatus* are also vectors playing important role in transmission of the virus.

Management . Virus free plant stocks should be used to establish strawberry plantation. Isolation of the plantation from potential source of infection and management of the vectors are the important measures to be followed for the management of the disease.

❍ Strawberry vein banding caulimovirus disease

This disease is most prevalent in Eastern and Western North America, Australia and Brazil where it was probably imported from infected planting material. Disease damage includes reduction in vigour, runner production and yield.

Symptoms. (1) Vein banding in tissue along primary and secondary leaf veins is an important symptom of the disease. (2) Besides these, yellowing, crinkling and curling of leaves may also be observed in infected plants. (3) *Fragaria vesca* and *F. virginiana* are suitable indicator plants that react with the production of mild leaf curl accompanied by chlorotic banding along the main veins. (4) Stunting of plants and necrosis of older leaves may also be observed as diagnostic characteristics of the disease.

The causal virus. *Strawberry vein banding caulimovirus.* The particles are isometric in morphology. Particles usually measure 40 to 50 nm in diameter, containing probably double stranded DNA. The sedimentation coefficient of the particles determined by co-sedimentation with *Cauliflower mosaic virus* is 200 ± 10 S. The virus can be detected directly by ELISA and serological specific electron microscopy (SSEM) using cauliflower mosaic antiserum. Several strains including leaf curl strain and vein banding strain are known to occur.

Disease cycle. The virus perpetuates in diseased plants. Initial infections in new strawberry plantations usually originate from diseased planting materials. Many aphid vectors have been reported to transmit the virus in non-persistent manner. The efficient vectors are *Chaetosiphon fragaefolii, C. jacobi* and *C. thomasi.* The virus is also transmissible through grafting and dodder *(Cuscuta subinclusa)* but not transmissible by mechanical inoculation through infected plant sap or by any other means.

Management. The use of healthy planting materials for establishment of new plantation represents a suitable control measure of the disease. Virus free mother plant can be obtained by thermal treatment for 10 days at 42°C or by tissue culture of runner tips.

❍ Strawberry latent ringspot nepovirus disease

The disease is widespread in occurrence. It causes considerable damage to the plants. Loss caused by the virus usually depends upon the severity of the disease. The disease usually occurs as mixed infection with some other viruses.

Symptoms. (1) The virus causes symptoms like leaf mottle and decline in strawberry and raspberry. (2) Reduction of growth, rosette appearance, dieback in peach, spots and occasional stunting in rose are the important symptoms of the disease. (3) *Chenopodium amaranticolor, C. murale* and *Chenopodium quninoa* are important indicator plants of the virus. (4) They exhibit chlorotic or necrotic local spots, systemic chlorosis, necrosis and mild chlorotic mottle. (5) Other indicator plant-*Cucumis sativus* may be observed with or without local spots, systemic chlorosis and necrosis between leaf veins. (6) Tobacco (*Nicotiana tabacum*) and Petunia (*Petunia hybrida*) are tolerant to this virus, producing no characteristic symptoms.

The causal virus. *Strawberry latent ringspot nepovirus*. The virus is isometric in morphology. It measures about 28 to 30 nm in diameter. Virus sediments contain three groups (T, M and B) of particles. These particle groups have sedimentation coefficients of 58 S (T), 94 S (M) and 126 S (B) respectively. The virus genome is composed of two RNA species of 2600 kDa (RNA 1) and 1600 kDa (RNA 2). Thermal inactivation point of the virus is 54 to 56°C, dilution end point in cucumber sap is 1×10^{-3} to 1×10^{-5} and longevity *in vitro* is 15 days to 13 months at 4°C.

Host range. Natural hosts are both cultivated and wild plants. Small fruit host species are strawberry, raspberry, blackberry, black currant, red currant and grapevine.

Disease cycle. The virus is preserved systemically in numerous herbaceous and woody hosts found in nature. In the soil it is transmitted by the nematodes-*Xiphinema diversicaudatum* and *X. coxi*. The virus has been observed to remain infective without its plant host for about 80 days in nematode-*Xiphinema diversicaudatum*. Both the larvae and the adult stages are known to transmit this virus. Virus transmission through mechanical means by sap, seeds from the infected plants and dodder (*Cuscutta subinclusa* and *C. californica*) have also been observed.

Management. Strawberry and plantations of other susceptible plants should be established with healthy planting materials. Infected plants from the plantations should be rogued out immediately on detection. If soil nematodes are known or suspected, the soil should be treated with suitable nematicide.

DISEASES ASSUMED TO BE CAUSED BY VIRUSES

A large number of strawberry diseases have been described by different workers but the causal agents of those diseases have yet to be identified. Some of the diseases of economic importance may be summarized as under.

❍ Strawberry chlorotic fleck disease

The disease causes reduction in yield, plant growth and fruits. The causal agent is transmitted by grafting and by cotton aphid-*Aphis gossypii*.

❍ Strawberry latent disease

The diseased commercial cultivars have erratic and non-diagnostic symptoms. The causal agent is transmitted by grafting, dodder and aphids.

❍ Strawberry stunt disease

Characteristic symptoms are stunting of plants, erect petioles and leaflets, seedy and hard fruits and papery appearance of the matured leaves. The causal agent is graft and aphid transmissible in nature.

STRAWBERRY AS ALTERNATE HOST

Arabis mosaic virus, Raspberry ringspot virus, Tomato ring spot virus, Tobacco mosaic virus and *Tobacco necrosis virus* are some of the important viruses that occur in strawberry as their alternate host.

VIRUS DISEASES OF RASPBERRY (*Rubus idaeus* and *R. occidentalis*)

❍ Raspberry vein chlorosis rhabdovirus disease (*Raspberry aphid-borne virus*)

The virus was first reported in Scotland and later detected and studied in Canada, continental Europe and New Zealand. The virus causes pathological changes resulting in weight loss of the fruit, formation of thinner canes, earlier maturation and increased pollen abortion.

Symptoms. (1) Yellow net pattern usually occurs along the smaller leaf veins. (2) Vein chlorosis may occur in patches and in some susceptible cultivars. Leaf deformity and epinasty are also observed. (3) Natural infection by the virus was observed only in red raspberry (*Rubus idaeus* and *R. idaeus* var. *strigosus*). (4) Many raspberry cvs. are susceptible to both natural and experimental infections. These plants include Golden queen, Great American, La France, Lloyd George, Malling Exploit, Malling Jewel and Malling Promise etc.

The causal virus. *Raspberry vein chlorosis rhabdovirus*. The virus particles are bacilliform with rounded ends at both the sides in morphology. Particles usually measure about 430 to 560 × 65 to 91 nm in size. Some particles may be shorter and rounded at only one end. Different strains are reported.

Disease cycle. Diseased raspberry plants are natural perennial source of inoculum. Infected nursery stocks are the important medium for the introduction of the virus in new plantation. *Aphis idaci* is a vector of the virus in the field. The vector requires 24 hours for acquisition which it retains for 24 hours to transmit it. The virus is neither transmitted by seed and nor by mechanical inoculation through sap.

Management. Use virus free planting materials for establishment of the new plantation. Potential sources of infection may be reduced by rogueing of the diseased plants from the plantation immediately on detection. Vector control can help to reduce the chances of disease spread to some extent.

❍ Raspberry ringspot nepovirus disease (*Raspberry nematode-borne virus*)

The disease was first observed in Scotland and later on in different countries including Great Britain, continental Europe and Turkey. The disease causes plant decline in susceptible cultivars, resulting in reduction in yield.

Symptoms. (1) Pale-green irregular spots and characteristic ringspots are usually observed on raspberry leaves of the infected plant. (2) Leaf curl is also observed on some susceptible cultivars. (3) Canes are stunted and brittle. (4) Infected plants may die after 3 to 4 years of appearance of the symptoms. (5) Some cultivars may not exhibit symptoms and remain less vigorous.

The causal virus. *Raspberry ringspot nepovirus.* The virus is composed of two single stranded RNA species (RNA 1 of 2400 kDa and RNA 2 of 1400 kDa and is isometric in morphology, measuring about 20 nm in diameter. Both RNA species are essential for infectivity. Particles are of equal size and they sediment in three components-Top, middle and bottom. Sedimentation coefficient of these components are 50 S, 92 S and 130 S respectively. The coat protein consists of a single species of 54 kDa. Thermal inactivation point in *Nicotiana rustica* sap is 65 to 70°C, dilution end point is 1×10^{-3} to 1×10^{-4} and longevity *in vitro* is 2 to 3 weeks at room temperature. Three strains of the virus are known to be important.

Host range. The virus has a broad host range. Potential hosts among small fruits and fruit trees are important as they play important role in providing reservoir for the virus.

Disease cycle. The virus is preserved in infected herbaceous and woody susceptible plants and in infected seed of many hosts. Soil borne nematode vectors have specific relationships in the transmission of the some strains of the virus. *Longidorus elongatus* is the most common nematode of the Scottish strain and *Longidorus macrosoma* and *L. attenuatus* are the natural vectors of the English or continental European strains.

Management. (1) Use of virus-free planting materials for establishment of new plantation is essential. (2) Nematodes should be managed by use of suitable insecticide and appropriate crop rotation. (3) Use of resistant cultivars should be preferred.

❍ Raspberry bushy dwarf virus disease (*Raspberry pollen borne virus*)

The disease was first described in red raspberry in Great Britain during 1951. Now it is known to occur in different countries worldwide including North America, New Zealand, Australia, South Africa and Chile. The virus contributes damage significantly in mixed viral infection.

Symptoms. (1) Plants of susceptible raspberry plants infected with this virus alone are usually observed to remain symptomless. (2) Mixed infections generally exhibit severe and characteristic bushy dwarf symptoms. (3) Besides bushy dwarf symptoms, shorter canes, chlorotic and red shoots and down curled leaves are also observed in infected plants.

The causal virus. *Raspberry bushy dwarf virus.* The virus is isometric in morphology, measuring about 33 nm in diameter. It consists of single type of identical particles with a sedimentation coefficient of 115 S. The protein coat consists of a single protein of 28 kDa and three single stranded RNA species of 2200, 900 and 400 kDa. Thermal inactivation point in *Chenopodium quinoa* sap is 65°C, dilution end point is 1×10^{-4} and longevity *in vitro* is 4 days at 22°C.

Disease cycle. The virus is transmitted through seed and pollen of infected raspberry plants. Propagation of infected planting materials also plays an active role in the infection of new raspberry plantation. The virus is also graft and infected plant sap transmissible.

Management. Use of virus free planting material and spatial isolation of plantation from infected cultivated and wild *Rubus* plant species are important measures to be followed for the management of the disease. The flowers should be regularly eliminated from the plants in cane nurseries in order to avoid infection through pollen. The use of resistant cultivars represents the most successful method of control.

RASPBERRY AS ALTERNATE HOST

Black raspberry necrosis virus, Rubus yellow net virus, Cucumber mosaic virus (all aphid borne viruses) and *Arabis mosaic virus, Cherry leaf roll virus, Strawberry latent ringspot virus, Tomato black ring virus, Tomato ring spot virus* (all nematode born viruses) are known to occur in raspberry.

RASPBERRY DISEASES ASSUMED TO BE CAUSED BY VIRUSES

❍ Raspberry leaf curl disease

Raspberry leaf curl disease occurs in nearly all regions where raspberries are grown. The disease is assumed to be caused by the virus. Natural hosts of the disease belong only to the *Rubus* species. Experimentally infected hosts belong to *Fragaria* and *Rubus* species. Infected plants remain symptomless or exhibit only slight down curling of apical leaves in the first year of infection. Next year, canes curl, leaves turn yellow and shoots proliferate, resulting in rosette appearance. Diseased plants are observed to remain stunted and are frequently killed. Fruits from such plants are small and crumbly with considerable reduction in yield. *Aphis rubicola* is considered as natural vector of the causal agent. Disease may be graft transmissible but not by mechanical transmission through infective plant sap. Use of healthy planting materials for planting, control of aphids and use of resistant cultivars are important measures to be followed for the management of the disease.

❍ Raspberry leaf mottle and raspberry leaf spot disease

Raspberry leaf mottle and raspberry leaf spot have been described as distinct diseases of this plant. Causal agents of these two diseases have not been identified and characterized by now. Causal agents of these two diseases are transmitted semi-persistently by the aphid-*Amphorophora idaei*. Both agents are also graft transmissible but not mechanically transmissible by infective plant sap inoculation.

VIRUS DISEASES OF BLACK RASPBERRY (*Rubus occidentalis*)

❍ Black raspberry necrosis virus disease

This disease was first recorded in British Columbia as the causal agent of severe tip necrosis in black raspberry seedlings. The disease ranks among the common virus diseases affecting raspberry and black raspberry crops.

Symptoms. (1) Characteristic symptoms of the disease are bending of shoot tips followed by its curling down and becoming brittle. (2) The leaves below the apex partially and gradually wilt. (3) In severe cases, there is necrosis in petioles, midribs and stem tips. (4) As a result of the disease, the affected plants usually wilt and die. (5) Leaves of surviving plants may exhibit mottling on leaves and produce smaller fruits alongwith thinner and shorter canes resulting in reduced yield.

The causal virus. *Black raspberry necrosis virus*. It usually occurs in low concentration in its natural raspberry and *Chenopodium quinoa* hosts. In partially purified preparation, few virus particles, measuring about 24 to 30 nm in diameter are observed. Thermal inactivation point in *Chenopodium quinoa* sap is 50 to 52°C, dilution end point is 1×10^{-1} to 1×10^{-2} and longevity of the virus *in vitro* is reported to be 6 to 24 days at 18°C.

Host range-Important natural hosts of the virus are raspberry, red raspberry and black raspberry. Other natural hosts are *Rubus fruitcosus, R. leucodermis* and *R. procerus*.

Disease cycle. Infected cultivated and wild natural host plants are important sources of virus preservation. The virus has been graft transmitted experimentally and aphid transmitted onto *Rubus albescens, R. henryi, R. laciniatus* and *R. molaccanus*. Herbaceous hosts infected mechanically by raspberry sap are *Chenopodium amaranticolor, C. quinoa, C. murale. Petunia hybrida, Spinacia oleracea* and *Gomphrena globosa*. Aphids-*Amphorophora agathonica* and its different other species usually transmit the virus in semi-persistent manner.

Management. Cultivars that resist aphid vector colonization represent the important control measure of the disease. Resistant cultivars should be grown for successful management of the disease.

❍ Black raspberry latent virus disease

The disease was first reported from Maryland and then is observed in severe form in different parts of Eastern U.S. The disease is known to be of minor importance.

Symptoms. Different black raspberry cultivars are natural hosts of the virus but with no visible symptoms. Diagnostic plants especially *Chenopodium quinoa, Nicotiana tabacum* and *Gomphrena globosa* exhibit characteristic symptoms of the disease. Local symptoms in *Chenopodium quinoa* may be observed as local vein chlorosis followed by necortic, chlorotic lesions and severe systemic infection symptoms. Local chlorotic, necrotic ring spots and line pattern in *Nicotiana tabucum* and in *Gomphrena globosa* small red rings and spots are observed.

The causal virus. *Black raspberry latent virus*. The virus particles are isometric in morphology, measuring about 26 nm in diameter. Particles usually sediment in three parts—top, middle and bottom. They have respective sedimentation coefficients of 81 S, 89S and 98 S at pH 7. Only particles of bottom appear to be infective. Thermal inactivation point in *Chenopodium quinoa* sap is 46 to 49°C, dilution end point is 1×10^{-4} and the longevity *in vitro* is few hours to 5 days at 20°C and 4°C respectively.

Disease cycle. The virus is seed borne in raspberry and seed and pollen borne in black raspberry. The virus is also transmitted into *Chenopodium quinoa* and other herbaceous hosts through the sap obtained from flower parts and young infected black raspberry plants. No vector has been reported.

Management. Healthy virus free seeds should be used and pollen transmission should be inhibited in order to avoid infection and spread of the disease.

BLACK RASPBERRY AS ALTERNATE HOST

Raspberry bushy dwarf virus, Rubus yellow net virus, Raspberry leaf mottle virus, Raspberry leaf curl virus, and *Tomato streak virus* are important viruses that occur in black raspberry, being their alternate host.

Black raspberry diseases assumed to be caused by the virus are Bramble yellow mosaic, Wineberry latent, Blackberry calico disease and ringspot disease. They have also been reported to cause diseases in blackberry.

VIRUS DISEASES OF GOOSEBERRY (*Ribes* species)

Till date no virus of significant importance has been reported in *Ribes* species (goosberry and currants) as its primary natural host. However, *Ribes* species are natural alternate hosts of many viruses. Some importnat viruses and diseases caused by them are summarized as under.

❍ Arabis mosaic virus disease

Arabis mosaic infected plants usually remain symptomless and the virus is detectable by mechanical inoculation of *Chenopodium quinoa. Chenopodium quinoa* serves as suitable indicator plant to be used in indexing and selection of healthy gooseberry stocks.

❍ Raspberry ringspot virus disease

Some cultivars remain symptomless and some other may exhibit symptoms like gooseberry deterioration, leaf mosaic and smaller malformed fruits. *Chenopodium quinoa* is as indicator plant and serological tests are used for detection and identification.

❍ Gooseberry vein banding disease

The disease was first reported in Czechoslovakia in 1987 and now is known to occur in different parts of the world especially Europe. No causal agent of this disease has yet been isolated and identified. The causal agent is known to be transmitted by chip budding and patch grafting but not by mechanical inoculation from infected plants. Aphids have been reported to transmit the causal agent in non-persistent manner.

❍ Gooseberry mosaic disease

The disease was first described in Poland during 1980. Infected plants exhibit blighting of leaves, yellow mosaic and yellowing of veins as its characteristic symptoms of the disease. The causal agent has not been reported and identified. The causal agent is gaft transmitted experimentally into other gooseberry and currants cultivars.

VIRUS DISEASES OF BLACK CURRANT (*Ribes* species)

❍ Aphid borne cucumber mosaic virus disease

Cucumber mosaic virus infected plants are observed to be stunted, resulting in reduction in yield. Scattered discoloration of leaves and appearance of pale chlorotic spots on the leaves along the midribs are the characteristic symptoms of the disease. The virus is both sap and graft transmissible from infected plants to the other herbaceous hosts and occasionally to black currant seedlings.

NEMATODE-BORNE VIURS DISEASES

Black currant serves as natural host of several nematode-borne viruses including *Raspberry ringspot virus*, *Strawberry latent ringspot virus*, *Tomato ringspot virus* and *Tomato black ring virus*. Due to limited occurrence and spread of these viruses, diseases so caused by these viruses have no great economic impact in black currant production.

BLACK CURRANT DISEASES ASSUMED TO BE CAUSED BY VIRUSES

Several diseases have been reported in black currant, but their causal agents have not been identified so far. Such diseases are black currant vein clearing disease, vein net disease, infectious variegation disease, reversion disease and yellows disease. These diseases are of minor importance.

VIRUS DISEASES OF RED CURRANT (*Ribes* species)

Red currant is alternate host for several viruses. Viruses known to be common in occurrence are Aphid-borne *Cucumber mosaic virus*, *Arabis mosaic virus*, *Raspberry ringspot virus*, *Strawberry latent ringspot virus* and *Tomato ringspot virus*.

Arabis mosaiv virus is widespread in several natural hosts including gooseberry, black currant and red currant but rare in occurrence in black currant.

Specific strain of *Raspberry ringspot virus* causes characteristic symptoms of spoon leaf and ringspot in leaves.

Strawberry latent ringspot virus is infective in red currant but does not occur naturally. Infected plants usually remain symptomless but occasionally display bright yellow symptoms.

Tobacco rattle virus has been isolated only from scattered and individual red currant bushes and is of minor importance.

Tomato ringspot virus is known to infect the currant plants but seldom causes considerable reduction in yield.

Interveinal white mosaic virus is experimentally graft transmissible and occurs in red currant occasionally.

Alfalfa mosaic virus is known to occur in red currant and usually causes necrotic local lesions in *Chenopodium quinoa*.

Besides these diseases, red currant is infected by some other diseases of unknown etiology. Such diseases include vein banding disease and yellow leafspot disease. Causal agents of these two diseases have not yet been identified and studied.

VIRUS DISEASES OF BLUEBERRY (*Vaccinium* species)

❍ Bluebery leaf mottle virus disease

The virus was first reported from Michigan, U.S.A. in 1977 and later was observed in the Jersey in severe form. A virus isolated from *Vitis labrusca* Concord grapevine in New York was determined to be closely related serologically with *Blueberry leaf mottle virus.*

Symptoms. (1) The virus causes leaf mottle and stunting of blueberry plants and such bushes become unproductive and die in few years. (2) Leaf mottle, leaf strap and curling are the characteristic symptoms of the disease. (3) Die back in older stems and stunting of new growth from crowns in bushes cease production in long run. (4) Suitable indicator plants are *Chenopodium quinoa* (chlorotic lesions, mottling and apical death), *C. amaranticolor* (systemic mottling) and *Niccotiana clevelandii* (pinpoint local lesions in inoculated leaves).

The causal virus. *Blueberry leaf mottle virus.* It is isometric in morphology, measuring about 28 nm in diameter. Sediments consist of three kinds of particles settled at top (T), middle (M) and bottom (B). These particle groups have sedimentation coefficients of 53 S, 120 S and 128 S respectively. The viral genome consists of two single stranded RNAs of 2150 kDa (component M) and 2350 kDa (component B). Protein subunits are of 54 kDa. Thermal inactivation point of the virus is 65°C, dilution end point is 1×10^{-4} and longevity *in vitro* is 5 to 14 days at 20°C and 4°C respectively. Blueberry and grapevine are natural hosts of the virus.

Disease cycle. Virus infected blueberry bushes represent permanent sources of infection. The virus is transmissible through pollen and sap inoculation.

Management. Only virus free planting materials should be used for establishment of plantation and infected plants should be rogued out immediately on detection.

❍ Blueberry red ringspot caulimovirus disease

The virus was first reported from U.S. and is now observed in New Jersey in severe form inciting considerable damage to blueberry.

Symptoms. (1) In high bush blueberry, the virus causes red spots and rings in older leaves especially in mid and late summer. (2) Red spots and rings also occur in one-year old and in other older canes. (3) Infected fruits are smaller and yield of the produce is reduced significantly. (4) Detection of the virus is done by early grafting, prior to bud break into highly susceptible cultivars.

The causal virus. *Blucberry red ringspot caulimovirus.* The virus is isometric in morphology, measuring about 42 to 46 nm in diameter. Two components are observed in the sediments. Virus particles consist of DNA and a 44 kDa protein. A faint protein band of 101 kDa has also been observed sometimes by some workers. The virus sample is moderately immunogenic.

Disease cycle. The virus perpetuates in infected plants and is suspected to be spread through aphids and mealy bugs. Spread through these vectors has not been confirmed.

Management. The use of virus free healthy planting materials and elimination of diseased plants immediately on detection are the important measures for the management of the disease.

❍ Blueberry shoestring virus disease

The disease is well known to occur in different countries causing considerable loss because the extent of damage is directly correlated with the number of diseased plants.

Symptoms. (1) Leaves in infected plants become strap-like and are malformed into curled and crescent shaped. (2) Red vein banding and red streaks along midribs and occasionally oak-leaf patterns may be observed on leaves of the infected plants. (3) Elongated red streaks may occur on 1-year old or in other older canes and on petals. (4) Reddish-purple coloration may also develop on the surface of immature fruits.

The causal virus. *Blueberry shoestring virus*. The virus is isometric in morphology, measuring about 27 nm in diameter with sedimentation coefficient of 120 S. It contains single stranded RNA of 1450 kDa and protein subunits of 30 kDa. It is strongly immunogenic in serological reactions.

Disease cycle. High bush blueberry (*Vaccinium corymbosum*) and low bush blueberry (*Vaccinium angustifolium*) are the natural hosts of the virus. It is transmitted by the some species of aphid and also transmitted mechanically into blueberry seedlings and young vegetatively propaged woody cuttings but not into herbaceous plants. The virus has also been transmitted experimentally by infected to susceptible goosberry by chip budding and whip grafting.

Management. (1) Use virus free healthy planting materials (2) Roguing of diseased plants from the plantation (3) Chemical control of vectors and (4) Replanting with immune bushes are useful for the management of the disease.

BLUEBERRY AS ALTERNATE HOST

❍ *Tomato ringspot virus*

Characteristic chlorotic spots and malformation of leaves in blueberry may be observed. Besides, characteristic circular and dark necrotic spots are also formed on the canes, twigs and branches.

❍ *Peach rosette mosaic virus*

Symptoms of infection have been observed in blueberry. However, these symptoms are not diagnostic. For diagnosis and detection of the virus indicator plants—*Chenopodium amarnticolor* and *C. quinoa* are used and then tested serologically to establish the presence of the virus.

❍ *Tobacco ringspot virus*

The virus displays necrotic ringspot symptoms in numerous host plants including blueberry. The virus is trnasmitted by infected plant sap through mechanical inoculation into herbaceous hosts and then tested serologically for confirmation.

BLUEBERRY DISEASES ASSUMED TO BE CAUSED BY VIRUSES

Some diseases such as blueberry mosaic disease and cranberry ringspot disease, both with unknown causal agents and etiology, have been observed in blueberry.

In **blueberry mosaic disease,** characteristic symptoms on leaves are mosaic pattern, yellow or yellow-green and mild to severe mottle. Vector for the transmission is not known. The causal agent is graft transmitted but is not transmissible mechanically by infective plant sap.

In **cranberry ringspot disease,** the unknown causal agent displays severe leaf and fruit symptoms. Fruits usually become necrotic at the end of blossom in this disease.

18

VIRUS DISEASES OF SPICES

Introduction; Diseases of black pepper—little leaf and mosaic; Ginger-mosaic; Cardamom—mosaic/Katte ; Chirkey disease of large cardamom; Diseases of chilli-leaf curl and mosaic ; Little leaf of clove.

Betel vine is known to be native of Malaysia and is cultivated widely in India. Different states in our country including Orissa, West Bengal, Tamil Nadu, Maharashtra, Kerala, Andhra Pradesh, Madhya Pradesh, Bihar, Karnataka, Assam and Meghalaya are well known for its production. However, no any important virus disease in betel vine has been reported. Several virus diseases have been reported to cause different diseases on other spices.

VIRUS DISEASES OF BLACK PEPPER
(*Piper nigrum*)

Black pepper is one of the most ancient spice crops. In our country it has probably originated from the hills of south-western regions. The plants are climbing perennial shrubs and seeds are used for different purposes. Seeds are used as an important component of culinary seasoning and are an essential ingredient in numerous domestic or commercial food stuff preparations. It has its important medicinal value in Indian medicine too.

❍ Little leaf of black pepper

The disease was reported from Sri Lanka and is assumed to be caused by the phytoplasma. The characteristic symptoms of the disease are chlorosis of leaves, shortening of internodes, proliferation of branches alongwith greening and enlargemnt of floral bracts. Number of flowers per spike and weight of the berry are reduced. Leaf size may also be reduced and malformed. Infected seeds usually germinate poorly.

❍ Mosaic disease of black pepper

The disease was first reported from Sao Paulo State of Brazil in 1972. Mosaic symptoms with chlorotic irregular yellowish areas are the characteristic symptoms of the disease. Leaves may be sunken with reduction in seed formation. Sap inoculation in different indicator plants usually produces symptoms resembling to *Cucumber mosaic virus*.

VIRUS DISEASES OF GINGER
(*Zingiber officinale* Rosc.)

The ginger is cultivated throughout in our country as perennial and rhizomatous spice crop. It is of great medicinal value especially used in respiratory and digestive diseases. Besides these, it is also used for culinary purposes and in the manufacture of different food products and soft drinks. Aroma of ginger is pleasant and spicy.

❍ Mosaic disease of ginger

Ganguly and Raychaudhary (1971) reported that *Wheat streak mosaic virus* usually occurs in ginger and causes considerable damage to the quality and yield of the ginger.

Symptoms. (1) The characteristic symptoms of the disease usually appear in younger leaves of the infected plants. (2) Appearance of chlorotic flecks which later change to spindle-shaped chlorotic streaks of discontinuous nature are usually observed. Chlorotic streaks seem running parallel to each other from midrib to the margins. (3) Several such streaks may coalesce forming larger yellowish stripes. (4) In severe cases, these stripes together with intervening green areas form a mosaic pattern. (5) Sometimes large patches of dark green and light green areas lie parallel to each other. (6) Commonly, small chlorotic specks may be observed which are distributed irregularly in between the streaks.

Causal virus. *Wheat streak mosaic virus* is thought to be the causal agent of the disease. The virus is preserved in infected rhizomes.

As high as 76.11% mosaic disease incidence has been reported in Pune variety of ginger.

DISEASES OF TRUE CARDAMOM
(*Elettaria cardamomum* Maton)

True cardamom also called lesser cardamom of commerce is popularly known as the queen of spices. It is one of the most important and costly spices in the world. India, Sri Lanka, Guatemala and Thailand are major cardamom producers of the world.

❍ Mosaic, marble or katte disease

The disease commonly known as Marble in Annamalais and Katte in North Kanara.

It is the most devastating disease in South India. It is prevalent in all the cardamom growing tracts, causing an extensive damage and crop yield loss. The disease is believed to be present for a very long time and the reference is available in ancient literature in our country.

Symptoms. (1) Cardamom plants may be infected at any stage of the growth. (2) The symptoms are first observed in young leaves, which show a general chlorosis of the entire blade with slender, interrupted, parallel streaks of pale green tissues running along the veins from midrib to the margin. (3) With the advancement of the disease, streaks of green tissue become evenly distributed exhibiting the characteristic mosaic symptoms. (4) As a result of the characteristic symptoms, the disease plants can be easily recognized even from some distance owing to their pale appearance. (5) No symptoms are observed in flowers. Pseudo-stems become stunted and leaves are reduced in size. (6) The rhizomes gradually shrivel and the entire clump dies eventually. (7) Infection in the seedling stage may result in the failure of diseased plant to bear flowers and fruits. (8) They may die before the time of bearing flowers and fruits.

The causal virus. *Cardamom mosaic virus* is the causal agent of the disease.

Transmission. It was recorded that virus transmission is done by banana aphid-*Pentalonia nigronervosa*. The vector also transmits the bunchy top virus in banana. The disease is not known to be transmitted by seed but was transmitted through infected clones. Seeds obtained from infected plants have been observed with very poor germination. By conventional sap inoculation method, it has not been possible to transmit the virus. Besides being transmitted through banana aphid, other aphid species such as *Aphis nerii, Macrosiphum sonchi,* and *Aphis gossypii* were also found to be present in the field.

Management. Use of healthy seed and management of the insect vectors should be done. Growing of resistant cultivars is the most suitable measure for the management of the disease.

❍ Chirkey disease of large cardamom

The large cardamom is a rhizomatic herb, usually 60 to 90 cm. in height and is indigenous to foot hills of Nepal. It is commonly grown in West Bengal, Sikkim and Assam hills of the Himalayas and other mountain ranges in the moist and shady sides of mountain streams and along hill slopes usually at an height of 765 to 1675 meters above sea level.

Symptoms. (1) The disease is characterized by mosaic streaks on the leaves. (2) These streaks usually coalesce and become brown in colour. (3) Leaves may ultimately dry and wither presumably due to secondary infection in later stages. (4) As a result of the disease, reduction in number of flowers in each inflorescence may be observed.

The causal virus. The virus is sap transmissible, It is also known to be transmitted through aphid vector especially *Rhopalosiphum maidis* and *Brachycaudus helichrysi*. The virus is transmitted non-persistently from cardamom to cardamom and wheat. The larger cardamom varieties such as Rammok, Ramsai, Kati, Hario Charumpha, the wild cardamom (*Amomum aromaticum*), arrowroot (*Curcuma angustifolia*), *Acorus calamus* and a number of varieties of ginger have been found to be attacked by the disease.

Management. (1) Disease free seedlings should be raised from true seeds. (2) Roguing of infected clumps should be carried out for a number of years and (3) Resistant varieties should be grown. Varieties like Swaney and Kopringey have been found to be resistant against the disease.

VIRUS DISEASES OF CHILLI (*Capsicum* species)

Chilli plants are small herbs, is native of tropical America. It is cultivated throughout the tropics including different parts of our country. The pungent fruits with thin and comparatively smooth pericarps are used as condiments in tropical countries for the preparation of hot sauces. The mildly pungent and non-pungent fruits are used in green condition for flavouring various food dishes and for making pickles. Dried red chilies are particularly used as condiment.

A large number of virus diseases are responsible for crop loss in chilli. Among the virus diseases, leaf curl and mosaic are two most important diseases known to cause considerable loss to the crop in our country.

❍ Chilli leaf curl virus disease

Leaf curl is the most destructive disease of chilli and it causes severe loss in yield every year in infected crop.

Symptoms. (1) The disease is characterized by the stunting of the plants with rolling and crinkling of leaves of the affected plants. (2) The newly formed leaves exhibit chlorosis and old curled leaves become leathery and brittle. (3) Dwarfing of the plants is usually due to shortening of the internodes. (4) Only few fruits are set and such fruits remain smaller and malformed.

The causal virus. *Chilli leaf curl virus.* The virus is successfully transmitted by wedge grafting and the whitefly-*Bemisia tabaci* also transmits the virus to *Capsicum* species and many other host plants. It has also been reported that the disease is also transmitted by the thrips- *Scirtothrips dorsalis* Hod. and mites-*Polyphagotars onemus latus*.

Host range. The virus has a wide host range. Transmission studies have showed that white flies can transmit the virus successfully to many hosts like *Nicotiana tabacum, N. glutinosa, Lycopersicum* species, *Petunia hybrida, Capsicum* species, and *Crotalaria juncea*.

Management. The crop must be protected from seedling to fruiting stage and diseased plants should be removed from the field on detection so as avoid spread of the disease. Judicious use of suitable insecticide is also recommended.

❍ Chilli mosaic virus disease

The disease is of great economic importance and is caused by the complex of viruses. As much as 90% loss in yield has been reported due to this disease.

Symptoms. (1) Characteristic symptoms in the field and in artificially inoculated plants are different types of abnormalities. (2) These include marked stunting in plants and poor development of the root system. (3) The flower buds abscise before attaining the full size and anthers do not contain pollen. (4) It leads to sterility as observed in inoculated plants under experiment. (5) Mosaic mottling, distortion and abnormal shape of leaves are the most common symptoms seen frequently in this disease. (6) Slight curling, marginal rolling and stunting of leaves are also observed sometimes. (7) Delayed embryo-sac development in mosaic infected chilli plants have also been observed in most cases.

The causal virus. The disease is caused by a number of viruses such as *Tobacco mosaic virus, Cucumber mosaic virus, Potato virus Y* and *Potato virus X.*

Transmission. The viruses are not transmitted by the seed and are usually transmitted by sap and by aphids like *Aphis gossypii, A. evonymi* and *Myzus persicae* in non-persistent manner.

Host range. In addition to chilli, the virus has been reported from a number of other hosts like *Nicotiana tabacum, N. glutinosa, Solanum nigrum, Petunia hybrida, Cucumis sativus, C. melo, C. utilissimus* and *Carthamus tinctorius* etc.

Management. The vector population should be kept under check by spraying suitable insecticides at regular intervals. Resistant/tolerant cultivars should be grown for the protection of the disease. Spraying of insecticide should not be done before a month of materity.

VIRUS DISEASES OF CLOVE
(*Syzygium aromaticum* (L) Merril et Perry)

The clove of commerce is the air dried, unopened flower bud. It is obtained from a handsome, medium sized, evergreen plant having straight stem tree growing to a height of 10 to 12.8 meters.

❍ Little leaf of clove

This disease, probably of Phytoplasma origin, was found in 1955- 56 affecting an old tree in Kanyakumari district of Tamil Nadu.

Symptoms. (1) The affected trees exhibited complete suppression of all tree and vegetative characters. (2) The trunk was observed to have numerous protuberances. (3) The branches of the affected trees grow at acute angle with the trunk giving the tree a cone-shaped appearance. (4) The leaves were reduced in size from the base to the apex of a shoot. Internodes were shortened and primary and secondary branches were also arranged closer and became shorter towards periphery. (5) The disease was noticed on the seedlings in the nursery also. (6) Shortening of the internodes and clustering of small and crinkled leaves were also noticed. (7) Growth of the seedlings was found to be arrested and fresh leaves did not emerge at all.

Causal agent. Phytoplasma as evident by its nature. The disease could not be transmitted either by sap inoculation or by grafting.

Management. Consequent sprayings of 200 ppm Tetracycline five times at biweekly intervals, have been found effective. As a result, normal leaves from the infected plants with normal elongated internodes were produced. Recovery of the disease after spraying with Tetracycline indicated the possibility for Phytoplasma as causal agent.

19

VIRUS DISEASES OF MUSHROOMS AND ORNAMENTAL PLANTS

Virus diseases of mushrooms, Types of viruses, Economic importance of viral diseases of mushrooms, Management of virus diseases of edible mushroms. Introduction of ornamental plants, Virus diseases of roses-mosaic disease; Tulip mosaic and Tulip necrosis; Dahlia mosaic, dahlia ring spot and dahlia stunting virus disease; Partial list of some important virus diseases of ornamental plants.

Mushroom is an indoor crop and is usually grown in rooms with some sort of control for maintenance of right environmental conditions. Cultivation of white bottom mushroom (*Agaricus bisporus*) was earlier confined to cooler regions chiefly because of availability of apppropriate environmental conditions for raising the crops. As early as 1948, a virus disease described by different names including 'La France disease' and 'Die-back' disease was first reported in United States. In 1950, much loss from similar disease was observed in Britain. This disease was much destructive in nature. In this disease it was observed that the causal virus could be transmitted by hyphal anastomosis. On examination, three types of particles associated with the diseases were observed. Disorder of this type was not reported in the Netherlands until 1964. Later on during 1966, disease occurred in severe form and significant yield loss was reported. In Australia, mushroom diseases of viral nature were observed probably dated back to the early days of mushroom growing in open ridges. In India also, spherical virus particles, measuring about 25-35 nm in size were reported in 1984.

VIRUSES AND VIRUS LIKE PARTICLES

Virus and virus like particles were commonly observed in *Agaricus bisporus* and few reports are available in *Pleurotus* species and *Lentinus edodes*. Club shaped virus particles which were 120-170 nm in length with a spherical body of about 40-50 nm and a cylindrical tail of 20-30 nm in diameter were reported in 1973. There have been only two other reports of such club shaped virus particles, one reported from Germany and other from South Africa. Different shapes and sizes of the viruses and virus like particles reported from different parts of the world may be summarized as under :

Mushroom & name of diseases	**Shape of particles**	**Size of particles**	**Name of countries reported**
1	**2**	**3**	**4**
Agaricus bisporus			
La France disease	Spherical	25 nm	Australia, England.
Watery stripe		29 nm	Holland, America.
Die back		35 nm	France.
Mushroom diseases	Spherical	40-45 nm	Germany and India.
	Bacilliform	18 × 50 nm	United Kingdom.
	Club-shaped	60-70 nm in diameter, 120-170 nm long with spherical body of 40-50 nm and a cylindrical tail of 120 nm in diameter.	France, West Germany and South Africa.
	Rods of varying length	19 × 9-90, 19 × 34 nm, 20 × 130 nm	Poland, Germany and China.
Pleurotus species			
Pleurotus colombinus	Spherical	26 ± 2 nm	France
P. ostreatus	—	—	—
P. pulmonarius	Spherical	24 nm	China
P. sapidus			
P. florida	Flexuous rods	40-600 nm long —	China —
Volvariella volvacea	Spherical	35 nm	China

1	2	3	4
Lentinus edodes	Spherical	29 nm	China, Japan.
	Spherical	23 nm	China, Japan.
	Spherical	36 nm	China, Japan.
	Spherical	45 nm	China, Japan.
	Spherical	30 nm	China, Japan.
	Stiff of flexuous rods	17 × 200 × 1200 nm	China
	Stiff of flexuous rods	15 × 700–900 nm	China
	Stiff of flexuous rods	18 × 1500 nm	Japan.
	Stiff of flexuous rods	15 × 16 × 200–300 nm	Japan.

CHARACTERISTIC SYMPTOMS

Characteristic symptoms of different virus diseases of mushrooms may be described as below :

* Mycelium does not develop or hardly develop in casing layer or may disapper after normal spread. Mushrooms appear only in dense clusters.
* Mycelium remains isolated from diseased sporophores in agar media and show slow and degenerated growth.
* Delayed appearance of the pinheads of the first flush or formation of fruiting primordia below the surface of casing layer can be an important indication of viral diseases.
* Symptoms on sporophores are highly variable and following abnormalities may be observed together or separately :
    (*a*) Off white colouration of the cap and early maturity.
    (*b*) Slow development of pin heads and dwarfing.
    (*c*) Elongated and slightly bent stipes or thin stipes.
    (*d*) Mushrooms are loosely attached to the substrate and at the slightest tough, they are pushed over.
    (*e*) Watery stipes and streaking in the stipes are usually observed.
    (*f*) Stipes are spongy and they quickly turn brown on wetting.
    (*g*) Thickened and barrel-shaped stipes may be observed.
    (*h*) Brown and slimy caps may be observed owing to a secondary bacterial rot
    (*i*) Abnormal or absent veils and hard gills may also be diagnostic symptoms of the viral diseases.
    (*j*) A specific musty smell in diseased mushroom may also be observed.

DISEASE SPREAD

Virus diseases in mushroom usually spread through (1) virus infected mushroom spores and (2) virus infected mycelium.

The spread of viruses through infected spores or mycelium can spread in many ways such as (1) through ventilation of air (2) through phorid and sciarid flies (3) through dirty containers (4) by means of transport which have not been disinfected (5) poor or no disinfection of wooden items, floor and or side planks after harvesting and (6) due to dirty clothings, smoking and footwear etc. Infected spores on germination produce mycelium which by anastomosis transmit the virus to healthy spawn and mycelium. Virus spread through mites has also been reported.

DIFFICULTIES IN DETECTION OF VIRUSES FROM MUSHROOM

Diagnosis of virus infection in mushroom is difficult because of the following reasons :

* Symptoms produced by viruses usually seem to be similar like symptoms produced by other biotic and abiotic agents.
* Elongation of stipes usually observed as a result of the virus infection may also be caused due to the presence of excess carbon-di-oxide.
* Losses in yield and appearance of bare patches may be induced by some other factors like poor compost and by mites.
* Watery stipes may also be due to the higher moisture content of the substrate.

DETECTION OF VIRUSES

Presence of viruses associated with the mushroom can be detected by the following methods :

(*a*) Symptoms in the bed.

(*b*) Growth characters in sterile cultures.

(*c*) Electron microscopy-ultra thin sectioning, dip method as well as purified preparations.

(*d*) Serological specific electron microscopy (SSEM).

(*e*) Polyacrylamide gel electrophoresis of viral dsRNA (PAGE), and

(*f*) Enzyme-linked immunosorbent assay (ELISA).

MANAGEMENT OF VIRUS DISEASES

❍ Preventive measures

1. Steam the compost for 1 hour at a temperature of 70°C. At emptying take away the compost quickly.
2. Spray the wood with 2% sodium pentachlorophenate to which 0.5 to 1.0% sodium carbonate has been added.
3. Disinfect doors, little holes in the floors, shutters, racks, floors and walls with formaldehyde but not with sodium pentachlorophenate. Also disinfect the manure yard and adjacent patches of ground with formaldehyde.
4. Use fan for exclusion of air and use spore filters during growing time.
5. After spawning, use pesticide against flies and then cover the compost with

paper. Always keep the paper moist and moisten the paper before removing it carefully.

6. Remove cuttings quickly and keep entire farm and its surroundings very clean. In the working corridor formaldehyde should be sprayed. Machines, refrigerators and other such items should also be sprayed with formaldehyde solution for disinfection.
7. At first contamination, the disease should be controlled by steaming out the concerned room immediately.

❍ Curative measures

1. Steam the compost for 1 hour at a temperature of 70°C. At emptying, take away the compost quickly.
2. Immerse the wood with 4% sodium pentachlorophenate solution to which 0.5 to 1.0% sodium carbonate has been added.
3. Disinfect doors, little holes in the floors, shutters, racks, floors and walls with formaldehyde but not with sodium pentachlorophenate. Also disinfect the manure yard and adjacent patches of ground with formaldehyde.
4. Use fan for exclusion of air and use spore filters during growing time.
5. Pick the mushroom when still closed.
6. Keep each room as a separate entity with separate clothes, shoes, steps, buckets, picking knives, and fans etc. Kill off diseased patches with salt and cover with plastic. First pick from healthy parts then from the diseased patches. Wash hands frequently with soap.
7. Allow rare visitors in the diseased rooms and keep the door towards the working corridors closed.

VIRUS DISEASES OF ORNAMENTAL PLANTS

Ornamental plants are also known to be infected by plant viruses. Some important diseases of ornamentals may be summarized as under :

VIRUS DISEASES OF ROSES

❍ Rose wilt and die back

This disease has been described to be popular in Australia. There seems to be two important types of virus diseases affecting the rose. One of these is known as 'rose wilt' and 'dieback' while the other is an infectious chlorosis or mosaic disease.

Symptoms. (1) In rose wilt, the characteristic symptoms include peculiar recurved appearance of the leaves of the young shoots. (2) The leaflets of infected plants may sometimes seem to be crowded together on the petioles and are very brittle. (3) Defoliation begins at the tip of the stems of affected plants. (4) The leaves sometimes turn pale green to brownish before dropping. (5) About a day later, the tips of the young stems begin to discolour and dieback for a distance of the 1 or 2 inches may take place. (6) The rest of the young stem develops a characteristic translucent, yellowish green appearance, turning the base brownish black within few hours. (7) Gradually the whole stem becomes discoloured and die back. In many cases, the plants send up one or more water-shoots after the stems have dried, but they soon become diseased.

Transmission. The virus has been shown to be filterable through a Seitz filter and is transmissible by niddle inoculation.

❍ Mosaic disease of rose

The disease is known to be prevalent in U.S.A. and Europe. Mosaic is another important disease, observed usually in some roses.

Symptoms. (1) Infected plants are dwarfed and such dwarfing is observed in all parts of the plant. (2) Buds of infected plants may be imperfect on short stems and bleached. (3) The normal colour of the flowers in certain varieties has been observed to be affected. (4) The leaves are variously distorted with midribs frequently bent and twisted. (5) The leaflets show distinct chlorotic areas especially along the midribs. It causes the leaflets to pucker and ruffle. (6) In most cases, vein clearing may be pronounced. (7) Usually all the leaflets of a leaf may show symptoms but in many cases some leaflets may show symptoms and some other may remain normal apparently. (8) When the chlorosis is confined to one side of the leaves, distortion may occur due to unequal growth of the two halves. (9) Symptoms vary considerably according to the variety ranging from minute speckling and occasional distortion. (10) In many species numerous minute chlorotic areas may be observed to be distributed over the entire leaflets or concentrated towards the tip or periphery of the leaflets with some of the chlorotic specks apparently interveinal.

Transmission. The virus causing this mosaic appear to be transmissible only by grafting. The insect vector transmission is not known.

DISEASE OF TULIP

❍ Tulip mosaic and tulip necrosis

The well known phenomenon of breaking in the garden tulip, whereby the flower becomes variegated, is due to a virus causing mosaic type symptoms. It is one of the few cases of a plant virus improving a plant from the aesthetic and commercial point of view, as the breaking of colour produces some attractive variegation. There are two types of colour breaking, the self (= red) and the clear (= white). The 'self' break consists of irregular areas of concentrated pigment on the original self ground. The 'clear' break consists of irregular areas of concentrated pigment and of self colour on a ground devoid of anthocyanin. The yellow and white ground colour depends upon the presence and absence of the yellow plastids in the mesophyll cells. The leaves of the affected tulip may also show mottling and irregular striping. The insect vectors were observed to be *Myzus persicae* Sulz., *Macrosiphum gei* Theob, and *Myzus pelargonii* Kalt. Theory has been advanced that tulip breaking is due to the interaction of two viruses. One of these viruses carries a colour adding factor and produces no visible effect on the leaves. The other virus removes flower colour and strongly stripes the leaves. It was also observed that certain varieties when 'broken' trend to segregate into plants or parts of the plants (clumps) bearing strongly darkened flowers. By encouraging this segregation through selection and by using inoculum prepared from the parts of flowers where the colour was removed and darkened respectively. It has been possible to secure the viruses in almost pure conditions. The colour adding virus has little effect on plant growth and may be of practical use in producing new varieties. The colour adding virus is so powerful in its action that it is possible to turn a white tulip to bright red. Colour removing virus is extremely virulent and reduces plant growth to a third of the normal plant.

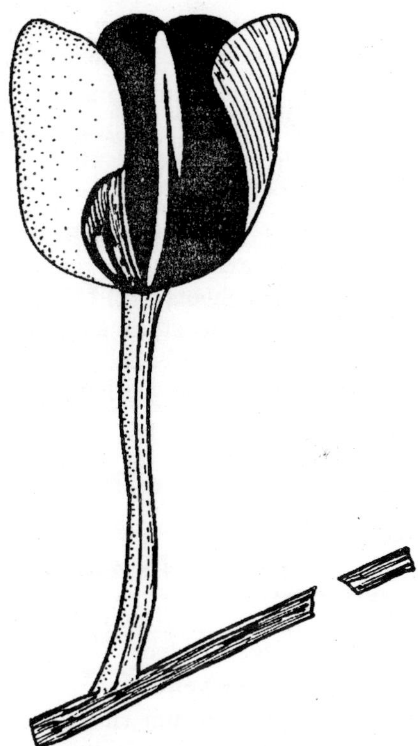

Fig. 19.1. Showing breaking in tulip

DISEASES OF DAHLIA

❍ Dahlia mosaic disease

Dahlia mosaic is prevalent in New York, New Jersey and probably throughout U.S.A. because of the suitable climatic conditions for the development of the disease. The dahlia is subjected to two or more viruses of mosaic types. Dahlia mosaic was first described in Germany.

Symptoms. (1) In this disease, the young leaves show an irregular pale dis-colouration especially near the main and lateral veins which gradually develops into tint symptoms. (2) Affected leaves are observed to be smaller and narrower than the normal. (3) Such leaves are found deformed and in flowers of some varieties colour change may be observed. (4) The most characteristic symptoms of the disease are the banding of the veins. (5) Some varieties show no appreciable dwarfing or distortion when affected with this virus.

Transmission. The virus was observed to be not sap transmissible and not transmitted by the aphid-*Myzus persicae*. However, American dahlia has been found to be transmitted by this aphid. Intracellular inclusion bodies have been found associated with mosaic of dahlia.

❍ Dahlia ring spot disease

Dahlia ring spot has been observed in many countries.

Symptoms. The disease is characterized by the zigzag or ring like markings in shades of green. The disease is not much distinct from mosaic.

Disease perpetuation. The viruses affecting the dahlia are carried with the tubers and so perpetuated year after year.

❍ Dahlia stunt virus disease

The so called dahlia stunting is also thought to be infected by the virus.

Symptoms. (1) Diseased plants are found to remain stunted from the beginning and often they form excessive number of shoots. (2) Leaves in infected plants are curled and numerous small cracks appear in the stem and also in the skin of the tubers whose development is much retarded. (3) Infected plants seldom produce flowers. (4) Presence of intracellular inclusions is strong evidence for being the causal agent to be a virus.

Table 19.1 Showing some other viruses of minor importance reported to occur in different ornamental plant species

S.No.	Name of the hosts	Virus/disease reported
1	Antirrhinum	Mosaic virus
2	Aster	Aster yellows
3	Delphinium	Delphinium ring spot, and Beet curly top *Cucumber mosaic virus*
4	Geranium or Pelargonium	Leaf curl, Curly top, Mosaic, Spotted wilt
5	Gladioulus	Ring spot, Mosaic
6	Lily	*Lily rosette virus*/rosette, *Tobacco ring spot virus*/Ring spot
7	Petunia	Aster yellows, Curly top virus disease
8	Phlox	Aster yellows
9	Sun flower	Mosaic, Aster yellows, Necrosis
10	Tulip	Tulip braking, Mosaic, Necrosis
11	Zinnia	Leaf curl

20

VIRUS DISEASES OF MEDICINAL PLANTS

✉ ***Belladonna diseases- belladonna mosaic; Datura diseases Datura distortion mosaic, datura mosaic disease and datura diseases of ,minor importance; Digitalis diseases-digitalis chlorotic mottle and digitalis diseases of minor importance; Hyoscymus diseases-henbane mosaic, yellow mosaic mottling disease and green mosaic; Opium poppy diseases - bean yellow mosaic disease, turnip mosaic disease and diseases of minor importance; Periwinkle diseases - periwinkle mosaic disease, periwinkle chlorotic stunt disease , cucumber mosaic disease, tomato spotted wilt virus disease and periwinkle phyllody; Plantago diseases; Rauvolfia diseases- rauvolfia mosaic disease, rauvolfia phyllody, rauvolfia yellow vein mosaic, rauvolfia ring spot and rauvolfia green mosaic; Withania diseases-withania leaf curl and withania witches' broom.***

BELLADONNA (*Atropa belladona* L.)DISEASES

❍ Belladonna mosaic

Symptoms- This disease was first described by Smith (1943) and is characterized by the appearance of characteristic mosaic pattern on the leaves of affected plants. Leaves and roots of belladonna contain pharmaceutically important alkaloids known as 1-hyoscyamine, atropine and hyoscine. As a result of the disease, qualities of these ingredients are affected.

Causal virus - *Belladonna mosaic virus.* The virus was reported to be inactivated at temperatures between 75 and 80°C. Sap extracted from infected plants may remain active for 6-11 days.

Transmission- The virus is sap transmissible to tobacco and other solanaceous plants. Belladonna acts as symptomless carrier of Hyoscyamus virus.

❍ Belladonna mottle

Belladonna mottle was first reported from Europe and then from Germany in 1968. The virus was also isolated from other plants in North America.

Symptoms-Characteristically, the virus causes mild mottling on leaves and sometimes deformation on other parts of belladonna. Naturally infected plants are often found. Infected plants may exhibit symptoms like severe mosaic, mottling and vein banding.

Causal virus- *Belladonna mottle virus.* Belladonna mosaic virus is a RNA group virus with isometric particles and angular polygonal outlines, measuring about 2 nm in size. When centrifuged, particles sediments as two components. The virus is strongly immunogenic. Serological relationship between the strains seems very close. Serological behaviour shows that this virus belongs to the *Turnip yellow mosaic virus.* Thermal inactivation point of the virus is 80°C and longevity *in vitro* varies from 5 days to 3 weeks depending on isolates. The virus is stable and appears similar to *Turnip yellow mosaic virus* in morphology.

Transmission- When tested by sap inoculation, most of the solanaceous plants were infected with variable symptom expression.

DATURA (*Datura* species) DISEASES

Different species of like *Datura innoxia* Mill, *Datura stramonium* L. and *Datura metel* L. are pharmaceutically important. Datura species are annual bushy herbs and are used both as crude as well as a sourse of tropane alkaloids.The seeds are used as a sourse of hyoscine.

❍ Datura distortion mosaic

Symptoms- Although most of the species are affected; however, characteristic severe mosaic with puckering and leaf distortion are usually observed on *Datura stramonium.* Yellowing of veins followed by slight inward rolling and distortion of leaves may also be observed. Symptoms of systemic mottling, leaf distortion and vein banding are commonly observed on *Datura stramonium.*

Causal virus- The disease was reported to be caused by a strain of *Cucumber mosaic virus* on *Datura innoxia.* This virus was observed to be flexuous particles and as single stranded RNA. However, a virus called as '*Datura yellow vein virus*' was isolated from *Datura stramonium* with symptoms of vein yellowing, leaf distortion and reduced leaf size. This virus was described as a new rhabdovirus.

Transmission- *Datura yellow vein virus* has been reported to be graft transmissible to several solanaceous hosts. However, it was not transmitted by mechanical inoculation and by insect vectors.

❍ Datura mosaic diseases

A number of mosaic diseases have been reported in different species of *Datura*. Symptoms appear as dark and light green patches on the leaves of the affected plants. Such symptoms are of varying shape and size. Growth of the affected plants was reduced significantly and the leaf lamina of such plant was retarded characteristically. Such symptoms were similar to those of tobacco mosaic virus disease. Electron microscopic studies showed straight, rod shaped particles similar to *Tobacco mosaic virus*.

❍ Virus diseases of minor importance

1. A strain of *Tobacco mosaic virus* was reported by Caponigro (1992) to incite systemic infection on *Datura metel*.
2. Two strains of sap transmissible aphid borne viruses were reported from Akola of the country producing mosaic symptoms on *Datura metel* and *Datura innoxia*. Naturally infected plants exhibited severe mosaic mottling accompanied with blistering, distortion and leaf deformities. Shoe string appearance was the distinguishing characteristic of this disease. These viruses were recognized as *Datura metel mosaic virus* and *Datura innoxia mosaic virus*.
3. A virus disease producing symptoms like vein clearing, mosaic pattern and leaf puckering were observed on *Datura metel* growing in waste land from Andhra Pradesh of India. The virus is known to be sap and insect transmissible. Characteristic cytoplasmic cylindrical inclusion bodies were observed in epidermal cells of infected *Datura metel* leaves under light microscope.
4. A potyvirus isolated from *Datura stramonium* from Yemen has been reported to be mechanically sap transmissible and also transmissible by aphid–*Myzus persicae* in non-persistent manner. The virus particles were flexuous rod shaped in morphology. The virus showed distinct serological relationship with *Pepper veinal mottle potyvirus* and *Potato virus Y*.
5. A mosaic disease causing symptoms like stunted growth, reduced leaf size and mosaic pattern on leaves of infected plants were also observed on *Datura metel*. The virus was observed to be mechanically transmissible on different hosts including *Datura stramonium, Petunia hybrida* and *Nicotiana plumbaginifolia*.

DIGITALIS (*Digitalis purpurea* L) DISEASES

Digitalis (*Digitalis purpurea* L) is a plant native of British Island and Western Europe. It is a herbaceous plant, cultivated for medicinal purposes in England, Germany, USA, Russia and India. Two main digitalis glycosides used in medicine are digitoxin and gitalin.

❍ Digitalis chlorotic mottle disease

Symptoms- This disease was first reported on *Digitalis lanata* in Germany. The disease exhibited systemic chlorotic mottling and ring like marking with characteristic chlorotic streak along the veins of the leaves of the infected plants. As a result of the disease, petioles are slightly twisted.

Causal virus- *Ribgrass mosaic virus* (Schumann, 1963). RNA containing virus particles consist of rod shaped particles, measuring about 18 nm X 300 nm in size. Different types of cytoplasmic inclusion bodies were observed in ultra-thin sections of *Digitalis purpurea* infected with different strains of the causal virus. Virus particles remain arranged in circular manner around a centre.

Transmission- The virus occurs in high concentration in sap, being very stable and readily transmissible by sap inoculation.

❍ Diseases of minor importance

A number of strains of viruses have been reported on *Digitalis purpurea*. Some important viruses may be summarized as under-

1. *Tobacco mosaic virus.*
2. *Cucumber mosaic virus.*
3. *Tobacco ring spot virus.*
4. *Beet curly top virus.*
5. *Broad bean wild virus.*

HYOSCYMUS (*Hyoscymus* species) DISEASES

Hyoscyamus niger and *Hyoscyamus muticus* are two important species known as sources for tropane alkaloids. The plant is erect tall herb commonly cultivated in USA, India and East European countries for medicinal purposes. Both the above species are known to be affected by important virus diseases described below.

Hyoscyamus species are susceptible for a number of viral diseases. Two viruses were frequently isolated from the leaves of *Hyoscyamus niger*. They were recognized as *Broccoli necrotic yellow virus* and *Cauliflower mosaic virus.* Belladonna plant has been reported to be the symptomless carrier of many such viruses as reported. Some other virus diseases may be summarized as under-

❍ Henbane mosaic disease

Henbane mosaic disease was an important viral disease incited by *Henbane mosaic potyvirus.* This virus was characterized by the presence of crystalline inclusions, measuring 12 nm in diameter (Stefanac et al, 1993). Presence of another mechanically and aphid transmissible virus disease on *Hyoscyamus muticus* was reported by Proctor (1944). He observed thermal death point of the virus to be between 60 and 65°C. He recommended control of this disease by weekly applications of the solution of nicotine and soft soap after a period of 8-9 weeks of appearance of the disease.

❍ Yellow mosaic mottling

This disease was first observed on *Hyoscyamus niger* by Shastry in 1977 from India. Symptoms of the disease consist of typical yellow mosaic mottling, vein clearing and vein banding. The first symptoms of the disease may appear 10-12 days after inoculation in the form of vein clearing followed by vein banding. Infected plants were observed to be stunted exhibiting yellow mosaic mottling. Electron microscopic studies revealed appearance of rod shaped particles of the virus, measuring 270-750 nm in length. Serological studies represented close resemblances of this virus in properties and host range with *Belladonna mosaic virus* and *Plantogo mosaic virus*. However, the virus was not related to *Tobacco mosaic virus* and *Potato virus X*.

❍ Green mosaic

Both *Hyoscyamus niger* and *Hyoscyamus muticus* were reported to be affected by this disease. Infected plants showed severe stunting and bushy appearance of the plants as characteristic symptoms of this disease. The leaves of the affected plants were reduced significantly in size with characteristic narrowing. In general, mosaic mottling symptoms were pronounced in younger leaves. Flowers were also found to be affected becoming discoloured, resulting in poor seed setting. Based on host range, physical properties and particle morphology, the virus was found to be a strain of *Cucumber mosaic virus*. The virus particles were observed to be isometric, measuring 27 nm in diameter. It was transmissible by mechanical inoculation and by aphid especially *Myzus persicae* but not by seed or soil.

OPIUM POPPY (*Papaver somniferum* L) DISEASES

Opium poppy is one of the most important medicinal plants used by the physicians as narcotic, sedative, analgesic, antispasmodic and hypnotic. Principal alkaloids exert both depression and excitement of the nervous system. Some believe that poppy was introduced in India by Alexander the Great in 300 B. C. A number of viruses have been reported from the plant. However, important viral diseases are as under-

❍ Bean yellow mosaic virus disease

The disease was first reported by Kovachevsky and Kovachevsky (1968) from Bulgaria. However, the virus is common in all other countries. Symptoms of the disease appeared as irregular chlorotic bands along the veins which spread very fast all over the inter-veinal areas. Green stripes along the veins of the leaves were also observed thereon. Infected plants are found stunted and the disease was mechanically as well as aphid transmissible from poppy to bean and from bean to poppy. Virus particles were found to be flexuous in morphology, measuring about 750 nm in length. Thermal inactivation point of the virus ranges between 50-70 0C and dilution end point was observed to be 10^{-3} - 10^{-4}. Longevity of the virus *in vitro* has been reported to be 3-4 days at 20°C.

❍ Turnip mosaic virus disease

Poppy plants are known to be infected by *Turnip yellow mosaic virus*. Infected plants exhibit characteristic symptoms like stunting of plants and chlorosis and distortion of leaves of the infected plants. Besides, considerable reduction in yield is most characteristic to the disease. The virus consists of flexuous filamentous particles, measuring 720 nm in length. The virus has world wide distribution and is transmissible through mechanical transmission by sap and also by insect transmission by aphids.

❍ Diseases of minor importance

1. *Cabbage ring spot virus* - The virus was found to infect opium poppy causing systemic infection.

2. *Beet yellow virus*- The virus is known to infect opium poppy and is transmissible by aphid-Myzus persicae.

3. **Sap transmissible poppy mosaic**- A mosaic disease of opium poppy was reported from India that caused vein banding, stunting and deformed capsule formation. The virus is rarely insect transmissible.

4. **Aphid transmissible mosaic**-This virus disease has limited host range.

5. **Phytoplasmal disease of poppy**- The disease incited by Phytoplasma was first reported by Muller *et al* (1974). The infection introduced dwarfing and witches broom appearance of the plants.

PERIWINKLE (*Catharanthus roseus* L) DISEASES

Tropical Periwinkle is known for its important medicinal value in folklore of a number of countries for a long period. More than 100 alkaloids have been isolated from this plant. The leaf alkaloids such as vincristine and vinblastine are potent anticancer drugs and root alkaloid- ajmalicine is used as hypotensive agent. Vinblastine sulphate is mainly used for the treatment of Hodgkin's disease and against lymphosarcoma, choriocarcinoma, neuroblastoma and carcinoma of breast, lung and testis. Some important viral diseases of this plant may be summarized as under-

❍ Periwinkle mosaic diseases

Three viruses causing different types of mosaic diseases of *Catharanthus roseus* are known to occur-

1. *Periwinkle mosaic virus* -Joshi and Raychaudhari (1964) reported a mosaic disease characterized by circular to irregular greenish yellow to green patches on leaves of the affected plants. Leaf malformation may also be observed in severe cases. The virus was designated as *Periwinkle mosaic virus.* The virus was transmitted by sap inoculation. The virus had an incubation period of 60-70 days in *Catharanthus roseus* and was not transmissible by insects. The virus produced greenish yellow spots followed by yellow streaks 8-10 days after inoculation.

2. *Periwinkle chlorotic stunt virus* - Zaidi *et.al.* (1978) reported a mosaic disease of *Catharanthus roseus* that produces yellow greeen mosaic symptoms followed by crinkling of the leaves and general stunting of the plants. The virus was transmitted by sap as well as by insect vector. The virus differed in its properties from *Periwinkle mosaic virus.*

3. *Cucumber mosaic virus* - A strain of this virus was found associated with another mosaic disease that produces severe mottling, blistering and distortion of leaves. The disease was first reported by Verma and Dwivedi (1971). The virus was easily transmitted by sap and insects to a large number of plants and was suggested to belong Cucumovirus group. The causal organism was identified as a strain of *Cucumber mosaic*

virus that consists of RNA genome with isometric particles, measuring about 30 nm in diameter. It has a wide host range. It is transmitted by many species of aphids in a non-perisistent manner and is readily transmissible by inoculation of sap. The virus is widespread and common in temperate regions. The virus is poorly immunogenic. Molecular weight of the virus has been estimated.

❍ Tomato spotted wilt virus disease

Periwinkle (*Catharanthus roseus*) was found infected with *Tomato spotted wilt virus* in Italy during the spring of 1992. The symptoms included leaf necrosis of the blade and margin. The virus was identified as *Tomato spotted wilt virus* (TSWV) on the basis of transmission studies, serological tests and electron microscopic studies (Davino *et. al.*, 1993).

❍ Periwinkle phyllody

The occurrence of phyllody or little leaf disease of *Catharanthus roseus* has been reported by several workers from India (Chakravarty *et.al.*, 1976, Kar et.al., 1982, Subba-Rao *et.al.*, 1983 and Sharma *et.al.,* 1993). The disease has also been reported from a number of other countries.

Symptoms- Characteristic symptoms of the disease were observed as reduction in the size of leaves, shortening of internodes, extensive branching and stunting with greening of flowers. When the disease is intensified, the plants turned vegetative with complete loss of flowering and fruiting may be observed. The diseased plants often looked like small bushes with stunted growth. Excessive branching was characteristically observed. In severe attack, leaves become chlorotic with pointed tips. There may be complete transformation of the infected plants beyond recognition. As a result, the disease causes considerable loss in the alkaloid content of the plant.

Causal organism - Phytoplasma. Electron microscopic examination of leaf tissue sections of infected plants revealed the presence of numerous pleomorphic bodies in the sieve tube cells of phloem elements. The bodies were of different sizes, most often circular and rarely oval. The bodies were bound by a unit membrane characteristic to the causal agent.

Transmission- The organism was not mechanically transmissible, but could be transmitted through grafts. Transmission of the disease by leaf hoppers to periwinkle has also been reported.

Management- Tetracycline treatment proved highly successful in limiting the disease symptoms. Treatment with oxytetracycline caused remission of the symptoms. Treated plants were found to produce normal leaves and flowers. Tetracycline and gibberellic acid therapy has been reported to be more effective.

PLANTAGO (*Plantago psyllium* Linn.) DISEASES

Plantago psyllium Linn. is well known to be commercially cultivated in Gujrat, Haryana and Rajasthan. *Plantago psyllium* has been used as traditional medicine in Middle East and India for several hundred years. Infusion and decoction of seeds is used to control chronic constipation. It is also used to control diarrhoea and dysentery. *Plantago* species are not known to be affected by any important virus disease. However,

Ribgrass mosaic virus and members of Potex virus group, Caulimovirus group, Potyvirus group, Tobacco necrosis virus group, Tombusvirus group have been reported from *Plantago psyllium*.

RAUVOLFIA (*Rauvolfia* species) DISEASES

This precious medicinal plant was named in honour of the sixteenth century German physician and botanist Leonard Rauvolfia. *Rauvolfia serpentine* and vomitoria are common species known to contain medicinally important alkaloids. In ayurveda, it was used for the treatment of snake bite, insect sting, epilepsy, diarrhea, dysentry and mental disorders. However, it is also effective as hypotensive and tranquilizer agent.

❍ Rauvolfia mosaic disease

This disease is characterized by the production of local necrotic lesions on the primary leaves of *Phaseolus vulgaris, Nicotiana glutinosa, Datura metel* and *Datura innoxia*. The isolated virus was observed to be sap transmissible, causing mosaic disease of *Rauvolfia serpentina*. The virus was identified as a strain of *Tobacco mosaic virus*. The virus infection was found to affect the alkaloid contents of the roots.

❍ Rauvolfia phyllody

Rauvolfia phyllody was first observed by Varadarajan (1967) who suggested the over wintering of the disease in *Catharanthus roseus, Nicotiana tabacum, Solanum melongena* and *Capsicum annum* in Gujarat (India). The disease was found to be transmitted by grafting and by stem parasite (*Cuscuta* species).

The causal virus was reported to resemble with *Aster yellow virus*. Characteristic symptoms of the disease were observed as retarded growth, shortened internodes and phyllody of flowers. The leaves became small and pale in colour; the floral parts of the infected plants were modified into leaf like structures, resulting into a cluster of small leaves in place of inflorescence. As a result of the disease, complete sterility of the affected plants may be observed. The disease adversely affected the alkaloid content of the plant.

❍ Rauvolfia yellow vein mosaic

A disease with characteristic of yellow vein mosaic pattern was observed on *Rauvolfia serpenttina* in experimental plantations of Jammu. Yellowing of young leaves and formation of yellow network in the back ground of green surface were observed as the important diagnostic symptoms of the disease. A minor retardation of growth of infected plants was also observed. Considerable reduction in root biomass and alkaloid contents of roots were recorded due to this disease.

❍ Rauvolfia ring spot

Rauvolfia ring spot was first reported from the experimental plantations of Jammu. Leaves of infected plants exhibited characteristic concentric yellow rings of different sizes usually scattered all over the surfaces of the leaves of infected plants. The rings gradually enlarged, coalesced and became necrotic in due course. As a result of the necrosis of entire leaves, defoliation was caused. It resulted in poor quality of roots and reduced alkaloid content. The virus pathogen was found be graft transmissible in nature.

❍ Rauvolfia green mosaic

Rauvolfia serpentina was reported to be affected by severe green mosaic, causing severe stunting of the infected plants with characteristic narrowing of leaves. Mosaic mottling symptoms were observed to be more pronounced in young leave as reported. The virus was identified as a strain of *Cucumber mosaic virus* (CMV) on the basis of studied made for host range, biophysical properties and serological relationship. The virus particles were isometric in morphology, measuring 27 nm in diameter. It was transmitted by aphid (*Myzus persicae*) but not by seeds or soil.

WITHANIA (*Withania somnifera*) DISEASES

In Ayurvedic literature it is commonly referred as Ashwagandha. *Withania somnifera* is an erect evergreen shrub distributed through out the drier parts of our country. It is cultivated at commercial scale in central parts of the country. Several alkaloids and non alkaloid compounds are isolated and used in different ailments including arthritis and inflammatory diseases. Leaf curl and witches broom are two important diseases of *Withania somnifera* incited by the virus and Phytoplasma respectively.

❍ Withania leaf curl

Occurrence of *Tobacco leaf curl virus* on this plant causing leaf curl was first reported by Pathak and Raychaudhari (1967). *Tobacco leaf curl virus* strain produces symptoms of the disease on the leaves as vein clearing, curling, puckering and occasionally rolling. The surface of infected leaves was observed to be characteristically wrinkled and malformed.

❍ Withania witches' broom

A witches broom disease of *Withania somnifera* was first reported from the experimental plantations of Lucknow (U. P.) India which later spread to commercial fields causing considerable damage. Characteristic symptoms of the disease were recorded as formation of small leaves, shortening of internodes and excessive branching. It resulted into witches broom appearance, causing premature drying and death of infected twigs and leaves. Typically infected plants remained stunted. The disease is incited by the Phytoplasma. On observation, ultra-thin sections of infected leaf tissue showed pleomorphic bodies, measuring 250-550 nm found in the sieve tubes of phloem. These pleomorphic bodies were densely stained. The organism was found to be very sensitive to tetracycline. The disease was transmitted from infected plants to healthy plants through grafting. Spraying of tetracycline in recommended dose was suggested for controlling the disease.

21

VIRUS DISEASES OF FORAGE FEED PLANTS

✉ ***Diseases of alfala—alfalfa mosaic and latent virus diseases; Brome grass diseases-brome mosaic, brome enation and mottle diseases; Different diseases of rye grass including mosaic, enation, mottle and diseases of weed grass-Johnson grass mosaic.***

Many forage feed plants are used both for animal feed and human nutrition. Such economically important plants are usually affected by a number of viruses. These viruses usually cause considerable damage to the plants. Economically important diseases incited by these viruses may be summarized as under :

VIRUS DISEASES OF ALFALFA (*Medicago sativa*)

Alfalfa is one of the important leguminous green fodders which is palatable feed for all domestic animals. Stems and leaves are used for processing several kinds of animal feed such as green fodder, hay, silage, and milled alfalfa. Alfalfa is natural host for *Alfalfa mosaic virus* and natural alternate hosts for several viruses. These viruses cause damage to the crop by reducing green matter, seed quality and yield.

❍ Alfalfa mosaic virus disease

Alfalfa mosaic virus is reported to occur in all the alfalfa growing areas of the world. A decrease of 11% has been reported in yield of alfala hay when 53% to 76% plants were observed to be infected. In addition to this crop, *Alfalfa mosaic virus* infects different other crops such as clover, pea, potato, tomato, pepper and celery etc. causing considerable damage to the crops.

Symptoms. (1) On young leaves, small, round and green-yellow spots are observed at the initiation of growth. (2) These spots become chlorotic and merge in the form of stripes and rings or remain uneven in shapes. (3) Leaves of early infected plants become crinkled and show retarded growth. (4) Chlorotic spots in older leaves may exhibit light yellow and white colouration. (5) At high temperature, the characteristic symptoms become masked and diseased plants may recover apparently. (6) Strains are known to exist.

The causal virus. *Alfalfa mosaic virus.* The virus particles are bacilliform in shape with multicomponent particles of different sizes. The three types of largest particles usually measure T (36 × 18 nm), M (48 × 18 nm) and B (58 × 18 nm). The virus particles contain single stranded RNA and three positive-sense RNA molecules are encapsulated in B, M and T particles consisting of RNA_{-1} (1100 kDa), RNA_{-2} (800 kDa) and RNA_{-3} (700 kDa) respectively. Thermal inactivation point of the virus is 50 to 70°C, dilution end point is 1×10^{-3} to 1×10^{-4} and longevity *in vitro* is 1 to 4 days at room temperature. Serologically, *Alfalfa mosaic virus* is weekly to moderately immunogenic.

Host range. More than 165 species are natural hosts of the virus. Some important hosts are *Apium graveolens, Beta saccharifera, B. vulgaris, Cannabis sativa, Capsicum annuum, C. frutescens, Daucus carota, Dianthus caryophyllus, Dolichos lablab, Glycine max, Lactuca sativa, Linum usitatissimum, Lycoperisicon lycopersicum, Nicotiana tabacum, Phaseolus vulgaris, Pisum sativum, Ribes rubrum, Solanum melongena, S. tuberosum, Trifolium hybridum* and *T. incarnation* etc.

Disease-cycle. The virus is preserved in natural hosts such as *Medicago* species, *Trifolium* species and *Stellaria media.* Potato tubers also serve as a reservoir from year to year.

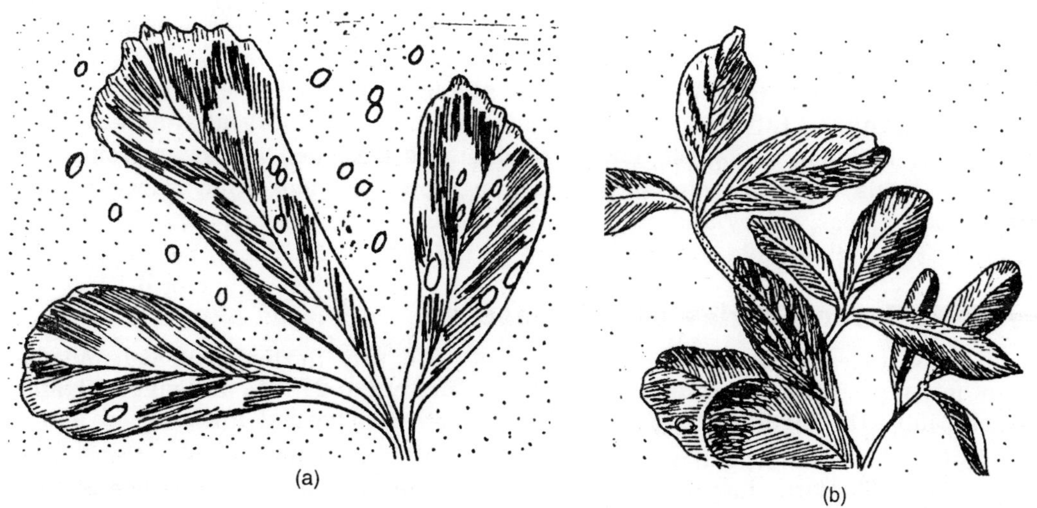

(a) (b)

Fig. 21.1 Alfalfa leaves infected from *Alfalfa mosaic virus* (*a*) and (*b*)

Transmission. The virus is known to be transmitted non- persistently by more than 15 aphid species especially *Acyrthosiphon pisum, A. solani, Aphis craccivora, Aphis fabae, A. medicaginis, Macrosiphum euphorbiae* and *Myzus persicae* etc. In nature, *Alfalfa mosaic virus* is preserved and transmitted with the seed of alfalfa, pepper, and weeds —*Datura stramonium, Solanum nigrum, Chenopodium quinoa* and possibly *Melilotus* species.

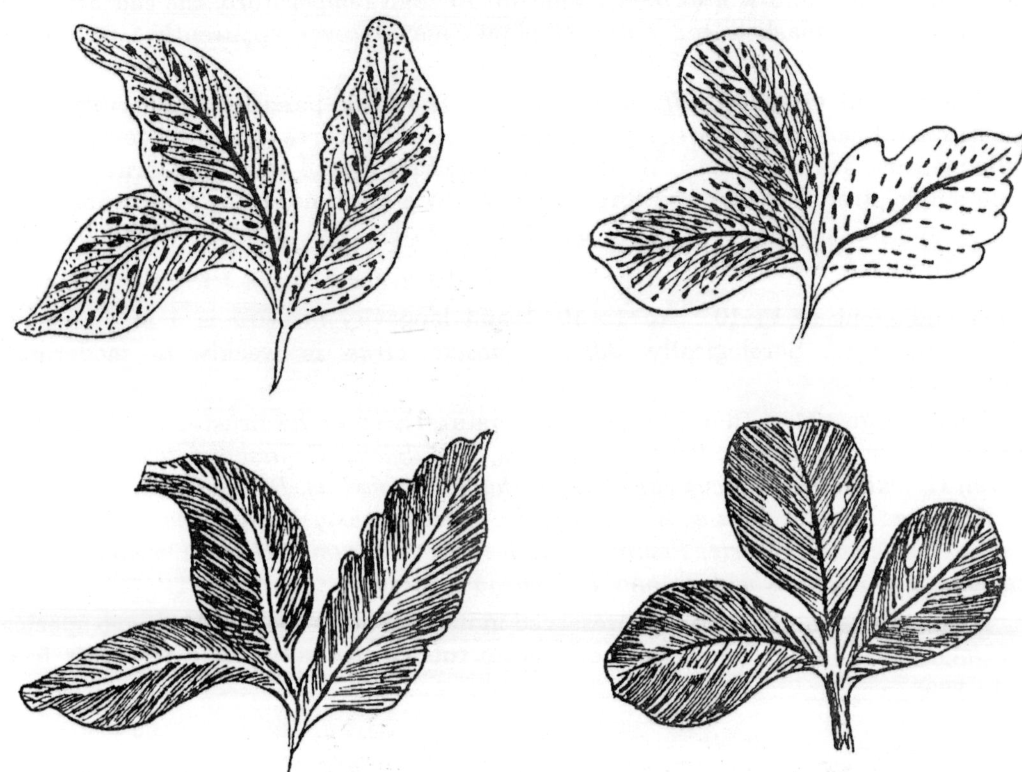

Fig. 21.2 Symptoms incited by *Pea leaf roll virus* on alfalfa leaves.

Management. Infection can be avoided by use of healthy alfalfa seeds. New alfalfa fields both for seeds and forage should be established far away from alfalfa and clover fields. Spatial isolation of the crop should be done from infected pepper tomato, potato, peas, celery and other naturally susceptible species. Aphids should be managed by using suitable insecticide time to time.

❍ Alfalfa latent carlavirus disease

The particles of the virus are rod shaped, slightly flexuous, measuring about 635 nm in length. They contain single species of protein of 27 kDa and single stranded RNA of 2450 kDa. Sedimentation coefficient is 38 S. Thermal inactivation point is 65 to 75°C, dilution end point is 1×10^{-3} to 1×10^{-4} and longevity *in vitro* is 4 to 6 days at 25C°. The virus has restricted host range and experimental infection has been observed mainly in some legume plants. Diagnostic plants are *Vicia fabae* producing red brown lesions and apical necrosis and *Pisum sativum* in which vein clearing and chlorosis of young leaves are observed as diagnostic symptoms. The virus over-winters in alfalfa plants, representing a perennial source of perpetuation. *Acyrthosyphon pisum* is commonly known vector which transmits the virus is non-persistent manner. No seed transmission is known to occur in nature.

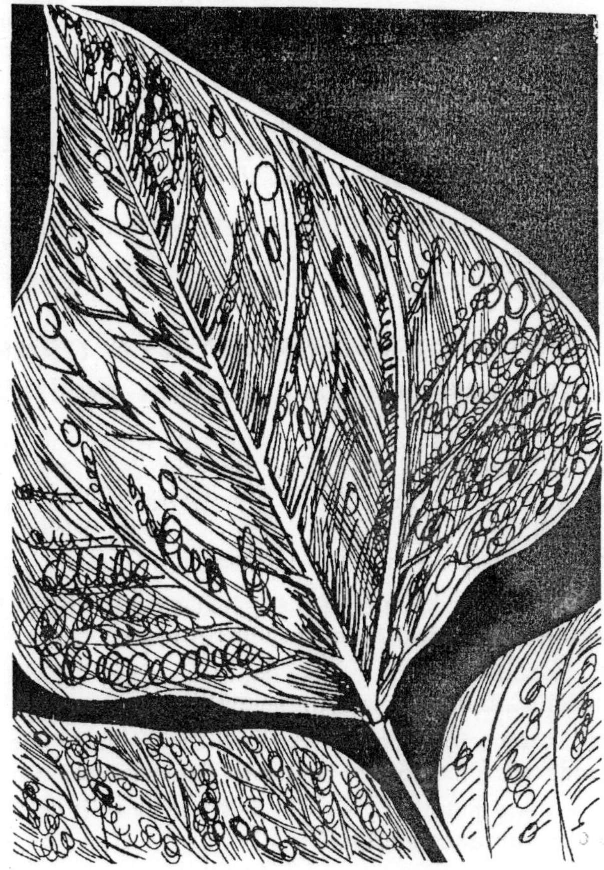

Fig. 21.3 Infected bean leaves showing yellow spottng incited by *Alfalfa mosaic virus*

SOME OTHER VIRUSES REPORTED ON ALFALFA

Lucern (Alfalfa) *Australian latent nepovirus, Lucern* (Alfalfa) *transient streak sobemovirus, Cucumber mosaic virus, Pea common mosaic virus, Bean ring spot virus, Peanut stunt virus* and *Pea leaf roll virus* are also known to occur on alfalfa causing considerable damage to the crop.

VIRUS DISEASES OF BROME GRASS (*Bromus inermis*)

Plants are perennial and they are natural primary host for the *Brome mosaic virus* and alternate host for some other viruses. *Brome mosaic virus* also called as *Brome grass mosaic virus* belongs to type member for the brome virus group. Several forage graminaceous species are known as natural hosts for this virus. Some researcher had inoculated mechanically many grass plants that become experimentally infected.

Such plants include *Agrostis gigantean, Alopecurus pratensis, Arrhenatherum elatius, Briza media* and *Bromus* species. Common symptoms on *Bromus inermis* leaves usually appear as light green or clear yellow mottling and striped spots. Dark-green stripes occurring first on the tips of the infected plant leaves gradually become darker leading to leaf tip necrosis, The leaves of infected *Hordium murinum* quickly turn paper white. The virus may cause yield reductions by 50 to 100% as well as considerable decrease in germination of seeds obtained from infected plants.

BROME AS NATURAL ALTERNATE HOST OF VIRUSES

Barley yellow dwarf virus, Cocksfoot mild mosaic virus, Wheat striate mosaic virus and *Wheat dwarf virus* are common viruses that survive in brome plants as their alternate hosts.

VIRUS DISEASES OF RYE GRASS (*Lolium perenne* and *Lolium multiflorum*)

Ryegrass (*Lolium* species) is a perennial grass, which inhabits mostly in pastures and is also grown as field crop. *Ryegrass enation virus, Ryegrass mottle virus* and *Ryegrass mosaic virus* have been described as important viruses occurring in this crop.

○ Ryegrass mosaic potyvirus disease

The virus is known to occur in ryegrass species especially in U.S., Canada, France, Holland, Germany, Denmark and Sweden.

Symptoms. It causes chlorotic streaks and stripes between leaf veins. Infected plants grow slowly and produce fewer secondary tillers.

The causal virus. *Ryegrass mosaic potyvirus.* The virus particles are tubular, fexuous rods of 700×15 nm in size. The thermal inactivation point of the virus is 60°C, dilution end point is 1×10^{-3} and longevity *in vitro* is 24 hours at 24°C. The virus is weak in immunogenicity.

Disease cycle. The virus perpetuates both in annual and perennial susceptible hosts. *Lolium perenne* is particularly important for the preservation of infectivity and transmission of the virus into next cropping season. Mites especially *Abacurushistrix,* acquire the virus from infected plants in 2 hours and remains effective for 24 hours. Development of mites from eggs to adults occurs in the same part of the plants from which they migrate to other leaves.

Management. All measures that contribute the reduction of population of mite vectors is suitable for management of the disease. Initial healthy plants may be obtained by both meristem-tip culture and by selection of resistant plants.

SOME OTHER DISEASES OF RYEGRASS OF MINOR IMPORTANCE

○ Ryegrass enation virus disease

The causal virus-*Ryegrass enation virus* was previously named as *Lolium enation virus* is a possible member of Reovirus group. The virus has limited distribution and characteristic symptoms are the formation of enations on the leaves of the infected plants.

❍ Ryegrass mottle virus disease

The causal virus-*Ryegrass mottle virus* was previously called as *Lolium mottle virus*. It has isometric particles of 27 nm in diameter. Its thermal inactivation point is 65°C, dilution end point is 1×10^{-3} and longevity *in vitro* is 10 days at 20°C. It is immunogenically active.

Natural alternate hosts of the virus are *Lolium perenne, Cynosurus cristatus, Avena sativa, Hordeum vulgare, Lagurus ovatus, Lolium multiflorum, Phleum pretense* and *Secale cereale*.

❍ Ryegrass bacilliform rhabdovirus disease

The virus-*Ryegrass bacilliform rhabdovirus* causes mild chlorotic symptoms on infected plants. Natural hosts are *Lolium multiflorum* and *L. perenne*. Mode of transmission in nature is not well known.

❍ Ryegrass cryptic virus disease

The causal virus-*Ryegrass cryptic virus* particles are isometric and measure about 29 nm in diameter. Chlorotic spots accompanied by necrosis particularly on older leaves are usually observed as characteristic symptoms of the disease. The virus is seed-borne and other modes of transmission are not known.

VIRUS DISEASES OF WEED GRASSES

Several species of *Agropyron, Anthoxanthum, Panicum, Setaria* and *Sorghum* are used both as grasses and as cultivated crops. As grasses they usually occur in the field along the main crops. Whether weeds or crops, such plants are known to act as reservoir of many viruses. *Agropyron repens* is a common weed in many crops specially cereals and maize. *Leersia oryzides* is widespread weed plant in the field of rice crops. This weed is propagated both by stolons and by seeds. It represents a key source of virus. *Sorghum halepense,* commonly called as Johnsongrass, is a perennial weed and the most important alternative host for many viruses. For the management of the virus diseases of main crops, elimination of these plants are essential.

❍ Johnson grass mosaic potyvirus disease

The disease has been reported from many countries especially from U.S. and Australia.

Symptoms. The virus produces mosaic, red stripes and ringspot symptoms in several *Sorghum* species. Necrosis and stunting may also be observed in cultivated species of *Sorghum*.

The causal virus. *Johnsongrass mosaic potyvirus*. The virus particles are flexuous filaments, measuring about 750 × 12 nm in size. The virus contains a single species of single stranded RNA of 3100 kDa with 9500 nucleotides. The coat protein is a single polypeptide species of about 33.5 kDa consisting of 303 amino acid residues. Thermal inactivation point of the virus is 60°C, dilution end point is 1×10^{-4} and longevity of the virus *in vitro* is 2 days at 20°C.

Disease cycle. Both Johnson grass and wild sorghum (*Sorghum verticilliflorum*) are permanent reservoirs for the virus. Other hosts including annuals are also important for providing secondary inocula. Aphids especially *Aphis craccivora, A. gossypii* and some other species are known to transmit the virus in non-persistent manner. Seed transmission has not been reported.

Management. Eradication of virus infected perennial hosts and control of vectors are the important measures for the management of the disease.

22

TISSUE CULTURE FOR ELIMINATING PLANT VIRUSES

Meristem immunity, Meristem sampling, Meristem culturing and development, Factors affecting meristem development, Culture containers, micro-grafting, Transplanting of plantlets, Indexing, Virus elemination and thermotherapy

Tissue culture, basically the culture of tissues in artificial media, is a biotechnological method for improvement and regeneration of plants. Plant tissue culture in its broadest sense usually refers to *in vitro* cultivation of all plant parts, whether a single cell, a tissue or organ under aseptic conditions. Principles involved in plant tissue culture may be explained as (1) a plant part from the intact plant and its inter-organ/inter tissue is isolated, (2) such plant part should be provided all necessary facilities with an appropriate environment in which it can express its instrinsic or induced potential, and (3) the above procedures must be carried out aseptically. As known to all of us that plant cell possesses a unique property called **Totipotency** or the property to produce a mature plant from its appropriate cell under suitable environmental conditions. This property was first explained by P.R. White (1934). This property was observed in case of tomato in which he developed tomato plant from root tip. Subsequently it was observed that plants can be produced from tissues of root, shoot, stem, flower or leaf in appropriate media under proper environmental conditions. This technique is also used to produce virus free plant in view of the general hypothesis that the rapidly dividing tissues do not contain any virus.

MERISTEM IMMUNITY

It is usually presumed that the meristem shoot tip in its stage of rapid growth usually remains devoid of any virus. It was white (1934) who first hypothesized that the plant meristem could be free from viruses. He studied the virus distribution in plants by inoculating *in vitro* grown tomato roots with aucuba strain of *Tomato mosaic virus*. He observed the presence of the virus in successive portions of plants by inoculating the extract from them in *Nicotiana glutinosa*.

Morel (1948) was the first to obtain virus free plantlets from diseased plant by carrying out the aseptic culture of meristem excised from shoot tips and proposed the hypothesis of 'meristem immunity' against viruses. It was also observed by applications of biological and serological methods of detection in other studies that the virus concentration in buds was 150 times lower than in developing leaves. No any virus was detected in the meristem in such studies and thus the hypothesis of 'meristem immunity' was supported by different experimentations. Holmes (1948) obtained *Dahlia* plants free from the *Tomato spotted wilt virus* by grafting meristem tips from infected diseased onto healthy root stocks. Similar results were also observed by Morel and Martin (1952, 1955) as they produced healthy plants from some virus infected cultivars of *Dahlia* and potato by excision and growth of meristem in a sterile synthetic medium.

DIFFERENT STEPS IN MERISTEM TIP CULTURE

Meristem tip culture usually consists of three major steps such as meristem sampling, meristem culturing and development in the culture medium. Besides these, other steps include transplanting of plantlets to plots and subsequent indexing.

MERISTEM SAMPLING

Different names have been used to indicate the explant suitable for virus elimination. Commonly used names are 'shoot tip', 'tip', 'meristem' and 'meristem tip'. The last two names indicate the explant made of meristematic dome and one or two leaf primordia (100/μm in diameter and 250/μm in length). 'Shoot tip' and 'tip' indicate part of the shoot apex including the meristem with several leaf primordia and adjacent differentiated stem tissue.

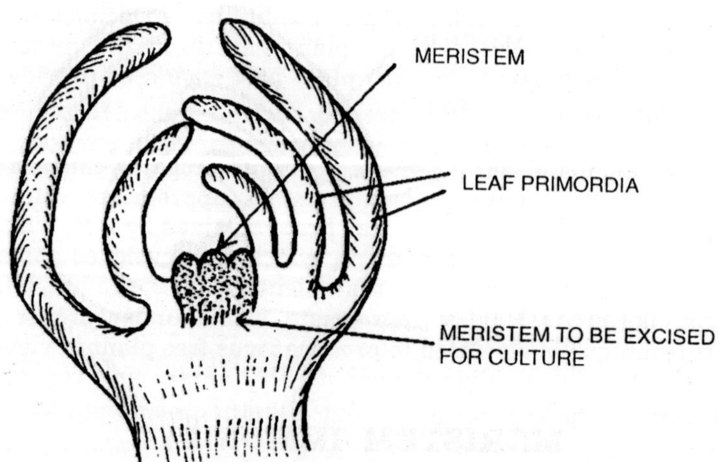

Fig. 22.1 : Diagramatic representation of a bud showing meristem dome, leaf primordia, and meristem to be excised for culture.

This kind of explant is usually removed from the heat-treated plants for clonal propagation, if freeness from virus is not required. Meristem-tip explants suitable for virus elimination are about 0.1 mm in diameter and 0.2 to 0.4 mm in length (apical dome plus one or two couples of leaf primordia).

These explants are normally dissected under aseptic conditions using a stereomicroscope fitted with cool light illuminator or glass fiber lamps to avoid desiccation during dissection. Dissection can also be performed in a petridish containing moist sterile filter paper to prevent drying.

The 'tip', however, should always be excised inside a laminar air-flow system. The first important goal in realizing meristem tip culture is to avoid explant's contamination by surface pathogens. If the meristem tips are collected after bud breaking from the bud sticks by placing them in sterile media, chances of obtaining contamination free meristem-tip is more.

Meristem-tips from underground plant organs, such as tubers, rhizomes, bulbs or corns from buds or from seeds should be dipped in 75% ethanol to remove trapped air, sterilized with sodium hypochloride or calcium chloride for 10 minutes and rinsed thrice in sterile water.

MERISTEM CULTURING AND DEVELOPMENT

Morphogenetic potential of meristem for culturing depends mainly on meristem size, plant species, physiological conditions of the donor plants and meristem position on the plant.

Meristem size. Most of the workers usually use tips between 0.2 to 1.0 mm of length, consisting of meristematic dome and two or more leaf primordia. As the number of leaf primordia per unit length vary remarkably, it is convenient to specify the number of primordia excised for culture instead of specifying the length. Selection of explant dimension is very important as it is to accomplish the development of a complete plant and virus elimination.

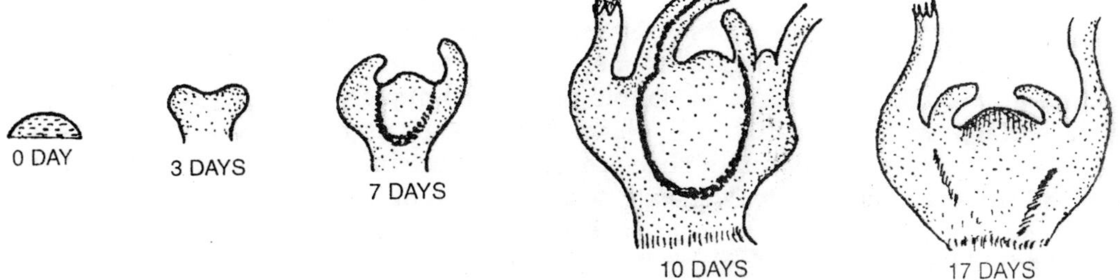

Fig. 22.2 : Diagramatic representation showing different stages of excised apical meristem of carnation.

Plant species. The regenerative potential of meristem is always related to the species or even to the cultivars. When 0.2 mm meristem of carnation cultivars is cultured, more than 68% regeneration was obtained. In general, high regenerative capacity is found in herbaceous plants. Bulbous plants such as iris, lily, gladiolus and fresia etc.

show very slow meristem growth than dicotyledonous plants and usually take a long period to become transferable to soil.

Physiological conditions of the mother plant. Physiological conditions of donor plants for meristem sampling should coincide with the highest vegetative activity. Full control of conditions may be obtained by using phytotrons or conditional green houses where light and temperature can be regulated. Light intensity and photo period are to be properly taken into account. Attention should also be given not to select sample from buds already induced to flowering, particularly in ornamentals. In carnation, meristem survives better when excised from plants in early spring and autumn. Shoot derived from winter culture, develop more easily than those cultured in summer but the latter originate more frequently virus free plants.

Meristem position on the plant. All plant meristem are thought to be suitable as starting material but morphogenetic potential and virus content depends on the position of existence of the virus. The viruses are known to exist in stems, leaves, phloem or roots etc. Meristem from basal buds of *Asparagus* develop into plantlets more easily than meristem of buds positioned near the apex. In gooseberry, successful culture is obtained only from apical bud. In rose, meristem obtained from mid part of stem develops faster. In carnation and *Chrysanthemum* meristem tips excised from apical buds give better results.

FACTORS AFFECTING MERISTEM DEVELOPMENT

❍ Tissue Culture Media

Tissue culture media usually consist of mineral salts, a carbon source of energy, vitamins, growth substances and many other minor components. Meristem development, therefore primarily depends on the composition of hormones as the meristem can not synthesize them. Shoot development usually depends upon cytokin in rich medium. Root formation has been observed to be stimulated by auxin-rich medium. In most cases, meristem usually grows well in nutrient media solidified with agar (0.6 to 0.8%) but in some cases liquid media is quite well. Difco Bacto agar, alternative products like biogel P 200 or alginate and Gelrite etc. are usually used as they do not contain inorganic contaminants toxic to meristem. In some cases liquid medium is also used, which require growth regulators at meristem. Use of liquid medium is suitable for rooting of woody species. Use of double phase technique (liquid above solid) is found to be suitable in some fruit trees. Normal pH range used in tissue culture is 5.0 to 6.5. pH lower than 5.5 inhibits shoot rooting. Other important components of media such as minerals, carbon and energy source, vitamins and growth regulators should be standardized for the development of meristem of different species. There are several standard media including 'Whites medium', commonly used in tissue culture of meristem.

❍ Light Factors

Light is an other factor which affects meristem organogenesis in a complex way through its various characteristics including its exposure time, intensity and wavelength. In most cases, 14 to 18 hours of day light with an intensity of 1.0 to 4.0 Klux of a cool fluorescent lamp, either alone or implemented by enrich-red fluorescent light (gro-lux) is adopted. Differentiated use of these parameters according to plant species and to the type of morphogenesis required, may improve or even elicit meristem development.

It is normally assumed that photo period requirement of tissue culture resembles that of the whole plant. Photo period and light intensity are interdependent requirements and therefore, they are always referred together. Wavelength requirement is usually similar for all plants.

❍ Culture containers

Dimensions of the containers can influence the type of meristem development. Cassava meristem has been observed to differentiate into plantlets when cultured in small tubes but produce callus in large containers. Most commonly used containers are glass tubes, measuring 10 × 120 mm in size closed with caps permitting air exchanges. Sealing of culture vessels to avoid contamination, may inhibit effective gas exchanges resulting in adverse morphogenesis.

❍ Micro-grafting

Micro-grafting is a convenient technique to raise virus free planting materials particularly in case of graft-propagated plants. In this case, the meristem (0.1 to 0.4 mm) excised from the infected cultivar, is grafted aseptically onto the vascular ring of a decapitated virus-free root stock, such as seedling or a shoot is propagated in culture. This technique was first used in *citrus* species to eliminate different viruses. This technique has also been tried in other fruits species including *Prunus persica* (peach), *Prunus amygdalus* (almond), *Prunus salicina* (Japanese plum), *Prunus domestica, Prunus insititia* and *Prunus armeniaca* with variable success.

Fig. 22.3 : Diagramatic representation showing filter paper bridge technique of culturing excised shoot tip in liquid medium. For the liquid culture, a filter paper bridge is prepared and inserted into the culture tube in such a way that the two arms are dipping into the medium and the platform on which the explant is placed remains above the medium.

❍ Transplanting of plantlets

After successful development of root system by the cultured shoots, they are transferred to well drained soil or special sand mixtures. At this stage, careful attention should be given to remove the agar sticking on the root surface, so as to avoid contamination. The most important requirement in this operation is to keep the plants under a very high humidity (90 to 100%) for at least two weeks. Humidity is decreased gradually so as to enable the plants to adjust to the normal humidity of the green house. Plants known to form resting organs such as tuber, corns, rhizomes and bulb-lets should be induced to produce these organs in culture.

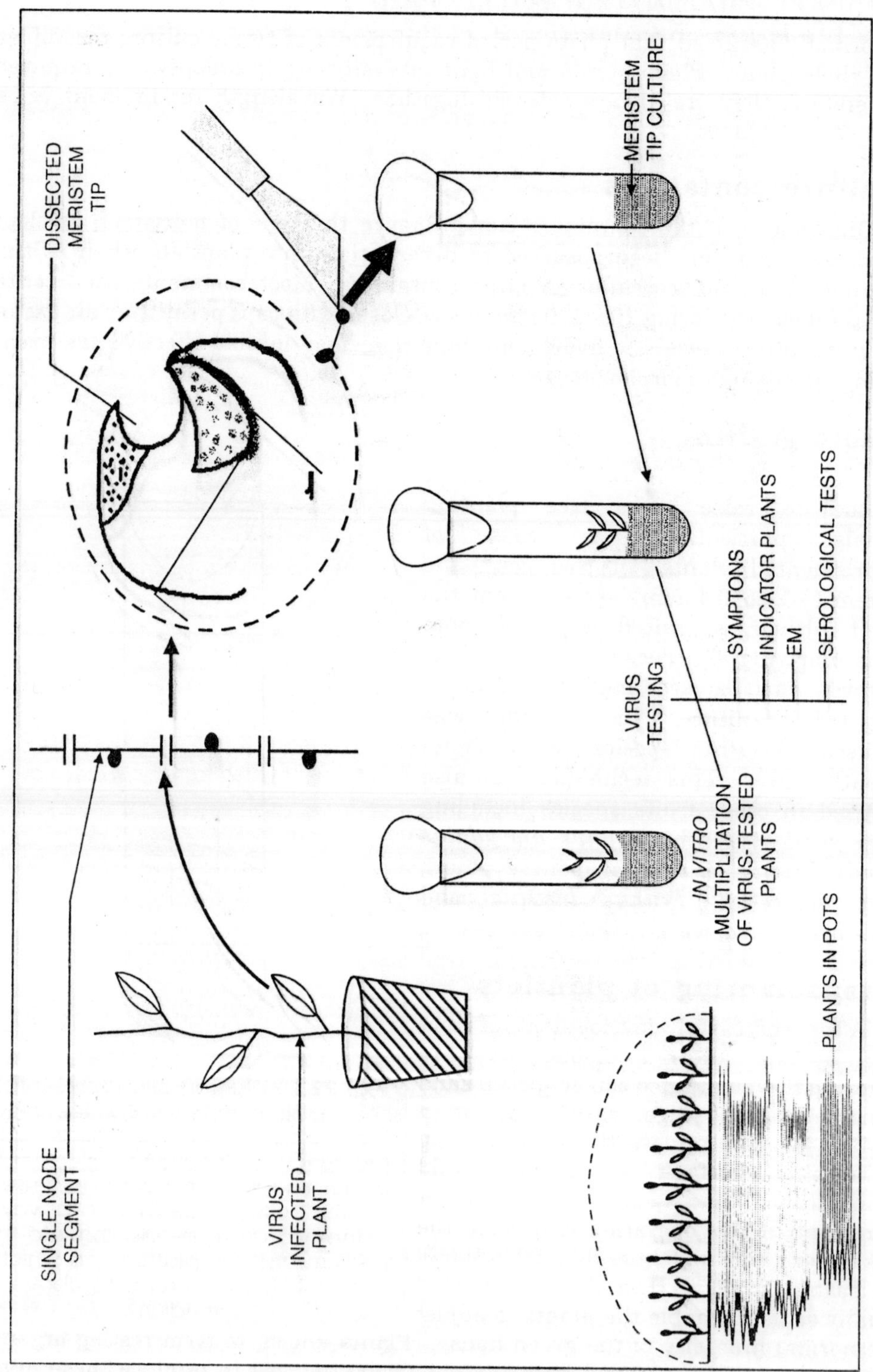

Fig. [illegible] 4 Diagramatic reprsentation showing method of production of virus free plants through shoot tip culture.

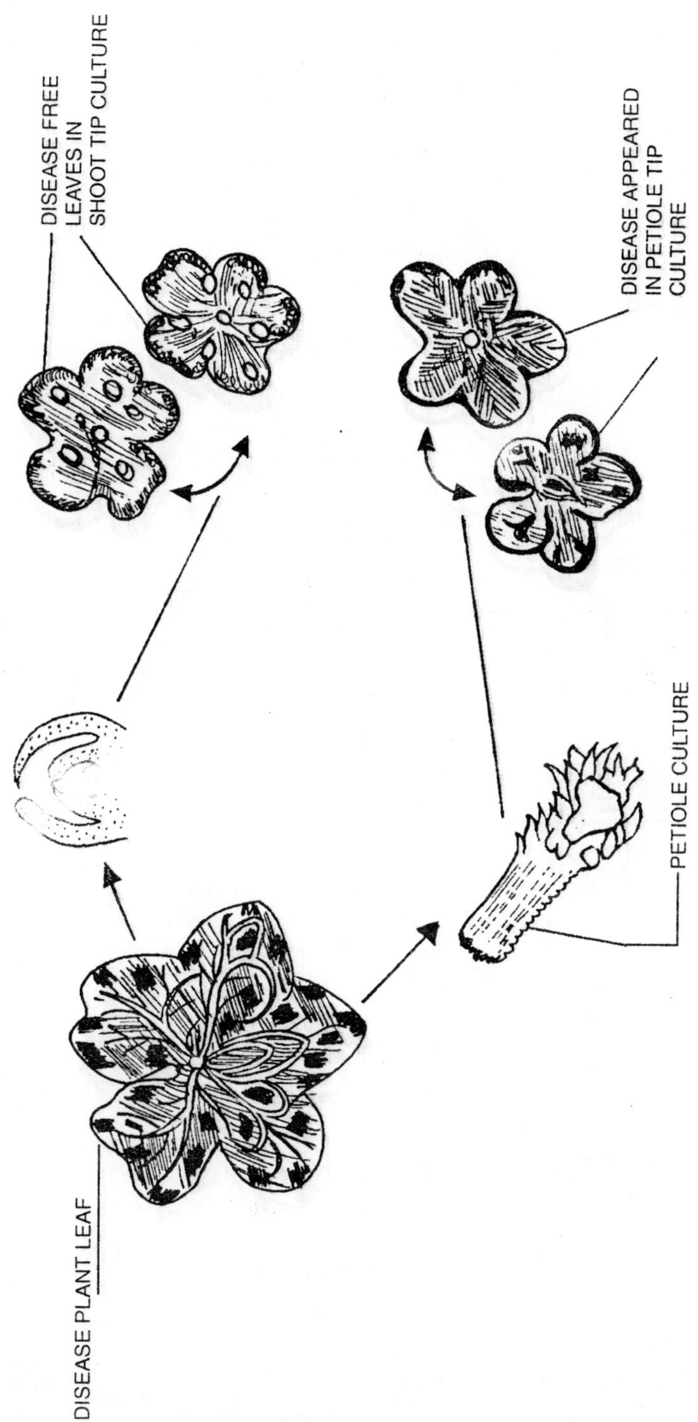

Fig. 22.5 Diagramatic representation of shoot tip culture and petiole culture showing that clear vein virus diseased character is transmitted in petiole segment culture but not in shoot tip culture.

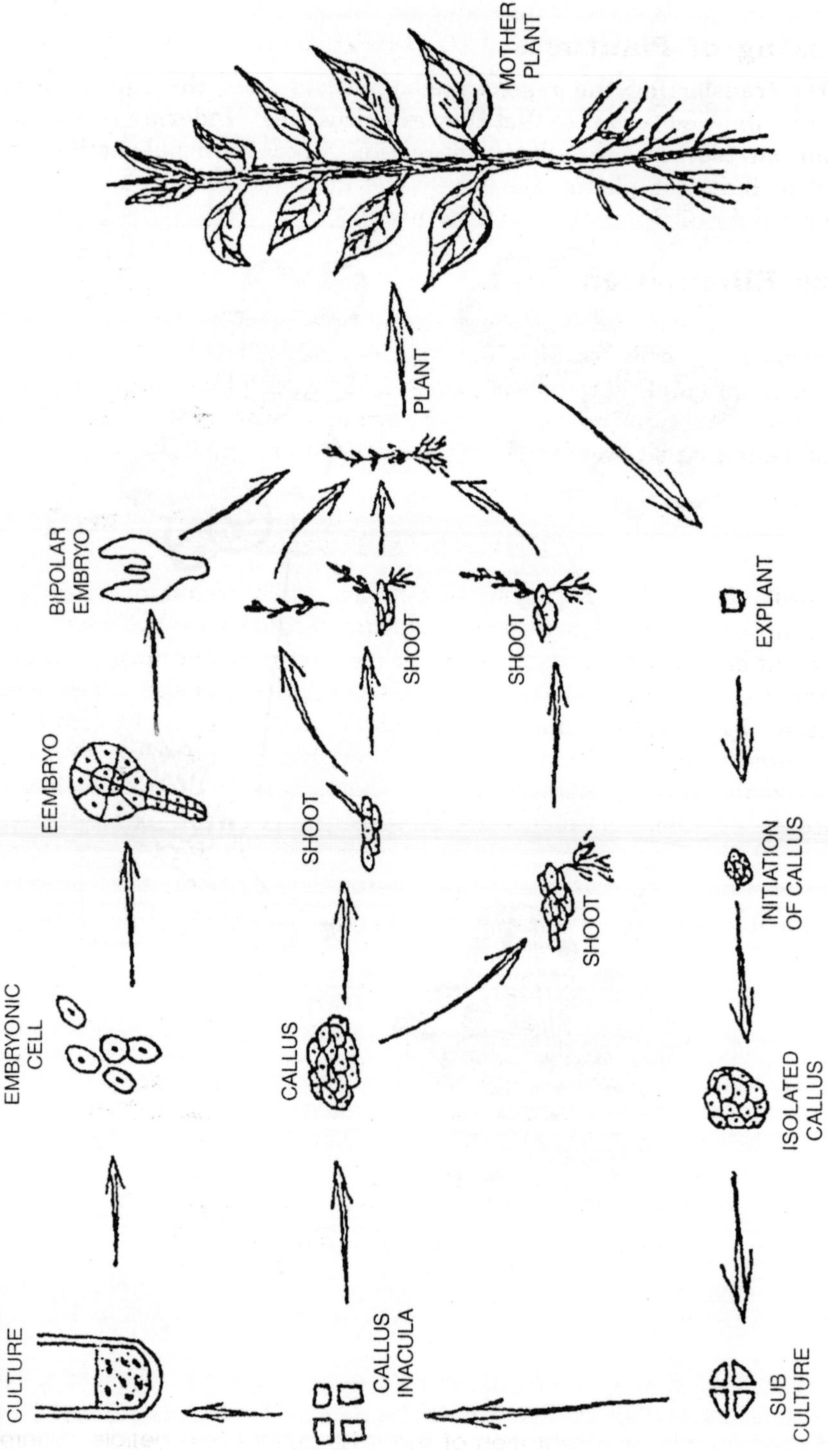

Fig. 22.6 : Diagramatic representation showing production of regenerated plants through tissue culture techniques

❍ Indexing of Plantnets

After transferring the regenerated plantlets from the culture medium to soil, they must be indexed to insure that they are virus-free. Indexing is to be done following more than one method. In addition of testing by conventional method and symptoms developed in indicator plants, sensitive serological methods such as ELISA, ISEM or nucleic acid hybridization etc. must be used.

❍ Virus Elimination

Virus elimination by meristem tip culture usually depends on meristem size, type of virus and virus strain, plant species and cultivar, physiological condition of the mother plants and meristem position on it. Each plant-virus combination exhibits a specific apical 'immunity' regarding a certain meristem size. Thus, before starting a successful elimination programme, virus distribution in meristem tip has to be precisely determined.

THERMOTHERAPY

In order to improve pathogen elimination, other techniques such as thermo and chemotherapy coupled with meristem tip culture should be used. Thermo-therapy should be carried out on mother plants, before meristerm excision or during the *in vitro* culture of meristem tips. Direct heat treatment in tissue culture is also effective in some cases. It has been observed to eliminate *Cucumber mosaic virus* and *Alfalfa mosaic virus* from *Nicotiana rustica* by treating at 30°C for 4 to 5 days or at 45°C for 9 days. In this way, virus infected plants may be inactivated by treating them at different temperatures for different times. Low temperature could also be utilized to free tissues from viruses before meristem sampling. It has been observed that *Potato virus A* and *Potato virus Y* may be eliminated from potato tissues grown at 5°C and *Potato spindle tuber viroid* has been observed to be eliminated from potato by cooling at 5°C for 3-6 months.

23

MANAGEMENT OF VIRUS DISEASES

Introduction, Epidemiology of viruses, General principles of disease management, Preventing infection from sources within the crop, Preventing the introduction of viruses, Control of incoming vectors. Use of virus resistant varieties, Biological methods of control, Immunization, Antiviral agents for disease management, Integrated management.

EPIDEMIOLOGY OF VIRUSES

The term epidemiology has been derived from the Greek world *epidemios* meaning prevalence or frequency. In other words, *"epidemics or epiphytotics may be defined as the phenomenon in which a pathogen spreads severely to and affects many plant individuals with in a population over a relatively large area and with in a relatively short time."* Similarly, *The study of epiphytotics in economic crop plants and of the factors that influence them is called as epidemiology.*

An epiphytotic (epidemic in case of animals and man) may be explained as any unusual increase of a disease in plant population which may occur occasionally in any crop in most parts of its cultivation.

Epiphytoties in some cases may cause moderate loss when they are kept in check either naturally or by the application of direct control measures (chemical sprays) or by the adaptations of some other effective and preventive control measures.

❍ Factors responsible for virus disease epiphytotics

Most important requirements for epiphytotics of plant virus diseases are abundance of virus inoculum and its sources, the presence of susceptible hosts during growth period and an adequate population density of vectors along with environmental factors suited to the vectors and disease development.

Specifically interactions of 5 factors are desirable for the development of epiphytotics. These factors are :

(1) The causal pathogen (the virus),

(2) the susceptible host,

(3) favourable environmental conditions,

(4) the virus vectors and

(5) sufficient time for disease development.

These factors should be studies simultaneously in virus disease epiphytotics. Study for the knowledge of all these factors is desirable for the management of such disease as well as for keeping these epiphytotic conditions under control. By the adaptation of suitable measures, severe losses due to the outbreak or increase and spread of the disease in question may be avoided.

❍ Conditions favourable for epiphytotics

1. Availability of susceptible hosts along with highest disease proneness of the hosts for disease development.
2. Presence of source of inoculum for the disease along with alternate and collateral hosts near the susceptible host.
3. Presence of aggressive pathogen with its high multiplication capacity and efficient and different means of spread with in the field and out side the field.
4. Adaptability of the pathogen in existing environment along with easy and efficient dispersal of pathogen through diferent vectors colonizing and multiplying easily in the manner of compound interest.
5. Optimum weather conditions for multiplication of vectors and diseases development.

All above factors are considered to be responsible for epiphytotics and must be taken into account well in time. Suitable control measures may be followed to interrupt these conditions to avoid the losses to great extent.

❍ Useful measures to avoid epiphytotics

1. Suitable crop rotation for 3-5 years with crops which are not the host of the same virus must be adapted especially in soil borne nematode and fungal transmitted viruses.
2. Field sanitation which includes destruction of refuge, diseased plant materials, alternate and collateral hosts, especially weed hosts should be done. Rogueing of infected plants in the field and weed hosts near and in the field should be done continuously.

3. Disease and their insect vectors, their natural host, alternate and collateral hosts must be kept in mind. On identification, such vectors should be managed through biological methods or by direct control through insecticide.
4. Large numbers of plant viruses are transmitted by aphids and they remain abundant in plains during winter but are destroyed automatically in summer. These aphids usually alternate between primary and secondary hosts and are polyphagus but prefer certain hosts for their survival. These aphids must be identified and destroyed with their alternate, susceptible and collateral hosts.

A partial lists of vectors with the host of preference and their role in epiphytotics may be summarized as under :

- *Aphis gossypii* is most common aphid in our country and is known to transmit a large number of viruses occurring on chilli, cotton and cucurbits. It looks creamy to greenish in colour.
- *Myzus persicae* is pale green to pinkish in colour and transmits more than 100 plant viruses in our country.
- *Aphis craccivora* is black in colour and usually transmits viruses occurring on plants belonging to leguminosae family.
- *Aphis fabae* is common bean aphid and *Toxoptera citricidus* affects certain crops.
- *Aphis rhamni* is common is potato whereas *Pentalonia nigronervosa* is common in banana.
- *Rhopalosiphum maidis* is common in maize and *Liaphis erysimi* is common and infects mustard.
- Leaf hoppers are more common as phytoplasma vectors. White flies are more common in legumes. Such vectors may retain the virus from few days to 25 days. These are important vectors and play role in epidemiology.
- Mealybugs, mites, thrips and beetles are not so common vectors, therefore, are not so important in disease epiphytotics.

5. Interference in environmental conditions for disease development may be created by irrigation or otherwise.
6. Suitable insecticidal sprays may be suggested for direct control of vectors, if so desired.
7. Any other suitable and effective measures, if any, suited to the locality or geographic area may be adopted.

❍ Importance of epidemiology in future

Due to the following reasons, epidemiological studies are important :

1. There is lack of information on viruses, disease prevalence and mode of perpetuation in many important crops.
2. Survival strategies of viruses are diversified and they have different methods of perpetuation and spread of invading new host plants and habitats through development of new strains.

3. Vectors behaviour is greatly influenced by complex implications of changes in crop population, spacing, thinning practices, size of fields and surrounding crops.

General principles for the management of virus diseases are almost the same as for the other diseases caused by fungi, bacteria and nematodes. Most of the methods described below are used for the general plant disease control and can be used in some cases for controlling more than one disease at the same time. The applicability of the methods depend upon the value of the crop, severity of the disease, the cost of labour and supplies and the care and efficiency with which they are used. Many methods have been used to break disease cycle and control virus spread, but not all the methods are completely successful.

❍ Diseases cycle

The disease cycle may be defined as the summary description of events involved in disease development. The term is similar to infection cycle and is usually used interchangeably. A life cycle trends to focus on the development of the pathogen with special attention on the various stages of the pathogen.

❍ Disease decline

Disease decline is an other term used commonly in its broadest sense. It can be explained as an overall reduction in the severity and incidence of plant disease over time. Several investigators include in their definition a requirement for an initial increase in disease severity over time followed by a subsequent decrease. In other words, disease decline denotes any measurable decrease in disease incidence over time as compared to an established baseline level of disease. Many factors can contribute to it and may exert either a direct effect on the pathogen itself or an indirect effect on the pathogen through changes in the microbial community.

These effects can be caused by changes in physiological and chemical composition in soil, changes in pathogen or alterations in the plant-pathogen relationship or in their structures. The nuclear phases of the pathogen and method of reproduction of the pathogen are involved along with the chain of disease development.

PLANT DISEASE CONTROL

Prevention, retardation or alleviation of disease by following five principal methods are known as disease control.·

(1) *Eradication*-desruction (rogueing) of infected plants or plant parts or killing of the pathogen or agent on or in the host; (2) *Protection*- application of a chemical or physical barrier to prevent entrance of the pathogen; and (3) *Immunization*-production of genetically resistant or immune plant cultivars, chemotherapy, or other treatment to inactivate or nullify the effect of the pathogen within the plant; (4) *Exclusion*-keeping the pathogen away from a disease-free area through quarantines, embargoes, and disinfection of plants and plant parts; plus a similar fifth method, (5) *Avoidance i.e.*, choosing cultural practices (*e.g.*, sanitation, rotation, choice of planting site and date, propagating and planting only disease-free material, etc.) that avoid disease.

❍ General principles for disease management

1. Preventing infection from sources within the crop

2. Preventing the introduction of viruses.
3. Control of incoming vectors.
4. Use of virus resistant varieties.
5. Biological methods of control.
6. Immunization.
7. Antiviral agents for disease management.
8. Integrated disease management.

1. PREVENTING INFECTION FROM SOURCES WITHIN THE CROP

This method can be applied by modifying the farming methods. Adjustment in crop management practices to prevent or minimize plant diseases is an important method of disease management. Such method of managing plant diseases may be called as cultural control.

It is the first and perhaps the most important of the major plant disease control strategies. As known to all of us the basic components of plant disease are host, pathogen and environment. Alteration in any of these components to disrupt their interactions could control or manage the disease. Cultural control involves principles of pathogen exclusion, pathogen eradication, disease avoidance and disease resistance. Restricting and reducing the amount of pathogen population to a level at which the pathogen may no longer cause any serious crop loss is the overall objective of most of the cultural practices.

DIFFERENT METHODS OF CULTURAL MANAGEMENT

This method of management usually includes crop rotations, crop free periods, tillage, sanitation, eradication of alternate hosts, selection of favorable conditions for planting, management of the environment, selection of resistant cultivars, nutrient management, management of farming systems, adjusting crop density, depth and time of planting, altering soil fertility, applying compost and pruning, optimizing soil drainage and soil pH, burning and eradicating volunteer plants, rougeing, fallowing, flooding, using high vigour seed, using light selective green house coverings, manipulating shade, modifying post-harvest environment, mulching, multiple cropping, organic soil amendment, pathogen-free planting material, planting diverse crops, planting in raised beds, using reflective mulches, altering row orientation, selecting suitable planting sites, solarizing soil, planting trap crops or toxic crops and control of weeds are important cultural measures.

All these cultural measures are not necessary to control any one disease of a particular crop but a few of these options should always be used for satisfactory control of many intractable diseases. Cultural control is a part of sustainable agricultural systems to achieve high crop yield and is an important tool to minimize disease losses in many crops.

Following methods are usually applicable for such modification.

1. Field sanitation and destruction of weed hosts. Sanitation is one of the important measures of defense against plant diseases. It eliminates or reduces the pathogen inoculum in the field, storage area, on a plant and prevents the spread of inoculum from infected plant material to healthy plants and plant products. It is well known that some virus diseases are carried in weeds and some other viruses are seed borne in weeds. Infected weed seeds can introduce viruses into fields and perpetuation of viruses. Weed control is also useful to limit the air borne viruses. Every possible precaution should be taken to keep the fields free from weeds. Perennial weeds/plants should be dug out and destroyed. Practices like ratooning in sugarcane should be discouraged.

2. Crop rotation. Mono-culture is a practice of growing a single plant species repeatedly on the same land. It is in contrast to inter-cropping (poly-culture) and crop rotation. In monoculture, an increase in pathogen poulations is usually observed. Monoculturing raises soil microflora and rhizophere microorganisms, build up their populations to cause more harm to the monocultured crop.

Crop rotation is the practice of growing a sequence of plant species on the same land. The benefits of crop rotation are to maintain crop yield and suppress soil borne diseases. The choice of crops for rotation depends on several considerations.

(1) Crop selected for rotation should fit into the current cropping systems.

(2) Crop rotation is not suitable in case of pathogens having wide host range of plants with certain exception.

(3) Crop rotation alone can not reduce the incidence of the disease caused by air-borne pathogens.

(4) Crop rotation may not result in dramatic reduction in the disease and increase in yield as observed in case of use of insecticides, fungicides or nematicides.

(5) Crop rotation is seldom practical for perennial crops such as orchard crops because they have longer growth cycle.

(6) Fields may contain virus infected plants or viruliferous vectors. Such plants and vectors must be destroyed before a new crop is planted. Crop rotation is important in the management of the some diseases incited by the viruses but in most cases this method does not play an important role because of the presence of the most of the viruses and vectors.

3. Green manuring. Green manuring is the practice of incorporating green biomass of a plant species into a field either by growing the crop in the same field or by bringing the crop residue from outside is usually referred to as green manuring. Green manuring has positive effects on soil fertility, prevention of nitrogen, leaching, modification of soil structure and texture, avoidance of soil erosion, decreasing soil infestation with pathogenic fungi, nematodes, bacteria and viruses and increasing soil microbial activity. Some data suggest that biological activity might be involved in the suppressive effect of green manure on soil-borne pathogens. Crops that are chosen for green manuring should have short growth cycles with abundant biomass with minimum input requirements like fertilizers and water.

4. Tillage is a cultural practice of fragmenting and burying plant residues through plowing. Tillage enhances the degradation of plant materials after harvest by mixing with soil and inverts the sub-soil to the surface. Tillage is useful to farmers for smooth farm operations by keeping the field clean and to reduce some of the weeds, insects and pathogens. Tillage practices can directly influence plant disease development.

5. Trap crop. Trap crop is a term used frequently in relation to insects and nematodes which are the important vectors of different viruses.

For insect management, trap crop can be planted alongside a field to lure pest insects away from the main crop. This practice works well to protect the crop and inhibit the transmission of the viruses from insect-pests. For nematode management trap cropping is aimed at egg hatch and nematode reproduction. First the trap crop stimulates the nematode eggs to hatch and promotes invasion of root tissue by juveniles. Then it limits the reproduction of the nematode by interrupting the nematode's life cycle or by increasing the ratio of males to females thereby reducing the number of new eggs produced. The trap crop is destroyed before the nematode can reproduce. Trap crops may consist of any of the two types of plants :

(1) Plants with root exudates that stimulate egg hatch but in which nematode reproduction does not occur.

(2) Plants that are destroyed before nematodes reproduction occurs.

Table 23.1 **Showing Trap Crops for Nematode Management**

Host	Target nematodes	Trap crops
Wheat	*Heterodera avenae*	Oat
Peas	*H. goettingiana*	Vetch
Sugarbeet	*H. schachtii*	Resistant radish, white, mustard, rape, and buck wheat
Potato	*Globodera rostochiensis*	Wild Solanum species.

A trap crop can reduce nematode population densities when nematode resistance is not available in the primary crop and when chemical control is unavailable, uneconomical and ineffective. Although the use of trap crop is beneficial in many respects, but there are four drawbacks in using trap crops :

(1) When the trap crop is a host of the nematode, timing of crop destruction is critical.

(2) If the trap crop is planted during the normal growing season, there is the expense of establishment sometimes without the economic benefit of a marketable crop.

(3) Like other control practices, reduction in nematode population density may not result in sufficient yield increase to produce an economic benefit.

(4) The reduction in nematode levels may not be consistent from year to year.

These drawbacks require careful monitoring of the management system.

6. Special cultivation. Cultivation of soil is known to affect the nematode vectors responsible for transmission of different viruses. A period of fallow may not necessarily decrease nematode population because many nematodes can survive many years without food under adverse conditions. Flooding of field by water is an age old technique for weed control in paddy. This method may be useful in the management of some nematodes.

7. Partial soil sterilization. Partial soil sterilization is known to affect the nematode population to some extent and this method can be applied by fumigation. Biocides used for fumigation are usually not selective; therefore, most of them also kill parasites as well as predators of the virus vectors. Such treatments have adverse effect on nematode and fungal vectors. Weeds are destroyed and nitrification is retarded. Besides these, mineralization of soil nitrogen is increased and damage caused by ectoparasite nematodes, fungi and other organisms are decreased.

2. PREVENTING THE INTRODUCTION OF VIRUSES

In order to prevent the introduction of viruses in the field, following methods may be applied.

1. Quarantine and seed certification

This method of prevention is very important for the management of the virus diseases. It is often very difficult to detect viruses in seed and in planting material because they rarely exhibit any significant symptoms. When growing planting materials or seeds of any desired plants are imported from any other place or country, these materials should be free from viruses and other micro-organisms responsible to cause diseases of different descriptions. As no symptoms on virus infected seeds or planting materials are observed quickly, therefore, such seeds/planting materials should be grown in virus free conditions and checked for virus infection. If no infection is observed these materials should be passed for exportation and information. Otherwise, infected seeds or diseased planting materials should be retained in quarantine in the respective country.

Like other countries, seeds/planting materials are grown in isolation by the seed producing units in our country to prevent virus infection. Such growing crop is examined again and again by the certifying authority certifying to be virus free.

2. Certified seed/planting materials

Certified seed/planting materials are usually advised to the farmers for crop protection from virus diseases. The basic seed/plant certification schemes consist of following three parts :

(1) Known pedigree or lineage of the seed,
(2) Third party field inspections, and
(3) Quality standards relating to purity, germination, weed seed and seed borne diseases.

The first part of seed certification is to provide a reliable and economical supply of seed. Most states have 'foundation' seed programmes, which takes over the multiplication of seed from the breeder and experiment stations.

The second part of seed certification is third party inspection of seed production fields. Certification standards establish minimum and maximum numbers and percentage of other contaminating crop, weed seeds and seed infected or contaminated by pathogens. Fields with plants infected with some seed borne diseases may be selected for certification if a chemical seed treatment is known to control the disease organisms.

The third part of a certification programme is that all certified seed should meet out minimum quality standards as determined by the National and State Seed Certification Directorate or Association.

Although majority of plant viruses are not seed borne, still it is better to select seeds from diseased free locations, fields and plants. If diseased free plants are not available in the market, the cultivators should grow their own seeds and produce diseased free planting materials with special care for individual plant health. Clonal selection of healthy plants is an important practice used in obtaining virus free healthy seeds. This kind of selection has been found very useful in case of potato viruses. When infected tubers are transplanted, viruses are transmitted generation to generation as long as such tubers are used for production. As a result of accumulation of infections in tubers year by year progressive decrease in yield of tubers are reflected. Thus the viruses associated with the tubers represent the major issue in potato production. This problem can be systematically solved by clonal selection of healthy plants.

3. Method of clonal selection in potato

The method of clonal selection is usually performed as under :

(1) *First year*. Visual selection and santitary control (biotests on diagnostic plants plus ELISA tests). Infected cultivars may be freed from viruses by the use of meristem tip culture and/or combined with thermotherapy.

(2) *Second year*. Initiations of clones starting with known healthy plants. Serological tests of all to eliminate infected plants.

(3) *Third year*. Multiplication of clones starting with healthy plants. Serological tests of most of the plants to eliminate infected plants.

(4) *Fourth year*-Multiplication of healthy clones and serological assays of a predetermined number of plants. Eliminate infected plants.

(5) *Fifth year*. Multiplication of healthy clones in field grown under isolated conditions. Serologial assays of a number of plants evenly distributed in a given space. Eliminate both infected and suspected diseased plants. Selected plants represent the super elite.

(6) Multiply super elite clones in isolated fields. Serological assays of a pre-determined number of plants. Eliminate infected and suspected to be infected plants. Continue to multiply elite plants, which represent the basic potato seed for continued reproduction; that is, the selection of virus free seed is in an ongoing process which is an important procedure for virus free potato production.

4. Cuttings, bulbs and tubers

Many virus diseases such as sugarcane mosaic and some viruses of potato are disseminated with their vegetative parts used as seed. In such cases, care should be taken to select these plant materials from such plants that are not infected. However, this method is not efective when the symptoms are not visible and when secondary infection through vectors is common to occur. In such cases, attempt should be made to grow a separate crop for seed purposes in a protected area with all possible means to protect the crop from vectors.

5. Rogueing of the field and surroundings

Removal of all diseased plants as soon as they are spotted has proved advantageous in many crops like sugarcane and potato. This method has been observed to be useful in controlling sugarcane mosaic provided

(1) The infection is less than 5%,

(2) The rougeing has been started at the right time and done frequently,

(3) Healthy seed cuttings are being used for planting and

(4) The fields and its surroundings are being kept free from weeds functioning as reservoir to the virus.

6. Field sanitation

Field sanitation is another line of defense against plant diseases as it eliminates or reduces the pathogen inoculum in the field, storage area or on a plant. It also prevents the spread of inoculum from infected plant materials to healthy plants. General sanitation practices include removing diseased plants or plant parts by pruning and rougeing; destroying plants and leaf debris along with leaf litter that may contain inoculum by composting and burning; removing alternate and reservoir hosts of pathogen; keeping the fields or gardens and its surroundings free from weeds; preventing introduction of pathogens and their spread by using pathogen free tools, equipment and clothes and planting pathogen free seeds and propagating materials in a pathogen free soil. In order to prevent the spread of a pathogen and to minimize post harvest diseases, it is also essential to wash hands when picking, packaging and handling fruits, flowers and vegetables. There are many problems with sanitation also. One of the problems in plant disease management is its inability to eliminate the pathogens completely through sanitation. The other problem is to keep the agricultural work area perfectly clean. Furthermore, sanitation is the labour intensive process and sanitation may not be effective when severe outbreak of a disease can develop from small amount of inoculum. Besides, sanitation is easy to follow in small area but very difficult in larger areas.

7. Restricted planting through legislation

Legislation may restrict the growing of those crops which are likely to become infected with virus diseases or act as sources of survival of diseases for other crops. Such restrictions have been imposed on certain crops in Australia and Philippines to prevent spread of bunchy top of banana.

8. Heat therapy for virus free seed material

Heat therapy has been found successful in some viral diseases usually transmitted through cuttings, bulbs and grafts. It has been observed that most of the viruses causing sugarcane diseases are adversely affected by heat treatments of seed cuttings. Sugarcane mosaic has been controlled by treating the cuttings at 53-54°C. Immersion of sets in water at 52°C for 20 minutes inactivate the virus to cause chlorotic streak of sugarcane. Similar results have been observed in many virus diseases of some fruits. In addition to the use of high temperature, low temperature can also be used in similar way. Temperatures of 5°C to 15°C followed by meristene tip culture have been used to eradicate potato virus A and Y from infected potatoes. In this treatment, low temperature stops virus synthesis, allowing virus free explants to be taken and tissue cultured into healthy plants.

9. Tuber indexing in potato

This method is used for production of virus free tubers of potato in large scale of seed production. Tuber indexing is done to discard virus infected clones. In recent years ELISA has been employed for tuber indexing which has replaced conventional chloroplast agglutination tests.

10. Tissue culture technique for virus eradication

Various types of tissues have been cultured to produce virus free plants from infected parent material including calls, protoplasts, various reproductive tissues and meristem tips.

3. CONTROL OF INCOMING VECTORS

This is one of the important steps in the prevention of plant virus diseases during growth of the crop. In order to prevent insect vectors from reaching the diseased or healthy plants, proper spraying with insecticides should be undertaken. Use of trap crops to attract and destroy the insect vectors is also recommended. Besides these, use of cages, barriers and cover crops are also useful to control spread of some virus diseases. Physical barriers such as tarred paper or coarse string netting have been tried to protect *Brassica* seedlings from aphid-borne non-persistent viruses. However, a narrow barrier of barley is more effective and cheaper.

Vector control in its broadest sense includes every thing that makes life hard for insects and tends to kill them and to prevent their increase or spread. The control of insects can be accomplished in many ways as classified as follows :

AN OUTLINE OF CONTROL MEASURES FOR VECTORS

Applied control. Measures to destroy insects that depend upon man for their application or success and can be influenced by him to a considerable degree, is called as applied control.

(i) Chemical control. Preventive or remedial operations which depends for their effectiveness upon the chemical action or chemical properties of the substances used. Different kinds of chemicals/substances are used as chemical control measures.

❍ A. Insecticides

Substances that kill insects by their chemical actions are called as insecticides. Insecticides are of three types.

1. Stomach poisons. Such as sprays, dusts, or dips that kill the insect when they are swallowed. Examples are lead arsenate, calcium arsenate, Paris green, sodium fluride, borax, thallium, phosphorus, mercury compounds, fixed nicotines and other organic toxicants.

2. Contact poisons. Sprays, dusts, or dips that kill the insect without being swallowed. Examples include Nicotine preparations, lime-sculpture, oil emulsions, pyrethrums, benzene hexa chloride and organic phosphates.

3. Fumigants. Chemicals used in the form of gas that kill insects. Fumigants are usually applied in an enclosure of some kind. Examples are hydrogen cyanide, carbon bisulfide, sulphur dioxide, para-dichlorobenzene, chloropicrin, ethylene oxide and methyl bromide etc.

❍ B. Auxiliary synergistic or supplemental substances

Materials added to sprays or dusts, which are not primarily toxicant but which make the insecticide cover more economical. Such materials stick or adhere better to plants and spread over plant surfaces more quickly and completely. Such material includes :

(*i*) **Carriers.** Such as water in a spray.

(*ii*) Talc or gypsum in a dust or bran in a poison

(*iii*) **Emulsifiers.** Such as soap, flours, calcium and potassium caseinate, blood albumin

(*iv*) **Stickers.** Such as lime, rosin and glues.

(*v*) **Spreaders, wetting agents and detergents**. Such as caseinates, oleates, stearates and variety of sulfated and sulfonated organic compounds.

(*vi*) **Stabilizers.** Such as caustic soda, glue and gelatin.

(*vii*) **Activators.** Such as sesamin and N-isobutyl- undecyleneamide.

❍ C. Attractants

Substances used in poisoned baits, sprays or dusts to induce insects to eat the poisoned material or to lure insects in to traps are called as attractauts.

❍ D. Repellents

Substances that keep insects away because of their offensive appearance, odour or taste such substances are called as repllants.

OTHER MEASURES FOR MANAGEMENT OF VECTORS

(ii) Mechanical and physical control

It includes special operations against insects that kill them by their physical and mechanical actions. Mechanical measures include operation of machinery or application of manual operations. Such operations include hand destruction (hand picking, jarring, swatting and worming), mechanical exclusion (screening, tree banding, linears barriers and fly nets), use of traps, suction and other collecting machines and use of crushing, dragging or grinding machines.

(iii) Physical measures

The application or manipulation of physical phenomena (opposed to chemical) are physical measures of insect control. Such measure includes manipulation of water or humidity (drainage or dehydration of breeding media or flooding and syringing), manipulation of temperature (superheating, burning, use of low temperatures), use of electric shock, electrostatic field, use of light and other radiant energy and use of sound waves.

(iv) Cultural control

Regular farm operations performed in such a way which are useful to destroy insects or prevent their injuries are called as cultural control. Such operations include crop rotation, variations in the time and method of planting or harvesting, destruction of crop residues, weeds and volunteer plants etc., use of resistant varieties, pruning and thinning, fertilizing and stimulating vigorous growth.

(v) Biological control

The introduction, encouragement and artificial increase of predaceous and parasitic insects, other animals and diseases to control the insect pests are called as biological control. Such practices include as under :

(1) Protection and encouragement of insectivorous wild birds and other animals. (2) Introduction, artificial increase and colonization of parasitic and predaceous insects, mites, worms, birds, fishes, toads and other animals. (3) The spread and increase of fungus, bacterial virus or protozoal diseases of insects and liberation of infected insects. (4) Use of growing plants to destroy, repel or prevent damage by insects.

(vi) Oil sprays

Spraying of paraffin or mineral oil on leaf surfaces of host plant has been found effective against aphids and white flies. However, problems associated with using oil sprays as a control measure, include phytotoxicity and failure to maintain continuous cover of oil over the whole surface of the plant. Besides, oil layer may be readily removed by rain or over head irrigation. However, oil sprays have been effective in controlling a number of vectors.

❍ E. Legal control measures

The control of insects by controlling human activities include (1) Inspection and quarantine laws to prevent the introduction of new insects/pests from foreign countries or their spread within the country. (2) Laws to enforce the application of control measures such as spraying, the cleaning up of the crop residues and eradication measures. (3) Insecticide laws to govern the manufacturer to sale and prevent the adulteration and misbranding of insecticides. (4) Poison residue laws should be imposed which fix a tolerance of various insecticides upon food products offered for sale and transportation.

❍ F. Natural control measures

All the measures are natural control measures that control, destroy or check insects which do not depend upon man and can not be greatly influenced by man. Such factors include climatic factors (rainfall, sunshine, cold, heat and wind), topographic features (as rivers, lakes, type of soil and other features that serve as barriers), predators and parasites already present in nature and insect diseases naturally present in the region.

4. VIRUS RESISTANT AND TRANSGENIC VARIETIES

Resistance is the capacity of the organism to withstand or oppose the operation of or to lessen or overcome the effects of an injurious and pathogenic factor. In other words, the term resistance can refer to the capacity of a plant to withstand damaging physical or chemical factors that cause physiological disorders or non-infectious diseases (drought resistance, frost resistance, salt resistance and herbicide resistance). In plant pathology, it usually refers to the capacity of a plant to lessen the activity or harmful effects of a pathogen or pathogens such as virus, fungus and bacterium.

The development of resistant varieties is the most satisfactory method of plant disease control but comparatively very few viruses have been controlled in this manner. The satisfactory control that has been achieved in our country through varietal resistance is that of sugarcane mosaic and some virus diseases of fruits, vegetables and mushrooms. Wild species of plants sometimes possess good tolerance to viruses and many other diseases. If these sources can be used to develop resistance in cultivated plants, a solution to the problem can be achieved. Plants can resist entry of virus or discourage vectors like aphids or white flies in diverse ways such as due to the biochemical nature of their sap, physical properties or due to the thickness of the waxy cuticles or because of the density of the glandular hairs on a leaf.

Resistance to viruses in varieties is the most dependable approach for controlling virus diseases but very few varieties are available in our country. CPRI hybrids in potato namely, VB-8, PH-12-22, 8-5 and 55-123 etc. possess resistance/tolerance to one or the other viruses. Resistance to vector aphids has been observed in potato cultivars like kufri badshah, kufri shakti, kufri jyoti and SLB Z/405-a have been reported from CPRI, Shimla. Tolerant varieties like kufri ashoka, kufri badshah and kufri sinduri are tolerant against PVX and PVY.

Transgenic resistance. The development of plant genetic transformation technology provides a powerful new tool for the development of disease resistant plants. Genetic enginering approaches allow the introduction of novel resistance genes, including genes from sexually incompatible and synthetic genes designed to interfere with specific pathogens or pathogenicity factors. Plants including new genes introduced by techniques other than hybridization with sexually compatible species is termed as transgenic. Transgenic resistance is usually based on expression of fully sequenced genes with thoroughly characterized resistance mechanism.

Pathogen-derived genes for virus resistance. The first commercial applications of transgenic resistance were against viral diseases which were built on an earlier approach of mild strain protection. This pathogen derived resistance has been developed using full or partial sequences from a range of viral genes that includes those encoding coat proteins and replicases. The same genes can be used as targets for inactivation by expression of antisense or ribozyme constructs in transgenic plants.

Pathogen derived resistance is a key concept in engineering of plant resistant to viral infection. Host expression of these pathogen derived genes can alter the life cycle of the virus in several ways and detailed understanding is the key factor in the abiity to design effective biological stategies for controlling plant diseases.

To date, the most convenient source of effective virus resistance, genes have been from viral genome. The construction of virus resistance genes from the virus own genetic material is commonly referred to as pathogen derived resistance (PDR). There is a major advantage in it because the viruses have relatively small genomes and it is simple to clone the potential resistant genes. Sanford and Johnston (1985) described the concept in *J. Theory. Biol.* that disruption of critical aspects of virus replication and/or movement should lead to an attenuated or aborted infection of a host, resulting in virus resistant phenotype. Virus activities can be disrupted by the expression of viral gene products in such a way that the gene products are disfunctional for the virus.

In a typical virus infection cycle, the RNA and protein products of viral genes interact with each other and with specific host cell proteins and structures, form the molecular machines that catalyze and regulate virus replication, gene expression and movement in an infected plant. One way to disrupt the normal activities of a virus is to disrupt these machines. If a plant cell is engineered to express a dysfunctional viral gene product, an invading virus may utilize this dsfunctional product. A machine (or virus) made with defective parts may not function properly. This can lead to a virus resistant phenotype in transgenic plants.

The PDR approach has proved to be very successful one and effective virus resistance genes have ben generated for more than nine different virus groups, using a variety of different virus derived sequences. The virus-resistant phenotypes observed in different transgenic plants ranged from a short delay in the appearance of virus-induced symptoms to apparent immunity.

❍ Transgenic sources

There are two important sources of transgenes. They are of (1) virus origin and (2) plant origin.

1. Transgenes of virus origin are coat protein, replicase protein, movement protein, proteases, antisense sequences etc.
2. Transgenes of host plant origin are R-genes and antiviral protein.

❍ Virus derived resistance (VDR)

The events that follow infection includes disassembly of virus particles, synthesis or transcription of mRNA where required, translation of proteins coded by viral genome for various functions, maturation of particles, systemic infection and vector transmission. Strategies directed to interfere with any of these functions, usually results in the development of virus resistant transgenic plants (VRTPs).

1. Coat protein gene mediated resistance - Coat protein (Cp) gene is the most commonly used transgene for developing virus resistant transgenic plants against viruses belonging to different groups. However, replicase protein gene and movement protein genes are also used as transgenes. Coat protein is most widely used transgene to generate virus resistant transgenic plants. The strategy is commonly referred to as coat protein mediated resistance (CPMR) and occasionally as genetically engineered cross protection. The mechanism of resistance induced by coat protein gene is either through the protein encoded by protein mediated transgene or by transcript of the RNA mediated transgene or both. Coat protein gene induced resistance is protein mediated when a single copy of transgene is inserted. This transgene undergoes transcription and translation, resulting in high levels of protein. This protein inhibits disassembly of infecting virus particles. It seems likely for the viruses belonging to potex-, tenui- and tobamovirus groups.

2. Replicase protein mediated resistance - Replicase protein mediated resistance is derived by replicase protein gene, which is the second widely used transgene to confer resistance against plant viruses. This strategy is referred to as replicase protein mediated resistance (RPMR). Molecular mechanism of replicase protein mediated resistance is not fully understood; however, it seems to be either protein or RNA mediated.

3. Movement protein mediated resistance-Cell to cell or long distance transport of viruses in plants is brought about by movement protein (MPs) or coat protein or helper component of protinase (Hc-pro) protein encoded by viruses. Interfering with cell to cell or long distance transport would thus be an ideal strategy for developing resistance.

4. Antisense RNA mediated resistance - Antisense technology provides protection either by inhibition of gene expression or viral replication. It is used against RNA/DNA viruses. Transgene engineered with gene replicase in antisense orientation show attenuated symptoms to the virus as reported.

❍ Host plant derived resistance or natural resistance

1. Resistance genes (R-gene) - Many plant genes have been reported and identified to impart resistance against viruses. A naturally occurring gene from tobacco and introduced in tomato has been reported to give good protection against TMV and *Tomato mosaic virus.*

2. Antiviral protein genes- Natural resistance to virus infection in non host has been attributed to the presence of antiviral proteins. The novel bio-molecules have been identified from several plant species and genes coding them have been transferred to the other desirable plants.

❍ Method of gene transfer

There are different methods of gene transfer. Some important methods are as under :

* Through use of vectors.
* Direct DNA uptake by cells.
* Polyethylene glycol (PEG) induced DNA uptake.
* Electroporation.
* Microinjection.
* Particle gene.
* Calcium phosphate precipitation and
* Liposome mediated DNA transfer.

Among all these, vector mediated gene transfer is most commonly used.

❍ Genome sequencing and its importance

A whole genome is the full genetic map of genes combined with a complete DNA sequence and other physical and linkage maps for a single organism. It is like a cartographic map that allows us to organize discovery into a database but also acts as a discovery tool at the same time. A complete genome is highly valuable because all the genes required to sustain life are known to be in the sequence. The physical arrangement of genes can provide clues to gene regulation and structure.

The technology for genome sequencing is dynamic and complex and a brief overview of the technology will highlight why the future looks so bright. There are two important methods that are represented in the diversity of genome sequencing projects being conducted today. The first strategy of The Institute for Genomic Approach, Shotgun sequencing is well known as the research (IGR) for sequencing microbial genomes. In this approach the whole genome is sheared into small pieces of DNA that are then cloned in to *Escherichia coli* and sequenced more or less randomly. Shotgun sequencing is fast and inexpensive but informatics support must be strong enough because DNA is sequenced in millions of small fragments of only a few hundred base pairs that must be reassembled into the whole genome.

The second major approach is clone by clone approach in which the genome is sequenced in a systematic way using some type of logical framework represented by yeast artificial chromosomes (YACs) or bacterial artificial chromosomes (BACs). These clones may be made from sequene tagged sites (STSs) or by amplification of known DNA sequences from sequence characterized maps. This approach is slower and expensive. There are more than 26 completed microbial genomes listed on the TIGR web site (www.tigr.org).

5. BIOLOGICAL METHODS OF CONTROL

This is usually taken to mean the release or encouragement of predators or parasites of the pests which have a limited host range to the pest species and its near relatives. They do not endanger beneficial species of these pests. This method of control is of great importance because it is economical, beneficial and simple. About 40-60% of aphids species are eaten by predators belonging to Coccinellid beetles and about 30 species of Hymenoptera are known to attack *Myzus persicae*, which is the most important aphid vector well known to transmit a large number of viruses causing diseases of economic importance.

6. IMMUNIZATION FOR MANAGEMENT

In human beings and cattles, immunization is a very successful method of managing virus diseases. Through vaccination the immunity is acquired against different virus diseases such as small pox, chicken pox, influenza and many other diseases. This method has not yet been very successful for controlling plant viruses.

Many mechanisms, operating at different stages in the sequence between contact with a pathogen and completion of the disease syndrome or pathogen life cycle can contribute to disease resistance. In some cases these mechanism operate so early and so effectively that the plant is exempt from infection by a particular strain or species of the pathogen or may exempt from detectable pathogen multiplication. Such plants are usually said to be immune to that particular pathogenic species or strain.

However, in some other cases, the mechanism operates later and reduces the extent of pathogenic multiplication or the severity of the pathogenic symptoms. In such case the level of resistance is expressed as high, moderate, or low; or by a score on a defined numerical scale. The term susceptiblity is commonly used to describe degree of non-immunity. It may be explained as high resistance corresponds with low susceptibility.

Susceptible plants may escape infection as observed in some cases. It is common for disease severity to vary in a genetically susceptible plant variety in different years or in different locations. In such case, individual plants or entire fields may fail to become diseased and remain free because they are not exposed to infective units of the pathogen under environmental conditions suitable for disease development. This phenomenon is known as disease escape. This condition is favourable for crop production and may be due to the following management strategies including :

1. Quarantine measures to exclude the pathogen.
2. Choice of planting time and location to avoid the pathogen.
3. Suitable treatment to protect the plants.

Failure of a plant to become infected by a compatible pathogen may be due to some quality of plant interfering with the operation of the vector is known as klendusity. It may be considered as disease escape.

As early as 1929, Mckinney, a scientist of U.S. Department of Agriculture, demonstrated that a plant infected with one virus was protected from infection by a second challenging (virulent) virus. It was called as cross protection. Cross protection is an important term, usually used in plant pathology. It refers to the ability of the plant infected with one virus to exhibit some degree of protection against challenged inoculation with another most severe strain of the same virus. This phenomenon should not be confused with antagonism, acquired or induced immunity. This term was introduced by Price in 1940. Now days, the term genetically engineered cross protection is being used to refer to plants protected from virus infection by the incorporation of viral sequences into the host genome.

In contrast to cross protection, the acquired or induced immunity response was first described a year before Mc Kinney's report. It was further observed that *Tobacco ringspot virus* which induced severe ring spot symptoms, usually recover as new growth showed no symptoms. In such case, virus could always be isolated from recovered tissue. This phenomenon is usually considered as self protection, rather than cross protection.

7. ANTIVIRAL AGENTS FOR DISEASE MANAGEMENT

No chemical substances (viricides) are yet available for controlling virus diseases of plants. Foliar application of certain growth regulating substances such as gibberalic acid has been effective in stimulating growth of the virus suppressed axillary buds in sour cherry yellows, resulting in increased fruit production. Similarly, sprays with gibberalic acid can be used to overcome stunting caused by the effect of some viruses as observed in case of severe etch virus on tobacco.

Effects of some antiviral agents have been studied. The antiviral agents when applied either to the infected plant before bud excision or incorporated into the culture medium, decrease the virus concentration without causing significant harm to the plant tissue. Elimination of *Potato virus S* is facilitated after the mother plants had been treated with anti-metabolites prior to meristem culture while incorporation of riboside in the medium greatly helps eradication of *Potato virus X, Potato virus Y* and *Potato virus M*.

Strong virus resistance inducing substances have been isolated from some plants especially *Clerodendrum aculeatum* and *Boerhavia diffusa* which are objects of special interest because they are excellent viral inhibitors. Analysis of such plant extracts has shown that the biological activity is due to the presence of potent basic proteins. Resistance reponse leading to immunity can be achieved by using high doses of systemic resistance inducing proteins (40 to 80 μg/ml.). No phytotoxic or otherwise deterimental effects are observed following applications of aqueous solutions of such proteins. Purified resistance inducers were identified as low molecular weight basic proteins of 30 kDa to 34 kDa. The proteins so isolated were not phytotoxic. Besides this, they improved the plant growth and yield. Proteins were purified using different liquid chromatography columns.

8. INTEGRATED METHODS OF DISEASE MANAGEMENT

Key concept of disease management are elimination or reduction of primary inoculum, delay the onset of disease, slow the secondary disease cycle and increase the host plant resistance. Because of the diversity of pathogens that attack nearly every plant, the plant pathologist should integrate all the strategies in addition to the economic loss, pathogen, epidemiology, history of disease and other important information in disease development programme.

The compexity of integrated disease management strategies depends on whether the crop is perennial or annual, its value, the range of economically important diseases present in the production area and options available for disease management. Disease management strategies must be compatible with management of insect pests, weeds, soil erosion, control practices and environmental factors.

No one method of control is likely to keep the crops entirely free from virus infection. Therefore, different methods of disease control are applied to the same crop based on profit and loss ratio. One of the main aims of integrated control is to avoid changing in balance of nature. In this method judicious use of chemicals in the form of insecticide to manage vectors and in the form of weedicide to manage weeds as alternate or collateral hosts are also used if so desired.

24

GLOSSARY

Acquired resistance : A resistance response developed by a susceptible host. This resistance is not inherited.

Adenosine 5′-triphosphate (ATP) : A compound of one molecule each of adenine and D-ribose with three molecules of phosphoric acid. It conveys energy needed for metabolic reactions. It loses an phosphate group to become ADP.

Adjuvant : In serology, a substance injected mixed with antigens which non-specifically enhances or modifies the immune response to that antigen.

Affinity : The strength of the antigen-antibody interaction. High-affinity antibodies have a higher rate of association with antigen.

Agar gel column : Agar gel columns are used in analytical processes where it is necessary to separate chemicals with different sized molecules. The process is used in the PAGE test for virus identification.

Agarose : A constituent of agar lacking inhibitors of virus development. It is usually used in gel electrophoresis.

Agarose gel electrophoresis : It is a technique used for separating proteins or nucleic acids by passage of an electric current through the gel.

Agent of disease : A pathogen.

Agent of inoculation : It transmits the inoculum from its source to the susceptible hosts to incite infection. Wind, water, rain splash, insects, mites, tools and equipments are some of the common agents of inoculation.

Agglutination : It is a serological test in which viruses suspended in a liquid collect into clumps whenever the suspension is treated with antiserum containing antibodies specific against these viruses.

Agglutinin : An antibody that causes another particular antigen to clump and settle out of suspension.

Aggregation : Intermolecular interactions that do not involve covalent linkage.

Agrobacterium tumefaciens **:** A species of gram-negative, rod shaped soil bacterium. It often contains copies of a large plasmid, designated Ti. A Ti containing strain can infect many plants and form crown gall tumors.

Alate : Winged, which is a form in the life cycle of certain insects such as aphids.

Allele : It is one of the several alternative forms of a gene occupying a given focus on a chromosome.

Alternate hosts : A plant, different from the principal host, on which a pathogen may survive to complete its life cycle.

Alternative host : One of the several principal hosts, the pathogen can survive. Alternative hosts are not required for completion of a pathogen's life cycle.

Amber mutation : Point mutation producing a UAG termination codon and thereby premature termination of translation.

Amino acid : Basic building block of proteins that contains amino and carboxyl groups plus a variable side chain that determines the properties of the individual amino acid. Twenty amino acids are known to occur in nature.

Amino acid sequence : Linear order of the amino acids in a peptide or protein.

Amino group : ($-NH_2$). A basic chemical group binds a protein to form $-NH_3^+$. The amino terminus of a polypeptide is the end with a free α-amino group.

Angstrom (Å) : A unit of length equal to 1/10 millimicron or nanometer (nm) = 1/10,000 micron or micrometer.

Annealing : is the pairing of complementary single strands of DNA to form a double helix.

Angular velocity : Rate of rotation measured in radians per second. Angular velocity ($a\upsilon$) = 0.10472 rpm.

Anodized coating : A thin, hard layer of aluminium oxide formed electrochemically on aluminum rotor and/or accessory surfaces as a protective coating for corrosion resistance.

Antibiosis : Antagonistic association exists between two organisms or between one organism and a metabolic product of another organism.

Antibiotic : A chemical compound produced by one microorganism which inhibits or kills other living organisms.

Antibody : A new or altered specific protein produced in blood in response to an antigenic stimulus.

Anticodon : A sequence of three nucleotides complementary to the codon triplet in mRNA.

Anticoding strand : Anticoding strand of duplex DNA is used as a tempelate to direct the synthesis of RNA that is complementary to it.

Antigen : Foreign viral protein occasionally a complex lipid or polysaccharide and some nucleic acids, that when injected in to living animal tissues, stimulates the production and release of specific antibodies in the blood stream antagonistic to the substance injected and capable of specifically binding to antigen binding sites of antibody molecules. In other words antigen is any molecule whose entry into an organism provokes synthesis of an antibody.

Antigen reaction : The specific interaction between an antigen and an antibody that recognizes a specific structural feature of the antigen and binds to it.

Antigen binding capacity : It is the measurement of the ability of an antibody to bind antigen.

Antigen binding site : The area of an antibody molecule that binds to antigen.

Antigenic determinant : The small site or epitope on an antigen molecule to which an antibody is specifically bound.

Antiserum (pl. **antisera) :** The blood serum of vertebrates that contains antibodies after inoculation of specific antigens.

Antiserum titer : The reciprocal of the highest dilution of an antiserum that can react with its homologous virus antigen.

Antisense gene : An engineered gene placed in inverted orientation relative to a promoter which when transcribed produces a transcript complementary to the mRNA transcribed from the normal orientation of the gene.

Aphid : A small sucking agent of the family Aphididae, order Homoptera capable of transmitting many plant viruses.

Apical : At or near the upper end or tip.

Apical meristem : A mass of undifferentiated cells capable of division at the tip of the root or shoot. These cells differentiate by division.

Apical dominance : The phenomenon of suppression of growth of an axillary bud in the presence of the terminal bud on the branch.

Apterous : Wingless stage in the life cycle of certain insects.

Arbovirus : A virus replicating both in an arthopod and vertebrate.

ATCC. Initials of the American Type Culture Collection which is located at 10801 University building, Manassas, V A 20110-2209. A large collection of bacteria, fungi, viruses, viroids and cells are available there. Any of these can be obtained on request on nominal fee. Address-(Telex - ATCCROVE 908-768, Telephone 703- 365-2700, Fax-703-365-2701).

ATP : Adenosine 5′-triphosphate.

Attenuate, attenuated : To weaken or decrease in virulence or pathogenicity. DNA sequences that retard or stop RNA transcription.

Attenuated virus strain : A seleted strain of a virulent virus that does not cause severe disease symptoms associated with the parent virus but still replicate.

Attenuation : The process of producing a weakened virus strain.

Aucuba : Bright yellow mosaic leaf variegation of genetic or virus origin.

Autoclaving : Sterlization by heat (dry or steam).

Auxins : a plant growth regulator that causes cell elongation.

Avidity : The stability of the antigen-antibody complex as governed by the affinity of the antibody for the antigen.

Avirulent : Non-pathogenic. Virus strain lacking virulence.

Bacteriophage : A virus replicating in bacteria only.

Bacterium : A unicellular prokaryotic microscopic organism that lacks chlorophyll and multiplies by fission.

BAC : Bacterial artificial chromosome.

Badnavirus group : The type member of the group is *Commelina yellow mottle virus.* It is a new group and members of this group are known to cause diseases in clonally propagated tropical crops such as banana and sugarcane etc. Particles are bacilliform and have a genome consisting of ds DNA. Member viruses are usually transmitted by seed and mealy bugs.

Base analogue : A compound resembling one of the natural bases of RNA or DNA that is incorporated into newly synthesized nucleic acid by substituting for the normal base which can result in mutation or growth inhibition. Example : 5-fluorouracil. It is a substitute for uracil.

Base pair : A pair of nucleotides held together by hydrogen bonding and found in double stranded nucleic acids. The DNA contains the pairs A-T and G-C; RNA contains G-C and A-U.

Base ratio : The ratio of adenine (A) and thymine (T) to guanine (G) and cytosine (C) in the DNA in an organism.

Base sequences : The order in which the purine and pyrimidine molecules A, G, C, U (T) occur along the polynucleotide chain of nucleic acids.

B cells : Lymphocytes that produce antibodies.

Binary symmetry : Combination of cubic and helical symmetry.

Binomial nomenclature : The scientific method of naming organisms.

Biotransformation : The conversion of a small part of molecule in the structure and composition by means of biological systems.

Bioassay. Determining virus amount by measuring its biological activity/infectivity.

Biotechnology : The science which involves the use of genetically engioneered microorganisms and/or modern techniques and processes with biological systems for betterment and improvement of the plant.

Biomolecules : These are compounds that are produced by some type of biological source such as a plant, animal, microorganism or cultured cells.

Booster dose : A dose of immunogen given several days, weeks, months or years after the initial immunizing dose to stimulate production of antibody.

5-Bromo uracil : Mutagenic thymine analog in which the 5-CH group has been replaced by bromine.

Buoyant density : The density of a particle in a specified liquid medium. The density at which a virus or other macromolecule neither sinks nor floats when suspended in an aqueous solution of a heavy metal salt, calcium chloride or a sugar.

°C (Centigrade/Celsius) : Unit of temperature.

C-terminus : End of the peptide chain with a free alpha-carboxyl group.

Capsid : The protein coat of a virion composed of protein subunits or capsomeres forming a closed shell surrounding the DNA or RNA.

Capillovirus (capillo means hair) group : Type members of the group are *Apple stem grooving virus* and *Potato virus T*. The virus particles are filamentous particles forming clusters. They measure about 600-700 nm in length and 12 nm in width. The members are transmitted by seed and sap but not through any vector.

Capsid polypeptide : Protein forming part of the capsid structure of a virus particle.

Capsomer(s) : A protein sub-unit or a small protein molecule or group of molecules that is structural and chemical unit of the protein coat (capsid) of a virus.

Carboxyl group : COOH

Carboxy-methyl-cellulose : A cellulose derivative used to separate proteins by iron exchange chromatography.

Cucumber mosaic virus RNA 5 Syn. Carna-5 RNA : A satellite RNA of CMV dependent on the remainder of the CMV genome for its own replication but not essential for the replication of the CMV particle.

Carrier : Plant or animal harboring an infectious disease agent.

cDNA : Abbreviation for complementary DNA.

Cellular immunity : Immunity ascribed to various cellular functions other than those that produce antibody.

Cell culture : The growing of cells *in vitro.*

Cell line : Cells originating from a primary culture successfully subcultured for different items (first, second etc.).

Cellular response : Immune response which involves the interaction between cells and an antigen.

Central dogma molecular biology : The concept that the base relationship among DNA, RNA and protein is "one way". It can be explained that DNA serves as a template for both its own duplication and the synthesis of RNA. RNA in turn serves as messenger for protein synthesis.

Centrifugal effect : It is accumulated value of time and angular velocity.

Centrifugal force : In a centrifugal field, the force which causes a particle to move away from the centre of rotation.

Cesium chloride density gradient centrifugation : Method for separating viruses based on their density. Sedimentation ceases when the virus reaches a position in the gradient equal to their own buoyant density.

Chelating agent : A chemical such as sodium EDTA which will bind with bivalent and trivalent cations to assist in virus purification.

Chemotaxonomy : Taxonomy based on chemical characteristics.

Chemotype : Group of chemically differentiated individuals of a species of unknown or of no taxonomic importance.

Chloramphenicol : Antibiotic which acts as phenylalanine analog, is isolated from *streptomyces venazuelae.* It inhibits prokaryotic protein synthesis.

Chloroplast : Specilized cytoplasmic organelle (plastid) found in plant cells. It is the site of photosynthesis.

Chlorosis : Yellowing or whitening of plant tissues due to loss of chlorophyll.

Cistron : The basic unit of a genetic function. Sequence of nucleotides within a certain area of DNA or RNA that codes for a particular protein.

Classification : A systematic arrangement of names of organisms into categories on the basis of characteristics, usually divided into divisions, sub-divisions, classes, orders, families, genera and species.

Cloning Vector : is a plasmid or phase that is used to carry inserted foreign DNA for the purposes of producing more material.

Clone : A population of cells, viruses or organisms of identical genotype produced asexually.

Coat protein : The protective protein layer(s) surrounding the viral nucleic acid.

Coding capacity : The amount of protein that a given DNA or RNA sequence can encode.

Coding sequence : The process by which nucleotides within a certain area of RNA or DNA determine the sequence of amino acids in the synthesis of a particular protein.

Codon : Three adjacent nucleotides coding for either an amino acid or a chain termination.

Complementary DNA (cDNA) : ssDNA synthesized by reverse transcription from an RNA Template; if the cDNA is made double- stranded and cloned, it is labelled as cDNA clone.

Complementary RNA (cRNA) : A ssRNA molecule complementary in base sequence to the single strand from which it was transcribed. Most ssRNA viruses use complementary RNA as intermediates in replication.

Complementary strand : A double-stranded nucleic acid molecule complementary in base sequence to the single strand from which it was transcribed.

Complementation : Occurs when one virus is assisted by another (or a strain of the same virus) to replicate.

Complement-fixation test (CFT) : A sensitive test in which the antigen-antibody reaction can be detected and quantified. It is often used for comparing different or related antigens, *e.g.*, viruses.

Conjugate : The product of joining two or more dissimilar molecules by covalent bonds.

Conservative replication : Opposite of semi-conservative replication; whereby no displacement of single stranded form from the double-stranded genome occurs during replication.

Constitutive resistance : Genetically controlled, inherited resistance.

Covalent bonds : Strong bonds formed by the sharing of electron pairs between atoms; also termed as *primary bonds.*

Cross inoculation : Inoculation with one virus, then simultaneously or later inoculation with a second virus.

Cross protection : A susceptible host infected with a virulent pathogen (usually a virus), thereby resists infection by a second, usually related virulent pathogen in the same host. In such case, the host expresses relatively mild symptoms, lower virus concentration, and/or restricted virus movement.

Cross reactive antigen : Antigen capable of combining with antibody produced in response to a different antigen; may cross react due to sharing of determinants by the two antigens or because the antigenic determinants of each, although not identical, are related closely.

Cryptovirus group : It is a new virus group whose type members are *White clover cryptic virus* and *Beat cryptic virus*. Virus particles are isometric in morphology containing ds RNA genome divided into 10 segments. They measure 30—38 nm in length. They are usually transmitted by seed and pollen and are known to occur in very low concentration being apparently unable to move from cell to cell.

Cross reactive antiserum : Antiserum capable of combining with different antigens that share common epitopes; such antisera can be purified to isolate several specific antibodies.

Cubic symmetry : Form of capsid in which protein subunits are assembled to a compact shell with three axes of symmetry, passing through apices, edges, and faces.

Cultivar (cv.) : A cultivated variety.

Culture collection : It is a botanical herbarium and a zoological museum for bacteria, fungi, viruses, viroids, cells, and other organisms.

Cu m : (cubic metre) = 1.30794 cu yard = 35.3144 cu ft = 28.3776 bushels = 264.173 U.S. gal = 1056.7 qt (liquid) = 2113.4 pints (liquid).

Cycloheximide : Antibiotic isolated from *Streptomyces griseus* which reversibly inhibits eukaryotic (but not Prokaryotic) protein biosynthesis.

Cytopathic effect (cpe) : Change in the microscopic appearance or morphology of cultured cells following virus infection, *e.g.*, cell fusion, inclusion bodies.

CMI AAB : Initials of the Common Wealth Mycological Institute/Association for Applied Biologists situated in the United Kingdom.

Clarification. Clarification is the removal of unwanted solid matter usually by centrifugation or filtration.

Da : Dalton.

Dalton : Unit of atomic size equal to the mass of a proton or single hydrogen atom ; an expression of molecular weight. *see* kilo Dalton (kDa).

Damage threshold : The lowest pest population density at which damage occurs.

De-aminase : An enzyme involved in the removal of an amino group from a molecule, in which ammonia is liberated.

Deamination : Removal of an amino group, especially from an amino acid.

***De novo* :** Arising from an unknown source.

Decarboxylation : Removal of a carboxyl group—COOH.

Defective interfering (DI) particles : Virus particles that lack part of the genome nucleic acid of the standard virus and that often interfere with its replication.

Defective virus : A virus that lacks part of its genome, or some function, and is thus unable to replicate fully.

Denaturation : The destruction of secondary and tertiary (H- bonds) structure of a protein, nucleic acid, or virus by physical or chemical means.

Denatured protein : A protein that has been altered by treatment with a physical or chemical agent to change its properties.

Density : means mass per unit volume.

Density separation : A centrifugal separation process based on differences in particle densities.

Density gradient : A gradient of a solute in a solvent used to support macromolecules during fractionation. It is used for separation of macromolecular species by centrifugation or electrophoresis.

Density-gradient centrifugation : A method of centrifugation in which particles (or components) of a purified virus separate in layers based on differing buoyant densities in sucrose or cesium chloride.

Deoxyribonuclease (DNase) : An enzyme that degrades DNA.

Deoxyribonucleic acid (DNA) : The gene-bearing material of each DNA virus, plant and animal cell.

DNA polymerase : One of the several enzymes which synthesizes a new DNA strand complementary to a template strand by adding nucleotides one at a time to a 3′-OH end.

Deoxyribose : A five-carbon sugar being one of the components of DNA It has one oxygen atom less than its parent sugar ribose.

DEP : Dilution end point.

Dependent transmission : Transmission of a virus (by aphids) that occurs only when the vector feeds on a source plant jointly infected by a second virus. The second virus is referred to as a *helper virus,* and the virus not transmissible on its own is called the *dependent virus.*

Determinant : Antigenic determinant.

Diagnosis (pl. **diagnoses) :** Identification of the nature and cause of a disease problem.

Diagnostic : A distinguishing characteristic important for identification of disease or other condition.

Dicotyledon, dicot (pl. **diçotyledonae,** adj. **Dicotyledonous) :** A flowering plant having two cotyledons (seed leaves), in contrast to monocotyledons (grasses, cereals).

Differential centrifugation : Cycles of alternate low-(to clarify) and high-speed (to sediment) centrifugation used to purify a virus.

Differential separation : A centrifugal separation process based on differences in particle sizes.

Differential hosts : Special species, cultivars, inbreds, or isogenic plants varying from susceptible to one virus but not another, that express distinctive symptoms ; commonly used to separate a virus from a mixture to facilitate identification.

Differentially permeable : Referring to membranes that allow certain substances to pass through and that retard or prevent the passage of others.

Diffusion coefficient : A measure of the rate at which a solute moves along a gradient from a higher to a lower concentration.

Dilution : The process of increasing the proportion of solvent or diluent to solute.

Dilution end point : The last point at which a virus remains infective in a progressive dilution series ; the greatest dilution of an antibody that gives a measurable reaction with an antigen in a serological test.

Disease cycle : The sequence of events involved in disease development, including the stages of developmet of the pathogen and the effect of the disease on the host ; the chain of events that occurs between the time of infection and the final expression of disease.

Disease gradient : Change in incidence of a disease with increasing distance from the source of infection.

Disease pyramid : A concept describing the four factors needed simultaneously for a plant disease to occur; a susceptible host, presence of a virulent pathogen, a favourable environment for infection and time to develop a disese.

Disease, plant : Any disturbance in a plant that interferes with its normal growth and development *e.g.*, structure and function, economic value or aesthetic quality which leads to the development of symptoms. Injury, in contrast, results from a momentary damage.

Disease range : The geographic distribution of a disease.

Disease tolerance : Capacity of a plant to maintain fairly normal vigour, without excessive injury or loss in yield, although infection by a pathogen is established within the plant.

Disease triangle : A concept describing the simultaneous occurrence of three factors such as a pathogen, a susceptible host and a favourable environment resulting in disease development.

Dispersal : Dissemination.

Dissemination (dispersal) : In relation to plant diseases, the transfer (spread) or transport of infectious material (inoculum) to healthy plant tissue by wind, water, insects, animals, machinery, or other means.

Distribution : Spread of a pathogen to areas outside of its previous geographical range; "geographical distribution" is synonymous with "range."

Disulfide bonds : Chemical bonds that bind polypeptide chains together.

DMSO : Dimethyl sulfoxide.

DNA (deoxyribonucleic acid) : A molecule occurring in nuclei of plant and animal cells composed of repeating subunits of nucleotides containing deoxyribose (a five-carbon sugar), phosphoric acid, and one of four nitrogenous bases (adenine, cytosine, guanine, and thymine). Every inherited charateristics has its origin in the code of an individual's complement of DNA. The linear chain of deox-yribonucleotides is double-stranded in some DNA viruses (ds-DNA) and single-stranded in others (ss-DNA). ds-DNA is held together by bonds between base pairs of nucleotides (adenosine, guanosine, cytidine, and thymidine); bonding occurs only between A-T and G-C; thus, one can determine the sequence of either strand from that of its partner. Also, in ds-DNA, the two strands are antiparallel in a double helix.

DNA-binding protein : A protein that binds directly to DNA; often determined by specific amino acid sequences.

DNA cloning : Means of isolating individual fragments from a mixture and multiplying each.

DNA-dependent DNA polymerases (I, II, III alpha, beta, gamma) : Enzymes that synthesize DNA from a DNA template.

DNA ligase : An enzyme that catalyzes phosphodiester bond formation between the 3-phosphate of one oligonucleotide and the 3′-hydroxyl of another involved in DNA synthesis and in linking DNA in genetic manipulation.

DNA-RNA hybrid : Double helix containing one strand of DNA hydrogen-bonded to one stand of RNA.

DNAse : An enzyme that breaks down DNA by hydrolysis.

DNA sequencing : The relative order of nucleotide pairs in a stretch of DNA, a gene, a chromosome, or an entire genome.

Dioecious aphid : An aphid whose life cycle alternates between a primary and secondary host plant.

Dorsal : Referring, to the back or upper surface of an organism.

Double antibody sandwich (DAS) : Methods in enzyme-linked immunosorbent assay (ELISA) in which the reactants are added to the test plate in the order or antibody, virus, antibody-enzyme complex, and enzyme substrate.

Doun stream process : (of protein) is the amount (or units) of the protein of interest divided by the total amount of protein in a sample.

Double-diffusion test : Antigen-antibody precipitation reaction in agar or a similar gel in which antigen and anitbody are allowed to diffuse toward one another and react at equivalence in the agar.

ds : Double-stranded (nucleic acid).

Durable resistance : It is used to deserible resistance that is long lasting.

Early genes : Viral genes expressed early in the replication cycle, usually involved in the replication of the viral nucleic acid.

EBIA : Electro Blot Immuno Assay (***See*** Western blot). A technique that combines polyacrylamide gel electrophoresis and ELISA on nitrocellulose or nylon membranes.

Ecdysis : The moulting of the integument of an insect.

Economic injury level : The lowest population density of pests that will cause economic damage.

Economic threshold level : The density of pests at which control measures should be used to prevent an increasing pest population from reaching an economic injury level.

Ecosystem : A community of living things and its environment.

ED : Effective dose.

ED50 : The dose that gives a 50% response.

Electro-focusing : Separating protein molecules by gel or density-gradient electrophoresis where a pH gradient exits. Each protein moves to a pH at its isoelectric point.

Electronic microscope serology : *See* immunosorbent electron microscopy (ISEM).

Electronic microscopy : Use of an elelctron microscope, in which a focused beam of electrons produces a greatly enlarged image of minute objects (such as virus particles).

Electrophoresis : The differential migration of charged molecules and macromolecular ions (e.g., fragments of nucleic acid or proteins) in a free solution or through a porous medium in an electric field; the porous supporting, medium may be filter paper, cellulose acetate or a gel.

Eloctrophoretic mobility : The relative rate of movement of a charged particle or virus per unit potential gradient where mobility is toward the cathode or the anode, depending on its net positive or negative charge at the pH used.

Electroporation : A method using an electric pulse, whereby nucleic acids or virus particles can be introduced into protoplasts or cells by creating transient pores in the plasma membrane.

ELISA : Enzyme-linked immunosorbent assay.

Empty virus particles : Virions-absent nucleic acid, which can be identified by negative staining and electron microscopy and of lower buoyant density than complete virus particles.

Embryo Culture : The culture of embryos in nutrient medium.

Epitope : An antigenic determinant of defined structure, *e.g.,* an identified oligosaccharide, or a chemical hapten that elicits the formation of antibodies.

Epidermal strip test : An electron microscope technique by which a virus can be quickly examined in crude-sap extracts. Quick leaf dip and quick dip techniques are the same.

Equilibrium density gradient centrifugation : Isopycnic gradient.

Equilibrium dialysis : A technique used to measure the affinity of antibody-antigen binding, based on diffusion of unbound antigen across a dialysis membrane.

Equivalence : The ratio of antibody to antigen that gives the maximum precipitation in a quantitative precipitation reaction.

Escape : A condition in which a susceptible plant avoids infectious disease through some character of the plant or its location.

Etiologic agent : The parasite or virus causing a disease in a plant or animal.

Etiology : The science of the causes or origins of disease ; the study of nature of the causal factor and its relations with the host.

Ethium bromide : is a fluorescent orange dye used commonly in the separation of DNA and in gel electrophoresis.

Evolution : The development of a species, genus, or other larger group of plants, animals, or other organisms over a long period of time.

Excise : Cut out and prepare a tissue for culture.

Exclusion : Control of disease by excluding the pathogen or infected plant materials from crop production areas (*e.g.,* by quarantines and embargoes).

Exonuclease : An enzyme requiring a free end in order to digest an RNA or DNA molecule both 5 -or 3′-exonucleases.

Extraction buffer : The buffer used in grinding of infected leaves during the initial stages of virus purification.

Fab fragment : Two Fab fragments constitute each 7S-antibody molecule. A Fab contains one antigen-combining site and can combine with antigen, as a univalent antibody but cannot form precipitates.

Fahrenheit (F) : A thermometer scale in which the freezing point of water (ice point) is set at 32° and the boiling point (steam point) is 212°. To convert from Fahrenheit to celsius, subtract 32° the Fahrenheit reading, multiply by 5, and divide the product by 9, Example : 132°F — 32 = 100 × 5 = 500 ; 500 / 9 = 55.5°C.

Filamentous : Composed of long thread-like structures, often used to describe bacterial colonies or virus particles.

Filter, bacterial : A special type of filter through which bacterial cells cannot pass.

Filterable virus : Capable of passing through the pores of a bacterial filter; applies to most viruses.

Fingerprinting : A procedure for characterizing DNA, RNA or proteins using electrophoretic or chromatographic analysis of specific fragments.

Flexuous : having turns, bends or windings alternately in opposite directions ; capable of bending.

Floating genera : Unassigned genera not placed in any families by the ICTV in its 7th Report (Van Regenmortel etal, 2000) are called as floating genera.

Flocculate (n: flocculation) : To precipitation reaction of antibody and antigen in which the precipitate appears as flakes of insoluble protein.

Fluorescence microscope : A compound light microscope arranged to emit radiation of specific wavelengths such as UV to the spectrum, which then fluoresces.

Fluorescent antibody : An antibody conjugated with a fluorescent dye, *e.g.*, fluorescein isothiocyanate, which then can be used in a fluorescent microscope to detect viral antigen in cells.

Foundation seed : Seed stocks increased from breeder seed and handled to maintain the genetic identity and purity of a cultivar.

Freezed-drying or lyophilization : Preservation of living microorganisms (or concentration of macromolecules with little or no loss of activity), by removing water under a high vacuum while tissue remains in a frozen state.

Freund's adjuvant : A substance containing an emulsifier (lanolin) and mineral oil that is mixed with an antigen then injected into muscles of an animal to produce antiserum. Adjuvant allows slow release of antigen-enhancing immune responses. Freund's complete adjuvant includes killed mycobacteria; Freund's incomplete adjuvant contains no mycobacteria.

Focus : The cite of initial disease infection from where secondary infection may occur (plural-foci).

G and C content : The total guanine (G) and cytosine (C) content of a nucleic acid, usually refers to double-stranded DNA. The G and C content is a good measure of such physical properties as melting temperature.

Gamma globulin : A fraction of serum proteins containing antibodies. The term for Immunoglobulin G (IgG) is used.

Gel : A jelly-like colloidal mass; coagulated colloid.

Gel chromatography : A molecular sieving (purification) procedure that separates viruses or proteins of different sizes when passed through the pores of gel beads such as agarose.

Gel double-diffusion : A serological test in which the antibody and antigen reactants diffuse toward each other in gel and react to form a visible precipitation line.

Geminivirus sub groups : Recently geminivirus group has been divided into three subgroups designed as I, II and III on the basis of host range, type of vector and genome fragmentation. Subgroup I—has monocotyledonous hosts, leaf hopper vectors and monopartite genome; subgroup II—has dicotyledonous host, leaf hopper vectors and monopartite genome; and subgroup III—has dicotyledonous hosts, whitefly vectors and bipartite genomes.

Gel electro diffusion : Electrophoresis of macromolecules in a matrix of agarose, polyacrylamide, or similar gel.

Gel filtration : A type of column chromatography that separates molecules on the basis of size.

Gene : The base triplets of the DNA molecule in a chromosome that determines one or more hereditary characters. The smallest functioning unit on a chromosome; bearer of an inherited factor ; an ordered sequence of nucleotides that specifies the manufacture of a single type of protein.

Major gene : Many genes that have large obserable effects on the phenotype.

Minor gene : One gene that has a specific effect on the phenotype.

Gene cloning : The isolation and multiplication of an individual gene sequence by its insertion, usually into a bacterium, where it can multiply.

Gene expression : Expression of genetic material as specific traits; transcription of mRNA from the DNA sequence of a gene; mRNA then translates into a protein = gene product.

Gene therapy : Insertion of more desirable DNA into cells to correct a given genetic defect.

Gene-for-gene hypothesis : The concept that corresponding genes for resistance and virulence exist in the host and pathogen, respectively.

Genetic code : The sequence of nitrogen bases in a DNA molecule that codes for an amino acid or protein. More broadly, the sequence of all events from translation of chromosomal DNA to the final synthesis of an enzyme.

Genetic engineering or genetic manipulation : Nucleotide insertion into or removal from an organism so that a cell can produce more or different chemicals or perform new functions.

Genetic map : A graphic representation of the linear arrangement of genes on a chromosome or genome by nucleotide sequence analysis.

Genetic marker : A mutation in a gene that allows its phenotypic identification.

Genetic variability : The ability of an organism to change inherited characteristics from one generation to the next.

Genetics : The science or study of patterns of inheritance of specific traits.

Genome : The complete genetic complement of an organism or virus; size is usually denoted in gene pairs ; in viruses the nucleic acid component, either DNA or RNA, which may consist of one (monoparite), two (bipartite), three (tripartite), or more (multipartite) molecular species.

Genomic library : Several clones of overlapping DNA fragments representing a genome.

Genotype : The set of genes that influences phenotype; individuals sharing a specific genetic makeup; the genetic constitution, expressed and latent of an organism.

Germplasm : Material capable of transmitting heritable characteristics sexually or asexually ; the total genetic variability available within an organism; a pool of germ cells or seed.

Glycoprotein : A conjugated protein with at least one carbohydrate covalently attached to an amino acid.

gp : Gene product.

Graft, grafting : Transfer of aerial parts of one plant (*e.g.* buds or twigs — the scion) into close cambial contact with the root or trunk (the rootstock) of a different plant ; a method of plant propagation. Also, the joining of cut surfaces of two plants so as to form a living union.

Graftage : Method of inserting buds, twigs, or shoots in other stems or roots for fusion of tissues.

Graft indexing : A procedure to determine the presence or absence of a virus, phytoplasma in a plant. The plant is grafted to a healthy plant known to show symptoms if infected. Used to detect disease agents not readily transmitted mechanically.

Green islands (in virology) : Non-chlorotic region in a leaf showing mosaic or ringspot symptoms.

Group-specific antigen : An antigen specific to a group of virus.

Guanine : One of the purine bases found in DNA and RNA.

Guanosine : A nucleoside of guanine and ribose.

Hapten : A partial antigen; substance that can combine with antibody but can initiate an immune response only if bound to a carrier before injection into an animal. Most hatpen molecules (M < 1000) carry only one or two antigenic determinants.

HAT medium : A cell culture medium (containing hypoxanthine, aminopterin and thymidine) used in monoclonal antibody production to select hybridomas from unfused myeloma cells.

Helenin, helenine : An antiviral antibiotic from *Penicillium funiculosum* which is considered to be an RNA of viral origin.

Helical symmetry (of virology) : A form of capsid structure in many RNA viruses in which the protein subunits interact with the nucleic acid to form a helix. The only axis of symmetry is the length axis of the particle. All rod-shaped plant viruses have coat portein subunits arranged in helical symmetry.

Helix (adj. **helical**) **:** Coiled or spiral in shape with a repeating pattern. It is often used in reference to the double spiral of the DNA molecule.

Helper virus : A virus required for replication of defective or satellite virus or a satellite RNA.

Heterologous : Derived from a different type or species.

Histopathology : Microscopic study of diseased tissues.

Homologous, homology : In serology, the specific relationship between an antigen and the antibody induced by its interaction with animal immune systems; likeness in structure ; degree of relatedness between two nucleic acids or amino acid sequences.

Homologous antiserum : A serum containing antibodies raised against a specific antigen and that will react with that antigen.

Homologous reaction : A serological reaction in which an antiserum reacts positively with the antigen used for its preparation.

Hopperburn : Marginal yellowing, scorching, and curling of leaves (*e.g.*, alfalfa, dahlia, potato) due to the feeding of certain leafhopper species.

Horizontal resistance : Resistance that protects a host against all genetic variants of a pathogen to a greater degree.

Host : A living organism (*e.g.*, a plant) harboring or invaded by a parasite and from which the parasite obtains part or all of its nourishment.

Host indexing : (1) A procedure to determine if a plant is a carrier of a virus, phytoplasma, or spiroplasma : (2) a procedure in which material is transferred from one plant to another that then will develop characteristic symptoms if infected by the pathogen in question.

Host range : The complete range of plant species susceptible to a virus.

Hybridoma : A hybrid animal cell or cell line produced from the fusion of a spleen cell (lymphocyte) and a tumor (immortal mouse mycelome) cell able to multiply *in vitro* to produce monoclonal antibodies.

Hyperchromicity : Increase in UV absorbance resulting from the denaturation of a macromolecule : provides an indication of the amount of base-pairing in a nucleic acid.

Hyperimmune serum : Serum from an animal that has received two or more injections of a foreign antigen to produce a reagent for use in serology.

Hyper immunization : A condition resulting from immunization, usually with extensive booster doses, designed to stimulate the production of a high-affinity antibody relatively late in the immune response.

Hyperplasia (adj. **hyperplastic) :** A plant overgrowth (gall, enation, tumor, witches' broom) due to increased cell division ; excessive, abnormal usually pathological multiplication of the cells of a tissue or organ.

Hpersensitive (in virology) : An extreme reaction to a virus, *e.g.*, the production of local lesions or the necrotic response of a leaf to a plant virus.

Hypertrophy (adj. **hypertrophic) :** A plant overgrowth such as gall or tumor due to abnormal cell enlargement ; excessive, abnormal, usually pathologically induced enlargement of individual cells in a tissue or organ.

Hypoplasia (adj. **hypoplastic) :** Underdevelopment (malformation) of plant tissue due to decreased cell division.

Hypotrophy : Underdevelopment of plant tissue due to reduced cell enlargement.

Hypovirulence : Reduced virulence of a pathogenic strain.

Icosahedral (n. **icosahedron) :** A regular polyhedron with 20 equilateral traingular faces or sides, 30 edges, 12 apices, and two-, three-, and fivefold axes of symmetry ; the symmetry forms the basis for the arrangement of the protein subunits of isometric virus particles.

ICTV : It stands for International Committee on Taxonomy of Viruses. It was formed in 1966.

ID : Infective dose. Number of units of a pathogen required to infect a host.

Identification : The study of the characters of an organism to determine its name.

Idiotope : An antigenically distinct region associated with an immunoglobulin paratope or hyper variable region.

Ig : Immunoglobulin.

IgE : Immunoglobulin class that fixes to most cells and is responsible for anaphylactic and allergic sensitivity.

IgG : The major Immunoglobulin class in the serum human ; found in most species from amphibians upward, but not in fish. Human IgG molecular weight = 150,000, S20w = 7S.

IgM : Pentameric Immunoglobulin; first class of antibody produced to most antigens during an immune response.

Immortaliztion : Growth of cells in culture long after normally expected to cease; cloning of cDNA in a bacterial plasmid or production of monoclonal antibodies in a hybridoma.

Immune (n. **immunity) :** Not affected by or responsive to disease; exempt from infection due to its inherent properties (*e. g.,* tough outer wall, hairiness, nature of natural openings, waxy coating, thick cuticle, etc.).

Immune response : The ability of an animal to produce antibodies to foreign antigens, such as proteins or carbohydrate, introduced by either infection with a pathogenic agent or artificial injection. The antigen ability to induce this response is referred to as immunogenicity. The substances capable of inducing the response are called immunogens.

Immune serum : The liquid portion of blood containing one or more specific protein antibodies.

Immunity : The natural or acquired state of being immune, exempt from infection.

Immunization : The process of increasing or of giving resistance to a living organism. In serology injection of an antigen into an animal in order to induce antibody production.

Immunoblot (Western blot) : Reaction of labelled antibodies with proteins adsorbed to nitrocellulose paper.

Immunochemistry : The identification of the sites of antigens in cells using antibodies to which a reporter molecule, *e.g.,* ferritin, gold, or a fluorescent dye, is attached.

Immunocytological methods : Procedures used to study cytopathological disorders in ultra thin sections of virus diseased tissues, using labelled antibodies to diagnose the virus.

Immunodiffusion : A serological procedure in which the antigen- antibody reaction occurs by allowing the reactants to diffuse toward each other in a gel matrix.

Immunoelectrophoresis : A technique involving separation of proteins in a gel, using an electric field followed by a precipitation reaction in the gel with antibodies to the separated proteins.

Immunogenic : Causing immunity ; a protein's (antigen) ability to induce antibody production.

Immunoglobulin classes : Subfamily of proteins produced by B cells based or large differences in H-chain amino acid sequence : isotopes IgA, IgD, IgE, IgG, and IgM.

Immunoglobulin G (IgG) : Serum globular glycoprotein with least mobility to the positive electrode during eletrophoresis, constituting a distinct class of antibodies.

Immunoglobulin subclasses : Subpopulations of an Ig class based on more subtle structural or antigenic differences in the H chains than are class differences (*e.g.,* IgG1, IgG2, IgG3, IgG4).

Immunology : A study of acquired immunity in animals and men against infection disease.

Immunosorbent electron microscopy (ISEM) (syn. **Electron microscope serology and immunoelectron microscopy) :** Techniques to identify viruses involving the visualization of the antibody-antigen reaction in the electron microscope (EM) to detect viruses. These include :

Trapping : The EM grid first coated with antiserum, referred to as an antibody-coated grid (ACG), which then attracts virus particles from a virus preparation placed on it.

Decoration : Virus particles are attached to the EM grid and antiserum is then added. Homologous antibodies react with the particles to coat or "decorate" them.

in vitro : Applied for growth of a tissue in any type of culture container.

in vivo : Applied for any process occuring in a whole organism with in the living organism.

Inactivation : The loss of the ability of a virus to initiate infection.

Inbreeding depression : It is a loss of yield and vigour caused by inbreeding.

Intellectual Property Rights (IPR) : It is a general term covering copyright, trade mark, industrial designs, geographical indications, lay- out design of integrated circuits and protection of undisclosed information (trade secrets).

In-apparent infection : An infection that does not give obvious symptoms.

Inarch (adj.) **:** A type of plant graft often used to detect plant viruses, phytoplasmas and viroids with an indicator plant(s). Cut diseased stem (scion) upward and healthy stem (stock) downward. One-third of each stem of similar diameter cut diagonally ; both bound at this point with grafting tape.

Incidence of disease : Number of plants affected within a population ; disease incidence should be distinguished from disease severity.

Inclusion body : Sub-cellular structures any matrix or array of virus particles, abnormal bodies or areas of abnormal staining in the cytoplasm or nucleus of virus-infected plant cells.

Incomplete antibody : An antibody that binds antigen but did not precipitate or agglutinates the antigen.

Indicator : A plant that reacts to certain pathogens or environmental factors, producing specific symptoms and used to detect and identify these factors; a substance that changes colour as conditions change. *e.g.,* pH indicators reflect changes in acidity or alkalinity.

Indicator plant or host : A plant that responds specifically to certain viruses, other pathogens, or environmental factors with specific characteristic symptoms ; used for identification of the specific pathogen(s) or environmental factor(s); also used in diagnosis of pathogens.

Induction : The activation of a latent virus infection ; an increased rate of synthesis of an enzyme caused by a small molecule generally the substrate or a closely related compound.

Infected (of an organism) : Successfully attacked by a pathogen.

Infection (*v.* **infect**) **:** Process or act of a pathogen entering (invasion, penetration) and establishing an infection in a host plant ; after entry, multiply (viruses replicate), and persist in a carrier.

Infection court : Site of a host plant where infection can occur: root, shoot, leaf, flower, or fruit.

Infectious : Capable of infection and spreading disease (a pathogen) from plant to plant.

Infectious disease : A disease caused by a pathogen that can multiply and spread from a diseased to a healthy plant.

Infectious unit : The smallest number of virus particles that, in theory, can cause infection.

Infective (*n.* **infectivity**) **:** (Of a pathogen) able to infect a living organism ; (of a vector, medium, etc.) having the ability to transmit a pathogen.

Infectivity assay : A bioassay using mechanical sap transmission which quantitatively determines the number of infectious virus particles.

Initiation : The start of synthesis of a polypeptide or nucleic acid chain ; or an infection.

Injury : Momentary (transitory) damage by a causal agent, *e.g.* insect feeding, action of a chemical, physical, or electrical agent, or an adverse environmental factor.

Inoculate (*n.* **inoculation**) **:** (1) artificial introduction of a pathogen at the site of infection of a host (the infection court) to induce disease or into a culture medium. (2) to treat seeds of leguminous plants with bacteria to induce nitrogen fixation in the roots.

Inoculation access period : The time that vectors are caged on test plants.

Inoculation feeding period (syn. test feeding period) : The lengths of time to feed on a test plant during pathogen transmission experiments.

Inoculation threshold period : The minimum feeding period an inoculative vector need on a susceptible test plant to transmit a disease agent.

Inoculative insects : Infective insects that will transmit during a given test access period.

Inoculum (pl. **inocula**) **:** The pathogen or its parts (*e.g.,* fungus spores, mycelium, bacterial cells, nematodes, virus particles, etc.) used for inoculating to produce disease.

Inoculum potential : The number of independent infections induced by the inoculum and amount of tissue invaded per infection that may occur in a population of susceptible hosts at any time or place.

Insect : Member of the class Hexapoda (phylum Arthropoda). In the adult stage, true insects have six walking legs, wings, and three body divisions.

Insect vector : An insect that transmits a disease. Plant viruses are transmitted by insects in three ways : (1) mechanically or stylet-borne (also termed nonpersistent or nonpropagative) : (2) semipersistent or circulative indicating an ability to transmit over longer periods of time, but the virus does not replicate in the insect; and (3) persistent or propagative for virus that replicate in the vector as well as in the host plant.

Integrated pest management (IPM), integrated control : The use of all available methods (biological, chemical, cultural, genetic, legal, and physical) to control diseases weeds and pests for best results with least cost and damage to the environment.

Integration (in virology) : Insertion of viral DNA into the host genome, usually involving a virus-coded enzyme, integrase.

Interference (in virology) : Effect of the replication of one virus on another.

Interferon : Proteins released by animal cells in response to viral infection that protect other cells from infection.

Intermolecular recombination : Recombination due to the re- assortment of species of nucleic acid between viruses whose genomes are segmented.

Intramuscular : A route in muscle commonly used for injection of purified viruses usually prepared with Freund's adjuvant.

Intraperitoneal : A route commonly used for injection (*e.g.*, antigens and viruses) into an animal via the peritoneum.

Intravenous : Describing a route sometimes used for the injection of antigens into the venous blood system of an animal.

Introns : DNA sequences that interrupt the protein-coding sequences of a gene ; introns are transcribed into mRNA but eliminated from the message before translation to protein.

Invasion (*v.* **invade) :** Entry of a pathogen into a plant.

Invasion court : The place on the host where the pathogen enters.

Isoelectric focusing (electro focusing) : A separation technique where mixtures of proteins and/or viruses are resolved into their components by subjecting them to an electric field in a supporting gel or stabilized solution in which a pH gradient is established.

Isoelectric point : The pH at which a virus particle or protein molecule has a zero net charge ; the point of highest probability of crystallizing or precipitating out of solution.

Isolate : To separate a culturable microorganism from an infected suspect and grow it in the absence of other organisms ; (noun) a sample (*e.g.*, a virus) from a defined source.

Isolation : (1) Prevention of crossing among plant populations due to distance or geographic barriers (2) securing an organism or virus into pure culture, or the culture itself.

kb : Kilo base ; refers to single-stranded nucleic acid.

kbp : Kilobase pairs ; refers to double-stranded nucleic acid.

kDa : Kilo Dalton ; molecular weight designated per 1000 units.

kilobase (pairs) (kb, kbp) : 1000 nucleotides in a polynucleotide chain ; a measure of the size of a nucleic acid molecule.

Kinase : Enzyme catalyzing phosphorylation reactions.

Koch's postulates : Rules by Robert Koch to prove the pathogenicity of a microorganism modified for plant viruses are : (1) isolation of the virus from a diseased host ; (2) cultivation of the virus in experimental hosts or cells ; (3) purification or filterability following inoculation of the filtered or purified virus of the pathogen ; (4) production of a comparable disease in the original or related host species following inoculation with the processed virus ; and (5) re-isolation of the virus.

Late genes : Genes in a viral nucleic acid that are expressed late in the virus replication cycle ; often those coding for capsid proteins.

Latency : Stage of an infectious disease, other than the incubation period, where no symptoms are expressed in the host.

Latent : Present but not manifested or visible.

Latent infection, latency : Infection in a plant without visual symptoms.

Latent period (phase) : Period after a vector acquires a virus before it can transmit, as in persistent or propagative transmission : (in virology) the time between the apparent disappearance of the infecting virus and the appearance of newly synthesized virus.

Latent virus : A virus that does not induce symptom development in its host ; often used to describe in apparent virus infection.

Leafhopper : Active insects (order Homoptera, family Cicadellidae) with sucking mouth parts ; a vector of pathogens, especially persistent viruses ; may cause direct plant injury during feeding, even in the absence of virus.

Lesion : Well-marked, localized area of diseased or disordered tissue; a wound.

Life cycle, life history : Cyclical stages in the growth of an organism (plant, animal, or pathogen) between the appearance and reappearance of the same stage ; not so obvious for virus replication.

Liner DNA : One of several forms of DNA. The two linear strands of double-stranded DNA may be free, bound to a specific protein, or closed by a hairpin loop.

LIV : Longevity *in vitro*.

Local lesion : A small, localized, chlorotic or necrotic spots produced on a leaf upon mechanical inoculation with a virus (*e.g.,* a hypersensitive reaction).

Longevity end point or longevity in vitro (LIV) : The time a virus in plant sap diluted 1/10 in a buffer retains its infectivity.

Lyophilization, lyophilize (syn. **freeze-drying**) **:** A technique for water removal under high vacuum while tissue is frozen. Used for long-term preservation of antisera, viruses, and types of pathogens.

Macroscopic : Visible to the naked eye.

Macromolecules : Molecules with molecular weight of a few thousand to hundreds of million Daltons.

Masked : Pertains to symptoms absent under certain environmental conditions but apparent under other conditions ; a condition whereby a virus-infected host exhibits no disease symptoms due to unfavourable environment for disease expression.

Masked virus : A virus carried by a plant that shows no symptoms.

Mealy bug : Small, oval insects (family Pseudococcidae, superfamily Coccoidea) with sucking mouth parts and a cottony, scale like covering. unlike scale insects, mealybugs possess functional legs and reproduce by producing eggs or living young. Mealybugs transmit a number of plant-infecting viruses.

Mechanical injury : Injury of a plant part by abrasion or wounding.

Mechanical transmission (or inoculation) : Artificial introduction of inoculum in presence of mild abrasive. It includes when a virus is transmitted from one plant to another by machinery, leaves rubbing, or root contact.

Median effective dose : The amount of a substance required to produce a response in 50% of the hosts (subjects) to which it is given.

Median effective time (ET50) : The amount of time for a substance to produce a response in 50% of the hosts (subjects) to which it has been given.

Median ineffective dose (ID50) : The dose of a chemical, pathogen, etc. that, on average, will infect 50% of the hosts (individuals) to which it is administered.

Median inoculation access period (IAP50) : Inoculation access period during which 50% of the inoculative insects will transmit.

Median lethal dose (LD50) : The dose of a substance that is fatal to 50% of the test population.

Median lethal time (LT50) : The period of time required for 50% of a group of organisms to die following a specific dose of an injurious agent, *e.g.,* virus, radiation, drug, etc.

Median Survival Time (ST 50) : The period of time at which half the subjects have died following the administration of an injurious agent *e.g.* virus, radiation, drugd etc.

Meristem : Localized region of active cell division in plants from which permanent tissue is derived. It occurs at the tips of the stems and roots between Xylem and phloem of vascular bundles.

Messenger RNA (mRNA) : A chain of ribonucleotides that codes for a specific protein. Messenger RNA by definition + sense moves from nucleus to ribosomes, where protein is synthesized in the cytoplasm.

Microbial control : Use of microorganisms and viruses as biological control agents for pests and diseases.

Microbiology : The science or study of microorganisms, *e.g.,* bacteria, actinomycetes, fungi, algae, viruses and protozoa.

Micrometer (μm) : A unit of length = one-thousandth of a millimetre (0.001 mm or 1 micron {μm}).

Micron (μm) : One millionth of a metre (m) = 0.001 mm = 0.00003937 of an inch. Same as micrometer.

Microscopic : Too small to be seen except with the aid of a microscope.

Millimicron (mμm) : One-thousand of a micron or 10Å ; a nanometer (nm).

Mite : Minute (1/64-to1/32-inches long) animals divisions ; (order Acarina, families Tetranchidae and Eriophydae) without evident body ; six-legged as larvae and eight-legged as adults. Red spider mites commonly cover leaf surface with fine webbing. Eriophyid mites transmit a number of plant-infecting viruses.

Mitomycin C : Antibiotic ; selectively inhibits DNA replication by cross-linking the single strands.

Model length : The length that occurs most frequently in a population of virus particles ; a criterion used when classifying rod-shaped viruses.

Mode infection (in virology) : Inoculation of cells or an organism with a solution that lacks virus particles ; a control in virus infection experiments to ascertain any possible side effects of materials in the inoculum other than infectious particles.

Molecular biology : A field of biology concerned with the interaction of biochemistry and genetics in the life of an organism. Molecular techniques in use include DNA-DNA hybridization, DNA fingerprinting, PCR (polymerase chain reaction), RFLP (restriction fragment length polymorphisms), RAPD (random amplified polymorphic DNA), and DNA sequencing.

Molecular radius (Mr) : The radius of the space occupied by a molecule and is considered a more correct term for macromolecules than molecular weight, as it allows for hydration.

Molecular weight (mw) : Sum of the atomic weight of constituent atoms in a molecule.

Molecule : A unit of matter ; the smallest portion of an element or a compound composed of one or more atoms that retains the chemical identity with the substance in mass. A molecule usually consists of the union of two or more atoms ; some organic molecules contain hundreds to a million or more atoms.

Monoecious aphid : An aphid that spends complete life cycle on a single plant species.

Monoclonal antibody : A homogeneous antibody population specific to a single antigenic epitope. Produced by fusing specific antibody-producing cells (in a single clone of lymphocytes) with immortalized tissue culture cells ; synthesized and secreted by clonal populations of hybrid cells (hybridoma) prepared by the fusion of individual B lymphocyte cells from an immunized animal (usually a mouse or rat) with individual cells from a lymphocyte tumor (*e.g.,* myeloma).

Monocotyledoneae, monocots (pl. **monocotyledonae,** adj. **monocotyledonous) :** The subclass of flowering plants, including the grasses and cereals, having one cotyledon (seed leaf) in the embryo ; characterized by parallel-veined leaves and fibrous roots. *See* Dicotyledon.

Monolayer cells : Animal cells grown in culture while attached to a solid surface, in contrast to cells grown in suspension culture.

Monomer : A single polypeptide chain.

Morphological subunit : The structural subunit of a virus particle viewed by electron microscopy ; often clusters of protein subunits (capsomeres) especially in isometric particles.

Morphology : Study or science of the form, structure, and development of organisms.

Mosaic : Disease symptom characterized by a clearly differentiated patchy mottling of the foliage or by sharp variegated patterns of dark and light green to yellow ; disarrangement or unequal development of the chlorophyll content ; symptomatic of many viral infections.

Mottle, mottling : Disease symptom of alternate light/dark irregular patterns differentiated from mosaic, often symptomatic of viral diseases.

mRNA : Messenger ribonucleic acid.

Multicistronic messenger RNA : An m RNA that contains the coding sequences for two or more proteins.

Multicomponent virus : A virus whose genome, required for infection, consists of two or more parts, each separately encapsidated ; differs from a multipartite genome.

Multipartite genome : A viral genome split between two or more nucleic acid molecules that may be encapsidated in the same particle ; if in separate particles, they are multicomponent.

Multipartite virus : Multicomponent virus.

Multiplicity of infection (m.o.i.) : Number of infectious virus particles added to a known number of cells required to cause infection.

MW : Molecular weight.

Mycovirus : A virus that replicates in fungal cells.

Naked virus : A virus without a lipoprotein (*See* also Viroid).

Nanometer (nm) : A unit of length equal to one-billionth (10^{-9}) of a meter (m) or one millimicron = 10 Å.

Necrosis (pl. **necroses,** adj. **necrotic)** : Localized or general death and disintegration of plant cells or plant parts, commonly a symptom produced by fungus, nematode, virus, or bacterial infection ; a symptom of disease or injury.

Negative contrast staining : Staining procedure used to prepare virus particles for examination in an electron microscope.

Negative-sense strand (negative strand) : Nucleic acid complementary to the plus strand.

Negative-strand virus : Virus whose genome is negative-sense RNA. Five familie of negative-strand viruses are recognized.

Nepovirus (NEPO) : Member of the tobacco ringspot virus group ; usually transmitted by nematodes : Nematode-transmitted Polyhedral- shaped viruses.

NET : A term used for Nematode-transmitted tubular-(rod) shaped viruses.

Neutralizing antibody : An antibody that inhibits virus infectivity.

Nomenclature : The system by which names are assigned to organisms and microorganisms. The name is governed by the International Code of Botanical Nomenclature. The Code is comprised of principles, rules, and recommendations. The names of viruses are governed by the International Committee on Taxonomy of Viruses (ICTV).

Nonpathogenic : Incapable of causing disease.

Non-permissive cells : Cells in which a specific virus will not infect and replicate.

Nonpersistent transmission (syn. stylet-borne transmission) : Type of insect transmission in which the virus is acquired by the vector after short (minutes) acquisition feeding times and is transmitted during short inoculation feeding periods. The vector (*e.g.,* aphid) remains viruliferous for only a short period (*e.g.,* a few minutes to perhaps 4 hours) unless it recharges by again feeding on an infected plant.

Nonproducer cells : Cells carrying all or part of a viral genome but not producing virus particles ; they are usually transformed by the virus.

Nonstructural protein : Protein encoded by a viral genome but not involved in the structure of the virus particle. The protein is usually functional (enzymatic) during replication.

Normal length (of virus particles) : The most common length, *i.e.,* the intrinsic natural length of rod-shaped virus particles.

Northern blotting : A procedure analogous to Southern blotting but involving the transfer of RNA to nitrocellulose or activated paper sheets.

Noisiness : Errors that may occur during the replication of a virus genome.

N-terminal : The portion of polypeptide chain ending with NH2, often surface located in the protein subunit of a viral capsid ; a site known to include a specific antibody response.

Nuclease : An enzyme that can hydrolyze the internucleotide linkages in a nucleic acid.

Nucleic acid : A compound of high molecular weight of pentose (ribose or deoxyribose), phosphate, and nitrogen bases (purines and pyrimidines) joined in a long chain of repeating units (nucleotide complex); present in all living cells ; constitute the infectious parts of plant viruses; all either DNA or RNA.

Nucleocapsid : The nucleic acid (RNA or DNA) of a virus particle or virion enclosed by a protein capsid.

Nucleoprotein : Referring to viruses or another complex consisting of nucleic acid and protein.

Nucleoside : The combination of a sugar (ribose or deoxyribose) joined to a base molecule.

Nucleotide(s) : The building blocks of DNA and RNA, consisting of a phosphate group joined to a base, a phosphate ester of a nucleoside. Thousands of nucleotides link to form a DNA or RNA.

Nucleotide phosphohydrolase : An enzyme that removes a phosphate group from the triphosphate end of nucleotides.

Obligate parasite : A parasite that can grow in nature only on or in living tissue ; not on an artificial medium.

Obligate pathogen : Viruses that replicate naturally only in living host tissue.

Occlusion body : Large virus-coded protein crystal containing viruses, referred to in the more general term "inclusion body".

Odontostyle : The feeding stylet of a nematode is called as odontostyle.

Okazaki fragments : Short pieces of DNA, with attached RNA primers, produced during DNA synthesis. The primers are later replaced by DNA and the fragments are joined together.

Oligogenic : Applied to a character determined by only a few genes as contrasted with many genes-polygenic.

Oligonucleotide : A short-chain nucleic acid molecule.

Oligonucleotide probe : A short DNA probe for which hybridization is sensitive to a single base-mismatch.

Open reading frame (ORF) : A set of codons for amino acids (usually encoding a protein) uninterrupted by stop codons.

Operon : A cluster (two or more) of functionally related genes in the chromosome, the function is subject to a common control mechanism ; regulated and transcribed as a unit.

Ouchterlony gel diffusion test : Serological test in which antibody and antigen are placed in separate wells in agar and allowed to diffuse toward each other. A positive reaction is a visible band of precipitate between the antibody and antigen wells. Serological relationships of viruses can be determined by the bands interacting with each other.

Oudin tube : Simple diffusion in agar. Antigen in solution is placed over agar containing antibody in a test tube. Antigen diffuses into agar and forms a preciptin band at equivalence.

PAGE : Polyacrylamide gel electrophoresis.

Partite : Suffix meaning "consisting of parts" ; *e.g.*, bipartite, tripartite.

Parts per billion (ppb) : A method of expressing the concentration of chemicals in a substrate or diluent.

Parts per million (ppm) : milligrams per litre ; 1 ppm = 1 mg l^{-1}

Passive hem agglutination : A serological test to detect virus- specific antigens by coating red blood cells with viral antigen. If viral antibody is present, red blood cells agglutinate.

Path-, patho- (prefix) **:** Suffering, hence disease.

Pathogen, pathogene : An organism or agent (*e.g.*, fungus, bacterium, nematode, virus, or viriod) capable of causing disease in a particular host. Most pathogens are parasites, but a few exceptions exist.

Pathogenesis : The sequence of processes in disease development from the time of infection to the final reaction to hypersensitive.

Pathogenic : Ability of a pathogen to cause disease ; the state of being pathogenic.

Pathogenicity : Causing or capable of producing disease.

Pathology, plant : Science or study of diseases, their nature and effects on plants, causes and their control.

Pathotoxin : A toxin or poison produced by a pathogen and/or its host within the infected plant that functions in the infected plant that functions in the production of disease, not itself the initial causal agent; vivotoxin. *Tobacco mosaic virus* was first labelled *contagium vivum fluidum* (Beijerinck, 1898) before viruses were named and known to be infectious.

Pathovar (pv) : Synonym for subspecies, strain, pathotype of infectious microorganism or virus.

PBS : Phosphate-buffered saline.

PEG : Polyethylene glycol.

Pelleting : A centrifugal separation process in which particles in a sample, sediment to the bottom of the tube.

Peplomer : Glycoprotein projection (spike, knob) located on the envelope.

Permissive cells : Cells in which infection results in production of infectious virus.

Persistent (*n.* **persistence) :** Of circulatory viruses that remain infectious within their living vector for long period without lysis, and are transmitted via salivary fluids.

Persistent transmission : Type of insect or nematode transmission in which a pathogen (*e.g.,* a virus or phytoplasma) is acquired by a vector only after a long time in minutes, hours, or days rather than seconds acquisition feeding period. A latent period usually follows the acquisition feed, before the vector can transmit the pathogen. The vector often remains inoculative its full life. The pathogen sometimes multiplies in the vector. Nematode vectors transmit immediatelty after acquisition; they lose the capacity to transmit when they molt.

Pesticide : [Note: no virucides are yet known]. Any chemical or physical agent that destroys, prevents, mitigates, repels, or attracts pests is called pesticide. It includes acaricide or miticide, bactericide, fungicide, herbicide, insecticide, nematicide and rodenticide etc.).

Phenotypic mixing (or **genomic masking) :** Individual progeny from a mixed viral infection encapcidated with structural proteins derived from both viruses; or the genome of one virus encapsidated in that of the other, which is called *genomic masking* or *transcapsidation*.

Phosphodiester bond : Linkage between nucleotides of polypeptide chains by covalent bonding of phosphoric acid with the 3-hydroxyl group of one ribose or deloxyribose sugar and the 5-hydroxyl group of the next ribose or deoxyribose ring.

Phospholipase : An enzyme that catalyzes the hydrolysis of a phospholipid and is used in the study of cytoplasmic membranes.

Phosphoprotein : A protein with one or more amino acids phosphorylated by a portein kinase.

Photo reactivation: The enzymes repair of DNA damaged by UV light. The enzymes involved are activated by exposure to long- wavelength light.

Physiogenic (physiological) disease : A disease (or disorder) produced by some unfavourable genetic, physical, or other injury, etc.

Phytopathogenic : Capable of causing disease in plants.

Phytopathology : Plant pathology ; scicence or study of plant diseases.

Phytoplasmas (Mycoplasma like organisms) are prokaryotic microorganisms and are morphologically identical with or similar to the members of Mycoplasmatales. Phytoplasmas (Mycoplasma like organisms) have been found to cause more than 75 distinct diseases to more than 200 plant species and a large number of artropods.

Pinwheel inclusions : Shape of some virus-induced, cytoplasmic inclusion bodies seen in cross and thin-section in an electron microscope, composed of sheets of virus-coded protein and found in cells of plants infected with potyviruses for which they are diagnostic.

Plant-disease interaction : The concurrent infection of a host by two or more pathogens in which symptoms are distinctive or other effects are greater than the sum of the effects of each pathogen acting alone; an example of synergism.

Plant hopper : Small, leaping, homopterous insects (family Delphacidae) with piercing-sucking mouth parts known to transmit plant-infecting virses and phytoplasma.

Plant pathology : The science or study of plant disease; also Phytopathology.

Plasmodesmata : The cytoplasmic connectious between cells are called as plasmodesmata.

Polyacrylamide gel electrophoresis (PAGE) : Electrophoresis in a gel of Polyacrylamide made by cross-linking acrylamide with N.N- methylene-*bis*-acrylamide; for separation of nucleic acid or protein molecules according to molecular size to estimate molecular weight.

Polyclonal antibody : Antibody produced at different sites and by different B-lymphocytes against more than one epitope of an antigen; rabbits preferred.

Polyhedron : Large many-sided or rounded occlusion body.

Polymerase : An enzyme that forms RNA or DNA by adding ribonucleotide or deoxyribonucleotide triphosphates.

Polymerase chain reaction (PCR) : The selective amplification of DNA by repeated cycles of : (1) heat denaturation of DNA; (2) annealing of the annealed primers with the heat-stable DNA polymerase; (3) to produce probes for virus diagnosis and amplify low copy number sequence; (4) to selectively amplify sequences of interest in the presence of irrelevant DNA(s).

Polynucleotide kinase : An enzyme that phosphorylates the 5′-OH terminal ends of RNA and DNA nucleotide chains.

Polynucleotide ligase : A generic term for enzymes that catalyze the linking or repair of DNA or RNA strands. *See* DNA ligase and RNA ligase.

Polypeptide : A chain of amino acids linked together by peptide bonds, either by synthesis or partial hydrolysis of a protein.

Polyploid virus : A virus that contains a variable number of genomes, depending on such factors as host cell and cultural conditions found in viruses of various groups.

Polyprotein : A large precursor protein later cleaved into two or more functional proteins.

Positive-sense strand (positive strand) : For RNA, the strand that functions as the messenger (mRNA) ; and for DNA, the strand with the same sequence as the mRNA.

Post-transcriptional cleavage : Cleavage of polyprotein or RNA into functional units, usually mono cistronic mRNAs.

Precipitation (syn. precipitin) reaction : In immunology, a visible fine precipitate when adequate quantities of soluble antibodies (precipitins) and soluble antigens form an insoluble lattice ; detected in test tubes as sediment or in agar gels as a white line appearing where equivalent amounts of antigen and antibody interact. Also termed as immunoprecipitation.

Precipitin : The reaction in which an antibody causes precipitation of soluble antigens.

Primary host : (1) The virus host of most economic importance and/or on which the virus was first observed. (2) Plant on which the sexual forms of an aphid mate and lay eggs to over winter. *See* Secondary host.

Primary symptom (syn. local symptom) : Symptom(s) produced immediately after infection at the site of entry, in contrast to a secondary symptom, which follows more complete invasion (colonization) of the host.

Primase : An enzyme that synthesizes the RNA primers for DNA synthesis on a DNA template.

Primer : Small fragment of nucleic acid with a free 3-hydroxyl group necessary for the initiation of DNA and, sometimes, RNA synthesis.

Prion : A "proteinaceous infectious particle", apparently absent nucleic acid, that causes certain neurological diseases of vertebrates.

Probe : A sequence of DNA or RNA used to detect complementary ones by hybridization.

Procapsid : A viral capsid lacking nucleic acid, possibly a stage in virion formation.

Propagative virus : A virus that multiplies (replicates) in its insect vector.

Proteases : Enzymes that digest protein by cleaving polypeptide chains into fragments ; involved in inactivating and degrading proteins; for peptide mapping or structural studies.

Protectant (of pesticides) : An agent, usually a chemical that tends to prevent or inhibit infection by a pathogen.

Protection : Placement of a chemical or physical barrier between the pathogen and the host that prevents infection.

Protein : Complex, high molecular weight, organic, nitrogenous substance (polymer compound), built up of amino acids joined by peptide bonds.

Protein kinage : Enzyme that catalyzes the phosphorylation of protein, usually in the presence of cyclic AMP or cyclic GMP.

Protein subunit : A small protein molecule that is the structural and chemical unit of the protein coat of a virus ; one or several subunits, depending on shape of the virus, comprise a capsomere.

Proteinase : An enzyme that hydrolyzes proteins to polypeptides.

Proteolytic cleavage : The splitting or digesting of polyproteins into simpler structural compounds.

Protective plant extracts : Certain plant extracts activate the normal defence mechanisms against viral infection in two ways of inhibitory response. (1) They reduce (*Dianthus caryophyllous* and *Phytolacca americana*) virus activity when co-inoculated with the virus into susceptible plants and (2) Extracts from some non-host plants

(*Clerodendrum aculentum* and *Mirabilis jalapa*) inhibit virus infection and symptoms by stimulating the production of virus inhibitory agents.

Provirus : A viral genome inserted into a host genome or a plasmid; DNA passively replicated by host and transmitted to the next generation.

Pseudo type : *See* Phenotypic mixing.

psi : Pounds per square inch.

Purification : To separate molecules, cellular components or viruses from cellular parts.

Purine : A heterocyclic compound containing fused pyrimidine and imidazole rings. The purine bases of nucleic acid are adenine and guanine.

Quarantine : A place of detention for animals, plants, or people coming from a place where a disease is known to exist ; place where people or animals are kept for inspection.

R-loop mapping : A technique where single-stranded RNA is annealed to the complementary strand of partially denatured DNA. The DNA segment complementary to the RNA can then be mapped.

Radial immunodiffusion : A serological test in which liquid antigen (or antibody) is placed in wells cut in agar gel containing the other reactant previously added to the warm gel prior to solidification and allowed to diffuse out into the gel. The resulting antigen-antibody complex forms a halo or ring of precipitate around the well.

Radioimmunoassay : Sensitive, versatile protocols similar to those of enzyme-linked immunosorbent assay (ELISA), with solid- phase binding of either antibodies or antigens.

Radioimmuno precipitation : A serological test in which a reactant, usually antibody, is labelled. The amount of isotope precipitated in the antigen-antibody, complex can be used to quantify immunoprecipitation. The antibody in the immunoprecipitate can also be measured using radiolabelled protein A.

Reflective mulch : A polythene or straw layer placed on the soil surface around the crop plant to control air borne insect vectors.

Rate zonal—A method of particle separation based on differential rate of sedimention, using a performed gradient with the sample layered as a zone on top of the gradient.

Reading frame : A sequence of codons in RNA or DNA beginning with the initiation codon AUG. *See* Open reading frame.

Read through : Reading (translation) of mRNA through a stop codon.

Re-assortment : Production of a hybrid virus that contains parts derived from the genomes of two viruses in a mixed infection. Also termed pseudo recombination.

Recognition factors : Specific molecules or structures in or on the host (or pathogen) that can be recognized by the pathogen (or host).

Recombinant (n. recombination) : A new strain of a virus resulting from the breakage and renewal of covalent links in a nucleic acid ; genes replaced with different alleles ; the exchange of genetic material from two or more virus particles into recombinant progeny virus during a mixed infection.

Recombinant DNA : A new hybrid DNA molecule produced by enzymatic insertion of one piece into another from a different source *in vitro*.

Reflective mulch : Plastic, aluminum, or straw layer placed on the soil surface around crop plants to control air-borne insect vectors.

Re-inoculation : Inoculated with the same virus a second or third time at successive intervals to ensure adequate test exposure to a virus when testing for host range or susceptibility.

Reiterated sequence : A nucleotide sequence that occurs many times in a nucleic acid.

Repeated sequence : A nucleotide sequence occurring more than once in a DNA or RNA sequence in the same or opposite orientation.

Replicase : The enzyme involved in the replication of viral genomic nucleic acids.

Replication (v. replicate) : Duplication of the genomic DNA or RNA molecule of a virus ; repetition of an experiment at the same time and place.

Replicative form (RF) : The intracellular structural form of viral nucleic acid active in replicate ; usually the double-stranded form in viruses with single-stranded genomes.

Replicative intermediate : Nucleic acid form produced during viral replication.

Replicon : A portion of DNA able to replicate from a single origin. Since most viruses have one origin of replication, the entire genome is a replicon.

Repressor : A regulatory protein that binds to a specific DNA sequence upstream of the transcription initiation site and that prevents RNA polymerase from starting RNA synthesis.

Rescue : The activation of a defective virus by recombination or by complementation of the defective functions.

Resistance : The inherent ability of an organism (host plant) to overcome or retard, completely or partially, the infective activity of a pathogen or other damaging factor.

Resistant : Possessing qualities not to be infected from a particular pathogen. A plant may be slightly, moderately, or highly resistant.

Restriction endonuclease map : The cutting sites for restriction endonucleases marked on a linear or circular representation of a ds-DNA molecule.

Restriction endonucleases : Enzymes, usually bacterial, that hydrolyze DNA at highly specific sites. In recombinant DNA experiments, restriction enzymes are used to cut ds-DNA from a given organism.

Restriction enzyme : Restriction endonuclease.

Restriction fragment : A polynucleotide fragment produced by cutting DNA with a restriction endonuclease.

Reverse passive haemagglutination : A serological test in which red blood cells coated with a virus-specific antibody are used to test for an antigen. If virus antigen is present, the red blood cells agglutinate.

Reverse transcriptase : An enzyme coded by certain viruses that make a DNA copy of a primed RNA molecule. The enzyme can also synthesize DNA from a DNA template.

Reverse transcription : Copying of the genetic information from RNA into DNA.

Ribonucleases (RNAses) : Enzymes that hydrolyze phosphodiester bonds of **RNA** : used to characterize and sequence RNA.

Ribonucleoside : A purine or pyrimidine base covalently bound to a ribose sugar molecule.

Ribonucleotide : A ribonucleotide with one or more phosphate groups esterified to the 5′ position of the sugar.

Ribose : A five-carbon sugar ; a component of RNA.

Ribosome : A sub-cellular ribonucleoprotein particle, made up of two sub-particles and several proteins, responsible for translating mRNA into protein.

RNA : Ribonucleic acid. A nucleic acid found in the nucleus and cytoplasm involved in control of cellular activities and protein synthesis; the genetic material of many plant viruses. Nucleotides with a ribose sugar and a base : A, G, C and U.

RNA ligase : An enzyme that can join RNA molecules and requires ATP.

RNA polymerase : An enzyme synthesizing RNA from a DNA or RNA template specific functions include DNA-dependent RNA polymerase and RNA-dependent RNA polymerase.

RNA processing : Modification of RNA after transcribing.

RNA replicase : RNA-dependent RNA polymerase.

RNA segment : A distinct piece of RNA ; frequently refers to genomic segements of segmented genome viruses.

RNA transcriptase : RNA-or DNA-dependent RNA polymerase.

RNA-dependent DNA polymerase : *See* Reverse transcriptase.

Rocket Immunoelectrophoresis : An immunological technique to determine a single constituent in a protein mixture in a number of samples. Diluted samples are applied side by side to circular wells in an agarose gel.

Rugose, rugous : Coarsely wrinkled surface ; covered with coarse, netlike lines ; roughened. Descriptive of certain virus diseases characterized by warty, roughened, or severely crinkled leaves or other plant parts.

Rugose mosaic : Striking mosaic accompanied by deformation such as leaf crinkling, curling, or roughening of the leaf surface.

Russet : Brownish, roughened surface areas (epidermis) of leaves, fruits, stems, and tubers resulting from abnormal cork formation ; may result from disease, insects, spray or other mechanical injury.

S : Sedimentation coefficient, coefficient of sedimentation velocity.

S20w : Sedimentation coefficient expressed in Svedberg units and adjusted to 20°C in water.

S-adenyosyl-L-methionine (ADO, SAM) : An intracellular source of activated methyl groups, including those used for RNA and DNA methylation ; stimulates transcription in some viruses ; required by class I restriction endonucleases for initial binding.

SAH : S-adenyosyl-L-homocysteine.

SAM : S-adenyosyl-L-methionine.

Sanitation (v. sanitize) : Destruction (removal) of infected and infested plants or parts ; elimination of disease inoculum and insect vectors ; decontamination of tools, equipment, containers, workspace, hands, etc. ; cultural methods of disease control that reduce inoculum.

7th Report of ICTV : In this report different virus groups listed earlier have been referred to as genera and viruses as species. In this report plant viruses have been classified into 14 families and 70 genera.

Satellite RNA : A small RNA packaged in protein shells of an unrelated helper virus, on which the satellite RNA depends for its replication, but with little or no sequence similarity to the genome of the helper virus.

Satellite virus : A small defective virus associated with *Tobacco necrosis virus* (TNV) that depends on the "helper" TNV genome to replicate it.

Schlieren optics : An optical system that detects gradients of concentration of a solute in a solvent using a phase plate.

Scientific method : Problem solving consisting of stating the problem, establishing one or more hypotheses as solutions, testing, hypotheses by experimentation/observation with controls, and accepting or rejecting the hypotheses.

Scion : Detected bud, twig, or shoot inserted by grafting into a stock (rootstock).

Scion-stock interaction : Effect of rootstock on scion and vice-versa, wherein a scion on one kind of rootstock grows differently than on its own roots or on a different rootstock.

Screening test : A test to observe the response of a range of plant cultivars or type to virus infection.

Scorch : Sudden browning and death (necrosis) of large, indefinite areas on a leaf, fruit, or stem from infection, lack or excess of some element, chemical injury, or unfavourable weather conditions.

SDI : Serological differentiation index.

SDS : Sodium dodecyl sulphate.

SDS-polyacrylamide gel electrophoresis : Electrophoresis in polyacrylamide gels of proteins denatured with SDS, which gives proteins equal charge per unit molecular weight, thus separates proteins by molecular weight.

Secondary host : A virus host usually of lesser economic importance, but one that adequately supports virus replication in nature. The host plant on which the asexual aphid form occurs ; also to indicate alternative hosts for pathogens. Do not confuse with alternate host, being required for completion of the life cycle of a fungus.

Secondary infection : Infection resulting from the spread of infectious material (inoculum) after a primary infection (the first infection by a pathogen after a resting period) or from subsequent infections without an intervening inactive period.

Secondary inoculum : Inoculum from primary infections or other secondary infections.

Sedimentation : The setting out particles from a suspension in the earth's field of gravity. In the centrifuge this process is accelerated and the particle move away from the axis of rotation.

Sedimentation coefficient : Influenced both by shape and molecular weight of a particle, determined by its rate of settling in a solvent ; the rate of sedimentation of a macromolecule, such as a virus, per unit centrifugal field is measured in *Svedberg units.*

Sedimentation rate : The rate at which a macromolecule (virus) moves in a standard gravitational field.

Seed-borne disease : Disease in which inoculum is borne in or on seed.

Seed-borne microflora : Bacteria, fungi, nematodes, phytoplasma or viruses associated with seeds.

Seed-borne pathogen : An infectious agent associated with seeds and having the potential of causing a disease of a seedling or plant.

Seed contamination : Seed contominated with pathogens.

Seed infection : Colonization of seed tissues by pathogens with or without conspicuous symptoms.

Seed infestation : Pathogen propagules carried on the outside of seeds or associated with seed lots.

Seed transmission : Passage of inocula from an infected/infested to its seedling plant.

Seed treatment : A chemical or non-chemical used to control pathogen propagules associated with true seeds and seed pieces.

Semi conservative replication : DNA-dependent DNA replication in which the synthesis uses both strands of dsDNA as templates, resulting in progeny, each comprising one parent strand and one new strand.

Semipersistent transmission : Transmission by a virus that circulates for a short time but does not multiply in its arthropod vector, intermediate between *nonpersistent* and *persistent* transmission. The acquisition feed by the vector is short, with no latent period ; it may transmit the virus for hours to days.

Self incompatible : The inability to produce seed by self pollination.

Sequence : The order of nucleotides in RNA or DNA or of amino acids in a polypeptide.

Sequencing : The determination of a sequence of a nucleic acid or protein.

Sequential epitope : An antigenic site composed of five to seven sequential peptides in an unfolded random coil.

Serological differentiation index (SDI) : A measure of the degree of serological cross reactivity of two antigens.

Serology : A method using the specificity of the antigen-antibody reaction to detect and identify antigenic (protein) substances and/or organisms that carry them ; the study, detection, and identification of antigens, antibodies, and their reactions.

Serum : The watery amber portion of blood remaining after coagulation of red blood cells. Serum contains no fibrinogen and thus is commonly used in immunological procedures becuase no clots are formed when other materials are added.

Serum neutralization : The inhibition of the infectivity of a virus by antiserum.

Shock (syn. **acute) symptoms :** The severe, often necrotic symptoms produced on new growth following infection with some viruses.

Shot-hole : Disease symptom in which small, roundish to irregular dead fragments drop out of leaves, making them appear as if riddled by shot.

Signal sequence : Signal peptide or the nucleotide sequence encoding a signal peptide.

Silent gene (message) : Gene not expressed ; ribosome-binding site is blocked/unavailable.

"Silent" infection : An infection with no detectable symptoms ; synonym for latent infection.

Somaclones : Plants produced by genetic engineering technique by which single cells or protoplasts are cultured to produce individuals which are geneticlly variable from their stable parent.

Single diffusion : A test in which antigen diffuses into agar containing antiserum, resulting in a ring of antigen-antibody precipitation.

Single radial diffusion test : Radial immunodiffusion.

Single-stranded (ss) : Nucleic acid molecules (DNA or RNA) as a single polypeptide chain.

Sodium dodecyl sulphate (SDS) : Syn : sodium lauryl sulphate (SLS), an anionic detergent capable of disruption of virus particles and cells, inhibiting nucleases during nucleic acid extractions and denaturing proteins for gel electrophoresis.

Southern blotting : A technique in which DNA fragments, separated by gel electrophoresis, are immobilized on a nitrocellulose or nylon-based membrane. The immobilized DNA is available for hybridization with a labeled ssDNA or RNA probe.

Specific absorbance (A) : Absorbance per unit mass of a substance. It is usually measured at the wavelength where absorbance is maximal.

Specific infectivity : The infectivity of a virus expressed as percent number or per unit weight of particles ; can be measured by plaque, pock, or local lesion assays.

Specificity (of serology) : A term defining selective reactivity between substances, *e.g.*, of an antigen with its corresponding antibody.

Starch lesion : Local accumulation of starch in a virus-infected leaf demonstrated by decolorizing the leaf and staining with iodine. It is useful to assay for virus concentration.

Strain : An isolate of one virus related closely to another determined by a combination of characteristics including serological or biophysical properties, amino acid sequences or host range and differential host reactions.

Structrual unit : Protein subunit, the basic building block of the capsid.

Stunted : Plant reduced in size and vigour due to unfavourable environmental conditions caused by a range of pathogens or a biotic agents.

Stylet : Relatively long, pointed, stuff, slender, hollow, feeding organ in the mouth portion of plant-parasitic nematodes and some insects (*e.g.*, aphids) for piercing and withdrawing nutrients from plant cells. Nematodes have three types :

1. *Stomatostyle* : A spear apparently developed through evolution by the fusion or sclerotization of the stomal wall, commonly in species of *Secernentea.*
2. *Odontostyle* : A spear evolved from a large tooth and derived prior to each molt from a single cell in the esophagus ; anterior aperature is broadly oblique ; found in some members of the *Adenophorea.*
3. *Onchiostyle* : Stiff, slender, curved, grooved, tooth-like structure found in the adenophorean genus *Trichodorus* ; derived evolutionarily from an onchium ; originating in the stomal wall.

Stylet-borne : A virus borne on the stylet of its insect vector ; a non-circulative virus.

Subcutaneous : Under the epidermis or skin.

Subcutaneous injection : Injection of antigens between the skin and underlying tissues used in the preparation of antisera.

Sub cuticular : Beneath a cuticle ; between the cuticle and the upper epidermal wall.

Sub genomic RNA : RNA less than the genomic length in infected cells, sometimes encapsidated. If encapsidated, not involved in natural infection. Each species of sub genomic RNA has a different cistron at the 5′ end, opening it for translation.

Sucrose : A sugar used in sepatating in RNA, subcellular organelles and cell membranes.

Sucrose gradient, sucrose density gradient centrifugation : Particles (*e.g.*, viruses) of different sedimentation coefficients are separated during centrifugation in gradient of sucrose concentrations, increasing from top to bottom, constructed in a centrifuge tube with the solution containing the test particles placed on top.

Super infection : Inoculation of a host with a second virus, usually a strain of the first infecting virus resulting in (1) interference between the two viruses, the first virus preventing replication of the second (Cross protection) (2) the two viruses replicating independently (Synergism) (3) recombination occurring between the two viruses and (4) phenotypic mixing.

Supernatant—It is the liquid above the sedimented material following centrifugation.

Suppressor tRNA : tRNA molecule containing an altered anticodon that either reads a mutated codon in the same sense as the original or introduces a different amino acid that does not abolish protein function.

Suscept : Any living organism susceptible to a disease, pathogen, or toxin ; an abbreviated term for "susceptible plant" or "susceptible species".

Susceptibility : The inability of a plant to resist the effect of a pathogen.

Susceptible : Not immune ; lacking resistance or with little resistance ; prone to infection.

Suspect : Any plant potentially subject to infection and colonization by a pathogen.

Svedberg equation : A formula for estimating the molecular weight of a macromolecule ; $S = (1/w^2r)\ dr/dt$; r = distance in cm of sedimenting boundary from the center of rotation, t = time in seconds, w = angular velocity in radians per second ; standard defined as 20°C in water.

Svedberg units (S) : The units used to measure the rate of sedimentation of a macromolecule, sub-cellular component, or virus to determine its *sedimentation coefficient.*

Svp : Sub viral particle ; devoid of outer capsomeres, the core containing the nucleic acid ; refers to isometric viruses.

Swing-out rotor : A centrifuge rotor with buckets free to swing out horizontally when the rotor is spinning. The gravitational force is thus along the long axis of the tubes.

Symmetry : Structural principle of viral capsid or nucleocapsid.

Symmetrical : Of equal morphology about a designated axis.

Symptom : Indication of disease ; visible effects produced in or on a plant by the presence of a pathogen.

Symptomatology, symptomology : The study of symptoms of disease caused by pathogens for the purpose of diagnosis.

Symptomless carrier : A plant infected by a pathogen (*i.e.,* a virus) with no visible effects.

Symptom less virus : A virus present in a plant that produces no visible symptoms.

Systemic infection : Infection resulting from the spread of virus from the site of infection to all or most of the cells of the host.

Tailing : The addition of stretches of nucleotides to the 3′-terminus of ds nucleic acid to facilitate cloning into a vector.

Taxon (pl. **taxa**) **:** A taxonomic group of any rank such as family, genus, species, etc.

Taxonomy : Science of systematically describing, naming, and classifying organisms (viruses) based on natural relationships.

Tablespoonful = 3 tsp = 14.8 ml or cc = $\frac{1}{2}$ fl. oz. = 0.063 cup.

TDP (thermal death point) : Thermal death (or inactivation) point.

TEM : Transmission electron microscope.

Temperature-sensitive mutant : A mutant not capable of infection at as high a temperature as its wild-type strain.

Template : A nucleic acid molecule from which a complementary nucleic acid molecule is being synthesized.

Terminal redundancy : Identical sequences at each end of a linear polynucleotide molecule.

Terminal repetition : An identical nucleotide sequence at each end of a nucleic acid molecule.

Terminal transferase, deoxynucleotidyl transferase : An enzyme that adds deoxynucleotide triphosphates (dNTP) to the 3′ hydroxyl groups of the DNA fragment used in 3′ end labeling of DNA and in tailing DNA fragments with complementary dNPSs to facilitate cloning.

Tenuivirus (Tenuis *means* thin) group : The type member of the group is *Rice stripe virus*. It is a new group of viruses whose particles are thin about 3.0 nm in width and coiled, having flexuous, filamentous particles. Such particles measure 950-1350 nm in length. The filamentous particles consist of multipartite non messenger (negative sense) RNA genome, usually transmitted by leaf hoppers in persistent manner.

Test plant : A plant species, variety, or cultivar used to diagnose the infectivity of a pathogen. *See* Indicator plant.

Thermal death (or inactivation) point : The lowest temperature at which death or inactivation of an organism occurs (after heating) for usually 10 minutes.

Thermotherapy : The curing of a host (or propagative part, *e.g.*, a seed, bulb, corm, tuber) or cell line of infection by a pathogen by heat treatment.

Thrips : Small slender insects (order Thysanoptera), usually with four long, narrow wings. Thrips have rasping-sucking mouthparts and a ten-segmented abdomen. They influence the development of disease in plants by acting as vectors of pathogens like fungi, bacteria, and the *Tomato spotted wilt virus*.

Thymidine kinase : An enzyme catalyzing the phosphorylation of thymidic acid.

Thymine : Pyrimidine nitrogenous base found in DNA.

Tiplasmid : A class of large, conjugative plasmids found in the soil bacterium—*Agrobacterium tumefaciens*.

Titer or titre (in serological reactions) : The antibody titer is the reciprocal of the highest serum dilution to produce a discernible antigen-antibody reaction. Virus ; the concentration of virus present in a preparation as measured by bioassay or a serological assay.

Titration : The measurement of titer.

Tolerance (adj. **tolerant**) **:** Ability of a plant to endure virus infection without serious damage or yield loss.

Ton (metric) : = 2,204.6 lb. = 1000 kg.

Transcript : The RNA molecule produced by transcription. The primary transcript is often processed or modified into mature functional RNA, *e.g.* mRNA, rRNA or tRNA.

Transcription : Synthesis of RNA with one strand of DNA as template, catalyzed by the enzyme DNA-dependent RNA polymerase ; to copy a gene into RNA.

Transcapsidation : Encapsidation of nucleic acid of one virus with the protein of another strain during simultaneous replication of two strains.

Transfection : Virus infection of cells after inoculation with viral nucleic acid.

Transfer RNA (tRNA) : The RNA that moves amino acids to the ribosome in order prescribed by the messenger RNA (mRNA). Each tRNA has a specific trinucleotide sequence that interacts with a complementary sequence in mRNA. Also called soluble RNA (sRNA) and acceptor RNA (aRNA).

Transformation of DNA : A technique wherein cell properties can be modified by insertion and expression of foreign DNA.

Transgressive segregation : Genetic mechanism transferring, characters to progeny not expressed by parents.

Translation (adj. **translational**) **:** Synthesis of proteins on ribosomes as directed by successive triplets of nucleotides moved along mRNA.

Transmission : The transfer of virus from an infected plant to a healthy plant.

Transmission electron microscope (TEM) : An electron microscope in which an electric beam passes through a thin specimen (*e.g.,* a preparation of virus particles negatively stained or shadowed), or a thin section of tissue mounted on grid. The image of the specimen is magnified with electrostatic lenses, observed on a fluorescent screen, or photographed.

Transport protein : A protein involved in the transport of small molecules around the cell.

Trapping : A procedure in which EM grid is first coated with antiserum.

Treehopper : Small, jumping, homopterous insects of the family Membracidae with piercing-sucking mouth parts ; known to transmit several plant-infecting viruses.

Triangulation number : Number of identical equilateral triangles composing, a face of a given icosahedron, *e.g.,* T = 4, 9, or 16.

Tris : common biological buffer with pH range of 7.0 to 9.2.

Triton 100 : A nonionic detergent for disruption of cells, stabilizing proteins, solubilizing aqueous samples in scintillation fluids, etc.

Triturate : To grind, as with a mortar and pestle.

Trypsin : A proteolytic enzyme that catalyzes hydrolysis of peptide bonds on the carboxyl side of arginine, lysine, and aminoethyl cysteine residues.

Tryptic peptide : A peptide formed from a protein by the action of trypsin. It has arginine, lysine or aminoethyl cysteine at the C-terminus.

Tuber indexing : Propagation of a plant from a tuber assesses presence of a tuber-borne disease.

Type (in nomenclature) **:** A specimen is the type for a species, a species for a genus, a genus for a family, etc.).

Type-specific antigen : An antigen specific to a certain type of virus.

Ultracentrifuge : A high-speed (up to 70,000 rpm and 5000,000 g) centrifuge.

Ultracentrifugation : Processing in a high-speed centrifuge capable of sedimenting small particles.

Ultra filtration : A method for the removal of all but the very smallest particles (*e.g.,* viruses) from a fluid gradient.

Ultramicroscopic : Too small to be seen with a light microscope.

Uncoating : The removal of the outer layers of a virus particle on infection, thus releasing the viral nucleic acid. Ribosomes may be involved in uncoating the particles for some plant viruses.

Upstream processes—produce the starting material of interest.

Uracil : One of two pyrimidine nitrogenous (cytosine) bases found in RNA.

Uranyl acetate : A negative stains to aid visualizing viruses in an electron microscrope ; often used as a 1% solution, natural pH 4.0.

URF : Unidentified reading frame deduced from a DNA sequence but in which not protein or genetic function is known. *See* Open reading frame.

Urea : Low molecular weight compound used to denature proteins and nucleic acids.

Uridine : The nucleoside of **uracil** and ribose.

Uridine 5′-triphosphate (UTP) : A pyrimidine nucleotide, one of the four major constituents of RNA.

UV : Ultraviolet (radiation).

Valence (of antibody) : The number of epitopes with which one antibody can combine.

Valid (of taxonomic epithets) : Names published in accordance with the Code.

Van Regenmortel *et al* (2000) : Virus Taxonomy : Classification and nomenclature of viruses. 7th Report of the International Committee on Taxonomy of viruses. Academic Press, San Diego, New york.

Variability : The ability of an organism to change its characteristics from one generation to another due to adaptation to the environment or a mutation. *See* Genetic variability.

Variant : An organism showing some variation from the parent culture.

Vector : A living organism (*e.g.,* insect, mite, bird, higher animal, nematode, parasitic plant, human, etc.) able to carry and transmit a pathogen (virus, bacterium, fungus, nematode). In genetic engineering a vector or cloning vehicle is a self-replicating DNA molecule, such as a plasmid or virus, used to introduce a fragment of foreign DNA into a host cell (as the receptor for DNA molecules).

Vector efficiency : Usually expressed as percentage, indicating the proportion of vectors among a population tested.

Vector propensity : Probability that a vector with opportunity to acquire a pathogen in nature will transmit it ; *i.e.,* it probes a non-infected plant.

Vector resistance : Resistance of a host plant to the vector of a virus.

Non-preference : Resistance because a vector prefers not to feed on a host ; the vector may probe-feed a few times after landing, then move on, which may reduce the transmission of a persistent virus, but increase the spread of a nonpersistent virus.

Tolerance : Ability of a host plant to withstand a vector's attack without damage does not control virus spread.

Vein banding : Symptom of a virus disease in which regions along the leaf veins remain darker green than the tissue between the veins.

Vein clearing : Disease characterized by the disappearance of green colour adjacent to the veins of young leaves.

Ventral : Front or lower surface, as opposed to dorsal.

Vertical resistance : Resistance with complete protection of a host only against specific strains of a pathogen. *See* Gene- for-gene hypothesis.

Vertical transmission or genetic transmission : Passage of a viral genome from host generation to the next, either as a provirus or associated with the gamete genome, *i.e.*, transovarial transmission in insect vector, or seed transmission of plant viruses.

Virion : Complete infectious virus particle.

Viroid : An infectious pathogen smaller than a virus ; unencapsidated, free-floating, circular, single-stranded, 247 to 374 nucleotides, ribonucleic acid (RNA) that can infect certain plant cells, directs its own replication from host metabolites, and causes disease. Replication in the nucleus occurs by rolling circle-producing, oligomeric forms processed to unit length. The nucleic acid cannot code for proteins. Heat stability for viroids range from narrow to wide.

Viroplasm : An amorphous, usually proteinaceous, cytoplasmic inclusion body absent membrane, associated with virus infection in plant cells infected with wound tumor, cauliflower mosaic, and other viruses.

Virosis (pl. **viroses) :** Any virus disease of plants.

Virucidal : Describing a virus-inactivating agent, *e.g.*, formalin and chlorine.

Virucide : A chemical or physical agent capable of inactivating or permanently suppressing virus replication.

Virulence : The degree of pathogenicity of a virus ; capacity to produce disease.

Virulent : Highly pathogenic, the capacity to cause a severe disease; able to produce the symptoms typical of the disease in a susceptible host.

Viruliferous : Term applied particularly to virus-laden insect and nematode vectors capable of transmitting the virus.

Virus : A submicroscopic, filt'erable agent that causes disease and multiplies (actually replication) only in living cells ; intracellular, obligate parasite consisting of a core of one or more infectious nucleic acids (either RNA or DNA) encapsidated by protein. Viruses contain no energy-producing enzymes, no functional ribosomes or cellular organelles; all are supplied by the cell in which viruses replicate.

Virus assembly : The coming together of the constituent parts of a virus particle and the formation of that particle. The process varies from autoassembly of protein subunits around nucleic acid.

Virus cryptogram : A descriptive code summarizing the main properties of a virus.

Virus inactivator : A chemical that inactivates a virus, causing loss of infectivity.

Virus inhibitor : A chemical that prevents virus transmission without inactivating the virus.

Virus particle : The morphological form of a virus. In some viruses, it consists of a genome surrounded by a protein capsid.

Virus replication : The process of forming progeny virus from input virus. It involves the expression and replication of the viral genomic nucleic acid and the assembly of proc ny virus particles.

Virus-like particle : A structure resembling a virus but pathogenicity is unproven.

Virusoid : The very small circular RNA component of some isometric RNA viruses.

Virustatic : Able to inhibit viral replication, which can be resumed once the virustatic agent is removed. Actinomycin D and 5-fluorodeoxyuridase inhibit DNA viruses. Thiouracil, 5- fluorouracil and puromycin inhibit RNA viruses.

Viviparously : A method of a sexual reproduction occuring in aphids by which the young are borne alive and active.

von Magnus phenomenon : The increase in the proportion of defective virus particles produced during the repeated passage of a virus at a high multiplicity of infection.

VPg : A genome-linked virion protein.

Western blotting : The transfer of proteins, separated on a polyacrylamide gel, to an immobilizing matrix, often nitrocellulose. Proteins are frequently transferred using electrophoresis, called electroblotting.

Witches' broom : Disease symptom with an abnormal, massed, brush- like development of many weak shoots or roots of mainly woody plants, arising at or close to the same point or resulting from the proliferation of buds.

X bodies : Inclusion bodies in *Tobacco mosaic virus* (TMV)- infected plant cells.

Yd (Yard) : = 36 in. = 3 ft = 0.181818 rod = 0.9144 m.

Yellowing (distinct from chlorosis) : To make or render tissue yellow that once was green due to the under-development or partial distruction of chlorophyll.

Yellows : A plant disease characterized by yellowing and stunting of the host plant usually caused by xylem-limited fastidious bacteria or elemental deficiencies ; yellows of the cabbage family (Brassicaceae) is caused by *Fusarium oxysporum* f. sp. *Conglutinans* ; peach yellows is caused by a virus.

Zonate : Marked with concentric zones (bands or lines) of different colors and/or textures ; target-like ; any leaf or stem development appearing in concentric rings.

Zoochoric : Dependent on animals for dissemination or dispersal.

(+) sense : Plus-sense or positive-sense. In RNA viruses, the strand that functions as a messenger (mRNA).

(-) sense : Minus-sense or negative-sense ; nucleic acid complementary to the + strand.

SUGGESTED READING

Author thankfully acknowledges having consulted, reviewed and abstracted following books, journals and research papers listed below, in addition to many others not included in this list.

Aapola, A.A. and Mink, G.I. 1973. Potential aphid vectors of pea seed-mosaic virus in Washington. *Pl. dis. Reptr.* 57:552.

Agrawal, H.O. 1964. Identification of cowpea mosaic virus isolates. *Meded. Landbourwhogesch. Wageningen* 64 (5)

Agrios, G.N. 1988. Plant Pathology, Third edition, Academic Press, New York.

Ahlawat, Y.S. 2001. Characterization of viruses and diagnosis of viral diseases of plants. *Practical training manual.* Advanced Center for Plant Virology, Division of Plant Pathology, IARI, New Delhi—110012.

Ashby, J.W. 1984. Bean leaf roll virus. *CMI/AAB Descriptions of Plant Viruses,* No. 286.

Bancroft, J.B. 1968. Tomato top necrosis virus. *Phytopathology* 58:1360-1363.

Bancroft, J.B. 1971. Cowpea chlorotic mottle virus. *CMI/AAB Descriptions of Plant Viruses,* No. 49.

Baranwal, V.K., Sridhar and Puri, S. N. (1996). Leaf curl disease of tobacco and its management N.C.I.P.M. *Tech. Bull.* No. 1, p.1.

Bawden F.C. *et al.* 1951. Some properties of board bean mottle virus. *Ann. Appl. Biol* 38:774-784.

Beier, M. *et al.* 1977. Survey of susceptibility to cowpea mosaic virus among protoplasts and intact plants from Vigna sinensis lines. *Phytopathology* 67:917-921.

Bercks, R. 1960. Serological relationship between beet mosaic virus, potato virus Y and bean yellow mosaic virus.*Virology* 12:311-313.

Best, R.J. 1968. Tomato spotted wilt virus.*Adv. Virus Res.* 13:65-146.

Bird, J. and Maramorosch, K. 1978. Viruses and virus disease associated with whiteflies. *Adv. Virus Res.* 22:55-110.

Black, I.M. 1940. Strains of potato yellow-dwarf virus. *Am. J. Bot.* 27:386-392.

Blattny, C. and Janeckova, M. 1980. Apricote bare twig and unfruitfulness. *Acta Phytopathol. Acad. Sci. Hung.* 15:383-390.

Blodgett, E.C. and Aichele, D. 1976. Spur cherry. In: *Virus Diseases and Noninfectious Disorders of Stone Fruits in North America.* USDA *Handb.* 437:252-253.

Bock, K.R. 1966. Arabis mosaic virus and Prunus necrotic ringspot virus in hop (*Humulus lupulus L.*). *Ann. Appl. Biol.* 57:131-140.

Bock, K.R. and Conti, M. 1974. Cowpea aphid-borne mosaic virus. *CMI/AAB Descriptions of Plant Viruses,* No. 134.

Bodine, E.W. and Kreutzer, W.A. 1942. Ring spot of apricot. *Phytopathology.* 32:333-335.

Bos, L. 1970. Bean yellow mosaic virus. *CMI/AAB Descriptions of Plant Viruses,* No. 40.

Bos, L. 1972. Soybean mosaic virus. *CMI/AAB Descriptions of Plant Viruses,* No. 93.

Bos, L. 1973. Pea streak virus. *CMI/AAB Descriptions of Plant Viruses,* No. 112.

Bos, L. 1976. Onion yellow dwarf virus. *CMI/AAB Descriptions of Plant Viruses,* No. 158.

Bos, L. 1981. Leek yellow stripe virus. *CMI/AAB Descriptions of Plant Viruses,* No. 240.

Bos, L. 1984. Spinach latent virus. *CMI/AAB Descriptions of Plant Viruses,* No. 281.

Bos, L. 1996. Research on viruses of legume crops and the International Working Group on Legume Viruses; historical facts and personal reminiscenses. *Intl. Work. Group Legume Vir.,* c/o ICARDA, P.O. Box 5466, Aleppo Syria.

Bos, L. and Van der Want, J.P.H. 1962. Early browning of pea, a disease caused by a soil-and seed-borne virus. *T. Plantenziekt.* 68:368-390.

Bos, L. ***et al.*** 1974. The identification of bean mosaic, pea yellow mosaic and pea necrosis strains of bean yellow mosaic virus. *Neth. J. Pl. Pathol.*80:173-191.

Bos, L. ***et al.*** 1978. Leek yellow stripe virus and its relationships to onion yellow dwarf virus; characterization, ecology and possible control. *Neth. J. Pl. Pathol* 84:185-204.

Bos, L. ***et al.*** 1978a. Further characterization of celery latent virus. *Neth. J. Pl. Pathol. 84:61-79.*

Bos, L. ***et al.*** 1980. Spinach latent virus, a new ilarvirus seed-borne in *Spinacea oleracea. Neth. J. Pl. Pathol.* 86:79.

Bos, L. ***et al.*** 1984a. Further characterization of melon necrotic spot virus causing severe disease in glasshouse cunumbers in the Netherlands and its control. *Neth. J. Pl. Pathol.* 90:55-69.

Boscia, D. ***et al.*** 1990. Association of a phloem-limited nonmechanically transmissible isometric virus with fleck disease. (Abstr.) *10th Meeting ICVG,* Volos, Greece, Setp. 3-7, p. 22.

Bovey, R. and Cazelles, O. 1978. Alfalfa mosaic virus on grapevines. *Proc. 6th Conf. Virus and Virus Dis. Grapevine,* 13-21 September, 1976, Madrid, p. 131-134.

Bozarth, R.F. and Shoyinka, S.A. 1979. Cowpea mottle virus. *CMI/AAB Descriptions of Plant Viruses,* No. 212.

Bradford, F.C. and Joley, L. 1933. Infectious variegaton in the apple. *J. Agric. Res. 46:901-908.*

Brandes, E.W. 1919. The mosaic disease of sugarcane and other grasses. *Tech. Bull. U.S. Dept. Agric.* 829.26 pp.

Break, J. 1975. Garlic mosaic virus particles and virus infections of some wild *Allium* species. *Sbornik UVTIO chrana rostlin* 11:(XLVIII) 237-242.

Broadbent, I. 1964. The epidemology of tomato mosaic. VII. The effect of TMV on tomato fruit yield and quality under glass. *Ann. Appl. Biol.* 54:209-224.

Broadbent, I. 1965. The epidemology of tomato mosaic. XI. Seed- transmission of TMV. *Ann. Appl. Biol.* 56:177-205.

Broadbent, L. 1961. The epidemology of tomato mosaic: A review of the literature. *Rep. Glasshouse Crops Res. Inst.*, 96-116. (Abstr. In *RAM* 41/1962/:271).

Broadbent, L. 1964. Control of plant virus diseases. In: Corbett, M.K. and Sisler, H.P., Eds. *Plant Virology* University of Forida Press, Gainesville, p. 330-364.

Broadbent, L. 1965. The epidemiology of tomato mosaic. XI. Seed transmission of TMV. *Ann. Appl. Biol. 56:177-205.*

Brown, J.K. *et al.* 1984. Irrigated corn as a source of barley yellow dwarf virus and vector in eastern Washington. *Phytophthology* 74:46-49.

Brunt, A.A. and Kenten, R.H. 1971 Pepper veinal mottle virus, a new member of the potato virus Y group from peppers (*Capsicum annuum* L. and C. *frutescens* L.) in Ghana. *Ann. Appl. Biol.* 69:235-243.

Brunt, A.A. and Kenten, R.H. 1972. Pepper veinal mottle virus. *CMI/AAB Descriptions of Plant Viruses,* No. 104.

Brunt, A.A. and Kenten, R.H. 1974. Cowpea mild mottle virus. *CMI/AAB Descriptions of Plant Viruses,* No. 140.

Buck, K.W. and Coutts, R.H.A. 1985. Tomato golden mosaic virus. *CMI/AAB Descriptions of Plant Viruses,* No. 303.

Butler, J.P.G. 1970. Structures of turnip crinkle and tomato bushy stunt viruses. *J. Mol. Biol.* 52:589-593.

Cadman, C.H. 1963. Biology of soil-borne viruses. *Annu. Rev. Phytopathol.* 1:143-172.

Cameron, H.R. 1954. A bark splitting virus disease of Montmorency sour cherry. (Abstr.) *Phytopathology* 44:484.

Campbell, R.N. 1971. Squash mosaic virus. *CMI/AAB Descriptions of Plant Viruses,* No. 43.

Campbell, R.N. 1973. Radish mosaic virus. *CMI/AAB Descriptions of Plant Viruses,* No. 121.

Campbell, R.N. and Lin, M.T. 1972. Broccoli necrotic yellows virus. *CMI/AAB Descriptions of Plant Viruses,* No. 85.

Campbell, A.I. 1962. The effect of some apple viruses on the growth of *Malus* species and varieties. *J. Hort. Sci.* 37:239-246.

Campbell, A.I. 1962a. Apple virus inactivation by heat therapy and tip propagation. *Nature* 195:520.

Campbell, A.I. 1968. Heat sensitivity of some apple viruses. *Tagungsber. DAL DDR, Berlin,* 97:311-316.

Campbell, A.I. and Best, M.W. 1964. The effect of heat therapy on several apple viruses. *Rep. Long Ashton Res. Sta.* 1963:65.

Campbell, A.I. and Bould, C. 1970. Virus, fertilizer and rootstock effects on the nutrition of young apple trees. *J. Hort. Sci. 45:287-294.*

Carroll, T.W. 1980. Barley stripe mosaic virus: its economic importance and control in Montana. 64:136- 140.

Castellano, A.M. *et al.* 1983. Virus-like particles and ultrastructural modifications in the phloem of leaf roll-affected grapevines. *Vitis* 22:23-39.

Cation, D. 1949. Transmission of cherry yellows virus complex through seeds. *Phytopathology* 39:37-40.

Cation, D. 1952. Further studies on transmission of ringspot and cherry yellows viruses through seeds. *Phytopathology 42:4.*

Cech, M. *et al.* 1980. Strawberry latent ringspot and cucumber green mottle mosaic viruses in apricot with bare twig and unfruitfulness disease syndrome. *Acta Phtopatol. Acad. Sci. Hung.* 15:391-396.

Cesati, R.R. and van Regenmortel, M.H.V. 1969. Serological detection of a strain of tobacoo necrosis virus in grapevine leaves. *Phytopathol* 64:362-366.

Chamberlain, E.E. *et al.* 1959. Two diseases of plum, causing distortion and internal necrosis of fruits *N.Z.J. Agric. Res.* 2:174-180.

Cheney, P.W. *et al.* 1967. Graft transmissioin of the flat apple disease. *Plant Dis. Reptr.* 51:509-510.

Cheney, P.W. *et al.* 1976. Black canker. In *Virus Diseases and Noninfectious Disorders of Stone Fruits in North America. ARS.* USDA *Agric. Handbook,* No. 437:209-210.

Chod, J. 1965. Studies of some ways in which carrot mosaic virus can be transmitted. *Biologia Plantarum 6:463-468.*

Chod, J. 1988. Carrot mosaic virus. In: Smith, I.M. *et al.*, Eds. *European Handb. Pl. Dis.,* Blackwell Sci. Publ., London P. 38.

Christ, E.G. 1960. New peach tree problem. Stem pitting. *Hort. News N.J. Hort. Soc.* 41:4006.

Clark, M.F. and Adams, A.N. 1977. Characteristics of the microplate method of enzyme-linked immunosorbent assay for detection of plant viruses. *J. Gen Virol* 34:475-483.

Cochran, L.C. and Smith, C.O. 1938. Asteroid spot, a new virosis of peach. *Phytopathology* 28:278-281.

Cohen, S. 1982. Control of whitefly vectors of viruses by color mulches. In: Harris, K.F. and maramorosch, K., Eds. *Pathogens, Vectors* and *Plant Diseases, Approaches to Control,* Academic Press, New York. P. 45-46.

Cohn, E. *et al.* 1970. *Xiphinema italiae,* a new vector of grapevine fanleaf virus. *Phytopathology* 60:181- 182.

Cole, A. *et al.* 1982. Location of Prunus necrotic ringspot virus on pollen grains from infected almond and cherry trees. *Phytopathology* 72:1542-1545.

Conover, R.A. 1964. Mild mosaic and faint mottle ringspot, two papaya virus diseases of minor importance in Florida. *Proc. Fla. State Hort. Soc.* 77:444-448.

Conover, R.A. 1964a. Distortion ringspot, a severe virus disease of papaya in Florida. *Proc. Fla. State Hort. Soc.* 77:440-444.

Conti, M. 1969. Investigations on a bullet-shaped virus of cereals isolated in Italy from planthoppers *Phytopathol.* Z. 66:275-279.

Conti, M. 1972. Barley yellow striate mosaic virus isolated from plants in the field. *Phytopathol.* Z. 73:39-45.

Conti, M. 1980. Vector relationships and other characteristics of barley yellow strate mosaic virus (BYSMV). *Ann. Appl. Biol.* 95:83-92.

Conti, M. 1988. Barley yellow striate mosaic virus. In: Smith. I.M. *et al.*, Eds. *European Handbook Plant Diseases,* Blackwell Sci. Publ., London. p. 76.

Conti, M. and Plumb. R.T. 1977. Barley yellow striate mosaic virus in the salivary glands of its planthopper vectors *Laodelphax striatellus* Fallen. *J. Gen. Virol.* 34:107-114.

Conti, M. *et al.* 1980. A closterovirus from a stem- pitting-diseased grapevine. *Phytopathology* 70:394-399.

Cooper, J.I. 1988. Brome mosaic virus (BMV). In: Smith, I.M. *et al., European Handbook Plant Diseases.* Blackwell Sci. Publ., London p.69.

Cooper, J.I. and Harrison, B.D. 1973. The role of weed hosts and the distribution and activity of vector nematodes in the ecology of tobacco rattle virus. *Ann. Appl. Biol* 73:53-66.

Corbett, M.K. and Grant, T.J. 1967. Purification of citrus variegation virus. *Phytopathology* 57:137-143.

Corbett, M.K. and Sisler, H.D. 1964. *Plant Virology*. University of Florida Press. 527 pp.

Cordy, C.B. and MacSwan, I.C. 1961. Some evidence that bark measles is seed borne. *Plant Dis. Reptr.* 45:891.

Costa, A.S. and Muller, G.W. 1980. Tritezas control by cross protection. *Plant Dis. Reptr.* 64:538-541.

Crescenzi, A *et al.* 1995. Plum pox virus (PPV) in sweet cherry. *Acta Hort.* 386. Fruit Tree Virus Diseases XVI.

Cropley, R. 1960. Pear blister cankers a virus disease. *Ann. Rept. East Malling Res. Sta.* : 43-159.

Cropley, R. 1961. Cherry leaf roll. *Ann. Appl. Biol.* 49: 542-549.

Cropley, R. 1963. Apple star crack. In: *Virus Diseases of Apples and Pears. Techn. Commun. Bur. Hort. E. Malling* 30:47- 49.

Cropley, R. 1968. The identification of plum pox (Sharka) virus in England *Pl. Pathol* 17:66-70.

Cropley, R. 1968a. Varietal reactions to viruses causing star crack and russet rings on apple fruits. *J. Hort. Sci.* 43:157-165.

Cropley, R. 1968b. Testing cherry rootstocks for resistance to infection by rasberry ringspot and cherry leaf roll viruses. *Rept. East Malling Res. Stn.* 1967:141-143.

Cuozzo, M. *et al.* 1988. Viral protection in transgenic tobacco plants expressing the cucumber mosaic virus coat protein or its antigens RNA. *Biotech.* 6:549.

Currie, J.A. 1971. A short history of striate mosaic disease. *Cane Grow. Q. Bull.* 35(1): 12-13.

Arcy. D.J. and Burnett, P.A. 1995. *Barley yellow Dwarf* : 40 Years of Progress, APS Press, St. Paul. MN, 374 pp.

Da Camara Machado, A *et. al.* 1991. Coat protein-mediated protection against plum pox virus (Abstr.) *XVth Int. Symp. in Virus and Virus Diseases of Temperate Fruit Crops.* 8-13 July, Vienna, Austria.

Dale, J.I. *et al.* 1994. Banana Virus Research at the Centre for Molecular Biotechnology. Queensland University of Technology, Brisbane, Australia.

Davidson, T.R. and Allen, W.R. 1976. Fruit pitting of sweet cherry. In: *Virus Diseases and Noninfectius Disorders of Stone Fruits in North America. USDA Handb.* 437:227-230.

Davidson, T.R. and George, J.A. 1965. Effects of necrotic ringspot and sour cherry yellows on the growth and yield of young sour cherry trees. *Can. J. Pl. Sci.* 45:525-535.

Davis, R.M. *et al.* 1997. *Compendium of Lettuce Diseases.* APS Press, St. Paul, MN, 79 pp.

De Bokx, J.A. 1965. Hosts and electron microscopy of two papaya viruses. *Plant Dis. Reptr.* 49:742-746.

De Jager, C.P. 1979. Cowpea severe mosaic virus. *CMI/AAB Descriptions of Plant Viruses,* No. 209.

De La Rosa, and Lastra, R. 1983. Purification and partial characterization of papaya ringspot virus. *Phytopathol* Z. 106:329-336.

De Leon, D. 1952. Cadang-cadang disease of coconuts in the Philippines. *Foreign Agric.* 16:103. {Abstr. In *RAM* (1954) 33:152)}.

De Sequeira, O.A. 1967. Purification and serology of an apple mosaic virus. *Virology* 31:314.

De Zoeten, G.A. and Reddick, B.B. 1984. Maize white line mosaic virus. CMI/AAB *Descriptions of Plant Viruses,* No. 283.

Demski, J.W. 1981. Tobacco mosaic virus is seed borne in Pimiento peppers. *Plant Dis.* 65 : 723-724.

Dercks, A.FL.M. and Van den Abecle, J.L. 1980. Bean yellow mosaic virus in some iridaceous plants. *Acta Hort.* 110 : 31-38.

Derrick, K.S. 1975. Serological relationships among strains of sugarcane mosaic virus. *Proc. Am. Phytopathol.* Soc. 2.42.

Desvignes, J.C. 1971. Observations on some pear virus diseases, vein yellows, quince sooty ringspot, ring pattern mosaic. *Ann. Phtopathol. No. hors serie* 295-304.

Desvignes, J.C. 1980. Different symptoms of the peach latent mosaic. *Acta Phytopathol. Acad. Sci. Hung.* 15 : 83-190.

Desvignes, J.C. 1988. Peach latent mosaic disease. In : Smith, I.M. et al., Eds. *European Handb. Pl. Dis.,* Blackwell Sci. Publ., London, p.111.

Desvignes, J.C. 1988a. Cherry green ring mottle disease. In : Smith, I.M. *et al.,* Eds. *European Handb. Pl. Dis.,* Blackwell Sci. Publ. London, p. 103-104.

Desvignes, J.C. and Boye, R. 1988. Different diseases caused by the chlorotic leaf spot virus on the fruit trees. (Abstr.) *XIVth Int. Symp. on Fruit Tree Virus Diseases,* 12-18 June, Thessaloniki, Greece.

Desvignes, J.C. and Savio, A. 1971. A virus disease causing necrosis on *Prunus insititia* L. var. Krikom. *Ann. Phytopathol.* 1 : 75-84.

Desvignes, J.C. *et al.,* 1991. Quick detection of the principal apple and pear virus diseases (Abstr.). *XVth Int. Symp. Virus and Virus Dis. Temp. Fruit Crops.* 8-13 July, Vienna, Austria.

Dias, H.F. 1975. Peach rosette mosaic virus. *CMI/AAB Descriptions of Plant Viruses,* No. 150.

Dias, H.F. and Mckeen, C.D. 1972. Cucumber necrosis virus. *CMI/AAB Descriptions of Plant Viruses,* No. 82.

Diener, T.O. and Raymer, W.B. 1967. Potato spindle tuber virus. A virus with properties of a free nucleic acid. *Science* 158 : 378-381.

Diener, T.O. and Raymer, W.B. 1971. Potato spindle tuber "virus". *CMI/AAB Descriptions of Plant Viruses,* No. 66.

Dimitrijevic, B. 1980. Some properties of the new latent virus from grapevine rootstocks in Yugoslavia. *Proc. 6th Mtg. Int. Conf. Study Viruses and Virus-like Disease of the Grapevine,* Niagara Falls, Can., Sept. 8-12, p.21-24.

Dodds, J.A. and Bar-Joseph, M. 1983. Double stranded RNA from plants infected with Closteroviruses. *Phytopathology* 73 : 419-423.

Dodds, J.A. and Mirkov, T.E. 1983. Association of double-stranded RNA with lettuce big vein disease. In : *4th Int. Cong. of Plant Pathology*, Abstract 113, Melbourne.

Dosba, F. *et al.* 1991. Breeding for resistance to sharka in apricot trees. (Abstr.). *XVth Int. Symp. Virus Dis. Temp. Fruit Crops,* 8-13 July, Vienna, Austria.

Dowson, G.W. *et al.* 1986. Antifeedants ; a new concept for control of BYDV in winter cereals. *Br. Crop Prot. Conf. Pests and Dis.* : Proc. 3 : 1001-1008.

Duffus, E.J. and Russel, G.E. 1962. Serological relationship between beet western yellows and turnip yellows viruses. *Phytopathology* 62 : 1274-1277.

Duffus, J.E. 1961. Economic significance of beet western yellows (radish yellows) on sugar beet. *Phytopathology* 51 : 605- 607.

Duffus, J.E. 1965. Beet pseudo-yellows virus, transmitted by the greenhouse whitefly (*Trialeurodes vaporiorum*). *Phytopathology* 55 : 450-453.

Duffus, J.E. 1972a. Beet yellows stunt, a potentially destructive virus disease of sugar beet and lettuce. *Phytopathology* 62 : 161-165.

Duffus, J.E. 1973. The yellowing virus diseases of beet. *Adv. Virus Res.* 18 : 347-386.

Duffus, J.E. and Rochow, W.F. 1978. Neutralization of beet western yellows virus by antisera against barley yellow dwarf virus. *Phytopathology* 68 : 45-49.

Duffus, J.E. and Russell, G.E. 1975. Serological relationship between beet western yellows and beet mild yellowing viruses. *Phytopathology* 65 : 811-815.

Dunez, J. 1972. Beet western yellows virus. *CMI/AAB Descriptions of Plant Viruses,* No. 89.

Dunez, J. and Sutic, D. 1988. Plum pox virus (PPV). In : Smith, I.M. *et al.*, Eds. *European Handb. Pl. Dis.,* Blackwell Sci. Publ., London, p. 44-46.

Dunez, J. *et al.* 1976. Myrobalan latent ringspot virus. *CMI/AAB Descriptions of Plant Viruses,* No. 160.

Dunez, J. *et al.* 1982. Detection of virus and virus-like diseases of fruit trees. *Acta Hort.* 130 : 319-330.

Edwardson, J.R. and Christie, R.G. 1991. *CRC Handbook of Viruses infecting Leguines,* CRC Press LLC, Boca Raton, FL, 504 pp.

Elnagar, S. and Muant, A.F. 1976. Relations of the semi- persistent viruses, parsnip viruses, yellow fleck and anthriscus yellows with their vector, *Cavariella aegopodii. Ann. Appl Biol.* 84 : 169-181.

Elnagar, S. and Muant, A.F. 1978. Aphid-injection experiments with carrot mottle virus and its helper virus, carrot red leaf. *Ann. Appl. Biol.* 89 : 245-250.

Eslick, R.F. 1953. Yield reductions in Glacier barley associated with a virus infection. *Pl. Dis. Reptr.* 37 : 290-291.

Fagbenle, H.H. and Ford, R.E. 1970. Tobacco streak virus isolated from soybeans *(Glycine max.) Phytopathology* 60 : 814-820.

Faggioli, F. ***et al.*** 1990. Further characterization and serology of closterovirus type III isolated from grape in Italy, (Abstr.) *10th Meeting ICVG,* Volos, Greece, Sept. 3-7, p.76.

Falk, B.W. and Purcifull, D.E. 1983. Development and application of an enzyme-linked immunosorbent assay (ELISA) to index lettuce seeds for lettuce mosaic virus in Florida. *Plant Dis.* 67 : 413-416.

Fauquet, C.M. and Beachy, R.N. 1993. Status of coat protein- mediated resistance and its potential application for banana viruses. *Proc. Workshop Biotech. Appl. Banana/Plantain impvt., INIBAP,* Montpellier, France, 1992, p.69-84.

Fawcett, H.S. 1932. New angles on treatment of bark diseases of citrus. *Calif. Citrograph* 17 : 406-408.

Fawcett, H.S. 1933. New symptoms of psorosis, indicating a virus disease of citrus. *Phytopathology* 23 : 930.

Ferro, D.N. *et al.* 1980. Effect of mineral oil and a systemic insecticide on field spread of aphid-borne maize dwarf mosiac virus in sweet corn. *J. Econ. Entom.* 73 : 730-735.

Findley, W.R. *et al.* 1977. Breeding corn for resistance to virus in Ohio. In : Williams, L.E. *et al.,* Eds. *Proc. Maize Virus Dis. Colloq. Workshop.* Ohio Agric. Res. Dev. Cent., Wooster, OH, p. 123-127.

Finley, A.M. 1957. Wheat streak mosaic, a disease of sweet corn in Idaho. *Pl. Dis. Reptr* : 41 : 589-591.

Flock, R.A. and Wallace, J.M. 1955. Transmission of fig mosaic by the eriophyid mite *Aceria ficus. Phytopathology* 45 : 52-54.

Flores, R.C. ***et al.*** 1991. Studies on detection, transmission and distribution of peach latent mosaic viroid in peach trees. (Abstr.). *XVth Int. Symp. Virus and Virus Diseases of Temperate Fruit Crops,* 8-13 July, Vienna, Austria.

Ford. R.E. and Tosic. M. 1972. New hosts of maize dwarf mosaic virus and sugarcane mosaic virus and a comparative host range study of viruses infecting corn. *Phytopathol.* Z. 75 : 315- 348.

Ford. R.E. ***et al.*** 1970. New hosts and serological identity of bromegrass mosaic virus from South Dakota. *Pl. Dis. Reptr.* 54 : 191-195.

Ford. R.E. *et al*. 1989. Maize dwarf mosaic virus. CMI/AAB *Descriptions of Plant Viruses,* No. 341.

Fox, P.N. and Tola. J. 1990. Barley yellow dwarf in the Andean countries of South America. In : Burnett, P.A., Ed. *World Perspectives on Barley Yellow Dwarf.* CIMMYT. Mexico, D.F., Mexico.

Frankel. M.J. *et al.,* 1991. Sequence diversity in the surface- exposed amino-terminal regions of coat proteins of sugarcane mosaic virus strains correlated with natural host specificity. (Abstr.) *Phytopathology* 81 : 1155.

Franki, R.I.B. and Randles, J.W. 1970. Lettuce necrotic yellow virus. *CMI / AAB Descriptions of Plant Viruses,* No. 26.

Frederiksen, R.A. 1986. *Compendium of Sorghum Diseases.* APS Press, St. Paul, MN, 82 pp.

Freitag, J.H. 1956. Beetle transmission, host range, and prospectives of squash mosaic virus. *Phytopathology* 46 : 73-81.

Fridlund, P.R. 1966. Transmission and lack of transmission of seven viruses through *Prunus seed. Plant. Dis. Reptr.* 50 : 902-904.

Fridlund, P.R. 1976. Pear vein yellows virus symptoms in greenhouse-grown pear cultivars. *Plant Dis. Reptr.* 60 : 891-894.

Fridlund, P.R. and Bottorf. F.O. 1968. Virus gummosis of apricot caused by some prune dwarf virus strains. *Phytopathology* 58 : 119-120.

Fuchs, E. 1980. Serological detection of apple chlorotic leaf spot virus (CLSV) and apple stem grooving virus in apple trees. *Acta Phytopathol. Acad. Sci. Hung.* 15(1-4) : 69-73.

Fujikawa *et al.* 1972. *Ann. Phytopathol. Soc. Japan* 38 : 213.

Fulton, J.P. 1967. Dual transmission of tobacco ringspot virus and tomato ringspot virus by *Xiphinema Americanum. Phytopathology* 57 : 535.

Fulton, R.W. 1948. Hosts of the tobacco streak virus. *Phytopathology* 38 : 421-428.

Fulton, R.W. 1968. Serology of viruses causing cherry necrotic ringspot, plum line pattern, rose mosaic and apple mosaic. *Phytopathology* 58 : 635-638.

Futrell, M.C. and Scott, G.E. 1969. Effect of maize dwarf mosaic virus infection on invasion of corn plants by *Fusarium moniliforme. Pl. Dis. Reptr.* 53 : 600-602.

Gallitelli, D. *et al.* 1984. Aritchoke vein banding virus. *CMI / AAB Descriptions of Plant Viruses,* No. 285.

Galvez, G.E. 1967. Frecuencia de *Sogata oryzicola* and *S. cubana* en campos de arroz y *Echinochloa* en Colombia. *Agr. Trop., Bogota, Colombia* 23 : 384-389.

Galvez, G.E. 1971. Rice tungro virus. CMI/AAB *Descriptions of Plant Viruses.* No. 67.

Gamez, R. 1982. Bean rugose mosasic virus. *CMI / AAB Descriptions of Plant Viruses,* No. 246.

Gardner, M.W. and Kendrick, J.B. 1921. Soybean mosaic. *J. Agric Res.* 22 : 111-114.

Garnsey, S.M. and Gonsalves, D. 1976. Citrus leaf rugose virus. *CMI / AAB Descriptions of Plant Viruses,* No. 164.

Garnsey, S.M. *et al.* 1981. Application of serological indexing to develop control strategies for citrus tristeza virus. In : *Proc. Int. Soc. Citrus culture.*

Geelen, J.L.M.C. *et al.* 1972. Structure of capsid of cowpea mosaic virus. The chemical subunit : molecular weight and number of subunits per particle. *Virology* 49 : 205-213.

George, J.A. and Davidson, T.R. 1963. Pollen transmission of necrotic ring spot and sour cherry yellows viruses from tree to tree. *Can. J. Plant Sci.* 43 : 273-288.

George, J.A. and Davidson, T.R. 1964. Further evidence of pollen transmission of necrotic ring spot and sour cherry yellows viruses in sour cherry. *Can. J. Plant Sci.* 44 : 383-384.

George, J.A. and Davidson, T.R. 1966. Virus assay of seeds from selected Montomorency cherry trees. *Can. J. Plant. Sci.* 46 : 501-505.

German, S. *et al.* 1991. Genomic organization of apple chlorotic leaf spot closterovirus (ACLSV). *XVth Int. Symp. Virus and Virus Dis. Temp. Fruit Crops,* 8-13 July, Vienna, Austria.

Ghabrial, S.A. and Lister, R.M 1974. Chemical and physiochemical properties of two strains of tobacco streak virus. *Virology* 57 : 1-10.

Gibbs, A.J. 1972. Board bean mottle virus. *CMI/AAB Descriptions of Plant Viruses,* No. 101.

Gibbs, A.J. and Harrison, B.D. 1964. A form of pea early-browning virus found in Britain. *Ann. Appl. Biol.* 54 : 1-11.

Gibbs, A.J. and Harrison, B.D. 1964. Viruses in sugar beet. *Rep. Rothamsted Exp. Sta. For* 1963, p. 106.

Gibbs, A.J. and Harrison, B.D. 1973. Eggplant mosaic virus. *CMI/AAB Descriptions of Plant Viruses,* No. 124.

Gibbs, A.J. and Smith. H.G. 1970. Board bean stain virus. *CMI/AAB Descriptions of Plant Viruses,* No. 29.

Gibbs, A.J. *et al.* 1963. The relationship between barley stripe mosaic and lychnis ringspot viruses. *Virology* 20 : 194-198.

Gildow, F.E. 1990. Current status of barley yellow dwarf in United States : a regional situation report. In : Burnett, P.A., Ed. 1990-*World Perspectives on Barley Yellow Dwarf,* CIMMYT, Mexico, D.F., Mexico, p. 11-20.

Gildow, F.E. *et al.* 1983. Identification of double-stranded RNAs associated with barley yellow dwarf virus infections of oats. *Phytopathology* 73 : 1570-1572.

Gill, C.C. 1969. Variation in strains of barley yellow dwarf virus in Manitoba and the occurrence of green-bug-specific isolates. *Can. J. Bot,* 47 : 1277-1283.

Gill, C.C. 1976. Oat necrotic mottle virus. CMI/AAB *Descriptions of Plant Viruses,* No. 169.

Gilmer, R.M. 1958. Two viruses that induce mosaic of apple. *Phytopathology* 48 : 432-434.

Gilmer, R.M. 1961. A possible history of sour cherry yellows. *Phytopathology* 51 : 265-266.

Gilmer, R.M. 1967. Apple chlorotic leaf spot and tobacco mosaic viruses in cherry. *Plant Dis. Reptr.* 51 : 823-826.

Gilmer, R.M. and Kelts, L.J. 1965. Isolation of tobacco mosaic virus from grape foliage and roots. (Abstr.) *Phytopathology* 55 : 1283.

Gilmer, R.M. and Kelts, L.J. 1968. Transmission of tobacco mosaic virus in grape seed. *Phytopathology* 58 : 277-278.

Gilmer, R.M. and Uyemoto, J.K. 1972. Tomato ringspot virus in "Boconoir" grapevines in New York. *Pl. Dis. Reptr.* 56 : 133-135.

Gilmer, R.M. *et al.* 1970. A new grapevine disease induced by tobacco ringspot virus. *Phytopathology* 60 : 619-627.

Gilmer, R.M. *et al.* 1976. Prune dwarf. In : *Virus Dis. Noninfec. Disorders Stone Fruits North America,* USDA *Handb.* 437 : 179-190.

Gingery, R.E. *et al.* 1978. Maize chlorotic dwarf virus. CMI/AAB *Descriptions of Plant Viruses,* No. 194.

Giorda, M.L. *et al.* 1986. Identification of sugarcane mosaic strain H isolates in commercial grain sorghum. *Plant Dis.* 70 : 624-628.

Giunchedi, L. *et al.*, 1987. Correlation between tolerance and beet necrotic vein virus in sugar beet genotypes. *Phytopathol. Mediter.* 26 : 23-28.

Goheen, A.C. 1970. Grape leafroll. In : Frazier, N.W., Ed. *Virus Dis. Small Fruits Grapevines,* University of California, Dacis, Div. Agr. Sci., p. 209-212.

Goheen, A.C.1977. Virus and virus-like diseases of grape. *Hort. Sci.* 12 : 465-569.

Goheen, A.C. and Cook, J.A. 1959. Leafroll (red or rougeau) and its effects on vine growth, fruit quality and yields. *Ann. J. Enol. Vitic.* 10 : 173-181.

Goheen, A.C. *et al.*, 1965. Inactivation of grapevine viruses *in vivo.* In : *Proc. Int. Conf. Virus Vectors Peren. Hosts Spec. Ref. Vitis.* University of California, Davis, *Div. Agr. Sci.* p. 255-265.

Gonsalves, D. 1988. Control of papaya ringspot virus : a case study. *Annu. Rev. Phytopathol.* 36 : 415-437.

Gonsalves, D. and Garnsey, S.M. 1975. Nucleic acid components of citrus variegation virus and their activation by coat protein. *Virology* 67 : 311-318.

Gonsalves, D. and Ishii. M. 1980. Purification and serology of papaya ringspot virus. *Phytopathology* 70 : 1028-1032.

Gonsalves, D. *et al.* 1978. Purification and serology of citrus tristeza virus. *Phytopathology* 68 : 553-559.

Gooding, G.V. and Hewitt, W.B. 1962. Grape yellow vein : Symptomatology, identification and the association of a mechanically tranmissible virus with a disease. *Am. J. Enol. Vitic.* 13 : 196-203.

Gooding, G.V., Jr. 1963. Purification and serology of a virus associated with the grape yellow-vein disease. *Phytopathology* 53 : 475-480.

Gooding, G.V., Jr. 1965. The reaction of grapevines and herbaceous plants to grapevine yellow-vein virus. In *Proc. Int. Conf. Virus Vector Peren. Hosts Spec. Ref. Vitis,* University of California, Davis, Div. Agr. Sci. p. 211-222.

Goodman, R.M. and Bird, J. 1978. Bean golden mosaic virus. *CMI/AAB Descriptions of Plant Viruses,* No. 192.

Gordon, D.T. and Nault, L.R. 1977. Involvement of maize chlorotic dwarf virus and other agents in stunting diseases of *Zea mays* in the United States. *Phytopathology* 67 : 27-30.

Gordon, D.T. *et al.* 1981. Introduction : history, geographical distribution, pathogen characteristics and economic importance. In : Gordon, D.T. *et al.,* Eds. *Virus and Virus-like Dis. Maize United States. South. Coop. Ser. Bull.* 247, June, OARDC, OH, p. 1-12.

Gordon, D.T. *et al.* 1984. Maize chlorotic mottle virus. *CMI/AAB Descriptions of Plant Viruses,* No. 284.

Govier, D.A. and B. Kassanis. 1974. A virus-induced component of plant sap seeded with aphids acquire potato virus Y from purified preparations. *Virology* 61 : 420-426.

Graniti, A. and Martelli, G.P. 1965. Further observations on legno riccio (rugose wood) and graft-transmissible stem-pitting of grapevine. In : *Proc. Int. Conf. Virus Vector Peren. Hosts Spec. Ref. Vitis,* University of California, Davis, Div. Agr. Sci. p. 168-179.

Grant, T.J. and Corbett, M.K. 1964. Properties of citrus variegation virus. *Phytopathology* 54 : 946-948.

Greber, R.S. 1977. Cereal chlorotic mottle virus (CCMV) a rhabdovirus of Gramineae transmitted by the leafhopper *Nesoclutha Pallida. Aust. Pl. Pathol. Soc. Newsl.* 6 : 17.

Greber, R.S. 1977a. A severe stunting virus disease of maize in Queensland. *Aust. Pl. Pathol. Soc. Newsl.* 10(2) : 29-30.

Greber, R.S. 1979 Cereal chlorotic mottle virus—a rhabdovirus of Gramineae in Australia transmitted by *Nesocluthà pallida (Evans.). Aust. J. Agr. Res.* 30(3) : 433-443.

Greber, R.S. 1981. Ecological aspects of cereal chlorotic mottle virus. *Aust. Pl. Pathol. Soc. Newsl.* 10(2) : 29-30.

Greber, R.S. 1982. Cereal chlorotic mottle virus. *CMI/AAB Descriptions of Plant Viruses,* No. 251.

Greber, R.S. 1982a. Maize sterile stunt—a delphacid transmitted rhabdovirus disease affecting some maize genotypes in Australia. *Aust. J. Agr. Res.* 33(1) : 13-23.

Grorda, L.M. *et al.,* 1986. Identification of sugarcane mosaic virus strain H isolate in commercial grain sorghum. *Plant Dis.* 70 : 624-628.

Gross, H.J. *et al.*, 1982. Nucleotide sequence and secondary structure of citrus exocortis and chrysanthemum stunt viroid. *Eur. J. Biochem.* 121 : 249-257.

Grumet, R. 1994. Development of virus resistant plants via genetic engineering. *Plant Bred. Rev.* 12 : 47-79.

Gumpt, D.J. 1971. Purification and properties of soil-borne wheat mosaic virus. *Virology* 43 : 588-596.

Gupta, K.C. 1981. Studies on the identity of sunflower mosaic virus. *Abstr. 3th Int. Symp. on Plant Pathol.,* New Delhi, December 14-18, p. 117.

Haber, S. 1990. Situation review of barley yellow dwarf in Canada. In : Burnett, P.A. Ed. *World Perspectives on Barley Yellow Dwarf,* p. 7-10.

Hadidi, A. 1991. Detection of fruit crop viroids by reverse transcription polymerase chain reaction (Abstr.), *XVth Int. Symp. Virus and Virus Dis. Temp. Fruit Crops,* 8-13 July, Vienna, Austria.

Hadidi, A. *et al.*, 1990. Homology of the agent associated with dapple apple disease to apple scar skin viroid and molecular detection of these viroids. *Phytopathology* 80 : 263-268.

Hagborg, W.A.F. 1954. Dwarfing on wheat and barley by the barley stripe-mosaic (false stripe) virus. *Can. J. Bot* 32 : 24-37.

Hagedorn, D.J. 1984. *Compendium of Pea Diseases,* APS Press, St. Paul, MN, 57 pp.

Hagedorn, D.J. and Walker, J.C. 1949. Wisconsin pea streak. *Phytopathology* 39 : 837-847.

Hall, R. 1991. *Compendium of Bean Diseases,* APS Press, St. Paul, MN, 73 pp.

Hamilton, R.I. 1965. A embryo test for detecting seed-borne barley stripe mosaic virus in barley. *Phytopathology* 55 : 798-799.

Hampton, R.O. 1975. The nature of bean yield reduction by bean yellow and bean common mosaic viruses. *Phytopathology* 65 : 1342-1346.

Hampton, R.O. and Mink, G.I. 1975. Pea seed-borne mosaic virus. *CMI/AAM Descriptions of Plant Viruses,* No. 146.

Hansen, A.J. and Stace-Smith, R. 1971. Properties of a virus isolated from golden elder berry. *Phytopathology* 61 : 1222- 1229.

Hansen, A.J. *et al*. 1976. Apricot ring pox. In : Virus Diseases of Noninfectious Disorders of Stone Fruits in North America. *USDA Handb*. 437 : 45-48.

Harpaz, I. and Klein. M. 1969. Vector-induced modifications in a plant virus. *Ent. Ann. Appl.* 12 : 99-106.

Harpez, I. 1972. Maize Rough Dwarf Virus, Israel University Press, Jerusalem.

Harris, H.B. and Kuhn, C.W. 1971. Influence of cowpea chlorotic mottle virus (soybean strain) on agronomic performance of soybeans. *Crop Sci.* 11 : 71-73.

Harrison, B.D. 1957. Studies of the host range, properties, and mode of transmission of beet ringspot virus. *Ann. Appl. Biol.* 45 : 462-472.

Harrison, B.D. 1958. Relationship between beet ringspot, potato bouquet and tomato black ring viruses. *J. Gen. Microbiol.* 18 : 450-460.

Harrison, B.D. 1964. The transmission of plant viruses in soil. In : Corbett, M.L. and Sisler, H.D., Eds. *Plant Virology.* University of Florida Press, p. 118-147.

Harrison, B.D. 1970. Tobacco rattle virus. *CMI/AAB Descriptions of Plant Viruses,* No. 12.

Harrison, B.D. 1973. Pea early-browning virus. *CMI/AAB Descriptions of Plant Viruses,* No. 120.

Harrison, B.D. 1984. Potato leaf roll virus. *CMI/AAB Descriptions of Plant Viruses,* No. 291.

Harrison, B.D. and Robinson, D.J. 1978. The tobraviruses. *Adv. Virus Res.* 23 : 25-77.

Harrison, B.D. *et al.* 1972. Two properties of raspberry ringspot virus determined by its smaller RNA. *J. Gen. Virol.* 17 : 137 : 141.

Harrison, B.D. *et al.*, 1972. Evidence for two functional RNA species in ringspot virus. *J. Gen. Virol.* 16 : 339-348.

Haseloff, *et al.* 1982. Viroid RNAs of cadang-cadang disease of coconuts. *Nature* (London) 299 : 316-321.

Heagy, **J. and Rochow. W.F.** 1965. Thermal inactivation of barley yellow dwarf virus. *Phytopathology* 55 : 809-810.

Hendre, R. *et al.* 1975. Growth of mosaic virus free sugarcane plants from apical meristems. *Ind. Phytopathol.* 28 : 175-178.

Hendre, R.R. *et al.* 1979. The effect of sugarcane mosaic virus on the yield of eleven gain sorghum *(Sorghum bicolor)* cultivars. *Aust. J. Exp. Agric. and Anim. Husb.* 19(97) : 225-232.

Hernandez, C. *et al.* 1991. Evidence supporting a viroid etiology for pear blister canker disease (Abstr.). *XVth Int. Symp. Virus Dis. Temp. Fruit Crops,* 8-13 July, Vienna, Austria.

Hewitt, W.B. 1954. Some virus and virus-like diseases of grapevines. *Bull. Ca. Dept. Agr.* 43 : 47-64.

Hewitt, W.B. 1956. Yellow vein, a disease of grapevine caused by a graft-transmissible agent. *Phytopathology* 46 : 15.

Hewitt, W.B. 1968. Viruses and virus diseases of the grapevine. *Rev. Appl. Mycol.* 47 : 433-455.

Hewitt, W.B. 1970. Virus and virus-like diseases of the grapevine. In : Frazier, N.W. Ed. *Virus Diseases of Small Fruits and Grapevines,* University of Calfornia, Davis, Div. Agr. Sci., p. 195-196.

Hewitt, W.B. *et al.* 1958. Nematode vector of soil-borne fanleaf virus of grapevirus. *Phytopathology* 48 : 586-595.

Hibi, T. and Kameya-Iwaki, M. 1988. Soybean chlorotic mottle virus. *CMI/AAB Descriptions of Plant Viruses,* No. 331.

Hibi, T. *et al.* 1984. Double-stranded RNA of rice gall dwarf virus. *J. Gen. Virol.* 65 : 1585-1590.

Hibino, H. 1979. Rice ragged stunt, a new virus disease occurring in tropical Asia. *Rev. Pl. Prot. Res.* 12 : 98-110.

Hibino, H. *et al.* 1979. Reovirus-like particles associated with rice ragged stunt diseased rice and insect vector cells. *Ann. Phytopathol. Soc. Japan* 45 : 228-239.

Hiebert, E. and McDonald, J.G. 1973. Characterization of some proteins associated with viruses in the potato Y group. *Virology* 56 : 349-361.

Hill, J.H. *et al.* 1974. Seed transmission of maize dwarf mosaic and wheat streak mosaic viruses in maize and response of inbred lines. *Crop Sci.* 14 : 232-235.

Hohn, T. *et al.* 1982. Cauliflower mosaic virus on its way to becoming a useful plant vector. *Curr. Topics Microbiol. Immunol.* 96 : 193-236.

Hollings, M. 1963. Cucumber stunt mottle, a disease caused by a strain of arabis mosaic virus. *J. Hort. Sci.* 38 : 138-149.

Hollings, M. 1964. Some properties of five viruses of celery (*Apium graveolens* L.) in Britain. *J. Hort. Sci.* 39 : 130-141.

Hollings, M. *et al.* 1969. Celery Yellow vein and Hungarian chrome mosaic viruses. *Res. Glasshouse Crops Res. Inst.,* 1968, p. 102-103.

Holmas, F.O. 1937. Inheritance of resistance to tobacco-mosaic disease in the pepper. *Phytopathology* 27 : 637-642.

Holmes, E.O. 1960. Rose mosaic cured by heat treatments. *Plant Dis. Reptr.* 44 : 46-47.

Homes, F.O. 1932. Symptoms of tobacco mosaic disease. *Contr. Boyce Thomp. Inst.* 4 : 323-357.

Honda, Y. and Ikegami, M. 1986. Mung bean yellow mosaic virus. *CMI/AAB Descriptions of Plant Viruses,* No. 323.

Hooper, G.R. and Wiese. M.V. 1972. Cytoplasmic inclusions in wheat affected by wheat spindle streak mosaic. *Virology* 47 : 664-672.

Horvath, J. 1979. New artificial hosts and non-hosts of plant viruses and their role in the identification and separation of viruses. XIII. Nepovirus group (CLRV sub-groups) : cherry leaf roll virus. *Acta Phytopathol. Acad. Sci. Hung.* 14 : 319-326.

Howell, W.E. and Mink, G.I. 1980. Carrot thin leaf virus. *CMI/AAB Descriptions of Plant Viruses,* No. 218.

Hsieh, S.P.Y., *et al.* 1970. Transmission of rice transitory yellowing virus by *Nephotetrix impicticeps.* (Abstr.) *Phytopathology* 60 : 1534.

Hu, J.S. *et al.* 1990. Characterization of grapevine leafroll disease associated closteroviruses. (Abstr.) *10th Meeting ICVG,* Volos, Greece, Sept. 3-7, p.5.

Hughes, C.G. 1961. Striate mosaic virus : a new disease of sugarcane. *Nature* 190(4773) : 366-367.

Hull, R. 1972. The multicomponent nature of broad bean mottle virus and its nucleic acid. *J. Gen. Virol.* 17 : 111-117.

Hull, R. and L ane, L.C. 1973. The unusual nature of the components of pea enation mosaic virus. *Virology* 55 : 1-13.

Hutchinson, P.B. and Francki, R.I.B. 1973. Sugarcane Fiji disease virus. *CMI/AAB Descriptions of Plant Viruses,* No. 119.

Hutchison, P.B. *et al.*, 1972. Corn, sorghum and Fiji disease. *Sugarcane Pathol. Newsl.* 9 : 12.

Huth, W. 1980. The occurrence of barley yellow mosaic virus in Germany. (Abstr.) *3rd Conf. Virus dis. Gramineae Europe,* Rothamsted, May 28-30.

Huth, W. 1988. Barley yellow mosaic virus (Bar YMV). In : Smith. I.M. et al., Eds. *European Hand. Pl. Dis.,* Blackwell Sci. Publ., London, p. 89-91.

Huttinga, H. 1969. Interaction between components of pea early- browning virus. *Neth. J. Pl. Pathol.* 75 : 338-342.

Huttinga, H. 1975. Properties of viruses of the potyvirus of the group 3. A comparison of buoyant density. S value, particle morphology, and molecular weight of the coat protein subunit of 10 viruses and virus isolates. *Neth. J. Pl. Pathol.* 81 : 58-63.

Iizuka, N. *et al.* 1984. Natural occurrence of a strain of cowpea mild mottle virus on groundnut *(Arachis hypogaea)* in India, *Phytopathol.* Z. 109. 20/45.

Ikata, S. and Kawai, I. 1940. Studies on the wheat yellow mosaic. *Bull. Japan Min. Agr. Forest* 154 : 1-123.

Ikegami, M. and Francki. R.I.B. 1976. RNA-dependent RNA Polymerase associated with subviral particles of Fiji disease virus. *Virology* 70 : 292-300.

Inouye, T. 1976. Wheat yellow leaf virus. *CMI/AAB Description of Plant Viruses,* No. 157.

Inouye, T. and Fujii, S. 1977. Rice necrosis mosaic virus. *CMI/AAB Descriptions of Plant Viruses.* No. 172.

Inouye, T. and Nakasone, W. 1980. Broad bean necrosis virus. *CMI/AAB Descriptions of Plant Viruses,* No. 223.

Inouye, T. and Omura, T. 1982. Transmission of rice gall dwarf virus by the green vice leafhopper. *Plant Dis.* 66 : 57-59.

Ito, S. and Fukushi, T. 1944. Studies on northern cereal mosaic. *J. Sapporo Soc. Agric. For.* 36 : 62-89.

Ivanovic, D. 1979. Investigation of Beet Necrotic Yellow Vein Virus. M.Sc. thesis, Fac. of Agric., Univ. of Belgrade, Beograd, Zemun, p.1-46.

Iwasaki, M. *et al.* 1980. Influence of rice grassy stunt disease on the yield components. *Proc. Assoc. Pl. Prot. Kyushu* 26 : 7-9.

Jackson, A.O. and Brakke, M.K. 1973. Multicomponent properties of barley stripe mosaic virus ribonucleic acid. *Virology* 55 : 483-494.

Jafarpour, B. *et al.* 1979. Serologic detection of bean common mosaic and lettuce mosaic viruses in seed. *Phytopathology* 69 : 1125-1129.

Jafri, A.M. 1972. Localization of virus and ultrastructural changes in sugarbeet leaf cells associated with infection by a necrotic strain of beet mosaic virus. *Phytopathology* 62 : 1103.

Jang, X. *et al.* 1991. Nucleotide sequence of apple scar viroid reverse transcribed in host extracts and amplified by the Polymerase chain reaction (Abstr.) *XVth Int. Symp. Virus and Virus Dis. Temp. Fruit Crops,* 8-13 July, Vienna, Austria.

Janson, B.F. and Ellett, C.W. 1963. A new corn disease in Ohio. *Pl. Dis. Reptr.* 47 : 1107-1108.

Jarjees, M.M. and Uyemoto, J.K. 1984. Serological relatedness of strains of maize dwarf and sugarcane mosaic viruses as determined by microprecipitin and enzyme-linked immunosorbent assays. *Ann. App. Biol.* 104 : 497-501.

Jedlinski, H. 1976. Oat striate mosaic, a new virus disease in Illinois spread by the leafhopper, Graminella nigrifrons (Forbes). (Abstr.) *Proc. Am. Phytopathol. Soc.* 3 : 19.

Jensen, D.D. 1949. Papaya virus diseases with special reference to papaya ringspot. *Phytopathology* 39 : 191-211.

Jensen, S.G. *et al.* 1986. Size variation among proteins induced by sugarcane mosaic viruses in plant tissue. *Phytopathology* 76 : 528-532.

Jones, A.T. and Duncan, G.H. 1980. The distribution of some genetic determinants in two nucleoprotein particles of cherry leaf roll virus. *J. Gen. Virol.* 50 : 269-273.

Jones, A.T. and Mayo, M.A. 1975. Further properties of black raspberry latent virus, and evidence for its relationship to tobacco streak virus. *Ann. Appl. Biol.* 79 : 297-306.

Jones, J.B. *et al.* 1991. *Compendium of Tomato Diseases,* APS Press, St. Paul, MN. 73 p.

Jones, R.K. and Tolin, S.A. 1972. Factors affecting purification of maize dwarf mosaic virus from corn. *Phytopathology* 62 : 812-816.

Joubert, J.J. *et al.* 1974. Purification and properties of tomato spotted wilt virus. *Virology* 57 : 11-19.

Joyce, P.A. *et al.*, 1997a. Mosaic resistant transgenic sugarcane. *Proc. ISSCT 5th Pathol. and 2nd Mol. Biol. Workshop.*

Joyce, P.A. *et al.*, 1998. Transgenic sugarcane resistant to sugarcane mosaic virus. *Proc. ASSCT* 20 : 204-210.

Juarez, J. *et al.* 1988. Recovery of virus-free peach trees from selected clones by shoot-tip grafting in vitro (Abstr.). *XIVth Int. Symp. Fruit Tree Virus Dis.,* 12-18 June, Thessaloniki, Greece.

Juarez, J. *et al.* 1990. Shoot tip culture and the recovery of viroid-free grapevines. (Abstr.) *10th Meeting ICVG,* Volos, Greece, Sept. 3-7, p. 40.

Juarez, J. *et al.* 1991. Recovery of virus-free almond plant by shoot-tip grafting *in vitro* (Abstr.) *XVth Int. Symp. on Virus Dis. Temp. Fruit Crops,* 8-13 July, Vienna, Austria.

Kahn, R.P. 1956. Seed transmission of the tomato ringspot virus in the Lincoln variety of soybeans. (Abstr.) *Phytopathology* 46 : 295.

Kaiser, W.J. Wyatt, S.D. and Pesho, G.R. 1982. Natural hosts and vectors of tobacco streak virus in eastern Washington. *Phytopathology* 72 : 1508-1512.

Kalashjan, J.A. *et al.* 1988. Cytopathology of apple stem grooving virus and the methods of its diagnostics (Abstr.) *XIVth Int. Symp. Fruit Tree Virus Dis.,* 12-18 June, Thessaloniki, Greece, p. 30.

Karayiannis, I. 1991. Susceptibility of apricot cultivars to plum pox virus natural infection. *XVth Int. Symp. Virus and Virus Dis. Temp. Crops* (Abstr.), 8-13 July, Vienna, Austria.

Karle, H.P. and Nyland, G. 1959. Yellow bud mosaic virus in almond. *Plant Dis. Reptr.* 43 : 520-521.

Kassanis, B. 1947. Studies on dandalion yellow mosaic and other virus diseases of lettuce. *Ann. Appl. Biol.* 34 : 412-421.

Kassanis, B. 1954. Heat-therapy of virus-infected plants. *Ann. Appl. Biol.* 41 : 470-474.

Kassanis, B. and Govier, D.A. 1972. Potato aucuba mosaic virus. *CMI/AAB Descriptions of Plant Viruses,* No. 98.

Kassanis, B. and MacFarlane, I. 1965. Interaction of virus strain, fungus isolate and host species in the transmission of tobacco necrosis virus. *Virology* 26 : 603-612.

Kassanis, R. and Phillips, M.P. 1970. Serological relationships of tobacco necrosis virus and their ability to activate strains of satellite virus *J. Gen Virol.* 9 : 119-126.

Katwijk, van W. and Meijneke, C.A.R. 1963. Apple rough skin. In : Virus Diseases of Apples and Pears. Techn. Commun. *Bur. Hort. E. Malling* 30 : 43-44.

Kegler, H. 1965. Bark split and decline in "Beurre Hardy" pear trees. *Zastita bilja* 16 : 311-316, Beograd.

Kegler, H. and Schade, C. 1971. Plum pox virus. *CMI/AAB Description of Plant Viruses,* No. 70.

Kegler, H. and Schimanski, H.H. 1988. Pear stony pit disease/Pear vein yellows disease. In : Smith, I.M. *et al.*, Eds. *European Handb. Pl. Dis.,* Blackwell Sci. Publ., London, p. 111-112.

Kerlan, C. and Dunez, J. 1976. Some properties of plum pox virus and its nucleic acid protein components. *Acta Hort.* 67 : 185-191.

Kerlan, C. *et al.* 1981. Immunosorbent electron microscopy for detecting apple chlorotic leaf spot and plum pox viruses. *Phytopathology* 71 : 400-404.

Khush, G.S. and Ling, K.C. 1974. Inheritance of resistance to grassy stunt virus and its vector in rice. *J. Hered.* 65 : 135-136.

Kimura, I. 1962. Further studies on the rice dwarf virus. *Ann. Phytopathol.* Soc. Japan, 27 : 197-203.

Kingsland, G.C. 1980. Effect of maize dwarf mosaic virus infection on yield and stalk strength of corn it the field in South Carolina. *Plant Dis.* 64 : 271-273.

Kirkpatrick, H.C. *et al.* 1965. Purification of a second mechanically transmissible virus latent in apple. *Phytopathology* 55 : 386-390.

Kishi, K. *et al.* 1973a. Studies on virus diseases of stone fruits. IV. New virus diseases of peach, yellow mosaic, oil blotch and star mosaic. *Bull. Hort. Res. Stn.,* Japan A-12 : 197-208.

Kishi, K. *et al.* 1976. Pear necrotic spot, a new virus disease in japan. *Acta Hort.* 67 : 269-273.

Kleinhempel, H. *et al.* 1980. Investigation of carnation ringspot virus in fruit trees. *Acta Phytopathol. Acad. Sci. Hung.* 15 : 107-111.

Klos, E.J. 1976. Rosette mosaic. In : Virus Diseases and Noninfectious Disorders of Stone Fruits in North America. USDA *Handb.* 347 : 135-138.

Klos, E.J. and Parker, K.G. 1960. Yields of sour cherry affected by ringspot and yellows viruses *Phytopathology* 50 : 412- 415.

Klos, E.J. *et al.* 1967. Peach rosette mosaic transmission and control studies. *Michigan Agric. Exp. Sta. Quart. Bull.* 49 : 287-293.

Klos, J. 1976. Rosette mosaic. In : Virus Diseases and Noninfectious Disorders of Stone Fruits in North America. *U.S. Dept. Agr. Handbk.* 347 : 135-138.

Knesek, J. *et al.* 1974. Purification and properties of pea seed- borne mosaic virus. *Phytopathology* 64 : 1076-1081.

Knoke, J.K. *et al.* 1974. Distribution of maize dwarf mosaic and aphid vectors in Ohio. *Phytopathology* 64 : 639-645.

Koganezawa, H. *et al*. 1982. Viroid-like RNA associated with apple scar skin. *Acta Hort.* 130 : 193-197.

Koike, H. and Gillaspie, A.G. Jr. 1976. Strain M, a new strain of sugarcane mosaic virus. *Pl. Dis. Reptr.* 60 : 50-54.

Kojima, M. *et al.,* 1969. Purification and electron microscopy of potato leaf roll virus. *Virology* 39 : 162-171.

Kolte, S.J. 1985. Diseases of Annual Edible Oilseed Crops. Vol. III : Sunflower and Nigerseed Diseases, CRC Press LLC, Boca Raton, FL.

Kondaiah, E. and Nayudu, M.V. 1984. A Key to the Identification of Sugarcane Mosaic Virus (SCMV) strains. *Sugar Cane* 6 : 3- 8.

Krake, L.R. and Woodham, R.C. 1983. Grapevine yellow speckle agent implicated in the etiology of vein banding. *Vitis* 22 : 40-50.

Kristensen, H.R. 1963. Apple green crinkle. In : Virus Diseases of Apples and pears. Techn. Commun. *Bur. Hort. E. Malling* 30 : 33-34.

Kristensen, H.R. and Thomsen, A. 1962. Apple mosaic virus host plants and strains, *Proc. 5th Eur. Symp. Fruit Tree Virus Diseases,* 21-26, Bologna.

Kubo, S. 1981. Tobacco necrotic dwarf virus. *CMI/AAB Descriptions of Plant Viruses,* No. 234.

Kunze, L. 1988. Prune dwarf virus (PDV). In : Smith, I.M. et al., Eds. *European Handb. Pl. Dis.,* Blackwell Sci. Publ., London, p. 15-17.

LaFlucer, D.A. ***et al.,*** 1996. Portions of the banana streak badnavirus genome are integrated in the genome of its host Musa sp. (Abstr.). *Phytopathology* 86 : S100.

Laird, E.F. ***et al.*** 1969. Attempts to transmit citrus exocortis virus by insects. *Plant Dis. Reptr.* 53 : 850-851.

Lana, A.F. ***et al.,*** 1983. Association of tobacco ringspot virus with a union incompatibility of apple. *Phytopathol. Z.* 106 : 141-148.

Lane, L.C. 1974. The components of barley stripe mosaic and related viruses. *Virology* 58 : 323-333.

Lange, L. 1978. *Synchytrium endobioticum* and potato virus *X. Phytopathol. Z.* 92 : 132-142.

Langenberg, W.G. and Schroeder, H.F. 1973. Endoplasmic reticulam- derived pinwheels in wheat infected with wheat spindle streak mosaic virus. *Virology* 55 : 218-223.

Lee, P.E. 1964. The extraction of wheat striate mosaic virus from diseased wheat plants. *Can. J. Bot.* 41 : 1617-1621.

Lee, P.E. and Bell, W. 1963. Some properties of wheat striate mosaic virus. *Can. J. Bot.* 41 : 767.

Legg, J.T. 1959. A mild strain of hop mosaic virus. *Annu. Rept. East Malling Res. Sta.* 46 : 116-117.

Lemaire, O. ***et al.,*** 1988. Effect of beet necrotic yellow vein virus RNA composition on transmission by *Polymyxa Betae. Virology* 162 : 232-235.

Lesemann, D. 1972. Electron microscopy of maize rough dwarf virus particles. *J. Gen. Virol.* 16 : 273-284.

Lesemann, D.E. ***et al.*** 1983. Natural infection of cucumbers by zucchini yellow mosaic virus in Lebanon. *Phytopathol. Z.* 108 : 304-313.

Lin, M.T. ***et al.*** 1970. Lettuce big vein virus transmission by single-sporgangium isolates of *Olpidium brassicae. Phytopathology* 60 : 1630-1634.

Lindsten, K. 1959. A preliminary report on virus diseases of cereals in Sweden. *Phytopathol. Z.* 4 : 420-428.

Ling, K.C. ***et al.*** 1970. A mass screening method for testing resistance to grassy stunt disease of rice. *Pl. Dis. Reptr.* 54 : 565-569.

Lisa, V. and Lecoq H. 1984. Zucchini yellow mosaic virus. *CMI/AAB Descriptions of Plant Viruses, No. 282.*

Lisa, V. ***et al.*** 1981. Characterization of a polyvirus that causes zucchini yellow mosaic. *Phytopathology* 71 : 668-672.

Lister, R.M. 1970. Apple chlorotic leaf spot virus. *CMI/AAB Descriptions of Plant Viruses,* No. 30.

Lister, R.M. ***et al.*** 1965. Some sap-transmissible viruses from apple. *Phytopathology* 55 : 859-870.

Lister, R.M. ***et al.,*** 1972. Evidence that particle size heterogeneity is the cause of centrifugal heterogeneity in tobacco streak virus. *Virology* 49 : 290-299.

Lizarraga, R.E. *et al.,* 1980. Elimination of potato spindle tuber viroid by low temperature and maristem culture. *Phytopathology* 70 : 754-755.

Lockhart, B.E.L. 1986. Purification and serology of a bacilliform virus associated with banana streak disease. *Phytopathology* 76 : 995-999.

Lott, B. and Keane, F.W.L. 1960. The host range of the virus of twisted leaf of cherry. *Plant Dis. Reptr.* 44 : 240-242.

Lovisolo, O. and Acimovic, M. 1961. Sorghum red stripe disease in Yugoslavia. *FAO Plant Prot. Bull.* 9 : 99-102.

Luckwill, L.C. and Campbell, A.L. 1959. Malus platycarpa as an apple virus indicator. *J. Hort. Sci.* 34 : 248-254.

Luckwill, L.C. and Campbell, A.L. 1963. Apple chlorotic leafs spot. In : Virus Diseases of Apples and Pears. Tech. Commun. *Bur. Hort. E. Malling* 30 : 7-9.

Luckwill, L.C. and Campbell, A.L. 1963b. Platycarpa dwarf. In : Virus Diseases of Apples and Pears. Tech. Commun. *Bur. Hort. E. Malling* 30 : 59.

Luisoni, E. *et al.* 1973. Serological relationship between maize rough dwarf virus and rice black streaked dwarf virus. *Virology* 52 : 281-283.

MacFarlane, I. and Plumb, R.T. 1978. A new soil-borne virus of winter oats (oat goldenstripe virus-OGSV). (Abstr.) *3rd Int. Cong. Pl. Pathol.,* Munchen, August 16-18.

MacKenzie, D.R. *et al.,* 1966. Differences in maize dwarf mosaic virus isolates of the Northeastern United States. *Pl. Dis. Reptr.* 50 : 814-818.

Macovei, A. 1970a. The results concerning influence of plum pox virus on plum pollen morphology and germination. *Biol. Ser. Bot.* 22(4) : 325-328.

Macovei, A. *et al.* 1971. New development of the study in influence of *Prunus spinosa* L. on the appearance of Sharka symptoms. *Ann. Phytopathol.* H.S., 171-178.

Magee, J.P. 1940. Transmission studies on the banana-top virus. *J. Austr. Inst. Agric. Sci.* 6 : 109-110.

Magyarosy, A.C. and Duffus, J.E. 1977. The occurrence of highly virulent strains of the beet curly top virus in California. *Pl. Dis. Reptr.* 63 : 248-251.

Mahmood, K. *et al.* 1972. Pea symptomless virus, a newly recognized strain of red clover mottle virus. *Neth. J. Pl. Pathol.* 78 : 203-211.

Malathi, V.G. *et al.* 2001. Applications of molecular techniques in Plant Pathology. *Practical training manual.* Center of Advanced studies in Plant Pathology, Division of Plant Pathology, IARI, New Delhi—110012.

Marenaud, C. *et al.* 1976. Identification and comparison of different strains of apple chlorotic leaf spot virus and possibilities of interactions. *Acta Hort.* 67 : 219-226.

Martelli, G.P. 1965. Preliminary report on the purification and serology of a virus associated with Hungarian grapevines showing macroscopic symptoms of fanleaf and yellow mosaic. In : *Proc. Int. Conf. Virus and Vector Per. Hosts Spec. Ref. Vitis,* University of California, Davis, Div. Sci., p. 402-210.

Martelli, G.P. 1988a. Pea enation mosaic virus (PEMV). In : Smith, I.M. *et al., European Handb. Pl. Dis.,* Blackwell Sci. Publ., London, P.75.

Martelli, G.P. 1988b. Artichoke Italian latent virus (AILV) In : Smith. I.M. et al., Eds. *European Handb. Pl. Dis.,* Blackwell Sci. Publ., London. P. 25-26.

Martelli, G.P. 1988c. Artichoke yellow ringspot virus. In : Smith, I.M. et al., Eds. *European Handb. Pl. Dis.,* Blackwell Sci. Publ., London. P.26.

Martelli, G.P. and Cirulli, M. 1969. Mottled dwarf of eggplant (*Solanum melongena*) a virus disease. *Ann. Phytopathol* 393-397.

Martelli, G.P. and Conti, M. 1988. Grapevine stem pitting disease. In : Smith, I.M. et al., Eds. *European Handbk. Pl. Dis.,* Blackwell Sci. Publ., London.

Martelli, G.P. and Quacquarelli, A. 1972. Grapevine chrome mosaic virus. *CMI/AAB Descriptions of Plant Viruses,* No. 103.

Martelli, G.P. and Russo, M. 1973. Eggplant mottled dwarf virus. *CMI/AAB Descriptions of Plant Viruses,* No. 115.

Martelli, G.P. ***et al.*** 1971. Tomato bushy stunt virus. *CMI/AAB Descriptions of Plant Viruses,* No. 69.

Martelli, G.P. ***et al.*** 1977. Artichoke Italian latent virus. *CMI/AAB Descriptions of Plant Viruses,* No. 176.

Martyn, E.B. Ed. 1971. Plant virus names. Supplement No. 1 Addition and corrections to Phytopathological Paper No. 9, 1968 and newly recorded plant virus names. *Phytopat. Pap.* 9, Suppl. 1, p.41.

Mathews, R.E.F. 1980. Turnip yellow mosaic virus. *CMI/AAB Descriptions of Plant Viruses,* No. 230.

Mayo, M.A. ***et al.,*** 1982. Evidence that potato leaf roll virus RNA is posotive-stranded, is linked to a small protein and does not contain polyadenylate. *J. Gen. Virol* 59 : 163-167.

McDaniel, L.L. and Gordon. D.T. 1985. Identification of a new strain of maize dwarf mosaic virus. *Plant Dis.* 69 : 602- 607.

Mac Donald, D.M. (1973). Heat treatment and meristem culture as a means of freeing potato varieties from viruses X and S. *Potato Res.* 16 : 263-269.

Mcgrum, C.R. ***et al.*** 1963. Dapple apple. In : Virus Diseases of Apples and Pears. *Tech. Commun. Bur. Hort. E. Malling* 30 : 29-30.

Mc grum, C.R. ***et al.*** 1963. Dapple apple. In : Virus Diseases of Apples and Pears. Tech. Commun. *Bur. Hort. E. Malling* 30 : 29-30.

McKinney, H. 1925. A mosaic disease of winter wheat and rye. *Bull. U.S. Dept. Agric.,* 1361, 1-10.

McKinney, H.H. and Greeley, L.W. 1965. Biological characteristics of barley stripe-mosaic virus strains and their evolution. *Bull. U.S. Dept. Agric.* 1324, 84 pp.

McKinney, H.H. ***et al.***, 1965. Longevity of some plant viruses stored in chemically dehydrated tissues. *Phytopathology* 55 : 1043.

McNeal, F.H. ***et al.*** 1976. Barley stripe mosaic virus data from six infected spring wheat cultivars. *Pl. Dis. Reptr.* 60 : 730-733.

Meijneke, C.R. ***et al.*** 1963. The economic importance of virus diseases of apples and pears. Tech. Commun. *Bur. Hort. E. Malling* 30 : 1-4.

Mikel, M.A. ***et al.*** 1984. Seed transmission of maize dwarf virus in sweet corn. *Phytopathol. Z.* 110 : 185-191.

Mikel, M.A. *et al*. 1984a. Genetics of resistance of two corn inbreds to maize dwarf mosaic virus and transfer of resistance into sweet corn. *Phytopathology* 74 : 467-473.

Milbrath, J.A. 1957. The relationship of peach ringspot virus to sour cherry yellows, prune dwarf and peach stunt. *Phytopathology* 47 : 529.

Milbrath, J.A. 1966. Severe fruit necrosis of sour cherry caused by strains of green ring mottle virus. *Plant Dis. Reptr.* 50 : 59-62.

Millikan, A.A. *et al.* 1964. A wood-pitting symptom in pear ; its occurrence, distribution and association with certain pear virus diseases (Abstr.). *Phytopathology* 54 : 1435.

Millikan, F.D. 1963. Apple scar skin. In : Virus Diseases of Apples and Pears. Tech. Commun. *Bur. Hort. E. Malling* 30 : 51- 52.

Milne, R.G. and Conti. M. 1986. Barley yellow striate mosaic virus. *CMI/AAB Descriptions of Plant Viruses,* No. 312.

Milne, R.G. and Luisoni, E. 1977. Serological relationships among maize rough dwarf-like viruses. *Virology* 80 : 121-20.

Milne, R.G. and Luisoni, E. 1977a. A serological investigation of some maize rough dwarf-like viruses. *Annales de Phytopathol.* 9 : 337-341.

Milne, R.G. *et al.* 1973. Partial purification. Structure and infectivity of complete maize rough dwarf virus particles. *Virology* 53 : 130-141.

Milne, R.G. *et al.* 1984. Closterovirus-like particles of two types associated with diseased grapevines. *Phytopathol. Z.* 110 : 360-368.

Milne, R.G. *et al.* 1986. Serological relationships between the nucleocapsids of some planthopper-borne rhabdoviruses in cereals. *Intervirology* 25 : 83-97.

Mink, G.I. and Aichele, M.D. 1984. Detection of Prunus necrotic ringspot and prune dwarf viruses in Prunus seed and seedlings by enzyme-linked immunosorbent assay. *Plant Dis.* 68 : 378-381.

Mircetich, S.M. *et al.* 1970. Peach stem pitting : transmission and natural spread. *Phytopathology* 60 : 1320-1334.

Mircetich, S.M. *et al.* 1982. Seed and pollen transmission of cherry leaf roll virus (CLRV-W) the causal agent of the blackline (BL) of English walnut trees. (Abstr.) *Phytopathology* 72 : 988.

Mirkov, T.E. *et al.* 1997. Transgenic virus resistant sugarcane. *Proc. ISSCT 5th Pathol. and 2nd Mol. Biol. Workshop.*

Mirkov, T.E. *et al.,* 1997. Transgenic virus resistant sugarcane. *Proc. ISSCT 5th Pathol. and 2nd Mol. Biol. Workshop*.

Moghal, S.M. and Francki, R.I.B. 1976. Towards a system for the identification and classification of potyviruses. I. Serology and amino acid composition of six distinct viruses. *Virology* 73 : 350-352.

Moletti, M. *et al.* 1990. Some agronomic traits affected by rice giallume virus inoculated at two phenological stages in 11 Italian rice varieties. In : Burnett, P.A., Ed. *World Perspectives on Barley Yellow Dwarf,* CIMMYT, Mexico, D.F., Mexico, p. 464-467.

Moline, H.E. 1973. Mechanically transmissible viruses from corn and sorghum in South Dakota. *Pl. Dis. Reptr.* 57 : 373-374.

Montllor, C.B. and Gildow, F.E. 1986. Feeding responses of two gain aphids to barley yellow dwarf virus-infected oats. *Entomol. Exp. Appl.* 42 : 63-69.

Moore, D.J. and Keitt, G.W. 1944. Host range studies of virus disease necrotic ringspot and yellows of sour cherry. (Abstr.). *Phytopathology* 34 : 1009.

Morinaka, T. *et al.* 1982. Transmission of rice gall dwarf virus by cicadellid leafhoppers *Recilia dorsalis* and *Nephotettix nigropictus* in Thailand. *Plant Dis.* 66 : 703-704.

Morris-Krsinich, B.A.M. *et al.* 1983. The synthesis and processing of the nepovirus grapevine fanleaf proteins in rabbit reticulocyte lysate. *Virology* 130 : 523-526.

Morton, D.J. 1961. Host range and properties of the globe artichoke curly dwarf virus. *Phytopathology* 51 : 731-734.

Mowaz, W.P. 1962. Other soil-borne viruses. *Annu. Rep. Scot. Hort., Res. Inst.* 9 : 69.

Mulligan, T.E. 1960. The transmission by mites, host-range and properties of ryegrass mosaic virus. *Ann. Appl. Biol.* 48 : 575-579.

Mukhopadhyay, S. Rai, Jaishree, Sharma, B.C., Gurung, Anita, Sengupta, **R.K. and Nath, P.S.** (1997). Micro-propagation of Darjeeling orange (*Citrus reticulata* Blanco) by shoot tip grafting. *J. Hort. Sci.* 72(3) : 493-49.

Muniyappa, V. and Reddy. D.V.R. 1983. Transmission of cowpea mild mottle virus by *Bemisia tabaci* in a nonpersistent manner. *Plant Dis.* 67 : 391.

Murant, A.F. 1974. Carrot mottle virus. *CMI/AAB Descriptions of Plant Viruses,* No. 137.

Murant, A.F. 1974a. Parsnip yellow fleck virus. *CMI/AAB Descriptions of Plant Viruses.* No. 129.

Murant, A.F. 1981. Nepoviruses. In : Kurstak, E. Ed. *Handb. Pl. Virus Infec. Comp. Diag.,* Elsevier/North-Holland Biomedical Press, p. 197-238.

Murant, A.F. and Goold. R.A. 1968. Purification, prospectives and transmission of parsnip yellow fleck, a semi-persistent, aphid- borne virus. *Ann. Appl. Biol.* 62 : 123-137.

Murayama, D. and Kojima, M. 1965. Studies on the properties of potato leaf roll virus by the aphid-infection method. *Ann. Phytopathol. Soc.* Japan 30 : 209.

Nagel, J. *et al.* 1983. Strains of bean yellow mosaic virus compared to clover yellow vein virus in relation to gladiolus production in Florida. *Phytopathology* 73 : 449-454.

Nault, L.R. *et al.* 1964. Biological relationship between pea enation mosaic virus and its vector, the pea aphid. *Phytopathology* 54 : 1269-1272.

Nault, L.R. *et al.* 1973. Semipersistent transmission of leafhopper-borne maize chlorotic dwarf virus. *J. Econ. Entomol.* 66 : 1271-1273.

Navarro, L. and Pino. 1988. Citrus vein enation disease (Wallace and Drake, 1953) and Citrus woody gall disease (Frazer, 1958). In : Smith, I.M. *et al. European Handb. Pl. Dis.,* Blackwell Sci. Publ., London, p. 108-109.

Navarro, L. *et al.* 1982. Shoot tip grafting in vitro for elimination of viruses in peach plants. *Acta Hort.* 130 : 185-192.

Nayudu, M.V. *et al.* 1971. Striate mosaic of sugarcane in India. Sugarcane Pathol. Newsl. 7 : 24. {Abstr. In *Rev. Pl. Pathol.* (1972) 51 : 2810}.

Nel, A.C. and Engelbrecht, J.D. 1972. Grapevine virus diseases in the nursery. *Ann Phytopathol. (No. hors serie),* I.N.R.A. Publ. 72-4 : 47-74.

Nelson, M.R. *et al.* 1982. Pepper mottle virus. *CMI/AAB Descriptions of Plant Viruses,* No. 253.

Nelson, R.M. 1932. Investigation in the Mosaic Disease of Bean *(Phaseolus vulgaris L.) Mich. Agric. Exp. Sta. Techn. Bull.,* No. 118.

Nemeth, M. 1963. Field and greenhouse experiments with plum pox virus. *Phytopath. Medit.* 2(3) : 162-166.

Nitzany, F. 1975. Tomato yellow leaf curl virus. *Phytopathol. Mediter.* 14 : 127-129.

Nyland, G. 1959. Hot water treatment of Lambert cherry bud sticks infected with necrotic rusty mottle virus. *Phytopathology* 49 : 157-158.

Nyland, G. 1976a. Almond virus bud failure : In : Virus Dis. Noninfec. Disorders of Stone Fruits in North America. *USDA Handb.* 437:33-42.

Nyland, G. and Lowe, S.K. 1964. The relation of cherry rugose mosaic and almond calico viruses to Prunus ringspot virus. (Abstr.). *Phytopathology* 54 : 1435-1436.

O'Brien, M.J. *et al.,* 1963. Symptomless hosts of the potato spindle tuber virus (PSTV). (Abstr.) *Pytopathology* 53 : 884.

Ohki, S.T. *et al.* 1976. Beet yellows virus and beet western yellows virus isolated from spinach and fodder beet plants affected by yellowing diseases. *Ann. Phytopathol. Soc. Japan* 43 : 46.

Ohki, S.T. *et al.* 1978. Carrot latent virus, a new rhabdovirus of carrot. *Ann. Phytopathol. Soc. Japan* 44 : 202.

Omura. T. *et al.* 1985. Location of structural proteins in particles of rice gall dwarf virus. *J. Gen. Virol.* 66 : 811-815.

Orellana, R.G. and Quacquarelli, A. 1968. A sunflower mosaic caused by a strain of cucumber mosaic virus. *Phytopathology* 58 : 1439-1440.

Osaki, T. and Inouye, T. 1978. Resemblance in morphology and interanuclear appearance of viruses isolated from yellow dwarf diseased tomato and leaf curl diseased tobacco. *Ann. Phytopathol. Soc. Japan* 44 : 167-178.

Paliwal. Y.C. 1968. Changes in relative virus concentration in Endria inimica in relation to its ability to transmit wheat mosaic virus. *Phytopathology* 58 : 386-387.

Paliwal. Y.C. *et al.* 1968. Some properties and behaviour of maize mosaic virus in India. *Phytopathology* 58 : 1682-1684.

Palmer. L.T. *et al.* 1978. Rice yield losses due to brown planthopper and rice grassy stunt disease in Java and Bali. *Pl. Dis. Reptr.* 62 : 962-965.

Panjan. M. 1966. About some manifestations of mosaic on corn in Yugoslavia. *Rev. Roum. Biol. Botanique* 11 : 159-162.

Paulesen, A.Q. and Fulton, R.W. 1968. Hosts and properties of a plum line pattern virus. *Phytopathology* 58 : 766-772.

Pearson, R.C. and Goheen, A.C. 1990. *Compendium of Grape Diseases,* APS Press, St. Paul. MN. 93 pp.

Pelham, J. 1972. Strain-genotype interaction of tobacco mosaic virus in tomato. *Ann. Appl. Biol.* 72 : 219-228.

Persley, D.M. *et al.* 1972. Research notes : A new source of mosaic resistance in sorghum. *Austr. Pl. Pathol. Soc. Newsl.* 1 : 11-12.

Pesic. Z. *et al.* 1977. Influence of maize mosaic virus on total oil content and fatty acids ratio in corn grain. *Ann. Phytopathol.* 9 : 357-360.

Peters, D. and Goldbach, R. 1995. The biology of tospoviruses. In : R.P. Singh *et al.*, Eds. *Pathogenesis and Host Specificity in Plant Diseases. Vol. III. Viruses and Viroids.* Pergamon press, P. 199-21.

Peters, D., 1982. Pea enation mosaic virus. *CMI/AAB Descriptions of Plant Viruses,* No. 257.

Pfeilstetter, E. *et al.* 1991. Occurrence of petunia asteroid mosaic (PAMV) and carnation Italian ringspot (CIRV) viruses in cherry orchards in northern Bavaria (Abstr.). *XVth Int. Symp. Virus and Virus Dis. Temp. Fruit Crops,* 8-14 July, Vienna, Austria.

Phatak, H.C. 1974. Seed-borne plant viruses—identification and diagnosis in seed health testing. *Seed Sci. and Tech.* 3 : 155.

Pierce, N.B. 1892. The California vine disease. *Bull. Div. Veg. Physiol. Pathol.* U.S. Dept. Agr. 2 : 222.

Pine, T.S. 1964. Influence of necrotic ringspot virus on growth and yield of peach trees. *Phytopathology* 54 : 604-605.

Pirone, T.P. 1972. Sugarcane mosaic virus. *CMI/AAB Descriptions of Plant Viruses,* No. 88.

Pirone, T.P. *et al.* 1972. Virus-like particles associated with a leafhopper-transmitted disease of corn in Kentucky. *Plant Dis. Reptr.* 56 : 652-656.

Pirone, T.P. *et al.*, 1973. Tobacco vein mottling virus on burley tobacco in Kentucky. *Pl. Dis. Reptr.* 57 : 841-844.

Pitre, H. N. 1968. A preliminary study of corn stunt vector populations in relation to corn planting dates in Mississipi. Notes on disease incidence and severity. . *Econ. Entomaol.* 61 : 847-849.

Plumb, R.T. 1974. Problems and possibilities for control of BYDV in Britain. *Mikrobiologija* 11 : 41-47.

Polak, J. 1988. Apple stem grooving. In : Smith, I.M. et al., Eds. *European Handbook of Plant Disease,* Blackwell Sci. Publ., London. P.89.

Posnette, A.F. and Cropley, R. 1959. Transmission of virus causing star crack of apples. *J. Hort. Sci.* 34 : 126-129.

Posnette, A.F. and Cropley, R. 1959a. The reduction in yield caused by apple mosaic. *Annu. Rep. East Malling Res. Sta.* 1958, 89-90.

Posnette, A.F. and Cropley, R. 1963. Apple stem pitting. In : *Virus Diseases of Apples and Pears. Commun. Bur. Hort. E. Malling, Techn. Comm.* 30 : 77.

Posnette, A.F. and Cropley, R. 1965. The growth of apple trees with and without latent virus infection. *Annu. Rep. East Malling Res. Stn.* 1964, 150-151.

Posnette, A.F. 1951. Virus diseases of sweet cherries. *Annu. Rep. East Malling Res. Sta.* 1950, A 34 : 209-210.

Posnette, A.F. *et al.* 1962. Heat inactivation of some apple and pear viruses. *Annu. Rep. E. Malling Res. Sta.* 1961, 94-96.

Price, W.C. 1940. Comparative host ranges of six plant viruses. *Ann. J. Bot.* 27 : 530-541.

Price, W.C. 1970. Citrus tristeza virus. *CMI/AAB Descriptions of Plant Viruses,* No. 33.

Probasco, E.G. and Scotland, C.B. 1978. Host range, general properties, purification, and electron microscopy of hop latent virus. *Phytopathology* 68 : 277-281.

Prusa, V. *et al.* 1959. Oat sterile-dwarf virus disease. *Biol. Plantarum* 1 : 223-234.

Purcifull, D. *et al.* 1984. Papaya ringspot virus. *CMI/AAB Descriptions of Plant Viruses,* No. 292.

Purcifull, D.E. and Hiebert, E. 1979. Serological distinction of watermelon mosaic virus isolates. *Phytopathology* 69 : 112- 116.

Purcifull, D.E. and Hiebert, E. 1982. Tobacco etch virus. *CMI/AAB Descriptions of Plant Viruses,* No. 258.

Putz, C. 1977. Composition and structure of beet necrotic yellow vein virus. *J. Gen. Virol.* 35 : 397-401.

Ragozzino, A. *et al.* 1991. Apricot ring-pox-like disease and related disorders of apricot fruits in Gampania (Abstr.). *XVth Int. Symp. Virus and Virus Dis. Temp. Fruit Crops,* 8-13 July, vienna, Austria.

Ramsdell, D.C. *et al.* 1979. A comparison between enzyme-linked immuno-sorbent assay (ELISA) and *Chenopodium quinoa* for detection of peach rosette mosaic virus in "Concord" grapevirus. *Plant Dis. Reptr.* 63 : 74-78.

Rana, G.L. *et al.* 1982. Artichoke latent virus : characterization, ultrastructure and geographical distribution. *Ann. Appl. Biol.* 101 : 279-289.

Randles, J.W. and Imperial, J.S. 1984. Coconut Cadang-Cadang Viroid. *CMI/AAB Descriptions of Plant Viruses,* No. 287.

Rankovic, M. and Sutic, D. 1986. Resistance of some peach cultivars and variable pathogenicity of the Sharka (Plum pox) virus. *Acta Hort.* 193 : 193-199.

Rao, S.A. 1968. Biology of *Polymyxa graminis* in relation to soil- borne wheat mosaic virus. *Phytopathology* 58 : 1516-1521.

Rao, S.A. and Brakke, K.M. 1969. Relation of soil-borne wheat mosaic virus and its fungal vector *Polymyxa graminis. Phytopathology* 59 : 581-587.

Rast, A.T.B., 1972. M II-16, An artificial symptomless mutant of tobacco mosaic virus for seedling inoculation of tomato crops. *Neth. J. Pl. Pathol.* 78 : 110-112.

Rast, A.T.B., 1975. Variability of tobacco mosaic virus in relation to control of tomato crops by resistance breeding and cross protection. *Agric. Res. Rep. (Neth.)* 834 : 1-76.

Ravelonandro, M. *et al.* 1991. Transgenic tobacco plants that contain the plum pox virus (PPV) coat protein gene (Abstr.). *XVth Int. Symp. on Virus and Virus Diseases of Temperate Fruit Crops,* 8-13 July, Vienna, Austria.

Raymer, W.B. and O'Brien, M.J., 1962. Transmission of potato spindle tuber virus to tomato. *Am. Potato J.* 39 : 401-408.

Reddy, D.V.R. 1991. Groundnut viruses and virus diseases : Distribution, identification and control. *Rev. Pl. Pathol.* 70 : 665-677.

Reddy, D.V.R. 1998. Contrul measures for the economically important peanut viruses. In : A. Hadidi *et al.*, Eds. *Plant Virus Disease Control,* APS Press, St. Paul, MN. P. 541-546.

Reddy, D.V.R. and Richins, R.D. 1998. Plant pareretro viruses : Legume caulimo viruses. *Encyclopedia of Virology*. 2nd Edition. Academic Press, New York, (in press).

Reddy, D.V.R. ***et al.,*** 1998. Pecluviruses, ***Encyclopedia*** *of Virology.* 2nd Edition. Academic Press, New York (in press).

Refatti, E. and Osler, R. 1975. Possible relationships among some fruit viruses detected in graft transmission trials. *Acta Hort.* 44 : 201-208.

Reijinders, L. ***et al.*** 1974. Molecular weights of plant virus RNAs determined by gel electophoresis under denaturing conditions. *Virology* 60 : 515-521.

Rezaian, M.A. ***et al.*** 1990. Grapevine viroids. (Abstr.) *10th Meeting ICVG,* Volos, Greece, Sept. 3-7, P.41.

Roberts, I.M. and Brown. 1980. Detection of six nepoviruses in their nematode vectors by immunosorbent electron microscopy. *Proc. 15th Int. Symp. Eur. Soc. Nematol.,* Bari, 1980.

Rochow. W.F. 1969. Biological properties of four isolates of barley yellow dwarf virus. *Phytopathology* 59 : 1580-1589.

Roland, G. 1960. A contribution to the study of the viruses of chrysanthemum. (Abstr.) *Rev. Appl. Mycol.* 39 : 584.

Rose, D.J.W. 1978. Epidemiology of maize streak disease. *Annu. Rev. Entomol.* 23 : 259-282.

Rosenberger, D.A. and Jones, A.L. 1976. A graft-transmissible agent associated with bark and woodgrooving disease of peach and nectarine. *Phytopathology* 66 : 729-730.

Rosenkranz, E. 1969. A new leafhopper-transmissible corn stunt disease in Ohio. *Phytopathology* 59 : 1344 - 1346.

Rosenkranz, E. 1983. Susceptibility of representative native Mississippi grasses in six subfamilies to maize dwarf mosaic virus strains A and B and sugarcane mosaic virus strain B. *Phytopathology* 73 : 1314-1321.

Rosenkranz, E. 1987. New hosts and taxonomic analysis of the Mississippi native species tested for reaction to maize dwarf mosaic and sugarcane mosaic viruses. *Phytopathology* 77 : 598-607.

Rosenkranz, E. and Scott, G.E. 1984. Determination of the number of genes for resistance to maize dwarf mosaic virus strain A in five corn inbred lines. *Phyopathology* 74 : 71-76.

Rosner, A. ***et al.*** 1983. Molecular cloning of complementary DNA sequences of citrus tristeza virus RNA. *J. Gen. Virol.* 64 : 1757-1763.

Rowhani, A. and Stace-Smith, R. 1979. Purification and characterization of potato leaf roll virus. *Virology* 98 : 45-54.

Russell, G.E. 1962. Sugarbeet mild yellowing virus : a peristent aphid-transmitted virus. *Nature* 195 : 4847, 1231.

Russell, G.E. ***et al.*** 1975. An aphid transmitted yellowing virus disease of sunflower. *Plant Pathol. (U.K.)* 24 : 58.

Russo, M. ***et al.*** 1979. Comparative studies on Mediterranean isolates of watermelon mosaic virus. *Phytopathol. Medit.* 18 : 94-101.

Russo. M. and Rana. G.L. 1978. Occurrence of two legume viruses in artichoke. *Phytopathol. Mediter.* 17 : 212-216.

Saito, Y. ***et al.*** 1962. Electron microscopy and purification of soil-borne wheat mosaic virus. *Ann. Phytopathol. Soe. Japan* 26 : 16-18.

Sanger, H.L. 1982. Biology, structure, functions and possible origin of viroids. In : Parthier, B. and Boulter, D., Eds *Nucleic Acids and Proteins in Plants,* Vol. 2, Springer- Verlag, Berlin, p. 368-454.

Sanger, H.L. *et al.* 1976. Viroids are single-stranded covalently closed circular RNA molecules existing as highly base-paired rod- like structures. *Proc. U.S. Natl. Acad. Sci.* 73 : 3852- 3856.

Saric, A. 1971. The occurrence of sowbane mosaic in sour cherry. *Ann. Phytopathol.* 71 : 155-158.

Sasaki, M. and Shikata, E. 1978. Studies on hop stunt disease. II. Properties of the casual agent, a viroid. *Ann. Phytopath. Soc. Japan* 44 : 570-577.

Scalla, R. and Rochow, W.F. 1977. Protein component of two isolates of barley yellow dwarf virus. *Virology* 78 : 576- 580.

Scheifele, G.L. and Wernham, C.C. 1969. Further evidence supporting the hypothesis that two genetic systems control disease reaction to maize dwarf mosaic virus strain A and strain B. *Pl. Dis. Reptr.* 53 : 150-151.

Scheller, H.V. and Shukle, R.H. 1986. Feeding behaviour and transmission of barley yellow dwarf virus by Sitobion avenae on oats. *Entomol. Exp. Appl.* 40 : 189-195.

Schmid., G. 1980. Transmission experiments with pseudo-pox and similar disorders of plum. *Acta Hort. Fruit Virus Disease* 94 : 159-165.

Schroeder, W.T. and Barton, D.W. 1958. The nature and inheritance of resistance to the pea enation mosaic virus in garden pea (*Pisum Sativum L.*), *Phytopathology* 48 : 628-632.

Schroeder, W.T. and Provvidenti, R. 1971. A common gene for resistance to bean yellow mosaic virus and watermelon mosaic virus 2 in *Pisum sativum. Phytopathology* 61 : 846-848.

Schwartz. H.F. and Mohan, S.K. 1995. *Compendium of Onion and Garlic Diseases.* APS Press, St. Paul, MN. 54 pp.

Scott, H.A. 1961. Serological detection of barley stripe mosaic virus in single seeds and dehydrated leaf tissues. *Phytopathology* 51 : 200-201.

Scott, H.A. and Hoy, J.W. 1981. Blackgram mottle virus. *CMI/AAB Descriptions of Plant Viruses,* No. 237.

Sehgal, O.P. 1966. Host range, properties and partial purification of a Missouri isolate of maize dwarf mosaic virus. *Pl. Dis. Reptr.* 50 : 862-866.

Semancik, J.S. 1972. Bean pod mottle virus. *CMI/ABB Descriptions of Plant Viruses,* No. 108.

Semancik, J.S. and Kajiyama, M.R. 1967. Properties and relationships among RNA species from tobacco rattle virus. *Virology* 33 : 523-532.

Semancik, J.S. and Szychowski, J.A. 1990. Comparative properties of viroids of grapevine origin isolated from grapevines and alternate hosts. *10th Meeting ICVG,* Volos, Greece, Sept. 3- 7, p. 37.

Senevirante, S.N. and Posnette, A.F. 1970. Identification of viruses isolated from plum trees affected by decline, line pattern and ringspot diseases. *Ann. Appl. Biol.* 65 : 115- 125.

Shepherd, R.J. 1964. Properties of a mosaic virus of cowpea and its relationship to the bean pod mottle virus. *Phytopathology* 54 : 466-473.

Shepherd, R.J. 1965. Properties of a mosaic virus of corn and Johnson grass and its relation to the sugarcane mosaic virus. *Phytopathology* 55 : 1250-1256.

Shepherd, R.J. 1981. Cauliflower mosaic virus. *CMI/AAB Descriptions of Plant Viruses,* No. 243.

Shepherd, R.J. *et al.* 1966. A severe necrotic strain of the beet mosaic virus. *J. Am. Soc. Sugar Beet Tech.* 14 : 97-105.

Shukla, D.D. *et al*. 1989. A novel approach to the serology of potyviruses involving affinity-purified polyclonal antibodies directed towards virus-specific N termini of coat protein. *J. Gen. Virol.* 70 : 13-23.

Shukla, D.D. *et al.* 1989a. Taxonomy of potyviruses infecting maize, sorghum and sugarcane in Australia and the United States as determined by reactivities of polyclonal antibodies directed towards virus-specific N-termini of coat proteins. *Phytopathology* 79 : 223-229.

Sill, W.H. 1958. A comparison of some characteristics of soil-borne wheat mosaic virus in the Great Plains and elsewhere. *Pl. Dis. Reptr.* 42 : 912-924.

Sill, W.H., JR. 1966. Maize dwarf mosaic virus in Kansa. *Pl. Dis. Reptr.* 50 : 11.

Singh, J.P. 1979. Mechanical and seed transmission of the causal agent of sunflower rugose mosaic in Kenya. *Sunflower Newsl.* 3 : 13.

Singh, R.P. and Bagnall, R.H. 1968. Infectious nucleic acid from host tissues infected with the potato spindle tuber virus. *Phytopathology* 58 : 696-699.

Singh, B.R. ; Gupta, S.P. and Tripathi, D.P. (1990). Response of some chilli lines to mosaic and leaf curl diseases. *Indian J. Virol.* 6 : 133-115.

Singh, B.R. and Tripathi, D.P. (1991). Occurrence of tomato spotted wilt disease of tomato. *Madras Agricu. J.* 1-4 : 34-36.

Singh, B.R. and Tripathi, D.P. (1993). Reaction of pea lines to mosaic disease. *Madras Agricul. J.* 7 : 399-400.

Singh, B.R. ; Gupta, S.P. ; Tripathi, D.P. and Yadav, M.D. (1994). Response of groundnut lines to bud necrosis disease. *Madras Agric. J.* 10 : 577.

Sinha, R.C. 1968. Serological detection of wheat striate mosaic virus in extracts of wheat plants and vector leafhoopers. *Phytopathology* 58 : 452-455.

Sinha, R.C. and Chiykowski. L.N. 1967. Multiplication of wheat striate mosaic virus in its leafhooper vector Endria inimica Say. *Virology* 32 : 402-405.

Sinha, R.C. *et al.* 1976. Chemical composition and some properties of wheat striate mosaic virus. *Phytopathol. Z.* 87 : 314- 323.

Slykhuis, J.T. 1962. Wheat striate mosaic, a virus disease to watch on the Prairies. *Can. Plant Dis. Surv.* 42 : 135-142.

Slykhuis, J.T. 1962a. An international survey for virus disease of grasses. *F.A.O. Pl. Prot. Bull.* 10 : 1-16.

Slykhuis, J.T. 1963. Vectors and host relations of North America wheat striate mosaic virus. *Can. J. Bot.* 41 : 1171-1185.

Slykhuis, J.T. and Polak. L. 1971. Factors affecting manual transmission, purification and particle lengths of wheat spindle streak mosaic virus. *Phytopathology* 61 : 569-574.

Slykhuis, J.T. and Sherwood, P.L. 1964. Temperature in relation to the transmission and pathogenicity wheat striate mosaic virus. *Can. J. Bot.* 42 : 1123-1133.

Smith, K.M. 1946. Tomato black ring, a new virus disease. *Parasitology* 37 : 126-130.

Smith, K.M. 1972. *A Textbook of Plant Virus Diseases.* 3rd Edition. Longman Group, Ltd.

Smith, P.R. and Challen, D.I. 1972. Aetiology of the rosette and decline disease of peach and interactions between *Prunus* necrotic ringspot, prune dwarf and dark green sunken mottle viruses. *Austr. J. Agric. Res.* 23 : 1027-1034.

Snazelle, T.E. *et al.* 1971. Purification and serology of maize dwarf mosaic and sugarcane mosaic viruses. *Phytopathology* 61 : 1059-1063.

Stace-Smith, R. and Melior, F.C. 1968. Eradication of potato viruses X and S by thermotherapy and axillary bud culture. *Phytopathology* 58 : 199-203.

Stellmach, G. 1970. Tomato black ring in *Vitis.* In : Frazier, N.W. ed. Virus *Diseases of Small Fruits and Grapevines,* University of California, Davis, div. Agr. Sci., p. 234-236.

Stellmach, G. *et al.* 1965. Tomato black ring virus on grapevine. In : *Proc. Int. Conf. Virus and Vector Peren. Hosts Spec. Ref. Vitis.* University of California, Davis, Div. Agr. Sci., p. 234-236.

Stoner, W.N. 1949. Virus diseases of Corn with Special Reference to Insect Transmission of Leaf Fleck and Western Cucumber Mosaic. Ph.D. thesis, Univ. of California, Berkeley, 49pp.

Stoner, W.N. 1952. Leaf fleck, an aphid borne persistent virus disease of maize. *Phytopathology* 42 : 683-689.

Stubbs, L.L. 1947. A destructive vascular wilt disease of board bean (Vicia fabaL.) in Victoria. *J. Dept. Agr.* Victoria 46 : 323-332.

Stubbs, L.L. and Barker, D. 1985. Rapid sample analysis with a simplified ELISA. *Phytopathology* 75 : 492-495.

Stubbs, L.L. and Smith, R.P. 1971. The association of prunus necrotic ringspot, prune dwarf and dark green sunken motle viruses in rosetting and decline of peach. *Austr. J. Agric. Res.* 22 : 771-781.

Sun, M.K.C. *et al.* 1974. Properties of tobacco vein-mottling virus, a new pathogen of tobacco. *Phytopathology* 64 : 1133- 1136.

Sutic, D. 1961. Assay of the transmission of Sharka virus disease by sap inoculation to herbaceous plants. *T. Planteavl.* 65 : 138-146.

Sutic, D. and Rankovic, M. 1981. Resistance of some plum cultivars and individual trees to plum pox (Sharka) virus. *Agronomie* 1(8) : 617-622.

Sutic, D. and Rankovic, M. 1983. Sensitivity of some stone fruit species to Sharka (plum pox virus) disease. *Zastita bilja* 34 : 241-348.

Sutic, D. and Sinclair, J.B. 1991. *Anatomy and Physiology of Diseased Plants,* CRC Press, Boca Raton, FL.

Sutic, D. and Tosic, M. 1966a. Transmission of mosaic virus by barley seeds. *Adv. Frontiers Pl. Sci., New Delhi* 17 : 205- 208.

Sutic, D. and Tosic, M. 1966b. A significant occurrence of maize mosaic virus on Johnsongrass *(Sorghum halepense Pers.)* as a natural host plant. *Rev. Roum. Biol. Ser. Bot.* 11 : 219- 224.

Sutton, W.S. 1955. Yellow top disease of tomatoes. *Agric. Gaz. N.S.W.* 66 : 655-658.

Sweet, J.B. 1980. Fruit tree infections of woody exotic and indigenous plants in Britain. *Acta Phytopathol. Acad. Sci. Hung.* 15 : 231-238.

Sweet, J.B. and Campbell, A.I. 1976. Pome fruit virus infection of some woody ornamental and indigenous species of Rosaceae. *J. Hort. Sci.* 51 : 91-97.

Sweet, J.B. ***et al.*** 1978. Improving the quality and the virus status of hardy ornamental trees and shrubs. *Rept. Long Ashton Res. Stn.* 1977, p. 36-37.

Sylvester, E.S. 1954. Yellow-net virus disease of tomato. *Phytopathology* 44 : 219-220.

Tamada, T. and Baba, T. 1973. Beet necrotic yellow vein virus from Rizomania-affected sugarbeet in Japan. *Ann. Phytopathol. Soc. Japan* 30 : 325-331.

Tamada, T. ***et al.,*** 1969. Soybean dwarf, a new virus disease. *Ann. Phytopathol. Soc. Japan* 35 : 282-285.

Tandon, J.P. ***et al.*** 1990. Status of barley yellow dwarf virus research in Asia, with special emphasis on India. In : Burnett, P.A., Ed. *World Perspectives on Barley Yellow Dwarf*, CIMMYT, Mexico, D.F., Mexico, p. 81-84.

Tanne, E. and Meir, E. 1990. Double-stranded RNA associated with the corky bark disease in grapevines. (Abstr.) *10th Meeting ICVG,* Volos, Greece, Sept. 3-7.

Tanne, E. ***et al.*** 1978. Further studies of a leaf roll-associated virus : transmission from herbaceous plants, purification and characterization. *VIth Meeting ICVG*, Madrid, Sept. 13-21, p. 213-215.

Taylor, C.E. and Raski, D.J. 1964. On the transmission of grapevine fanleaf by *Xiphinema index. Nematologica* 10 : 489-495.

Taylor, C.E. and Raski, D.J. 1964. On the transmission of grapevine fanleaf by Xiphinema index. *Nematologica* 10 : 489-495.

Taylor, R.H. and Stubbs, L.I. 1972. Board bean wilt virus. *CMI/AAB Descriptions of Plant Viruses,* No. 81.

Taylor, R.H. ***et al.*** 1968. Purification and properties of board bean wilt virus. *Aust. J. Biol. Sci.* 21 : 929-935.

Teakle, D.S. 1962. Transmission of tobacco necrosis by a fungas *Olpidium brassicae. Virology* 18 : 224-231.

Teakle, D.S. 1962. Transmission of tobacco necrosis by a fungas *Olpidium brassicae. Virology* 18 : 224-231.

Teakle, D.S. and Grylls, N.E. 1973. Four strains of sugarcane mosaic virus infecting cereals and other grasses in Australia. *Aust. J. Agric. Res.* 24 : 465-477.

Teakle, D.S. and Pritchard. A.J. 1971. Resistance of Krish sorghum to four strains of sugarcane mosaic in Queensland. *Pl. Dis. Repr.* 55 : 596-598.

Teakle, D.S. ***et al.*** 1972. Transfer of sugarcane mosaic virus resistance from Krish sorghum to inbred lines. *Sorghum Newslett.* 16 : 2-3.

Teakle, D.S. et al. 1989. Sugarcane mosaic virus. *CMI/AAB Description of Plant Viruses,* No. 342.

Teycheney, P.Y. and Dietzgen, R.G. 1994. Cloning and sequence analysis of the coat protein genes of an Australian strain of peanut mottle and an Indonesian "blotch" strain of peanut stripe potyviruses. *Virus Res.* 31 : 235-244.

Thomas, A. 1975. Cross-protection experiment with apple mosaic virus. *Acta Hort.* 44 : 119-122.

Thomas, H.E. and Hildebrand, E.M. 1936. A virus disease of prune. *Phytopathology* 26 : 1145-1148.

Thomas, H.E. and Rawlins, T.E. 1939. Some mosaic diseases of *Prunus* species. *Hilgardia* 12 : 623-644.

Thomas, J.E. and Bowyer, J.W. 1980. Properties of tobacco yellow dwarf and bean summer death viruses. *Phytopathology* 70 : 214-217.

Thomas, P.E. and Bowyer, J.W. 1984. Tobacco yellow dwarf virus. *CMI/AAB Descriptions of Plant Viruses,* No. 278.

Thornbury, D.W. and Pirone, T.P. 1983. Helper component of two potyviruses are serology distinct. *Virology* 125 : 487-490.

Thresh, J.M. *et al.,* 1972. The spread and control of nettlehead and related diseases of hop. *Annu. Rep. East Malling Res. Sta.* 59 : 155-162.

Timian, R.G. 1960. A virus of durum wheat in North Dakota transmitted by leafhoopers. *Pl. Dis. Reptr.* 44 : 771-773.

Timian, R.G. 1964. Dodder transmission of barley yellow dwarf virus. (Abstr.) *Phytopathology* 54 : 910.

Timian, R.G. and Sisler, W.W. 1955. Prevalence, sources and inheritance of resistance to barley stripe mosaic (false stripe). *Pl. Dis. Reptr.* 39 : 550-552.

Toler, R.W. 1985. Maize dwarf mosaic virus the most important virus disease of sorghum. *Plant Dis.* 69 : 1011-1015.

Tomlinson, J.A. 1970. Lettuce mosaic virus. *CMI/AAB Descriptions of Plant Viruses,* No. 9.

Tomlinson, J.A. 1988. Beet western yellows virus (BWYV). In : Smith, I.M. et al., Eds. *European Handb. Pl. Dis.,* Blackwell Sci. Publ., London, p. 21-23.

Tomlinson, J.A. *et al.,* 1983. Chenopodium necrosis : A distinctive strain of tobacco necrosis virus isolated from water. *Ann. Appl. Biol.* 102 : 135-147.

Topchiiska, M. 1977. Preliminary studies on a strain of apple mosaic virus isolated from almond. *Hort. Vitic. Sci. (Sofia)* 14(1) : 37-43.

Topchiiska, M. 1983. Effect of *Prunus* necrotic ringspot virus (PNRV) and prune dwarf virus (PDV) on some biological properties of peach. *Acta Hort.* 130 : 307-312.

Topchiiska, M. and Topchiiski, I. 1976. Isolation of cucumber mosaic virus from almond (*Prunus amydalus* Stocks). *Hort. Vitic. Sci. (Sofia)* 13(3) : 44-54.

Tosic, M. and Ford, R.E. 1972. Grasses differentiating sugarcane mosaic and maize dwarf mosaic and sugarcane mosaic viruses. *Phytopathology* 64 : 312-317.

Tosic, M. and Sutic, D. 1977. Investigation of maize virus transmission through corn seed. *Ann. Phytopathol.* 9 : 403- 405.

Tosic, M. *et al.* 1977. Effect of previous mosaic virus infection on corn susceptibility to the stalk and ear rot caused by *Gibberella zeae. Ann. Phytopath.* 9 : 395-401.

Tosic, M. *et al.* 1980. Transmission of tobacco mosaic virus through pepper (*Capsicum annuum*) seed. *Phytopathol.* Z. 97 : 10-13.

Tosic, M. *et al.* 1990. Differentiation of sugarcane, maize dwarf, Johnsongrass and sorghum mosaic viruses based on reactions of oat and some sorghum cultivars. *Plant Dis.* 74 : 549-552.

Traylor, J.A. *et al.* 1963. Studies on the passage of prunus ringspot virus complex through plum seed (Abstr.) *Phytopathology* 53 : 1143.

Tosic, M. *et al.* 1977. Effect of previous mosaic virus infection on corn susceptibility to the stalk and ear rot caused by *Gibberella zeae, Ann. Phytopath.* 9 : 395-401.

Tosic, M. *et al.* 1980. Transmission of tobacco mosaic virus through pepper (Capsicum annuum) seed. *Phytopathol.* Z. 97 : 10-13.

Tosic, M. *et al.* 1990. Differentiation of sugarcane, maize dwarf, Johnsongrass and sorghum mosaic viruses based on reactions of oat and some sorghum cultivars. *Plant Dis.* 74 : 549-552.

Traylor, J.A. *et al.* 1963. Studies on the passage of prunus ringspot virus complex through plum seed (Abstr.) *Phytopathology* 53 : 1143.

Trefzger-Stevens, J. and Lee, P.E. 1977. The structural properties of wheat striate mosaic virus, plant rhabdovirus. *Virology* 78 : 144-149.

Tremaine, J.H. and Hamilton, R.I. 1983. Southern bean mosaic virus. *CMI/AAB Descriptions of Plant Viruses,* No. 274.

Trifonov, D. 1971. Bud drop of pear. *Ann. Phytopathol.* 3 : 285-294.

Tripathi, D.P. (1970). Scientific research in Plant Viruses (*Paudhon ke visanuo par bagyanik parikshan*). *Vigyan Pragati.* Feb. 1970, India.

Tripathi, D.P. (2005). Mushroom Cultivation, Oxford & IBH Publishing Co. New Delhi.

Tu, J.C. *et al.* 1970. Effects of soybean mosaic virus and/or bean pod mottle virus infection on soybean nodulation. *Phytopathology* 60 : 518-523.

Tu. J.C. and Ford, R.E. 1971. Maize dwarf mosaic virus predisposes corn to root rot infection. *Phytopathology* 61 : 800-803.

Tu. J.C. *et al.* 1968. Comparisons of chloroplasts and photosynthetic rates of plants infected and not infected by maize dwarf mosaic virus. *Phytopathology* 58 : 285-288.

Turner, N.W. *et al.* 1987. Expression of alfalfa mosaic virus coat protein gene confers cross protection in transgenic tobacco and tomato plants. *EMBO J,* 6 : 1181.

Usugi. T. and Saito, Y. 1979. Relationship between wheat yellow mosaic virus and wheat spindle streak mosaic virus. *Ann. Phytopathol. Soc. Japan* 45 : 397-400.

Uyemoto, J.K. 1970. Symptomatologically distinct strains of tomato ringspot virus isolated from grape and elderberry. *Phytopathology* 60 : 1838-1841.

Valleau, W.D. 1932. A virus disease of plum and peach. *Ky. Agr. Exp. Sta. Bull.* 327 : 89-103.

Van der Meer, F.A. 1975. Plant species outside the genus Malus as indicators for latent viruses of apple. *Acta Hort.* 44 : 213-220.

Van der Meer, F.A. 1976. Observations on apple stem grooving virus. *Acta Hort.* 67 : 293-304.

Van Dorst, H.J.M. and Peters, D. 1974. Some biological observations on pale fruit a viroid incited disease of cucumber. *Neth. J.Pl. Pathol.* 80 : 85-96.

Van Kammen, A. and De. Jager, C.P. 1978. Cowpea mosaic virus. *CMI/AAB Descriptions of Plant Viruses,* No. 197.

Van Oostea. H.J. 1971. Further information about herbaceous host range of Sharka (plum pox) virus. *Ann. Phytopathol.* H.S. 195-201.

Van Oostea. H.J. 1976. The importance of virus-free apple trees for fruit growing. *Gewasbescherming.* 7 : 1-15.

Verhoyen, M. and Meunier, S. 1988. Bean common mosaic virus (BCMV). In : Smith, I.M. et al., Eds. *European Handb. Pl. Dis.,* Blackwell Sci. Publ., London, P. 26-35.

Verma, H.N. 2003. Basics of plant virology, oxford & IBH Publishing Co. Private Ltd. India.

Vogel, R. and Bove, J.M. 1980. Pollen transmission to citrus of the agent inducing cristacortis stem pitting and psorosis young leaf symptoms. In : Calavan, et al. *Eds. Proc. 8th Conf. Int. Organ. Citrus Virol.,* Univ. Calif., Riverside, p. 188-190.

Wadley, B.N. 1966. Apricot leaf pucker, a virus-induced disorder (Abstr.). *Phytopathology* 56 : 152.

Wagnon, H.K. ***et al.*** 1958. Stubby twig, a new virus disease of peach and nectarine in California. *Phytopathology* 48 : 465- 468.

Wagnon, H.K. ***et al.*** 1960. Observations on the natural spread of the so-called peach stunt virus in California peach orchard. *Plant Dis. Reptr.* 44 : 488-490.

Walker, J.C. and Larson, R.H. 1939. Yellow dwarf of potato in Wisconsin. *J. Agric. Res.* 59 : 259-280.

Walkey, D.G.A. 1968. The production of virus-free rhubarb by apical tip-culture. *J. Hort. Sci.* 43 : 283-287.

Walkey, D.G.A. and Neeley, H.A. 1980. Resistance of white cabbage to necrosis caused by turnip and cauliflower mosaic viruses and pepper spot. *Ann. Appl Biol.* 95 : 703-713.

Walkey, D.G.A. ***et al.*** 1973. Serological, physical and chemical properties of strains of cherry leaf roll virus. *Phytopathology* 63 : 566-571.

Wallace, J.N. and Darke, R.J. 1953. A virus-induced vein enation in citrus. *Citrus Leaves* 33 : 22-24.

Wallace, J.N. and **Darke, R.J.** 1960. Woody galls on citrus associated with vein enation virus infection. *Plant Dis. Reptr.* 44 : 580-584.

Walter, B. ***et al.*** 1990. The use of a green-grafting technique for the detection of virus-like diseases of the grapevine. *J. Phytopathol.* 128 : 137-145.

Waterhouse, P.M. and Murant, A.F. 1982. Carrot red leaf virus. *CMI / AAB Descriptions of Plant Viruses,* No. 249.

Waterworth, H.E. 1981. Bean mild mosaic virus. *CMI/AAB Descriptions of Plant Viruses,* No. 231.

Waterworth, H.E. 1965. Some properties of an unidentified virus latent in pear introduction (Abstr.). *Phytopathology* 55 : 1081.

Waterworth, H.E. and Fulton, R.W. 1964. Variation among isolates of necrotic ringspot and prune dwarf viruses from sour cherry. *Phytopathology* 54 : 1155-1160.

Watkins, T.C. 1941. Clover leafhooper *(Aceratagalia sanguinolenta Prov.). Bull. Cornell Univer. Agric. Exp. Stn.* 758, 24 pp.

Watson, M. 1962. Yellow-net virus of sugar beet. I. Transmission and some properties. *Ann. Appl. Biol.* 50 : 451-460.

Watson, M.A. 1963. *Annual Report. Rothamsted Exp. Sta. Rep.* 1962.

Way, R.D. and Gilmer, R.M. 1963. Reductions in fruit sets on cherry trees pollinated with pollen from trees with sour cherry yellows. *Phytopathology* 53 : 399-401.

Webb. R.E. and Scott, H.A. 1965. Isolation and identification of watermelon mosaic viruses 1 and 2. *Phytopathology* 55:895-900

Weber, I. 1986. Cucumber leaf spot virus. *CMI/AAB Descriptions of Plant Viruses,* No. 319.

Wellman, F.L. 1934. Infection of Zea may and various other graminaea by the celery virus in Florida. *Phytopathology* 24:1035-1037.

Welsh, M. F. and Keane, F.WL. 1963. Leaf Pucker and associated fruit disorders. *Techn. Comm. Commonw Bur. Hort. Plant. Crops.* 30:11-15.

Welsh, M. F. and May, J. 1973. Suppression of the symptoms of apple leaf pucker disease in an occurrence pettern that indicates virus infection. *Can. J. Plant Sci* 53(1) : 137-145.

Welsh, M. F. and Nyland, G. 1965. Elimination and separation of viruses in apple clones by exposure to dry heat. *Can. J. Plant Sci.* 45:443-454.

Wetter, C. and Conti, M. 1988. Pepper mild mottle virus. *CMI/AAB Descriptions of Plant Viruses* No. 330.

Wetter, C. *et al.* 1969. Purification and serology of maize rough dwarf virus from plant and vector. *Phytopathol. Z.* 66:197-212.

Whited, R. A. and Fischbach, R.A. 1973. An X-ray scattering investigation of board bean mittle virus in solutions of various electron densities. *J. Mol. Biol. 75:549-558.*

Whitney, W. K. and Gilmer, R M. 1974. Insect vectors of cowpea mosaic virus in Nigeria. *Ann. Appl. Biol.* 77:17- 21.

Wilde, W.H.A. 1960. Insect transmission of the virus causing little cherry disease. *Can. J. Plant Sci.* 40:407-712.

Wilks, J.M. and Welsh, M. F. 1965. Freckle pit-a virus disease of "Anjou" pears. *Can. Plant Dis. Survey* 45:90-91.

Williams, L. E. and Holdeman, G.L. 1970. American current mosaic. In: Frazier, N.W., Ed. *Virus Dis. Small Fruits and Grapevine.* University of California, Berkeley.

Williams, L.E. *et al.* 1967. A virus of corn and small grains in Ohio and its relation to wheat streak mosaic virus. *Pl Dis. Reptr.* 51:207-211.

Williams, L. E. *et al.* 1968. Seed transmission studies on maize dwarf mosaic virus. In corn. *Pl. Dis. Reptr.* 52:863-864.

Wood, G. A. 1975. Some bud transmissible disorders in Prunus. *N. Z. J. Agr. Res.* 18:255-259.

Wu, G. J. and Bruening, G. 1971. Two proteins from cowpea mosaic virus. *Virology* 46:596-612.

Yamashita, S. *et al.* 1976 *Ann. Phytopathol. Soc., Japan* 43:46.

Yarwood, C.E. 1995. Mechanical transmission of an apple mosaic virus. *Hilgardia* 23:613-628.

Yoshikawa, N. and Takahashi, T. 1988. Properties of apple stem grooving and apple chlorotic leaf spot viruses (Abstr.). *XVth Int. Symp. Fruit Tree Virus Dis., 29, 12-18 June,* thessalonik, Greece.

Yot-Danthy, D. and Bove, J. M. 1968. Purification and characterization of citrus crinkly leaf virus. *Proc. 4th Conf. Int. Organ. Citrus Virol.,* p. 255-263.

Younkin, S. G. 1942. Weed suscepts of the potato yellow dwarf virus. *Am. Potato J.* 19:6.

Zaumeyer, W. J. and Goth, R. W. 1964. A new severe symptom -inducing strain of common bean mosaic virus. *Phytopathology* 54:1378-1385.

Zaumeyer, W.J. and Thomas, H.R. 1948. Pod mottle, a virus disease of beans. *J. Agr. Res.* 77:81-96.

Selazny, B. *et al.* 1982. The viroid nature of the cadang-cadnag disease of coconut palm. *Scientia Filipinas* 2:45.

Zitter, T. A. *et. al.* 1996. *Compendium of Cucurbit Diseases,* APS Press, St. Paul, MN, 87 pp.

SOURCES OF INFORMATION ON PLANT VIRUSES

❍ Books–

(*a*) **Plant Pathologist's pocket book-*Publisher* : CAB International, U. K.**

(*b*) **Handbook of plant virus disease.** CRC Press, Boca Raton London, New York, Washington D.C.

(*c*) **Virus and virus like diseases of potato.** *Publisher* : Kluwer Academic Publishers, London.

(*d*) **Recent trends in disease management of fruits and seeds** *Publisher* : Scientific Publishers, Jodhpur (Raj.).

(*e*) **Encyclopedia of Virology.** Vol. 1,2 and 3. *Publisher* : Academic Press.

(*f*) **Basic and Laboratory Methods for Biotechnology.** *Publisher* : Prentice Hall International, New Jersey.

❍ Journals–

(*g*) **Archives of Virology.** *Publisher* : Springer Verlogwien, Austria.

(*h*) **Phytopathology.** *Publisher* : American Phytopathological Society.

(*i*) **Indian Phytopathology.** *Publisher* : Indian Phytopathlogical Society, IARI.

(*j*) **Microbial Ecoloy.** *Publisher*: Springer Verlogwien, Austria.

(*k*) **Journal of Plant Biochemistry and Biotechnology.** *Publisher* : Soc. of Plant Bio Chemistry and Biotechnology, IARI.

(*l*) **Plant Diseases.** *Publisher* : Prentice Hall International, New Jersey.

❍ Other Journals

1. Intervirology
2. Journal of General Virology
3. Indian Journal of Virology
4. Virology
5. Journal of Virological Methods
6. Annals of Applied Biology
7. Journal of Molecular Biology
8. Molecular Plant Pathology
9. Nature
10. Plant Cell
11. Plant Molecular Biology
12. Science
13. Virus Research.

❍ Abstracting Journals

Review of Plant Pathology
(Formerly, Review of Applied Mycology)
Biological Abstract

❍ Review Journals

Advances in Virus Research
Annual Review of Microbiology
Annual Review of Phytopathology
Annual Review of Plant Physiology and Molecular Biology.

PLANT VIRUSES ON LINE-QUICK INTRODUCTION

Mirror plant viruses online provides descriptions and lists from the VIDE (VIRUS IDENTIFICATION DATA EXCHANGE) which includes as alphabetical index of virus species, virus genera, virus acronyms, host plant species and host families. We may also view notes about the data and its presentation and view the character list used to generate the descriptions.

www.image.fs.uidaho.edu

* DIR : Internet IPM Resources on plant viruses
  www.ippc.orst.edu
* All the virology
  www.tulane.edu
* Plant viruses
  www.micro.msb.le.ac.uk
* ICTV Approved plant virus families and genera

A large database containing descriptions of all viruses has been divided into several categories according to the type of viral genomic nucleic acids. Throughout this document, each type species name is preceded by the name of the order, family and genus it belongs to.

www.ag.arizona.edu

* The best source of plant pathology information on web : **The plant pathology internet guide book.** It is a subject oriented internet guide book on plant pathology and related fields with regular updates is available at

  www.bspp.org.uk / ppigb

* Another important web site with hyperlinks to different societies/organizations on plant pathology is :

  www.uct.ac.za / microbiology / saspbook.htm

* The international society for plant pathology could be accessed at the site :

  www.ispp.org

* Search on terminology in the field of plant pathology could be done at :

  www.academicpress.com / pmpp

* The American Phytopathological Society publishes four Journals and a news letter. The publications are : Plant Health Progress, Plant Diseases, Phytopathology, Molecular Plant-Microbe interactions & Phytopathology news. All these publications are available in electronic format on APS net-Plant pathology Online at site :

  www.apsnet.org

* British Society for Plant Pathology

  www.bspp.org.uk

* Indian Phytopathological Society

  www.ipsdis.org

* Plant Pathology Internet Guide Book

  www.ifgb.uni-hannover.de

* International Mycological Institute

  www.cabr.org / institute / imi / grc.htm

* Molecular Plant Pathology

  www.bspp.org.uk / mppol

* Plant Pathology

  www.scisoc.org

* Annual Review of Phytopathology

  www. phytoannualreview.org

* Plant Virus

  www.biology.amu.edu.au / groups / mes / video

Some of these on-lines are paid sites and could be accessed only by subscribers.

ONLINE VS. CD-ROME DATABASE SEARCHES

Following are the important differences between Online and CD- ROME searches.

1. Up-to-date information : Online search provides uptodate information on subject whereas CD-ROME can not because of its production time.

2. Time and cost : CD-ROME searches can be conducted as many times as required with one time payment but online search costs money for every search.

3. Resource sharing and CD Networking : Information on CDs can be shared by the participating agencies.

4. Searching of information : C-ROME search is menu driven and does not require any online connection. Online search is command based and require online connection. In both the forms, searching of information can be made according to fields such as keyword, author, journal name, publication year, type of document (book, paper or report etc.), country of publication, subject description and classified codes. The user can also limit the search to specific fields and modify the search with additional terms as required.

5. Sorting, printing and down-loading of information : Records of information retrived from search output can be sorted by author, title, year, journal, type of document and number of occurrences etc. Desired information viewed may be marked for printing and can be saved on disk or transferred on to a floppy.

In the wake of agricultural developments through scientific means, the need for information and data has also increased manifolds. The ever growing amount of data needs to be stored, accessed and manipulated in order to be of use in answering various questions. The solution to this problem lies in exploitation of power of computers to manipulate data. For this purpose, we need relevant software. Extensive databases now store information in powerful computers. There are databases known to contain information on most species of viruses known to infect plants. Additional databases store ribosomal RNA sequences. As these form part of the genetical material of plant viruses, information on these is extremely useful. This information could be accessed using the **World Wide web (WWW)....**

Thus information gathering, storage and analysis etc. is only possible with the help of computers and use of information technology. The application of this technology can better be appreciated through practical demonstration than oral explanation. The recent advances in computers and communication technology have resulted in faster movement of information and its utilization.

Relevant Information on Measurements

Weight	**Metric units**	**in grams (g)**
	Kilogram (kg)	10^3
	Gram (g)	1
	Milligram (mg)	10^{-3}
	Microgram (μg)	10^{-6}
Volume	**Metric units**	**in litre (l)**
	Kilolitre (kl)	10^3

	Litre (l)	1
	Deciliter (dl)	10^{-1}
	Centilitre (cl)	10^{-2}
	Millilitre (ml)	10^{-3}
	Microlitre (μl)	10^{-6}
Length	**Metric units**	**in metres (m)**
	Kilometre (km)	10^{3}
	Metre (m)	1
	Decimetre (dm)	10^{-1}
	Centimetre (cm)	10^{-2}
	Millimetre (mm)	10^{-3}
	Micrometre (μm) or micron (μ)	10^{-6}
	Nanometer (nm) or millimicron (mμ)	10^{-9}
	Angstrom (Å)	10^{-10}

Conversion in Measurements

1 gram	=	1000 mg
	=	0.035274 oz.
	=	0.0222046 lb.
	=	0.001 kg.
1 kg	=	1000 grams
	=	35.273957 oz.
1 lb	=	453.59 grams
1 hectare	=	2.471 acres
	=	10,000 m^{-2}
	=	0.01 km^{-2}
1 Millilitre	=	0.01 litre.
1 Millimetre	=	0.1 cm.
	=	0.01 decimetre
	=	0.001 m
	=	1000 μm.
1 Ounce (oz)	=	437.5 grains
	=	28.349527 grams.
	=	0.0625 pounds
Parts per million (ppm)	=	miligrams per litre.
One ppm	=	1 mg l^{-1}